← After writing an essay in my first book *Artificial Arcadia*, Lars invited me to give a lecture at Rice. As a matter of payment for the lecture he rented me a car to roam the Houston area. These are the photographs that came out of of that short trip through the hurricane struck city and along the coastline.
—**Bas Princen** is a Rotterdam-based architect and photographer.

Everything Must Move.

Documenting a decade-and-a-half of propositions about the suburban city in general, and Houston in particular

This city—shapeless, polluted, traffic-clogged, water-logged, limitless—is a workshop for testing ideas about operating in impossible situations.

Edited and designed by
Thumb/Luke Bulman and Jessica Young

Architecture at Rice 44

Everything Must Move

Published by:
Rice University School of Architecture
6100 Main Street, Mailstop 50
Houston, Texas 77005-1892 United States
www.arch.rice.edu

Distributed by:
Actar D
Roca i Batlle 2
08023 Barcelona
t: +34934174993
f: +34934186707
office@actar-d.com
www.actar-d.com

Super Houston, from *The City, Seen as a Garden of Ideas* by Peter Cook, copyright
©2003 by The Monacelli Press, a division of Random House, Inc. Used by permission
of Monacelli Press, a division of Random House, Inc.

All images courtesy of the authors unless otherwise noted. All reasonable attempts
have been made to identify owners of copyright. Errors or omissions will be corrected
in future editions.

Printed and bound in Hong Kong

First edition, 2009
ISBN-13: 978-1-885232-11-3
Please contact the publisher for Library of Congress catalog-in-publication information.

Editors: Luke Bulman and Jessica Young
Copy editor: Polly Koch
Data analyst: Trevor Coe

Design: Thumb

This book is set in the typefaces Helvetica Neue, Dolly,
Courier New, Courier Sans, and Wingdings.

Endpapers: Andrew Albers, *Parking Pattern*

About this book
Luke Bulman and Jessica Young

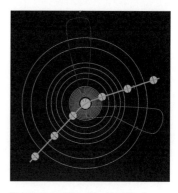

Early diagram of *Everything Must Move*'s structure based on a series of "trips."

All utopias are depressing because they leave no room for chance, for difference, for the "miscellaneous." Everything has been set in order and order reigns. Behind every utopia there is always some great taxonomic design: a place for each thing and each thing in its place.
—George Perec, "Think/Classify"

Everything Must Move is, in many ways, an archival project. However, as we built the book from the bottom-up, by infusing the archival material from the last 15 years with new perspectives and projections we sought to keep the project "alive," poly-vocal, diverse, and open. We asked current and past students, faculty, and visitors to Rice School of Architecture to contribute fresh material until the last possible moment before we went to press. This editorial flexibility has kept the book "loose" in its view and nature, forestalling closure and finality. In a way, this approach reflects the optimism of the school's project: to embrace the improvisational and prepare to find an opportunity to intervene whenever and wherever it might arise.

Although the contents of this book range widely, we could not possibly incorporate the full scope of contributions made by the community at Rice over so many years. At best, *Everything Must Move* demonstrates some of the ideas that we pursued together and in which each of us might be able to identify a bit of our own interests and passions.

This body of material required an organizational principle to sort ideas, but we wanted one that would productively—even promiscuously—make connections among the kaleidoscope of work drawn from a 15 year history. The book is organized into clusters that are roughly analogous to the typological geography of the contemporary city, in general, and Houston, in particular. This organizing principle produces surprising juxtapositions, and some possible contradictions, yet presents with clarity many of the issues raised by the interactions of architecture and the metropolis.

In the end, it is our hope that this book will open the ideas produced during this period to a wider audience. While always familiar with the ideas being explored at other schools, Rice always had its own approach to dismantling them. In reassembly some parts needed to be customized, jacked up, spray-painted, or just simply discarded in order to work in such a place as Houston—shapeless, polluted, traffic-clogged, water-logged, limitless. In retrospect, we think that process was pretty spectacular. Everything Must Move aspires to reflect the recklessness with which the project at Rice has been pursued.

Houston is no utopia, nor maybe even a "nice place" for that matter, but in its rowdy, soggy, excess it presents a sublime environment for testing ideas about operating in seemingly impossible situations. During Lars Lerup's time as dean at Rice School of Architecture, the imperative of engagement was clear: "get off your ass, do something!" he might say. We think we'll do just that.

LUKE BULMAN and **JESSICA YOUNG** are partners at Thumb, a Brooklyn-based design office. They both received M.Arch. degrees from Rice School of Architecture and were consecutive Directors of Publications and Exhibtions at the School from 1998-2007.

Contents

It's Still Architecture to Me

John J. Casbarian, FAIA

On a hot and steamy August afternoon in 1965, my plane landed at Houston's Hobby International Airport, the last leg of an episodic journey that began a week earlier in Beirut, Lebanon. My brother was at Hobby to meet me and drive me directly to Rice in his shiny new Ford Mustang. We drove on streets with such evocative names as Old Spanish Trail, Telephone Road, Stella Link, Blodgett and Binz, ending up at Entrance Number One to Rice University on Main Street. I was dropped off at the Sallyport of Lovett Hall, the symbolic gateway to the academic world of the university. So began my forty-four-year history with the School of Architecture, first as a student, then junior faculty and finally associate dean. The following is my personal and anecdotal narrative.

In 1965, the School of Architecture was mostly an undergraduate professional program under modernist influence, directed by Bill Caudill, partner of Caudill Rowlett and Scott (CRS), who ran it like his office. He had rescued the School from near ruin in 1961 when the program lost its accreditation, and built the foundation for its future success. Many of the young faculty, like Paul Kennon, also worked for CRS and the "team" approach to design found its way from CRS to the School. Bill Caudill's educational philosophy was based on his so-called Triad Theory—Design, Technology and Management, which permeated all studio and support courses. Paradoxically, the grounding for this architectural curriculum was a Bauhaus-based abstract design freshman studio taught by a disciple of Joseph Albers, Elinor Evans. Her influence continues to this day in the undergraduate curriculum. Bill Caudill also established the Preceptorship Program in 1996, which has grown from a limited and optional opportunity to the centerpiece of the undergraduate program. Andy Todd was the keeper of the Meisian flame at the School and Jack Mitchell was at the forefront of urban design. Toward the end of his deanship, Bill Caudill hired a new breed of young faculty, less professionally oriented and more academically focused. Peter Papademetriou introduced a more rigorous approach to history and was a leader in chronicling Houston's architectural heritage. My own odyssey through the School at that time led me, in 1969, to Los Angeles on the Preceptorship Program to work for a little known architect at the time, Cesar Pelli a partner at Gruen Associates. I remained an additional year to attend the California Institute of the Arts, returning in 1971 to the School to complete my Fifth Year. During this final year the opportunity to teach Miss Evans freshman studio arose, and I thus embarked on my teaching career while simultaneously founding my own practice with Danny Samuels and Bob Timme, Taft Architects.

Bill Caudill's lasting legacy was the formulation of a plan of action for the significant expansion of the graduate program. By the time the first dean of the School of Architecture, David Crane, was appointed in 1970, this growth was well underway. Under his leadership the graduate urban design program was established and became the strength of the School. Additionally, he established the beginning graduate program in architecture—named the Qualifying Graduate Workshop and headed by the Miesian Andy Todd. An attempt by the dean to dismantle the five-year Bachelor of Architecture program was thwarted by the faculty who affirmed its commitment to both undergraduate and graduate architectural education. David Crane was also responsible for establishing the very successful community outreach organization the Rice Design Alliance, which continues to this day as a leader in design awareness and advocacy in Houston. He also hired me to teach the sophomores in a tenure-track posititition.

David Crane was succeeded by the in-house candidate Jack Mitchell, who had been the director of the graduate urban design program under Crane. He consolidated all of Crane's initiatives and oversaw the continued growth and success of the School. His greatest legacy was the implementation of the remodeling and extension of Anderson Hall by James Stirling and Michael Wilford which resulted in their first completed U. S. building. The new building greatly enhanced the prestige of the School and led the way for other world-class architects to produce buildings at Rice University.

Jack Mitchell's terms as dean ended in the late 80's with the appointment of the team of Paul Kennon, head of CRS and former professor, as dean, and Alan Balfour, as associate dean. During his first semester Paul Kennon brought in many leading young architects and the stage was set for the School to return to a new and updated version of the Caudill model. His untimely death led to the appointment of Alan Balfour as dean, who was less interested in the professional aspects of architecture and more focused on history and theory. His departure after one year, followed by yet another untimely death of interim dean Jack Mitchell, led to the appointment of Lars Lerup.

Lars, who had previously guest taught at the School, was not only a good friend, but very familiar with the culture of the School. He appointed Albert Pope director of graduate programs and I became the director of undergraduate programs upon his arrival. For five years this triumvirate ran the School. Lars brought several young faculty with him, and the graduate program underwent radical change with the establishment of the design thesis and a new rigorous focus on design research. Digital media was introduced across the curriculum, and an emphasis on prototyping and fabrication was implemented through the introduction of the new fabrication lab. In 1998, Lars asked me to collaborate more closely with him and appointed me as associate dean to oversee with him all aspects of the School. Since then, we have placed particular emphasis on enriching the curriculum and in particular, on international programs. In 2002 we founded the Rice School of Architecture Paris (RSAP), the only satellite campus of the university.

What has emerged over the past fifteen years at RSA is the innovation in the simultaneity of design research and architecture, a focus on the study of new forms of urbanism, particularly in Houston and other new cities, and an interest in technological and material advancements in fabrication and construction. At first glance this may appear to be radically different than the School I arrived at in 1965, but in reality its still about architecture.

JOHN J. CASBARIAN, FAIA is a partner at Taft Architects. He is the associate dean and a professor at Rice School of Architecture and the director of Rice School of Architecture-Paris.

Among Houses and Trees
Lars Lerup

The most startling encounter between Nature and culture is found in suburban conurbations. Here trees and houses face each other in simultaneous combat and amorous conjunction. Yet the persistent demonizing of this form of co-habitation encumbers both the present reflection and its theorizing, a demonizing not by suburban inhabitants, but by those observers who normally do not take phenomena of such scope and prevalence for granted. Under the rubric of sprawl, a city like Houston has been repeatedly treated with disdain, sarcasm, and dismissal. This treatment greatly inspired my contrarian nature and led me to move to Houston and to bring the city to the foreground in my role as the new dean of the Rice School of Architecture. That is now fifteen years ago.

The foregrounding of something that is either taken for granted or dismissed as an unfortunate development was met by colleagues and students with an enthusiasm I found surprising until I realized that timeliness is of the essence. As one of my favorite informants—the German philosopher Peter Sloterdijk—has recently suggested, my introduction of the "silent background" of the city was not revolutionary, but rather the result of a shift that had interrupted the giant real estate game silently chugging away on the checkerboard at the edge of the vast city. It was as if its air were "no longer breathable." The twentieth century, Sloterdijk continues, was filled with these encounters with "thematic latecomers," be it noxious atmospheres, our bodies, or today most obviously Nature and the energies we extract from it. The encounter between the suburban conurbation and the faculty and our students is recalled in the book at hand—not fully, not without its own mythologies, and not without its lacunas, conveniently forgetting some of its mishaps, but roughly making its own landscape of projects and reflections. My claim on this immense effort must remain utterly modest. RSA has the benefit of a spectacularly loyal and productive faculty, a student body of enviable energy and quality, and my friend and comrade John Casbarian, whose intelligence, fairness, and steady hand have persistently inspired us all to keep our eyes on the project. This book is the culmination of, as well as a shorthand for, how we as a collective have seen architecture under acute metropolitan conditions. Yet we have just begun: the suburban project is no longer a peculiar phenomena—the mere result of an assembly of rubber, steel, and federal programs—but an integral and dynamic component of the nomadic urge that has motivated this country since its humble beginnings in the first clearings of the great wilderness. We now cast this same light with skeptical intensity over the millions of cul-de-sacs, suggesting two trajectories.

The first is a return to what has been almost forgotten in the enthusiastic pursuit of the suburban city—the reinvention of architecture. But this time, leaving decades of formalistic pursuits behind, we hope to find new inspiration precisely in the noxious atmospheres that brought the discontinuous conurbation to our attention. We see this new enlightenment emerging in many of the School's student projects, sparkling with ingenuity and hope.

The second trajectory is no less ambitious and, like it, a return, this time to the clash between Nature and culture cited at the beginning of this text—a separateness that is no longer acceptable. So, how are we to join the wondrous natural richness of the plants (however pushed and pulled into brilliant lawns and friendly hedges) and the sinuously curving bayous inscribing themselves on the stark flatness of the moist prairie with the crass market machine that produces millions of housy-houses? Can we find in this unholy union the tail of the nomadic urge that with a firm grip on its inherent enthusiasm, will allow us to recover the hopes and dreams that motivated the first generation of suburban denizens?

LARS LERUP is the dean and William Ward Watkin Professor of Architecture at Rice School of Architecture.

The Primacy of Space

Albert Pope

1. ALTER-URBANISM.

The contemporary city, the city that is, at this moment, under construction, is invisible. Despite the fact that it is lived in by millions of people, that it is endlessly reproduced, debated in learned societies, and suffered on a daily basis, the conceptual framework that would allow us to see it is conspicuously lacking. While the contemporary city remains everywhere and always seen, it is fully transparent to the urban conceptions under which we continue to operate.

These conceptions—the way we actively "think" the city—seem, at present, incapable of expanding to include the radically divergent formations of contemporary urbanism. The result is a brutal world of collective neglect, very nearly dropped from the consciousness of its inhabitants. Viewed out the window of a train or plane, in the background of televised newscasts, or through the ubiquitous windshield, what passes for the city is a field of unloved buildings persisting at the edges of a heedless and distracted vision. The Megalopolis has been not so much forgotten or deliberately ignored, as it has gone unseen.

The inadequacy of a conceptual framework is tied to the process of urban production that has been underway for the past fifty years. The contemporary city is, for the most part, understood as a sub-set of known urban conventions in the process of formation. Read as a literal extension of the conventional prewar urban core—as a sub-urb—it is implicitly understood to carry, in premature formation, the qualities and characteristics of the more mature form of urbanism found in the core. Yet, as suburban growth continues, it is apparent that the urban/sub-urban dynamic is failing. Contemporary urban development is not sub-development rather it is alter-development. As time passes, and the sheer size of new construction approaches a critical mass, it becomes less and less plausible to regard the contemporary city in a subordinate relation to anything at all. It must finally be recognized that new

development is less an extension or outgrowth of the core than a unique organism, presently at the brink of overwhelming its host.

As a form of parasite, the contemporary city possesses characteristics completely alien to its conventional urban sponsor. What was yesterday an innocuous extension of conventional form today turns out to be, not a "suburb," but an entirely unprecedented type of urban development. The contemporary city is much less about an extension of known convention than its antithesis, an inversion driven by rapidly accelerating curves of development, unprecedented demographic shifts, unique political catastrophes, and exotic economies of desire, all foreign to the forces which drove traditional urban development. It is necessary to separate this new parasitic city from its identification with the host, from its conceptual moorings as mere urban supplement and, after nearly fifty years of construction, attempt to raise it into discourse.

2. THE ECLIPSE OF FORM.

There remain, however, serious blockages to such a conceptual re-orientation. Among the greatest is that the contemporary city is not an identifiable object or "entity." Its characteristic dissipation and dispersion establish a complexity that is difficult to grasp as anything other than a statistical construct. As such, it remains conceptually transparent to participants of a discourse bound to the analysis and design of discrete and identifiable objects and spaces.

As proposed many times, from *Garden Cities of Tomorrow*, to *The New City*, to *Learning from Las Vegas*, to *S,M,L,XL*, it is not built form which characterizes the contemporary city, but the immense spaces over which built form has little or no control. These spaces, which overwhelm the architectural gesture, ultimately dominate the contemporary urban environment. Vast parking lots, continuous or sporadic zones of urban decay, undeveloped or razed parcels, huge public parks, corporate plazas, high speed roads and urban expressways, the now requisite *cordon sanitaire* surrounding office parks, industrial parks, theme parks, malls and subdivisions are characteristic spaces which have failed to become the focus of significant investigation. As a result the characteristic spaces of contemporary urban production remain virtually unseen and under-theorized. Without adequate conceptual access to these amorphous, unquantifiable spaces, the contemporary city remains inaccessible not only to those who live in it, but to those who design it.

This inaccessibility exists for the simple reason that the characteristic spaces of the contemporary city are not identifiable entities, but rather are absences, gaps, lacunae, hiatuses, or ellipses that our commodity-bound words, buildings and places are unable to account for. Architects and planners stick to the discrete and the designable, even if their efforts prove to be undermined by forces beyond their control. Against such forces, designers must retreat to myopic self-examination or, more frequently in urban discourse, to a time when form was indisputably privileged. What the city has been or could be, as a formal entity, dominates academic and professional thinking. This retreat to the logic of form is a transparent attempt to retain our professional prerogatives, our fixation with the known and designable, to the neglect of the actual state of the contemporary urban environment. There often seems no greater priority than to preserve, against all evidence to the contrary, the primacy of built form.

The difficulty in generating discourse around the actual qualities of the contemporary city stems from a near universal inability to abandon a preoccupation, not with form itself, but with the primacy of form in the contemporary urban environment. This insistence on primacy preempts the ability to conceptualize any characteristic absence or lack without transforming it into something else, that is, into something architectural. The characteristic absence of contemporary urban space cannot be confronted directly by design discourse. Despite all claims to the contrary, nothing could be farther removed from contemporary urban realities than the old avant-garde tendency (operating at least since Piranesi) to construct absence, or to articulate, with all metaphysical ostentation, the architectural "Void." Such exercises imply direct design intervention into a space that, by granting priority to design of form, becomes the kind of fixed and determined entity that the contemporary city conspicuously lacks.

The fallacy of constructing such a model of absence is that it produces something other than what the city is. Attempts to reinstate the privileges of design in the contemporary city do not correspond to the unconstructed kind of absence characteristic of megalopolitan production. This absence, like chaos, is not susceptible to conventional design intervention. It cannot be set up as an analytic or a design model. To state the obvious, when absence is focused on, it loses its distinguishing qualities and becomes presence. Ignoring this situation leads to the familiar, futile exercises in which developers and architects seek to formally intervene in the contemporary environment. The attempt to affect vast expanses of space with ineffectual "design" gestures ignores rather than confronts the overwhelming scale of the context. This constitutes a paradox for the discipline, where the quality of space that is most characteristic of contemporary urbanism ultimately remains inaccessible to direct design intervention.

3. SPACE/FORM.

A critique of the primacy of built form in the contemporary urban environment need not lead to the paralysis, absurdity, nihilism, irony, commercial prostitution, or the despair of an aspiring form-maker. A rejection of the primacy of form is not a rejection of urban form itself, but of its privileged status in an environment where it clearly has none. Acceding to this diminished status is not a capitulation of professional prerogatives, nor is it a betrayal of the discipline's principles. On the contrary, it opens up another set of possibilities that a continuing denial of the contemporary situation otherwise obscures. Only by abandoning the primacy of built form is it possible to reposition form so that it may effectively respond to a city dominated by space.

One of the most basic relations in the logic of conventional urban development is the working dialectic between built form and urban space. This subtle and shifting dialectic is best expressed in, for example, the association between a piazza and a campanile, a cathedral and a *parvis* or, more simply, the association between an urban street and a façade. This particular dialectic establishes, in large part, the autonomous logic of historical urban development. Despite the more recent dominance of space, such logic obtains in the contemporary city of space. The interaction between space and form continues to be a vital urban relation, but this relation may be exploited only if the recent and radical shift toward the spatial is acknowledged. The potential of significant architectural intervention in the contemporary city lies in the assertion that form can yet effect space as space continues to effect form.

The dramatic skewing of the dialectic toward the spatial is key to a revised strategy of urban intervention. Out of a rigorous analysis of the contemporary city, a so-called "post-urban" strategy of intervention emerges. Given the continued interrelation between contemporary space and form, it is possible to draft an "oblique" urban strategy that aims indirectly at the primary target of space through a secondary intervention of form. While built form is clearly subordinate, the dialectic between space and form remains operative, if not actually heightened, by the primacy of space. By forgoing attempts to regain its privileged status, built form can emerge as a strictly secondary or subordinate intervention that is nevertheless capable of engaging the primacy of space.

The idea presented in *Ladders* aims precisely at this inverted status between contemporary urban space and form. The intent is to identify and elaborate an operative dialectic and reposition contemporary urban space in relation to it. What would otherwise be an obvious course of action is blocked, however, by the inability to see and understand the qualities of contemporary urban space. While a coherent logic between urban space and form may exist in the contemporary city, the traditional primacy of built form must be reversed. It is interesting today to see the most strident polemicists—many of them unabashed formalists—privileging built form in complete disregard for the dominance of space. Regardless of whether specific architectural vocabularies are revolutionary or reactionary, the privileging of form amounts to a certain paralysis with regard to effective intervention. To deny the primacy of space is to sustain a blindness to the greater urban realities whose effects remain transparent to contemporary imagination.

4. SPACE / TIME.

Before outlining a more informed version of space/form, it is necessary to note another strategy that forcefully challenged the privileged status of architectural form. As far back as 1932, a critique of conventional urban strategies emerged from the familiar if still surprising urban polemic of Frank Lloyd Wright. In his book, *The Disappearing City*, Wright advocated an extreme dispersion of urban form into a continuous landscape, far more radical than any proposed before or since. Broadacre City rejected not only the centralization and monumentality pursued by Le Corbusier and others, but any significant urban aggregation whatsoever. The project suggested not simply deurbanization, but an evanescent regional dispersal—the complete disappearance of the city. In support of the disappearance, Wright articulated a new analytical formulation: "… not only have space values entirely changed to time values, now ready to form new standards of movement measurement, but a new sense of spacing based upon speed is here… And, too, the impact of this sense of space has already engendered fresh spiritual as well as physical values."[1] This polemical association of urban space with time was for Wright a necessary conceptual reorientation to contemporary urban development, a reorientation still remarkably convincing. Reiterated in the 1950's by Melvin Webber (1963) and again in the 1970's by Paul Virilio (1991), this conjunction of space and time through the agency of "speed" remains powerful in its challenge to traditional urban form.

As it has evolved, the proposition suggests the dissolution of urban form into the temporal vectors of transportation and communication networks. The speed of a vehicle on a freeway, of radio and television transmission, or of digital communication has usurped the territorial domains established by form. In this regard, the contemporary urban environment is composed and recomposed by each individual everyday around literal and virtual itineraries, and not in relation to a fixed arrangement of places. The city is tied together, not by space and built form, but by this itinerary executed through space in real time. In this way, time is affirmed as the legitimate increment of contemporary urban "dimension." The disappearance of the city occurs when form completely dissolves as it is disengaged from space and space is engaged by speed as it is measured over time. As space/form becomes space/time, new rules of urban development

emerge supplanting the traditional dialectic between space and built form. On the overthrow of form, Virilio is clear:

> Are we prepared to accept a reversal of all philosophical meaning… to consider movement and acceleration not as displacement but rather as emplacement, an emplacement without any precise place, without geometric or geographic localization, as with the particles of quantum mechanics? We must at least resolve ourselves to losing the sense of our senses, common sense and certainties, in the material of representation. We must be ready to lose our morphological illusions about physical dimensions. [2]

This seemingly inevitable abdication of physical form is the flip side of the privilege of form. The extremes being promoted range from the absolute primacy of built form to the absolute irrelevance of built form. There is little doubt that form is dissolving, that the city is in fact disappearing into the periphery, and that the dynamic of speed has overwritten our most fundamental urban certainties. Yet, it is also true that this dissolution of form will never be complete, that urban substance will not dissolve to zero. Form will never become fully transparent to our activities, be those activities muscular, mechanical, electronic or cerebral. We must remain skeptical of the Ultimate Liquidation— of "losing the sense of our senses, common sense and certainties"—and of whom this liquidation actually serves. Until the body becomes finally and fully digitized, there must always be an accounting of form and an effort to enlist its remainder into positive outcomes. No matter how intense the maelstrom of modernization becomes, how fully colonized by technologies, or how subjected we are to scientific analyses, industrial processes, corporate power, demographic upheavals, cataclysmic growth, digital revolutions, bureaucratic organization, global economic transformations, there is always a remainder of form, and this remainder belongs to us. If only it can be effectively seen, understood and engaged. The city—under the dramatic and often disastrous process of transformation—will not be replaced by nothing.

At this point, it is perhaps clear that the oblique strategy outlined above lies somewhere between the primacy of form and the irrelevance of form. In addressing the radical skewing of the dialectic between form and space, we are affirming the validity of formal strategies; simply because built form is subordinate to space, it is not irrelevant. In this case, we have chosen an approach that prefers space over time in its ability to enter into a material relation with form, these diminished formal prerogatives constitute the basis of architectural activity.

5. AUTONOMOUS FORM IN A CITY OF SPACE.

While it is clear that built form is secondary to the primacy of space, the logic of form itself has never been more apparent than in the patterns of contemporary urban expansion. It is necessary to emphasize this distinction between built form, which is actual construction, and form itself, which constitutes the abstract, autonomous logic of the city that both precedes and succeeds built form. This definition of urban form specifies the important distinction between form and a specific design based on that form. The logic of the urban grid, for example, precedes specific grid design. An actual city grid may be rectilinear or square, it may be based on regular or irregular intervals, or it may not even be orthogonal at all. It may be curvilinear, skewed or wracked. Whatever the particular design, it remains a grid as long as it maintains the independent, internal logic that is unique to the grid form. Precisely how such an internal logic is established is a recurrent subject of architectural debate. The logic is sometimes thought to be transcendent, always indexing "first causes" or the origins of urban form (Rossi). At other times the logic is established as it evolves over time and constitutes a codified urban typology unique to the discipline and its traditions (Argan). At still other times, the logic is seen to arise, not from urban construction at all, but from mimetic procedures that engage a wide range of natural phenomena, specifically from biological forms or biological "systems" (Thompson). Whether typology is justified by first causes, customary usage or mimesis is not the point. Each of these formal approaches attempts to discern the continuity of self-governing forces existing beneath the apparent order of things. The bottom line is that urban form and thus the city is always imagined to be, to some degree, autonomous.

In modern architecture, autonomy has always been regarded skeptically. In the context of functional and technical determinism, the idea is practically laughable. Given the apparent irrelevance of design interests in the decisive processes of megalopolitan development, the idea that "form follows form" strikes one as an extravagant academic conceit. In the face of such skepticism, it will be argued that urban form maintains a degree of autonomy that operates beneath the apparently comprehensive economic and bureaucratic contingencies that drive its realization. It will be argued that contemporary urban form—in this case the urban grid itself—is presently undergoing a relatively *autonomous process of transformation*. The step-by-step fragmentation transforms the continuous *gridiron* organization into a discontinuous *cul-de-sac* organization. This staged fragmentation is the autonomous process. It is grid fragmentation that has altered the conventional relation between contemporary urban space and built form and brought about, not only the primacy of space, but also a dramatic reversal of the grid's traditional organizational properties. This brought on the emergence of an altogether separate and distinct form of urban organization that I have identified as the "ladder."

Ladders traced the autonomous attrition of the grid through 20th-century urban development and identified the precise point in that process when the contemporary dialectic between urban space and built form first emerges. It is possible to reduce this evolution to a series of precise stages. The first stage involves an analysis of the qualities of the prewar gridiron city and the existence of universal open space from 19th-century gridded construction. The second stage describes a process of grid "implosion" and the transformation of open urban systems into closed ones. This implosion involves the fragmentation of the continuous grid and the consolidation of a new form of organization based on the ladder. The third stage concerns the inundation of space into conventional urban fabric resulting in the creation of a new bureaucratic battlefield, the "inner city." The final stage of development traces the evolution of the grid in greenfield sites where it transforms into a new type of urban organization. Beneath these surface transformations, the ladder is seen to be asserting itself in ever-greater clarity up to the final stages.

Traditional formal analyses have been regarded as instrumental inasmuch as they have distilled design strategies down to an established typological base. Such is not the case here. Typology derives from the dominance of form. It is simply not meaningful to establish a typology of form in a city of space. The value of the analysis thus derives, not from explicit intervention strategies, but from the identification and elaboration of the unseen potential of Megalopolis. It is most urgent that contemporary urban space and form be seen, and that a coherent identity can be conceptualized or "thought." If the city cannot be thought then, regardless of the quality of its interventions, it ceases to be an object of individual or collective concern. In the end, such indifference only promotes an unspoken acquiescence to the forces which otherwise drive its development.

Notes

1. Robert Fishman, "Space, Time and Sprawl." (London, *Architectural Design*. Vol 64; No. 3/4, 1994) p. 46.

2. Virilio, Paul. *Lost Dimension*. (New York: Semiotext(e), 1991) p. 19.

This essay originally appeared in *Ladders*, Architecture at Rice 34, co-published with Princeton Architectural Press, 1996.

ALBERT POPE is the Gus Sessions Wortham Professor of Architecture at Rice School of Architecture.

Everything must move

Ambiguous destinies

"The one who owns the sewage owns the city."—Dick Tracy

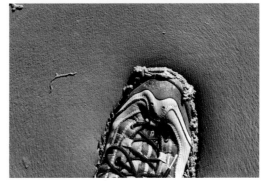

Selection of photos taken on various trips (above and previous spread)

←Houston, Inside Slowly

These images were located and selected, through a combination of mapping investigations and an informed personal curiosity, to act as potential destinations in an itinerary of walking the city. Typically, I began a trip with a Metro bus ride to the far terminus of the route, which at times positioned me over thirty miles from downtown, but never outside of the city limits. Then I headed home, so to speak.

When Houston looks at itself, it is usually through a windshield. As Reyner Banham realized in Los Angeles, one must learn to drive in order to experience the city at the rate and scale for which it is designed. The car is an appropriate analytical tool for investigating an urban condition in which large distances must be traversed quickly in order to maintain urban cohesion and experiential continuity.

It is not necessary to slow oneself down in order to recognize the existence of other spaces, spaces that do not conform to general urban use patterns. One can "see" them at seventy miles per hour. Yet what if the object of research is not spatial continuity, but rather the very thing that this continuity divides, omits, and jumps over? Such an urban residuum is not designed for, or used at, breakneck speeds. It must be examined at a much slower pace, the speed of a bulldozer, or perhaps a pedestrian—a relative crawl. To actually enter and investigate this space requires a wholesale elimination of the mechanisms that allow the city to operate in the first place. There are significant breaks in urban space that cannot be understood from the thirtieth floor or even from the sidewalk.

We must go inside slowly...

By analyzing this fragmentary void space from within, it may be possible to create scenarios through which we can relate these spaces to the spaces we "use" daily, thereby creating a complex understanding of Houston as a whole. Can we conceptualize the city beyond the series of paved zones that we use every day? Could Houston function on a day-to-day basis if we eliminated these residual zones altogether? What if we filled them all with middle-income housing stock? Where would we put all of the cows?

LEE MOREAU / M.Arch. Thesis, 1999 / Albert Pope, director

Lee Moreau got in touch with Houston the hard way: by riding METRO busses to the ends of their routes and then walking back home. He constructed this grid of images of Houston to prove it.

Moreau's presentation is graphically elegant and urbanistically vacuous. He's showing Houston as it is. If you've spent any time in the "greater" metropolitan area, you'll definitely recognize the landscapes he walked through. Even if they're not there anymore, they haven't changed. Fragmentation, discontinuity, signs conveying stern social directives, signs broadcasting happy subjectivities, abuse of prescriptive and attractive signs alike, mute infrastructure, animals adjusting to given conditions, reeds, mud, muck, dead vegetation, discarded whiskey bottles, vacant space, and what I take to be Moreau's exhausted sneaker—all look like Houston to me. (The only thing missing is the humidity.)

When Frederick Law Olmsted, still a social critic and not yet a landscape architect, traveled across Texas by horseback in 1854, he found here—as he had in other southern states—a slovenly, wasteful attitude toward the landscape that scandalized him. It was, he asserted, a reflection of the demoralizing impact of slavery on an entire culture. Only in German settlements and a Mexican border community did he encounter domestic landscapes where diligence, economy, and conscientiousness appeared to be held in collective esteem, attitudes that he could detect by reading the local landscape. Olmsted did pronounce Houston "agreeable," finding its streets "shaded," if also busy. His broader perspective, though, makes one realize that the vistas Moreau documented represent historical patterns, not just the effect of rapid and careless modernization. Houston isn't this way by accident. It perpetuates collective practices affecting the landscape that are rooted in popular tradition.

Olmsted, who died in 1892, was one of the founders of the Progressive Movement in the United States. His invention of the profession of landscape architecture combined his criticism of landscape management practices, his scientific regard for public health and communal well-being, and his faith in nature into an instrumental practice capable of systematically integrating natural and sociopolitical processes in the new City Beautiful. It is this vision, which is to be achieved by public planning, that Houston rejected again and again in the twentieth century. Moreau's 1999 status report demonstrates that the landscapes he traversed reflect the southern populist inclinations toward truculent independence and impulsive expediency. This observation imbues these landscapes with the dimension of social class. Moreau's grids of images remind Houstonians that what sets Houston apart from other large Texan cities is its perennial resistance to efforts to manage and shape the city to reflect elite spatial preferences and priorities.

Students are not taught in architecture schools to design and construct elite priorities. Yet the city Moreau mapped has so little need of architects and what they have to offer that it implies a link between elitism and architecture nonetheless. A commitment to comprehensiveness, order, a cultural context, conceptual rigor, material economy, and ecological sustainability (what design faculty like to think they are instructing their students to value and produce) doesn't look too relevant to the city through which Moreau slowly rode and trudged. Inside that city, there is no whole, and even if there were, as Moreau's signs warn, it wouldn't be a pretty picture (think: happy subjectivities—like the advertising graphics).

Moreau's humorous photographs of dystopian Houston challenge academic studio culture to commit to the discipline of research to document and analyze the historical processes through which specific places evolve. To function as criticisms of the status quo and as alternatives to what Lars Lerup calls the "drosscape" of Houston, design interventions must be grounded in a dialectical engagement with these processes, as Olmsted—and Rem Koolhaas, and Andrés Duany and

Observation towers are located in the open, in-between spaces of Dublin offering views of previously under-utilized landscapes

Elizabeth Plater-Zyberk—have demonstrated. Critics and students alike have to recognize and confront an ingrained tradition of populist suspicion and defiance of reason and culture if they are to formulate dialectical antitheses to the Houston Moreau shows us.
—**Stephen Fox** is a fellow of the Anchorage Foundation and a lecturer at Rice School of Architecture.

↑ Escape

This is an attempt to embrace a new city and a new consciousness. It began with the sudden realization that the city I thought I knew did not exist. The sprawling periphery of Dublin, Ireland, is the site. It is a field of contradictions created seemingly unconsciously to accommodate emergency housing needs. Now, thirty years since the first of these endless housing estates was built, the permanence of the condition needs to be recognized.

Against all odds, in this depressed landscape of dead-end streets, unemployment, isolation, and alienation lies an explosive energy. This energy, this gritty fight for survival and a desire not to be forgotten, has been extensively expressed in recent literature, music, and film, but it remains unmarked in the physical environment. This energy is the motivation for the project.

Characters in the books, films, and music relentlessly pursue a momentary dream of getting away. There is always a desire to escape—to escape yourself and escape this place. This dream of escaping is another motivation for the project. The project attempts to capture the dream and the energy, and express both. It is the open spaces, the in-betweens, and the leftovers that remain free enough for this expression. It is here, with this available freedom, that this letting go or escaping can happen.

The primary move has been to define the open spaces that have avoided the trap of daily life. They are marked and preserved as free zones. They are marked by both chosen field boundaries and constructed pieces within the fields. The constructed pieces are experienced from near and far as either

Free zones, formerly voids, are opened up to use by a system of fields, paths and destination

a totality or a fragmented form, as tactile pieces, distant markers, mental probes, or physical adventures. The individual is manipulated by the repeating elements of field, path, and destination. The constructed pieces become "vehicles" for this escape experience.

These vehicles can be social condensers or distant markers. They should stimulate, disturb, and pose questions about self, the community, alienation, individuality, position, displacement, life, and the city... The act of leaving these marks in this invisible zone will make visible the previously invisible. This field of leftover ground will be seen with new eyes as full of potent possibility. These areas become available as a kind of escape valve, a vent for frustration, joy, or other emotions.

The field boundaries will move with the season; the structures will change, be added to, or gradually fall into disrepair. Nothing is finished. Nothing is ever complete. If something exists as perfectly complete, it becomes nothing. These fields and structures will only be something with use. It is through use that they exist. This use will define their value for a particular time, in this place, even if only as ruins.

A deliberate open-endedness and lack of inevitability characterize the final work. In somewhat the tradition of the storyteller or the ballad singer, the story is not complete but is left open for return and possible reinterpretation.

This project will not go away. It poses many questions that can probably not be answered. They will return. This project is not concluded but only begun.

ANN DOYLE / M.Arch. Thesis, 1997 / Albert Pope, director

↓ Bayouniverse
Keith Krumwiede

Looking back on old words written in another context can be a frightening but also cathartic experience. The words below, written nine years ago about a then two-year old studio project, remind me of what was possible, or of what we thought was possible, at Rice, and in Houston. They remind me of the long reach of some of studios and thesis projects, of the willingness to leave typical architectural and pedagogical methods behind, and of the desire to try to come to terms with a plan-less suburban city that seemed to be mapping out our collective urban future while the discipline stood idly by making plans. Taking on what was then a still surprising artifact of the explosion of metropolitan edge development, this studio, originally entitled Box___Box, asked students to collectively rethink the space of shopping, to break the big out of the box and imagine a porous, metropolitan-scaled, ecological realm that brought slow civic functions to the fast space of the discount retailer, combing luxury and efficiency, green virtues with black asphalt, neighborhood and freeway, and cold hard cash with good clean fun. As such, it can, I think, but perhaps immodestly, be seen to usher in a new type of architectural design studio, a studio of collaborative metropolitan research and unified design action with the aim of identifying ways we might productively inhabit a world driven by forces beyond our control but not immune to a nudge or bump delivered with some intelligence and humor. It's perhaps best to let the words I used then describe the specifics of the process and the project. So, in a condensed form, and with only some mild reservations born of the years, I present Bayouniverse (trademark pending):

Architectural education has long suffered an ill-defined relationship to the culture at large, reflecting a deeper, long-standing dilemma regarding architecture's position as either an autonomous critical discipline or a client-dependant service profession. The resulting opposition between progressive (white hat) and commercial (black hat) practice generates an educational vacuum that leaves us unable to prepare students to act both critically and concretely in the world "beyond the hedges." The typical design education tends to simultaneously induce a moral seriousness verging on zealotry and a passivity resembling somnambulism. Younger architects and students have begun to recognize the affliction with which they have been burdened and are seeking ways to blur disciplinary and professional boundaries. In the process they are establishing new methods of practice that expand architecture's creative opportunities. Consumer society resides in a continuously constructed environment that flows freely across various milieus, both virtual and physical. Our experience of any part of this realm inherently involves our exposure to the whole. In order to operate productively within this realm, it is necessary to rethink the conventions of design studio education.

Bayouniverse is the result of an effort to formulate a pedagogical method that would situate the design studio within a larger, more inclusive cultural context—to take the studio out into the world to engage the programs and practices that drive metropolitan development. It is common within design education to look beyond the limits of architecture proper for material with which to supplement its tools and methods. In this studio, however, the interest was to expand the limits of what might constitute architectural or, as we came to see it, design practice in general. Shopping, as a cultural process and as an architectural program, was investigated collaboratively within a complex matrix of communications, systems, urban, landscape, and architectural design. No area of action or method of practice was considered off limits.

It is increasingly common within industrial and commercial spheres to operate in an interdisciplinary and collaborative manner. The fluid environment of shopping that the studio addressed is built through a conscious (at the level of the specific project, product,

Partial view of Bayouniverse model (park)ing area

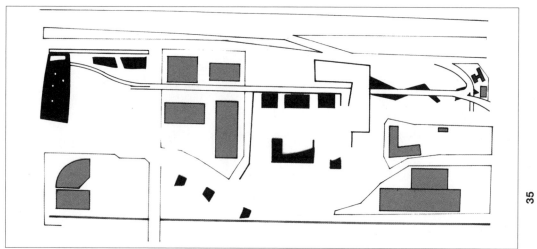

Bayouniverse footprints

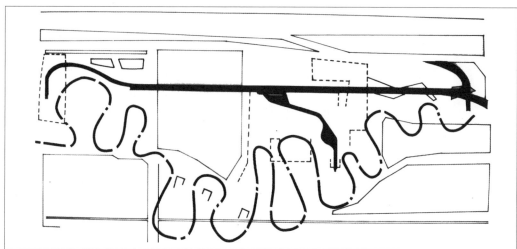

Bayouniverse access speeds

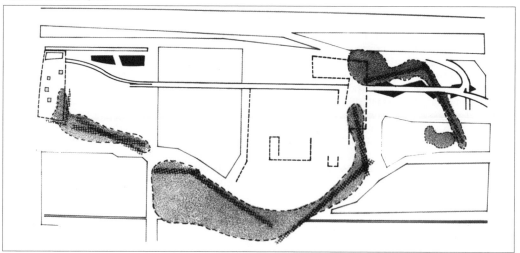

Bayouniverse green space

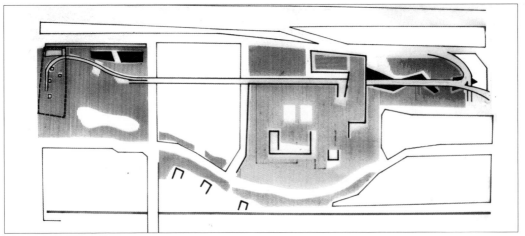

Bayouniverse park space

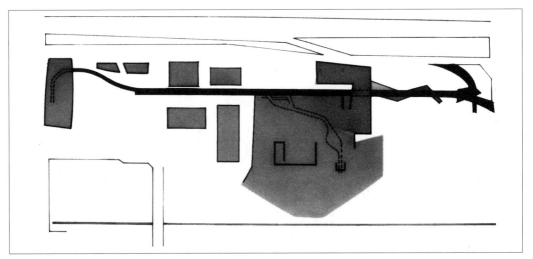

Bayouniverse shopping

or service) or unconscious (at the level of the total agglomeration) collective operation. An appropriation of this model suggested a studio situation in which an open and operative exchange of information demanded continuous critical inquiry from, and negotiation between, the participants. The collaboration operated mimetically relative to the object of inquiry; it demanded a reconceptualization of shopping.

Consumption, in its many forms, shapes the suburban metropolis. Consumerism permeates all aspects of contemporary life, including architectural production. It is impossible to escape its influences—there is no consumption shadow, free from the glare of capital…. If escape is futile, then what lies within?

It is no longer possible to engage in any serious inquiry regarding the current state of urbanism and architecture without coming to terms with the economic rationale that underpins all development. Architects typically face a moral crisis of the first order when they are confronted with clarifying their position relative to the twin demons of production and consumption. Indeed, if we are to believe what we are told, there

seem to be only two alternatives available: resistance or capitulation.

Is it possible to locate other positions in the space between? Can architecture negotiate the borderlands between commerce and culture without being swallowed whole by capital? More importantly, can architecture afford not to construct a place for itself in the act of city building? This is not to suggest an uncritical relationship to commerce, which is already and everywhere occurring. It is, however, to propose a reappraisal of our role as image and place makers in a world where image and place are being constructed ad infinitum while we look on from the sidelines with a moral paralysis born of an "exaggeratedly Calvinist sense of sin."[1]

As architects, we have become accustomed to calls for a reconstitution of what is termed Public Space. The differences between the actual public place of retailing and the ideal public space of architecture are revealing, however. The "public place" of retailing is specific. Its public-ness recognizes the desire to see and be seen (or sometimes to see and not be seen), while its place-ness defines a locale that is unique even as it combines elements or conditions that are known. A "public place" is fun, fast, artificial, and cool. It is an attraction and an intersection, one embedded in the everyday. And, lest we forget, a "public place" is typically private.

As understood within the tradition of architecture, Public Space, on the other hand, is generic. Its public-ness refers to the noble interaction of citizens in pursuit of the greater good. Space, that wonderful, vaporous abstraction, provides a forum that valorizes civic virtue. Public Space is polite, slow, authentic, and proper. It is a shelter, a retreat from the quotidian. Commerce here is verboten.

How can we bridge this gap between "public place" as it is currently constructed and Public Space as an ideal democratic forum? Sanford Kwinter's description of the city's impact on life is particularly helpful in this light: "Did not the city permit the explosive diversifica-tion of personality, raise the chance encounter to a sublimated art form, break the stranglehold of church and family on private practice and public morality? Did it not inject a critical dimension of 'play' into the social mechanism—in the double sense of 'free action' and 'a sanctified space of pure hypothesis'—did it not, in fact, eroticize the public sphere?"[2] Perhaps, and this is what the studio investigated, if we insert the notions of play, desire, and sensuality into the project of urban-ism, free from moral qualifications of what constitutes proper human interaction, it may be possible to come to terms with the city as it stands and deflect it toward other, heretofore unknown configurations.

While architecture busied itself with concerns about the elimination of Public Space and the decline of the city, the world of retailing was reinventing itself and, as a matter of course, the metropolis. In the face of an onslaught of new modes of commerce fostered by the new media, retailing built.

Over the course of the last fifty years, consumption or, shall we say, shopping has become the dominant activity in the shaping of the contemporary American city. The superstore is merely the latest phase in the continuing development of shopping typologies. Cut loose from the armature of the mall, these big boxes float freely in the exurban field, reshaping it as they drift. These stores, and the conditions they generate, were the focus of Bayouniverse.

As conventionally understood, big boxes are responsible to nothing save the market. Simply stated, they operate on one basic premise: pack as much stuff as possible into the biggest building you can afford and provide parking. Specifically, however, they present a broad range of retailing strategies, including the price-busting, catalog-like megaliths of Wal-Mart and Home Depot, the comfortable, domestic boxes of Borders and Barnes and Noble, the spectacular, entertainment-oriented media environments of Virgin Megastores and Niketown, and the free-for-all play spaces of Toys-R-Us and REI. Far from homogeneous, these stores position themselves strategically in order to capitalize on distinct, and often divergent, markets. In the process, they respond to as well as generate different lifestyles.

In his 1967 text "The Right to the City," Henri Lefebvre argues: "Imagination must be deployed, not the imaginary which allows for escape and evasion, which is the conveyor of ideologies, but the imaginary which is engaged in appropriation (of space, of time, of physiological activity, of desire). Why not counter the idea of the eternal city with ephemeral cities, the fixed center with multiple moving centers? Every daring gesture is permitted. Why limit these proposals to the single morphology of time and space? Why not include in this plan proposals for lifestyles, for ways of living in the city, for development of the urban?"[3]

What are the retailers doing if not deploying an imagination that, while not free of ideologies, is engaged in the appropriation of space, time, activ-ity, and desire? Don't we live in ephemeral cities of "multiple moving centers"? And as for the proposal of

Partial view of model

lifestyles, we are constantly purchasing new lifestyles. In a perverse turn of events, these stores are executing what architects have failed to even recognize as a possible course of action. While obviously at ideological odds with Lefebvre's philosophy, the operative modes of retailing correspond at multiple levels with the "procedures" that he outlines in his text. He specifically locates two methods with which to reinstate what he terms a "right to urban life": transduction and experimental utopia. "Transduction," he writes, "constructs and develops a theoretical object, a possible object on the basis of information that applies to reality as well as to a problematic raised by that reality. Transduction entails a constant feedback between the conceptual framework and empirical observation."[4] "Utopia," he continues, "should be considered experimentally, by studying its implications and consequences in the field. They may surprise."[5]

The correspondence between the actuality of retail development practice and Lefebvre's by now thirty-year-old (forty-year-old at this remove) theory of new urban procedures suggested a means by which we could interrogate shopping. The studio focused on both the physical urban residue of retail environments as well as their ephemeral, ever-changing media presence. Initially, the students worked in small teams to analyze and speculate upon a series of individual megastores. They examined everything from the type and quantity of products, and their methods of display, to the construction methods, formal characteristics, and siting of the buildings. They also studied the marketing and advertising strategies as they related to the specific physical environments. One student noted that the media of the circular and catalog operated in parallel with the actual stores, both exhibiting the same display logic. He found that the IKEA catalog shares its organizational structure with the actual store: each incorporates a series of initial image showrooms to situate the shopper. Home Depot's circulars are as packed with product as its

aisles. The media design of the retailers reflects the spatial logic of the stores themselves. This insight not only informed the conceptualization of the project but also manifested itself in the utilization of the circular as a presentation tool.

Working collaboratively, the students ultimately brought several big boxes together on one site in an effort to generate a new suburban landscape. A process of perpetual negotiation and exchange allowed the students to pursue the most interesting and productive trajectories en masse as proprietary interests were suspended in favor of collective critical appraisal and projective action.

The collaboration ultimately took the form of an interdisciplinary team, with different students taking on specific and varied responsibilities: operations, marketing, advertising, product display and distribution, engineering, and architectural development. These various areas of concern grew out of the particular interests of each team member. The diversity of approaches and outlooks resulted in the design of a new entropic shopping terrain that collects a variety of both urban and suburban activities and environments. In the end, this mixture produced Bayouniverse, a kind of multifaceted suburban "lustgarten" that integrates authenticity and artificiality, permanence and transience, originality and convention, fast and slow, big and small, nature and artifice.

Notes

1. Jonathan Raban, *Soft City* (New York: Dutton, 1974), 11.
2. Sanford Kwinter, 'Play Time' in *Games of Architecture, Architectural Design Profile* No. 121 (London: Architectural Design, 1996), 65.
3. Henri Lefebvre, "The Right to the City," in *Architecture Culture 1943-1968: A Documentary Anthology*, ed. Joan Ockman (New York: Columbia University Graduate School of Architecture, Planning, and Preservation, and Rizzoli, 1993), 433.
4. Ibid., 430.
5. Ibid., 431.

Partial view of model

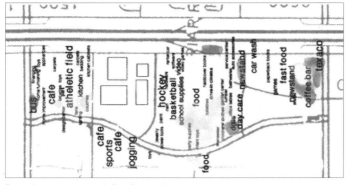

Bayouniverse programmatic flux diagram 1

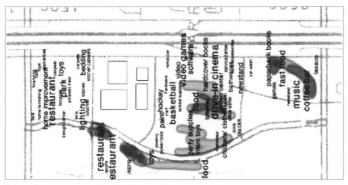

Bayouniverse programmatic flux diagram 2

Bayouniverse programmatic flux diagram 3

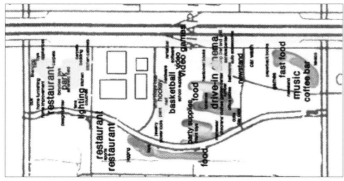

Bayouniverse programmatic flux diagram 4

KEITH KRUMWIEDE is an assistant dean and an assistant professor at Yale School of Architecture. He was an assistant professor at Rice School of Architecture from 1996-2003.

STUDIO TEAM: Andrew Albers, Gail Borden, Lucia Cheung, Gerard Chong, Caryn Dietrich, Laura Dougherty, William Hall, Brooke Johnson, Matt Seltzer, Mary Springer, Rusty Walker / Graduate Option Studio, 1999 / Dave Hickey, Keith Krumwiede, Lars Lerup, critics

Partial review transcript, 1999, Dave Hickey, Wes Jones, Keith Krumwiede, Sanford Kwinter, Lars Lerup, Detlef Mertins and Bayouniverse studio members

Wes Jones: When I heard you say Bayouniverse, I thought bottom-up versus top-down. Hyper-functionalist design tends to fragment itself down into a lot of cool or clever or brilliant little sub-moves and stuff, but I'm curious: what are some of the bigger ideas, if there are any? Or maybe that's the whole point: big ideas are not appropriate.

Studio: You would interact with Bayouinverse as a total site: the nature and the different types of programs that are present there. We're not putting a value judgment on shopping versus the park. It's a complete experience. You can choose your own path.

Wes Jones: The critique is that the obverse is negative?

Studio: I think we all believe that right now you have complete freedom. That's why these places are successful and that's why everybody loves them. Rather than use that as a critique or rather than to say that this place is neces- sarily worse or better because of that, we've embraced it instead of condemning it. Then we tried to pump it up a little bit. Not in order to denigrate what's there, but to try to explore the potentials, the impli- cations of what's already there.

Wes Jones: See, that's an inter- esting theoretical proposition. Here you are using theory and criticism, not as a resistive practice, but in fact as a means of enhancement, a celebratory practice. You see that to me is a big break from what may have happened here or anywhere else as recently as last year. You guys are kids—you're supposed to be the ones rebelling, right? Maybe this is your rebellion against received wisdom.

Dave Hickey: Yeah, it's the locus of resistance. I got something in the mail about young architects embracing the culture of consumption… and the first things that comes to mind is that "oh, what other culture is there?" Everybody that hasn't consumed something this morning raise your hand. I mean, that is the definition of culture. It doesn't matter if it is being celebrated, it's just that the culture of consumption is a rather redundant term. It presumes that there is some residual modernist disinterested position floating up there.

Sanford Kwinter: And you presume there isn't?

Dave Hickey: Yeah.

Sanford Kwinter: I would just like to go on the record right now and perhaps for the rest of the afternoon, as taking the opposite position.

Dave Hickey: OK, I've just never discovered how you can have anything without taking or trading it, to take Jane Jacob's position. You either take it from someone or you trade it for something.

Sanford Kwinter: But certainly there are other aspects of human life that are not reducible to the marketplace even if they are, like you say…

Dave Hickey: I didn't say marketplace, I said consumption. The idea that there is some institutional refuge from the market place—I grew up with all the people who paid for this beautiful campus. They aren't disinterested modernist critics of culture. They're capitalists, and this institution is a product of their capitalism.

Wes Jones: Would you say that cities are the products of an infrastructure? They are slowly put together by the advent of increasingly sophisticated economies. That's something that I think we would all agree with. But to say that capitalism has, sometime in the last 20 years, shut down and excluded everything that through history was

not reducible to exchange. That's a strong statement.

Dave Hickey: Well, no, but my experience in this culture has led me to generally believe that. There are certainly fissures, to use Foucault's term, and that's about as far as I am willing to go.

Wes Jones: I'm a little confused, when did consumption turn into capitalism?

Dave Hickey: That's right. That's my point. It's just that you get and spend, and it's just the pejorative association with the term consumption that I have a lot of trouble with… Architecture is the primary object of consumption. It is the thing that the prince wants; it is the thing that the capitalist wants. Now whether he gets a good one or a bad one is up to you, but it is the primary object of consumption at the high levels of culture. It seems to me more like a defection to sort through the contingencies of everyday life. In other words it doesn't really seem so much like an embracing. It may be an embrace of capitalism. Most of the architecture I see is an embrace of capitalists. Perhaps a distinction could be made there.

****

Sanford Kwinter: You're taking a huge piece of the city and privatizing it, including a lot of natural aspects: the bayou, the park…

Detlef Mertins: It blurs the distinction between public and private, between landscape and building

Dave Hickey: What is it now? Is it now a sylvan glade? I mean, in it's present state. Is it public property?

Studio: Absolutely not. It's BMC software country. Software and banks.

Sanford Kwinter: What we have here is the production of a new kind of, what Urban Goffman used to call, total institution. This is culture, as Dave would have said it. It's a kind of nightmare at the same time. But the fact is that this kind of economic rationality is spreading and we think of shopping malls as parks or places of leisure. It's an important thing to understand the way that we have sort of sold out, as citizens, our claim to a certain kind of space because we basically have agreed that there is no culture left besides the culture of consumption. Therefore we create consumption parks.

Lars Lerup: I'd like to venture a proposition here that I think has underlined some of the values of this studio—please correct me if I'm wrong. I think there is a kind of Buddhist proposition here. If you fall in the river and you're a Buddhist, you don't swim upstream you swim downstream. Then you have a chance to veer off and do something kind of nice by yourself on the shore. That's why there at least two things going on here: speed and slowness. It's program and counter program. In other words, this is what's left of the former resistance, it's a resistance that actually takes time from shopping and places you in an area of elevated consumption… My sense is that the park, the green space, is the thing that has grown the most. It has proliferated, taking on all kinds of qualities it didn't have before. It has become more and more intense. If they had worked another six weeks all of the shopping would have fallen away and it would only be park. But, there was an internal understanding of a necessity to bring these forces (shopping and the park) together and allow for a time out, each for the other. I think it is extremely pragmatic.

Wes Jones: But shopping and the park remain two separate forces. It is still too easy to separate the innovations that Detlef is looking for from each other and reduce this to a hyper-functionalist, high-modernist, game of program manipulation, which I enjoy. I mean, that's what I do and I think it is the most bitchin' thing in the world. But it doesn't seem to be coming from the same place as program-based design, which is a political argument toward empowerment and emancipation. A modernist would gather all of these innovations into a master plan that would cause all of them to be related to the next in a fairly classical hierarchy of value. The criticism that this project is supposed to be a project that proposes a blur of these distinctions, and further, smears them to the point of non-recognition, so that each person, in theory, becomes responsible for authoring their own experience through this place.

Model showing various "destinations" in the Superstore

↑The Mass-Democratic-Collagist-Superstore, or, Confronting Wal-mart

This [international luggage company] prototype will be a Superstore. It will be the place to go when you plan to travel. [The international luggage company]'s market will open up to include all the things you didn't know you needed for traveling—the new necessities. It will include multiple lifestyles subscribed to by the advertising and target groups to which the company will market. These groups will include the ultra-high end traveler, the business traveler, the leisure traveler, the spontaneous traveler, the sports traveler, the beach bum, the wine-country tourist, and the Air Stream tourist.

The store will be a destination, a place to travel to before you "really" travel. It will be spectacular and ironic. Travel gear will include food, clothing (from $250 T-shirts to cheap plastic visors), containers (from mahogany wardrobes to

Styrofoam ice chests), pet carriers, playpens, attaches, pillows...

This prototype big box store will use mechanisms of tourism to convert the shopping experience into a trip itself. There will be a historical marker for the first shelf in the store, scenic overlooks in the parking lot and inside the store, and themed rest stops located ten seconds apart.

The merchandise will be limited to all things travel-related. [The international luggage company] does not make all the merchandise, but they will continue to make their luggage and now sell it in this store. What is [the international luggage company]'s role in this? Their luggage will be sold here just as it's sold now in department stores, but the store will be named after [the international luggage company], so their image will change even if their products won't necessarily.

Why a superstore? Spectacle. [The international luggage company]'s background is missing competitors. So they should create some, such as Wal-Mart, Niketown, or Gallery Furniture. To be a healthy business, they must change, wildly. They must be their own Tax Increment Reinvestment Zone, funneling money into this zone to stimulate growth in their market neighborhood.
SARA STEVENS / Undergraduate Option Studio, 1999 / Luke Bulman, Dawn Finley, critics

→The Urbanism of the Interior

In 1996, this studio examined a swath of land northwest of Fort Worth, Texas, that was connected to the world through its own airport, rail line, and network of highways, a place where corporations could store goods, tariff-free, for up to thirty days. Within the context of this dynamic site and its at the time radical program, students were asked to develop a site-specific, large-scale building with a hybridized program. Students identified lists of pairings between infrastructural programs (relating to the site's transportation networks) and commercial programs (relating to its thirty-day, tariff-free loophole). Through scenario writing and diagramming, students speculated on delivery paths for products that might move through such a site. How could a new, invented program tap into both the private and the public potentials of the site? How might this new program be informed by both global interconnectedness and local idiosyncrasy? Dallas and Fort Worth were at the time, and are today, growing metropolitan areas with huge populations. While the zone of land immediately adjacent to the site did not have population density in 1996, it was speculated that in a few short years Fort Worth would grow and engulf it, bringing residential neighborhoods smack up against an industrial shipping and storage yard. New intertwined programs would arise.

The project shown here is such a speculation. It is a hybridization between a storage warehouse for Target Corporation, a post office, and a conventional Target store. Today this is commonplace, but in 1996 the innovation in the project was that people could order products on-line, have them delivered to the "postal warehouse" within the Target store, and then pick up those products, tax-free, within thirty days.
MARK SWACKHAMER / Graduate Option Studio, 1996 / Mark Wamble, critic [See also *The Circuit and the Cell*, page 81]

Exterior view of post office / Target store / Target warehouse

Section view of post office / Target store / Target warehouse

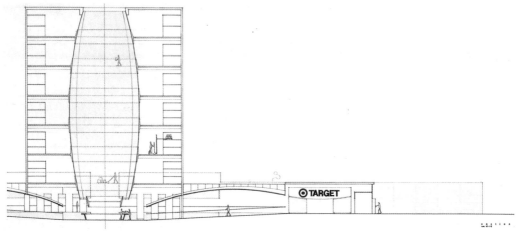

Section view of post office / Target store / Target warehouse

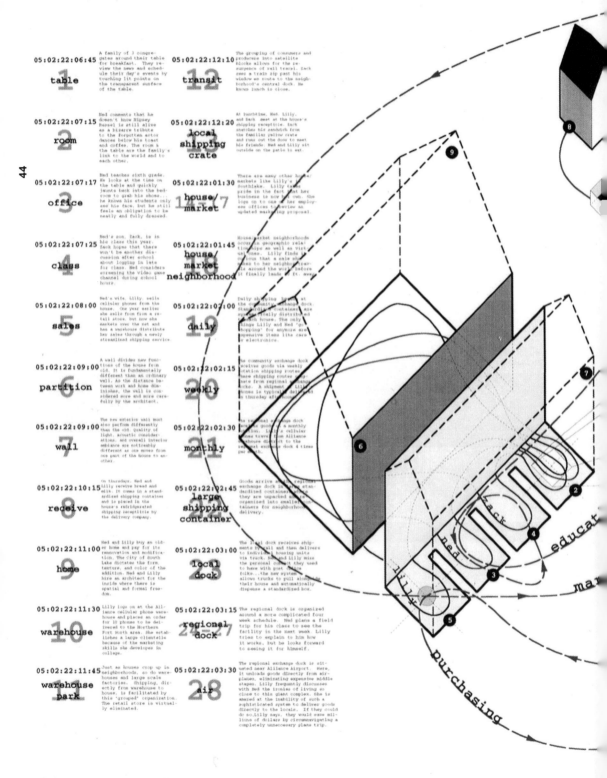

05:02:22:06:45 — table 1
A family of 3 congregates around their table for breakfast. They review the news and schedule their day's events by touching lit points on the transparent surface of the table.

05:02:22:07:15 — room 2
Ned comments that he doesn't know Nipsey Russel is still alive as a bizarre tribute to the forgotten actor dances below his toast and coffee. The room & the table are the family's link to the world and to each other.

05:02:22:07:17 — office 3
Ned teaches sixth grade. He looks at the time on the table and quickly jaunts back into the bedroom to grab his shoes... he knows his students only see his face, but he still feels an obligation to be neatly and fully dressed.

05:02:22:07:25 — class 4
Ned's son, Zack, is in his class this year. Zack hopes that there won't be another discussion after school about logging in late for class. Ned considers screening the Video game channel during school hours.

05:02:22:08:00 — sales 5
Ned's wife, Lilly, sells cellular phones from the house. One year earlier she sells from from a retail store, but now she markets over the net and has a warehouse distributes her sales through a newly streamlined shipping service.

05:02:22:09:00 — partition 6
A wall divides new functions of the house from old. It is fundamentally different than an ordinary wall. As the distance between work and home diminishes, the wall is considered more and more carefully by the architect.

05:02:22:09:00 — wall 7
The new exterior wall must also perform differently than the old. Quality of light, acoustic considerations, and overall interior ambience are noticeably different as one moves from one part of the house to another.

05:02:22:10:15 — receive 8
On thursdays, Ned and Lilly receive bread and milk. It comes in a standardized shipping container and is placed in the house's refridgerated shipping receptacle by the delivery company.

05:02:22:11:00 — home 9
Ned and Lilly buy an older home and pay for its renovation and modification. The city of South Lake dictates the form, texture, and color of the addition. Ned and Lilly hire an architect for the inside where there is spatial and formal freedom.

05:02:22:11:30 — warehouse 10
Lilly logs on at the Alliance cellular phone warehouse and places an order for 10 phones to be delivered to the Northern Port North Area. She establishes a large clientele because of the marketing skills she developes in college.

05:02:22:11:45 — warehouse park 11
Just as houses crop up in neighborhoods, so do warehouses and large scale factories. Shipping, directly from warehouse to house, is facilitated by this 'grouped' organization. The retail store is virtually eliminated.

05:02:22:12:10 — transit 12
The grouping of consumers and producers into satellite blocks allows for the resurgence of rail travel. Zack sees a train zip past his window en route to the neighborhood's central dock. He knows lunch is close.

05:02:22:12:20 — local shipping crate 13
At lunchtime, Ned, Lilly, and Zack meet at the house's shipping receptacle. Zack snatches his sandwich from the familiar yellow crate and runs out the door to meet his friends. Ned and Lilly sit outside on the patio to eat.

05:02:22:01:30 — house/market 17
There are many other house/markets like Lilly's in Southlake. Lilly takes pride in the fact that her business is now her own. She logs on to one of her employees offices to review an updated marketing proposal.

05:02:22:01:45 — house market neighborhood 18
House/market neighborhoods occur in geographic relationships as well as virtual ones. Lilly finds it curious that a sale she makes to her neighbor travels around the world before it finally lands 40 ft. away.

05:02:22:0?:00 — daily 19
Daily shipping level at the community exchange dock. Standardized containers are systematically distributed to each house. The only things Lilly and Ned 'go shopping' for anymore are expensive items like cars or electronics.

05:02:22:02:15 — weekly 20
The community exchange dock receives goods via weekly rotation shipping routes hate from regional exchange docks. A shipment Lilly phones is typically delivered on thursday afternoon.

05:02:22:02:30 — monthly 21
The regional exchange dock goods on a monthly rotation. Lilly's cellular phones travel from Alliance warehouse district to the regional exchange dock 4 times per month.

05:02:22:02:45 — large shipping container 22
Goods arrive at the regional exchange dock in large standardized containers where they are unpacked and organized into smaller containers for neighborhood delivery.

05:02:22:03:00 — local dock 23
The local dock receives shipments by rail and then delivers to individual housing units via truck. Ned and Lilly miss the personal contact they used to have with post office folks...the new system allows trucks to pull alongside their house and automatically dispense a standardized box.

05:02:22:03:15 — regional dock 24–27
Lilly logs on at the Alliance cellular phone ware... The regional dock is organized around a more complicated four week schedule. Ned plans a field trip for his class to see the facility in the next week. Lilly tries to explain to him how it works, but he looks forward to seeing it for himself.

05:02:22:03:30 — air 28
The regional exchange dock is situated near Alliance Airport. Here, it unloads goods directly from airplanes, eliminating expensive middle stages. Lilly frequently discusses with Ned the ironies of living so close to this giant complex. She is amazed at the inability of such a sophisticated system to deliver goods directly to the locals. If they could do so, Lilly says, they would save millions of dollars by circumnavigating a completely unnecessary plane trip.

Program diagram of post office / Target store / Target warehouse

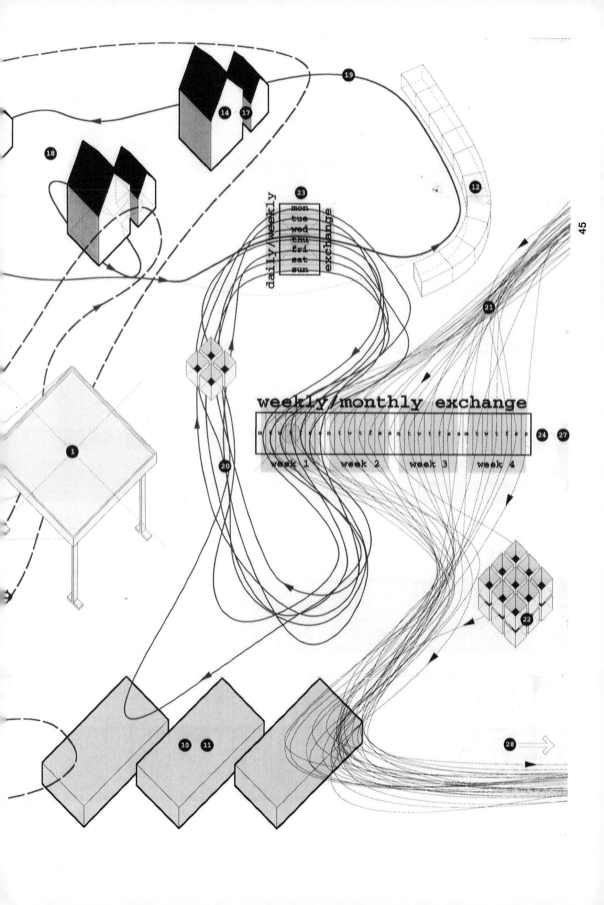

Section perspectives of prototyping facility

↗ Terra-Industrial: A Prototyping Facility for North Face in Don Guang, China

Terra-Industrial proposes that the infrastructure required of a modern industrial production facility produces climatic and experiential conditions whose uncertainty and instability can be utilized. The site is divided into climatic zones for prototyping products according to their required environmental conditions. Each climatic/prototype zone contains as many biotopes as possible. Diversity within each system will promote emergent stability and activity. A "thick roof" holds utilities, waste lines, and heavy traffic, folding to wrap over and around offices and housing, laboratories and manufacturing, canteens and computer labs. This elevated surface warps in response to needs for entry, drainage, and light, while containing disparate programs. The undulating roof catches and filters storm water (cleaning it as it drains), reduces the urban "heat island" effect that occurs with dark rooftops and pavements, and produces a cooling effect through the evapo-transpiration of the foliage.

JONATHAN LAROCCA, BEN REGNIER / Graduate Option Studio, 2005 / Clover Lee, critic

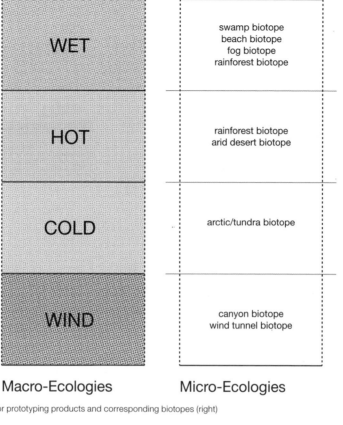

Macro-Ecologies	Micro-Ecologies
WET	swamp biotope beach biotope fog biotope rainforest biotope
HOT	rainforest biotope arid desert biotope
COLD	arctic/tundra biotope
WIND	canyon biotope wind tunnel biotope

Site climatic zones (left) for prototyping products and corresponding biotopes (right)

Circuits   Manufacturing   Prototyping   Living

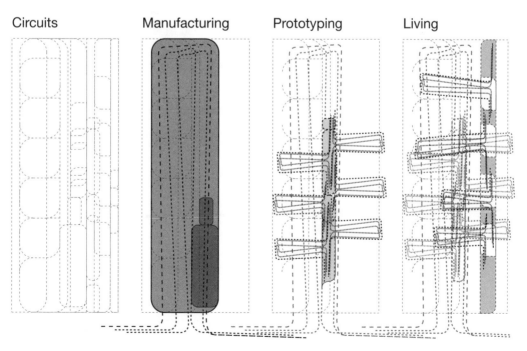

Programmatic zones in prototyping facility

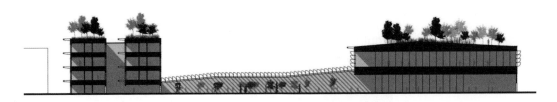

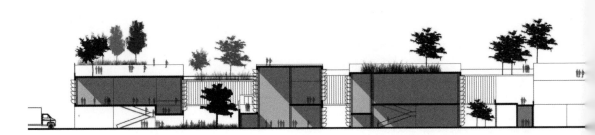

Transverse sections of prototyping facility

Longitudinal section of prototyping facility

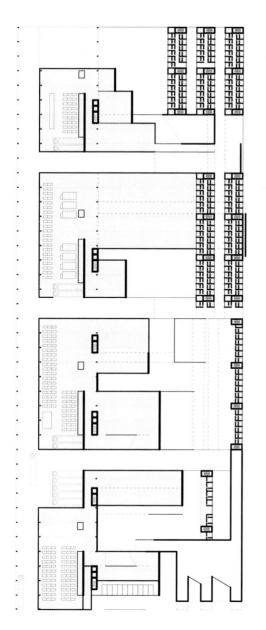
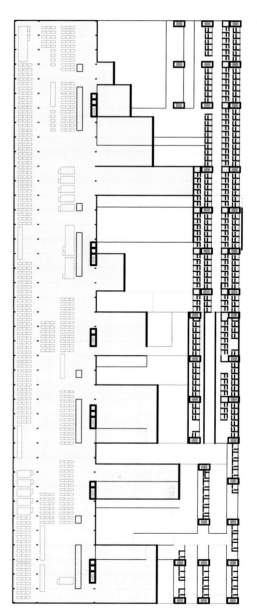

Ground floor plan (left) and first floor plan (right)

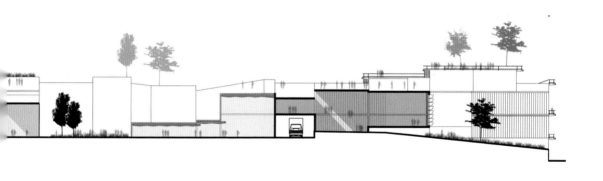

Winter Texans congregate for an event at the San Bernard River

↑ Sweeny, TX

Sweeny, Texas, a small town of approximately 5,000 citizens located in the upper Gulf Coast region, approached Rice School of Architecture, seeking to devise a strategy for redefinition and growth that would revitalize its community and downtown central business district. A studio collectively worked to understand and develop a path of action for the town.

It became clear that forces larger than local commerce and "historical" aesthetics had already been shaping Sweeny, and the project expanded beyond the boundaries of the small town. What began as an effort of city and regional planning became a project to formulate a contextual overview of what Sweeny currently is and what its possibilities are for the future. The ensuing methodology began by formulating an initial series of hypotheses, then aggressively questioned these possibilities through scenarios. From these, several overriding issues emerged to structure the proposal: connectivity, sustainability, legibility, community, and flexibility. Outlining the basic requirements, desires, and structures for a comprehensive plan, the project provided Sweeny with the elements necessary to establish itself within its own context—to be recognizable to both itself and the outside world as 29.04° N, 95.69° W, TX.

Above: One possible Sweeny future, developed through scenario planning, is Flexible Sweeny, which repeatedly remakes itself to best attract cyclical residents and visitors. **STUDIO TEAM: Darshan Amrit, Hite Billes, Theo Calvin, Lian Chang, Wyatt Frantom, Tilly Hatcher, Brian Huffines, Justus Kessler, Pete Koehler, Angela Loughry, Kyle Martin, Nikki Mellado / Graduate Option Studio, 2000 / Keith Krumwiede, critic**

→ Tearing a Cleft in the Continuous Surface of Reality

A participant in the world and yet disjunctive with it, the Barcelona Pavilion tears a cleft in the continuous surface of reality.
—*K. Michael Hays*

Representation and manipulation of spatial conditions intrinsically links the visual perception of materials to surfaces. Developing architecture from the visual relationships between materials and light (and the eye) has required that the objective viewpoints of models, plans, sections, and elevations be circumvented. As an alternative

to conventional methods, photographs have been constructed directly from compositions of surfaces and light. These images are photographs of spaces that one perceives as inhabitable; the spaces are no longer tied to the size and scale of the compositions from which the images were derived.

With this method, an approach to architecture develops that is able to transcend a purely perspectival or figure/ground understanding; it is an architecture that implies space beyond its own physical limits. Its surfaces consist of pigment, aluminum, steel, glass, and plastic laminate, but they have multiple readings when seen in different lighting conditions and from different vantage points. Sometimes these surfaces dematerialize, while at other times they are recognizable, altering our perception over time and in space as conditions change. The images suggest moments of material transcendence where surfaces stop being seen only as definitive limits to space and become visually spatialized—with the view of the landscape and horizon, when present, offering a space within which to posit oneself. This architecture is activated by its subjects and their optical interrogation of surfaces, which results in complex relationships between viewer and space. **BEN THORNE / M.Arch. Thesis, 1998 / Michael Bell, director**

In the eighties and nineties, the work on theorizing vision by Jonathan Crary, Norman Bryson, and Rosalind Krauss influenced my own work and my teaching. For me this was an extension, if not by logic, then by the scarcity of theory on vision in architecture, aside from that by Robert Slutzky and Colin Rowe on transparency. Rice, as I knew it then, was in turmoil—caught at a threshold moment between Manfredo Tafuri's and Gilles Deleuze and Félix Guattari's work on urban subjectivity or on urban life in the metropolis. Everyone was searching for a response, mounting a reaction to the city, to themes of the metropolis as predatory, whose operations were less then formal. No one at Rice expressed overt faith in

Untitled 11

form, though everyone was capable of an inordinate propensity to search for it. If the Deleuzean realm tended to be enacted in the mode of the diagram—as immanent or pre-formal—my own direction was more inclined to using form to enact or precipitate rapid, instantaneous change, to create instability in the visual field and leverage this emergence of experience. I was obsessed by form, by aspects of form that could be discussed in light of "style," meaning aspects that seemed to hold qualities that while self-evident were also non-consumable.

Ultimately, I was interested in using architecture to affect the wider field, to act as an enzyme.

Ben Thorne's thesis fit here. It was not the out-of-focus aspect of, or even the depth-of-field issues in, his photographs or the potential kitsch of the oversaturated images (à la David LaChapelle) that interested me, but the issue of their chemical development, the thermodynamics of color emerging from halides, the exposure processes, the development process, and finally the search for a human figure (or plastic figurine)

in his Cibachrome prints: there was someone in the picture (the plastic figure à la OMA models), someone taking the picture. What made working with Ben exciting was that he was making the work physically real. Saturated in light, the chemistry of film and paper produced figures and forms, but the photograph was also saturated by money and the commodity aspects of making a quasi-vulgar Pop image. The popular aspects of a picture were here—a low-quality Polaroid and an instant picture of a cardboard study model.

Untitled 03

Thorne's work was a vertical project of elevation. It was perspectival and monocular in its outline. But by administering and even pushing light—allowing it to fall, to be absorbed, or to be almost rubbed into his colored surfaces—Thorne forced the artificiality of his models to give palpability to the effervescence of his tungsten lights. Light hit a Cibachrome film and paper—the models were vertical structures, the prints were horizontal processes—then the paper was put back in a vertical position and returned to the eye of the author or photographer.

From Slow Space to 16 Houses to my own work in a series of glass houses and in looking at premanufactured building parts, the visual was always essential: if you could turn visual comprehension into material comprehension, you could momentarily reconstruct a material history of a city that most people saw as a fast-buck sprawl or laissez-faire urban detritus. You could visually adore something that was easy to find homely. It was a struggle to make a case for a material city in a place infused by money and chemical intelligence—it looked like junk-space. Thorne tried to thread a line that skipped past the semiotics or codes of branding—or other outward signifiers of metropolitan structure—and so could allow a reading of junk or salvage a coherence that might be extended. The work could never have happened within the

Untitled 12

current theoretical work on vision, which ultimately was tied to ideas of an afterimage, to work on matter and intuition. Thorne's photographs were just that: photographs. There never was another step or other medium. His work did not quite allow you to design a house, and he presented the photographs as direct experience.

The phrase "to tear a cleft in the surface of reality" comes from an essay by K. Michael Hays. Hays's early critical writing saw in Mies van der Rohe's work a simultaneous empirical clarity and factual presence; in its occupation, however, it became surreal: it refuted visual clarity or logical consumption. It was real, but it tore at the real. It participated in material culture and the monetary systems that infused it, and it also became an objection to, and refuge from, that consumption and its predatory means. It had the immanence of a diagram and the real/stillness of spent money and real material.

—**Michael Bell** is an associate professor at Columbia Graduate School of Architecture, Planning and Preservation and a principal at Visible Weather. He was an associate professor at Rice School of Architecture 1994-1999.

Mixed metaphors: A mini-Vatican hosting a Mexican protestant sect

Architecture stripped bare by the franchise

The penultimate link in the consumer assembly: highway, automobile, parking tarmac, box store, credit card, consumer satisfaction

Kids to come

Fences make good Paranoians

Estate sale photos, by Alex O'Briant

Claiming a Stake in the Limitless City

Carlos Jiménez

In the summer of 1982, I began to look for a site where I could build a house and studio. Since graduating from architecture school the year before, I had been intent on finding a site where I could test my design and building skills. Searching the neighborhoods around my Montrose apartment, I looked for an inexpensive residual lot, an abandoned garage, or a corner site of unwanted dimensions, but to no avail. While doing this, I was setting up a design office with a friend and developing some prospects. Things did not work out for our fledgling partnership, and by the year's end we went our separate ways. I instead set up a design/build studio in the dining room of my apartment with two remodeling jobs to complete, always with my garage-sized house and studio in mind. (I say "garage-sized" as I had heard that such structures tended to be around half the cost of typical house construction. Besides, I had no problem with exiling the car to its proper place—outside—and turning 500 square feet into a living and working space.)

I had practically given up on finding a site when one day, on my way to Texas Art Supply, I accidentally turned onto Willard Street from Montrose Boulevard. I soon caught sight of a painted For Sale sign in the middle of what appeared to be a parking area shaded by a marvelous pecan tree. The empty site was covered with seashells and oyster shells, which in my excitement I took as a good omen. I called a classmate and friend who had become an enterprising realtor to help me through the process of securing the 50-by-100-foot lot.

I was able to obtain a $2,000 loan by putting up my 1964 Volkswagen Beetle as collateral, after convincing the skeptical banker that the car was an antique worth at least the needed down payment. The mother of my friend the real state agent, in a true act of faith and trust, co-signed the loan as I not only was recently self-employed but had a minimal amount of work. To celebrate the occasion of my closing, I slept that night in the bartered VW beneath what I considered to be the most amazing pecan branches.

I soon learned that one of the great benefits of being a recent graduate and of having some credit history was the influx of credit card invitations I received in the mail. I still remember the enticing letters hinting at new-found wealth as I naively mistook these cards as an expedient way to achieve my building dreams. The first credit card that I received and put into action was an American Express card, and I would do the same with the others that soon followed. I began to order precise amounts of materials, having them delivered to the site. I decided from the first day to build with concrete blocks, a material that culturally I was very familiar with and one that I much preferred to the "fast and furious" wood-framed construction.

My native Spanish language turned out to be a great asset in negotiating the best price for the concrete work as bids came in quite high. I remember the building inspector telling me that I could build a high-rise with the foundation I was about to pour (as I could not afford an engineer, I had dramatically increased the size of everything to make sure that the slab did not move). I was also told that the oyster shells and seashells on the site were a proven stabilizer for the notoriously expansive soil conditions of Houston.

I managed to reduce costs further by getting involved practically in every aspect of the construction, while expanding my Tex-Mex vocabulary to full advantage. I would help tie the steel bars to make the beams or stack the concrete blocks for the mason during the night so that he was ready to start early the next morning. The mason took off so many cents per block in the exchange, and so it went.

I believe that the total construction cost came out less than half of the going construction rate. This bargain entailed no air conditioning, and for two and a half years I survived the extreme Houston heat with

two fans and the benefits of the proverbial orientation, cross-ventilation, and ample insulation.

The house and studio comprised 500 square feet of ground floor area, with living and dining, and a linear kitchen and bathroom opposite, flanking a central library and studio space in between. A 200-square-foot open attic loft became a sleeping alcove. The concrete blocks were insulated and painted inside and out. The floors were 1-by-6-inch tongue-and-grove yellow pine boards for the ground floor, marble tiles for the kitchen, and wool carpet for the loft. The latter two were minor extravagances in an otherwise spartan construction.

The house and studio were built on half of the 50-by-100-foot lot as I thought I could sell the other half or develop it in the future. At one time I even considered building a small cinema club to show films to other film enthusiasts. When I finished the construction in 1984, it included a 200-square-foot library/studio tower at the back of the property, a customized barbeque pit, and an enclosed and lushly planted courtyard. By this time I had tapped all of eight or nine credit cards to their maximum and in some cases had gone beyond their set line of credit. I found myself floating their minimum monthly payments from one card to the other. It worked for a while, but I was going to collapse if I did not soon remedy the accelerating financial snowball. I tried to get another bank loan, but no one would hear of backing an already built concrete block complex the size of a Houston garage. I was eventually able to refinance the original site loan and add the credit card debt and their strangling high interest. The bank that had the lien on the property probably realized that they had no choice but to help me out as now I was living (courtesy of multiple credit cards) on their financed site, which by proxy had become my legal homestead.

Ever since completing this first phase of construction, I have seen my house and studio through many transformations, expansions, and alterations. The two original units remain and reappear as if nothing has changed, yet everything has changed. Architecture is "built time" as much as it is "built thought." It is not a commodity for which a true price can be determined, and even if one could, how could it ever repay what is the priceless joy of its making or of its being?

CARLOS JIMÉNEZ is the principal of Carlos Jimenez Studio. He is a professor at Rice School of Architecture.

→ The Liquid House

A new understanding of domestic space may be found by dividing the house into two concepts—Liquid and Solid. While the Solid House has evolved reluctantly over the past century, the Liquid House has experienced revolution after revolution. Defined by market economies, construction standards, pop culture, etc., the Liquid House is an amorphous, constantly shifting figure that overshadows its Solid counterpart. The rise in prominence of the Liquid House is marked by astonishing statistics: The average single-family house has doubled in size in fifty years as lots have grown 25 percent smaller and households have decreased 15 percent. As per capita expenditures have tripled and credit card debt has more than doubled, average closet space has increased sevenfold. This thesis explores the ways in which the Liquid House, perpetuated by these statistics, has come to dominate, giving rise to contradictions and paradoxes that simultaneously define and confuse the very essence of domestic life.

Paper Covers Rock

I live in two houses. One has two bedrooms, one bath, a kitchen, a living room, a deck at the rear, and a porch in front. It is wooden with vinyl siding, perched atop brick piers. In the winter, the floor is cold. In the summer, the door frames shift and the drywall cracks. Out of each of nineteen windows, I can see my property and a neighbor's. It is the SOLID house.

The other house I live in has a television and a stereo, a painting by a friend, about half of the IKEA catalog, a computer, fine china still in boxes, and several hundred books and CDs. I send a little piece of it out every month to two different banks and another big piece out at the end of the year to the county tax assessor. Some parts of it I strap on my back every morning and cart across the city. Others I have not laid eyes on in years, although I know they are there. This house, the LIQUID house, I will take with me when I move away from Houston. The SOLID house will stay.

The LIQUID house is found in the pages of magazines or in a letter from a friend. Its "houseness" is about complex financial formulations and real estate deals. It is about standard construction processes and spontaneous deviations from these standards.[1] It is formulated by our spending habits and our predilections for things. The LIQUID house is mobile. It is stuffed in our pockets, strapped to the roofs of our cars, mailed to our families, forwarded to new addresses. It is the sum of its parts.

These parts that comprise the LIQUID house are dispersed across the metropolis. They are lightning fast, responsive to market forces, fickle attitudes, increasing demand, resource shortages, political crises. Vast amounts of capital, labor, time, and energy go into their assembly. More parts flow at faster rates year after year, bringing change upon change to our houses, both LIQUID and SOLID.

It is the process by which the LIQUID house is thought of, built, and lived in that is radical and radically changing with each passing day. The LIQUID house flows at such a rapid rate that it doesn't evolve—it mutates. It is pushed along by the speed of progress, marking time with bullet trains, specialized freeways, DNA sequencing, and the latest multi-gigahertz processor. The LIQUID house is caught up in what Manfredo Tafuri referred to as the "uncontrollable acceleration of time."[2] Form seems always sluggish in the face of rapid change; thus, as the LIQUID house has mutated, the SOLID house seems to have barely evolved. Material

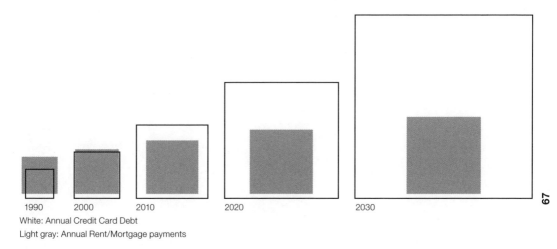

1990   2000   2010   2020   2030

White: Annual Credit Card Debt

Light gray: Annual Rent/Mortgage payments

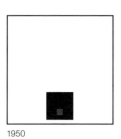 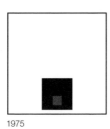 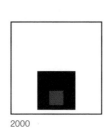 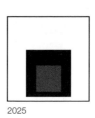 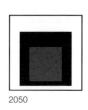

1950   1975   2000   2025   2050

White: Average Lot Size

Black: Average House Size

Dark gray: average closet space

A comparison, above 1950, below 2000

Dark gray: average home size

Light gray: average closet space

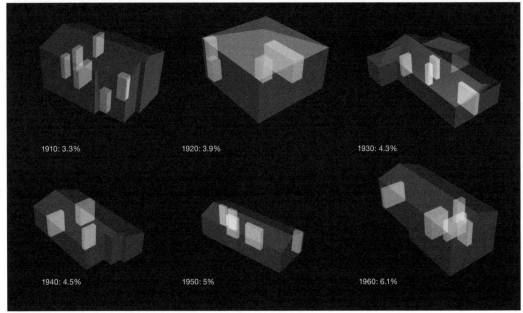

Storage as a percentage of the total volume of the house 1910-60

technologies have infiltrated it, and stylistic alterations have updated it, yet it remains relatively static.

The primacy of process over form in the face of Tafuri's accelerated time has reshaped the domestic landscape in important ways. The house is no longer tethered to its site with such fixity; new media such as the credit card have changed the way we shape domestic space; economies of scale now challenge spatial relationships and test our capacity to push the domestic envelope ever outward and upward. Essentially, the SOLID house has given way to the LIQUID house.

Paradox 1: Here and Elsewhere

The LIQUID house is both here and elsewhere. Its interior has been given over to the global surfaces of communication and exchange, making it reliant more on its relationship to styles, trends, and global market forces than to its site. As technologies and behaviors minimize the importance of physical context, the house becomes an object—one that is temporary, mutable. As an object, it can accessorize, update, unload, reload. For its identity, the LIQUID house relies on the pages of the latest style magazines, on the hippest of new television shows, on the displays at Target or Pottery Barn. It has found a place within the market, and thanks to this, it enjoys a relative placelessness, where it rests precariously and temporarily. It is the LIQUID house's ability to assimilate urban activities, to respond to market forces, to accommodate constantly changing projections of lifestyle, and to broadcast itself in thousands of fragments across the globe that makes it an ever-changing entity that is always somewhere, just beyond.

The television, found in 98 percent of American homes, is one of the many factors that serve to tie the LIQUID house to global networks and sever its relationship to its immediate surroundings. Email, the telephone, and the internet have allowed us to develop "communities without propinquity"[3] that free the LIQUID house to float across boundaries, exercising its relative formlessness in a constant undermining of here in favor of elsewhere.

Paradox 2: Mobile and Stabile

The LIQUID house is mobile, and this mobility shifts its emphasis from the realities of its geography to the possibility of an infinite set of futures.[4] True, it does not (usually) float about, and the images of mobility in housing projected in the thirties and forties have never quite come to fruition: Fuller's Dymaxion house is nowhere to be found. These experiments grew from the desire to make the SOLID house move. Instead, the SOLID house has remained where it lies, only occasionally being hoisted rather awkwardly onto a truck to find its way to a new site. The LIQUID house, on the other hand, is constantly moved about in fragments, disassembled, packed up, shifted around, relocated, and reassembled. It travels with its owners, who are increasingly likely to move out within six years of moving in.[5] Because it is an amassing of gear, a process of negotiation, a fluidity of finance, the LIQUID house is resilient, assuming similar forms in ever-changing locations, leaving only a trace of itself behind. It is a process of relocation—a certain cultural lightness that gives its inhabitants ultimate freedom to move about the metropolis.

Paradox 3: Density and Dispersion

The LIQUID house is dense with activities previously associated with public space. Increasing levels of disposable income have facilitated its assimilation of elements of the city, such as the office, the library, the swimming pool, or the gym, allowing it to achieve a programmatic density. This is evidenced both in the

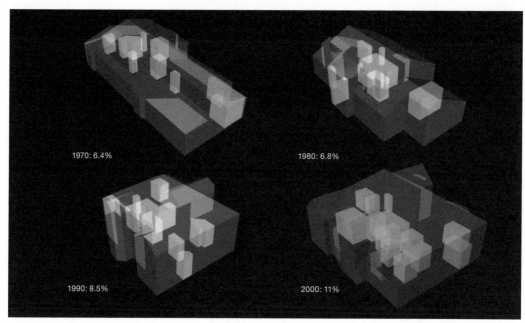

1970: 6.4%   1980: 6.8%

1990: 8.5%   2000: 11%

Storage as a percentage of the total volume of the house 1970-2000

gear of the house (software) and the house's spatial configuration (hardware). As the envelope of the house has expanded outward, larger amounts of space have generated a more complex system of public and private zones. The "retreat" spaces found in new builder homes recognize a desire, at least in name, to be able to "escape" from one's own private domestic world within its very confines.[6]

Concurrent with this densification is the dispersion of the LIQUID house across an array of media networks and channels. The surface of the house is projected upon the city, available in the aisles of Wal-Mart and in internet chat rooms, reassembled in coffee shops and in sophisticated automobiles. Our most private realm can be pieced together, in all its intimacies, by collecting the fragments that we spread across a multitude of public media. The simultaneous density and dispersion of the LIQUID house blurs the edges of "houseness" and allows houses to act like small cities and cities to act like large houses,[7] attenuating domesticity and atomizing the public realm.

Paradox 4: Container and Contained

The LIQUID house upends the static relationship between house (container) and goods (contained). Traditionally, we have conceived of the house, specifically the SOLID house, as a container for the goods that we accumulate. The LIQUID house calls into question the hierarchy that privileges domestic space over its contents, instead elevating the status of the contents and diminishing the importance of the container. The concept of the LIQUID house dissolves the traditional distinction between container and contained by revealing the relationship between the two—the goods within are not contained by, but are constituent of, the modern house, the LIQUID house. A key element in dissolving the boundary between container and contained is

credit. Our purchases achieve the same status as the space they occupy through our willingness to mortgage our future to them.

As the SOLID house has become an increasingly large repository for our burgeoning amounts of stuff, the LIQUID house has itself been contained by the very forces that enable us to amass so many things. The LIQUID house takes on the form of its container, succumbing to dominating market forces, economic trends, and stylistic change.

Notes

1. Keller Easterling, "A Short Contemplation on Money and Comedy," *Thresholds* 18 (1999): 12–16.

2. Manfredo Tafuri, "There Is No Criticism, Only History," *Design Book Review* (Spring 1986), no. 9: 8–11.

3. Lars Lerup, quoting Melvin Webber.

4. Initial thinking on this issue stems from J. B. Jackson's "The Movable Dwelling and How It Came to America," in *Discovering the Vernacular Landscape* (Westford, MA: Yale University Press, 1984). Jackson is fixated on the ephemeral quality of the American dwelling.

5. Rough estimation based on U.S. Census Bureau statistics.

6. This phenomenon is quite prevalent in industry literature and building practices. Regardless of whether the space of the house has actually changed, that space is being represented entirely differently—as an insular world large enough to make possible a retreat from itself.

7. Subsequent to writing this passage, I learned that I was actually sampling Aldo Van Eyck, who quipped, "a city is not a city unless it is also a huge house / a house is a house only if it is also a tiny city." This poem can be found, among other places, on page 45 of Herman Hertzberger's *Aldo van Eyck: Hubertushuis = Aldo van Eyck Hubertus House* (Amsterdam: Stichting Wonen/Van Loghum Slaterus, 1982).

ALEX O'BRIANT / M.Arch. Thesis, 2001 / Keith Krumwiede, director

↑Gray Space

This project, part of ongoing research, has its origins in a photography exhibition exploring the subject of junk. In the fall of 2000, the project evolved into a master's thesis document on the state of the American house. During research for this thesis, the subject of storage in general and closets in specific emerged as an important theme. New research focused on this topic and yielded a seminar on the subject in the spring of 2002. It was in this seminar that the arguments and information presented here were explored and developed. Most of the recent dialogue on the closet is related specifically to issues of sexuality, and there appear to be no available resources that deal with the closet as an important spatial phenomenon or that track its growth. Clearly, closets remain under our critical radar, and it is in hopes of diversifying the discourse that this research is undertaken. The text ends with speculation about a super-domestic condition in order to suggest how the research might further evolve to investigate the ways in which domestic behaviors have been inscribed upon the public sphere: i.e., the way in which the transformation of the closet from residual to instrumental is mirrored at the urban scale in the evolution of parking lots and other instrumental residuum. Perhaps gray space is even bigger than we thought.

ALEX O'BRIANT / Seminar Brief, 2001

Although the trends outlined in Gray Space have continued more or less unabated over the past six years, it's hard not to speculate that the current extreme duress in the U.S. housing markets, increasing energy costs, and a burgeoning interest in sustainable building practices might finally slow or reverse some of these trends. One could imagine that over the coming years the average American single-family house will actually decrease in size below its 2007 benchmark of 2,587 square feet (National Association of Home Builders). Present circumstances mark a potential watershed moment for domesticity in America. Somehow the situation today seems different from the myriad postwar recessions, wars, and political crises, none of which stemmed the consistent growth of the American domestic landscape. It now seems evident that the house and its closets can't possibly grow in the next fifty years the way they did in the last fifty. Current economic discomfort notwithstanding, this has to be a good thing.

—**Alex O'Briant** is an associate at Polshek Partnership Architects. He was the Wortham Fellow at Rice School of Architecture in 2002.

↓Starting with Seven Suburban Houses

The suburban house in its mass production represents a condens-ation of what we as an American culture want, need, and look for in a house. Regardless of their differences, the typical home accommodates the same set of people: the single family. However, there are other growing segments of the population that could potentially locate themselves in suburbia. There are single people, extended families, stepfamilies, and roommate situations, to name just a few alternatives to the single family. The primary concern becomes: What would have to happen to the single-family house in order for it to accommodate these alternatives? The immediate answer is nothing. Nothing would have to happen. These houses are flexible in their innocuous gypsum-board rooms, which can be renamed and given over to any function depending on the stuff you put in them. In fact, the suburban house could be seen as the equivalent of loft spaces

Views of three suburban house proposals

be determined by the occupant. The house is merely an exterior envelope, leaving the structure of the neighborhood and the anonymity of the occupant intact.

The second response to the question is that changes needed to be effected. The single-family house is very prescribed in its interior room arrangements. A range of spatial types and qualities are not offered, pigeonholing specific activities into rigidly defined rooms. The houses often have too much overall space in too many rooms that aren't big enough. This eventually led to the design of the three houses represented here. While these houses seem to make a case for architecture, in that it is still a useful tool for making meaningful spaces, their very existence seems to indicate a choice, rather than a necessity, for architecture.
LAURA DOUGHERTY / M.Arch. Thesis, 1999 / Farès el-Dahdah, director

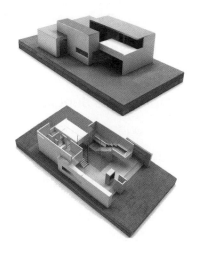

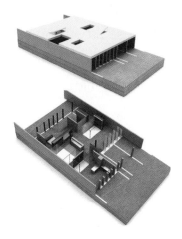

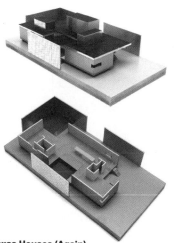

Texas Houses (Again)

The reworking of Hejduk's Texas Houses through diagrams, drawings, and models allows for a set of principles and concepts for organizing material, surface, volume, and space into architecture to emerge.
MATTHEW RADUNE (above), JAMIE FLATT (top), CHRISTIAN SHERIDAN (middle), MEGAN BRADY (bottom) / Graduate Core Studio, 2001 / Keith Krumweide, Blair Satterfield, critics

The Law of the Street: Six Split Statements

Luis Fernández-Galiano

Domestic Discipline: the Jungle or the Lounge

Neither jungle nor lounge: the city is ruled by the law of the street. This unraveled and abrasive norm governs the physical and social spaces of coexistence, joining security and freedom in a fragile balance. The law of the street is not the law of the jungle, because the urban foundation rests precisely on its condition of precinct protected from the arbitrary disorder or inhuman logic of hostile nature; but the law of the street is not the law of the lounge either, because urban substance demands the haphazard drift of unexpected encounters and fertile findings rather than the encoded ritual of social choreography. Urbanity as the domestication of behavior that protects us from each other is complemented by the hygienic anonymity demanded by the old saying, "city air makes one free"; and the submission to the discipline of collective living is compensated by the molecular multi-plication of collisions, exchanges and bonds.

The City of Risk: Danger and Shelter

Our lives are exposed to a dizzying cocktail of danger and shelter: we experi-ence alternately the intoxicating euphoria of the adrenaline released by threat and the distressing nausea of the hang-over that locks us up in a self-absorbed fortress. This is probably the meaning of the "risk society" theorized by Ulrich Beck, half-way between the "ecology of fear" coined by Mike Davis and the institutional "re-embedding" described by Anthony Giddens. If contemporary urbanity lies somewhere between the cocooning brought by the insecurity of the new ecology of fear and the reconstruction of a network of post-tradi-tional links and certainties that permits the re-embedding of individuals, perhaps the bittersweet acceptance of everyday risk may be able to recon-cile taxonomy and therapy. Our chaos, after all, is a product of success: it does not come from the slow degradation of waste, but from the confused acceleration of prosperity.

Urban Mutations: Anomie and Identity

This accelerated mutation of the urban condition, which consumes territory at an unprecedented pace, producing both indifferent anomie and thematic identity, is a process without governance that cannot be easily described with the analytical tools of Simmel or Benjamin, because our anomie is no longer that which wears out the fading appetite of the *flâneur*, and our identity is not one to threaten the narcissistic individuality of the *fin-de-siècle* dandy, hesitant between Marx and Baudelaire. We are not referring to the insomniac buzz or the relentless swarming of the metropolis—with that reassuring reference to the discipline of social insects so dear to 19th-century social sciences—because our unruly times cannot be shaped with ethological metaphors—and also because the totalitarian collectivisms of a past still too present have left their crop of scars and vaccines.

Policies of Space: Sound or Silence

The anxiety caused by this mutation produced an endless variety of images that oscillated schizophrenically between the frenzied sound of hyper-urbanity and the narcotic or metaphysical silence of city landscapes devoid of figures, and it is in that polarity between the noise that prevents hearing and the desolation where nothing can be heard that the path of the arts circulated at the dawn of the metropolis. Today, when the city shattered in fragments tolerates no more representation than the shard nor more narrative than that of the kaleidoscope, the gaze of the arts becomes etiologically political in order to recover the sociability of public space through urban form, and the so-called "policies of space" acquire a greater cultural relevance than the sterile symbolic explorations of architects locked up with the only toy of the seismographic register of stylistic tremors and the atmospheric detection of the trends of taste.

The Human Landscape: Babylon and Jerusalem

Beyond the self-referential universe of the 'cool hunters,' pursuers of evanescent preys and painters of vanishing faces, the effort to place architecture at the heart of contemporary artistic practices does not spring from the fleeting popularity of fashion, or from the late-Romantic reconstruction of a *Gesamtkunstwerk* of jaded profiles, but from the strictly political message of an essential axiom: "we make the city and the city makes us." This statement, good both for built territory and human landscape, governs critical thinking on the city, an archipelago of precarious islands separated by abysses and currents, or a chimera of badly restitched anatomical fragments: a *cadavre exquis* that pretends to be a new Babylon in downtowns of skyscrapers, and a new Jerusalem in the anonymous extension of suburban horizontality.

Organic Metaphors: Sustainability or Metastasis

The new discourse on sustainability, which is the new name given to the ecological concerns brought about by the energy crises of the 1970's, and even farther back in time, the organic metaphors engendered by the hostility to the paleoindustrial modernity of the 19th century, is plagued by a new disurbanism—not very different from the Russian of the 1920's that, before the regime defined Communism as "the Soviets plus electricity," found the source of all social inequality and hierarchy in urban privilege—which sees the city as a metastasis, and considers urban development as a form of cancer. But the uncontrolled growth of the urban tissue is also, paradoxically, a reluctant growth of the public domain, where the iron law of nature has been replaced by the artifice of the law of the street: a rough and complex norm that, without accepting the sweetened fiction of indoors protocols, does not yield either to the ultimate paranoia of the split between friend and enemy that rules the society of exclusion and panic.

LUIS FERNÁNDEZ-GALIANO is a professor at the School of Architecture of Madrid's Universidad Politécnica and editor of the journal *AV/Arquitectura Viva*. He was a Visiting Cullinan Professor at Rice School of Architecture in 1996.

↓Differentiated Bigness, Houston Skyscraper

With increased mobility in communications and transportation, the traditional central business district has lost favor to peripheral centers. There land is cheaper and office parks are closer to residential areas. This trend is especially salient in Houston. This project takes as its premise that for the skyscraper to develop there, builders must be motivated by a new factor: the skyscraper's potential to house a wide variety of spatial conditions, sizes, and programs, all within a very high-density, and small, footprint.

With this in mind, the project is sited in the Greenspoint district of Houston at the intersection of I-45 and Beltway 8 in close proximity to the George Bush Intercontinental Airport and a sprawling business district. The site's cultural and economic value lies in its proximity to the airport and the subsequent potential for attracting and servicing business travelers and conventions. While Greenspoint may be successful as an office park, it lacks public and cultural space and an urban identity. It fails to provide Houston with a landmark to serve as a gateway to those visiting for conventions or events. These visitors represent a clear opportunity for that area, and the skyscraper could take advantage of that opportunity. As a building type, it has the ability to unify programs related to both travel and to short-term use. It can also house steady local programs and offer a more sustainable alternative to the existing exurban sprawl.

In this proposal the circulation and mechanical cores, structure, envelope, and program are all interrelated. The distributed core arrangements and the double-skin facade become the main organizers of the project, both in plan and in section. To allow for different building types to coexist in one enclosure, the cores move from a central layout at the ground level to a peripheral one at the top. This allows small programs (hotels, apartments, offices) to cluster around the cores, and large ones (atrium, retail) to span the space in between them. The double skin reflects these programmatic changes both visually and mechanically. Further, by decreasing the spandrel dimension and increasing floor-to-floor heights while moving up the tower, the architecture becomes lighter and volume expands as elevation increases. Mechanically, the skin acts as a ventilation shaft for the hotel and offices. For example, in the upper floors, the double skin expands, becoming a return air plenum that can be occupied, and a public atrium and garden. The public space is thus given the most privileged view and takes full advantage of the skyscraper's design to achieve and express height.

MICHAEL KROSS / Graduate Option Studio, 2005 / Clover Lee, critic

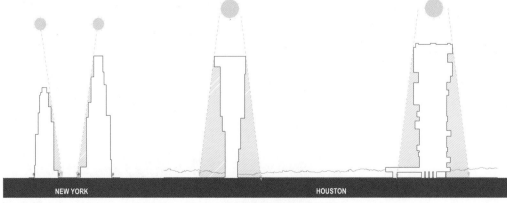

THE NEW, VERTICAL GREENSPOINT

EXISTING GREENSPOINT MODEL

| PUBLIC SPACE | RETAIL / LIGHT COMMERCIAL / RESTAURANT | RESIDENTIAL | HOTEL / CONVENTION FACILITIES | OFFICES |

Existing and proposed program distribution

NEW YORK   HOUSTON

Sun-shade studies related to mass distribution, existing model (left), proposed model (right)

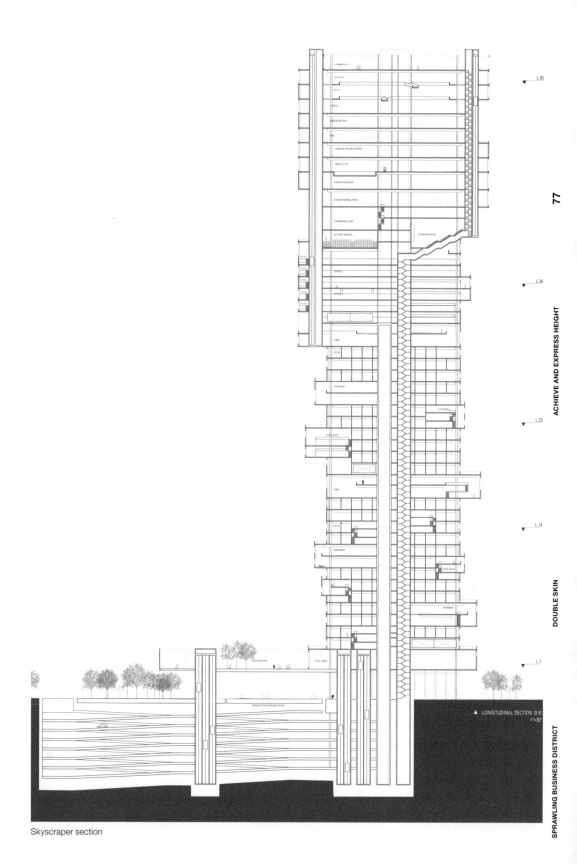

Skyscraper section

ACHIEVE AND EXPRESS HEIGHT

DOUBLE SKIN

SPRAWLING BUSINESS DISTRICT

▲ LONGITUDINAL SECTION B-B
1"=30'

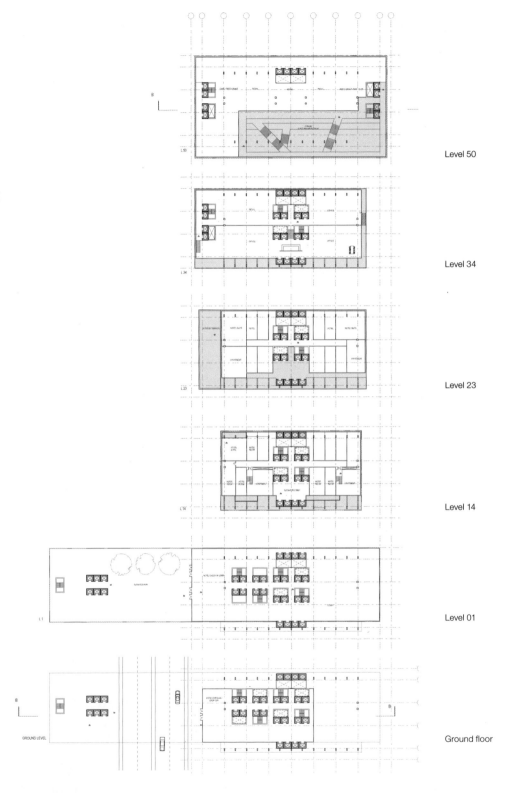

78

Level 50

Level 34

Level 23

Level 14

Level 01

Ground floor

Skyscraper floor plans

↓Tidal Flux

Since its beginnings, Austin, Texas, has seen development directly linked to the control of its various water sources. While this rational approach has indeed ensured the city's growth and prosperity, it does not take advantage of the city's qualitatively ever-changing environment, denying the chance for engaging with these potentially new conditions.

This project begins by first developing a programmatic strategy tied to the seasonal flooding of a creek running through the site, and then linking it, with a similar approach, to other cyclic urban behaviors that also affect the site. Based on a stable programmatic spine along the perimeter of the site, different uses (i.e., library branch, extended-stay facility, outdoor performance space, etc.) seasonally bleed onto the property of this former estate. In this way a variety of adjustable nodes improvisationally engage the performative surface of the site, activating an infinite interplay between natural and programmatic tides.

MARC FROHN / Graduate Option Studio, 2002 / Carlos Jimenez, critic

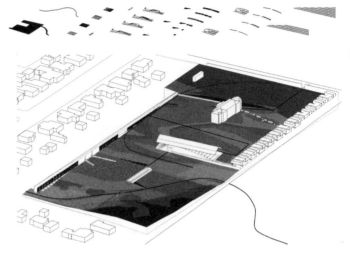

Seasonal site plan and inventory of programmatic pieces and topography

Site model showing stable programmatic spine

NATURAL AND PROGRAMMATIC TIDES

CYCLICAL URBAN BEHAVIORS

SEASONAL FLOODING

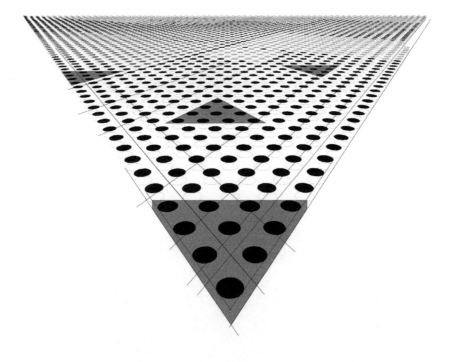

↓The Circuit and the Cell

Mark Wamble
Critic, Graduate Option Studios, 1996-2008

When a circuit is open it is invisible. Only when it is closed does it impact the overall shape of a system. Once re-opened, the shape vanishes again but its impact is factored into the dynamic of the field, the moment is factored into the system's memory. The cell feigns a less important role. Hilberseimer saw the cell as elementary, a reproducible building block of the city. While we can challenge this reading of the cell in its relation to the city (or any network of distributed spaces), it should be remembered that there was also a reciprocal relationship between the two that recognized, as Hilberseimer did, the cell's metabolism. In an attempt to understand the extreme conditions under which contemporary architectures must perform, the studio begins with this simple relationship between the circuit and the cell.

The metaphor of the circuit and the cell allows us to comprehend a quality of architecture that expands the consequences of building. In architecture, the circuit and the cell work together. They are, to extend the metaphor a little further, "alive". They help us to imagine the qualities of operational complexity and fixed materiality together. Neither the circuit, nor the cell can be understood without the other. Combined they describe field and object, energy and resistance, movement and stasis, connectivity and isolation, fluidity and incrementation, expansion and contraction. These attributes enable design to influence quantitative and qualitative developments as they occur over time and through form. It is important that we think of architecture as having these attributes as we engage the prospects of a deliverable architectural product to better understand how buildings perform, and architecture can be alive.

Scrounger
Mark Wamble and R.E. Somol in Conversation

res said... Attending your "Circuit and Cell" final review seven years ago was one of those rare instances of witnessing the potential realignment of a discipline and its pedagogy, at once optimistic and humorous, speculative and materially precise. Embarrassing as this is to admit, I finally "got" what you had been talking about all those years before. On the one hand, the "circuit-cell" approach to understanding the metropolis through an architectural lens not only displaced the more static (and formal) figure–ground opposition, but equally swerved from the activity-oriented alternative Lars had established with "stim-dross." Moreover, it capitalized on an "organic" (biological or animate) understanding, but in a quite divergent way from the other

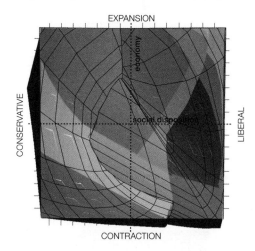

EXPANSION

economy

CONSERVATIVE

social disposition

LIBERAL

CONTRACTION

↑Architecture as Product—On System Form
Economy, vertical axis: The condition of the economy is the most influential force on the condition of architectural production. Social Disposition, horizontal axis: Conservative and liberal are terms used to describe both different political agendas within the government and the atmosphere that is typified by those particular political agendas. Mass Customization and Mass Production scenarios combined: Neither mass production nor mass customization exists in isolation (as indicated by their relative transparency above). Rather, one will be more prevalent than the other, thus defining the ideological atmosphere in which production occurs. The scenario of mass customization and mass production combined shows that the transition between ideologies depends on a particular expression of the critical contingencies.
KEN ANDREWS / Graduate Option Studio, 2001

architectural manifestations of that organic model dominant at the time with its digital mimicry of "life." The promise of the studio was that one could, even (if not necessarily) in an amateurish and gerry-rigged way, think through the problems of program and form, scenario and design, simultaneously. What has been the legacy of that early insight and opportunity for you and, maybe more so, for the discipline generally? Or, to be more pointed, what went wrong in the last seven years?

January 7, 2009, 7:15 pm

wamble said... So maybe I should start by listing the ideas that persist in the studios. 1. When we look at an object we see a process. 2. Time should always be understood as a dimension of form. 3. The circumstances that produce the opportunity for architecture never repeat themselves or occur twice in the same way. 4. The difference between a stroke of genius and a boondoggle is the presence (or absence) of one simple detail. 5. We should not always design for people. 6. Contingency is not the enemy. In one way or another students have always encountered

these ideas in the studios. And you're right, aspects of these ideas can be found in those architectures involved in the "digital mimicry of life" project. The common thread is the parsing eye notion described in the article in *Slow Space* about the same time as the studios began. For either project to work; whether it is the aforementioned mimicry project or the work in the studio, we have to bring the conventions of form into new sets of relational influence.

January 11, 2009, 9:09 pm

res said... The principles you've set out in the studios are a useful corrective to what I've been discouraged by in the field recently. Namely, architecture as a product and/or as a guarantor of certainty. For me, the signature products of the mimicry work simply reproduce the same image at all scales and operations, much as their postmodern predecessors did: the household product is the same as the house is the same as the institutional building, and so on. On the other side of this signature work, there are those who promote a universal method of optimization and efficiency

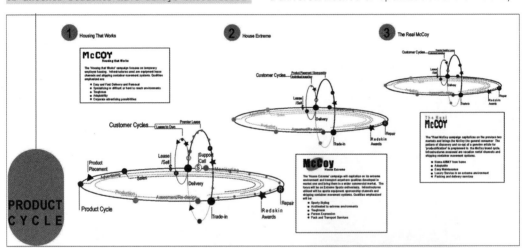

↑Architecture as Product—The Perishable Object

The Real McCoy: The McCoy project is the immersion of an architectural product in the hubris of a Super Brand. The launching product for the McCoy Super Brand is temporary housing for extreme environments. The McCoy's trade dress is a play on the plastic high-performance aesthetic of extreme sports equipment and the frontier myth of rugged independence. The McCoy utilizes high-tech, impact-resistant plastics. The combined durability and transparency of the material is key to the McCoy "look." It allows occupants to choose and display a system of branded accessories—from the original McCoy blind to designer faux finishes (everything from suburban clapboard to rustic log). Of course, the customer can eschew the McCoy finishes altogether and line the McCoy with his/her personal collection of products or original creations. The service system associated with the McCoy allows it to move beyond object and begin to reflect the complex interaction of consumer and branded product.

ANGLEA LOUGHRY / Graduate Option Studio, 1999

82

for all problems, whether from the academic side (the cult of the voronoi from the parametricists, the honeycomb crowd) or from the commercial-professional world (the marketers of BIM). To me, these three reductions of architecture to product would eliminate the central aspect of the discipline—the possibility of failure. They all confirm an existing market.

In your studios and work, the product orientation avoids the above three reductions by capitalizing on contingency. The product is really a conceit, a maguffin to get the action started, a boondoggle that is utterly without usefulness in the present context, or even a "gizmo" à la Banham: the potential "GO" button for an as yet unmapped territory. In this way, your "cell" is not an embryo blob or totalizing hexagon or data entry on a project spread sheet. For all of the rhetoric of movement, dynamism and interactivity that these diverse contemporary positions trumpet, the fix is always in. And it is a fix I always associated with the move to seeing architecture as a product, eliminating the risk that architecture is often well-situated to unleash. When you invoke the product (or cell) how do you avoid the extremes of either signature object or collectively negotiated and value-engineered construct? Do you think we need an alternative to the market model as an instigator of future speculation that has been dominant for the last decade given the recent economic collapse?

wamble said... The idea of contingency is important. Levi-Strauss talked about it in a way that stuck. He described the production of basic, primitive implements as an acknowledgement of everything you cannot know. So in order to push through in the face of uncertainty you do a lot of hedging. If the club you need to hunt fish doesn't work so well (the tlinglit club from the "Science of the Concrete" essay, 1967) you carve the image of a fish-hunting beast onto the base of it to pin down the intention even though the technical part isn't sorted out yet. Levi-Strauss describes specific points in the process of creating basic cultural objects as moments of contingency. For me, the goal is to keep these "moments" open—to work on them all without the objective of closing any of them down. Students are asked to operate on sets of objects and operations to perpetuate the contingency. Some parts are recast. Others are borrowed to introduce new combinations. If you can invent a gizmo that induces a new flow of capital, that connects isolated corners of the city, that maps out new geographic precincts, that identifies a feral movement, all operating in the open and in plane view, then you have invented something; a kind of shape. It may be a virtual shape but it started with a very specific material innovation—a gizmo as you put it. Levi-Strauss was an anthropologist, and a structuralist, so he was interested in observing from a distance and annunciating underlying causes. I don't share his philosophical project. But I do like the idea that there are multiple points along the way worth operating on.

So this idea about contingency is more a way of deciding where the project is, and on how many levels you want to address it. And, it is a kind of ethic. Knowing that on some

↑**Architecture as Product—Pre-Fabricated Housing**
Repetitive felt modular system (left) and Action Plastic pre-fab building system (right)
SUSANNAH HOHMANN / Graduate Option Studio, 2003

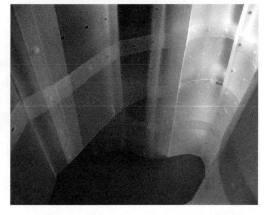

MAGUFFIN TO GET THE ACTION STARTED

ONE SIMPLE DETAIL

BOONDOGGLE

level it is all in play and the first design project is locating the toggles that effect change in a system.

January 16, 2009, 11:36 pm

wamble said… The product orientation is hard to pin down easily because it revolves in some ways around the original definition of the boondoggle. I rely upon this definition in the studios. It is a definition based upon the use of the word from the 1930's rather than the more common understanding derived from the Savings and Loan debacle of the 1980's. A boondoggle was the term given to a meticulously constructed object belonging to no stated purpose or utility. Some associate it with depression era job creation. In reality it was an exercise in discipline and focus given to scouts as a rite of passage. As the term evolved over time it came to resemble the definition I gave earlier, above. In the studio the boondoggle is a well constructed set of relationships that provide context for a new product. The context is real and the relationships are researched and sampled from plausible and specific scenarios. Of course some of them seem completely crackpot – but that is a matter of perspective. Elements of these scenarios are taken directly from the headlines. Scenarios allow the designer to work on sets of objectives, projected into the future, without relying upon a fixed, functional program. We borrowed Lawrence Wilkinson's scenario planning strategy developed in the early 90's for the Global Business Network. It is a strategy devised to help capital investors assess the potential risks and exposures related to a proposed product or service. A good set of scenarios (they are always produced in plural) enable you to act now, and move forward into a murky future even though you cannot know which of the scenarios will unfold most accurately. Not acting in the face of uncertainty is the architects' worst nightmare.

So the difference between a stroke of genius and a boondoggle is the presence (or absence) of one simple detail, or the vantage point on the scenario you have constructed. Any product resulting from the development of the scenarios is linked to the specifics of that scenario set. In a small and incremental fashion each product (cell) and operation (circuit) provides a shift and new degree of definition to the city and landscape. It is never repeated twice in the same way. To my way of thinking this idea of product thwarts the signature object because it cannot be easily commodified or mediated, and it requires a designer's vision. We all have witnessed how good ideas falter under the (supposed)

↑**Architecture as Product—The Perishable Object**
Subdelivery: A global directory and delivery service for Arctic Circle settlements
GUNNAR HARTMANN / Graduate Option Studio, 1999

84

scrutiny of the collectively negotiated and value-engineered construct.

January 21, 2009, 3:09 pm

res said… What's useful in the boondoggle version of the cell is that it retains an open-endedness, a requisite degree of slack. By contrast, the parametricist's cell (e.g., the voronoi hex) is too tightly scripted, too shrunk-wrapped to some presumed reality principle. Of course, in the end this is really a procrustean reality-principle, a formal *a priori* that requires a faith in that high-definition ("hot") geometric protocol to be able to "solve a problem" at every scale of operation. Their belief in a meta-geometric project blinds them to the experience that an identical geometry will operate to very different ends at varied scales of application. So, I think one thing that needs to be differentiated is the parametric form of scripting from the scenario-writing that you have helped bring to the forefront. This is why I've been trying to articulate a new genre of architectural production that I call "poli-fi," or political fiction (or maybe as well

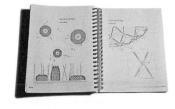

↑**Architecture as Product—Strategies for Structural Skins**

Flat-pack modular building component system for temporary use

EMILY KIRKLAND / Graduate Option Studio, 2002

↑**Architecture as Product—Studio Research and Design Book**

Graduate Option Studio, 2002

↑**Architecture as Product—The Perishable Object**
WYATT FRANTOM / Graduate Option Studio, 1999

"many fidelities"), the projection of alternative plastic arrangements in the world.

It's a funny moment, because having been at GSD thesis reviews recently, what one is witnessing is a critical reassessment of the 60's techno-utopians (of various stripes, but let's broadly include Fuller, Archigram, Superstudio, etc.), and that revival is being wed to a contemporary standard of visualization and production technique. Again, a strange marriage between the neo-critical scholars (read: *Grey Room*) and the neo-shop guys (read: CNC-milling). It's about "hotting up" the space-frames, bucky-balls, walking cities, etc. But it's exactly the plastic political project that gets abandoned in this higher resolution of the technical apparatus. They remove all the cartoon quality of the original moment with this earnest technicality and somber sociality of the current situation.

This is why I appreciate your very different take on the cell. At the same time, I wonder if we could focus equal attention on the circuit, and would that entail a renewed attention to new scripting techniques, or political fictions and stories as a corollary to the new product-gizmo-boondoggle-cells. We share an enthusiasm for the "make-do" opportunism of James Garner's "scrounger" character in the *Great Escape*. To me, this relates to an on-going interest in the caper film: the hyper-calculation of probabilities that ends up producing a chain of totally unpredictable events and coincidences, that liberates a new territory by virtue of trying to insist on a different story-line for the city, for its materials and players (see, e.g., *The Italian Job*). I was talking to Sam Jacob (of FAT) recently, and he was

also discriminating between stories and codes. Clearly, both the parametric digerati and New Urbanists have gone to the side of code-writing. But it leaves open the possibility for injecting new stories, false memories, political fictions that would fashion an unlikely collective. In a way, it was Obama's story that undid the seemly rigid parameters of red and blue. It's a shift from *langue* to *parole*, from representation to performance, structure to event. In this mode of design as speech act, saying makes it so.

February 2, 2009, 5:06 pm

wamble said... Maybe the circuit deserves the last word. Circuits are subject to aesthetic evaluation. There are beautiful and not-so-beautiful circuits that work in conjunction with the cell, as we've discussed. I think of them as inseparable. Evaluation of the circuit is a discussion relating to system form. So when we look at an object we see a process. This process is as much a part of the design project as the material facts we often focus on. Scripts, scenarios and fictions are all equal partners in this part of the endeavor.

****

R.E. SOMOL is the director of the University of Illinois at Chicago School of Architecture. He was a Visiting Cullinan Professor at Rice School of Architecture in 2001.

MARK WAMBLE is a principal at Interloop—Architecture. He is a Cullinan Visiting Professor at Rice School of Architecture.

↑Menil Remix

The site strategy devises new spatial relationships for the current Menil buildings, future institutional buildings (deemed "Proposed Improvements"), the surrounding neighborhood fabric, and the vegetated landscape. On the one hand, we sought to create a subtle yet compelling series of forms around the idea of an emblematic campus. On the other, we pursued the formation of an original neighborhood fabric that respects its surroundings, promoting urban continuity.

The proposed site strategy recomposes the existing site (above ground), reweaving existing pathways and roads. All parking is located underground and is accessed from Sul Ross Ave., Branard St., West Main Ave., and Colquitt Ave., which remain continuous but ramp below grade from the east and west flanks of the site. This creates a continuous central greenscape that runs unimpeded from the northern to the southern edge of the site. Circulation atriums are scattered throughout the site, bringing visitors and residents up from the parking level. The site is thus divided into four strips (two residential blocks each) bisected by a central green space.

Each strip is divided into two "sectors," which equate to one residential block at the neighborhood scale. The residential component of this site strategy has been resolved into small, narrow towers or "Spires." All preexisting institutional buildings, such as the Cy Twombly Gallery and Rothko Chapel, are left in place. In the remaining sectors, the aging vernacular Houston bungalows are replaced with a cluster of housing Spires networked together by a common canopy. The Proposed Improvement buildings are set at the inner edge of the sectors, creating an institutional buffer between the private residential Spires and the central green space. The heights of the Spires vary according to their location relative to Piano's Menil Collection building, growing taller as they radiate outward from the museum. The tallest of the Spires are situated along the highly trafficked southern edge of the site.

Landscape design is of great importance to the overall site strategy. Currently, various types of vegetation around the Menil engage the visitor. Oleander arches over sidewalks and rows of bamboo direct movement and filter vision. The large canopies of oaks shade many spaces from the harsh Houston sun. The strategy reduces vehicular traffic to a minimum, transforming

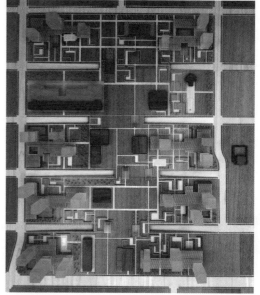

Aerial view of site model

the site into an open pedestrian surface. We propose to activate this contiguous open surface with different types of landscape amenities. Small ponds, exterior sculpture, and public benches are networked together with vegetation and pathways. These features are intended to diversify the pedestrian experience and allow for engaging moments in which to meander, pause, and discover. Rows of trees are also placed strategically throughout the site to accentuate edges, encourage movement, and create a visual canopy that disperses the imposing heights of the Spires from the grade-level pedestrian experience. The strategy immerses residential occupants and museum visitors in a vegetated pedestrian environment, a rarity in Houston.

JUSTIN HOLDAHL, RUYA SANER / Graduate Option Studio, 2007

The last pedestrian hitching a ride

The death of the street

↓Land Bank

David Brown
Critic, Graduate Option Studios, 2003-2004

The ongoing processes of the contemporary city often generate disparate, non-idealized sites and conditions that elude conventional architecture, planning, and development practices. Physically too fragmented for master planning efforts and economically unviable for infill construction, the land sits idle and vacant to the continued detriment of the surrounding area. However, by working organizationally and managerially, as well as materially and physically, architecture can elicit latent urbanisms from such situations. These studios pursue new or transformed organizational logics, structuring networks, systems, and shifting modalities that can work generatively to enable those latent urbanisms to unfold in time.

→Plans of Action in Fourth Ward: A Community Land Trust

This studio responds to an effort by a community organization to develop a community land trust in Houston's Fourth Ward. A community land trust is a non-profit organization that purchases and holds land for the benefit of community residents. The organization maintains ownership and responsibility for the land, but sells the house or any built structure to individual members. As a result, the cost of the land does not appreciably enter into the purchase price of the house.

While the principal purpose of such a trust is to provide and preserve long-term affordable housing for low- and moderate-income families, this collective holding of land (and its attendant restructuring of relations between, and configurations of, buildings, lots, and blocks) seems to offer an opportunity to consider a number of other factors—such as community identity and legibility, sustainability, adjacency, outreach, and connection—that contemporary development strategies do not typically take into account. The site for this investigation, Fourth Ward, foregrounds these additional considerations: because of prolonged contestation and failed speculation, the area is more vacant than built. A land trust would, therefore, consist of land for future development of housing and/or commercial services more than land with existing structures. Additionally, planning in this area is filled with contingency, as the trust would be the latest of

many organizations developing property within the ward.

Working, both individually and collaboratively, with planning and design guidelines as well as processes and frameworks, students seek to develop comprehensive, yet flexible plans of action that the trust might initiate as a participant in the generation of new development in this area.
DAVID BROWN, critic, Graduate Option Studio, 2003

In its heyday in the 1930's, Fourth Ward thrived as the center of African-American culture in Houston. Today the land in Fourth Ward remains 52 percent vacant. Developers and city institutions have recently taken notice of this inner city area with its proximity to downtown Houston and low land costs. Area residents are primarily in a low-income Hispanic and African-American demographic. New townhomes and lofts popping up along its borders, however, are quickly changing the character and costs of living for the ward. As a result, Fourth Ward is currently in an interesting position in its development. It lies mostly vacant and largely neglected. Capitalizing on this state of limbo, powerful forces are acting to both develop the area as a hotbed for young professionals and improve living conditions and services for its original residents.

Throughout Fourth Ward, artifacts remain embedded in the land. We found that these forgotten, re-appropriated, and reused objects and sites had incredible potential as readings of past use as well as indicators of future use for the land. They were our launching point for conceiving of a Community Land Trust (CLT) in Fourth Ward: a way of developing the land as a network of structures and infrastructure that show the potential for the creation of

community resources. A number of these resources were identified as long-term goals that the CLT could accommodate (in their various degrees of formalization) through specific interventions on a site. The project looked at these programmatic interventions through time, mapping present and possible future conditions caused by external forces (i.e., developer initiatives, city regulations), community needs, and circumstances (i.e., plant growth, community resources, site constraints), and identified various critical moments for the CLT to respond and so initiate change within Fourth Ward.

We developed programmatic interventions through two palettes—one of building specifications and the other of plantings—addressing their possible physical manifestations from a less formalized to a more formalized state. The palette of building specifications reflects the various sensibilities of land ownership, foundation load capacities, material maintenance cycles, structure mobility, city regulations, facility of delivery and assembly, and environmental conditions in regard to building materials. The second palette deals with growth cycles and types of plants, discussing the claiming of vacant lands through growth and alternatively the types of short- and long-term crops that could be cultivated by and for the community. We explored these palettes together by unfolding the cycles of design intervention that could occur on various sites the CLT developed, choosing possible strategies for initial acquisitions, slow-paced acquisitions, and special projects acquisitions.
QUYEN LUONG, DELIA WENDEL, KATHY WILLIAMS / Graduate Option Studio, 2003

1005 Saulnier Ave. Site was completely vacant, and facing new urban loft townhome development on Buckner St. Site is seeded and reinforced with concrete pavers. Scenario shows squatting on the site by an adjacent informal car wash / auto repair program.

1005 Saulnier Ave. A new structure, partially funded by special grants, is built, responding to initial site moves. Structure is built on site to accommodate leasing space for small minority businesses. Spaces are purchased by proprietors, although the land remains with the CLT.

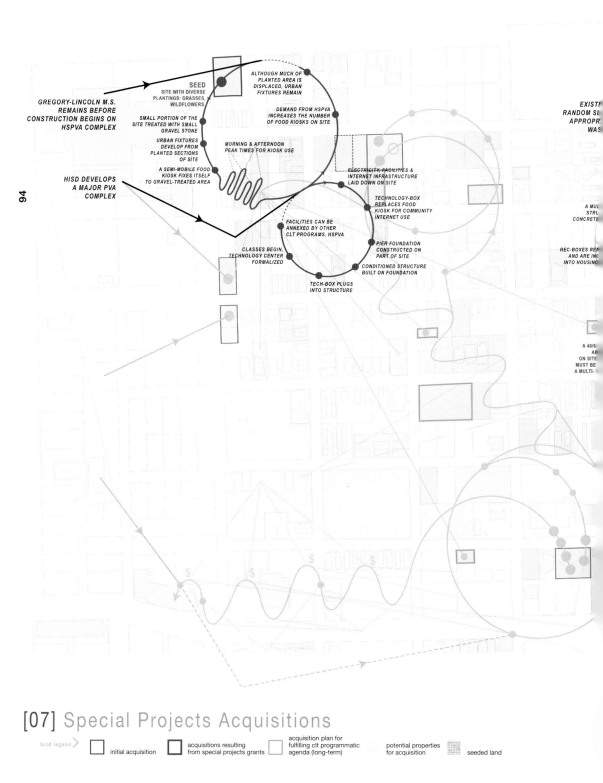

GREGORY-LINCOLN M.S.
REMAINS BEFORE
CONSTRUCTION BEGINS ON
HSPVA COMPLEX

SEED
SITE WITH DIVERSE
PLANTINGS: GRASSES,
WILDFLOWERS

ALTHOUGH MUCH OF
PLANTED AREA IS
DISPLACED, URBAN
FIXTURES REMAIN

SMALL PORTION OF THE
SITE TREATED WITH SMALL
GRAVEL STONE

DEMAND FROM HSPVA
INCREASES THE NUMBER
OF FOOD KIOSKS ON SITE

URBAN FIXTURES
DEVELOP FROM
PLANTED SECTIONS
OF SITE

MORNING & AFTERNOON
PEAK TIMES FOR KIOSK USE

HISD DEVELOPS
A MAJOR PVA
COMPLEX

A SEMI-MOBILE FOOD
KIOSK FIXES ITSELF
TO GRAVEL-TREATED AREA

ELECTRICITY, FACILITIES &
INTERNET INFRASTRUCTURE
LAID DOWN ON SITE

TECHNOLOGY-BOX
REPLACES FOOD
KIOSK FOR COMMUNITY
INTERNET USE

FACILITIES CAN BE
ANNEXED BY OTHER
CLT PROGRAMS, HSPVA

PIER FOUNDATION
CONSTRUCTED ON
PART OF SITE

CLASSES BEGIN,
TECHNOLOGY CENTER
FORMALIZED

CONDITIONED STRUCTURE
BUILT ON FOUNDATION

TECH-BOX PLUGS
INTO STRUCTURE

EXISTI
RANDOM SI
APPROPR
WAS

A MUL
STRL
CONCRETE

REC-BOXES REI
AND ARE INC
INTO HOUSING

A 40/6
A
ON SITE
MUST BE
A MULTI-

94

[07] Special Projects Acquisitions

land legend

☐ initial acquisition   ☐ acquisitions resulting
from special projects grants   ☐ acquisition plan for
fulfilling clt programmatic
agenda (long-term)   potential properties
for acquisition   seeded land

The special projects acquisitions diagram addresses site and program types that might be developed under a directed funding source,
and also incorporates ideas for site interventions that might be developed either after or in conjunction with the seeding and material
change that might occur during a slower paced site development.

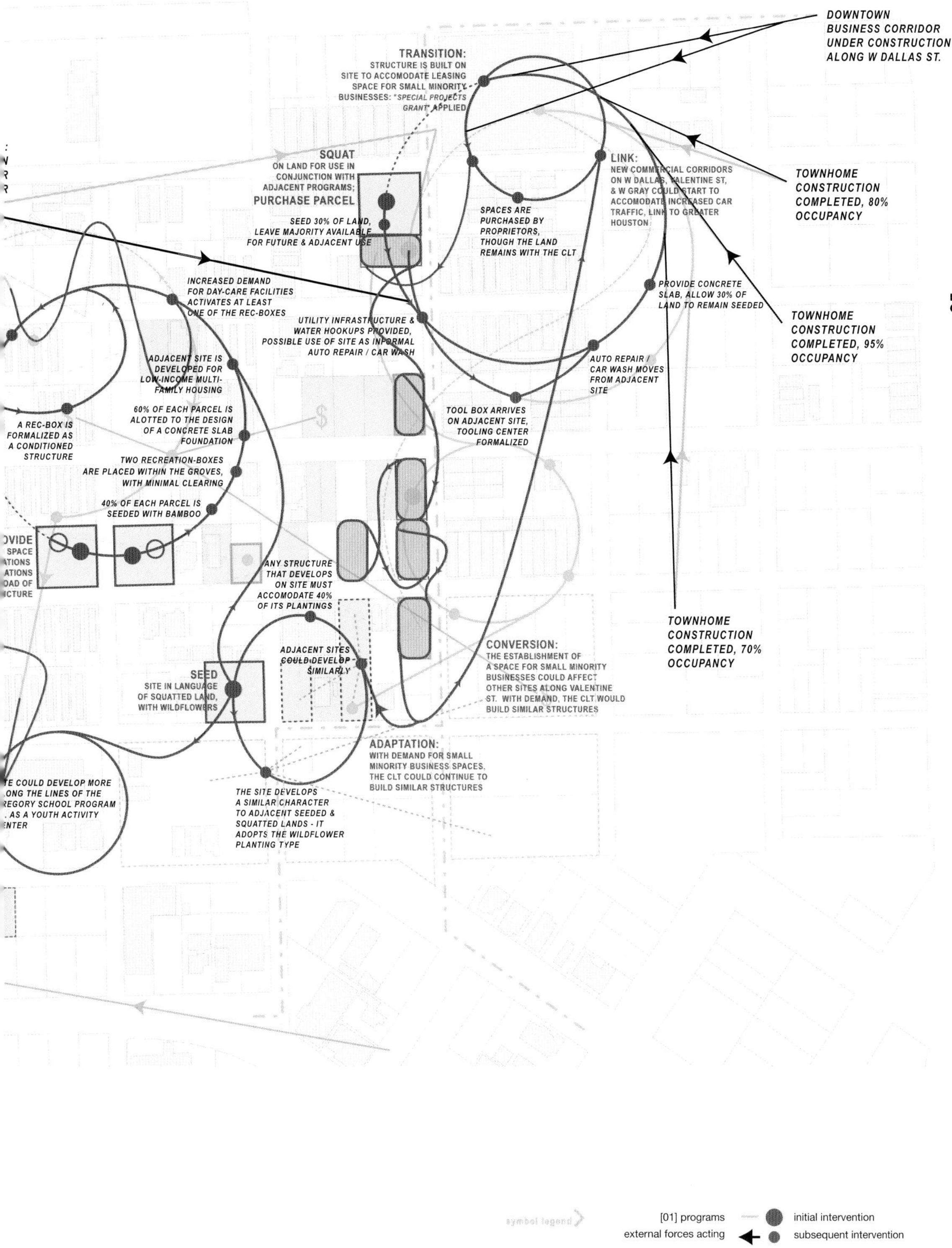

DOWNTOWN BUSINESS CORRIDOR UNDER CONSTRUCTION ALONG W DALLAS ST.

TOWNHOME CONSTRUCTION COMPLETED, 80% OCCUPANCY

TOWNHOME CONSTRUCTION COMPLETED, 95% OCCUPANCY

TOWNHOME CONSTRUCTION COMPLETED, 70% OCCUPANCY

TRANSITION:
STRUCTURE IS BUILT ON SITE TO ACCOMODATE LEASING SPACE FOR SMALL MINORITY BUSINESSES; "SPECIAL PROJECTS GRANT" APPLIED

SQUAT
ON LAND FOR USE IN CONJUNCTION WITH ADJACENT PROGRAMS;
PURCHASE PARCEL

SEED 30% OF LAND, LEAVE MAJORITY AVAILABLE FOR FUTURE & ADJACENT USE

SPACES ARE PURCHASED BY PROPRIETORS, THOUGH THE LAND REMAINS WITH THE CLT

LINK:
NEW COMMERCIAL CORRIDORS ON W DALLAS, VALENTINE ST, & W GRAY COULD START TO ACCOMODATE INCREASED CAR TRAFFIC, LINK TO GREATER HOUSTON

INCREASED DEMAND FOR DAY-CARE FACILITIES ACTIVATES AT LEAST ONE OF THE REC-BOXES

UTILITY INFRASTRUCTURE & WATER HOOKUPS PROVIDED, POSSIBLE USE OF SITE AS INFORMAL AUTO REPAIR / CAR WASH

PROVIDE CONCRETE SLAB, ALLOW 30% OF LAND TO REMAIN SEEDED

ADJACENT SITE IS DEVELOPED FOR LOW-INCOME MULTI-FAMILY HOUSING

A REC-BOX IS FORMALIZED AS A CONDITIONED STRUCTURE

60% OF EACH PARCEL IS ALOTTED TO THE DESIGN OF A CONCRETE SLAB FOUNDATION

AUTO REPAIR / CAR WASH MOVES FROM ADJACENT SITE

TWO RECREATION-BOXES ARE PLACED WITHIN THE GROVES, WITH MINIMAL CLEARING

TOOL BOX ARRIVES ON ADJACENT SITE, TOOLING CENTER FORMALIZED

40% OF EACH PARCEL IS SEEDED WITH BAMBOO

PROVIDE
SPACE
ATIONS
OAD OF
CTURE

ANY STRUCTURE THAT DEVELOPS ON SITE MUST ACCOMODATE 40% OF ITS PLANTINGS

ADJACENT SITES COULD DEVELOP SIMILARLY

SEED
SITE IN LANGUAGE OF SQUATTED LAND, WITH WILDFLOWERS

CONVERSION:
THE ESTABLISHMENT OF A SPACE FOR SMALL MINORITY BUSINESSES COULD AFFECT OTHER SITES ALONG VALENTINE ST. WITH DEMAND, THE CLT WOULD BUILD SIMILAR STRUCTURES

ADAPTATION:
WITH DEMAND FOR SMALL MINORITY BUSINESS SPACES, THE CLT COULD CONTINUE TO BUILD SIMILAR STRUCTURES

TE COULD DEVELOP MORE ONG THE LINES OF THE REGORY SCHOOL PROGRAM . AS A YOUTH ACTIVITY NTER

THE SITE DEVELOPS A SIMILAR CHARACTER TO ADJACENT SEEDED & SQUATTED LANDS - IT ADOPTS THE WILDFLOWER PLANTING TYPE

symbol legend

[01] programs
external forces acting

initial intervention
subsequent intervention

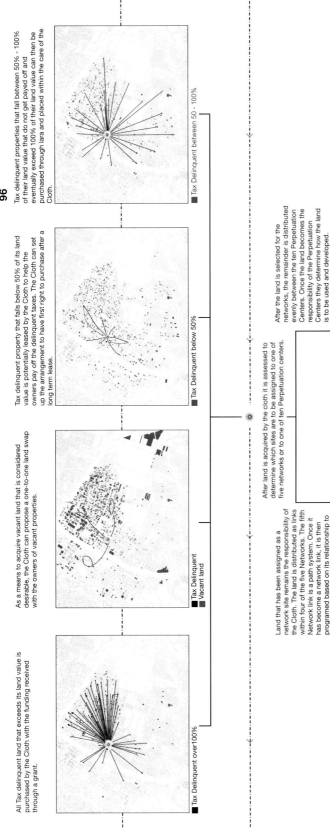

All Tax delinquent land that exceeds its land value is purchased by the Cloth with the funding received through a grant.

Tax Delinquent over 100%

As a means to acquire vacant land that is considered desirable, the Cloth can propose a one-to-one land swap with the owners of vacant properties.

Tax Delinquent
Vacant land

Tax delinquent property that falls below 50% of its land value is potentially leased by the Cloth to help the owners pay off the delinquent taxes. The Cloth can set up the arrangement to have first right to purchase after a long term lease.

Tax Delinquent below 50%

Tax delinquent properties that fall between 50% - 100% of their land value that do not get payed off and eventually exceed 100% of their land value can then be purchased through lara and placed within the care of the Cloth.

Tax Delinquent between 50 - 100%

After land is acquired by the cloth it is assessed to determine which sites are to be assigned to one of five networks or to one of ten Perpetuation centers.

Land that has been assigned as a network site remains the responsibility of the Cloth. The land is distributed as links within four of the five Networks. The fifth Network link is a path system. Once it has become a network link, it is then programed based on its relationship to the nodes within its respective networks.

After the land is selected for the networks, the remainder is distributed evenly between the ten Perpetuation Centers. Once the land becomes the responsibility of the Perpetuation Centers they determine how the land is to be used and developed.

☐ Tax delinquent sites selected for Networks
◀ Vacant sites to be acquired through land-swap
◇ Tax delinquent sites to be swapped for vacant sites
⬚ Tax delinquent sites selected from second round

◇ Education held sites
◈ Cultural Arts held sites
◻ Social Services held sites
◆ Economic held sites
◇ Spirituality held sites

◇ Comprehensive Health held site
◈ Housing held sites
◇ Political Empowerment held sites
◆ Children & Family held sites
▨ Recreation held sites

All tax delinquent land that exceeds its land value is purchased by the Cloth with the funding received through a grant. Tax delinquent property that falls below 50% of its land value is potentially leased to the Cloth to help the owners pay off the taxes. After land is acquired by the Cloth it is assessed to determine which sites are to be assigned to one of five networks or to one of ten Perpetuation centers.

←Exploring the Potential of LARA: Third Ward Community Cloth

In 1995, Houston's Department of Planning and Development began developing plans for reclaiming and revitalizing tax delinquent properties. The result of that effort was a proposed organization, the Land Acquisition Redevelopment Authority (LARA), that would oversee the identification, reclamation, and redevelopment of long-term tax delinquent properties. Currently, LARA remains a proposed organization. However, the Houston City Council has just agreed to start LARA, pending approval from the Houston Independent School District, Houston Community College System, Harris County Education Department, and Port of Houston Authority.

The studio studies the potential of LARA activity in the context of Third Ward. While the city intends to utilize reclaimed properties for affordable housing, such housing is but one of many potential uses that emerge when these properties are examined from the perspectives of various area, city, and regional organizations. In the studio, these potential uses are investigated and developed to indicate ways that LARA might address a range of needs within the ward and in its relationships to the metropolitan area.

The studio begins with an analysis of Third Ward and of organizations that might oversee the planning, development, and management of sites reclaimed by LARA. Students are asked to develop a design project based on the identification of sites and the selection of the organizational processes through which those sites could be developed. In each phase students have the opportunity to work both individually and collaboratively.
DAVID BROWN, critic, Graduate Option Studio, 2003

For better or worse, the found conditions of Third Ward are integral to its character. It is our intent to understand this fabric and to encourage a natural evolution by basing our proposal in the cultural, historical, and existing influences of the area.

Recreation and green space—community activity and outdoor center

The purpose of our proposed networks is to call attention to and preserve the history and culture of Third Ward as it appears, both formally and informally (buildings and events), and to maintain the ratio of vacant to built property. Each network is made up of two parts—the node and the link. The nodes are a group of historical and/or cultural sites that are located throughout Third Ward and are related to one another indirectly by program, activity, or events held within each site. The links act as connectors for the nodes in three ways—corridor, path, or point. The corridor establishes an area for the development of business. The path marks historically significant routes and provides the connection between historically significant places. The points are a series of informally programmed sites that relate to and connect their respective network's nodes. The links can be preexisting, or acquired and programmed by the primary network tracker the Cloth.
DAN BURKETT, ANDREA DIETZ / Graduate Option Studio, 2004

The moment for these particular sites and, as a result, these particular projects has passed. The proximity of both wards to downtown Houston has led to economic conditions in which infill construction becomes viable. However, the idea that a dispersed set of sites can work dynamically in relation to one another to generate alternative urbanisms is still relevant. Houston, as well as other cities, continues to encounter similar situations. In Chicago, for example,

the city owns vacant land spread across its wards that equals the size of the Loop.

The projects effectively reveal that by working incrementally and with variability, efforts at a small scale can operate urbanistically on a greater area. The extended range of such work, in terms of both distance between sites and the scale of the area that they might work upon, remains unknown, as do the limits of the urbanisms that can be derived. As a set, the two projects suggest that the alternatives that can be generated are perhaps as diverse as the organizations that might provide oversight and the organizational logics that they would introduce. However, the focus on developing generative potential from the modification of those existing activities of residents in their locations that could provide the immediate activation of the area leaves open the question of whether or not work from such situations can operate across a range of scenarios.
—David Brown is the associate director of graduate studies and an associate professor at University of Illinois at Chicago School of Architecture. He was an assistant professor at Rice School of Architecture from 1996-2003.

↓Rice Building Workshop Projects 1996-present

Nonya Grenader and Danny Samuels

Directors, Rice Building Workshop, 1996-present

In 1996 Dean Lars Lerup instigated the Rice Building Workshop (RBW) with the goal of bringing students of architecture out of the studio and into the larger community, where their creativity could be challenged by the demands of real-life practice. Ten years and some two hundred students later, we have designed and built more than a dozen projects, each one indeed challenging Rice students in novel ways.

The educational benefits to the students are clearly evident. Working at various scales and in diverse situations, RBW students explore the processes of building and allow the act of making to inform all aspects of design. Budget, schedule, and construction constraints test conceptual ideas as students work together to transform designs into built contributions to a community beyond their classrooms.

Architecture students at all levels, from second year through graduate, participate in the workshop, where projects range in scale from furniture to neighborhoods and involve different stages in the process of design and making. Some projects reach fruition in one semester; others may require several years to move from idea to reality. In the design stages, the seminar works much like an architect's office: students meet with community clients to develop programs; small teams propose and develop a variety of design solutions; the choices are narrowed down; and budget, technical detail, and code compliance assume greater importance. When building begins, a weekly seminar class is used as a "job meeting" while construction takes place on Saturdays.

Every building is evidence of the collaborative process—a shared vision among client, architect, consultants, and contractors. Unlike the typical emphasis in architecture school on the fiercely held individual idea, RBW emphasizes the possibilities of collaboration. The student architects work with each other, as well as with consultants, contractors, suppliers, and crafts-people, to develop their visions. But of all the valuable learning opportunities offered by the workshop, it is our engagement with community clients that has been most rewarding.

The Collaboration

The relationship between Rice Building Workshop and Project Row Houses began in 1997 with the design and construction of a low-cost house prototype on the Project Row Houses campus—the first new construction on that

↑Core
completed 2008

A modern core was designed for one of the original shotgun-style row houses at 2501 Holman Street in Houston's Third Ward. Though designed for the individual house, the project was seen as a prototype that could be applied to the numerous neighborhood shotgun-style houses in need of renovation. A Project Row Houses' visiting artist is currently using the house.

site—and has continued through numerous design, planning, and building projects. Now RBW is completing a new home base, a research and development facility, on the campus.

Project Row Houses and its surrounding community form a coherent and instructive example of vernacular architecture and urbanism. The shotgun house, a type that migrated from Africa to the Caribbean, then to the south coastal United States, is a gem of programmatic compaction and architectural exuberance. Here, such houses – (almost) strictly repetitive cellular units of about 500 square feet—were built in long rows as homes for generations of African-Americans. As reinterpreted by Houston artist John Biggers, the shotgun house can now be seen as the generator of a rich environment, accommodating the family as part of the larger community.

When students work within the fabric and social life of this community, subtle learning opportunities emerge. As students frame, sheetrock, paint, or redesign a detail, they appreciate the context of their actions in ways that would never be possible during a brief site visit. They understand the vital sounds and textures of a place that is informed and enlivened by its inhabitants.

The community of Project Row Houses—the staff, artists, and residents—has been an ideal client for young architecture students. In

↑ Workbox and Workyard
completed 2007

Somewhere between a lunar lander and a manufactured home, a toy box and a job trailer, the Workbox is a functional home away from home for the Rice Building Workshop. This project anticipated our need for mobility and convenience during the on-site construction process. The Workbox utilizes a modified freight container to create a two-part workshop and a secure storage unit that has been outfitted with metal and woodworking tools. The Workbox is easily transported to virtually any site. Once it is on-site, the Workbox's two large doors open to become work platforms and reveal a fully equipped workshop that is ready for use.

After ten years of nomadic existence, the Rice Building Workshop is coming home. We will soon complete a permanent research and development facility to explore further ideas in affordable housing and other construction research. This facility is located in the community where we have done much of our work: the Third Ward, right in the middle of the Project Row Houses campus.

The new workshop facility occupies an urban lot, 50' x 100', and incorporates two existing components: Workbox, a woodshop in an adapted 20' shipping container, and a 40' container with metal tools. A 34' x 68' roof that is two stories high shelters the Workyard from sun and rain. The steel structure is conceived as a full-size "erector

set," with standardized column and beam components that can be deployed as a kind of scaffolding to facilitate future projects, as well as support the roof. The students have also designed a small (8' x 20') office module. A movable perimeter both provides security and suggests space usable by the community during RBW off-seasons.

many design critiques, members have exhibited a real sympathy for the students' intentions, while still arguing for the constraints of maintaining a strong contextualism. This has encouraged the students to work within a given design framework and still find the means (and the appropriate scale) to express their own ideas. This approach is more akin to participating in a continuing vernacular tradition than to espousing the modernist ethos that the students practice in the studio.

The continuing nature of this collaboration means that students not only learn from individual projects, but are able to participate in a longer arc of development than is usual in the school experience. This is an adaptive regime, where lessons are learned, absorbed, and applied to subsequent projects, so that the evolutionary development of design is able to occur over an extended period.

NONYA GRENADER, FAIA is a principal at Nonya Grenander Architect and a professor in practice at Rice School of Architecture.

DANNY SAMUELS is a partner at Taft Architects. He is the Smith Professor of Architecture at Rice School of Architecture.

↑ **XS House**
completed 2004

As we worked in the community, we observed that many shotgun-style houses were being torn down and their dwellers displaced. This led us to focus on a segment of today's housing market that is often neglected—an extra-small house for one or two people.

The challenge was to design and build a dwelling of modest size (500-square feet) with a small projected budget ($25,000) while implementing innovative design and construction techniques. Our goal with this project was to suggest that this housing type was still viable for those with limited funds, limited land, or a desire to live simply and use fewer resources.

Again, the design of this house is sensitive to its surroundings and borrows design concepts found in neighboring homes. Features such as generous porches, deep overhangs, and aligned openings for greater cross-ventilation are rendered with modern construction methods and materials. These concepts are by their nature energy efficient. A thickened wall provides additional insulation from the western sun exposure and provides the house with ample space for storage and services.

The house is a modern interpretation of the shotgun-style row house that once populated many areas in the southern United States. An adjustable footing/ foundation system lifts the building off the ground, much like the concrete block footings that are used to support the original row houses located within this community. Hardiplank walls and metal windows are used in place of wood products to minimize maintenance and upkeep. The core of the house is wrapped in translucent polycarbonate which distributes light throughout the structure. The core contains the bathroom and houses the kitchen along its outer edge. The placement of this single element divides the interior into "large" and "small" spaces that may be furnished in a variety of ways. Porches offer places for gathering and extend the interior areas into the surrounding community.

↑ **Duplexes**
completed 2004

After the completion of the Six-Square
House, Project Row Houses, recognizing
the pressing need for rental apartments in
the neighborhood, asked us to proceed
with the design of duplex units on the
remainder of the site. After an exploration
of design alternatives that focused on the
Houston prototype of the freestanding
duplex apartment in its various configurations (one-story and two, side by side, up
and down), the students decided to adhere
closely to the Six-Square type in concept
and detail. The design as it developed
placed two two-bedroom units in the Six-
Square format (of 10'-8" squares under a
large roof), one above the other, accessed
by exterior stairs, and each with its own
front porch. The design character was consistent with that previously developed. The
full site plan envisioned four such units.
The students prepared working drawings
as part of the course, while Project Row
Houses pursued possibilities for funding.
There matters stood for five years until,
in the spring of 2004, the financing package came together, and a neighborhood
contractor constructed eight new apartments. These have been so successful
that Project Row Houses is now pursuing
the construction of sixteen more two- and
three-bedroom apartments.

↑ Six-Square House
completed 1999

Project Row Houses uses eight existing
shotgun houses for a "Young Mothers'
Residential Program" offering transitional
housing and services for families in crisis.
One-year residencies provide young
mothers with the opportunity to develop
the skills needed for independent and self-
sufficient lives while becoming a part of the
social network of neighbors and services.
Our program goal was to provide a next
step for those families—affordable housing
within their familiar neighborhood context.

Our first design/build project, a 900-
square-foot house, was conceived as a
low-cost prototype that may be configured

in a variety of ways. This modular house,
six over six square units that measure

10'-8" at each side, utilizes materials
and concepts found in neighboring homes,
such as deep overhangs and double-hung
windows that are aligned for cross-
ventilation. Shaded porches extend living
spaces and allow traditional community
relationships to develop. Modular floor
and framing panels were constructed on
the Rice campus and taken to the site for
assembly.

Completed in 1999, the Six-Square
House has become the home of a mother
and her two children; as a prototype, it
generated a range of variations.

Shotgun houses awaiting relocation, Houston, photograph © Lewis Watts

The Shotgun House in Houston

Stephen Fox

The shotgun cottage has been a characteristic Houston house type for over a hundred years. Associated especially with working class African-American neighborhoods in Houston and the South, it was a local, vernacular house type that in the last decades of the nineteenth century made the transition to a widely diffused, mass-produced, popular house type.[1]

The shotgun cottage did not figure among Houston's earliest house types. The grid-iron town plan of Houston, surveyed in 1836 at the confluence of Buffalo Bayou and White Oak Bayou, was improved with a variety of other house types. Almost all were of wood construction, with gabled or hipped roofs, as depicted in sketches from Mary Austin Holley's diary of late 1837 and early 1838.[2] A sketch by Holley of Barnard Bee's dwelling illustrates a familiar house type of the southern coastal lowlands: a two-room cottage, raised above grade, with a full-width front veranda inset beneath its side-gabled roof. This type, the Gulf Coast cottage, became the most representative vernacular house type of nineteenth-century Houston. It was adaptable for middle-income housing, as exemplified by the Ruppersberg-Meyer House of 1868, originally on West Dallas Avenue in Fourth Ward

Shotgun cottages, 2011-2013 Decatur Street, Houston, c. 1895.

and now located in Sam Houston Park. The Gulf Coast cottage lent itself as well to smaller houses, such as the Levy House of about 1866 at 1910 Decatur Street in Sixth Ward. It could become a double house, as at the cottage at 1909 Decatur Street, dated to about 1870. And it was flexible enough to be a tiny house, like the Castanie-Fromm House formerly at 809 Robin Street in Fourth Ward. Part of a row of shotgun cottages until moved from its site in 2002, this appears as a freestanding house on the W. E. Wood Map of Houston of 1869, which shows the outline of buildings on their lots.[3]

In contrast to the Gulf Coast cottage, the most representative elite house type in Houston during the third quarter of the nineteenth century was the three-bay wide, side-hall southern town house, prefaced by a double veranda and in Houston capped by a shallowly

pitched hipped roof. One of the few surviving examples is William M. Rice's house of about 1850, now in Sam Houston Park. The earliest house in Houston known to have been built by an African American, the house of the Rev. Jack Yates of about 1870, which stood at 1318 Andrews Street in Fourth Ward until it was moved to Sam Houston Park in 1994, is a three-bay, side-hall southern town house.[4] Although exceptional, both in its size and early date of construction (Yates himself was exceptional; although enslaved until 1865, he had persuaded the family that held him to teach him to read and write), the Yates Homestead indicates that African Americans did not stand outside the mainstream of contemporary material culture, despite the asymmetries that characterized their relationship to the dominant white culture in the South.

Louise Passey's master's thesis of 1993 on the development of the Freedmantown neighborhood in Fourth Ward contains descriptions from Houston's newspaper, the Telegraph, of this newly established African-American neighborhood. Typically, the reports employed derogatory rhetoric, characterizing the dwellings of recently emancipated African Americans as "miserable hovels" and "shanties" (1865) and "huts built of planking and waste timber," although acknowledging that "…a few Negroes… have bought lots and erected some very nice cottages" (1866).[5] An unusually favorable article in 1875 reported "many evidences of thrift and prosperity in Freedmantown. New houses have been built, and still others [are] in course of con-

Shotgun cottages, Sixth Ward, Houston, c. 1910.

struction."[6] None of the accounts describes the types of cottages under construction. The Wood Map of 1869 does not illustrate houses exhibiting the oblong shape of the shotgun type, although it does show what were clearly houses built in a row as multiples. But by the time the first Sanborn's fire insurance map for Houston was published in 1885 (the Sanborn maps also show the outlines of buildings on their lots and contain written notations about properties), what seem to be shotgun cottages had been built in Houston. A pair of shotgun cottages on the block of Capitol Avenue downtown, now occupied by Jones Plaza, is annotated with the words "Negro tenements."

The shotgun cottage originated as a U.S. house type in New Orleans, according to the pioneering research of John M. Vlach.[7] Vlach traces the shotgun type to the Yoruba dwellings of Nigeria, via the indigenous *bohío* of Santo Domingo and the *maison basse* of Haiti. Vlach found an example of the shotgun type recorded as early as 1833 in the New Orleans Notarial Archives.[8] On the northern periphery of the French Quarter, one still finds block fronts composed of New Orleanian variations of the shotgun cottage, both single and double houses, with the overhanging Creole *abat-vent* sheltering the sidewalk in place of a front veranda. The transformation of the shotgun from a localized New Orleans vernacular house type to a popular southern house type corresponded chronologically to the extension of railroad networks through the South in the last quarter of the nineteenth century.

This can be seen in the Texas-Mexico border city of Brownsville, which the railroad—and shotgun cottages—did not reach until 1904. Brownsville's geopolitical situation on the edge of the South had earlier enabled African Americans to challenge the social construction of racial superiority/inferiority that white southerners had encoded in architecture as in all other facets of daily life. Just across the Rio Grande from Brownsville, in the Mexican city of Matamoros, Tamaulipas, the grandest Victorian house in the city was built in 1885 by the Anglo/Afro-American merchant Melitón H. Cross, whose father, Juan S. Cross, was a South Carolina plantation-overseer-turned-wholesale merchant, and whose mother had been enslaved. The façade and towers of Matamoros's parish church, Nuestra Señora del Refugio, were built in the 1850's to the design of the architect and engineer

A pair of shotgun cottages at 2011 and 2013 Decatur Street in Houston's Sixth Ward, which appears in the Sanborn's map of 1896, illustrates the way in which vernacular house types were adapted to popular architectural trends. The decorative screening and turned posts of the veranda, and the gablets beneath the peak of the roofs, surfaced with fish-scale shingles, represented Victorian flourishes that did not disrupt the spatial and constructional economy of the type. Reproduction in multiples suggests the extent to which such houses were built and identified as tenant (that is, rental) housing. The Stiles Row at 1501-1519 Victor Street in Fourth Ward, owned by a woman, Miss Lauretta Stiles, who was white, seems to have been built in stages between 1914 and 1922, to judge from listings in the Houston City Directory. By the first decade of the twentieth century, whole block fronts, sometimes entire blocks, in the southwest quadrant of Fourth Ward were under single ownership and built out with repeating rows of cottages, both shotguns and the older type of square-planned cottage.[10] These contrasted with such houses as the Rutherford B. H. Yates House of 1912 at 1314 Andrews Street, a late Victorian L-front cottage, and the bungalow type house at 2209 Dowling Street in Third Ward, built next door to Wesley Chapel A. M. E. Church in 1926 as the pastor's house and designed by the African-American architect W. Sidney Pittman. Houston African-American families who attained middle class status during the segregation era embraced middle-income house types. In the

Shotgun cottage, West End, Houston, c. 1915.

Frank Cash Row (Project Row Houses), 1939.

Bártolo Passement, who immigrated to Matamoros from New Orleans in 1832. The U.S. Census of 1830 identifies Passement as a brick mason and a free man of color.[9] Where people of color were not systematically excluded from civil society, those who attained middle class status appear to have gravitated to the mainstream of contemporary material cultural expression. The shotgun cottage is fascinating because, as it made the transition from a local New Orleans-based vernacular house type to a popular southern house type, it became implicated in the dominant culture's social construction of superiority/inferiority. From a white perspective, the shotgun cottage was socially constructed as "Negro"; from a white *and* black middle class perspective, it was socially constructed as "working class."

Detering Addition in West End, west of Sixth Ward, there are extremely narrow shotgun cottages. One is the house at 707 Reinicke Street (moved to another site in 2003), perhaps acquired as surplus from the decommissioned World War I U.S. Army training camp, Camp Logan, in what is now Memorial Park.

Houston's cycles of population expansion created a constantly growing market for new housing at all income levels. Working class African-American families seem to have been the primary (although not exclusive) clientele for tenant row housing, whether composed of shotgun cottages, L-plan cottages, or square-plan cottages. The location of rental housing in rows suggests how patterns of residential racial segregation were reinforced, particularly with respect to working class neighborhoods. The African-American neighborhoods in Third Ward and Fourth Ward were the primary locations of housing built in rows. Shotgun cottages were built in other Houston neighborhoods, but rows of such housing were the exception rather than the rule. In such predominantly white working class neighborhoods as Sixth Ward and the West End, shotgun cottages tended to be built singly or in pairs. Thus the row also seems to have acquired racial and class overtones.

In the 1920's, one sees the beginning of a systematic effort by Houston's elite, carried out under the guise of reform, to erase the culture and urbanism associated with the shotgun cottage. The *Report of the City Planning Commission* of 1929 contains two examples. In one the evidence is indirect: drawn from a comparison of an aerial photograph, looking west toward Fourth Ward, showing the new Central Library of 1926 facing Hermann Square, with a perspective rendering showing a proposed Civic Center of public buildings grouped around the library and Hermann Square.[11] The rendering treats the blocks of cottages in Fourth Ward (as well as in Sixth Ward north of the bayou) as a generalized street grid lined with trees but devoid of buildings. The newly-constructed Allen Parkway, a parkway drive following the course of Buffalo Bayou westward from the Civic Center to the gates of River Oaks, appears to run through open countryside. The second example is more explicit.[12] A pair of maps in the report deals with the continued problem posed by the expansion of existing African-American residential neighborhoods once the elite garden-suburban neighborhoods of River Oaks

housing complex in the South. It was restricted to white occupancy only.[13]

What became Project Row Houses, the Frank Cash row in the 2400 and 2500 blocks of Holman and Division avenues in Third Ward, was built about 1939 as planning began for Allen Parkway Village. Although its five-room houses conform to the iconic image of the shotgun cottage with their front-facing gables (reiterated in the decorative gablet framing the front porch) and bungalow-style brackets, they deviate from the pure type by being one-and-a-half rooms wide rather than the single linear file of rooms historically associated with the shotgun type. The repetition of house fronts along the block faces speaks to what is so compelling about the organization of this house type in rows: the capacity of a house so narrow that alone it would be spatially insignificant to form a collective that shapes space urbanistically. It is the strong form of the shotgun cottage that endows these small houses with the presence and dignity that are essential attributes of urban architecture.

The proximity of the cottages to each other reveals their status as economic instruments, built four to a lot (two facing the street, two facing Division, which is actually an alley through the center of a standard sized Houston city block) to maximize site coverage and the investor's return. The narrow intervals between the houses make visitors aware of the closeness with which African-American working class renters were compelled to live, in contrast to owner-occupied

Street elevation, Project Row Houses.

Detail of porch, Project Row Houses.

and Riverside Terrace began to be developed in their paths of growth in the mid 1920's. One map shows the "as is" concentration of African-American neighborhoods in Houston. The second shows what supposedly ought to be, including a dramatic contraction of Fourth Ward, pulled sharply back from Allen Parkway, where it grazed the north edge of the original Freedmantown. The 1929 report, however, could recommend no legally acceptable methods for achieving this urban disappearing act. Ten years later, when the Housing Authority of the City of Houston was constituted, the means were at hand. Using funds from the U. S. Housing Authority, the Houston Housing Authority acquired seventeen blocks of Freedmantown by eminent domain and replaced them with the one-thousand unit Allen Parkway Village public housing complex. Built in stages between 1940 and 1944, Allen Parkway Village was the largest public

houses along Holman Avenue, built one to a lot. Necessity begot ingenuity: the porches and kitchens were located on the west side of the houses, and the bedrooms and bathrooms on the east where they would have access to the prevailing southeast breeze. As bell hooks described in her talk "House Art," necessity also begot the social rituals that domesticated rented houses and turned them into people's homes.[14] The back porch was a space of domestic sociability related to the shared back yard, where the clothesline now memorializes the work that transpired in such spaces, visible in a photograph from the *Report of the City Planning Commission* of 1929 with its disapproving caption, and documented by Ellen Beasley in her book on working class urban space in a southern city, *The Alleys and Back Buildings of Galveston*.[15]

This type of urban housing proved amazingly durable in Houston. Row houses were built as rental housing in working class African-American neighborhoods through the 1950's. These houses were adapted, however, to successive trends in the production of domestic architecture and space in Houston, metamorphosing into mini-ranch houses, built at grade on concrete slab foundations, with walls of brick-veneered wood stud construction and interior rooms lit by high-set horizontal windows. Rather than facing the street, rows of such houses tended to cluster around a paved driveway and parking apron. But it was not unusual for these houses to retain small front porches that continued to be used for socializing. Although these ranch houses no longer

Common back yard, Project Row Houses.

qualify typologically as shotgun cottages, their descent from the shotgun row is obvious.

PRH has been a catalyst. At the turn of the twenty-first century, it has forced a reappraisal not just of the shotgun cottage but also of "shotgun" culture: of southern working class African-American culture. As Sheryl Tucker de Vásquez observed in her essay on PRH in the journal *Places*, it has been a catalyst for thinking about how architecture can make connections to the places where it is built, as well as addressing such issues as the provision of affordable housing. This effort is represented by the Six Square House of 1998 on Division, designed and built by the Rice Building Workshop of Rice's architecture school.[16] The Six Square House makes connections to other Houston buildings whose designs were predicated on claiming a place culturally through architecture:

the house of the architect William F. Stern, The Menil Collection museum by Renzo Piano, and the Live Oak Friends Meeting House by Leslie K. Elkins. These buildings participate in a dialogue on local culture that, while not dependent on the shotgun cottage, engages and includes it rather than excluding and segregating the shotgun as culturally inferior. The sculptor Mary Miss affirmed the necessity of such connections in her 1998 installation *One Hundred Chairs* at the University of Houston. Evoking an academic symposium, her aluminum chairs also call to mind the shotgun sociability of the sidewalks and front porches of nearby Third Ward, making this the only instance in which the University of Houston spatially acknowledges its connection to Third Ward.

The connection between art and life that PRH makes was a constant theme in the art of John T. Biggers. One sees in his painting, *Shotgun, Third Ward #1* of 1966, a row of cottages strikingly similar to those at PRH. In his *Shotguns* series of 1987, Biggers treated the shotgun cottage iconically rather than naturalistically. He frequently composed the fields of these paintings with repeated, flat, frontal gables to imply the density and weight of African-American culture in the South. Robert Farris Thompson calls attention to Biggers' equally iconic treatment of household items associated with everyday domestic life, reinforcing the representation of the shotgun as a symbol of collective dignity and cultural identity.[17] Biggers' paintings challenge the social construction of the shotgun row as an icon of inferiority by insisting that viewers who might construe it as such reevaluate their own judgments and critically examine their prejudices.

Biggers painted the *Shotguns* series in the midst of a contentious debate in Houston, lasting from the late 1970's through the end of the century, over the fate of Fourth Ward. That his efforts, and those of other artists and architects, to make connections across boundaries of social class and race were exceptional is tragically apparent in how this debate was resolved. Three successive mayors of Houston—Lee Brown, Bob Lanier, and Kathy Whitmire—spared no effort to destroy Fourth Ward, which, when it was listed in the National Register of Historic Places as the Freedmen's Town Historic District in 1985, was one of the last intact late nineteenth- and early twentieth-century African-American neighborhoods in a large southern city. Paul Hester's poignant photographs convey the violence wreaked on the low-income residents of Fourth Ward, many of whom had lived in the neighborhood as renters for generations, as the engine of state-sponsored "revitalization" displaced them and, between 1999 and 2003, eradicated an irreplaceable cultural landscape.[18]

I conclude with Houston's newest shotgun cottage, designed and built by the architect George G. McMillin and his wife, Elizabeth, as rental housing in the Sixth Ward Historic District in 2001. The McMillin cottage is one of several neo-shotguns built in Sixth Ward since the late 1990's. Brett Zamore's radical reconstruction of a double-wide shotgun cottage at 4739 Buck Street in Fifth Ward as House 00, completed in

1999 and now occupied by the artist Bert L. Long, Jr., was undertaken with the Fifth Ward Community Redevelopment Corporation to demonstrate the feasibility of preserving and rehabilitating shotgun cottages rather than scrapping them.[19]

Thanks to John Biggers, Rick Lowe and Deborah Grotfeldt at PRH, and those whom they have inspired, the shotgun cottage has gradually been transformed from an architectural emblem of poverty and shame into an icon of Houston. An overview of its development highlights the ways in which a house type that has more often seemed like an economic instrument than a work of architecture accrues cultural density and meaning. Its material economy, its reproducibility, its adaptability to changes in architectural style and the organization of domestic space indicate the qualities that made the shotgun cottage such an enduring popular house type. Examined historically, what is so intriguing is the way in which the shotgun cottage has come to be valued for the very attributes that caused it to be scorned for much of the twentieth century. This process of examination and reevaluation is especially notable in Houston because at PRH the shotgun cottage has come to stand for an alternative vision of Houston, not as an abstract field for pursuing profit, but as a city in which people might live lives of mutual enjoyment, edification, and respect.

Notes

This paper is dedicated to the memory of V. Nia Dorian Becnel, historian of African-American material culture in Houston, ardent historic preservationist, and assistant professor of architecture at the University of Houston. It is also dedicated to four Houstonians who have struggled diligently to preserve the contributions of African Americans to the history of Houston: Gladys M. House, Lenwood E. Johnson, Ngeri Shakur, and Catherine M. Roberts.

1. Distinctions between "vernacular" and "popular" often prove elusive. "Vernacular" generally connotes patterns of cultural transmission based on local communal influence. "Popular" generally connotes patterns of cultural transmission based on mass dissemination. In Texas, the arrival of the railroad usually marked the beginning of the transition from vernacular culture to popular culture.

2. Mary Austin Holley, Mary Austin Holley: The Texas Diary, ed. J. P. Bryan, (Austin: University of Texas, 1963), 38-39.

3. Matthew B. Cox, "Bettie E. Williams House, 1910 Decatur," City of Houston Archeological and Historical Commission Landmark Designation Report (16 January 1997). Thanks to Randy Pace, Historic Preservation Officer, City of Houston, for making information on 1909 and 1910 Decatur available. Pace's extensive research on the house at 809 Robin Street suggests the possibility that it could have been built as early as 1848. It seems to be a one-room house with a one-room outbuilding, which was eventually attached to the front house by the construction of additional rooms.

4. Rutherford B. H. Yates, Sr., and Paul L. Yates, The Life and Efforts of Jack Yates, (Houston: Texas Southern University Press, 1985) 19.

5. M. Louise Passey, "Freedmantown: The Evolution of a Black Neighborhood in Houston, 1865-1880," (master's thesis, Rice University, 1993), 55 and 53.

6. Passey, 117.

7. John Michael Vlach. "The Shotgun House: An Architectural Legacy." In, editors. Common Places: Readings in American Vernacular Architecture, ed. Dell Upton and John Michael Vlach (Athens GA: University of Georgia Press, 1986), 58-78.

8. Vlach, 62.

9. The racial origins of Melitón Cross parents are based on local oral tradition in Brownsville. Juan S. Cross' biographical entry in John Henry Brown's Indian Wars and Pioneers of Texas (Austin TX: L. E. Daniell, Publisher, n.d. [c. 1891]), 481-82, refers to Cross' children but not his wife. On Passement, whose racial origin was not commented upon when he was memorialized in the Brownsville newspaper at the time of his death in 1868, see "Don Bártolo Passement," Daily Ranchero, August 2, 1868, and the Census of 1830, Orleans Parish, Louisiana.

10. Kenneth A. Breisch, Freedmen's Town Historic District, Houston, Harris County, Texas" United States Department of the Interior, National Park Service, National Register of Historic Places Inventory-Nomination Form, November 1984, Item 8, pp. 6-7.

11. Report of the City Planning Commission of Houston, (Houston: The Forum of Civics, 1929),.84-85.

12. Report of the City Planning Commission of Houston, 25-27.

13. Stephen Fox and V. Nia Dorian Becnel, "San Felipe Courts Historic District, Houston, Harris County, Texas," United States Department of the Interior, National Park Service, National Register of Historic Places Inventory-Nomination Form, December 1987, Item 8, 4-5.

14. bell hooks, "House Art: Merging Public and Private," (lecture delivered at Rice University, October 11, 2001, in conjunction with the exhibition and symposium Shotguns 2001).

15. Report of the City Planning Commission of Houston, 102; and Ellen Beasley, The Alleys and Back Buildings of Galveston: An Architectural and Social History, (Houston: Rice University Press, 1996).

16. Sheryl G. Tucker, "Reinnovating the African-American Shotgun House," Places 10 (Summer 1995): 64-71.

17. Robert Farris Thompson. "John Biggers's Shotguns of 1987: An American Classic," in The Art of John Biggers: View from the Upper Room, ed. Alvia J. Wardlaw, (New York: Harry N. Abrams, Inc., and The Museum of Fine Arts, Houston, 1995), 108-111.

18. Dana Cuff has coined the term "convulsive urbanism" to describe the process of state-subsidized urban transformation, which since 1996 has entailed the destruction of Allen Parkway Village and Fourth Ward, and the displacement of their residents. See Dana Cuff, The Provisional City: Los Angeles Stories of Architecture and Urbanism, (Cambridge: MIT Press, 2000).

19. Deborah K. Ditesch, "Blast from the Past: Return of the Shotgun," Washington Post, 29 July 2000, C-2.

This essay originally appeared in Row: Trajectories Through the Shotgun House, Architecture at Rice 40, 2004.

STEPHEN FOX is a fellow of the Anchorage Foundation and a lecturer at Rice School of Architecture.

→House 00

The shotgun house is a distinct American house type associated with African-American communities in the South. It derives its power and timeless universal appeal from the rhythmic recurrence of simple geometric forms. The Texas shotgun type, which was built as an affordable housing solution, still offers qualities we can appreciate today. This project rethinks this house type as an alternative to suburban domesticity.

In Houston's Fifth Ward, an existing double-occupancy shotgun-style house was rehabilitated and reprogrammed as a viable space for a single family of low income. Removing its parting walls and allowing its modules of space to flow into one another simplifies the plan and organization of the house. The interior is not overprescribed, allowing for a greater flexibility, and while respecting the existing house as a duplex, the refill weaves the opposing two sides into a single home. Yet, the central dividing wall remains as the driving force of the design, allowing the two sides to take on the roles new tenants give them: through the use of a central core, the house becomes open. Miesian in conception, this central space concentrates all technology into one spot. It contains the kitchen, bathroom, and closet space, with storage space above where the hot water heater and the HVAC unit are hidden on top of the central core, keeping the space below free from the service systems. The core has three sliding doors that allow the bathroom to service the house for different situations. This space allows the functions of the house to remain flexible.

BRETT ZAMORE / M.Arch. Thesis, 1999 / Lars Lerup, director

For his thesis project, Brett Zamore bought a derelict shotgun house in Houston's Fifth Ward and imaginatively restored it into a home now occupied by artists Bert Long and Joan Batson. Constructing a real building for a thesis project, turning a thesis project into a real estate development project, and reusing a building in a city that has consistently erased everything over a generation old—any of these would have made an improbable thesis project. Doing all of them together distinguished House 00 and made it an influential project out of which Zamore was able to launch a successful career designing and building kit and conventional small houses that draw on the architectural heritage of the rural South.

It would be a mistake, however, to see this exclusively as an interest in historical restoration or context. It is really more an essay on the use of resources, even the use of architectural style as a resource. The exterior was simply repaired and repainted. One has the feeling that the "double porch" version of the standard shotgun was interesting enough without additional architectural commentary. The interior of the house is also a collage of old and new, bought and donated, finished and unfinished, so that the house is as much a timely commentary on the ethos of recycling and reuse as historical architecture.

—**Gordon Wittenberg** is the principal of Gordon Wittenberg Partnership. He is a professor at Rice School of Architecture.

COLLAGE OF OLD AND NEW

FINISHED AND UNFINISHED

House 00 under construction

AFFORDABLE HOUSING SOLUTION

Bert Long in the completed interior of House 00

Completed exterior of House 00

John Biggers, *Shotguns*, 1987, ©John T. Biggers Estate/Licensed by VAGA, New York, NY. Estate Represented by Michael Rosenfeld Gallery

→ Third Ward Projects
William D. Williams and
Rick Lowe in Conversation

William Williams: In 1994, there was a renewed focus on audience, I was in Los Angeles during the 1992 civil unrest or riots, depending on your politics, and we were all searching for ways to make a difference. The goal was to rethink the role of design in social justice and in building communities. We should all be better citizens, but I think architects were starting to believe that design, and I mean design with a big "D," could make a difference. At the very least, we realized that architecture had been contributing to many of our social problems. There was also a growing suspicion of "ism's" and a belief that it was reflected in our professional detachment as well as a distinct move towards diagramming and various notational systems. In many ways it seemed as though we were desperate for a new language to address the problems facing our cities. I am not totally convinced that we have moved beyond the discourse we were having in the

mid-nineties except that some think technology will save us while others believe the answer rests with economies of scale or restraint. It is probably the case that both approaches will have to find a way to merge — this will require designers to rethink the way buildings are conceived and fabricated and recycled.

Rick Lowe: It was audience that guided my interest in issues of architecture, planning, and urban design. Back in 1994, I didn't have any appreciation for the importance of architecture. My interest at that time was centered on trying to create a safe and nurturing environment within the northern part of Third Ward in Houston, Texas, a neighborhood that was troubled by decaying building structures. Dilapidated buildings were the breeding grounds for all sorts of criminal activity. So buildings in the northern part of Third Ward were seen as problems, not assets. As an artist, my natural instinct was to focus on the people and generating activity that would foster a better community. During the early developmental stages of Project

Row Houses (PRH), around 1993, I began to see how the architecture reinforced the programs and activities that were being developed. In fact, the architecture shaped the identity of the project which has continued to shape the identity of the broader community. It wasn't until then that I understood the critical role architecture played in building good communities. I have to emphasize "role" in that statement because I understood architecture to not be an end but a part of the process of building good communities.

I think the relationship between the physical and social environments continue to be challenging for architecture. For some years now, a conversation on this relationship has lead to better understandings about how the social impact of physical environments and vice versa. However, there are still challenges. What interests me going forward is how designers address issues affecting low-income communities, from urban planning to the design of the living unit. From my perspective, most design for low-income communities seems to trickle down from design for higher income communities. Suburban-style master planned communities may work for higher income communities, but in cities where public transportation is poor, suburban design does not work. The same with the living unit. Upper income developments have pushed the scale of the living unit up to fit their needs. This has shifted the whole thinking around size of low-income living units.

WW: What do you define as the "project," and how do you know if you have been successful?

RL: I think of the "project" in two distinct ways. One is a "project" for me as an artist. The other is the "project" as something is separate from me. As an artist, for my own artistic and aesthetic reasons, I look at the project through an artistic conceptual framework on the one hand, while stepping back and looking at it from the perspective of the community on the other. So from an artistic perspective, I continue to find ways to infuse my creative impulse into the project. Sometimes in obvious ways, sometimes it's very subtle. So as an art project, I define success based on my ability to keep the project aesthetically relevant. As a community project, outside of my aesthetic goals, I think the project is defined by it's physical and social impact upon the community. Architecture has certainly become a key component in defining PRH physically. The engagement of community residents, volunteers, supporters, visitors, et cetera, all contribute to defining the project socially. Success is difficult to measure.

WW: What role if any do you feel aesthetics plays in the design of affordable housing? There are certainly architects that look at the local context, and try to fit in, but that seems complacent if not complicit. Of course, we all know examples where effete formal exercises seem masturbatory. Do you see value in formal invention? Or is style only a developer's way of accessorizing, or only an architect's brand?

RL: I think that aesthetics are extremely important in the design of affordable housing. However, I think it is rare that designers really grasp the aesthetic concerns and sensibilities of low-income populations. Mainly because it's hard for designers to have a genuine reciprocal dialogue about aesthetics within low-income communities because aesthetics generally just exist in the community without much deliberate conversation about it. Therefore authentic aesthetics generally come out of a co-mingling of aesthetics. Its hard for designers to deal with this because they are trained to design or impose an aesthetic. Whereas in most low-income communities aesthetics evolve over time out of complex mixing. As a result of this I think that much of the aesthetics of affordable housing is passed down from low-end market rate housing that does not really address the aesthetics or functions of low-income communities very well.

WW: Leonardo da Vinci once said "a work of art is never finished, only abandoned." How will you know when it is time to move on from PRH? Will you always be able to evolve at the same pace as the institution it has become?

RL: An artwork must continue to work. Otherwise it is abandoned. However, just because it is abandoned does not mean that it ceases to be an artwork. It can always regain it's relevance. As for PRH, I think that it can remain a vital and relevant artwork as long as there are creative participants who are willing to continue to challenge and question the existence of PRH. As an artist, my role with PRH is to continue to question it's existence, challenge the way the project moves forward, identify connections within and outside of the project that gives deeper insight into it's meaning, identify ways to build relationships that advance the complexity of meaning of the project, et cetera. Joseph Beuys, the German artist who came up with the theory of Social Sculpture, said that everybody is an artist. I think community building needs creative leaders involved to elevate the creative potential and engagement of others in the process. If at a point the creative engagement of a significant number of participants is present, then the need for the creative leader diminishes. There have been times when PRH has been in a place where my role has lessened. Other times my engagement has been deepened. So I think consistent creative engagement in the project will be a good signal that the time has come to move on.

WW: PRH and Houston seem to be a perfect fit, what influence do you think the city has played in its development?

RL: I hate to say it, but I think no zoning contributed to our ability to get PRH off the ground in Houston. To weave a housing program with education and artist's studio/workshop/gallery spaces into the block-and-a-half of 22 little houses would probably been difficult to get through zoning. The City's hands-off and wait-and-see approach was helpful. I also think that Houston starves for identity. PRH in a very small way contributes to the identity of the city.

WW: I have always felt that one of the reasons that PRH has been successful is because it is one of the few community organizations that was formed in order to create something. Unfortunately, many of our community organizations were first started in opposition to something. While they are necessary, and perform a vital community service, they also forge a very different coalition whose primary skill is keeping things from happening. When other communities ask you for advice about creating something like PRH in their community, what do you tell them? What is the one thing they must have? What is the thing they must avoid?

RL: I think you might be on to something. I understand completely what you are saying about formation of most community actions. It's usually a response in opposition. Many of those groups, if they are successful, find the need for the group effort no longer exists. The thing about PRH was that it had a physical component. The physical aspect of the project requires a constant engagement. It's hard to let the physical aspect of a socially engaged project just sit. It constantly requires some consideration. So it becomes a medium through which to continue to engage folks.

WW: I find it interesting that a place designed with a completely different purpose and, thinking back to our earlier comments, audience in mind, could evolve into such an essential component of community engagement in a way that the original Italian family could never have imagined when they built the worker housing that now houses PRH. But the way that the porches and the in-between social spaces work have become critical to the very nature of the place. In some ways it is an issue of scale that just seems appropriate to the mission. But if there were a couple of things that you would have preferred to inherit as an existing condition what would they have been? I am thinking about things that are not as easily replicated as new and seem forced, if not kitsch, when you try to reproduce them.

RL: The Italian family who built the houses appear to have had a keener understanding of the aesthetics and function of the community when they built the houses than we have today. The program of PRH is simply trying to understand what this family knew that we don't know today.

WW: One of the things I have always appreciated about PRH is its inclusiveness. Like jazz, it is a wonderful strategy of inclusion where different participants are allowed an occasional solo and even encouraged to improvise, but always in the context of building a stronger community. As PRH grows, so will its community. How has your understanding of the PRH community changed? Is the balance of the community still connected to the Third Ward? And, does it matter if it is not?

RL: Good analogy. I think creative energy is what keeps the project going forward. It's great when a creative force comes into the process and makes their offerings to elevate some aspect of the project. This creative force has come from many sources, from artists, architects, community members, et cetera. Some of these creative forces make their mark and move on. Others continue and demand higher levels of creative engagement from other participants. The PRH community has changed and will continue to change. It will be a challenge to keep the balance between our existing community and the new developments that are happening around and among us.

WW: As a follow up: The Rice Building Workshop has had a longstanding relationship with PRH. Have you ever been concerned that their solo might be going on a bit long, or just by the volume of their contributions, be becoming a bit too loud? As band leader, how do you continue to get others involved?

RL: The long-standing relationship has been great with Rice Building Workshop. The goal in our relationship with Rice is not of quieting that relationship but to build some stronger ones. For future developments there are potential limitations to how we can work with the Building Workshop on projects. Because it is student driven, there will be developments where we will have to bring on professional services because of the magnitude and timing of the project. So I think there is plenty of room for continued engagement with the Building Workshop. The potential future growth of our community holds lots of opportunities for broader architectural services.

WW: I was thinking more about the issue of balance between the old and new that you mentioned. Given the need for housing in the Third Ward in general, but in the area of development PRH is focused on in particular, is it possible that in filling the needs of residents with new housing and even commercial opportunities, that the identity of the place could be radically changed, not necessarily in a good way? Currently, growth has evolved at a scale and pace that makes it seem almost organic and slightly quirky, a lot like the city of Houston itself. But building on the Houston analogy, in times of tremendous growth, much of the city's organic quirkiness has been erased or at the very least, subsumed. How can that be avoided?

RL: You ask such difficult questions! There seems to be a momentary reprieve since the downturn of the market. In 2008 there seemed to be new townhouse projects popping up every week. I don't have high hopes of any kind for uniform planned development in the Third Ward. As you said, that's part of the quirky aspect of this city. But it is also a part of the aesthetic reality of low-income communities. Things are not particularly planned. In the best-case scenario, they evolve within the confines of the market in a way that it's aesthetics and identity are still readable within the new development. Our strategies have been to acquire land (that option is not so available since the cost of land has increased so much), build houses that reflect the existing housing stock to counter balance the new townhouses that are coming up, and currently, trying to acquire existing buildings that will help to symbolically hold onto the scale of the community. The real answer to your question is that I don't

know if the problems that face this community can be avoided. We can only hope that our efforts will nudge development in a way that honor this community as a place that has an aesthetic and an important history.

WW: In addition to the new Community Development Center (CDC), the afterschool program for kids and the residential program for young mothers, along with the artist exhibits, is there something else you would like to add on the programming side?

RL: At this point, we are focusing on pushing our programs deeper. In each program from our arts program to the residential housing program of the CDC, we are looking to maximize the benefit of these programs for community members. For instance, we are attempting to focus our arts program on things that add to the communication of the aesthetic and historic aspect of this community in a more literal way. For example, the artist Terry Adkins has focused his work on commemorating the legendary musician Sam Lightnin' Hopkins, a former resident of the Third Ward, by creating Lightnin' Hopkins bus stops. We are exploring commercial enterprises to serve our residents. Things like a community store and laundromat. So the idea is that if we have these tenants, how can we develop things with them to enhance their quality of life beyond the housing and cultural programs? How can we get more integrated work from artists that work in the arts program?

What we have realized is that there are now some 40 residents, multiple programs, existing within 50 buildings. The scale of the project is now affording the opportunity to think inward in terms of quality of programs as opposed to looking outward to increase scale.

WW: Lastly, if John Biggers were alive today, and he was going to do an updated shotgun painting featuring PRH how would it differ from his past investigations, and if you were doing one, how would yours?

RL: John Biggers was working from an image he had of the shotgun communities from the past, however, if he was adding to that historical context with consideration to PRH's contribution, I think he would probably eliminate the railroad tracks. They symbolically represented the segregation and isolation of these communities. I also think that he would probably identify ways to see the shotgun housing type within the context of the growth of the community. The formal structure of the shotgun housing type may no longer be relevant for contemporary design,

however, realizing that elements of its design could add value to new developments. As for me, I could never stand toe-to-toe with John Biggers when it comes to painting. So I'll just stick to exploring what he has already laid out in his shotgun paintings.

****

WILLIAM WILLIAMS is an associate professor at University of Virginia School of Architecture. He was the Brochstein Visiting Assistant Professor from 1999-2004.

RICK LOWE is a Houston-based artist and the founder of Project Row Houses.

"... It must be in the storage"

The alphabetics of suburban grammar: storage, street, bayou

Don't throw stones...

Texas Medical Center (green light in Sick City)

Nervous

substance

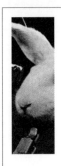

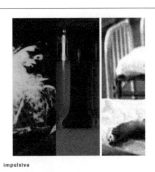

impulsive

action

tolerance

compulsion

↑**Nervous Substances**

A visual essay on the practices of research and development in the
pharmaceutical industry.
HEIDI WERNER / Undergraduate Seminar, 2001 /
Sanford Kwinter, Luke Bulman, instructors

response

depressive

dosage

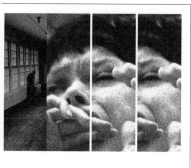

frequency

→Architectures of Pestilence: Smallpox, Tuberculosis, and the Spatial Control of Epidemic Disease

By examining the spatial dialogue that arose to reconcile the opposing figures of smallpox and tuberculosis treatment, it has been possible to trace a spatial or architectural transformation in which methods for protecting the body from disease have evolved into methods for protecting disease from the body. However, given that the threat of pestilence has always inspired defensive strategies based on redundancy, this transformation may be traced as it has unfolded not only at the scale of the individual body, but also at the scale of the building, the city, the international network, and the natural order. In separating out the products of these various scales of defense and allowing them to read independently, it is possible to show how solutions follow from the representation of the threat: the problem of pestilence, however, has always been that there was, at any one time, more than one such representation. Analysis has demonstrated that these physical structures and the spaces they create have been established within a reflexive geometry in which both the disease and the measures established against it have been complicit. With new infectious diseases emerging at rates never before seen and old ones returning with renewed vigor, what Michel Foucault called the "millennial gaze" has again paused over human suffering and made it necessary to speculate upon the space that the next response to epidemic disease will fashion.

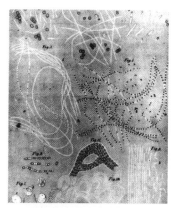

A drawing of anthrax bacilli by Robert Koch

Patients on the roof garden, House of Mercy, Philadelphia, in winter

The encapsulated structures that have historically followed from major epidemic outbreaks provide a context within which to analyze social response: by privileging the scale of the response and its operational strategy over its historical or sociological pedigree, the lineage of epidemic disease management may be studied much like a sophisticated architectural program.

DIANA DAVIS / M.Arch. Thesis, 1998 / Farés el-Dahdah, director

Politics and disease, or disease and politics? Just as the twentieth-century World Wars mutated into the Cold War and later the so-called War on Terror, today new forms of contagion have emerged. AIDS, SARS, and computer viruses infecting entire networks have progressively scrambled the boundaries of nation states and definitions of sovereignty. Architects and urbanists, no longer masters in their own houses, confront as a fundamental condition of their activity the opposition between friend and foe posited by political theorist Carl Schmitt. To dwell in the modern world has long meant to keep out or to maintain at a distance. Time will tell who or what might define space if and when these concerns become secondary.

—Ed Dimendberg is an associate professor at University of California at Irvine. He was a Visiting Cullinan Professor at Rice School of Architecture in 1999.

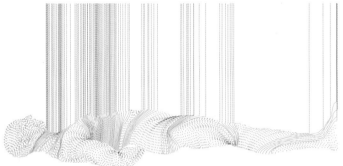

Proprietary Systems endo-dermal drug administration system

→Dispensary
Dawn Finley
Critic, Undergraduate Option Studio, 2001

Recent shifts in the medical industry and the business of beauty are creating interdisciplinary transitions in professional identity, products, and services that imply spatial and commercial practice innovations. These slippages between pharmacy and cosmetic practices are examined to understand their legislative, cultural, technological, and economic directives.

Pharmacy Practice
Technology and economics have brought pharmacists and the

pharmacy to a transitional crisis. Pharmacy has lost distinction as a professional medical trade by being absorbed within the stripped-down, bottom-line spatial productions known as discount drugstores, where primacy is given to convenience, price, and volume. Prescription counters are typically located at the back of drugstores, luring customers through numerous aisles of discount goods to be purchased on the way to and from the pharmacy: pick up some jujubes and a toilet scrubber with your Prozac. Pharmacists are identified as store clerks, stocking shelves in their spare time, rather than as trained medical physicians. Technicians with no formal medical training are replacing many pharmacists; hired to count pills and label prescriptions, they allow major chain retailers to cut their corporate costs in salaries

previously paid to pharmacists. Robotic prescription filling and labeling is now entering the market, promising greater speed and accuracy. On-line pharmacies, equipped with health information networks, are expected to decrease demand for physical transactions and face-to-face prescription advice. Members of the medical community are concerned about the future role of the pharmacist and pharmacy establishments in professional practice. The studio examines the regulatory, economic, and technological procedures shaping current pharmacy and drugstore practice today. Strategies could be for just over-the-counter medicine purchases and within the retail chain.

Cosmetic Practice
Increasingly, cosmetic companies are developing and emphasizing

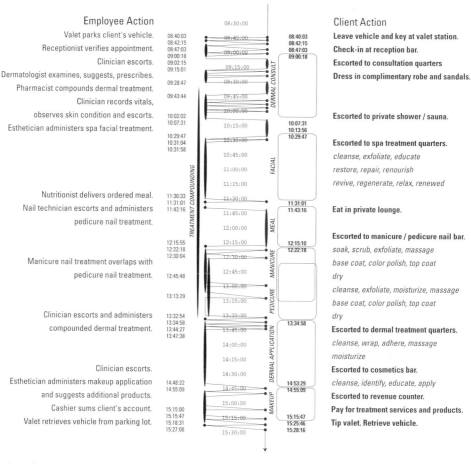

Employee Action			Client Action
	08:30:00		
Valet parks client's vehicle.	08:40:03	08:40:03	Leave vehicle and key at valet station.
	08:42:15	08:42:15	
Receptionist verifies appointment.	08:47:03	08:47:03	Check-in at reception bar.
	09:00:18	09:00:18	
Clinician escorts.	09:02:15		Escorted to consultation quarters
	09:15:01		
Dermatologist examines, suggests, prescribes.			Dress in complimentary robe and sandals.
	09:28:47		
Pharmacist compounds dermal treatment.			
	09:43:44		
Clinician records vitals,			
observes skin condition and escorts.	10:02:02		Escorted to private shower / sauna.
	10:07:31	10:07:31	
Esthetician administers spa facial treatment.		10:13:56	
	10:29:47	10:29:47	Escorted to spa treatment quarters.
	10:31:04		*cleanse, exfoliate, educate*
	10:31:58		
			restore, repair, renourish
			revive, regenerate, relax, renewed
Nutritionist delivers ordered meal.	11:30:33		
	11:31:01	11:31:01	Eat in private lounge.
Nail technician escorts and administers	11:43:16	11:43:16	
pedicure nail treatment.			
			Escorted to manicure / pedicure nail bar.
	12:15:55	12:15:10	*soak, scrub, exfoliate, massage*
	12:22:18	12:22:18	
	12:30:04		*base coat, color polish, top coat*
Manicure nail treatment overlaps with			*dry*
pedicure nail treatment.	12:45:48		*cleanse, exfoliate, moisturize, massage*
	13:13:29		*base coat, color polish, top coat*
Clinician escorts and administers	13:32:54		*dry*
compounded dermal treatment.	13:34:58	13:34:58	Escorted to dermal treatment quarters.
	13:44:27		*cleanse, wrap, adhere, massage*
	13:47:38		*moisturize*
			Escorted to cosmetics bar.
Clinician escorts.			*cleanse, identify, educate, apply*
Esthetician administers makeup application	14:48:22	14:53:29	Escorted to revenue counter.
and suggests additional products.	14:55:09	14:55:09	
Cashier sums client's account.	15:15:00		Pay for treatment services and products.
	15:15:47	15:15:47	
Valet retrieves vehicle from parking lot.	15:18:31	15:25:46	Tip valet. Retrieve vehicle.
	15:27:08	15:28:16	

A Proprietary Systems line of medicinal treatments infiltrates a day spa, relocating health care professionals such as dermatologists and pharmacists into a service-based environment.

health-related skin-care products (lotions enriched with vitamins, age-defying cremes, foundation with sunblock, etc.) in a strategic marketing attempt to link their identity and services with the medical industry. Overt changes in industry terminology, packaging, and retail strategies can be found at department store counters: cosmetic consultants (employees) wear white lab coats, carry clipboards, and are ready to add vitamin E-enriched nighttime moisturizer to your personal chart during this month's appointment. Cosmeticians are identified as medical practitioners, recommending innovative new treatments to cure your facial and body ills. This medical marketing image is furthered by the somewhat loose FDA restrictions placed on the substantiation of cosmetic performance claims. Cosmetic companies are investing tremendous resources into chemical research and material technology for the production of innovative, health-based cosmetic lines. Is this just a fashion trend? Or is there a future for beauty within the practice of medicine?

Dispensary

This studio investigates the pharmacy, the business of beauty, and health-care related practices through the development of a prototype commercial environment.

The invention of the caplet as a means of dosage measurement and dispensing transformed the commercial space of pharmacy retail and the role of the pharmacist. Will time-released implants and topical treatments shift the now commodity-focused industry into service-based, procedural environments?

DAWN FINLEY is a principal at Interloop—Architecture. She is an assistant professor at Rice School of Architecture.

↑ Proprietary Systems™

Patented molecules. Polymer technology. Performance delivery systems. Proprietary Systems seeks to "brand" at the scale of drug administration, specifically utilizing technological advances in the transdermal absorption of medication on the molecular level. Delivery efficiency is sevenfold in comparison to oral drug dosages that anticipate resistance from the body's defensive gastrointestinal system, while extended control over the temporal aspect of a drug's delivery into a patient's bloodstream has significant implications for society's current medicating cycles and rituals.

Proprietary Systems provides a spectrum of preprogramming and customization particulars based on factors of consumer commitment and product

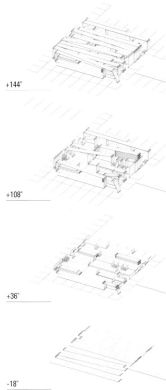

+144"

+108"

+36"

-18"

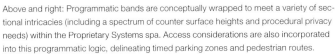

Above and right: Programmatic bands are conceptually wrapped to meet a variety of sectional intricacies (including a spectrum of counter surface heights and procedural privacy needs) within the Proprietary Systems spa. Access considerations are also incorporated into this programmatic logic, delineating timed parking zones and pedestrian routes.

marketability. A full-service surgical implant dispenses medication for up to a five-year period and relinquishes the patient from the monotonous prescription label regimen. Medicinal threads are implanted in bundles just beneath the skin in accordance with the tension lines structuring its dynamic capabilities. Compartmentalization across the dermal surface allows for localized treatments or simultaneous absorption of multiple molecular compounds into the bloodstream.

HEIDI WERNER / Undergraduate Option Studio, 2001

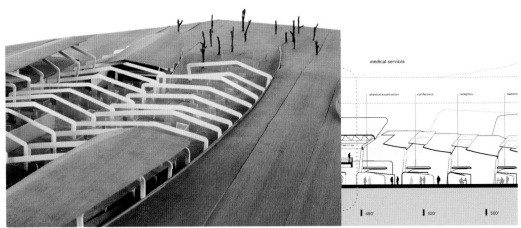

medical services

physical examination | conference | reception | classroom

480' | 520' | 560'

↑Feedback

In a wellness and community center for a new generation of technologically savvy senior citizens, the private, procedural components of the facility are organized as a gradient field condition of semi-enclosures suspended within public interstitial space. This "negative space" between components becomes the embodiment of the senior wellness center, as its gradually increasing density promotes the social interaction critical to maintaining physical and psychological longevity.

DAVID HERMANN / Undergraduate Vertical Studio, 2002

Interior Perspective at Prescription Drop-Off Counter

Interior Perspective at Consultation Counter

The PHARMETICS *junkie* drops her order at the prescription counter and continues on to the *shifting* stock display shelf to scan this week's product combinations. *Blue-Belly Pregnancy Stick?* After picking up her prescription - a refill of Prozac blended in a translucent pink dermal stick - she wanders over to the manicure/pedicure area for a clear coat.

The new customer is greeted by a *sideline* technician who conducts a brief consultation, explaining the product and service concepts at PHARMETICS. After purchasing a solid aftershave blended with *Nicoderm*, the customer checks in with a procedure technician, and is escorted to the second level for a two o'clock appointment.

Blue-Belly Pregnancy Stick

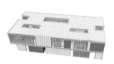

Ground Level Exploded Perspective

Solid Aftershave Blended with Nicoderm

Second Level Exploded Perspective

The PHARMETICS dispensary is sited as an operational component in commerce, utilizing economic and regulatory systems, marketing strategies, and cultural identification as means to investigate and articulate a physical retail environment

↑Capsizing the Flagship

Flagship and superstore are retail terms that refer to maximizing the amount and variety of different programs contained within one huge store, rather than providing unique consumer services with a strategic placement of specific quality programs. Numerous products and programs—grocery, pharmacy, video rental, clothing, bank, restaurant, liquor store, coffee shop, etc.—are all squeezed under a single roof. Big box supermarket, drugstore, and one-stop-shop retail for all home and body needs limits the consumer's tangible experience of the city primarily to a numbing interior repetition of generalized shopping. Discount drugstore chains are a primary example of this type.

Capsizing the flagship recognizes the potential of a strategic combining of programs to produce an innovative retail environment

that blends and mutually exploits different industries' operations (research, development, marketing, distribution). This sharing and borrowing of resources creates new hybrids of industry, product/service, and practice. It is through such a specialized reconfiguration that the environment of contemporary urban industry manifests itself.

This proposal rejects the dominant trend to absorb pharmacy into supermarket/general-store environments. Pharmacy is examined and developed through the strategic combination of potential adjacencies—transformative sideline programs that activate an experimental production component of pharmaceutical retail. Strategic business, operational, and spatial organization facilitates cross-industry sharing and borrowing to produce innovative product/service concepts that might never evolve if specialized industries remain competitively and operationally disconnected. The project blends pharmacy practice

with other categories to produce mutual industry (re)invention. The corporate drugstore chain and the international cosmetic company combine to establish PHARMETICS dispensary, a retail environment concept that capsizes the flagship.

DAWN FINLEY / M.Arch. Thesis, 1999 / Keith Krumwiede, director

↑**Waiting Room**
MARC FROHN / Graduate Core Studio, 2002 / Dawn Finley, Gordon Wittenberg, critics

→As Found: Space—Light—Situation

The montages shown here are not a representation of any design for architectural space or form, but are themselves a designed experience. By design these images are able to sustain a playful engagement with us because they interact with our cognitive mechanism of attention in specific ways.

Attention has many aspects, but it is generally defined as the process by which we selectively focus on one facet of the environment while ignoring others. I consider the montages as "playful" because they engender a prolonged interaction between these two subjects of attention: a viewer and the environment. They are continuously promoting our engagement with them while also demanding engagement from us.

The montages were produced simply, in multiple stages, in an environment simulating that of their ultimate viewing. This design process allowed my own mechanisms of attention to develop the content and experience of the images.

Each montage is a simple overlay of two photographs in Photoshop, with a layer filter applied to interlace them in a smooth way. This always left an incongruity in the spaces of the montages, but the simple procedure also allowed for the production of quite a few. In six stages I took over 12,000 photographs, performing over 7,000 overlays to produce 624 viable montages. The immediacy and unpredictable nature of working with this many images assured that I wasn't focused on designing them, but was only reacting to them. The montages that could captured my attention on their own, retaining subtle but recognizable artifacts in the process.

The montages were produced in multiple stages: photos were taken, then overlaid, then more photos were taken, and so on. The spaces I chose to photograph evolved throughout these iterations to become more and more mundane. To economize its resource of attention, our brain filters out visual patterns it finds recognizable. In this way we become habituated to our everyday environment. Parking garages, unoccupied office space, art galleries with blank walls—these simple spaces are recognizable patterns to our brains and so produced the most attractive overlays.

Which of the photos I selected to overlay also evolved, clarifying the figure/ground relationship of the montages in turn. Recognizing shapes in an environment is a basic human visual function, rooted in the cognitive ability to separate objects from their surroundings. The more successful montages accessed this basic drive. Doors, windows, and picture frames are recurring themes in the final images.

As I designed these montages, they filled my field of view, much in the way they do when viewed on a wall at a comfortable distance. As such, they were too large for my eyes to focus on in total. The area in the field of view that our focused vision covers is very small, leaving the majority to peripheral vision. These two kinds of vision correlate with two types of attention processing in our brains: focused vision with conscious attention, and peripheral vision with what is called "covert attention." Covert attention filters out the visual information our brain won't think is interesting, as well as alerting it to things it should focus on next.

Through the design process used to produce these montages, they evolved into a balanced tension between conscious and covert attentions. While our focused vision understands the spaces in the montages as ordinary, our covert attention is captured by what the peripheral vision sees as being slightly askew. When focusing on any part of the montages, the brain is constantly telling the eyes they should be looking elsewhere, providing for a continuous game of cat and mouse.

BRENT LINDEN / M.Arch. Thesis, 2004 / Nana Last, director

COVERT ATTENTION

A COMFORTABLE DISTANCE

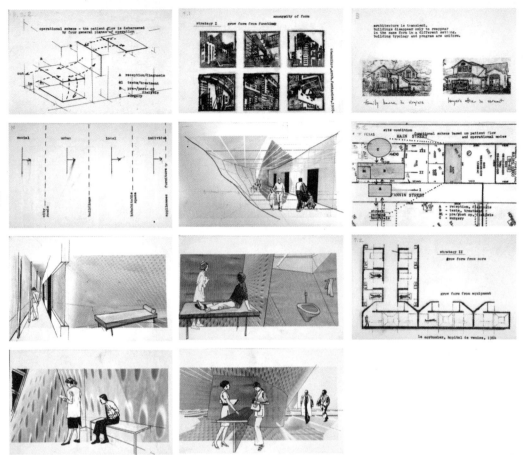

Possible interior scenarios and organization precedents for an ambulatory clinic

↑Ambulatory Clinic

The following is a letter: I am writing to you with an issue that causes a big part of the frustration that I have in studio.

Essentially I doubt the efficiency of our attempts to construct the "big picture" of architecture in the form of a building. An ambulatory service in the medical center, more than many other programs, like a movie theater, interweaves in itself as a concept of intricacy very difficult to grasp in a short two-or-three-or-four week period. I think it futile to try to envision all this complexity of politics, economics, sociology and esthetics on a sheet of paper—all this inevitably gets reduced to all-too-familiar diagrams. Such abstraction seems to me very unfair to the pretense of the program—to take into consideration the complexity of both the program and the site.

I don't want to make an argument against or for totality in design. My attempts have been to remove myself from the parts of the design process that I am simply not knowledgeable in and let other worry about them. Which in fact is closer to what happens in reality. Instead I want to try to orchestrate a number of scenarios along which the architecture could evolve.

Firstly I don't want to invent a new building typology. No need to re-invent the wheel—the building will be constructed along two principles: on one hand it will borrow an existing typology and on the other, its structural system will follow its internal organization. What that system can be will be defined when interior spaces take form.

Secondly I hope it is possible to design a part with regard to the whole. Not meaning a module that can be repeated and used as a structural element. The idea that building will be clothed in a skin, serving structural or esthetic purposes or both, seems to me insubstantial since it will cover a diverse system of activities. In other words the exterior will completely conceal its contents. In a highly technological and maintained environment as our program is, the contents of the building are what is valuable and where the investment goes. It looks like instead of putting on a friendly and inviting face, the building could expose its essence, its internal structure and declare an open invitation tot he activity that takes place inside. On the other hand who would care about the insides, if the building tells the story on the outside. It's a paradox.

I want to start with proposing that quality of space can be formed in a box of any size, in a space of any geometry. I will be staging an act and after that another act and another all in the same space.

My actors will be the trivial Light and Volume, with helpers like the necessary Furniture, the critical Hi-Tech Appliances, perhaps some irrational Decoration. Or maybe the arguments is: with the same actors I can stage many different acts, none of which is any better or worse than the other. The subject matter of space is essentially re-directed to equipment (by equipment I mean furniture, appliances, light fixtures, all sorts of interior devices).

I don't know.

In the end, that the design process ends up so fragmented, divided as responsibilities of many parties which all call themselves designers, seems only analogical to an uncontrollable conglomerate of pieces in a genetic whole. What if after we do that we find out that we haven't really constructed anything—instead some structure (not necessarily new), an unexpected architecture was created.

Maybe the designer's sole concern and responsibility can be the one detail, the small in view of the big whole… (how small is a good question—designing a door handle screw is as ridiculous as designing cities). Just like in some socialist utopia, humorously enough…

Part II

The point of all such concerns is that the building cannot be a singular statement. Simultaneously—yes, but never read as a book. More, it is experienced in a process, understood and then designed (with hope). Two things are inevitable: the human subject matter and the site.

A straightforward defiance: instead of a circulation ruled by the doctor's occupation and schedule, the program as priority has to stage the patient flow and time. A bridge: of course the money driven initiative in Medicare stimulates the specific kind of time management, i.e. shorter stay, more patients, more cash flow and better service. A more efficient model is proven to be: healthier environment, health education, patient self-care, better service, and cash of course. The context: as a site in the medical center, networking is a vital resource. The building cannot ignore its "habitat." At the same time, in addition to borrowing, it cannot afford to conform fully, due to the different time management on the inside.

Just like a virus, the program of the building affects the building's organism. Sometimes it moves silently, sometimes causes an infection. But every time the virus is visible, it only suggests something bigger underway. The building's integrity apparently remains, but there are signs that its constituency has been modified.

NIK NIKOLOV / Graduate Core Studio, 1998 / Keith Krumwiede, Gordon Wittenberg, critics

↑**Ambulatory Clinic**
JANELLE GUNTHER / Graduate Core Studio, 1998 / Keith Krumweide, Gordon Wittenberg, critics

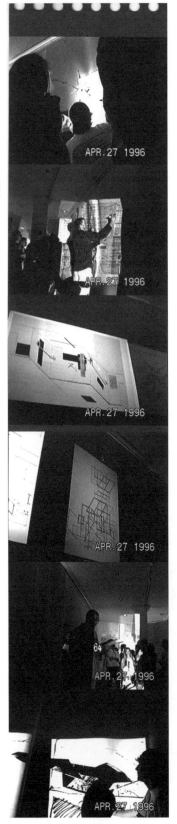

Performative drawing act of the thesis

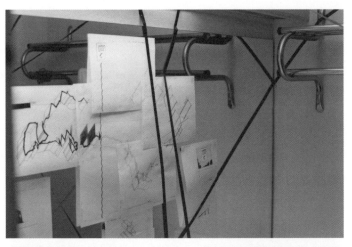

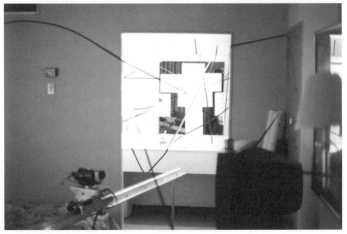

Occupation and redrawing in a hotel room

↑ Acting Space... Following the Line: Architectures of the Drawing Act

This thesis follows four lines of thought, which propose that drawing or more specifically drawing acts are the material practice of architecture. The first line studies the creation, development, and history of the clockwork, both as a conceptual order-imposer and later as an actual mechanism that began the quantification and routinization of time, technique, systems, art, science, and life in Western culture. The second line studies the effects the clockwork

had upon the development of rational techniques employed by the arts, philosophy, economic systems, perspective, cartography, and projective drawing systems, and how this systematization was essential in creating architecture as an autonomous and remote profession operating in incremental time and space. The third line develops a philosophy and alternate history of the drawing act or performative diagram that harnesses existing flows and systems to operate in the real time of the act and not in the incremental and rationalized time and space of the clockwork. The fourth and final line of the thesis involves a wide-ranging performative-based drawing: a road trip, field drawings, USGS re-mapping, simultaneous agents drawing in and between three cities, the performance of drawing over the facsimile machine, and the occupation of, and redrawing in, a hotel room, finally culminating in the performative drawing act of the thesis at Rice School of Architecture.

MARK KROECKEL / M.Arch. Thesis, 1996 / Michael Bell, director

↓Crash Hotel

Fifteen years ago, Yung Ho Chang directed a studio called Crash. The project took the ideas of J. G. Ballard's novels *Crash* and *Concrete Island* as a point of departure for programmatic investigation. Both books deal with perceptions and relationships that are altered by a violent act: a car crash. In the case of *Concrete Island*, a London family-man crashes his Jaguar and becomes trapped in a residual piece of urban infrastructure situated between freeway overpasses. The story follows the injured man's struggles to escape that isolated, forgotten, yet seemingly public urban space. Ballard recognized that we are often only an event away from having to completely reevaluate our relationship to our surroundings. Crash studio began with a violent act as well: a section cut through the body, a car, and a building. This cut began a family of drawings that took Ballard's ideas as a departure point. A series of drawings was constructed to test our preconceptions about program, space, and their relationship to urban infrastructure. The programs of hotel, tollway, body, and automobile were combined and reimagined. The experiment compressed related but often disconnected programs in an effort to find unseen opportunities that often hide in plain sight.

BLAIR SATTERFIELD / Graduate Option Studio, 1995 / Yung Ho Chang, critic

↑Jiffy Park
Parking provided for Enron, from your car to your cubicle 'in a jiffy.'
SCOTT ALLEN / Graduate Option Studio, 2000 / Jacob van Rijs, Kimberly Shoemake, critics

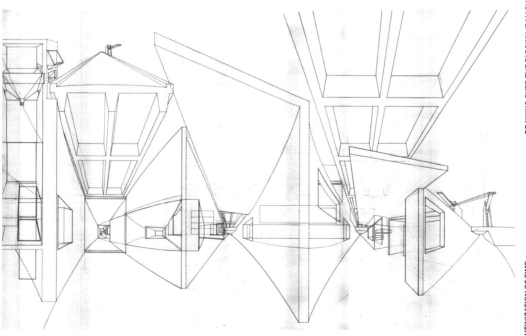

Multi-point perspectives of hotel "lanes"

Axonometric of hotel-tollway

10·18·95

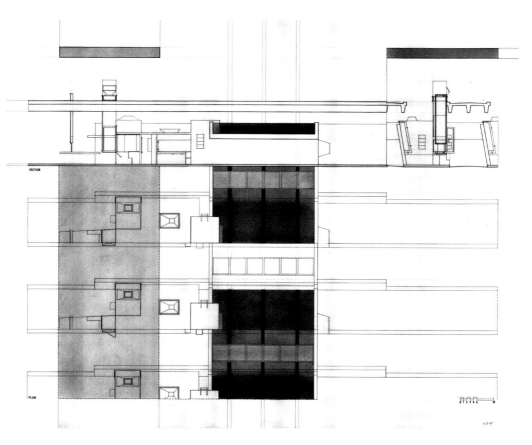

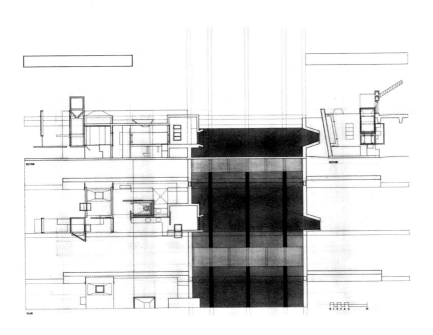

Hotel-tollway sections and plans

Maxi-Taxi transportation routes overlaying other city services

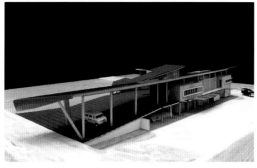

Service hub for Maxi Taxi system

↑Maxi Taxi

Houston's Fifth Ward is a residential neighborhood immediately adjacent to downtown, yet physically separated from it by freeway, rail, and ship traffic. A comparison of Fifth Ward data on demographics, pollution, employment, income, transportation, and communication access with like data from other neighborhoods found that concentrations of poverty, airborne pollutants, unemployment, and a lack of telephone and

Drivable surfaces extend through the Maxi Taxi service hub

vehicle ownership are endemic Fifth Ward characteristics. A latent strategy of resource sharing (carpooling, public transit, density of air-conditioning use, low yet concentrated population density) enables residents to navigate the dangers of the city even as it forces them to forego the "ideals" of house, lawn, and car.

The project proposes a system of independently owned and operated Maxi Taxis (decommissioned limousines, SUVs, and other oversized vehicles), each outfitted with telephony, internet access, and meeting space. Occupying a niche somewhere between taxis and buses, the Maxi Taxis follow fixed routes that may change as quickly as necessary. The system retains the quality of slow landscape changes, while working furiously and persistently to produce those changes. Because the system is fully plugged into the techniques of resource exploitation that give form to work (communication, transportation, mental confluence), it plays a major role in the development of the landscape. Large vehicles become destinations. They become a resource that is visible on the road, in the psychological map, and on the spreadsheet.

Maxi Taxi Central draws together a driving school, a transportation planning office, and a vehicle repair center. The building combines the typological associations of service stations, transit depots, industrial sheds, and small wood frame houses, with an architectural program related to the training, servicing, and administration of the system.

The site is modeled as a group of tile and grass-crete surfaces that mimic local industrial and infrastructure types. Habitable boxes compete with Maxi Taxis for space beneath the surfaces. Semiannually, the 200-foot-long shed roof of cerulean blue tile is handwashed to remove particle pollution, in emulation of washing one's car in public, while the small wood-sided buildings are painted with many thin, translucent coats, trapping the particle pollution in layers of gloss and producing deep, dirty, beautiful planes of color.

KENT FITZSIMONS, JON MCNEAL / Graduate Option Studio, 1999 / Michael Bell, Luke Bulman, critics

Today I look at this project with the concerns of a studio instructor. Throughout the project's development, two interweaving dynamics spun into what I consider to be a crucial moment in my understanding of architectural design. On the one hand, I recall feeling inhabited by a variety of interests:

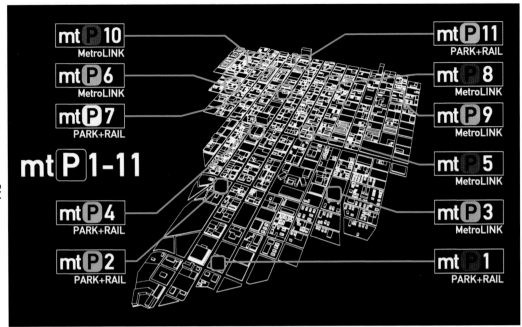

mtP system map

representation, individual and group identity, the architectonics of big roofs, natural and cultural cycles, the materiality of infrastructure, the politics of form... the list goes on. These concerns gravitated somewhat loosely and at times erratically around a personal agenda that I was trying to work out in the context of the studio topic. On the other hand, collaborating with Jon McNeal, who brought other concerns to the table, required that I organize and communicate this constellation of preoccupations. It also demanded that I let go of some obsessions and hop onto the project when it followed Jon's trajectory. The result was, I think, more than the sum of our contributions. Since then, I consider that fostering a student's personal drive and agenda while encouraging him or her to be open to a teammate's program is an obligation of design education.
—**Kent Fitzsimons** is the assistant director of Rice School of Architecture-Paris.

↗ mtP: an Urban Tactic

To operate at an urban scale in the contemporary metropolis requires a reassessment of forces too often considered beyond the grasp of the architect and too often ignored

by the planner. In Houston the difficulty of creatively engaging the disparate machinations of private development may constitute the greatest challenge to the project of urbanism. The redevelopment of Midtown Houston, a high-traffic corridor situated between the central business district and the Texas Medical Center, prompts us to create alternative tactics for reshaping the city.

Midtown Parking (mtP) is a system of eleven hybridized parking garages that uses the ever-present need for more parking as a means to intervene in the climate of private development, to organize existing potentials, and to influence the reshaping of the district. Based upon a flexible prototype, the garages respond to localized trends, needs, and paths. At a larger scale, they act together to focus the disparate field of Midtown. mtP offers a way of rethinking how urbanity might emerge from a private development paradigm and reflects a desire to make coherent and vital urban form.

The functioning of the transportation sector is central to the functioning of urban economies. Cities enable people to take advantage of economies of agglomeration, where spatial

proximity facilitates cooperation. Transportation defines proximity and determines how economies of agglomeration are realized.
MICHAEL MORROW / M.Arch. Thesis, 2000 / Keith Krumwiede, director

In a vein common to many of the best theses at Rice, Midtown Parking develops a line of research that seeks to leverage the commonplace but pervasive processes of the contemporary American city for the production of a civic infrastructure. In taking a dispassionate look at the typical development patterns that continually reshape Houston, Michael Morrow observed that an intelligent adjustment to one of Houston's most familiar building types—the parking garage—could rewire a district. Midtown Parking, in collectivizing the parking demands for an entire district, seeds the area with a civic garage in preparation for a projected wave of new residential development. The logic of the project hinges less upon the design of the garages themselves and more upon their potential to engender new urban typologies in the field that surrounds them. In this sense, the project builds upon the greater Rice project of delirious urban mapping in search of opportunities for the insertion of architectural change agents capable of

One of the eleven mtP hybridized parking garages

Zones of mtP influence, forming a calibrated field of parking structures

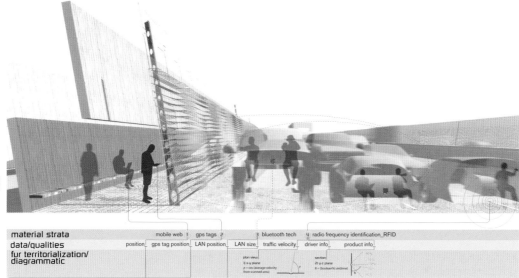

material strata		mobile web 1	gps tags 2		3 bluetooth tech	4 radio frequency identification_RFID	
data/qualities	position	gps tag position	LAN position	LAN size	traffic velocity	driver info	product info
fur territorialization/ diagrammatic			plan view			section	

redirecting the accelerating, but often dissociated forces that shape the city.
—**Keith Krumwiede** is an assistant dean and an assistant professor at Yale School of Architecture. He was an assistant professor at Rice School of Architecture from 1996-2003.

↑Tactile
Spectrum

This urban research studio examined the massively linked and synchronic global metropolis, approaching the urban field as a networking of heterogeneous, discrete systems—"small worlds" of social, political, and economic organizations. The "accidental" relations among these geographically adjacent but effectively disjunctive local-globals and global-locales produce a "shear space." More than a metaphor, shear is a material dynamic describing the spatial relationship of social and political forces in a built environment that literally radiates and pulses with information—where territory is defined not simply by walls but by access points, baud rates, and signal attenuation. Thus, the studio questioned how the twenty-first-century infrastructures that foster bottom-up organizations and global networking could be deployed within an urban field configured by the top-down

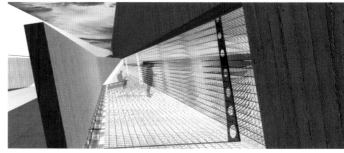

Points of view along the proposed spatial intervention, following the freeway

infrastructures of twentieth-century suburban processes.

The extreme freeway condition of Houston forces us to consider the following issues: Program (the freeway is not just about rapid transit anymore); Time (we spend more time in our cars than anywhere except work and home); and Place (the freeway complex occupies one-eighth of the Houston metropolitan area).

The typical reformer's approach to this situation is to find ways to "get freeways moving again." However, studies show that congestion persists in spite of our continual efforts to widen highways and create new ones. In the auto-based city, the traffic jam is a permanent condition. What if freeway paralysis is viewed not as an aberration from the working system, but as an integral element of that system? We could even say that within the urban freeway complex, rapid transit is the off-hour by-product of rush-hour congestion.

The team inversed the traditional concept of a network system as point nodes connected by vector links. The regularity of the traffic jam and the development of feeder roads as consumer strip centers allow us to see the vector-based freeway complex instead as a destination, with an address and hours of operation. Now the streets themselves are linear nodes, with their on/off ramps serving as linking connectivity.

Seizing the Highway 59 trench extension as a timely opportunity, our project reconstructs the freeway infrastructure to engage dynamically with the proliferating electromagnetic landscape of the city. Our intervention addresses three significant technology platforms: top-down mobile internet with GPS positioning; bottom-up Bluetooth-based local area networks; and passive RFID tags. Our scheme tracks these software/hardware packages as they are deployed amidst the field of the freeway traffic jam in order to observe and manipulate their capacity to incite new social, commercial, and formal realities.

Our attack redefines this infrastructural thread as a place of cultural exchange—a contemporary Agora—that frees the freeway from a rhetoric of rapid mass mobility. By forcing reinforced concrete to open up to interaction with the ever-thickening landscape of radio waves and digital communication, the intervention sketches the critical negotiations required of a twenty-first-century infrastructure.

SKY LANNIGAN, JUD MOORE, DAVID NEWTON / Graduate Core Studio, 2004 / Christopher Hight, Sean Lally, critics

→Mobile Event Structures

The sixties art movement Fluxus removed art from the traditional grip of prestigious isolation and placed it firmly into the everyday where any average Joe has the ability to participate in art's creation and its quirky development. An urban design project of a media center that both addresses the nature of the highways of Houston and heeds the Fluxus sentiment of art for all suggests that the architect must leave her ivory tower to engage the city streets—literally. The architect putting his money where his mouth is. A sample deployment of a traveling event bubble in the city.

MICHAEL SWEEBE / Graduate Option Studio, 1997 / Alex Wall, critic

Michael Sweebe's project is reminiscent of the brief interlude of a wind-blown plastic bag that appears in Alan Ball and Sam Mendes's 1999 film *American Beauty*. Like the film, the "situation" here is ambiguous, arbitrary, dark, and deeply ironic: the honor of its success ties back to the Situationists, those urban "guerillas" of the sixties and seventies.

The Situationists, like Fluxus—their better known peers and the group of radicals that Sweebe pays homage to—dealt an unmediated blow to the time-honored, immemorial nature of "master planning" by undermining the project of fixity, replacing it with fluidity. No longer was space concrete and immovable; it was transfigured into something more akin to a temporal series of circumstantial "Neubauten."

EVENT BUBBLE

LINEAR NODES

ELECTROMAGNETIC LANDSCAPE

Deploying the traveling event bubble; tea and chess inside the inflated bubble

Sweebe's project, however, is cautious nonetheless, since it does not admit exigencies, but rather seeks to control and counteract the environment in which it finds itself. Still, the spirit of Fluxus and the Situationists remains intact, a chimera of possibility, a moment exposed for what it is: an irrecoverable instant that resonates beyond its tentative aesthetic.
—**Elizabeth Gamard** is the associate dean of Tulane University School of Architecture. She was an assistant professor at Rice School of Architecture from 1990-97.

→ Many, Many, Many, Many Parking Spaces

The Puddle is the new American vernacular space. The Puddle is a secondary structure, the result of commercial development within the Ladder, the suburban structure described by Albert Pope. The individual parking fields of discrete commercial buildings bleed into one another, forming a continuous surface that short circuits the structure of the Ladder. The Puddle thus reorganizes the city. While the expanse of paved surface is what makes these places undesirable, it is this same interconnected surface that make these places interesting. This is where we shop, interact, exercise, socialize, scandalize...

The Puddle forms a secondary system of navigation that short circuits roads and provides new sites for programs. The ubiquitous space of the parking lot is navigable in almost any direction. Thus, it allows for programs to be dropped in without regard to traffic or street. By placing programs into the parking lot, one changes the navigation of that lot. The lot adjusts to the new program without changing its infrastructure. The ubiquitous space is one of endless potential. It allows for a "plug-in city" to actually become real.

This thesis attempts to address the Puddle and the parking lot without falling into the traps that formal games can create in this landscape. It is an experiment in

Collaboratively designed model combining continuous parking with other urban programs

planning a place—an attempt to redesign what the Puddle is and what it does. There are no formal dictates to the architecture, only guides to land use and urban growth. This thesis outlined a set of guides for the chosen site. These guides were given over to a set of individuals, along with an equally important set of "guides for the guides." The experiment was

conducted on a 1:100 scale model of the site. The scale was chosen because of the size of the site and to avoid formal games that might be played with the architecture of the individual buildings.
ANDREW ALBERS / M.Arch. Thesis, 1999 / Farès el Dahdah, director

On Touring Houston

Stephen Fox

I've acquired a certain reputation. I'm the go-to guy for tours of Houston architecture. That's how I first met Lars Lerup: taking him on an architectural tour of Houston with Sally Woodbridge in October 1983. The only thing I recall about the tour is lunch at Fuddruckers, a hamburger place on Chimney Rock in a building designed by Clovis Heimsath. Lars got mad at the waiter when he wouldn't let us sit where we wanted to. I don't remember now, but I think we did sit where we wanted. The semester after Lars came to Rice as dean, he got me to do a tour for him and Michael Bell. We stopped at Bolton & Barnstone's by then deserted (and now demolished) Winterbotham House on Briar Hollow and wandered around the outside, dismayed that such a beautiful modern house should be abandoned. In the back yard there was a swimming pool that had been drained. Michael saw a big turtle stranded on the floor of the pool and climbed down to rescue it, bringing it up to ground level and setting it loose.

Most of my tours with Lars have been in the twenty-first century: Saturday morning and afternoon expeditions to Houston's outer limits. I have photos of Lars taking photos of the Portofino Shopping Center near The Woodlands, a hysterical attempt to architecturally appropriate medieval Venice and remake it as a strip shopping center. It even has a canal. Lars and I spent hours (and many tanks of gas) prowling

and puzzling over Houston's endless periphery, marveling (Lars) and despairing (me) at the unconscionable incongruity of it all. We went to the Shri Swaminarayan Mandir in Stafford, Morton Cemetery in Richmond, and a Hispanic immigrant Saturday morning market in the Greenspoint area (thanks to Rafael Longoria), and we crossed the Houston Ship Channel on the Lynchburg Ferry. Yet, for me at least, the more I was exposed to outer Houston (visualize the endless retail corridor along Farm Road 1960 in the Champions area), the less comprehensible it became. There was something much more consoling about the economically depressed African-American, Hispanic immigrant, and Anglo-American working class neighborhoods of Houston's East End, Pasadena, and Baytown. Although in slow decay, they possess a sense of depth (what in any other city would be called "history") lacking in such economically vibrant but emotionally depressing planned communities as those west of Pearland.

The model for the kinds of tours I give is an all-day outing that Molly and Will Cannady organized one gray, overcast Sunday in February 1978. Reyner Banham, with whom Will had studied at The Bartlett in London, had come to Houston to speak to the RDA, bringing his wife, Mary, to see their friends Magda and John McHale, celebrated futurists who then taught at the University of Houston. Will asked me to come because he wanted to show the Banhams Galveston and I had been working with Drexel Turner on a Galveston project. Molly and Will put everyone (the Banhams, the McHales, and Mary Lynch, the president of RDA) into

Portofino Lifestyle Center, 2001, Hermes Architects.

Southern National Bank, Southwest Freeway, 1997, Kirksey.

Houston Ship Channel from the Lynchburg ferry.

Ching Hua Sheng Mwu Gong, Houston, 1995.

their cavernous Suburban, and Will piloted us through a Houston largely unknown to me. We went through the East End and Fifth Ward, where we rode *under* the Elysian Viaduct past housewives, ironing clothes on ironing boards set up in the street, who treated the overpass above them as a civic arcade. Will took us to the end of Harbor Street, the only place where you can get right next to the Houston Ship Channel, and then proceeded to drive along the loading docks between the wharf warehouses and the channel. We followed the awesome palisade of petrochemical refineries bordering the La Porte Freeway all the way out to Bay Ridge, and then turned south along Highway 146 to Galveston, ending up that night at John's Oyster Resort, a 1920's Spanish-style roadhouse on Offatts Bayou. Will's tour was not a tour of architectural monuments. It was a historical-topographical tour. It made you understand how these parts of Houston worked, why they were there, and how the pieces fit together.

Making Houston comprehensible is a challenge. Houston did not fascinate Reyner Banham the way Los Angeles had. Likewise, Rem Koolhaas seemed dispirited when I went with him and a group of Rice students from the observation deck of the Transco Tower eastward to Pasadena and refinery row, ending up in Clear Lake City—at rush hour. Los Angeles (a 1920's city with 1950's suburbs) and Atlanta (Koolhaas's choice for the representative U.S. suburbanized city) are more spatially legible, and more scenic, than Houston. Zoning and eighty years

of public sector planning have clarified their forms. Without a zoning code and the planning infrastructure its management would have required, Houston grew through the twentieth century the way U.S. cities did in the nineteenth century. It's just that here nineteenth-century heterogeneity was extrapolated to the scale of the suburbanized, sprawling postwar city, the kind Robert Bruegmann defends (he was very enthusiastic about Houston's urban mess).

In giving tours, I generally avoid the problematic outskirts and stick to the triangle between downtown, the Rice-Medical Center area, and River Oaks. Within this triangle, there is an amazing variety of landscape conditions that, when explicated historically, makes Houston's development patterns evident. This triangle also contains the great majority of Houston's architectural landmarks, both modern and pre-modern. For visitors, seeing how the buildings of Ludwig Mies van der Rohe, Renzo Piano, Philip Johnson, and Ralph Adams Cram fit into the city, how landscape conditions vary, and how certain adjacencies came into being brings the big picture of Houston into focus. The Tin Houses of the West End, Project Row Houses in Third Ward, the avenues of live oak trees lining North and South Boulevards, the Usonian houses of MacKie & Kamrath on Tiel Way, the flamboyant contemporary houses of Riverside Terrace, and Glendower Terrace, with its houses by Taft Architects, Carlos Jiménez, and Wittenberg Architects, are local surprises that attest to the vitality of Houston's architectural culture. Visitors are often surprised to discover that Houston just might be an interesting city, one with some historical grounding and architectural depth. (I have come to realize that it helps that visitors often arrive with low expectations.)

Of course, when Lars asked me to give Peter Cook a tour in March 2008, he specified that it was to be of the nastiest, vilest, most despicable parts of Houston. My dilemma was that I'd already given Peter Cook that tour in 1997 (which he remembered). So I connected the dots of out-of-the-way works of architecture in marginal neighborhoods (M+A Architects' Small House, Brett Zamore's Shot-Trot House, Stern & Bucek's Salazar House, MC2's Price/Martínez House, Michael Landrum's Balinskas House) along with some up-channel back roads off Clinton Drive (Emile Street is always good for a *frisson*) that seem to have entertained and amused. Twenty years earlier I felt similarly

Bellaire Medical Building under construction, Alief area, Houston, 2003.

The Quadruple Bypass pedestrian bridge in Texas Medical Center.

Aerial view of the Museum District and Hermann Park.

Downtown Houston.

Gulf Freeway and Beltway 8 interchange, Houston.

pressured when giving a tour to J. B. Jackson, then the Cullinan Visiting Professor, and his friend, Sheila Pellegrini, who had come from Santa Fe to visit him. Since Jackson had written an essay about architectural tours in which he decried those who would show him only posh neighborhoods, I was very careful to steer clear of such settings. Teasingly, and then with a rising note of exasperation, he continued to ask: "When are we going to get River Oaks? I want to show Sheila River Oaks." Not only did we make it to River Oaks, Jackson also insisted that we "show Sheila" the Bayou Club, where Anderson Todd had taken him to lunch. So much for anti-elitism.

Looking back on thirty years of architectural touring, I'm now amazed at some of the people I've shown around Houston: Pritzker laureates, philosophy luminaries, an English law lord, writer Andrei Codrescu and his wife (so far no movie stars, although Joanne Herring comes close). Interpreting the place where you live for outsiders not only makes you get your stories straight, but it also causes you to question the landscapes you know as you see them through other peoples' eyes and experiences. Try it.

STEPHEN FOX is a fellow of the Anchorage Foundation and a lecturer at Rice School of Architecture.

↑Supermundane
Exhibition of super-sized aerial photography
DAVID GUTHRIE / Farish Gallery, 2003

Promenade fragments

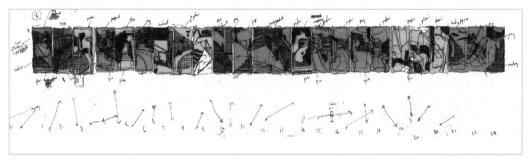

Translation sketch of promenade fragments

Strip model 1

Strip model 2

←Processing Context: Nice, France

Is there any difference between a length of 2x4 and the city of Nice? This project explores the process of translating experience into form through a continuous loop of abstracted self-reference. The underlying ambition is to fabricate a contextual vocabulary for the city of Nice that is based on the direct translation of sensory input. The experience of the European promenade—from medieval alleyway to seaside vista—is broken down, and its various components are reassembled into a catalogue of abstractions. Fragments of the experience are translated into drawing, where light, texture, and space are abstracted by graphite. From this drawing, spatial conditions are given simple material assignments—dappled light becomes pegboard, dark shadow becomes walnut, visual expanse becomes Plexiglas, etc. All of these meandering conditions are pulled taut and become subservient to the banality of the 2x4. This abstracted promenade is cut and carved to the point of failure, and then brought back to stability with the layering of materials. The collaged 2x4 becomes an object or site of its own, and its spatial conditions are translated once again through the process of drawing. The final model closes the loop of abstraction and delivers a vocabulary of contextualism.

BRETT TERPELUK / Graduate Option Studio, 1997 / John J. Casbarian, critic

↓MTA Lagos: Rethinking the Drive-through Market

In 2020, transportation infrastructure is projected as the only free and public space left, carrying thousands of people traversing the urban plane daily. It accumulates into a public realm of hyper-congestion. The drive-through market typology emerges from these zones of staccato flow, accommodating the multitude of transient consumers. By legitimizing the process of informal trade activity, the drive-through market offers Lagos the opportunity to regularize its economy and claim a shared public realm at the scale of the megalopolis it has become.

MTA is the future of mobile transactions allotments. Its new trading emporium, located at the base of the soon to be completed third mainland bridge, will facilitate an unprecedented magnitude of collective inhabitation and exchange. Just what Lagos needs: a drive-through market.

Street traders in Lagos have transformed the congestion of the rapidly growing city into a unique commercial condition where the zone of trading merges with the zone of highway traffic. Motor vehicle and pedestrian hawker coexist in a space of continuous transformation, organizing dynamically according to the flow of traffic. The structure of these markets is loose and undefined. Enclosure is generated by one or two elements, forming and reforming as transactions occur. Traders take advantage of the 10,000 passengers per hour riding the bus transit system that operates along the congested roads of an aging infrastructure.

NKIRU MOKWE / M.Arch. Thesis, 2008 / Lars Lerup, director

157

ZONES OF STACCATO FLOW

View of Lagos drive-through market

PULLED TAUT

2X4

The strands of hell (92 degrees and 100 percent humidity)

Megashape melting pot

Son & Lumière

Espresso Aven

The office workers' tunnel of love

Over Easy

Dawn Finley and Clover Lee in Conversation

November 22, 2008, 12:57 pm

clover said... Each generation of students have a few seminal projects that everybody looks at, talks about and references. I was a B.Arch student at Cornell in 1994 and there was clearly a disconnect between what I thought was interesting as a student and what my professors thought I should deem important and interesting. Regardless, I am trying to remember the projects we were all excited about then:

- Eisenman's Max Reinhardt Haus
- OMA's Villa dall'Ava and Jusseiu Library
- Zaha's Vitra Fire Station
- Tschumi's Le Fresnoy

I remember it being an exciting time when we finally got to see the built work of architects whose design work we had been familiar with. DF, what projects were you looking at then?

November 25, 2008, 1:50 pm

fin fin said... My list is strangely similar; with the addition of Toyo Ito's Tower of Winds (a slightly older project that was brought to my attention by my boss at the time). The tower project was critical and inspiring for me—overlapping, interdependent systems (material, environment, technology) that produced a dynamic affect.

In 1994, I was working in a tiny design office in New York City—reading a (dry) software manual, and trying to get the practice to "go digital." At that time, it simply felt like a way of shifting/transferring existing tools and techniques. What was important technically (and seemed radical) then is an even more pressing concern procedurally and organizationally now. Information and fabrication technologies are reshaping the tools used to design and the processes used to fabricate and deploy architecture.

November 28, 2008, 9:16 am

clover said... It is definitely the time when the promise of these technologies need to be fulfilled. In the past 10-15 years, every architecture school was trying to fill technology positions and a lot of people got teaching positions because of technical know-how. Today, there are still a lot of questions as to whether this technology should be folded into the design curriculum, or it should be used as a tool, just like the table saw or the plotter. So before these relationships can be tested and brought to fruition, every school is now scrambling to fill sustainability positions. How do these new inputs inform design? How do they relate to the autonomy of the discipline?

****

November 22, 2008, 11:55 am

clover said... A lot of schools are questioning whether or not students should be required to do a thesis for M.Arch. The premise of thesis is based on two assumptions: first, that students can and should work independently; second, that the work contributes to and advances the discipline. This second assumption puts research and innovation squarely on the table.

Other professional programs, such as MBA and MD degrees, focus on the apprenticeship model. These programs simulate the professional environment in teaching fundamentals with little expectation the work will involve innovation in their fields. In architecture programs, NAAB pushes for the apprenticeship model, which emphasizes competency, while thesis encourages innovation. Unfortunately, this model assumes that the core program, that addresses the HOW, will automatically lead to the question WHY.

November 26, 2008, 7:17 am

fin fin said... On top of it, the HOW is based on a limited, somewhat dated professional model that seems to be at an impasse with the way the rest of the world is operating—or at the very least moving. But on a side note to your mention of MD apprenticeship model and innovation—most medical innovations in modern surgery occurred during wartime—when doctors/physicians were confronted with large (vast) numbers of diverse injuries (problems) requiring fast action without sufficient medical equipment and support—prompting experiments, tests, and trial of new techniques.

Some of the schools questioning thesis for M.Arch. are looking to replace the first assumption (independent working) with team-based working/learning, while keeping the second assumption (advance the discipline) in tact. The set-up absorbs the pre-thesis semester into the "research studio," for a full academic year—endurance required. (Bear with me, CL. I'm trying to segue into the need for more interspersed "wartime" in architecture education—drastic conditions for fast action and innovation as a way to mediate the current disconnect in models... but need to log off again; LCW demanding that I draw a dinosaur).

November 26, 2008, 10:17 am

clover said... Hey, I want to draw a dinosaur too! I just got back to Rome today. I had a layover in Paris. I could see all the new buildings at CDG when the plane landed and the first impression I had was: Wow, the french sure takes infrastructure seriously. Needless to say, FCO at Rome was a stark contrast. Despite being the capital of Italy, the airport in Rome is a logistical and architectural mess… Rome has a new mayor... (oh i have to run. need to finish later. and sorry, i am a little off the talking points right now…)

Sorry… so the new mayor in Rome swears to demolish Richard Meier's project—the Ara Pacis, which was completed in 2005. The last new building to be constructed in the historical center of Rome was at least twenty years before the Ara Pacis. Despite my indifference towards the building, one cannot help but ask: How can a city be so hostile towards contemporary architecture? Who, in contemporary society, controls the reins in terms of design innovation?

November 30, 2008, 6:13 pm
finley said… Wait, that last question took a turn.

December 1 , 2008, 9:07 am
clover said… Sorry about the non sequitur. My rant regarding Fiumicino is only tangential to the earlier discussion. ALTHOUGH, I do think there is a question lurking in there regarding the relationship between innovation in architecture education and practice. Can a structured relationship between education and practice move innovation in a direction that breaks the apprenticeship/guru model of architecture education?

December 1 , 2008, 8:33 pm
finley said… Non sequitur = good.
One potential is to pursue more sponsored research for academic (research) studios—federal funding or speculative support from the private sector. This is a way to pull architecture innovation into public focus, as a resource for industries that drive and shape the built environment. This is procedurally complicated (stringent application and review process), but the norm for sciences and engineering. Most federal funding goes to universities, and the majority (if not all) of the research produced finds its way to the private sector. Projecting out —what new forms of professional practice might take shape around sponsorship, rather than the traditional client-based financing? Why am I know "finley" instead of "fin fin?"

****

November 22, 2008, 11:55 am
clover said… This question can apply to any thing and any discipline. DF, how about we come up with different iterations of the question that we think more specifically relates to architecture?
I will start: What is the percentage of well-designed, yet boring projects? Is it possible for a project to be the reverse—poorly designed, yet interesting?

November 25, 2008, 1:01 pm
fin fin said… Sure, I'm game - (Does this mean that we don't answer the questions, just generate them)?
How does time impact an interesting project? In other words, are projects actually better after 8 weeks; or 4 weeks?
What part of an interesting project is due to the architectural response to a situation? Or—what part is due to the situation that precedes the architectural response?

November 28, 2008, 9:32 am
clover said… Since this is our game, I assume it is up to us to set the rules. So I suggest we answer the questions only if we want to. Regarding your last question. I believe the architectural response trumps the situation. UNLESS the architectural responds by actively shaping the situation as part of the design project.

I remember a generation of projects where students were asked to design a house for a blind poet and the site is on a cliff facing the ocean. This type of project assumes that an interesting architectural response is dependent on the situation.

I am much more interested in studio projects based on generic building typologies that are not reliant on site or specific programmatic constraints. Such projects ask open-ended questions yet call for specific design strategies. They do not exclude site and program, but include them into the fold as part of the design agenda. You inevitably have to ask, what is the relationship between design, site and program?

December 1, 2008, 7:55 pm
finley said… At the end of the day, I think we have to believe that the architectural response trumps. (And I agree that it's not dependent on a prescribed "interesting" set-up). But, I'm often more interested in how the "situation" is defined, or redefined, through a design investigation/approach - and the extent to which it elicits a response. Or to say it another way, to find an architecture that acknowledges or is comfortable with looking for those other components that shape the situation (demographics, work and leisure, consumer patterns and practices, market forces, legislative directives and policies, etc.). Perhaps working in Houston has influenced this interest.

December 1, 2008, 8:59 pm

finley said... It may be helpful to clarify that I think of "situation" as an ongoing, evolving notion—not fixed.

December 2, 2008, 10:22 pm

clover said... Fin Fin (I can keep calling you Fin Fin regardless of what this blog 'thinks'), it is interesting that you brought up Houston. Is it fair to assume that Houston comes across as a *tabula rasa* if we consider it only as a context in the traditional sense? And that it is in fact a 'situation' that is laden with potential for design research?

****

November 24, 2008, 9:19 am

fin fin said... Okay, CL, first I'm revisiting (subjecting you to) a statement that I made years ago to a similar question—then moving ahead).

"Forget incrementalism. Forget refinement. Forget endurance. Move out of the modes of lingering and hesitation. Give your idea a temporary trajectory, and follow it out - quickly. And be prepared to change direction at any moment. Wayne Gretzky says you miss 100 percent of the shots you don't take; if this thought is applied as an attitude to design, quickness and quantity become primary factors of operation. Emphasis is placed not on a singular moment or solution, but on the accumulation of initiatives that isolate the particularities of complex design issues."

The assumption in my practice (and I believe yours as well, CL) is that innovation is an obligation. That said, innovation is not automatic - in any project. I think it requires discipline and the development of a critical sensibility for tracking the substantive threads or issues (however small or subtle) that might allow something new to emerge.

November 25, 2008, 5:18 am

clover said... Yes, I think the 'accumulation of initiatives' and the ability to 'track' them is critical. I am wondering how design methodologies come into play in this discussion. From the 9-square grid, to the diagram, to parametric design – these are all different methodologies that facilitate 'tracking'. These methodologies are not neutral, and should not be understood as such. But more importantly, they offer a frame work through which 'substantive threads and issues' can be explored in a critical manner.

In looking at design methodologies, it is interesting to see how they define or redefine the autonomy of the discipline in different ways.

November 30, 2008, 4:38 pm

finley said... Well, when I think of the 9-square grid, I think of a method that tracks the formal aspects of a design in relation to a primary template (formal template) when a design tends toward or away from the grid. But the diagram and parametric are both ways of "tracking" that suggest that there is no stable ideal—at all. i.e. I think of them as responses to the belief that there are not stable (templatable) formal models. When we use diagrams, it's a way to engage things in the world outside of the domains of architecture—trying to expand the field of influences in architecture. That said, I think architecture(s) of these methodologies (diagram, parametric —or performative architecture) are trying (in different ways) to move beyond issues of autonomy.

December 2, 2008, 10:28 am

clover said... I agree that tools such as the diagram are a way to engage issues that are 'outside' of the discipline. That said, I think these methodologies and tools are ways through which architecture stakes out its territory through manipulating the information in a specific and selective way. So maybe it is incorrect to say they reinforce the autonomy of the discipline, but it redefines and reinforces the boundaries of the discipline.

I realize we are totally off topic....

The best part of blogging (apart from having this discussion with fin fin), is the weird words that pop up for confirmation. I just got 'vimitsu'. They are all 'almost' words. I think we should add another level of difficulty to this blog by requiring us to fold these words into our entries!

****

DAWN FINLEY is a principal at Interloop—Architecture. She is an assistant professor at Rice School of Architecture.

CLOVER LEE is a principal of david clovers. She is an assistant professor at Rice School of Architecture.

→Scale vs. Size: Mass Housing Developments in Hong Kong

Clover Lee

Critic, Graduate Option Studio, 2007-2008

Charles Jencks once said there are architects who can build above 100,000 square feet and there are many that should not. Few straddle the in-between. Subverting this differentiation of small and large, the SCALE vs. SIZE studios (Spring 2007, Spring 2008) examined design opportunities that reside in the large-scale mass housing developments that are proliferating in hyper-dense cities such as Hong Kong.

The typical mass housing project accommodates 20,000 inhabitants in an area that is the equivalent of two Manhattan blocks. Such extreme density propagates disjunction at the building scale as well as the urban scale. At the building scale, the current design solution for mass housing relies on the strategic separation of two distinct building typologies—the tower and the podium. These two building typologies exemplify different models of efficiency—aggregation through vertical proliferation (the tower) and interiorized urbanity through horizontal expansion (the podium). Both models rely on the physical and programmatic separation of the two typologies, often at the expense of flexibility and differentiation. At the urban scale, with its increasing need for self-sufficiency, mass housing developments have become isolated islands, rendering the surrounding urban fabric and context irrelevant.

The SCALE vs. SIZE studios did not foreground the need to bridge these two scales of disjunctions, but instead embraced two opposing trajectories: one was to generate a new breed of urbanity within an autonomous building; the other was to create a singular, brand-able identity

that encapsulates both complex metropolitan forces and architectural organizations. To do so, the SCALE vs. SIZE studios explored the difference between size and scale—volume versus vastness, capacity versus content, spread versus scope. Working with 4.5 million square feet of mixed-use program, the studios studied the relationship between the strategies' scale and their methods of deployment. We asked questions, such as: Is there a one-to-one relationship between the scale of the diagram and the scale at which it is deployed? Can generative strategies be scaleless and deployed repetitively throughout a large-scale project? What are the repercussions of scaling up versus repeating a strategy for a large-scale project? With this expanded taxonomy, the studios examined various technical and organizational incarnations of the mass housing development within the context of a vacant site in Tseung Kwan O, Hong Kong.

With generous support from the Rice University Faculty Research Fund and Rice University School of Architecture, both studios visited Hong Kong and the Pearl River Delta in South China. Through firsthand experience of extra-large, multi-scalar projects in Hong Kong, the SCALE vs. SIZE studio bridged the gulf between the understanding of empirical information, such as size, and the experiencing of scalar and spatial aspects of extra-large developments. In addition, the studios gained a broader understanding of the dense urban environment in which such a typology exists, and the cultural and economic conditions from which it emerged.

↗ Lift/Tuck

Lift/Tuck was created to address many of the pitfalls of high-density housing projects in China and Hong Kong. The scheme concerns the tower/podium relationship and how it can work to form a landscape. The block is conceived as a solid that has been carved away so it has voids cut through the middle of it. The result generates a main promenade circulation that is obvious and global. One travels through the podium by

means of a secondary circulation system that is more circuitous and localized.

Sections of the building are lifted high off the ground plane, returning parts of the site to the city as ground-level public space. These spaces would be a gathering place for residents and visitors alike—used for concerts, markets, movies, beauty pageants, political gatherings, trade shows, and more. In addition, the residential

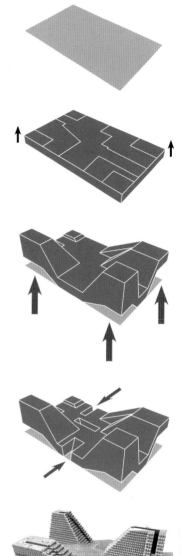

Overall site and development strategy, from top: raze, extrude and score, push and fold, cut out, final rendering

RAZE, EXTRUDE AND SCORE

VERTICAL PROLIFERATION

STRADDLE THE IN-BETWEEN

Market gathering at Lift/Tuck

towers are centered around communal open spaces.

Residential units collect at the corner towers, local retail clings to the residential towers, and destination retail pushes toward the exterior. The bi-level residential units lock into each other, and their relationship and configuration register on the towers.

MATTHEW CRNKOVICH, QUYEN MA, VIKTOR RAMOS, PETER

STANLEY / Graduate Option Studio, 2008 / Clover Lee, critic

This project redefines the relationship between mass housing developments and the street. Instead of an either/ or dialectic, where the building is Goliath and the street is David, Lift/ Tuck strategically intertwines the two. The street grid is no longer defined by the ground plane, but by

the underside of the plinth. I hope the reflected ceiling plan of the underside of the podium is as fantastical as the surface above: Aztec above, Mayan below.
—**Clover Lee** is a principal of david clovers. She is an assistant professor at Rice School of Architecture.

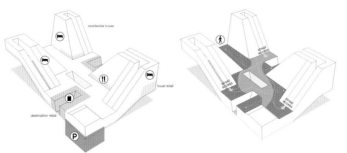

From left to right: Program distribution; Main promenade circulation; Vertical circulation

→The High Top

The High Top (THT) presents a new model for Hong Kong living. Unlike the existing mass housing schemes prevalent in the area, THT folds the fabric of the city into its interior. The affectionately termed "Strawberry Fields," a tectonic and formal intervention, pulls public access through the complex, varying in scale as it rises.

The public path begins by shearing up the ground plane, exposing a subterranean public bus interchange and metro connection. In its twists and turns, the pink path plugs into shared private amenities and plunges through private accommodation. It plays a major role in defining the characteristics of the "living zones" at any given moment. For example, in a city where soccer is the most popular sport, two junior soccer fields invite children from the many surrounding primary schools to play, train, and compete adjacent to the "family housing zone," where shared terraced gardens, game rooms, spa relaxation suites, and communal balconies blur the boundary between public and private spaces. Enjoy the action as public spectator seating folds into a sports bar adjoining the "young professionals zone." Or perhaps the privileged view from the outdoor public plaza, located on the forty-fifth floor, accessible directly from the central public core, can offer a brand new perspective on the game. Even here, when residents climb to the comfort of a novel "flex space," the vibrancy of the city is just a stroll away!

AMANDA CHIN, NKIRU MOKWE, BEATRICE ELEAZAR / Graduate Option Studio, 2008 / Clover Lee, critic

This project courageously takes on the possibility that a building of this size can and should absorb what

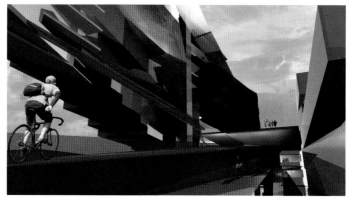

Public path departs from street level

Tracing "Strawberry Fields" through the High Top

we usually associate with public infrastructures such as transportation and parks. By absorbing these infrastructures, the project creates a new type of urbanity that is not nostalgic, but optimistic and opportunistic. The renderings are especially powerful in showing how unapologetic the project is with regard to its size. By inflating the building mass with vertical voids and "air bubbles," the project suggests a new urban perspective that is not only vertical, but contained within the building.

—**Clover Lee** is a principal of david clovers. She is an assistant professor at Rice School of Architecture.

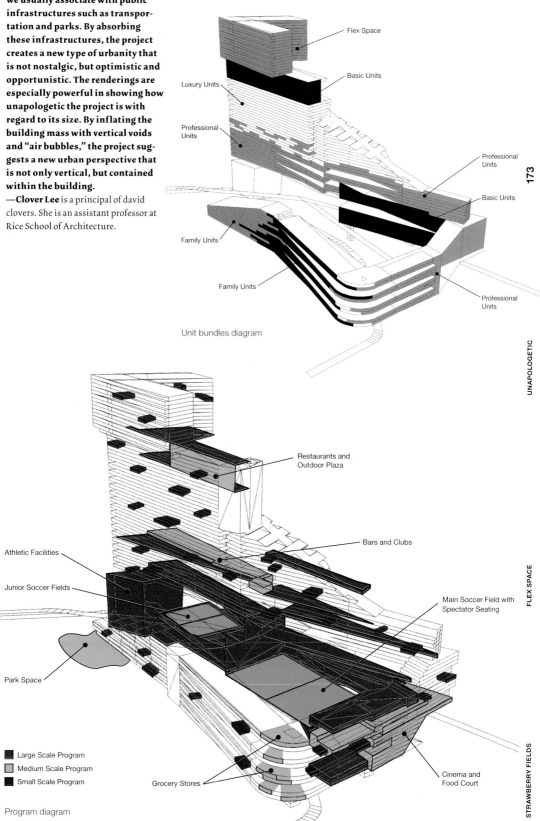

Flex Space

Basic Units

Luxury Units

Professional Units

Professional Units

Basic Units

Family Units

Family Units

Professional Units

Unit bundles diagram

Restaurants and Outdoor Plaza

Bars and Clubs

Athletic Facilities

Junior Soccer Fields

Main Soccer Field with Spectator Seating

Park Space

Cinema and Food Court

Grocery Stores

■ Large Scale Program
□ Medium Scale Program
■ Small Scale Program

Program diagram

↑ Double Stuffed

The intent of Double Stuffed was to implement a more suburban lifestyle into the dense vertical housing of Hong Kong. We did this in two ways. One was to break up the shared amenities typical of the tower/podium typology and distribute them directly to each living unit. This privatized the shared amenities, giving each unit (and resident) its own exterior space, something we noticed was lacking from existing residential types. Our second method explored the distribution of amenities by atomizing the shopping spaces and attaching them directly to the living units. The home/storefront is much more common in Hong Kong, with a prime example found in the Chungking Mansions. We assembled the two types into "landscapes" that would interact with each other across a central void. Various public programs would pierce these "landscapes" to connect the roof (which was open to various large-scale programs) back to the street level.

RICHIE GELLES, VIKTOR RAMOS / Graduate Option Studio, 2008 / Clover Lee, critic

SUPERBAN

CHUNGKING MANSIONS

TOWER/PODIUM

Double Stuffed gives a misleading first impression: you are led to believe that it is naïve in splicing a suburban organization into a high-density typology. But upon closer inspection, you realize its success lies in what and how it appropriates from the suburban model. It takes the individuated exterior space of the single-family home, but creates a shared spectacle out of its atomization and distribution.

As such, it does not subscribe to the utopia epitomized by the pitched roofs and white picket fences of the single-family home. Instead, those suburban icons are replaced by one that embraces a new utopia of density and congestion—superban!

—**Clover Lee** is a principal of david clovers. She is an assistant professor at Rice School of Architecture.

↓Edge of a City

In architecture, a concept can either be applied to a project or be derived from it. In this case, the methods and constraints of video-construction are the vehicles chosen to develop a concept, which is then applied to an architectural proposition. The design of the construction window of the video-editing software implies the possibility of a temporal construction of space as event/memory/image and action/ movement. Through this temporal construction, the project examines the rapidly disappearing courtyard spaces of Beijing, describing their place within the city and the movements of its citizens.

To open architecture to questions of perception implicit in the moving image requires the suspension of disbelief and rational thought to allow for simple exploration. Thus, this project begins with equal parts information and disorder, an indeterminacy of purpose, and a disjunction between program and space. Architecture is

Sequence of movement through old and new Beijing

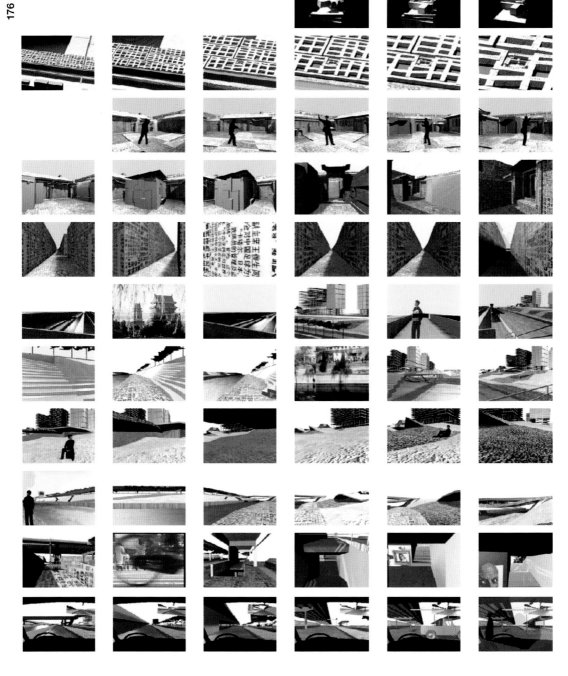

the result of acting on this realm of possibilities. Working in the video-editing software's spatial-temporal framework allows different aspects of the rapidly changing urban situation of Beijing to be projected onto each other to evoke a new understanding of their potential interrelationships. The results of this working method are gradually made clear by simultaneously constructing the space, event, and movement, thus exploring the links between memory and the city, its buildings and its people.

LI HU / M.Arch. Thesis, 1998 / Albert Pope, director

SPATIAL-TEMPORAL FRAMEWORK

SUSPENSION OF DISBELIEF

BEIJING

→ Infratecture

As a way to alleviate the record levels of urban congestion in Japanese cities, city planners have developed extensive land reclamation projects in Tokyo, Osaka, Nagoya, Kobe, and other major ports. Initially planned as centers for heavy industry and distribution, these landfill sites are gaining popularity as new live/work environments. Without the geographical constraints and overwhelming density of the mainland, these zones serve as a veritable tabula rasa for new waterfront development.

The port of Nagoya offers a particularly promising site for new city planning, as it has remained largely untouched by the kind of less-than-successful projects recently built in Tokyo and Osaka. However, current plans for a highly sophisticated enterprise zone, complete with a new international airport, train terminals, office parks, housing blocks, and hypermarkets, are characterized by the all-too-familiar imagery of the outdated Western city plan (as has already been implemented in Tokyo and Kobe).

In fact, one can generalize that large-scale development outside of every major city in the world has taken on a similar homogeneous, atomized quality. Yet a substantial amount of business is now conducted outside of traditional city centers by an increasingly itinerant work force. Moreover, the nature of construction in these environments has assumed a greater scale, an increased level of complexity, and a shorter time frame, with architects playing less of a role (if any) in the whole process.

In response to these challenges, I have attempted to develop a small, interdependent prototype for a business substation (BSP) within a proposed transportation terminal in Nagoya Port as a way to consolidate the various necessary programs into a recognizable unit. Conceived as the insertion of a new kind of urbanity into this

Exploded axon of business substation within Nagoya Port

horror vacui, the BSP would be inextricably tied to, and defined by, the greater infrastructure of the site, and as such would be merely a small hot spot of activity within the larger nervous system of the new city. The implementation of the BSP would require that the architect become a kind of specialist, working in conjunction with planners and engineers throughout the entire process of development. Thus, the potential for the architect is to help conceive the fundamental systems that shape the new city at a tangible level (rather than providing a rather limited cosmetic service toward the end of the process). In this way, the BSP is not only an attempt to provide an alternative live/work design model, but also a new strategy for architecture.

BLAINE BROWNELL / M.Arch.
Thesis, 1998 / Albert Pope, director

→ Intermodal Transit Center: Massy-Palaiseau, France

For the Massy-Palaiseau transportation center, we are proposing an architecture that bridges the rail bed while simultaneously occupying it. We are interested in the dichotomy that exists on the site between the grain of the transportation lines and the cross-grain of a bridging element that will reconnect the two sides of Massy-Palaiseau. The project follows a similar approach of juxtaposing opposites in order to create a station that addresses both the connection of the urban fabric and the needs of its inhabitants/users. The project intends to emphasize the clear interaction between the inherent grain and a potential cross-grain.

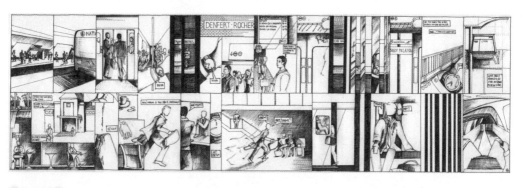

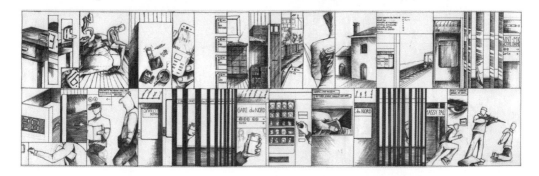

Intermodal Transit Center itineraries panel

Expounding upon the unique characteristics of the site, the transportation center unifies the multiple grains by interweaving them. The bridging across the rails acts as the transfer space from which the main program spaces are pulled along the grain of the tracks, allowing for direct occupation by the majority of the program. The two grains are further demarcated as "active" and "static." The bridge element (transfer space) breaks down into multiple trajectories, allowing for direct crossing of the rails or entrance into an "activity loop," which we have programmed with an array of fitness activities. The "static" areas are pulled from the "active" and contain slow-duration programs, such as restaurants, arcades, cinemas, and media services. This juxtaposition allows for quick transfer users to occupy the station in a different way than leisure users.

Due to the differing nature of the two sides of the site, the station addresses the urban fabric in opposing manners. At the southeast side, which sits upon a prospective commercial district, the station responds by presenting a commercial-scale front to maintain its importance in the urban fabric. Alternately, the northwest side of the tracks is occupied by mostly residential complexes and smaller single-family units. Thus, this area interacts in a more subtle way, blending into the ground, creating an urban plaza that spans out to converge and interact more directly with the surrounding fabric.

AMANDA CHIN, VIKTOR RAMOS / Graduate Option Studio RSAP, 2007 / John J. Casbarian, J. Kent Fitzsimons, critics

The final project's formal references might distract from the admirable recursive design process that led to it. Beginning with conventional analytical observations of site and program, overlaid by intuitive narratives and gestures, the early studies were articulated in a series of rich study models and diagrams. As the process moved forward, these investigations elicited questions about the substance and potential of the initial proposals,

Transportation center and activity loops

leading to a better understanding of the project's true limits. The formal language, therefore, is a natural evolution in this process, neither fixed from the start nor later applied. The final project captures the combination of intuitive moves and deduced principles laid out in the initial stages, the whole enhanced by layers of testing and pushing an architectural intention.

—**John J. Casbarian, FAIA** is a partner at Taft Architects. He is the associate dean and a professor at Rice School of Architecture and the director of Rice School of Architecture-Paris; **Kent Fitzsimons** is the assistant director of Rice School of Architecture-Paris.

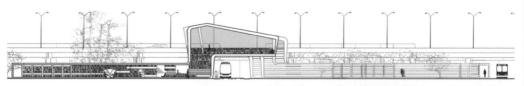

↓Mixed Use Developments: Urban Design and Investment Building Design

William T. Cannady
Critic, Graduate Option Studios, 1964–2008

This graduate studio typically focuses on the development of high-density, mid-rise, mixed-use complexes. A class of ten architecture students (Archies) and ten management students (MBAs) is divided into four project teams. Each team consists of two to three Archies and two to three MBAs. The Archies play the role of Project Design Architects and are responsible for assisting in constructing a pro-forma that establishes program and for developing the design concept. The MBAs play the role of Project Managers and are responsible for developing a market analysis, assessing economic feasibility, refining the program, and producing project budgets and loan packages.

↑A Metropolitan Library
A residual pocket of land defined by Downtown-Medical Center thoroughfares, the sweep of U.S. 59, and a proposed METRO light rail splice is further striated to receive a public library branch, newsstand, and transit facility.

HEIDI WERNER / Undergraduate Option Studio, 2001 / Carlos Jiménez, critic

↖**Mixed-Use Transit-Oriented Development Project**
Located on Main Street in Mid-town Houston
AXEL WEISHEIT, LINDSEY BRIGATI / Graduate Option Studio, 2006

—To give students the opportunity to fully develop a design for a project from the time the program is determined by a complex set of contradicting constraints, such as urban design considerations, site and code constraints, the client's goals, users' needs, existing building techniques, and economic realities (the organization of the studio requires students to complete a design including preliminary plans, outline specifications, cost estimates, and a project loan package)
—To provide students with a team of experts that includes a Rice School of Architecture design professor, a Jones Management School real estate development professor, developer clients, a project construction manager, a cost estimator, a mechanical, electrical, and plumbing engineer, a structural engineer, a landscape architect, an elevator consultant, and a curtain wall consultant
—To design a project where students strive to achieve a balance among the major characteristics of a good building: economy, utility, durability, and beauty.

Pedagogy

This comprehensive design studio, sadly one not required in a supposedly "professional school," has been well tested over four decades. It is organized to give RSA students the opportunity for an intense creative learning experience by investing long hours in the studio, sharing with classmates the frustrating search

An annual undergraduate vertical design studio is identical to the graduate studio, with the exception of the inclusion of MBA students and the use of a contractor providing cost-estimating services.

Each team initially develops several schemes from which the clients select a preferred scheme. The Project Design Architects and Project Managers are expected to coordinate their analyses and ideas so as to meet the requirements of the client/user/consultant team. The goal of the project is to combine a strong architectural design solution and an economic outcome that reflects adequate return for risks borne. A jury of both local and national leaders in real estate development and architectural design reviews final works of completed designs and mortgage packages.

Objectives

—To give students the opportunity to develop leadership skills while working in a team toward common goals

↑**Mixed-Use High-Density Development Project on Kirby Dr.**
Located next to River Oaks
JEAN-MARC TRIBIE / Undergraduate Vertical Studio, 2006

↑**Mixed-Use High-Density Development Project for Two Blocks**
Located on RIce Boulevard in the Rice Village
SCOTT STARK, RYAN LEMMO, MICHELLE ZUNIGA / Graduate Option Studio, 2008

↑**Mixed-Use High-Density Development Project for Two Blocks**
Located on RIce Boulevard in the Rice Village
KATHERINE McPHILIPS, LINH DAN DO / Graduate Option Studio, 2008

for ideas, discovering new methods of conceptual thinking and analysis, creating successful design projects that can be built, and doing all of this while having fun.

A good architect operates both as an artist and as a scientist. As David Edwards writes:

Art requires an aesthetic method, a process of thought guided by images, is sensual and intuitive, often thrives on uncertainty, and is 'true' in that it seems to reflect or elucidate or interpret what we experience in our lives, and is expressive of nature in its complexity, a basis of entertainment and culture.

Science requires a process of thought that is guided by quantification, is analytical, deductive, conditional on problem definition, is 'true' in that it is repeatable, is expressive of nature in its simplicity, a basis of technology and industry.[1]

Students are encouraged to incorporate both of these approaches in their work.

Note
1. David Edwards, *Artscience: Creativity in the Post-Google Generation* (Cambridge, Mass.: Harvard University Press, 2008).

After I arrived in 1963, my early professional experiences in Houston led me to an understanding that the fundamental forces of the city's pattern of urbanism were controlled by the real estate development industry, i.e., lenders, lawyers, developers, infrastructure engineers, and realtors. Architects, in practice and in the academy, had little impact on city planning, urban design, and city building in the early sixties. That still is true today. Early in my teaching and practice, I began exploring and attaining expertise in the real estate development process, including financial analysis, financing, and marketing, as well as design. In 1966, I began the Investment Building Design Studio that continues to the present. This studio includes many of the key players mentioned above. In order to deal with the problem that assistant professors of architecture have in finding clients and starting a serious practice, in 1970 I designed and built a house for my own family. At the same time, I became one of the first architect-developers in Houston, building several speculative modern town houses near Rice University. In 1983, at the suggestion of Rice School of Architecture Dean O. Jack Mitchell, I bought and renovated several mixed-use buildings in Rice Village. In addition to my interest in, and response to, Houston's urban development forces, another feature of my approach was to design buildings that respond positively to the automobile, one of the essential elements of Houston's lifestyle. I have always wondered what kind of architect / teacher I would have been if I had practiced / taught in Berkeley, Cambridge, or London.
—**William T. Cannady, FAIA** is principal at Wm. T. Cannady, Architect and a professor at Rice School of Architecture.

ECONOMY, UTILITY, DURABILITY, AND BEAUTY

CLIENT/USER/CONSULTANT TEAM

A Question about Thesis

M.Arch. thesis coordinators from the last 15 years were invited to participate in an online Q&A session on the status and role of thesis at Rice School of Architecture and in architecture education in general.

Keith Krumwiede set the stage with a general statement and a series of questions. Of the many questions asked and answered, one issue generated the most discussion.

Keith Krumwiede

Traditionally, the thesis project provides an opportunity for each student to stake their disciplinary claim by advancing an architectural proposition supported by original research and argued through design. As central as thesis is to the basic pedagogy and culture of some architecture programs, not least of which Rice, it is becoming increasingly marginalized at many other schools. While some programs have eliminated thesis work entirely, many have opted instead to require a final advanced design studio or, in a few cases, participation in a faculty-led research studio. There appears to be a growing dissatisfaction with the role, or perhaps just the results, of the thesis in architectural education. Philosophically, some find the architectural thesis project to be a self-indulgent relic of older pedagogical practices aimed at producing creative masters, and therefore not properly attuned to the dynamic and multi-disciplinary demands of contemporary practice. Others, realizing that only a small fraction of any batch of thesis projects will be truly exemplary, choose to hedge their bets and avoid the potential disappointment (or, perhaps for some, embarrassment) of public reviews by forcing everyone through one last controlled studio exercise.

Whatever the motivation, however, it seems essential that we ask what is lost in giving up thesis as the culmination of an architecture curriculum. Or, in light of the benefits accrued both individually and collectively in the best thesis work, what we stand to gain by continuing to see the thesis as a necessary right of passage. For in fact, if we can agree that a thesis project is driven as much by the particular culture of the school in which it plays out as by the individual objectives of its author then the strength of any program could be measured by the quality of the thesis work produced. A successful thesis therefore, in as much as success is measured by the impact of ideas on a particular culture, must feed back into the intellectual and creative life of its school as well as into the broader field of contemporary discourse. I think that this is particularly evident in the best thesis work at Rice which, as the culmination of a research driven and exploratory design curriculum, both builds upon the varied research investigations of the faculty and opens new avenues of exploration for the school as a whole. It is in this light that I would like to frame our discussion of the purpose and merits of thesis as both a pedagogical tool and method of design research.

Many of the thesis projects collected for *Everything Must Move* deployed architectural thinking and methods in what might be seen to be extra-architectural situations (uploading programmatic piggy-backs to the traditionally mono-functioning highway, choreographing a staged withdrawal of suburban houses from floodplains, developing a public and visible horticultural cleansing of urban air, recasting housing as an infrastructural sponge during storm events…

Is it necessary today to see architecture in this more extensive manner? Is this the best use of an architectural thesis?

Farès el-Dahdah

This "extensive manner" is a direct heritage of modern architecture, with which thesis students, declaredly or not, share paradigmatic values.

David Brown

I think thesis has been reconfigured at Rice by the fact that the School itself has had a thesis, variously investigated across the curriculum, raising questions, or presenting arguments and propositions that can be further pursued, extended or countered. The emphasis of an individual thesis shifts from the need to produce something new or make claims of mastery (two anxiety producing and often paralyzing, rather than liberating, concerns) to the opportunity to make a distinct contribution to the school's working proposition. The terms for defining a successful thesis also shift. A successful thesis can include work that describes or claims territory for architecture that has previously been unrecognized, if not ignored. At times, the best choice for a thesis could be to defer any design effort, beyond such description, in acknowledgment that no one design project could effectively address a subject's complexity.

In the sense, a thesis proposition should initiate an inquiry that exceeds the scope of what can be accomplished through one design argument. It should suggest more than one design argument, and the one to pursue is the one that will seemingly provide the greatest insight about the proposition. In this respect it is important to be attentive in both research and design activities. As the full scope of the proposition becomes apparent, an anticipated design argument might need to be dropped in favor of a different one. Similarly, the design argument might lead to the need for a shift in the proposition. The relationship between the two should be a dynamic one.

I remember [Rice M.Arch. thesis student] Alex O'Briant experiencing what I am talking about in terms of research and design. He began by thinking he was going to design a house, but soon realized that there was no way that one house, or even a set of houses, designed in a semester would be an effective argument relative to what his research revealed. Eventually, his design argument became a book that asks how does one design a house in light of the information it presents. It's a question about contemporary practice, which seems to be a good way to collectively describe the installation, exhibition, video, event, and book design modes of argumentation we see in thesis. To a certain degree they are all conjectures about ways of practicing or what a practice can entail, and they all contribute to Rice's thesis—a proposition that architecture, through a new set of techniques and practices, can effectively engage the contemporary metropolis.

Eva Franch

What is important to discuss in terms of poignancy and relevance in architectural thesis has little to do with questions of a disciplinary nature (many meta-discursive architectural theses are of little "use" today); what today is necessary in order for a thesis to become fully architectural is a social, political and formal awareness of the performative implications of thoughts, words and buildings. What I see as an emerging aspect of the thesis at Rice is a lineage of projects that try to envision possible futures (or possible pasts) with a full range of architectural decisions that have ecological, social, political and formal consequences.

Albert Pope

As we use the term today, "design research" is the way that we incorporate "extra-architectural" situations into the thesis project. Today at Rice, design research is broken out of the architectural thesis in the way that AMO is broken out of OMA. This expanded field of research started with "urbanism" and moved out into territory that is simply unrelated to building design. At Rice we have pushed this to an extreme, as the thesis projects in the book indicate.

This research agenda can be contrasted to the thesis research done only one generation ago. That way of doing design research eliminated any extra-architectural content by researching the design exclusively. Usually, the program came first: library, courthouse, museum, followed by case studies. These case studies included both modern precedents as well as pre-modern, typological analyses. After precedents came the site. A site was chosen and complete documentation followed—analysis of the urban district, specific site plans, photographs and models were all produced. This activity constituted the entire research effort and the design process moved on from this in the conventional way— schematic design and design development following on a solid foundation of research.

What changed that is hard to pinpoint. The Harvard Project on the City is one watershed, as was the recuperation of Buckminster Fuller's project. The Design Research Laboratory at the Architectural Association was another early manifestation. The explosion of resource material online coupled with print and web reproduction were all enablers. Sophisticated research, or at least the appearance of sophisticated research, came within reach of students and faculty. Research exploded and its link to building design became ever more tenuous or broken altogether in the case of the research thesis. I believe the reason for this is pretty straightforward. The need to state and restate the relevance of architecture and urbanism to a radically changing world ultimately drove the research project. I would argue that changes in technology

alone would have provoked these extra-architectural excursions, though they have gone far beyond that.

To succeed at research at the expense of design, however, only proves that we can do two things instead of one. The need to restate the relevance of architecture and urbanism to a radically changing world can lead to abandoning our expertise in favor of another (usually immaterial) expertise that is more demonstrably relevant. This, I believe, is where the project sits today. The present situation can be resolved into a simple, perhaps hackneyed, question. What is the relation of research to design? In the research seminar today we are directly concerned with locating a discursive space that acknowledges the fundamental difference between idea and object or concept and phenomenon and attempt to problematize their relation. We would like to figure out how a research agenda can be extended into material, form, space, geometry, fabrication, not to mention the ever-changing formal regimes which, like all necessary fashion, are never an end in themselves.

The specific relation between research and design is, of course, a much bigger problem than thesis. The separation of quantitative discourse from the objects it presumes to inform underwrote the entire postmodern reaction to modernism. The reaction did not result in solving the problem, however. It simply tipped the balance back in favor of the phenomenal object, privileging (again) design qualities over quantitative research. Thus we are still left trying to define that relation. The difficulty of relating quantitative analysis to the qualities of space and form has deep epistemological roots that cannot be underestimated. What it comes down to is the discipline must establish its own rigorous, internal logic in order to be. This is at odds with its relevance to an insanely changing world. It is important to recognize that we are setting the bar impossibly high before we go beating ourselves up for failing.

I would further argue for the "extra-architectural" thesis on the basis of the legacy of modern architecture and urbanism. At its inception, modernism itself was accused of being extra-architectural. Its utopian projections fell well outside the established role of the architect as the maker of tombs and monuments. Modernism was born out of a dystopian situation brought to a head by the First World War. To this situation the early modernists brought their utopian imagination. This dystopian/utopian cycle is exploited in many of the thesis projects. I will explain.

A good many of the thesis projects are blatantly dystopic. They are involved in highly problematic if not intractable situations: toxic tracts abandoned for decades, cities destroyed by acts of nature, megachurches that market salvation, subsistence farming in 'first world' cities. The dystopian thesis is, of course, only another way to describe a willingness to take on the most severe environmental problems of our day and to insist that architecture and urbanism are relevant to both the problem and the solution. Being part of the problem and the solution is another way to describe what these projects are—two sides of the same coined minted by the extreme conditions in which we live. Utopian dreams live on the other side of dystopian nightmares. This two-sided coin is one of the principal lessons of modern architecture and urbanism.

"Visionary" rhetoric once made utopian projection seem frivolous, arrogant, impractical and naively idealistic. I would argue that this is inaccurate because our utopian aspirations are, by now, integrated into the modernist legacy. It is in the best tradition of modern architecture that we project new worlds out of the dysfunction of the present. Modernism was born in the calamity of the First World War and widely adapted in the shadow of the second. Modernism taught us to perceive opportunity in advance of the rising need for radical change. We have learned to position ourselves at the forefront of that change in order to bend it toward progressive outcomes. Out of this process, utopian projection can be seen, not as an arrogant or misguided end in itself, but something that cycles, perhaps endlessly, between problem and solution, impasse and alternative, dysfunction and ideal. Engaging this cycle as the site for both urgent and meaningful work is second nature for the modern architect.

The irony of this method is that the techniques/ technologies used to find solutions to these problems are very likely to be their cause. For these dystopian scenarios evoke a catastrophe—frequently referred to as progress—that is itself the result of modernization. In this regard, architecture and urbanism might be thought of as the cause of these terrible problems rather than their cure. In other words, locate any dystopian situation, and beneath the surface you may find some apparently misguided utopian cause. For each dystopian problem we face, there is quite possibly a utopian projection behind it. This is not, however, offered up as a reason to abandon the utopian logic of modern architecture and urbanism. I would argue the opposite; the utopian cause beneath each dystopian situation can be exploited. The dystopian thesis becomes one of mining these intractable sites for their utopian residue or ballast and fabricating new projects out these residues. In this manner, utopian Modernism must confront its own compromised, yet concrete realization. It must constantly recycle its histories.

Such a program would sound remarkable were it not inevitable, for it merely makes explicit what we already know. Architecture is, by definition, a utopian enterprise. Without faith in the future, without a vision to animate that faith, and without the utopian tradition to turn vision into workable strategies, an architect would simply be paralyzed by the magnitude of the environmental problems we face today.

Helene Furjan

I agree with Albert's observation that "design research" is a key methodology in contemporary design thinking today. However, while I agree with much of what Albert says in his discussion of this design modality, I disagree with the exclusive—or even central—link to the academic model of the design thesis. While thesis is certainly a place in the academy

that research methodologies are explored, it is not exclusive. Indeed the inextricable relation between design and research is now the norm at progressive design schools to such an extent that it is demanding a wholesale revision of the Beaux-Arts pedagogical model that still dominates professional education.

The notion that architectural experimentation requires a rigorous feedback between design and research has been at play in design pedagogy since at least the 1960's and 70's. Albert is correct to note Fuller's project. But this moment also included the seminal research studio by Robert Venturi, Denise Scott Brown and Steven Izenour, *Learning from Las Vegas*; the rise of operations research and systems engineering; the urban networks research of Shadrach Woods, the Smithsons, Constantinos Doxiadis or Kenzo Tange; and the structure and materials research of Buckminster Fuller, Frei Otto and Robert Le Ricolais, to name but a few. Design research has been around for three or four decades already (with some hiccups and back-pedals of course), and has been linked to the innovative design practice (think Herzog & de Meuron's recent exhibition of countless test models and test materials at the Tate Modern), the commercial office committed to optimization (think the Advanced Geometry Unit at Foster+Partners), or, in the academy, the research studio (Harvard's Project on the City). Thesis is, in some respects, a late starter here, and while the Design Research Laboratory (DRL) post-professional program at the Architectural Association ends somewhat traditionally with thesis, it does so unconventionally and with a stronger allegiance to the research studio model: thesis projects are conceived and developed in teams run as mini-studios.

Indeed, it could be argued that the research studio expands a combination of feasibility study and market research already standard practice in commercial offices, simply learning from other disciplines—business, sociology, information sciences, graphic design—how to be smarter about this kind of research. We should bear in mind that Nicholas Negroponte came to "invent" the Media Lab at MIT through a vision of cybernetic architecture developed at MIT in the Architecture Machine Group's work of the late 60's and 70's, team-based post-graduate research that followed his architecture studies. This was the moment that cybernetics and architecture were closely related—a relation that lay at the base of systems thinking in architecture—and that much of this connection was centered around MIT, where Christopher Alexander was also exploring the connection between urban planning and computation (only to develop C++ computing language as a spin-off).

I will go further. The primacy of research—design as research and research as design—achieves two things: First, it has brought architecture back into the territory of graduate education demanded by the research university. Not merely "training" but neither eschewing critical thought and inquiry, the professional or post-professional degree program undertakes an experimental paradigm in which students and professors alike collaborate to push the boundaries of the discipline, allowing the pedagogical context to become a central stage in the development of new analyses, new techniques, and new theories. Collaboration rules out thesis to a large extent: thesis, an old model that was traditionally a rite of passage—the way the young scholar proved their readiness to graduate out of the academy (or upwards into a teaching position) through demonstration of their mastery of the discipline or profession—is an autonomous pursuit, one that can be directed or advised, but not collaborated on.

Second, research allows us to front-end our relationship with emerging technologies and processes, adapting both our field and these new tools in feedback, rather than simply applying the latter. Design-research follows a methodology that combines scientific rigor with innovation, intuition and opportunism: Design Research is a facilitator to jump-start future endeavors. But such an endeavor requires more than a hypothesis; it requires cross-disciplinary expertise, which in turn requires team building. Thesis preserves the Modernist myth of the designer as artist or creative genius. But practice—whether in the office or the school—is now a laboratory: group–oriented, open-source, networked and hybrid. As Brett Steele, founder of the DRL and now Chair of the AA, has put it, "Today's distributed design systems, and the forces shaping increasingly open, flexible, forms of collaboration are the result of both new technologies now routinely linking members of design teams (like software drawing and modelling applications, the web, and intranets) as well as the forms of professional specialization and management that transformed architectural offices during the latter half of the twentieth century." Research allows the architectural object to escape the bounds of an autonomous formalism, redefining its place in an intelligent landscape—or ecology—of interaction and immersion, and buildings as adaptive networked organizations that couple infrastructural, structural, circulatory, programmatic, environmental, informational, cultural, economic, historical or political systems in tightly interconnected but distributed formations.

Collaboration allows a socio-political form of "performance" to productively feedback with the scientific form of "performance" that now exerts so much sway on design thinking. Laboratories are process-oriented and operational; the experimental process is in part the production of disorder—the noise of accumulated data, records of events and traces of inscription—and in part the process of sorting, evaluating and pattern-finding within that disorder. Laboratories deploy multiple tactical operations alongside rational strategies: chance, mutation, niche-building, disorder, tinkering, informal communication. Tactics are dynamic and non-linear—they depend on time, noise and accident as much as reason and rational method, always "on the watch for opportunities that must be seized 'on the wing.'" They are covert, clandestine, make-shift, contingent, and on-the-fly, small subterfuges, ruses, and appropriations; the multitude of competing experiments, ideas, innovations, inventions, developments and proposals that together make up a map of the evolving and emerging design disciplines at any given moment.

This collaborative, interactive form of design research—of designing research and researching design—is what Michael Speaks calls "thinking as doing." His distinction between problem-solving and innovation looks a lot like the definition of thesis: "Problem solving works within given parameters to solve known problems." On the other hand, "innovation works by a different, more experimental logic where, by rigorous analysis, opportunities are discovered that can be exploited and transformed into design innovations… innovation risks working with existent but unknown conditions in order to discover opportunities that could not have been predicted in advance." Where the model of thesis is still relevant is in its reminder to us that disciplinary scope still matters. But for Speaks, "thinking as doing" can only take place in distributed and fluid hybrid organizations that form temporary alliances, and learn and adapt in response to changes in their environment; not in the older top-down models thesis is aligned with. While these practices are occupations of their disciplines, they are neither singular nor autonomous. They need what Bob Somol and Sarah Whiting have so neatly identified: conversation and co-conspirators. "Thinking as doing" involves transforming external information into "distributed intelligence": an open conversation, not an echo chamber. Nonetheless, research is nothing without analysis, projection, performance, organization, argument. Thesis is dead, long live thesis.

KEITH KRUMWIEDE is an assistant dean and an assistant professor at Yale School of Architecture. He was an assistant professor at Rice School of Architecture from 1996-2003.

FARÈS EL-DAHDAH is an associate professor at Rice School of Architecture.

DAVID BROWN is the associate director of graduate studies and an associate professor at University of Illinois at Chicago School of Architecture. He was an assistant professor at Rice School of Architecture from 1996-2003.

EVA FRANCH is an assistant professor at Rice School of Architecture.

ALBERT POPE is the Gus Sessions Wortham Professor of Architecture at Rice School of Architecture.

HELENE FURJAN is an assistant professor at University of Pennsylvania School of Design. She was an assistant professor at Rice School of Architecture from 2004-05.

From *The Image of Space/Space of the Image*: Houston Medical Center

↑ The Image of Space / Space of the Image

The growth of digital media in photography places photography in a crisis similar to that caused by the fixing of the chemical image in the mid-nineteenth century. Painting was forced to contend with its purpose as a medium to represent the image of the landscape, and modernism in painting was born.

In The Image of Space/Space of the Image, I have forced photography to contend with its purpose as a medium to represent the illusion of deep space. Through an awareness of the surface of the picture and the space within the view camera, the conventional image is dismantled and reassembled into a new representation.

CRAIG McCORMICK / M. Arch. Thesis, 1998 / Keith Krumwiede, director

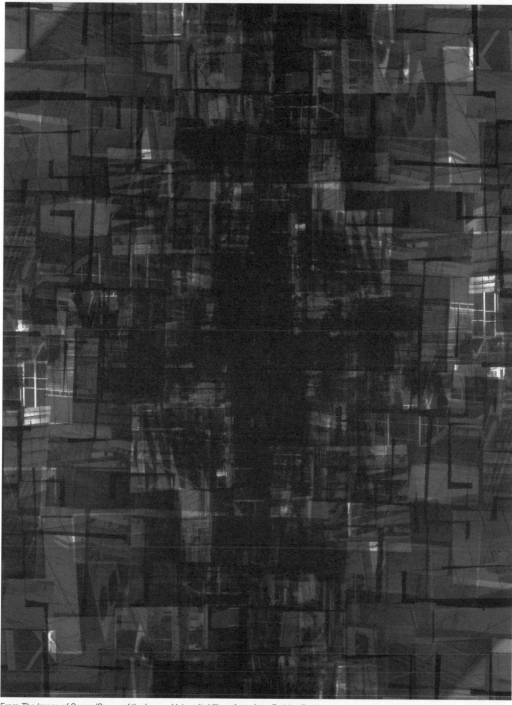

From *The Image of Space/Space of the Image*: University Village from Atop Parking Deck

↓Any Given Sunday

The megachurch is the ultimate convert in a typology that finds its ancestors within the very origins of architecture. It thrives as a collector of "seekers," creating enticing venues that capitalize on disconnected suburban environments to form a micro-city of services offered by the megachurch (such as gyms, daycare, and support groups). Currently, megachurches conservatively follow the organizational model of malls, restricting ownership to a single anchor church offering all services and products. This thesis suggests an alternative model, favoring the full inclusion of multiple tenant churches while maintaining a co-op of peripheral services. As an evolution of a prevalent form in suburban Houston, this megachurch has been recast as a vertical urban infrastructure that recontextualizes the mall section as a programmatic and filtering procession of services offered to the community. Exploiting the opposing time and scale of this daily service-based urbanism with the weekly worship service event, it redefines the relationship of worship spectacle to the anti-spectacle of community services.
ERIC HUGHES / M.Arch. Thesis, 2007 / Douglas Oliver, director

I'm a Believer:
Rock My Religion and the Medium Will be the Message
It may come as a surprise, but even if Houston is an eternally comatose city that for the most part consists of an endless sea of individual houses, covered by what Lars Lerup calls a "zoohemic canopy" of broccoli-like trees, it is also the birthplace of spectacular new forms of collective life, the success of which depends on a symbiosis between live and televised audiences. The buildings housing this new collective life are basically enormous television studios that can accommodate events from baseball to football, from Wrestlemania to rock concerts, and from demolition derbies to victims of a hurricane. The original 1965 Astrodome is still the most striking example. For a long time the biggest air-conditioned space in the world, this gigantic multifunctional building is at its versatile best during the Livestock Show & Rodeo, changing the arena for calf roping, bronc riding, or a country and western gig within minutes.

Houston also hosts two of the largest television churches in the U.S.: Lakewood Church, with an attendance

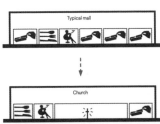
Reprogramming church using mall as model

Vertical organization of traditional church, suburban megachurch, urban megachurch

View of urban megachurch in midtown Houston

190

Siting of washateria/cafeteria, laundromat/automat on Richmond Avenue

of 25,000 per weekend, and the Second Baptist Church, with an attendance of 18,000 per weekend. Preaching that material and worldly success is a path to immortality—the only possible way to overcome Original Sin being hard work— these capitalist churches may not be so different from larger corporations, and they are taken very seriously in Forbes for their exemplary marketing methods. Housed in the Compaq Center—former home of the NBA's Houston Rockets—and making use of the most modern communication media, from television to streaming Internet, Lakewood Church reaches over 90 percent of American households and 140 countries with mass audiences like those at rock concerts. Dan Graham has already pointed out the relationship between American religion and rock music: "Rock performers electrically unleash anarchic energies and provide a hypnotic ritualistic trance basis for the mass audience."[1] The televised collective trance is transferred to the audiences at home. As an act of will, viewers can buy CDs, DVDs, and books from the services. "I am a big believer in the media," says Lakewood's pastor Joel Osteen. "That has always been my passion."[2]

—**Bart Lootsma** is the chair of architectural theory at the Leopold-Franzens-University Innsbruck.

1. Dan Graham, "Rock My Religion," in *Rock My Religion*, 1965–1990, ed. Brian Wallis (Cambridge, Mass.: MIT Press, 1993).
2. Tara Dooley, "Spreading Its Word," *Houston Chronicle*, September 26, 2004, sec. A, 1.

↑ washateria/cafeteria, laundromat/automat

Based on the idea of an architectural design thesis as praxis, two buildings were designed to both talk about and perform the thesis. The ideas at work in the project include consideration of objects, people, places, and things in shifting relationships with each other. Using collecting and collections as a starting point—the thesis building(s) is(are) a part of several larger collections within Houston—the project makes these relationships visible through moments of saturation, framing, exaggeration, and multiplication.

Initially the thesis collected a series of spaces and places within Houston. Called Marvels, they allowed for an exploration of marvelous characteristics and provided new terms specific to urban life in Houston. The thesis buildings were first understood as one of that series. They needed to be believable as actual spaces in Houston, but also marvelous. The buildings became part of a collection of buildings within their immediate neighborhood—a type (a Houston phenomenon modeled after Villa Savoye) and a strip (an urban situation found in many twentieth-century American cities).

The scales of the collections are embedded. Despite being singular things in a larger collection, the thesis buildings contain or enclose a series of

FROM WRESTLEMANIA TO ROCK CONCERTS

COLLECTION OF "SEEKERS"

Transmission Dome, 3420 Chimmney Rock, Houston, Texas. See *mini-astrodome, novelty and rarity, creative re-use, specificity of programming* (only transmissions)

Wig Mart, 1007 Eagle, Houston, Texas. See *saturation, sublime, intensive interior, simulacra*

Fiesta Supermarket, 6200 Bellaire Blvd, Houston, Texas. See *multiple program, variety, heterogeny*

Taqueria la Tapetia, Richmond Blvd, Houston, Texas. See *vividness and verisimilitude*

Miracle on Main Street, Main at Travis, Houston, Texas. See *imported climate, foreign and exotic, strange, and bizarre, creative re-use, temporal program*

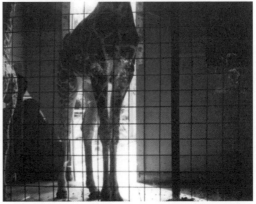

Giraffe Habitat, Houston Zoo, Houston, Texas. See *unusually large and unusually small*

smaller collections as well: a collection of experiences, views, and moments, a collection of activities in time (see Breughel), a collection of activities in time and in relationship to each other and to objects (i.e., food, laundry), and a collection of terms of engagement (i.e., the dial, the door handle). These collections are organized as a field with two enclosures—see The Museum of Jurassic Technology (a whole that contains multiple wholes)—or as three fields, two of which are interiors.

MARY SPRINGER / M.Arch. Thesis, 1999 / Keith Krumwiede, director

↘ Static Distorters:
An Economic Living Toy

An interest in Ed Ruscha's iconic 1970 book *Real Estate Opportunities*, which depicted twenty-five lots available for purchase in Los Angeles, led to similar research into available buildings in Houston's derelict Midtown district that could be adapted or reused for purposes other than their original intent. From a catalog of exhausted banks, dry cleaners, and apartment buildings, a defunct industrial laundry was selected for its flexible open structure, high ceilings, and proximity to developing nightlife.

At the center of the project is the belief that the city is energized by the unexpected collisions of activities and their various programmatic durations. Here, the proposed mixture combined a puppet theater, a nightclub, a copy center, and a shuffleboard and badminton court. Each was set in close proximity to the other, but still maintained distinct zones. Between each zone a transition was designed that visually blurred the threshold, encouraging a drift between zones. Thus a customer making copies might stop for a quick thirst-quenching beverage and consequently catch a portion of a puppet show. Drift, accident, mere circumstances were anticipated as the outcome of situations where individuals and groups with disparate needs and interests may overlap. The open city is where accidents are welcome and become opportunities.

LUKE BULMAN, KIMBERLY SHOEMAKE / M.Arch. Thesis, 1998 / Mark Wamble, director

Six real estate opportunites in Houston

The existing interior of the industrial laundry, an opportunity

Image multiplier between bar and copy shop

Pocket theaters for traditional puppet theater

EXHAUSTED BANKS

CREATIVE RE-USE

GIRAFFE HABITAT

↑Urban Showroom
NUNU CHANG / Undergraduate Option Studio, 2000 / Luke Bulman, Dawn Finley, critics

↑Urban Showroom
KATIE BENNETT / Undergraduate Option Studio, 2000 / Luke Bulman and Dawn Finley, critics

→Locus Moment

Locus Moment seeks out opportunity by making use of the latent dynamic properties of the Houston landscape. The aim is not to invent recognizable forms that alone operate as lasting figures in the landscape; Locus Moment instead is a stimulator, a momentary enacted form, and an afterimage. Like the great battles that were fought on sacred clearings of early medieval landscapes,

Locus Moment is situated within the urban wilderness of Midtown Houston.

Stimulated by vacancies and remnants, Locus Moment acts as a perceptual device. Vital for only a moment, it attempts to shape our understanding of these vacancies. As Locus Moment remains in the mind as an afterimage, one is encouraged to search for the latent potential that exists within the Houston landscape.

As a momentary enacted form, Locus Moment was an urban event that incorporated radio, live musical performance, and video. Broadcast over the airwaves at 9:00 p.m. on January 18, 2001, this event was the product of a collaboration between KTRU 91.7 FM Rice Radio, musician Jon Durbin, composer Jens Joneleit, and Gunnar Hartmann as coordinator. A soundfield, which functioned in part as accompaniment to the live performance, was broadcast to the site and elsewhere via KTRU. Members of the audience arriving at the site were asked to leave their car radios on.

"Scape Realizations" is a musical composition in which the performer tries to realize a landscape or cityscape for her/himself and/or the listening audience through sounds. The performer achieves this by utilizing her/his

vision of the surrounding environment, i.e., by looking at a greater "vision frame" and also reading certain focus areas. The performer uses the surrounding landscape as the score to play from, creating the sounds given through signs and symbols by the composer. In other words, the composer supplies only general guidelines with colored and shaped symbols, which are attached to certain pitches, as well as the symbols and signs needed to enable the performer to realize through sound the landscape from which she/he is reading it. In addition the soundfield should not be followed timewise: it only supplies a platform for the created sounds of the performer.[1]

1. Jens Joneleit, "Scape Realizations for Locus Moment," 2001.

STIMULUS
****
—1,000 cards mailed and posted
—one minute radio trailer played by KTRU 91.7FM Rice Radio
—two minute video trailer shown at the Media Center, Rice University

AFTERIMAGE
****
We arrived at the event and passed the site once, we could not find parking right away. So we parked behind the large garage across from the site. Just as we got out of the car, it started to rain very heavily so we stood underneath the parking garage and watched the large projection across the street. Felt like a drive-in movie theatre. I was there for about an hour.
A car pulled up, very slowly and eventually stopped—nobody got out. The people inside the car were observing us, wondering why we were standing in the rain and what was going on around them. While the car was stopped and still running, one was able to read the projected MOMENT in the exhaust smoke that came out of the car. It is hard to describe it. You could read MOMENT multiple times, like a mirage. It even seemed surreal as I saw it in person.

I really liked the fact that this was not a frontal performance, everybody looked into a different direction. We were surrounded by action. Even though I observed it most of the time from the parking garage, I eventually walked out after the heavy rain started to get lighter and slowly discovered that there were many little things waiting for me to discover. The projections and the sound made me aware of the environment that I was in. Both were very strange, how should I say, too slow. Not like in a movie, I had time to look around.

Who are these guys, they must be crazy!

I know this site very well—I've lived around here for five years or so. Before I used to live up on San Jacinto near the jail. There, every night I could hear the train passing by. Tonight during Locus Moment, I remember hearing the train and that is pretty much impossible, considering that we are on this side of town. It took me a while to realize this—I was actually listening to the sound that came out of the car radios.

I was there last night.

After I was soaking wet and cold, the performance still kept going. I got into my car and started up the engine. While listening to the radio, I was somehow still a part of this ongoing performance, even though I left the site. I decided to go home because it started raining even harder. Actually, I listened to the radio on my way home and somehow projected Locus Moment into these other vacant spaces that I saw.

The strongest memory I have is all the reflection of these projections. On the surfaces they were like mirrors. Then the trumpet player arrived out of nowhere and suddenly there was a dimension of depth. It just really made you enjoy being there especially out in the rain. It is strange I really do not know how to describe it.

I told you, I'd play! I never played in a context like this before. I felt as a part of the audience, we all were performers. Jens' composition

Event documentation of Locus Moment

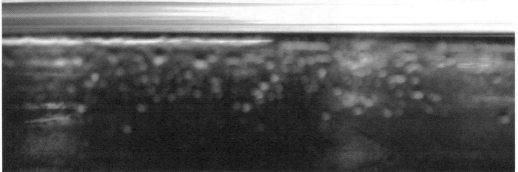

Event documentation of Locus Moment

guidelines helped me to not get stuck inside my own improvisation pattern. I searched within the landscape for the score. The whole environment— the rain, the wind, the people, all those cars and the atmosphere of lights—made the sound. It's tough to play the trumpet when it's cold.

Hey man, we just turned around onto Elgin and wanted to go up on Main. This looks great! We are really into graffiti. Man, you projected graffiti onto a wall. I was just talking to my friends how this is such a great idea. That means we could sketch and draw at home and project it without getting caught. You can project very large too.

Is this legal what you guys are doing? Are you the landlord? What are you doing out here? What is it for?

I was so busy making sure that everything was going well. The first time I looked up, I saw an audience standing to my right underneath

the large office building and then to my left there was an audience standing underneath the parking garage. For a moment, it appeared as both audiences were looking at each other.

I remember, WASTELAND was spelled into the air and Walt Whitman was projected onto the rough ground.

The walls and streets were these reflecting mirrors and the site was floating in between. Did you see those clouds passing by? What an atmosphere.
People stopping in the middle of the street to watch out of curiosity, almost causing an accident and creating traffic jam. Some cars honked their horns as they drove by —I guess they participated.

You should occupy this wall more than just one night. Do it every night for the next two weeks. Claim this wall. Make it your own. I think this has a lot of potential, the way that you invade these spaces.

If I would go out there today, would there be anything left to see?

Last week I wanted to meet a friend at Mai's for lunch. He couldn't remember where Mai's was at, so I told him it was a block down from the Locus Moment site.
GUNNAR HARTMANN / M.Arch. Thesis, 2001 / Keith Krumwiede, director

→Projection Bomb

The old drive-in theater is dead, so where do car culture, projection technology, and provisional communities converge in contemporary culture? On the street. In a parking lot. Around a second program. Three forms of guerrilla projection occur in three different urban conditions. But are the conditions mutually exclusive? Can guerrillas play together in overlapping urban instances? Can an institution cultivate these street artists without killing their street cred? It would take a new institution. Rumors of expansion at the Museum of Fine Arts, Houston, have pointed to property occupied by its parking garage as a potential site for new construction. But the parking garage may already be an ideal platform for the descendents of the drive-in. Framed by the limits of the existing garage, this thesis project proposes a small number of interventions to expand the potential for guerrilla occupation. The result is a moving target museum.

CLINT KEITHLEY / M.Arch. Thesis, 2008 / Carlos Jiménez, director

The reaction to and anticipation of a guerrilla action is what enables and empowers the act: What will it be? What is the potential risk for the creator and the participants? Will it be stopped? Can it be stopped? What if no one notices it? Can it be replicated, imitated, systematized, transferred to other sites? Are we complicit in the act with the creator if we participate in the action?

The replication of the drive-in: Sited in a parking garage for the Museum of Fine Arts required preliminary investigations of access and utilities, in particular when the viewing and projection could be located within the site itself. Determining the hours of accessibility to the garage and also if there was access to electricity to power the projection system and a façade that would function as a scrim to be projected on. A generator, like the ubiquitous leaf-blowers of Houston, generates an average decibel level of 70-75dB at 50 feet and would not have been an option, for obvious reasons. The MFA's providence revealed accessibility to space and power, two resources that could be utilized for a myriad of activities, legal and not, including the prescribed drive-in-theatre. The surrounding neighborhood structures were all unknowing participants.

In Houston, the lack of a formal zoning code, the only metropolitan area in the United States that is still holding out as an emblem of 'free enterprise' or a 'wild-catting' mentality provides this blank screen and what Projection Bomb presents us with is the question of retrofitting or redevelopment.

Guerilla projection event scenario

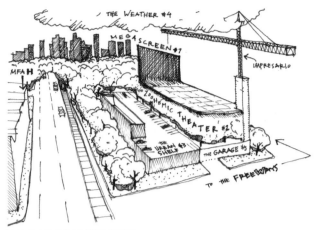

Apparatuses of the outdoor theater

At a moment of economic uncertainty, temporality is a focal point and what this intervention reveals and as an anticipatory act is how we can repurpose structures to become more productive in a capitalistic model that works on the factory's schedule of 24/7. Projection Bomb was an augur of the utilization of an existing structure as a machine that opens itself up to an activity that takes place at the site, but also leaks out into the rest of the city. An important element was the fact that administration of the museum was not complicit in the action, that the perpetrator did not seek their permission, but identified a possibility and took action upon the opportunity. This reflects back to Lars Lerup and his philosophy to get off your ass and do something.

–Architecture on paper is flaccid. And dead.

–Terrorism is eye-opening.

–Adrenaline feels better than Rhino.

–Snooze=Lose

—**Mary Ellen Carroll** is a New York-based artist. She was a Visiting Cullinan Professor at Rice School of Architecture in 2006; **Charles Renfro** is a partner at Diller Scofidio+Renfro. He was a Visiting Cullinan Professor at Rice School of Architecture in 2006.

Projection Bomb event at the Museum of Fine Arts, Houston

→Living Projection

Casting peers, faculty, and the odd passerby as integral parts of an open scripted system, the Living Projection is a multifaceted proposition. As a design for a physical library, it is equipped with theaters, production studios, stacks, and ticket booths. As a film, it freely engages in the visceral act of making time-based space, occupying the design with life and possibility. As an installation and event, it suspends disbelief and embraces the immersive collapse of the imagined virtual space with the physical space of the audience. Stepping forward and backward, framing and reframing, it becomes natural to not be sure where you are, effectively transforming the screening room into a component of the building.

No architects were harmed during the making of this project.

BRIAN WESLEY HEISS, MICHAEL MORROW / Graduate Core Studio, 1998 / Robert Mangurian, Mary-Ann Ray, critics [See also *Studioworks*, page 220]

Video stills from Living Projection

Living Projection vignette models

→ SoftCinema

"Cinemarchitecture" attends to the program of film (in general) and cinemas (in particular), investigating the complex relationship between film and architecture. Research into this relationship evolved into the concept of SoftCinema. From the start, the boundaries of bodies, buildings, and technologies were questioned, as explorations were conducted into how the softening of these boundaries might activate and enhance the cinema experience in the contemporary city.

A minimal apparatus remains intact in this proposal after a radical softening of the armature of normative cinema experience. Freed from the physical and social constraints of normative cinemas, which direct crowd circulation based on a formulaic, profit-driven arrangement, SoftCinema offers a terrain open for exploration and wandering by day and night. The temporal rhythms of the cinema are enhanced with programmatic shifts through the diurnal cycle. Hybridization occurs through time as programs occupy the same surfaces, rather than being projected simultaneously in separated spaces. As evening falls and the cinema becomes apparent, the programs begin to fuse. Mingled crowds become self-organizing, reacting to directional cues in the building.

The building is performative in its interactions with participants and with the city at large. As curtains fall to indicate the showing of a film, participants find themselves slowly removed from their orientation within the building and the surrounding city. Inside this film-viewing area, attention is focused on the film, while outside this space the film is visible and audible in combination with other activities, resulting in a more distracted viewer state. SoftCinema is extroverted: it participates actively in the urban landscape as an ever-changing, morphing body/building. It is both actor and set.

ELIZABETH MCQUITTY, NIKOLAI NIKOLOV, JESSICA YOUNG / Graduate Core Studio, 2000 / Robert

Softcinema video stills

Mangurian, Mary-Ann Ray, critics
[See also *Studioworks*, page 220]

For many years I have had a negative reaction to mixed media, feeling that any attempt to fuse two (confuse one for the other)—say cinema and architecture—would impoverish both. Each art has its own deeply imbedded media potentials and constraints that make it unique. "Architecture is not a radio" exclaimed the English critic Martin Pawley in the late 60's. Each art has is its own history, its own core-business with its own business potential. Nevertheless when a particularly inventive group of students in 1998 and 2000 presented their projects under the rubrics "Living Projection" and "SoftCinema" I remarked in the heat of a final project presentation, "Finally, I'm running a Film School." Since here both cinema and architecture were mixed, one juxtaposed on and inter-mingled with the other, my concern over fusion still

Softcinema study model and set

held. Many strands of memories came upon me at that moment. My very old interest in the Czech theater group Laterna Magika of 1958 (under the directorship of Alfred Rador and Josef Svoboda) in which projection and space were occupied by mute performers, mixed two medias. Again the discrete preservation of each media's potentials and constraints forced the viewers to perform the fusion—with spectacular results—at least for the nineteen-year-old Swedish Navy man. In addition, Mary-Ann Ray and Robert Mangurian's Grand Center Master Plan in St. Louis of much later, powerfully suggested that the entire city was a stage for a multitude of projections (it is therefore no surprise that both of these projects were done in their studio.)

In retrospect, our student's efforts were the precursor of the current intense interest in the animated surface, now already decades old. The desire to awaken architectural surface and space is architects' notorious dissatisfaction with its media constraints. The Rebellion Against the Limitations of Space—a worthy and longstanding struggle against spatial confinement. But also the desperate attempt to make "architecture move" (underlying the entire project of this book.)

But these student projects broke additional ground that, now lost, brings tears to my eyes. A wild enthusiasm in which space and cinema was the mere backdrop for human action. This was particularly apparent in the performance of SoftCinema. The students acted the occupation of space by actually and virtually appearing in both film projections and space. Here Svoboda's continued work in the luster of the magic lantern was awakened by a group of students who (probably) knew nothing of the Czech theater. Indicating that my hopes for an "endless seminar" had taken form, projecting both back and forward uncovering historical precedence just by understanding deeply the fecund natures of two medias; a type of Foucauldian archeology, uncovering (without knowing) artifacts from the past while projecting artifacts of the future. Heady times indeed!

—**Lars Lerup** is the dean and William Ward Watkin Professor of Architecture at Rice School of Architecture.

→Not a Box

David Erdman
Visiting Cullinan Professor, Graduate Option Studio, 2007

One thing that links the work of Josef Albers, Louis Kahn, James Turell, and Dan Flavin is the manipulation and illusive qualities light brings into their work. Each sees illumination as a medium, acting with matter, forming a larger environment, and producing optical and/or experiential effects.

Not a Box was a studio conducted at the Rice School of Architecture that, using these precedents (among others), sought out ways in which contemporary architecture can manage, integrate, and most importantly conceptualize the relationship of new media and architecture. The studio drew upon the rich relationship of architecture and painting by seeking out digital, rendering-like qualities in physically constructed environments. Like the use of perspective in the fifteenth century, the studio posited rendering as a contemporary and equally pervasive form of representation that can be made use of in architectural design.

The primary focus of the studio was to look at ways in which artificial light could take on extra-dimensional qualities and be encapsulated within architectural elements like corners, floors, walls, or columns. Students were asked to design a prototypical residence for an artist. Each unit had to be modular and accommodate a three-story live-work program consisting of a gallery, studio, living space, and roof terrace—each on separate floors. Units had to combine together into specific formations for an arts community of 200 units.

Working in teams, students researched and explored specific lighting effects and qualities through large-scale physical models. The investigations carefully considered how artificial light would impact materials and the overall mass of a prototypical unit. For instance, light was channeled through compressive columns forming a texture in the walls of one proposal; it pneumatically inflated roof-floor plates in another, while bending through the structural spine of another. In each proposal students were asked to develop daylight and artificial light environments, and conceptualize how circulation, program, and structure were organized within or through them.

Although the effects the students discovered were heavily influenced by a culture of rendering, one of the interesting things about this type of work is it is nearly impossible to investigate through the actual use of renderings. In fact, it reverses a typical order of operations. Where renderings are usually seen as a document produced at the end of a process, rendering-like effects were studied from the beginning of the process and used to guide design development. Students were asked to limit their work to the production of multiple study models and explore their effects through photography. In most cases these models mixed multiple processes and materials: 3D printed plaster, laser-cut plastics/wood, vacuum-formed plastics, and hand-cut rubber, foam, or wood. This type of aggressive and coarse mixing served as an extremely useful form of material intelligence and required students to examine design possibilities across these fabrication platforms and their associate software. Each model provided an analogical model for studying both the effects of the lighting (at scale) and its architectural consequences, serving as a rich tool for discussion and development.

The overall research offers some insight into the growing quantity of information that is rapidly being layered into our urban environments. Glowing architectural skins are emerging as an area of research in both architectural design and engineering. While promising to erode boundaries between inside and outside and to make altering realities and formal experiences present in the city, this trend of development (in cities such as New York, Shanghai, Hong Kong, and Tokyo) remains two-dimensional and frontal, where the skins act as signage or a TV screen displaying information. In most cases, the glowing surfaces are not only devoid of any relationship with the building mass (the Box), but are also spatially and experientially inert—the box stays dumb.

The research conducted by the RSA students in this studio if nothing else suggests that the boundaries between media and architecture can be more intensively related. By drawing upon our past and making use of contemporary representational tools like rendering, their projects push into an emerging territory of design research. The following images showcase examples of how a simple experiment using the medium of artificial light may reverse conventional flows or hierarchies. Here architecture emits, harnesses, and pushes media into its elements, producing effects that move across the street. It does specific work on floors, walls, and corners, examining blurry, conceptually translucent relationships between the inside and outside. In each case, the box changes: it becomes less legible and itself vibrates in and out of focus.

DAVID ERDMAN is a principal of david clovers and a faculty member at UCLA's Department of Architecture and Urban Design. He was a Visiting Cullinan Professor at Rice School of Architecture in 2007.

→ Video 1,2,3

Brian Wesley Heiss

Instructor, Seminar, 2002–05

The creation of architecture is founded in modes of 2D and 3D representation. With the ever-increasing presence of the video medium and accessibility to video editing tools, a light and flexible time-based mode of representation has become available to designers. Video 1,2,3 is an opportunity to experiment with the production of space given nothing but a video camera, the ability to edit footage, and a means of replaying footage in public space. Can the video medium be used to define space in ways that traditional architecture cannot? To answer this, we will look at the history of video art and deal directly with the issues of both representation and event in a hands-on manner.

The course will consist of three projects, each exploring different methodologies of using video as a tool to design and make space. The first project will focus on the content within a picture frame and deal with the use of filming techniques, editing, narrative, form, and juxtapositions in scale. The second project will deal with issues of filmic content through a site-specific video projection installation that must reprogram an existing space somewhere in the city. The final project will look at issues of content, site, and object by focusing on how the television functions physically and culturally in western civilization. Experimentation and invention of new apparatus and techniques for using/liberating/confining the gaze of the video camera will be encouraged.

BRIAN WESLEY HEISS is a professor of practice at Lehigh University Department of Art and Architecture. He was a visiting critic at Rice School of Architecture.

David Stockwell, Katherine Schoenfelder

Kari Smith, Dan Burkett

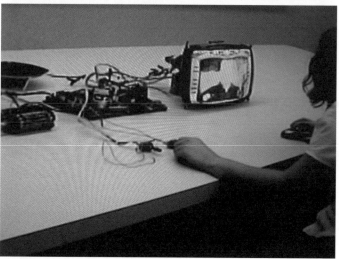

John Bacus

HOW THE TELEVISION FUNCTIONS

LIGHT AND FLEXIBLE

TIME-BASED MODE OF REPRESENTATION

Kayte Young, Matthew Radune

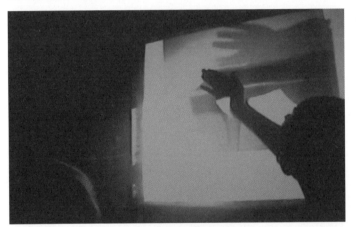

Nicole Blair

→Reactor

Point 1: Bodies, sounds, smells, hard work, sightlines, self-loathing, flesh, squeaky sneakers, bright fluorescent light, busy, meat market, willpower, sweat, lots of mirrors, music, self-improvement, CNN, spandex, repetition.

Point 2: The energy exerted in the improvement of one's body is valuable and can be focused to productive ends.

Reactor is a proposal for a fitness center that responds directly to the energy invested by its occupants. The outer skin of the building is made of fifty-three articulated panels that ride on protruding tracks. Rather than expending energy lifting a weight or compressing a spring, members of the club use the uniquely designed circuit training machines inside Reactor to open the façade of the building. Much in the way that one person lifts a car with a jack, a group of people in Reactor collectively lift the entire building. Each machine translates repetitive body motion into fluid pressure, which, in turn, is directed into hydraulic rams located near the exterior panels. A glazed skin sits just behind the moving panels to provide a weather barrier for the climate-controlled interior. Throughout the day the otherwise mute, opaque, and rectangular box opens and closes as a direct manifestation of how hard those inside are working.

BRIAN WESLEY HEISS / Graduate Core Studio, 1997 / Spencer Parsons, Gordon Wittenberg, critics

Reactor responding to fitness activity at various times of day

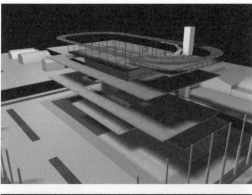
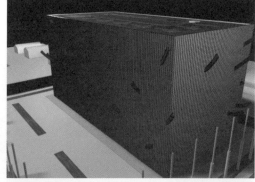

Structural layers and responsive skin system of Reactor

When the Wachowski brothers' *Matrix*, the resplendent if somewhat sophomoric science-fiction steamroller, premiered in 1999, it presented a grim analog to Brian Wesley Heiss's seemingly optimistic project of two years prior. In the film the "people as energy" proposition takes a dark turn.

As one looks back years later at Heiss's project, it would seem that it is the more difficult attitudes that Reactor betrays that give it a durable utility. A critical ambivalence about the contemporary condition is what, in retrospect, gives shape and depth to the progressive ideas that one finds upon first inspection. The animated spectacle of the building is actually the result of the metabolization of certain unsavory, unspoken urban realities that the project can address yet never quite dispel. Those realities remain our context.

Reactor is Barnum (P.T.) meets Banham (P.R.), but not without a healthy dose of Ballard (J.G.). From the hostile mechanized countenance of the building itself, with its haughty disregard for its context, to the disdain with which Heiss regards the image-obsessed users, Reactor deftly balances between an inspiring optimism and an unapologetically critical glare at inscrutable Houston, "America's Fattest City." A tense yet meaningful symbiosis is achieved. No pain, no gain.

—**Michael Morrow** is a principal at kinneymorrow. He is a visiting critic at Rice School of Architecture.

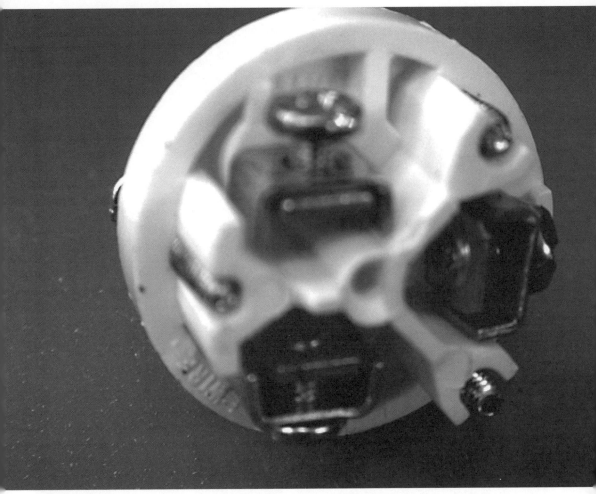

Electrical connector

→Hive Systems: Explorations into the Possibilities and Consequences of Behavioral Programming in Architectural Spaces

This is a project whose vision is to make visible the intersection between two worlds: (1) the world of media and information, and (2) the world of physical things as experienced by our bodies. A series of research projects investigated the possibilities of creating lifelike intelligence within architectural spaces. Various methods for applying behaviors to physical environments were explored, culminating in the design and creation of a mutually interactive website and physical installation. This installation allows users of the physical space to affect the experience of those entering the space virtually, and vice versa. A custom-programmed script allows web visitors to manipulate the atmosphere of the physical space and experience the effects through multiple views of streaming video and audio. The installation attempts to give a glimpse into the future of integrating information systems with architecture.

LOGAN RAY / M.Arch. Thesis, 2001 / David Brown, director

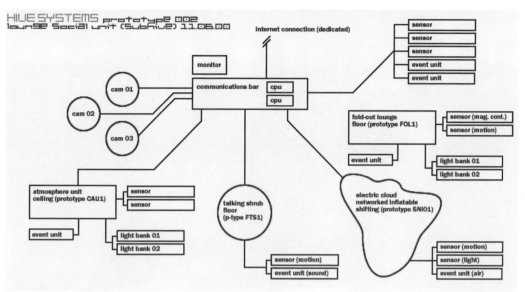

HIVE SYSTEMS prototype 002
lounge social unit (SubHive) 11.06.00

internet connection (dedicated)

sensor
sensor
sensor
event unit
event unit

monitor

communications bar | cpu | cpu

cam 01
cam 02
cam 03

fold-out lounge
floor (prototype FOL1)

sensor (mag. cont.)
sensor (motion)

event unit

light bank 01
light bank 02

atmosphere unit
ceiling (prototype CAU1)

sensor
sensor

talking shrub
floor
(p-type FTS1)

electric cloud
networked inflatable
shifting (prototype SNI01)

event unit

light bank 01
light bank 02

sensor (motion)
event unit (sound)

sensor (motion)
sensor (light)
event unit (air)

215

Hive Systems network diagram

Networked mobile electric units, powered
by ceiling panel

Internet controlled light wall set to "red and blue" (top), and just "red" (bottom)

very close   very close

Very Close: the camera moves within the crowd as an equal participant

↑ Incorporaiding City

Two distinctly different political ages in Eastern Europe are manifest simultaneously in shifting attitudes toward the body, toward communication, and toward taking action. The thesis provides the beginning of a genealogy of the crowd form, from the military marches and stadium spectacles characteristic of the hard totalitarian era of Eastern Europe to the crowd that gathered at the student and citizen protest in Belgrade in 1996–97. The protest persisted for four months and in its creativity managed to transcend the self-referential mechanics of a resistance project.

The formal manifestations of these general and specific attitude shifts toward the regime and toward the city allow one to believe that it is possible to visualize social phenomena and practices as "drawing machines" working at various scales, drawing by intervening in space the way that a dancing body describes its kinesthetic sphere. I have been drawing the protest event primarily in video to ensure that the experience of these mappings always fits the basic definition of an event.

ANA MILJACKI / M.Arch. Thesis, 1999 / Sanford Kwinter, director

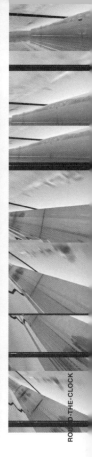

Each strip is an excerpt from a "studio"
that captures an aspect of the urban experience and translates it to a new spatial
sequence in the tower

↑Capturing the City, Spatializing the Captured

Both its incredible density and its ever-moving, round-the-clock public transportation system contribute to the vibrant character of Hong Kong. In this totally consumption-driven city, where the turnover rate is unbelievably fast, people have no time and no room to think. Compactness is no longer a function of lack of space, but has become a system of its own. A static representation is insufficient to document a city like Hong Kong, in which every single parameter is open to animation.

Various computer animation techniques were explored to spatial-ize the raw video footage of the city. These exercises sought to capture the ambiance rather than the physi-cal constructs of the city. "Studios" generated in the computer were stacked to form a tower in which the experiences and events of the city are encapsulated. The fixity and objectness of the tower (the object of architecture) is effaced by visually animating the surfaces. The tower also parallels the compactness of the city.

LUCIA CHEUNG / M.Arch. Thesis, 1999 / Albert Pope, director

ROUND-THE-CLOCK

KINESTHETIC SPHERE

GENEALOGY OF THE CROWD

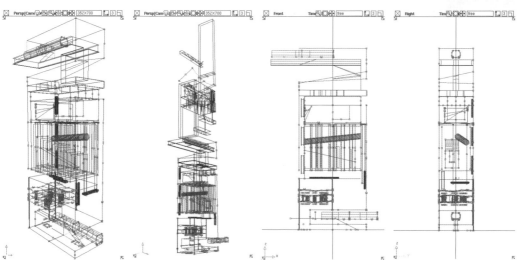

Above: more captured sequences of the "Studios"; below, wireframe views showing the assemblage of studios into the tower structure. Movement between levels is made thirough a variety of means: stair, ramp escalator, subway...

→ Frames
Farès el-Dahdah
Critic, Graduate Option Studio, 1997

These installations were produced during the last three weeks as a postscript to a semester-long project that considered downtown Houston as a singular (albeit gigantic) site for its design interventions, appropriations, reprogrammings, reinventions, etc. Having thus appropriated the whole of downtown in the form of design proposals, the studio subsequently (and physically) intervened within the interiors of two actual buildings found on its otherwise mega-site.

The garage installations as postscripts to the design proposals should not be regarded as miniature extensions of each project, but rather as temporary appropriations of an experiential condition that is constructed within the physical context of downtown Houston. Both the Travis Garage and the urbanity surrounding it were, in fact, regarded as "frames" that were qualified by the design interventions found in them, the act of framing having the virtue of reminding one that it is something we do, not something we find. These installations simply appropriated a building's interior, just as a design proposal seeks to reinvent its object of study. It was also the studio's concern to regard context as something that is produced rather than given, a stance opposed to the causal model of contextual reference wherein cause is the natural origin of effect. If the notion of context as cause and building as its effect was avoided, it was in order to grant design the possibility of "full causes without effects, immense effects with futile reasons, strong consequences from insignificant causes, rigorous effects from chance occurrences," thereby avoiding the positivistic connotations of "givenness," which are inseparable from the context idea.

FARÈS EL-DAHDAH is an associate professor at Rice School of Architecture.

Abandoned parking garage installations

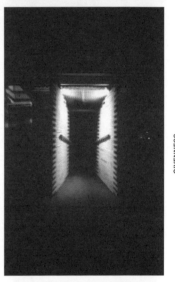

↓Studio Works

Robert Mangurian and Mary-Ann Ray

ROBERT MANGURIAN and MARY-ANN RAY are principals of Studio Works. They were Visiting Cullinan Professors at Rice School of Architecture from 1995-2006.

0605004

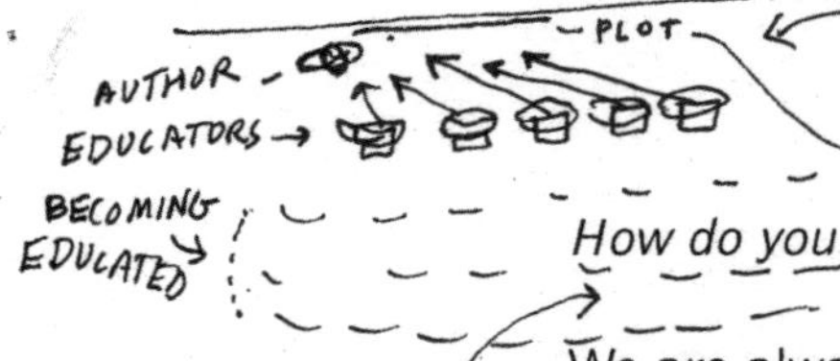

wall (white painted homosote)

AUTHOR —
EDUCATORS →
BECOMING
EDUCATED

PLOT

STRATIFIED STRUCTURE

"The Final Review"
DURATION: 20 MINUTES
(chopped lengths of shiny plot paper)

How do you see architecture education changing? WE DON'T

and "boards"

We are always surprised that the things that really need to be worked on aren't discussed. This has led to a defacto sitting at a table (often cluttered without direction) and staring into a much too small screen. Diversity of approach (working/designing method) is shrinking. Emphasis on the rendering seems to be in the forefront. Bow ties will follow.

HISTORY REPEATS + REPEATS ITSELF.

We actually see arch. education as stagnating and not changing while ripe for it,

Desk Crits, charettes, — chopped lengths old of rolls of glossy plot paper pinned to white painter sometime mounted on foam core or not

FUTURE POSSIBILITIES

PLAY + ACT OUT

homosote walls, authors backs pinned to the walls facing off against a line up of jury critics whose backs are turned to the "audience"... they are apparently teaching....... a dysfunctional ritual, a lame

repetition of architectural education habits, seeing work at ..... in other ways at

But, memories of Rice ..... thousands of candles positioned across an empty lot in the middle landscape of Houston producing a space, a plan viewed from the ground or from the top floor of the corporate towers across the street ....., a

book
a

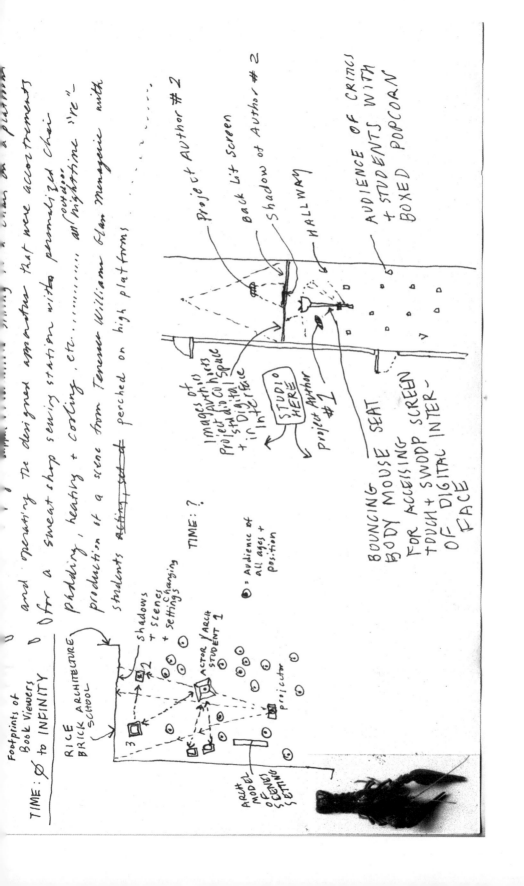

In 1994, what seemed important in architecture? What seems important now?

W E   A R E   N O T   R E A L L Y   S U R E   Y E T.

To us, in 1994 the 'deep' script that brought real content to work seemed important. Striking work explored formal/material issues, yes, and produced memorable works, while first and foremost producing within the works different ways of being - being in the works and being in the world. Really good work realized that the work could absorb enormous amounts of content.

To us, reclaiming the diversity of shaping, forming, designing, occupying, and thinking seems crucial. Architecture has always suffered from moving sideways, and not moving forward carrying much sometimes useful and sometimes not baggage.

@ this pivotal point in human history when
@ the world lives in cities already bursting @ the seams
50 % of the world + illegal city dwellers are pouring more concrete and building more sprawl area than world governments or corporations and

HOW DOES ARCH. REMAIN sq when the squatters
RELEVANT IN THE WORLD by 2050,
LIST e.g. winners ... one THIRD will be
MORE THAN one THIRD population will
of the worlds population of

architecture as building ..... ing
the city - the relationship of NOT
than + rural nature +

STRUCTURE or PROVIDING of
IN of the GOOD WORK
+ PROVIDING MORE
OF COURSE CHANGING UP
EXPANDING THE MEANING
LIMITED + PARTIAL + PROVISIONAL VIEW
HIGH COUNTRYSIDE AREA

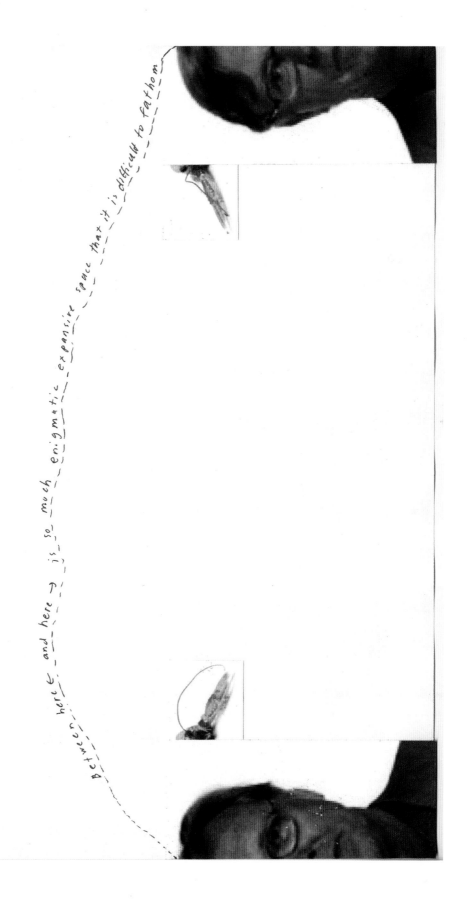

Between here← and here→ is so much enigmatic expansive space that it is difficult to fathom

What advice do you find yourself giving most often?

Use the hand (perhaps) to stimulate the brain. We have been shocked in recent years by an almost unthinking approach to 'tool/design skill' assessment when in the midst of designing. The hand has been mostly moved over to tapping on a keyboard, keeping track of too many commands. Much like the difference between flying a state of the art fighter aircraft and driving a car. Thinking (much) and conversations are not possible when managing a fighter aircraft.

We have been influenced heavily by Frank Wilson's The Hand, How its use shapes the brain, language, and human culture.

This is just a hunch on our part (and doesn't discount the possibility of working a completely (and handless) way, producing works held within the computer medium). Perhaps, for us, the 'time out' also includes 'slowing down' through the use of the hand making drawings and making things, to allow the brain to catch up with and ponder what the eyes see.

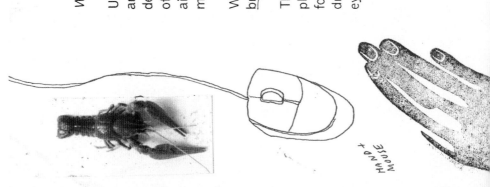

HAND + MOUSE

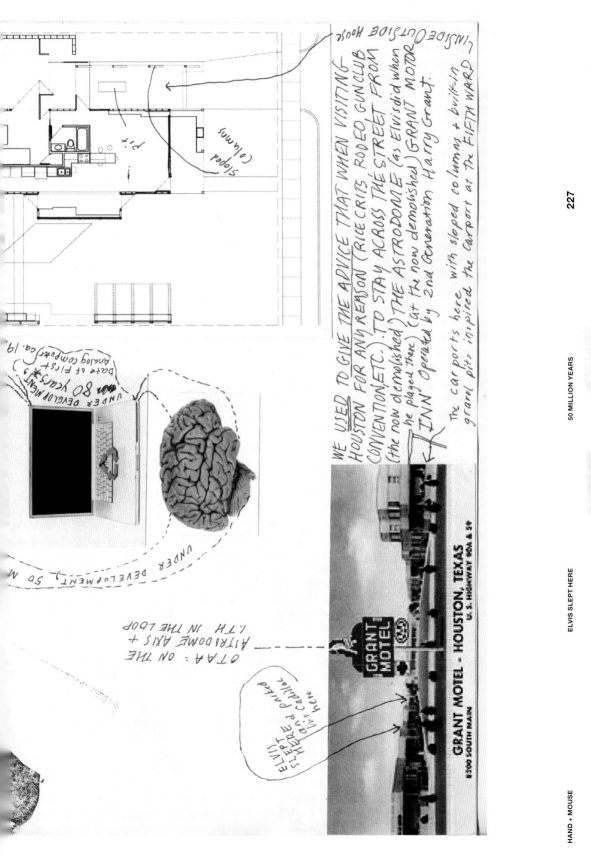

What makes an excellent project? and out
In school or out of school?
In school, the really excellent project is always the project that takes architecture to a place it hasn't been before. *Being involved as a teacher is being on a joy ride. It doesn't happen often.

tells architecture a little something it didn't know before

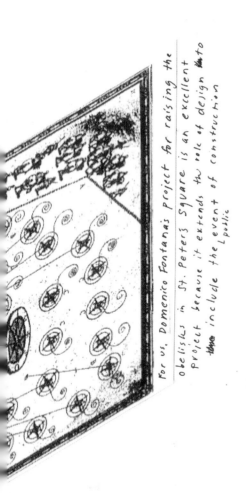

For us, Domenico Fontana's Project for raising the obelisks in St. Peters Square is an excellent project because it extends the role of design into include the event of construction [public]

* We don't always know it 'till we see it.

Lars propeller

Strangle hold

Why is the 'timeout' important? *

Our work at RICE was always excused (and perhaps praised with qualification) to be a timeout from the normative behavior - albeit quite exciting in the larsyears at RICE. We sometimes feel all our work is a 'time-out', and hopefully useful to the ongoing thrust that always seems to propel (and strangle) architecture.

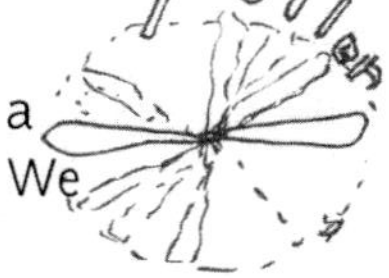

**

ARCHITECTURE IS SO

(INCESTUOUS) NEEDS — REFERENCE ITSELF — OTHERWISE IRRELEVANT

WE WILL MAKE ITSELF

NOT CODE IN REFERENCE ITSELF

BUT AN ARCHITECT 2 ACT IS READY 2 ACT

Lars once told us that what determined that he would be an architect

Naughty little
swaying pendant
hammock. (very DAPPER)

* Lars once ~~contacted~~ suggested at one of our final reviews at Rice that our studios were a kind of "time out" from Architecture

** would be great to have an L.L. Bobblehead w/ Bobble hand for drawing + writing activities

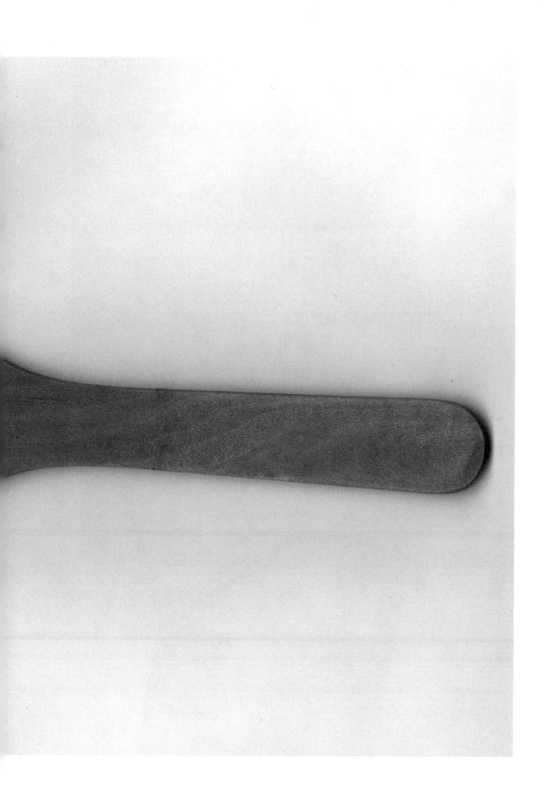

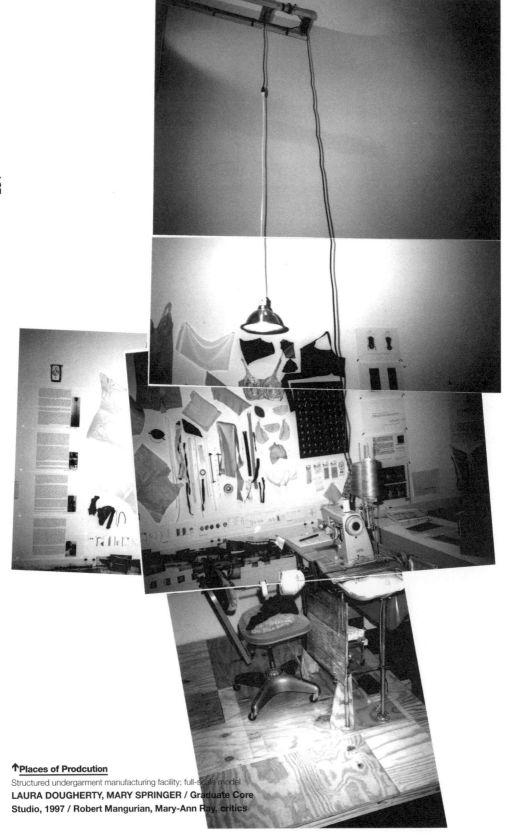

↑**Places of Prodcution**
Structured undergarment manufacturing facility; full-scale model
**LAURA DOUGHERTY, MARY SPRINGER / Graduate Core
Studio, 1997 / Robert Mangurian, Mary-Ann Ray, critics**

↑**City Seeing: the Long Books on Galveston Island**
Set of four, 72-inch long books
**LUKE BULMAN, KIMBERLY SHOEMAKE / Graduate Core
Studio, 1996 / Robert Mangurian, Mary-Ann Ray, critics**

↑**Living Projection**
Project screening and full-scale promotional items
**BRIAN WESLEY HEISS, MICHAEL MORROW / Graduate
Core Studio, 1999 / Robert Mangurian, Mary-Ann Ray,
critics**

↑**Scene Seen**
Theater vignettes
MERCEDES CORÑEJO, ANDREA MANNING /
Graduate Core Studio, 2004 / Robert Mangurian,
Mary-Ann Ray, critics

↑**The Glass Menagerie**
CALLIE BAILEY, DEWEY ERVIN, GABY FLORES, FRANK
GUITTARD / Ready Sets, Graduate Core Studio, 2004 /
Robert Mangurian, Mary-Ann Ray, critics

↑**Oedipus Rush**
ANDREW CORRIGAN, MERCEDES CORÑEJO, ANDREA
MANNING, MICHAEL SCHANBACHER / Ready Sets,
Graduate Core Studio, 2004 / Robert Mangurian,
Mary-Ann Ray, critics

↑**Ghost Trio**
SUSAN ARMSBY, BJ BEHN, JOHN HETTWER, SZE MIN
SOO / Ready Sets, Graduate Core Studio, 2004 / Robert
Mangurian, Mary-Ann Ray, critics

↓Play >Time

From the point of view of a world wholly determined by the operation of blind forces, play would be altogether superfluous.
–*J. Huizinga,* Homo Ludens: The Study of the Play Element in Culture

Play is the perfect creative act. It tears a cleft in the instrumentalized fabric of reality and offers up the liberation of pure experience. Excessive and unburdened by any claims to utility, play stands outside of the bonds of rationalized time. Duration dissolves into the eternal now—emergent, ripe, and sensual.

~~Did you find that (in the world) or did you make it up?~~

This question destroys play. Play makes no distinction between discovery and invention. It is a mobile activity, a state of flux where, as Christian Hubert has stated, "the boundaries between self and world remain labile and fluid." In this sense, traditional attempts to define play as beyond "ordinary life" or as "not work" fail to capture the full spectrum encompassed by play as a state of being—perhaps a state of grace—that finds itself paradoxically both within and beyond the "real" world. Playtime is an exploration into the space and time of play. Ten projects by twelve students test the limits of the architectural imagination as it runs headlong into the pleasures, and occasional horrors, of play. These toys twist, burrow, bulge, stand, flop,

hide, seek, open, close, shimmer, shake, swing, spin, knot, fold, gather, disperse, provoke, and react. They are full-scale models that represent, and simultaneously are, architecture.

STUDIO TEAM: Ken Andrews, Anne Buttyan, Jon Cherry, Laura Feist, Tony Hron, Kirsten Kinzer, Elizabeth Maletz, Nik Nikolov, Jin-Yeob Park, Fani Qano, Skye Smith / Graduate Option Studio, 2002 / Brian Wesley Heiss, Keith Krumwiede, critics

↑Carpet
ELIZABETH MALETZ

In this project, a familiar domestic object generates a flexible territory for play. Exhibiting obvious surface deformations and stresses, this carpet solicits direct exploration. Through play, it generates various topographies and yields access to inner realms that challenge conventional understandings of interior and exterior. It combines a variety of fabrics that exhibit distinct textures, weights, and colors. This mixture allows for a transformation from the banal to the flamboyant: flat, gray, and unobtrusive one moment, expansive and vividly colored the next.

←Surface/Space
KIRSTEN KINZER

A material investigation into the structural capacities of fabric creates a play environment that is both pure surface effect and mutable spatial envelope. Formless but not unformed, this project combines lush tactility with structural flexibility through the pleating and gathering of several layers of fabric. Potentially compact or expansive, it can be drawn together into a small backpack or deployed in an endless variety of tent-like configurations. As a toy it demands not only interaction but also creative appropriation in order to fully activate its latent energies.

LATENT ENERGIES

TWIST, BURROW, BULGE

INSTRUMENTALIZED FABRIC OF REALITY

→ Outpost Kitchen

The Outpost Kitchen is: simple, more than three minutes from a kitchen, low-input, fast, site-specific, warming/heating, storage, access to plumbing electricity, smaller than the nearest bathroom, access to disposal, familiar

The Outpost Kitchen is not: permanent, measuring, oven/stove, dishwasher, garlic press/pastry cutter/lemon zester, family, a primary tenant

ALEX KNAPP, SARA STEVENS / Graduate Option Studio, 2001 / Maria Nyström and Alex O'Briant, critics

Outpost Kitchen social area

← Product

Architectural education has a tendency to distance students from the harsh realities of production and profitability in design. The buildings, spaces, and objects that are represented in student projects typically stop at the point of representation. Although the critique of ideas and their means of representation is unquestionably valuable, there are ways of testing the success of an idea out in the world. We can, in fact, make real things.

By reducing the scale of our efforts from architecture down to the design of domestic products, and through a series of field trips to material suppliers, manufacturing facilities, and retail environments, this class will explore a means of production that enables a direct path to the market. Throughout the first half of the semester, students will be asked to generate ideas and develop prototypes. For the second half of the semester, each student will test his or her prototype, outsource the production of the selected design, and develop packaging materials. As a means of testing the success of these designs, all of the products will be for sale at Sunset Settings as retail products following the completion of the course.

All of the final items will be produced in a limited production run with the target of profitability at a maximum retail price of $50. Any profits made through the sale of these items will be used to recoup development and material costs.
BRIAN WESLEY HEISS, instructor, Seminar 2004–05

Clockwise from upper right: Felt Lamp by Matthew Radune; Bent Plywood Clutch by Kari Smith and Dan Burkett; Gasket Bag by Andrea Dietz; Pen Ball by Brian Baldor; Wobbowl by Mark Watabe

Outpost Kitchen preparation area

Stim and Dross:
Rethinking the Metropolis

Lars Lerup

stim
As in *stimulation* (William Gibson in *Mona Lisa Overdrive*) *Stimme*: voice, *Stimmung*: ambiance

dross
1. *Waste product* or *impurities* formed on the surface of molten metal during smelting.
2. Worthless *stuff* as opposed to valuables or value. *Dregs*.

rethinking
To *change one's point of view*, find a new vocabulary

Metropolis
No definition

Houston, 28th floor. At the window.

The sky is as dark as the ground; the stars, piercingly bright like a million astral specks have all fallen onto the city, rendering all else pitch black. On this light-studded scrim the stationary lights appear confident, the moving ones, like tracer bullets, utterly determined, while the pervasive blackness throws everything else into oblivion. The city like a giant switch-board, its million points switched either on or off.

Yet behind this almost motionless scene hovers the metropolis, and the more I stare at it the more it begins to stir.[1] A vast psychophysical map rolls out to fill my window like Marcel Duchamp's *Large Glass*, cut here at midpoint by a bright horizon: a dense band of lights flickering hysterically, like a great milky way sending a myriad distress signals about its impending demise. Enter the chocolate grinder, the bride and her nine bachelors, and yet a third field speedily emerges: Pulsating from below, the flurry momentarily draws the attention from Duchamp's frozen figures to the dynamics of their interactions—the abrasive motions of work and the throbbing tensions of sexual strife. Visible patterns in the glass may be few, but the individual points, and their various qualities and constellations are many, and their various qualities and constellations are many: cool and warm, some red, some green, but mostly yellow. Closer—or better, in the lower portion of the Glass—the moving lights easily match the intensity of the far more numerous immobile ones, suggesting the monstrous possibility that none are definitively fixed. All is labile, transient, as if it were only a question of time before all these lit particles would move—billiard balls on a vast table—unless *the table is not in itself a fluid in motion?* Physicist abstract from these flux-fields features such as: smoothness, connections to points-particles and rules

of interaction (between sources, sinks, cycles and flows.) "*Where space was once Kantian, [embodying] the possibility of separation, it now becomes the fabric which connects all into a whole.*"[2] Nothing on the plane is stationary, everything is fluid—even the ground itself on which the billiard balls career. The bio-vehicular, electro-commercial, socio-electronic and optico-ocular metropolis knows no steady state. In a city predominantly constituted of motion and temporalities, space itself is about deformation and velocity—*constantly being carved out in front of one and abandoned behind*—the end—definitive now—of the Corbusian promenade, and the Corbusian subject as the gentleman puppet on the architect's string.[3] The post-Corbusian subject emerges here as a complex amalgam of Benjamin's *Angelus Novus "a storm irresistibly propels him into the future to which his back is turned, while the pile of debris before him grows skyward. This storm... we call progress"* and an omni-gendered drifter—the wo-man-vehicle—whose subjectivity engulfs both the futurist reflections of Duchamp's descending nude (and the subsequent bachelors), and the tuned-out yet wired-in driver cruising along the superhighways of the Metropolis.

The European metropolis-without-crowds has skipped Westward while radically transforming itself into a new creature, leaner, meaner and more superficial, but harder to catch, at once simpler and less bearable to live in. This shift was prefigured by Robert Smithson in 1972 (in an interview with Paul Cummings) while discussing the New Monuments article: "I was also interested in a kind of suburban architecture: plain box buildings, shopping centers, that kind of sprawl. And I think this is what fascinated me in my earlier interest in Rome, just this kind of collection, this junk heap of history. But here we are confronted with a consumer society. I know there is a sentence in "The Monuments of Pessaic" where I said, "Hasn't Pessaic replaced Rome as the Eternal City?""[4]

Megashape

Back at my window the palimpsest of a new city flaunts its hypertextuality in black and light; its mental map of diverse subjectivities rarely operates while one is on foot, a predicament that hints at the possibility of a new visibility, a new field with emergent, unexpected, *megashapes* newly apprehensible but only at

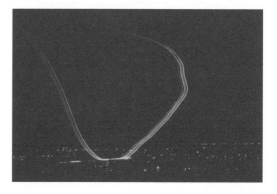

vastly different scales of motion.[5] And we can expect megashapes to be quite complex. One the one hand we have a megashape such as the *Zoohemic Canopy*, constituted by a myriad of trees, of varying species, size and maturity, and on the other, we have *Downtown*[6] that is formed by the tight assembly of skyscrapers. Both shapes rely on repetition, one of many small elements, the other on the repetition of a fairly small assembly of large elements. Though the two megashape examples seem different both are apprehended and appreciated only through shifts and distortions of scale and speed. Downtown relies less on speed than on distance. Both would require modern mathematics for analytical description. The Canopy demands a special kind of attentiveness since it operates truly on the periphery of everyday vision. However, once focused on, trees "get counted," and form with time and repetition a Zoohemic appreciation—even the pedestrian gets a sense of the forest. More intriguingly, the canopy is understood from within, from the counting of trees, not from the realization of the whole. More correctly, there are two ways of seeing the canopy, one from within and the other from the perspective of the *Aerial Field* (such as the 'space' all across the city viewed from the 28th floor.) Radically different, they don't lead to the same appreciation (form?) one is close and intimate, the other cool and distant. This double-reading brings Downtown and Canopy conceptually together since driving inside Downtown may lead to an appreciation of its megashape, and again, that would be quite different from the shape gathered from a distant position in the aerial field). There seems then, to be at least two readings of any megashapes, one from the *inside* leading to an appreciation of the algorithm of the shape (or its *taxis*, to borrow from Classical thought), and one from the *outside*, which leads to an understanding of the whole—the *figure* (the result of the algorithm, once solved.) The inside appreciation may well be the more interesting because it suggest that a megashape may be *imagined* through a fragment, and thus does not require completion, while the outside view both requires the more traditional perspective as well as a literal apprehension of the whole. The *fieldroom*, for example (literally simultaneously a field *and* a room, as will be discussed later) thus consists of one *actual* dimension—the room—and one imaginary or *extrapolated* dimension—the field. How we reconstruct or think about Downtown's megashape may be similarly developed.

Intention

The task at hand is—in a most rudimentary way—to trace the lineaments of this city. The desire to capture this elusive creature forever on the run, is however both audacious and presumptuous, offered in the spirit of the great Reyner Banham whose ruminations on the *Four Ecologies* of Los Angeles serve as a constant inspiration.[7] Because Houston, most perplexingly (and despite its deeply conservative and

isolating tendencies), is still a Metropolis waiting and poised for the great adventure.

The Plane, The Riders and Airspace

Houston is a different planet. Here space in the European sense is scarce—even nonexistent. With neither sea, nor confining walls to define it, it consists only of a mottled plane to navigate.[8] By turns smooth, undulating and choppy, this surface-medium appears endless—oceanic literally so during a downpour—a periodic, torrential "pouring" constitutes one of the critical affects of this (en)Gulf(ing) city. Its plane is also crude and wild, marked by fissures, vacated space and bits of untouched prairie, aptly describes by what Robert Smithson found in New Jersey: "Pessaic seems full of "holes" compared to New York City, which seems tightly packed and solid, and those holes… are the monumental vacancies that define, without trying, the memory-traces of an abandoned set of futures."[9] Patently unloved yet naturalistic, this *holey plane* seems more a wilderness than the datum of a man made city. Dotted by trees and criss-crossed by wo/men/vehicles/roads, it is a surface dominated by a peculiar sense of ongoing struggle: the struggle of economics against nature. Both the trees and machines of this plane emerge as the (trail or) *dross* of that struggle. In New York and Paris such a precarious, unstable status of the city is unthinkable. There nature has been defeated, erased or domesticated to a degree that ensures it will never return. In Houston however, schizophrenia rules: By proximity, or *synomorphy* (similarity of form), the *rider of the plane* drifts along, (in contradistinction to the pedestrian, the ruling subject of the old city) as morphing extensions of the machines, forming with technology a shifting and uneasy coalition. Yet, the same drifters coalesce with the biota and trees, particularly when (even for the briefest of moments) they walk the plane. The trajectories along which riders move follows at least two speeds, both of which are ballistic in nature: Along the first, bullet cars with their cooled interiors push through the thick, humid phlegm; Along the second even more viscous one, that of fear—*urban fear* (driving one to the false safety of closets, behind the barricades in one's enclaves)—another kind of bullet propels the action, but is now aimed back at the rider. It is no wonder that the commanding machine of this

plane is the *Chevy Suburban*, named appropriately, for all but achieving the dimensions of a suburban house, and by providing a protective, mobile, exoskeletal enclave (almost safe) along that tortuous trajectory of fear.

Fields

The commingling of machines and nature, be they houses, cars, or skyscrapers, set on a prairie, on this crudely gardened version thereof, results in a Houston that is neither fully city nor tree (*pace* Christopher Alexander). Yet all the things that constitute the specific territory are more or less *organically* related, such that we can assume that it is, if not strictly or classically a city, then certainly an *ecology*—or more theatrically, a flat planet—suggesting that it is the powerful web of *organic relations* that make Houston a palpable, cohesive reality.[10] Here *variously gendered* machines rather than pedestrians are the predominating species, and clean and cool air (rather than the *atmosphere* of Paris or the *energy* of New York) is the determinant commodity. The plane, with its *zoohemic canopy* of trees, forms a carpet-like *sub-ecology*[11] dominated by dappled light, the collective purring of a panoply of machines, the invincible stings of mosquitoes. The planetary impression becomes even more compelling as the reader ascends: suspended overhead in a skyscraper two distinct *strata* or *fields* are apprehensible, one sandwiched atop the other: *the zoohemic field below, the airspace—the aerial field—above.*

This huge bag of air is articulated by airplanes, helicopters and the grandiose machinations of weather, which roll into the upper strata either quietly or with terrifying fanfare. Shaped like wacked-out species of an exotic aquarium: huge partially disintegrated flounders, schools of drunken piranhas, bloated whales, slow, fast, frazzled, mostly opaque, and surrounded by whisps of indecisive greyish-brown mists, clouds often operate in opposite directions. Distemper: entire seasons pass, in minutes, raising or dropping the temperature, making the surprised and totally innocent drifters under the canopy change their clothes as if models working the runway. Or thunder poised to deliver. Flashes that like a giant Pert chart draw the most random connections, cloud to cloud, cloud to building, cloud to ground, independent along the horizon, hideous verticals etching cracks in the black heavens destined for human disaster. Or rain, totally ignoring gravity by operating in any conceivable direction, up, down, sideways, towards you, and away from you sucking you into its destiny. *Nature rampant.* Unlike the lower strata, this huge stadium seems underdeveloped—begging for more towers, more air traffic, more lights, introduced, if for nothing else, to counteract the forces of nature, to challenge its total dominance. As it stands now, nature shares equally the ground with artifice, while the bag of air above rules—if it wasn't for pollution.

Brown fumes. Fiery sunsets. Pollution fills the days when the weather rests. The yellow, totally still girdle of haze binds together the sky and the ground. Creating a third ecology, the vapor drops invisibly through the canopy of trees to slip into the drifter's nostrils, lungs and eyes. Sinus capital of the world. Yet it is only above the canopy with the benefit of foreshortening that pollution builds its body, and makes its demanding

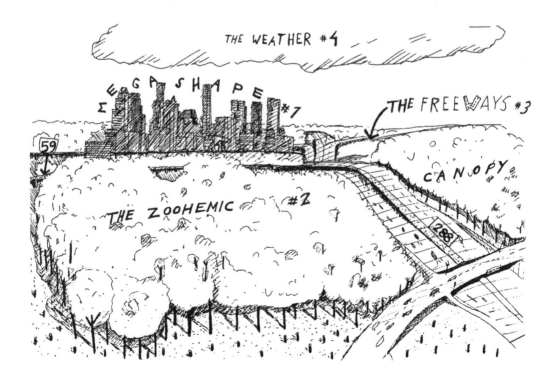

presence visible. Like some immense unwanted backlash the pollution-as-surplus reminds us of the price of our total mobility.

Two ecologies, two modalities of circulation and appearance (speeds). The two strata touch, as do the two speeds, when the freeway hews its way through the green carpet to merge with the airspace. In these gashes the two worlds are sutured together, or more precisely, the motorway adjoins the airspace by delaminating from the plane. Submerged in the lowest strata of a major freeway intersection, literally driving (at warp-speed) on the underside of the ground-ecology of the city, the rider is brought to a realization. In fact, all brushes with the outer margins of the various ecologies of the city, whether here at the base of the hierarchy or at its very top, hovering in an air vehicle while rapidly traversing both ecologies, tend to throw the whole in focus. Such realizations, frog-eye or soaring eagle perspectives, are *shapeful* and at least partially extra-spatial. They bring out of the scattered suggestions of wholes or *megashapes* that the rider senses while operating on freeways, or arriving at large openings in the ground plane such as an airfield, a sensation of traveling along the tangent of the very definition of the ecological envelope. While this may appear more evident in an airplane, it is in fact more sensational when you dip underneath the ground ecology (as in the great freeway cloverleaf), possibly because the vehicle operates along a curve whose origin is somewhere above the driver swinging him out of, yet against and into, the crust of the earth that serves as the carpet's ground.

Sprawl

Flying in over Houston, a late winter afternoon, with the Western light rushing in parallel to the ground, creating endless shadows, (and the Gulf vs. Canada weather-war cooperating by staying away,) *the holey plane* in all its tattered, uncouth ungainliness emerges gloriously. Simultaneously, the very material that defines the holes come into focus. Known as *Sprawl*, units, swatches, zones, and domains come to the fore, and since the Zoohemic Canopy is on its lowest photosynthetic self, the observer can read through the trees for the hundreds of thousand houses themselves. The meandering streets, the cul de sacs, the arteries and the sinuous freeways. Sprawl is the very motor of this entire plane. Sprawl's erratic, leap-frogging across the protean field, is the energy behind.[12] Combine weak controls, a huge domestic economy, and the will to live accordingly and you have Sprawl: the show—*Go West Young Man* (and all itinerant family members and paraphernalia.)

****

One of the most dominating megashapes in the suburban Metropolis is both to close to home and hard to see: the vast agglomerations of almost identical single family houses[13] on various lot sizes and shapes. In fact, at first we may hesitate to refer to them as shapes,

since it is only the interior reading that is distinct and clear while at the perimeter, at the locus of the figure, total formlessness prevails. Furthermore, the tentative shapeliness is only readable from an eagle's perspective. In the final analysis, *Sprawl*, just like the Zoohemic Canopy, is a *megashape* because of the prevalence, and predictability of the internal equation: many houses and lots, held loosely together with curving streets often ending in cul-de-sacs and with one outlet to an artery.

The common view of Sprawl is that it is chaotic, disorderly, ugly and confusing—an additional example of the bias in favor of totalizing views of the environment. This doesn't negate the potential of increasing shapeliness, or better, finding more effective uses or functions for the ungainly in-between, at the perimeter of each unit of Sprawl.

The internal nature of the Sprawl unit is both rudimentary and crude, and in much need of evolution. The orientation of the house is totally dependent on the platting with no regard for the compass, the landscape and prevailing ecology. Inefficient, and wasteful, Sprawl's true power and success lies in its economic and social effectiveness. Consequently it will take a lot of Jeffersonian (agararian) persuasion to transform this Hamiltonian (mercantilist) success story. Put differently, Sprawl is much like the Jeffersonian Grid, 'Hamilton doing Jefferson,' and the next evolutionary stage may be to tamper with this bias.

Oceanic Grammar

In the air or on the road, the clashes between the *Zoohemic* and the *Aerial* may be putting the drifter in touch with what Baudrillard calls the "astral."[14] This may also be particularly European (Eastern too?) but the sensation one has, when for the first time a tumble weed crosses the highway somewhere on former route 66 with no other car in sight, makes one's ancestral home burst, releasing the rider within or from its (oppressive) security into the open—never to return. "How can anyone be European?."[15] The sensations referred to here cluster around the notion of speed,

THE OCEANIC

or better, *the notion of motion*. In Houston, it is not an exaggeration to suggest that the prosthetic is neither the car nor the air vehicle *but the drifter's legs*. Thus coming from a pedestrian past bursting onto the scene of the vehicular (and its associated velocities) clearly demarcates a take-off that is *beside reality* as one once knew it; it lurches one not just into a more rapid disappearance of that which is seen in the rear-view mirror but also, *into the future* (Virilio). Not withstanding Baudrillard's point that "driving produces a kind of invisibility"[16] the shape of the setting for those "pure objects" become more visible. This is of course more truly the case when the trip is repeated, over and over again—a sensation Baudrillard clearly experienced. The shape of the city's ecologies appear at its margins but maybe more importantly during the *repeated* trips along those same margins. Yet this exterior shapefulness is more conceptual than actual, held in place by mental constructions made up of sporadically gathered shape-fragments rather than actual physical continuities. However, these external visions of shape are propped up, but now from the *inside* by additional visions of shape, both more contiguous and pervasive. To drive inside the zoohemic ecology—which includes, trees, incessantly drawn at the periphery of one's vision—builds an additional understanding of shape that may not be exactly synomorphic with the external shape of the ecology. However, counting the particles of a field, rather than establishing the parameters of the field itself, touches on another grammar of shape— *a grammar that has been called oceanic*. However fractal and seismic the oceanic experience may be, its is also smooth and voluptuous. The almost continuous underside of the leafy canopy supported by the countless tree trunks form an inverted mountain-chain of green that begins to build—once again through repetition—*a conception of an inside*. This inside is in no way trivial, particularly since it substitutes structurally for the actual loss of European city form. As city form, the Houstonian interiority is very different from, say, the Parisian. Where the latter is constituted by the street, the verticality established by the perimeter block, and propelled by a pedestrian subjectivity, the low-slung green canopy establishes a pervasive almost-domestic intimacy that in the European city can only be had inside the residential block—in the warmth of a house. Thus Houston is at any one location both a giant *room* as well as an ocean of endless surfaces. This inner

field-and-room, produced through a trajectorial subjectivity, is held in place by two planes: the ground and the canopy of trees. Both planes undulating, the *field-room* is not a space in the European (Euclidean) sense but a constantly warping and pulsating fluidity. The pedestrian, painstakingly, circumscribes the blocks of the old city, harbors no doubt about what moves and what is fixed. In Houston however, the speeding car projects itself into a space that is never yet formed, forever evolving and emerging ahead, while disappearing behind. This creates a liquidity in which the dance and the dancer are fused together in a swirling, self-engendering motion promoted by the darting of the driver's eyes, touching (because so intimate, so familiar): street, canopy, house, adjacent car, red light, side street, radio station: Tejano 106.5, car upon car, instruments, tree trunks, joggers, barking dog, drifting leaves, large welt and dip, patch of sunlight. This is a navigational space, forever emerging, never exactly the same, liquid rather than solid, approximate rather than precise, visual but also visceral in that it is felt by the entire body—not just through the eyes and soles of the feet. The body in this liquid space is suspended, held and urged-on by the trajectory.

The Zoohemic and the Aerial fields, invested by various velocities ranging from Suburbans to helicopters, pop out and disappear. At rare occasions nature itself draws the two strata clearly and distinctly, and for a brief moment their innate fluidity is arrested. 7 AM DECEMBER 29: a weather front has drawn a blanket of clouds across the metropolis, so low that the tops of skyscrapers brush it. Not yet completed, the blanket gapes to the East, and the sun, like a child's flashlight illuminates (not his momentary tent but) the airbag between the top of the zoohemic and the underside of the cloud-cover. The light from the sun paints all the Eastern facades of the skyscrapers—giant pilotis-candles supporting the sky. The huge window to my East burns bright red, while the sun rises up and out to create an eventual Arctic-scape of the cloud-cover's upper surface. The sun has literally drawn a new section of the city.

The similarity in form between the two assemblies (tree trunk/canopy and skyscraper/cloud-cover) posits the first determining structure or shapefulness of the two ecologies. First like stacked tables, one sits on top of the other, then at closer scrutiny, the upper table pokes its skyscraper trunks down through the

THE OCEAN OF ENDLESS SURFACES

zoohemic canopy to the ground, thus originating in the lower ecology—literally growing out of it. The clear definition of the two fields, and the air space in particular with its momentary ceiling forces the intimacy first established under the trees now to include the entire metropolis. Air and biota are merged to form a double-space, in which elements (tall buildings and certain vehicles) and fluids (air, sound and smell) circulate freely.

Back on the ground, driving across the zoohemic field the conceptual mingling of ecologies provokes additional cross-readings but now horizontal: the freeway underpass, laminated away from the ground (that barren forest of concrete columns-and-canopy) takes on new value as the petrified token of the dominating ecologies of the metropolis—the concrete columns as so many artificial limbs mending the rift in the green hewn by the freeway itself.[17]

Entortung

J. B. Jackson's Westward-moving House haunts Houston.[18] While driving East-West along a street of modest houses two remarkable rhythms occur . The street begins to roll like an ocean. Long shallow swells threaten to bounce riders from their seats while the houses, of which many are partially overgrown with vines, tilt ever so slightly, (further) revealing the tropic instability of the ground. The combination of the rolling street and the tilting houses is deeply unsettling. Everything moves (as in a sped-up geological flow). Every element is detachable—ready to go. The Westward-moving House could have originated in some Heideggerian clearing in the Schwartzwald, but Jackson choose to begin the story on America's East Coast. At the beginning of its trajectory the house still had a basement. As it migrated further West, and it often did so literally because the settlers brought their houses with them, the more it was modified to respond to the next move. Among the first modifications was leaving the cellar behind, replaced by a set of rocks placed simply on the ground to serve as point supports. The final transformation of the frontier *Urhaus* is the contemporary mobile home, still the cheapest and fastest way to "own a home," since it can be delivered like a car the following day on the basis of a loan amortized over a ten year period. The tendency to make things lighter and more mobile

goes hand in hand with what Karl Popper called the *ephemeralization of technology*, the suggestion that all technology will evolve from clocks to clouds. The titling houses encountered at the outset (they sit on the same type of supports as the Westward Moving House now made of mass produced concrete blocks) are both an expression of the emphemeralization and an *uprooting* of the house, here literally severed from the ground thereby shifting its status from building to furniture—the house can now be part of the next move. The rolling street (a reminder of the swamp out of which Houston arose) gives the experience of driving in this flat city a quality of being held hostage on a subdued roller coaster. The rolling is not at all confined to the poorest parts of the city but characterizes the entire secondary street grid—and every house has had or will have "a bad foundation day." Unsettling as it may seem, the rolling rhythm of the road and the racking of the houses (real or imagined) produce on the one hand, a strange echo of what in New York would constitute a city beat, though here it is not Be Bop but Blues, Zydeco and Cumbia; and on the other hand, this rolling of the ground, suggests that not only are the elements upon it unstable (and rhythmic) but the very field itself is the ultimate demonstration of *Metropolitan Entortung* (uprootedness,) that Georg Simmel began to map out in his famous essay "The Metropolis and Mental Life" and Massimo Cacciari used as one of the bases for his *Architecture and Nihilism: On the Philosophy of Modern Architecture*.[19]

In Houston, the entire foundation of the ground-level ecology is soft, rhythmic and unstable, held together by the roots of the canopy of trees, creating the absurd impression of a city suspended from the treetops from which its cars, riders and roads gently swing. At any rate, the ground is a detached ground, the house, an infinitely migrating detached house that follows in a slow attenuated progression the same Brownian trajectories as do its associated deputy paraphernalia—the car and the dweller—emblems of a restless urban matrix continually on the move.

Stim and Dross

Space is granted little physical presence on the plane of this planet. Dominated by motion, time and event, all components of this complex hide an essential vulnerability—trees die, cars and markets

crash, and the air slowly kills. In fact, in Houston, air functions much like our skin, an immense enveloping organ, to be constantly attended to, chilled, channeled and cleaned. Pools of cooled air dot the plane, much like oases in deserts. Precariously pinned in place by machines and human events these become points of stimulation—*stims*—on this otherwise rough but uninflected hide, populated only by the *dross*—the ignored, undervalued, unfortunate economic residues of the metropolitan machine. Space as value, as locus of events, as genius loci, is then reduced to interior space—a return to the cave. In these enclaves or Stims, time is kept at bay, suspension is the rule, levitation the desire—be it the office, the house, the restaurant, the museum or the ever-marauding *Suburban*. Outside, the minimization of time is the dominant force that both draws lines on this erratically littered surface and gathers its pools of energy. Because once the time lines are seen to coincide and overlap, they begin to curl and twist. Our plot thickens at the Galleria—Houston's giant shopping spree, where the pistons and cranks of the metropolis have compressed more buying-power into one single horizontal concatenation than in the entire region—and at the oil company office-park euphemistically known as Downtown, where again the metropolitan muscle is flexed, but now vertically to sculpt the ultimate urban physique. The entire Downtown as megashape is the token for all of America's Downtowns. In a less obvious manner, time dominates still other forms of thickening in the ecology. Many of these bulges are less physical than virtual, noted in remarks by the rider: "...there, another Exxon station, another Target."—subtle, ever-multiplying as market bytes whose recurrences follow the logic both of the cash flow and the catch basin. Outside, these Stims, at once retinal and rhythmic, like mild electroshocks on the plane, now join to become the extended skin of the rider.

The new space emerging from the impulses of this huge envelope is transient, fleeting, temporary and biomorphic rather than concrete, manifested, or striated. Barely visible to the classical eye these forms appear as expanding ripples in one's consciousness, swellings, bumps and grinds coursing through the nervous system. Erratic, unpredictable, the time line for the spatial event jumps, twitches, hums and wiggles like an erratic hose in a gardener's grip. *Yet the flow encourages, the speed comforts, the ride heals.* The chorus of the multitude of familiar Stims forms a signifying beat, tapping gently on the rider's visual domain—*the optic pouch*—which replaces the cone of vision of a more mechanistic time. This pouch is always changing its size sometimes confined, such as when one throttles through a tunnel of trees, at other times expanded to amorphousness as it fills out an abandoned lot, a leftover plot of prairie, or when, in a flash, the pouch explodes like a parachute to include a stretch of sky.

Yet urban threats prevail in this huge ecological envelope. Largely hiding out in the spaces between, the threats are kept away from the Stims. (They must not be implicated or soiled by any harsh realities.) Consequently, clandestine at first, yet ultimately as palpable as the humidity, the threats rush to the surface: environmental ones—made apparent by the metropolis as a large unified ecology, an envelope with its own air, a sloppy organ whose precarious health is clearly in question. Here the fear of miasma is real—Houston is one of the most polluted cities in the nation; and that of *urban fear*—the insidious force that atomizes the city like a scatter bomb into a myriad cells each surrounded and enclosed by various forms of callused protective tissue (physical prowess, power in numbers, rent-a-cops, walls, gates, distance, electronics, guard dogs, lot size, borders, rail-road or freeway barriers)—an entire physics of enclavism. We are talking warfare here. This strife propels and animates the ecology, much more than Ecology itself, maybe as much as the market force. Like a myriad invisible nano-machines clandestinely at work undermining metropolitan sanity, fear has de laminated the Stim from the plane—*Entortung* efficiently at work. In gaggles, Stims agglutinate, skip, and leap-frog once the barometer of fear passes the critical mark of 103 degrees. Yet among the middle class, the fear remains unspoken, silenced, merely illustrated in passing by the antiseptic crime statistics of the news media. In the street it speaks loud and clear. In fear's wake, in addition to *the great suburban escape*, come deed restrictions, restricted numbers of sewer hook-ups, zoning, alarms, and armaments onehundredthousandandfourhundred registered guns. Guns and gas—the propellants of the Metropolis on the run. To what end all this paraphernalia when according to recent polls Houston ranks as the fourth most livable city in the United States? The answer surely leads us to the Stims themselves, to their internal strength and alas, to their vulnerability.

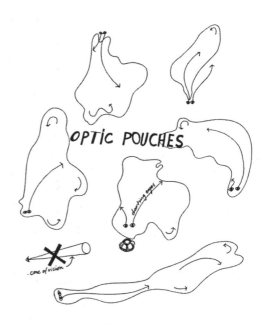

OPTIC POUCHES

cone of vision

Stimulators

A colleague invites us to a reception given by an art patron. We traverse the plane and navigate the dross: A mental map, an address, a curving road, large lots and gigantic houses, the *de rigeur* smiling rent-a-cop. Our destination is a marvel of a house, a fantasy sustained by a spectacular architectural scenography, various addenda (arresting decoration, whimsical furniture, subdued music, et cetera) and the glamour of the party itself. Truly stimulating. The collusion is in fact a perfect one, between architects (the curved interior street), decorators (the towels arranged on the floor in the bathroom), caterers (the glutinous loot of shrimp), the art patron (her son's taxidermic hunting trophies) and her own overflowing enthusiasm. Suspended, the audience hovers in the fantasy. The House itself is a miniaturized Siena, (turning abruptly I search for a glimpse of the Palio,) though not Siena at all, a marvelous polyphonic concoction that threatens all analogy in favor of the authenticity of the bristling Stim itself. Here critique and skepticism must fade in favor of the materiality of this specific event. It is an audacious one, surely costly, and marvelously intoxicating. Yet how does it hold up, or rather how is it held in place? Where are the invisible wires, the conceits of this theater of events? How and where does the dross come into play? After all, this fragment of Siena is held in place not by a city, by streets, piazzas, walls, or a city-state and its culture. Dislocated, the Stim is suspended in the ocean of the city, but also suspended in time and out of context (Tuscany is far away.)[20] When toggled on, the Stim's shimmering lights attract its participants like moths sucked out of the darkness of the city. However, the smiling guard suggests that the suspense is not only momentary but precarious. And when the lights are turned low, the guests and caterers departed, the Stim is turned off and the house and its occupants are again mere dross on the littered city floor. Indeed, light and darkness are inextricably bound together. Like a cyberspace, the Stim is anchored in place by much technology and machines of every type, mechanical, electronic and biological.[21] The *imbroglio* is vast, ranging from the Mexican laborers that tend the gardens to the architects' studies at the academy in Rome—it gathers, in a single sweep, lawnmowers and airplanes, but also sewage pipes, floral designers, pool installers, electrical power grids, telephone calls, asphalt, automobiles, the birds drawn to birdfeeder hubs, deathly silent air conditioners, mortgage banks, hunting rifles, and the little pink shrimps from the Gulf of Mexico. Many of these components and interlocking systems have in common architectural practice been taken for granted and ignored, while others have been dealt with as a kit of parts, each component neatly defined and rendered independent. This array forms a complex *body* that must, in the wet of the postwar city, be seen for what it is, a partially self-steering, partially spontaneous, yet cybernetic agglutination of forces, pulsations, events, rhythms and machines. The neglect of any of its interlocked systems may, despite a multitude of checks, locks, gates and balances, threaten its existence. The *Age of Integration* has come to call.

stimdross

The metropolis, like the surface of a lake during a rainstorm pocked by thousands of concentric ripples, is bombarded by a million Stims that flicker on and off during the city's rhythmic cycles. These Stims steam and stir, oscillate and goad, yet each specific *stimme* (voice) reverberates throughout the metropolis in a most selective manner: the "art party" visited above draws a very narrow audience just as the Zydeco Dance halls in East Houston. Both are essential and vital elements of the full-fledged Metropolis. The *Stimmung* (ambience) projected by each Stim is fully understood and fully had by insiders only. Although as a *stimulus* the Zydeco Dance occasionally draws a group of (slumming?) upper-middle class guests (and they are graciously tolerated) they remain aliens, however touched and moved they may be by the dance and its inert *stimulantia*. And there is *Hugo's Garage*, a stim that lasts for an hour or two on Friday afternoons when his clients come to pay their respect. He is the much beloved and respected mechanic (he works on imports too) whose greatly diverse clientele come to stim: beer and cars, and car-as-transport is parked and briefly elevated to car-as-art setting-aside all class and money distinctions between the aficionados. Simultaneously, a block away the trunk-hoods on a dozen of cars go up (and the tiny lights turn on) to wire the iron-clad Hispanic Parking Lot Stim. Men gather around, the echo of a Cumbia projected from several car radios envelops the momentary brotherhood like

HOUSTON'S 'SLOPPY ORGAN'

HUMAN COMFORT ZONE

open treasure chests the stationary cars, now project back in time and place (to common culture and history)—*Boulevard de Suenos*. A telling balance to the *carro's* otherwise futuristic prowess. A tiny sampler from the menu of "a million Stims."

Ranging from the Family Dinner to the Card Game all Stims are held precariously in place, in intensity, and in motion by the metropolitan physics of "walls, particles and fields." Metropolitan Life is concentrated in all these Stims, and we live as if our life depended on them.[22] The common tendency to focus all attention on the Stim itself ignores that it is a *living organism*, machines, a behavior setting, in short, *a many-fold shale of wonderful complexity*. As such it is dependent on its talons and its backwoods—first, the ocean of the metropolis—then the world. The inadequacy of the binary opposition of Stim and dross is becoming evident (the legacy of our stale language and its profound grammatical limitations). Only in the hybrid field of *stimdross* may we begin to rethink and then to recover from this *holey plane* some of the many potential futures.

****

Driving along Highway 59, one of the central freeways in Houston, going West (or South), the roadway suddenly drops below grade, and the neighboring streets bridge over. While drivers race down a concrete canyon, crossed over by overpasses counting some four or five blocks. This is the result of neighborhood action. A group of well-to-do citizens convinced the city to sink the freeway to lower the noise (and maybe put an open trench between them and their less affluent neighbors).

Driving the freeway you may see one of them. A lone observer. Just as you begin the decent into the canyon the observer looks right at you, then down at you, until he disappears above you. Invariably they are alone, often leaning on the balustrade, not moving. Or they walk back and forth, agitated, gesturing, and since their mouths seem to open and close, their heads are turning, fast, back and forth, up and down, they may be screaming, or haranguing you. You cannot hear. They are the *overpass people*. Where they come from, who they are, no one seems to know. At first, you may think that they are people from the neighborhood, looking down at you with a certain smug satisfaction.

But in this town the well-to-do are not idle. So they come from somewhere else. Who is to know? They are clearly too few for a sample, or a sociologist. The range from the quiet kibitzer to the enraged, suggest that they are here for the action—for the movement—clearly not for the attention. Some may be students of motion, others radicals protesting our daily commute, or aficionados of the noise and smell of motor cars, or transcendentalists in search of a continuous external and loud mantra—an artificial river.

For us, the drivers of the superhighway, they are the others. Those who have time to spare. Those who don't have to (bikes are often held or parked next to the observer). Those who don't. Those who refuse. Not the leisure class, not the vagrants, maybe the mad, but mostly those who fall in between, those who refuse to be counted.

Notes

1. The city we face at the dusk of the century is infinitely more complex than the night suggests. We must close the book on the City and open the manifold of the Metropolis. Behind this melodramatic pronouncement lies the hypothesis that our customary ways of describing, managing, and designing are now outmoded. Though the world is mutating at a dizzying speed we remain mesmerized by the *passeiste* dream of the City. Contemporary metropolitans must confront a series of givens that radically change the equation of the old city. Perhaps nowhere with more intensity than in Houston, is the full set of these revolutions being cinematically played out: *Demographic*: the emerging metropolis is giving way to a truly multiethnic continuum. *Economic*: global integration threatens not only to extend but to continuously redraw the boundaries of the city's hinterland. *Domestic*: both parents have absented themselves from the household semi-permanently to enter the marketplace, both despite and because of chronic and massive unemployment. While in the shadows hover AIDS, homelessness, substance abuse and epidemic violence. *Resources*: emphasis has shifted from raw and manufactured materials to "immaterials" such as knowledge, services, management. *Ecology*: a science, a politic, and an ethics that is simply no longer a fad . (Drawn from a lecture by Stephen L. Klineberg, "Making Sense of Our Times: Five Revolutionary Trends")

2. The entire section of the relationship between physics and the metropolis is drawn from Martin Krieger's *Doing Physics: How Physicists Take Hold of the World*, Indiana University Press, Bloomington and Indianapolis: 1992, p.25.

3. Lars Lerup, "At The End of the Architectural Promenade", in *Architecture and Body*, eds. Scott Marble et al., Rizzoli, New York: 1988, see essay four.

4. Interview with Robert Smithson for the Archives of American Art/Smithsonian Institute, Paul Cummings in *The Writings of Robert Smithson*, New York University Press, New York: 1979, p.154.

5. Kevin Lynch's work in *The Urban Image* (1960) on cognitive mapping, in which he distinguishes "districts, nodes, landmarks, edges and paths" prefigures notions such as the megashape. The radical difference is that he concentrated on mapping techniques, while megashape probably found its inspiration in cinematography. Someone may find it fruitful to marry the two.

6. …at night the disembodied city reveals itself. Especially during the holidays when the wattage is radically increased as each building is lit like a Christmas tree. This custom may be 'learning from Las Vegas', whose casino operators are known to create "highs" with a mixture of light and oxygen, presumably the Houston version is to induce shopping-euphoria.

From the 28th floor, the towers of Downtown glow in their erect priapic elegance, while 120 degrees due West the spread out buildings of the Galleria, accented with horizontal bars of light running along the eaves, highlight their low-slung horizontally. As two ends of a spectrum displaced by *a certain distance*, the separation (at birth) between the vertical and the horizontal is eerily graphic. The decision to literally remove the commercial ground-floor business from downtown and to relocate it on the grounds of the Galleria, is the most dramatic display of the demise of the City and the raise of the Metropolis. The instigators, Gerald Hines and his real estate movers, did in one single Monopoly move, what Alexander may have achieved by chopping off the Gordian knot. Those nostalgic for the City that could have been, are still smarting. For the suburbanite the logic was clear: by separating the oil business from shopping, the male would get his world and the female hers. In the process we would avoid, congestion, traffic snarls, parking problems and street life, all the components that make up the 'wicked' 20th-century Downtown.

Nostalgic attempts to return downtown to Downtown are not only futile but ill-advised since they obscure the fact that Houston is not a city, but a multi-centered metropolitan domain in which each center has to fend for itself. In other words, when Houston Industries light up downtown in a huge multi-million dollars fire work, they are much closer to a more productive strategy: as the potential contender as the energy capital of the world, Houston's downtown needs to be in a perpetual light-high, only then will it be able to fictionalize its true characteristics.

In the mean-time the third-world surface of downtown, occupied by service workers, derelicts, and other marginals, is carefully avoided by the vertical axis of the members of the first world, who slip into their elevators, out through their under-ground tunnels to the parking lot, via the freeway to their home-sweet-home only a gallon of gas away. This part of Downtown's 'horizontality' was left behind to linger in the shadows of the remaining towers.

7. It is ironic at the end of a century characterized by the most dizzying urban transformations in human history that academic readings (apart from writers like Banham and Koolhaas) and projects of the city (particularly in postwar cities like Houston) remain haunted by the irrelevant ghost of the historically outdated European center city. A distinctly European view of our cities have made them embattled, ridiculed and flat—too often conceived as mere Monopoly games. The hegemony of the pedestrian, the plaza, the street and the perimeter block must be challenged not because the "values" they embody are no longer valid, but rather because they are suffused with a set of fundamental misconceptions about the nature of contemporary civilization and its *outside*, leading to a

false understanding of the whole. More pointedly, even the most sophisticated readings (and the occasional building) of the American city and its postwar expansions (whether haunted and paranoid [as in Baudrillard's *America*] or openly nostalgic for the *eternal return* of the bourgeois pedestrian [Krier, Duany and Plater-Zyberk, Calthorpe, Solomon] are predicated upon a more or less hidden positivity, that,if fulfilled, would bring us Community—or better bring us back to the American version of the European City. Yet the City is forever surpassed by the Metropolis and all its givens (a steadily globalizing economy, demographic changes, AIDS, unemployment, violence and so on) all which will make any return to the past both impossible and undesirable. The obsession in valorizing the pedestrian over the car, hides and ignores the fact that there is a driver (and passengers) in the car—a roving subjectivity whose *body phantom* apprehends the world in a vastly different manner. A manner, that in turn will, and must, have consequences for the way the metropolis is designed. More importantly, however, to hinge all judgments about the city on the forlorn pedestrian and all his requirements, avoids tackling the fact that the Metropolis is driven-in and driven-by not only the pedestrian and the driver but a myriad of subjectivities ranging from the old (and possibly infirm) to the young (and equally vulnerable), men and women, African-American and White, as well as less human "objectivities" such as the economy, public opinion, and the market place.

8. The stabilities of the old City, its buildings, monuments, and city fabric, are rapidly loosing their firmness (if not their delight). Buildings, in cities like Tokyo and Houston, are likely to disappear before their mortgage runs out and long before the companies that occupy them. New street systems are broken, cul-de-sac-ed, and largely incoherent, leading somewhere but never everywhere. Monuments, often

built for enormous sums of money, are so completely idiosyncratic, and out of date, because they serve so few, that the publication in various media is more consequential than the monument itself. In the Metropolis, absurdly, shockingly, a series of radical reversals of stability has taken place.

Aspects and characteristics, that in the City were the mere back-drop of everyday life, have been rudely foregrounded as new stabilities. Stabilities that are not known or characterized by their firmness but rather by their dynamic, unpredictable instability. I am thinking about the pollution, weather, vegetation, and water. None of these are under the demanding auspices of the Metropolis truly natural, but complex compounds or admixtures of nature and artifice. Yet in their persistent return or foregrounding, we know that they will be all here when we leave. Despite often valiant attempts to reverse its presence, pollution is here to stay. It will come and go. But if one type is held back, pollution as a fixture of metropolitan life will return, be it in the air, water, food or our bodies. Pollution, slows imperceptibly between nature and artifice. And on the side of artifice flows other stable instabilities, such as electricity, and gas and their transformation into lights and vehicles. The 'astral specs' of the artificially lit Metropolis brings at night the entire conurbation under the same spell. It is as if nocturnally the metropolis counts itself—one light for every event. Traffic flows, peaking twice a day, and amounting to thirty man-years per day in Houston, are as predictable the profile of downtown. Yet this flow is also highly unstable. This goes also for weather, vegetation, and the water—which is particularly true in Houston where the water table often shows its sudden destructive power on the ground floor of the city—the sudden liberation of all bathtub rubber ducks. Sooner or later these instabilities will bring all of us into their momentary orbits.

The nature of all these 'new' stabilities are their catastrophic instability, their dynamic flux, that like the Metropolis itself immerse everyday life in their only semi-predictable power games—semi-natural or semi-artificial. When the rain storm, the morning commute, the steady TV signal, and the open telephone line—and of lately, bandwidth—have become our only stability, the City as we have known it has truly disappeared. Firmitas has become stochastic and conjectural.

9. op.cit. Smithson. p.55.

10. The city must be seen as an organism, but as such a deeply perplexing one because it is simultaneously a machine, or rather a series of disconnected (nano-) machines running their own determined and reckless courses—the combined result of which we will never fully fathom. Drifting, the procedure of preference for this reading, is umbilically connected to the Metropolis, via Baudelaire and the ultimate *flaneur* Walter Benjamin (although he would agree that in Houston the car rather than pedestrian locomotion is the a drifter's vehicle-par-excellence.) Benjamin began his drifting across the metropolis on the back-porch overlooking the inner court of his parents' apartment in Berlin. Here he has his first encounters with the Other. And learns that the bright lights of the city, are not only lights but tokens of the many pistons that drive its motors—the multitude of languages at work—whether under his bedroom door (when his emancipated Jewish parents entertain friends on Saturday night) or the mesmerizing red light signaling the district of prostitution. Despite the semantic luminosity of the many city lights there is no sense that Benjamin finds anything but tensions, ruptures and catastrophic leaps. The more he seems to grasp of the metropolis the faster he sees it slip away, until he finally escapes, by his own hand, in distant Port Bou.. This text is ostensibly being a drift along Houston's many physical trajectories—like

gossip or commentary the many oddities and kinks on the hide of this otherwise "lite city" (Koolhaas) leads to descriptions that warp and bend, while hopefully making the physical reverberate with all the other not-so-physical frameworks and constructions that shape the metropolis, ranging from the House to the Office to the circulation of Money. Drifting-as-text is more about departures than arrivals, more about movement and change than fixedness, but also about a desire to cover more with less, of leaving lacunae to be filled later—with the help of others.

11. The *subecology* applies to large domains in Houston, but a narrower band can be defined that roughly surrounds the old Downtown and reaches out to the first beltway—an example of the middle landscape.

12. "The holes —the empty lots—," writes Michael Benedikt, dotted about the landscape have to do with the use of land as speculative investment vehicle[s] by banks, real estate consortia [REITS], and even individuals, with deep enough pockets to wait for more favorable… market conditions." quoted in "Beautiful Cities, Ugly Cities: Urban Form as Convention", by Michael Storper, *Value: Center 10/ Architecture and Design in America*, University of Texas, Austin, 1998: p.122.

13. The American Dream always includes the suburban house more or less directly. The distance and its itinerant subjects, as they march out of the first clearing in the aboriginal forest, are inscribed everywhere in the suburban house, from the front lawn to the size of the master bedroom and the three-car garage. Architecture has always had a troubled relationship to Suburbia. Maybe because architecture is profoundly and fundamentally a product of city culture, which at first posed no serious problems since there was plenty of work and plenty of city to build. However, with the continued loosening of what the historian Grady Clay calls "the old grip of centrality," the centrifugal force of dispersion has turned the city into a Metropolis possibly dominated by the suburban subjectivity. Which in turn, brings us to a very insinuating and troubling question: is architecture possible in an empire of Suburbs?

14. Beaudrillard, Jean. *America*, Transl. Chris Turner, Verso, New York: 1988, p.27.

15. ibid. p.105.

16. ibid. p.7.

17. The two dominating ecologies harbor a multitude of sub-ecologies or *biotopes* (limited ecological regions or niches in which the environment promotes and supports certain forms of life.) These *topoi* are the often the growing grounds for the Stim, whose *biotic potential* (the likelihood of survival of a specific organism in a specific environment especially in an unfavorable one) is as I hope to show highly dependent on both Stim and surrounding Dross.

18. J. B. Jackson, "The Westward-moving House," in *Landscapes: Selected Writing of J.B. Jackson*, ed. Erwin H. Zube, The University of Massachusetts Press: 1970, p.10.

19. "In the Entortung it is the destiny of the West itself that runs from the rooting of the *Nomos* in the *justissima tellus*, through the discovery and occupation of the new spaces of the Americas ("free" spaces, that is, considered totally available for conquest, totally profanable: devoid of places), up to the universalism of the world market… "(a total mobilization of an intensive kind, a universal displacement.)" Transl. Stephen Sartarelli, Yale University Press, New Haven: 1993, p. 169.

20. The issue of appropriateness is evident here. However, the complexity and multitude of cultures and concerns in the manifold of the Metropolis force us to seriously question contextualism, or to elevate this issue to environmental *contextuality* leaving the issue of style to the beholder.

21. The Stim's apparent mixture of program and building on the one hand and all the support structures (people and machines) one the other, makes evident that the designer can but maybe should not exclude the latter from the design equation. Interior designers frequently cross the line between hardware and software. This attitude becomes even more relevant when environmental issues are brought up, since they have direct bearing on the life cycle and life span of the building (and all its elements and systems) and thus directly with its life (use)…

22. In attempting to find a narrow definition of the Stim, I have at this point excluded the workplace, although, clearly stimming takes place here too. The subject of the *suburbanization of work* and the increased need for Stims to compensate for the *loss of the office* is a chapter in itself in need of extensive exploration.

This essay originally appeared in *Assemblage 25*, 1994, and also appears in *After the City*, the MIT Press, 2001.

LARS LERUP is the dean and William Ward Watkin Professor of Architecture at Rice School of Architecture.

15
Responses

Houston's continuing lesson is that the metropolis is formed by default rather than by design—resulting from varied, autonomous, and disparate organizational and operational logics that are social, economic, and political, as well as physical. I am now in Chicago and find that there is more Houston in Chicago than one thinks.
—David Brown

Without zoning and topography, Houston is the ultimate tabula rasa. This blank slate not only liberates architecture from the baggage of site and context, but pushes form, mass, program, and typology to the foreground and to fertile ground.

Focusing on the typology of big buildings, my research explores the potential of large-scale developments' generating their own context. While hyper-dense cities in China, such as Hong Kong, epitomize the vertical model of densification, Houston is the prototypical model of horizontal expansion. Both models are facilitated by scales of development that render context irrelevant.
—Clover Lee

Even though Houston does not belong to the geography of my research, it does offer a great deal of support in terms of local patronage willing to fund cultural projects related to Latin America in general, and the history of Brazilian modern architecture in particular.
—Farès el-Dahdah

It has a large influence on me, as a native Houstonian. Houston has always been wide open with a diverse mix of people and ideas—that diversity is its greatest strength. In my own work (teaching and practice), I have had building sites and clients that have offered a rich variety of projects.
—Nonya Grenader

-

I tend to think of Houston and Rice as presenting what one might call an anamorphic perspective. The Rice School of Architecture is one of the leading schools in terms of research and innovation, but it is not located in one of the hubs of architectural culture (e.g., New York, London, LA). This means one is at once a part of the discourses of disciplinary advancement, but from a different point or view, that of distance from the manner in which problems appear within those centers. The brutal reality of Houston—a city rather indifferent to architecture—is integral to that, of course, but not in the touristic or ironic way in which those who visit the School often approach it. Houston is at once very specific and a prototype of contemporary patterns of urban processes and manifestations, and it therefore raises questions as to the modern practices and knowledges of "architecture" more or less calibrated to the problems of the nineteenth century metropolis rather than places such as Houston. In that sense, I see Houston/Rice as presenting an anamorphic view, not unlike the way Jacques Lacan presented the anamorphically distorted skull in Hans Holbein's *The Ambassadors* as a mark inscribing the dissolution of the subject—in this case, the historical construction of the "architect" and his practice.
—Christopher Hight

Houston completely changed my way of looking at cities. I now observe them from a different speed. I wrote quite a lot about it back then, mostly published in Cite. My recent book, Sprawltown: Looking for the City on its Edges (2006), was inspired by the contrast of commuting between two urban cultures, Houston and Montevarchi. As I have not been present for the last ten of these fifteen years, I really have no idea. I don't think people, except for Stephen Fox, remember anything in Houston. That's one of its charms—there is no resistance because there is no memory.
—Richard Ingersoll

Houston is a frontier city, a territory more than a city, where one can simultaneously explore the potentials and shortcomings of architecture. I am influenced by the city's open spirit and can-do attitude. In my opinion this openness is both an opportunity and a cautionary tale. Just because we can build practically anything in this city, it does not mean that everything is valid.
—Carlos Jiménez

I've heard Houston de-
scribed as a city that's only
emerged as a metropolis
in the last sixty years.
Architecturally speaking,
I've heard it described as
one of the most capitalisti-
cally transparent cities in
the U.S., and when friends
and colleagues visit, I know
that it's a city that can only
be experienced to be un-
derstood... statistics never
do it justice.
—Sean Lally

With so many miles of freeway, some might say Hous-
ton is all connective tissue,
no bone. If one is just passing through, its interstitial
vastness is forgettable—regrettable, even. But closer
scrutiny exposes the com-
plex ecologies (Banham),
megashapes (Lerup), and
middle landscapes (Rowe)
that comprise a city. Living,
working, and teaching in
Houston train one to keep
an eye on what's going on
in between, like learning to
notice the spaces between
letters. The city serves as
a constant reminder, in a
form-obsessed profession,
that the seemingly formless
"middle" is where every-
thing happens.
—Alex O'Briant

Houston's influence was
very enlightening. The
answer to why this is
would take many pages,
but to summarize I root the
development of my thinking
on Houston's urbanism in
two people: Lars Lerup and
Albert Pope. From them I
learned of the power and
limitations of urban poetics.
Were I to write something
serious on this issue, it
might be called something
like "The Long View," where
I would contrast the sub-
lime beauty of Lars's vision
of Houston (which is no less
detailed and compelling
than Ridley Scott's vision
of LA) with the profoundly
different view "from the
ground." While Lars's
vision is crystal clear and
deeply moving from the
twentieth floor of a tower
on Westheimer Blvd., it
utterly disappears at street
level. This does not negate
Lars's version of Houston...
if anything, it amplifies it.
Because my background is
deeply rooted in the "close
reading" mentality of Peter
Eisenman, I found Lars's
approach to "seeing" the
city both radically new and,
at the same time, utterly
foreign.
—Jason Payne

My work focuses on the
intersection of natural,
infrastructural, and cultural
systems, typically at the
metropolitan scale, so
Houston becomes incred-
ibly fascinating for me. The
scarcity of public space,
coupled with the extreme
climate, produces a condition where infrastructure
holds a rich potential to be
reconceived as a place of
collective occupation and
formal experimentation
that is guided, in terms of
design, by relatively strict
performance criteria.
—Michael Robinson

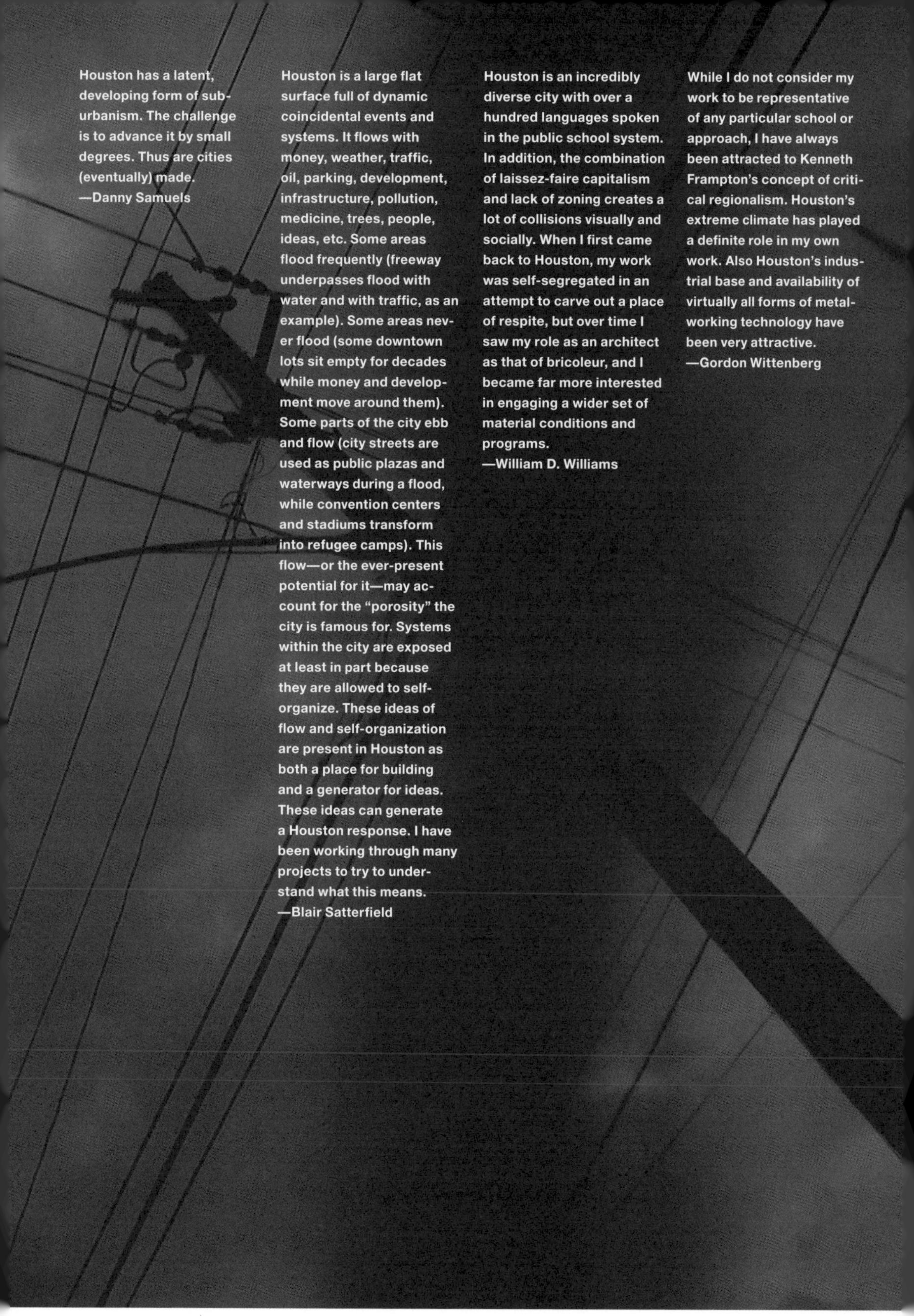

Houston has a latent, developing form of sub-urbanism. The challenge is to advance it by small degrees. Thus are cities (eventually) made.
—Danny Samuels

Houston is a large flat surface full of dynamic coincidental events and systems. It flows with money, weather, traffic, oil, parking, development, infrastructure, pollution, medicine, trees, people, ideas, etc. Some areas flood frequently (freeway underpasses flood with water and with traffic, as an example). Some areas never flood (some downtown lots sit empty for decades while money and development move around them). Some parts of the city ebb and flow (city streets are used as public plazas and waterways during a flood, while convention centers and stadiums transform into refugee camps). This flow—or the ever-present potential for it—may account for the "porosity" the city is famous for. Systems within the city are exposed at least in part because they are allowed to self-organize. These ideas of flow and self-organization are present in Houston as both a place for building and a generator for ideas. These ideas can generate a Houston response. I have been working through many projects to try to understand what this means.
—Blair Satterfield

Houston is an incredibly diverse city with over a hundred languages spoken in the public school system. In addition, the combination of laissez-faire capitalism and lack of zoning creates a lot of collisions visually and socially. When I first came back to Houston, my work was self-segregated in an attempt to carve out a place of respite, but over time I saw my role as an architect as that of bricoleur, and I became far more interested in engaging a wider set of material conditions and programs.
—William D. Williams

While I do not consider my work to be representative of any particular school or approach, I have always been attracted to Kenneth Frampton's concept of critical regionalism. Houston's extreme climate has played a definite role in my own work. Also Houston's industrial base and availability of virtually all forms of metal-working technology have been very attractive.
—Gordon Wittenberg

Seventh wonder of the world (in retirement)

Almost-nature (golf on the moist prairie)

Stim

Suburban respirator

1994

Graduates

M.ARCH.

Raed Al-Rabiah
Catherine Murray Bird
David Alfred Brothers
Ginette B. Castro
Matthew Preston Greer
Nonya S. Grenader
Jeffrey Michael Guga
Alexandra Howland Hussey
John Michael Jenkins
Michael John Kuchta
Stephanie Dean Law
Jennifer Frank Lucchino
Mark Andrew Oberholzer
Tze-Boon Ong
Athena Pervanis
Julian Ross Pittan
William Crabtree Rosebro
Francis Xavier Rudloff
Elizabeth Dawn Songer
Christopher Charles West
Jean Chih-Pin Wu

B.ARCH

Merrill Elbert Christopher
Aldrich
Stephanie Arwen Bassler
Eva Belik
Stephanie Kathryn Christoff
Jerome Uy Del Fierro
Joshua Henry Firebaugh
William Keoni Fleming
Matthew Eugene Harvey
Mary Schmidt Holmes
Lonnie Darren Hoogeboom
Timothy Duane Howell
Jeffrey Sterling Lewis
Walter Haertel Lorenzut
Robert Charles Mankin, Jr.
Amy Brooke Noble
Kristina Elizabeth Prokop
Daniel Uoo-Suk Suh
Georgeen Ann Theodore
Jill Anne Webb
Gina Sheng-Chi Yu

Faculty

Natalye Appel
Visiting Critic
Michael Bell
Assistant Professor
James Blackburn
Lecturer
William T. Cannady
Professor
John J. Casbarian
Associate Dean and
Professor

Yung-Ho Chang
Assistant Professor
Joseph Colaco
Lecturer
Louis DeLaura
Lecturer
Farès el-Dahdah
Visiting Critic, Caudill
Matthew Preston Greer
Lecturer
Alan Fleishacker
Lecturer
Stephen Fox
Lecturer
Wally Ford
Lecturer
James Furr
Lecturer
Elizabeth Gamard
Assistant Professor
Nonya Grenader
Visiting Critic
David Guthrie
Visiting Critic
Richard Ingersoll
Associate Professor
Carlos Jiménez
Visiting Critic
Sanford Kwinter
Visiting Cullinan Professor
Lars Lerup
Dean and Professor
Tom Lord
Lecturer
Spencer Parsons
Associate Professor
Albert Pope
Associate Professor
Eric Ragni
Wortham Fellow
Danny Samuels
Visiting Critic
Charles Tapley
Lecturer
Mark Wamble
Assistant Professor
Frank White
Lecturer
Gordon Wittenberg
Associate Professor

Staff

Doris Anderson
School Administrator
Rob Christie
Woodshop Manager
Molly Cumming
Program Administrator,
RDA
Dung Ngo
Director of Publications
and Exhibitions

Joan Reid
Assistant to the Dean
Kathleen Roberts
Graduate Coordinator
Elaine Sebring
Accounting Assistant
Mary Swift
Office Assistant, RDA
Linda Sylvan
Executive Director, RDA
Shisha van Horn
Information Technology
Specialist
Janet Wheeler
Office Assistant
Diania Williams
Receptionist

Awards

Edward B Arrants Award
John Lee
Gene Hackerman Award
(graduate)
Sommer Schauer
John Crowder Traveling
Fellowship
Stephen Engbloom
John T Mitchell Traveling
Fellowship
Duncan Davidson
Margaret Everson Fossi
Traveling Fellowship:
- 1st place
Matt Greer
MN Davidson Fellowship
Ari Seligmann
Morris R Pitman Award in
Architecture
Thad Briner
Rice Visionary Project
Ginette Castro
Tau Sigma Delta
Kelly Ann Boston, Sherry
Lin, Olaf Recktenwald, Lisl
Sollner, Eric Stotts
William Ward Watkin Awards:
- Mary Alice Elliott Award
Nina Murrell
- Honorable Mention
Stuart Bauer, John Clegg,
Ari Seligmann, Eric Stotts,
Jennifer Wlock
- Rosemary Watkin Barrick
Traveling Fellowship, 2nd
place
Sherry Lin
- William Ward Watkin
Traveling Fellowship
Joy Yoder

Thesis Titles

Catherine Bird—
The American Catholic
Church in the Public Realm
David Brothers—
A Concept of Home for the
Modern Urban Stranger
Ginette Castro—
Anti-Monument—Weak
Form
Matthew Greer—
The Architecture Machine
in the Age of Invisible
Technology
Nonya Grenader—
The Porch as Middle
Ground
Jeffrey Guga—
A Dynamic Figure Ground
Alexandra Hussey—
Secular Spiritualism
Evolved: The Market As
Communal Sanctuary
John Jenkins—
The New School: Creating
A Role For The Architect In
America's Urban
Landscape
John Kisner—
Mandatory National
Service: An Antidote For
Declining Egality In
Contemporary Society
Michael Kuchta—
Daylighting In American
Industrial Architecture:
Three Investigations
Stephanie Law—
Memory And Imagination
Jennifer Lucchino—
An Architecture of
Information Technology
And Place
Mark Oberholzer—
Wall
Tze Boon Ong—
Music As A Generative
Process In Architectural
Form/Space Composition
Athena Pervanis—
Adapative Reuse of Aircraft
Carriers
Julian Pittman—
Inhabiting The Threshold:
Space And Mora
Will Rosebro—
Ecological Architecture:
Redefining The American
Organic Tradition

Lectures

Exhibitions

Publications

The Little Books that Could

Thumb in conversation with Dung Ngo

Thumb: *The publication program at Rice School of Architecture, Architecture at Rice (AAR), had existed since 1961, but it really seemed to raise its profile in 1994. What had changed? The publication program seemed to be part of a developing "book culture" at the School. Was this unique to Rice, or was it that the era of the "big monograph" was felt across all segments of architecture culture?*

Dung Ngo: The first iteration of the Architecture at Rice series (which was active for roughly a decade) was fairly radical in its day. Until the early 80's architecture school publications tended to be year-end reviews or academic journals, and existed only at a handful of schools. AAR was one of the first—if not the first—to publish publications on discrete, focused topics, often with the design or thinking process of a single architect as the subject matter. The Louis Kahn and Shadrach Woods books were perhaps two of the more interesting AAR publications in this vein.

When Lars Lerup came to Rice, it must be remembered that at the time only a small group of architecture schools had their own publication programs, and those tended to be at the larger and more high-profile schools. Lars realized that by (re) starting the publication, two of his important goals would be achieved: (1) publications can help raise the profile of the of the school, circulating the Rice brand nationally and internationally through the most efficient channel possible at that time (in the early 90's few schools had websites that highly trafficked or had content beyond the basic school information); (2) more importantly, the AAR publications had the potential to present the current thinking and working process at the school, in the spirit of the original program. The partnership with Princeton Architectural Press was key in the wide dissemination of theses publications, allowing a school not located on either coast, with about 125 students, to be seen as a key center of architectural thinking and production at that moment.

T: *When Koolhaas came to Houston as part of his* SMLXL *tour more than ten years ago people waited on line for hours to get a seat. Do you think the book contributed to that phenomenon? Could something like that happen today or has the status of the architecture book changed since then?*

DN: Koolhaas had taught at Rice while working on *SMLXL*, and Houston—which both Koolhaas and Lars realized could be a new model for contemporary urbanism—was highly instrumental in Koolhaas's thinking at the time. In many ways his experience in Houston informed his work on Beijing and Lagos. *SMLXL* was also a new model for the architectural publication: a new hybrid or mash-up of monograph and manifesto, it has become a model for so many publications of younger architects, but at the time no one had seen anything like it. On top of this novel structure was Bruce Mau's fully integrated graphic co-authorship of the book—for many of us it was the first instance in a long time that form and content became one and the same.

The Koolhaas speaking events on the publication of *SMLXL* were a victory tour, rock tour, and site-specific engagements rolled into one. Koolhaas selected U.S. cities that informed his architectural thinking, past and present: New York, Houston, and Los Angeles. In Houston I was completely unprepared for the rock-star hysteria that surrounded the event. We booked one of the largest venues available, the auditorium at the Museum of Fine Arts, Houston (it was also important to Koolhaas that it was in a Mies building). Hours before the event there was a line around the block—students from all the architecture programs around the state have driven to Houston for the event—and we were only able to accommodate about half of the crowd. All this for a book. But we haven't seen such a book for a long time, and have yet to see one like it since.

The physical heft and theoretical density of *SMLXL* has made it the architectural equivalent of James Joyce's *Ulysses*—few people have really been able to consume the whole without a stomachache. At the same time as the release of *SMLXL* was the AAR publication *Rem Koolhaas: Conversations with Students*, which can be seen as the distillation and exegesis of the larger book. It remains the best selling AAR publication.

T: *Where should AAR (or other small/academic publishing programs) go today?*

DN: Despite the participation of various significant architectural personas with the AAR series, the most important outcome of the publication program has been to provide an alternative outlet to the voices of the day. Since the revival of AAR in 1994, many other media channels have appeared. At the same time, print media has become more costly to produce and environmentally questionable. All publishing programs should examine these newer channels, and take advantage of their speed and flexibility. The printed book will never go away, but their primacy as the disseminator of thought will. As long as AAR retains its original goals, there is no doubt interesting, quirky, and significants publications will continue to issue from Rice.

DUNG NGO is a Senior Editor of Architecture and Design at Rizzoli International. He was the director of publications and exhibitions at Rice School of Architecture from 1994-98.

270

Jury Room, Anderson Hall

1995

Graduates

DR.ARCH
David Gray Lever

M.ARCH.
Thaddeus Mies Briner
Peter Chen Chia Mien
Marana Chow
John Duncan Davidson
Jonathan L. M. Greene
Timothy Fowler Hagan
Douglas E. Hill
David James Marini
Jan Eran Montoya
James Patrick Powell
Joseph Lee Powell III
Peony Letitia Quan
Michael Robert Radeke
Blair Harold Satterfield
Sommer Leigh Schauer
Daniel Joseph Silver
Karin Elise Taylor
Dana Sundt Weeder
Bernardo Zavattini

B.ARCH
Craig Dale Bangart
Jody Justin Beck
Andrew W. Benner
John Miller Brookby
Heidi Elizabeth Bullinga
Andrew Carl Burnmeister
Susan Noelle Gruel
Jill Louise Harmon
Charles Christopher Clinton Hight
Davin Sock-Yong Hong
Collin C. W. Kemberlin
Cynthia Marie Labelle
Christian Davies Nixon
Lisa Joy Ross
Tuong-Vi Phan Tran

Faculty
Merrill Aldrich
  Visiting Critic
Jay Baker
  Visiting Critic
Michael Bell
  Assistant Professor
James Blackburn
  Lecturer
William T. Cannady
  Professor

John J. Casbarian
  Associate Dean and Professor
Yung-Ho Chang
  Assistant Professor
Joseph Colaco
  Lecturer
Karl Chu
  Visiting Critic
Louis DeLaura
  Lecturer
Farès el-Dahdah
  Assistant Professor
Sohela Farokhi
  Lecturer
Alan Fleishacker
  Lecturer
Stephen Fox
  Lecturer
Wally Ford
  Lecturer
James Furr
  Lecturer
Diane Ghirardo
  Visiting Critic
Elizabeth Gamard
  Assistant Professor
Nonya Grenader
  Visiting Critic

David Guthrie
  Visiting Critic
Gavin Hogben
  Caudill Visiting Lecturer
Richard Ingersoll
  Associate Professor
Sanford Kwinter
  Visiting Cullinan Professor
Lars Lerup
  Dean and Professor
Tom Lord
  Lecturer
Robert Mangurian
  Wortham Visiting Professor
Laura Miller
  Visiting Critic
Mark Oberholzer
  Lecturer
Spencer Parsons
  Associate Professor
Gary Poole
  Lecturer
Albert Pope
  Associate Professor
Eric Ragni
  Wortham Fellow
Mary-Ann Ray
  Wortham Visiting Professor
Lindy Roy
  Assistant Professor
Danny Samuels
  Visiting Critic
Blair Satterfield
  Visiting Critic
Roberto Segre
  Visiting Cullinan Professor
Adi Shamir
  Visiting Critic
Scott Strasser
  Visiting Critic
Charles Tapley
  Lecturer
Shisha van Horn
  Lecturer
Mark Wamble
  Assistant Professor
Frank White
  Lecturer
Gordon Wittenberg
  Associate Professor

Staff
Doris Anderson
  School Administrator
Rob Christie
  Woodshop Manager
Molly Cumming
  Program Administrator, RDA
Dung Ngo
  Director of Publications and Exhibitions

Joan Reid
Assistant to the Dean
Kathleen Roberts
Graduate Coordinator
Elaine Sebring
Accounting Assistant
Ann Sieber
Managing Editor, Cite
Mary Swift
Office Assistant, RDA
Linda Sylvan
Executive Director, RDA
Shisha van Horn
Information Technology
Specialist
Janet Wheeler
Office Assistant
Diania Williams
Receptionist

Awards

AIA School Medal
Carice Pengenot
AIA School Certificate
James Michael Evans
Alpha Rho Chi Medal
James Morris Spearman
Chillman Prize:
- 1st Prize
Wen-Kai Zhong
- Honorable Mention
Katherin B. Dy
Darden Award
Kelvin Brian Hall
Edward B Arrants Award
Katherine B. Dy, Diane
Theresa Golomb
Gene Hackerman Award
(undergraduate)
Karin Elise Taylor
John Crowder Traveling
Fellowship
Kerry Whitehead
John T Mitchell Traveling
Fellowship
Mark Kroeckel
Louis Sudler Prize in the Arts
Carice Pengenot
Margaret Everson Fossi
Traveling Fellowship:
- 1st place
Chris Hight, Daniel Silver
MN Davidson Fellowship
James Michael Evans,
James Moris Spearman
Morris R Pitman Award in
Architecture
Otto Driessen
Rae Jacobs Memorial
Scholarship
Carice Pingenot

Ralph S Herman Memorial
Scholarship
Stephen Traeger
Rice Visionary Project
Bernardo Zavattini
RTKL Traveling Fellowship
Wen-Kai Zhong
Tau Sigma Delta
Katherine B. Dy, James
Michael Evans, Diane
Theresa Golomb, Carice
A Pingenot, Niel Hanson
Prunier, Wen-Kai Zhong
Texas Architectural
Foundation Scholarships:
- Southwest Terrazzo
Association Scholarship
Constance Lai
William Ward Watkin Awards:
- Mary Alice Elliott Award
James Michael Evans
- Honorable Mention
Carice Pingenot, Brent
Edward Revis
- Rosemary Watkin Barrick
Traveling Fellowship, 2nd
place
Wen-Kai Zhong
- William Ward Watkin
Traveling Fellowship
Adam T Hayes

Thesis Titles

Thaddeus Briner—
Infrastructural/Spatial
Mediation in Mega Sites
Peter Chia-mien Chen—
Phenomenological Process
in Mapping The City:
Projective and Representa-
tional Alternatives
Marana Chow—
Exploration of Alternative
Space Through Perception
of the Real and the Illusory
John Duncan Davidson—
The Necessity of Hallways:
Path Making And The Re-
Formation of a Japanese
Tea Garden Into An East
Texas Roadhouse
Jonathan Greene—
The Journeyman And The
Bivouac: The Reinvention
of The American Pioneer
House
Timothy Hagan—
Urban Reinvention
Douglas Hill—
Extended Family
Housing: On Suture in the

Formal and Social Con-
struction of Housing
David Lever—
Local Domains: Neigh-
borhood Planning and the
Interests of Cities
David Marini—
Inhabiting Downtown
Houston: Density and
Hollowness in the
Contemporary City
Eran Montoya—
Emframements: Valuating
Decay in the City
James Patrick Powell—
Residential Framework
For The Transient: A
Critical Analysis of Object
Event Relationships in
Transient Residential Sites
Joseph Lee Powell—
The Museum Typology
Under Stress: A Design
Proposal For A Scattered
Site Jazz Museum In New
Orleans
Peony Quan—
Hilltop Housing:
Reconfiguring the Subur-
ban Condition
Michael Radeke—
Urban House: The Ultra-
sonic Blender Confusion of
Twenty-First Century
Society
Blair Satterfield—
Crash Motel, Perception
and Process: Machines for
People Who Still Walk
Sommer Schauer—
Physical and Real Time
Delineations on the
Electromechanical
Threshold
Daniel Silver—
The Formative Field

Tony Song—
Mechanization of the Eye
As An Architectural
Paradigm
Karin Taylor—
Infinite Projections for
Atopic Landscapes
Dana Weeder—
Time and Movement: A
Proposal for Drift
Bernardo Zavattini—
Five

Lectures

02.06
Robert Mangurian
Studio Works, Los Angeles
and Visiting Wortham
Professor
Recent Work

02.13
Mary-Ann Ray
Studio Works, Los Angeles
and Visiting Wortham
Professor
Recent Work

02.28
Peter Zumthor
Atelier Peter Zumthor,
Switzerland
Recent Work

03.13
Daniel Libeskind
Daniel Libeskind Architect,
Los Angeles & Berlin
Recent Work

03.27
Toyo Ito
Toyo Ito & Associates,
Architects, Tokyo
Recent Work

Jury Room in use, Anderson Hall

04.03
Charles Gwathmey
Gwathmey Seigel &
Associates, New York
Recent Work

04.06
Diane Ghirardo
Architectural Critic and
Historian, Los Angeles and
Visiting Professor
Recent Work

10.19
Stanley Tigerman
Tigerman McCurry Architects,
Chicago
Recent Work

10.23
Gisue Hariri
Hariri & Hariri, New York
Recent Work

11.06
David Lake & Ted Flato
Lake Flato Architects, San
Antonio
Recent Work

12.07
Ricardo Scofidio
Diller + Scofidio, New York
Recent Work

Exhibitions
*Luigi Snozzi: Buildings and
Projects 1972-1992*

Publications
AAR 35
Citta Aperta—Open City
Luciano Rigolini

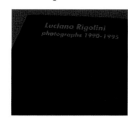

1996

Graduates
M.ARCH.
Carlos Andres Bruderer
Angel Javier Cormenzana
Baltza
Eric Otto Driessen

Stephen Carl Engblom
Kyle Ross Fisher
Richard Mansfield Graves II
Kelvin Brian Hall
Lonnie Darren Hoogeboom
Matthew E. Juros
John Leonard Kisner II
Mark Roderick Kroeckel
Petia Dorian Morozov
Alfons Poblocki Jr.
James W. Powell
Peter Lund Rockrise
Christian Schmidt
Tony Song
Niall Quin Washburn

B.ARCH
Mark David Adams
Stuart William Baur
Kelly Anne Boston
John Thomas Clegg
Angelo Agulto Directo
Constance Chunlan Lai
John Hans Lee
Sherry Yi-Chung Lin
Meredith Elise McCree
Enrique Montenegro
Garrett Evan Mosiman
Nina Linette Murrell
Julie Elizabeth Nymann
Margaret Lois Oakes
Robert Matthew Plummer
Olaf Lewis Recktenwald
Ari D. Seligmann
Eric Rollin Shamp
Lisl Alden Sollner
Eric William Stotts
Bradley Paul Taylor
Joy Virginie Yoder

Faculty
Merrill Aldrich
    Visiting Critic
Jay Baker
    Visiting Critic
Michael Bell
    Assistant Professor
James Blackburn
    Lecturer
David Brown
    Assistant Professor
William T. Cannady
    Professor
John J. Casbarian
    *Associate Dean and
    Professor*
Yung-Ho Change
    Assistant Professor
Joseph Colaco
    Lecturer
Bill Conte
    Lecturer

Louis DeLaura
    Lecturer
Farès el-Dahdah
    Assistant Professor
Sohela Farokhi
    Lecturer
Alejandro Ferdman
    Lecturer
Luis Fernandez-Galiano
    Visiting Cullinan Professor
Alan Fleishacker
    Lecturer
Stephen Fox
    Lecturer
Wally Ford
    Lecturer
James Furr
    Lecturer
Elizabeth Gamard
    Assistant Professor
Nonya Grenader
    Visiting Critic
David Guthrie
    Visiting Critic
Gavin Hogben
    Caudill Visiting Lecturer
Mark Holzbach
    Lecturer
Lonnie Hoogeboom
    Visiting Critic
Richard Ingersoll
    Associate Professor
Keith Krumwiede
    Wortham Fellow
Sanford Kwinter
    Assistant Professor
Lars Lerup
    *Dean and William Ward
    Watkin Professor*
Tom Lord
    Lecturer
Robert Mangurian
    Wortham Visiting Professor
Bruce Mau
    Visiting Cullinan Professor
Mark Oberholzer
    Lecturer
Spencer Parsons
    Associate Professor
Gary Poole
    Lecturer
Albert Pope
    Associate Professor
Mary-Ann Ray
    Wortham Visiting Professor
Lindy Roy
    Assistant Professor
Danny Samuels
    Visiting Critic
Charles Tapley
    Lecturer

A disrespectful stack, with model

Shisha van Horn
    Lecturer
Alex Wall
    Visiting Critic
Mark Wamble
    Assistant Professor
Frank White
    Lecturer
Gordon Wittenberg
    Professor

Staff
Doris Anderson
    School Administrator
Rob Christie
    Woodshop Manager
Molly Cumming
    *Program Administrator,
    RDA*
Dung Ngo
    *Director of Publications
    and Exhibitions*
Kathleen Roberts
    Graduate Coordinator
Barrie Scardino
    Managing Editor, Cite
Elaine Sebring
    Accounting Assistant
Mary Swift
    Office Assistant, RDA
Linda Sylvan
    Executive Director, RDA
Shisha van Horn
    *Information Technology
    Specialist*
Janet Wheeler
    Office Assistant
Diania Williams
    Receptionist

Awards
AIA/AAF Scholarship
    Carice Pengenot
AIA School Medal
    Jon McNeal
AIA School Certificate
    Gail Borden
Alpha Rho Chi Medal
    Matthew Seltzer
Chillman Prize
    Gail Borden
Darden Award
    Otto Driessen

272

Edward B Arrants Award
Victor Sheen
Gene Hackerman Award
(undergraduate)
Heather Coyne
John Crowder Traveling
Fellowship
Ben Thorne
John T Mitchell Traveling
Fellowship
Blaine Brownell
Margaret Everson Fossi
Traveling Fellowship:
- 1st place
Luke Bulman, Kimberly
Shoemake
- 2nd place
Eric Stotts
Mary Ellen Hale Lovett
Traveling Fellowship
(graduate)
Ana Miljacki, Robert Sheh
Mary Ellen Hale Lovett
Traveling Fellowship
(undergraduate)
James Evans, Adam
Hayes, Jim Spearman, Jon
McNeal
MN Davidson Fellowship
Emily Sing
Morris R Pitman Award in
Architecture
Ann Doyle
Ralph S Herman Memorial
Scholarship
Christina Letourneau,
James Evans
Rice Visionary Project
Branden Hookway
Tau Sigma Delta
Gail Borden, Heather
Coyne, Caryn Dietrich,
Jon McNeal, Victor Sheen,
Emily Sing
Texas Architectural
Foundation Scholarships:
- O'Neil Ford Traveling
Fellowship
David Parke
- Jesse H Jones Scholarship
Wen-Kai Zhong
- E.G. Spencer Memorial
Scholarship
James Evans
- George F Harrell II Memorial
Scholarship
Carice Pengenot
- Southwest Terrazzo
Association Scholarship
Brent Revis
William Ward Watkin Awards:

- Mary Alice Elliott Award
Emily Sing
- Honorable Mention
Heather Coyne, Jon
McNeal
- Rosemary Watkin Barrick
Traveling Fellowship, 2nd
place
Brooke Johnson
- William Ward Watkin
Traveling Fellowship
Gail Borden

Thesis Titles

Carlos Bruderer—
A Plan for the Urban
Expansion of La
Democracia, Escuintla
Angel Cormenzana—
When Form Resists
Program
Otto Driessen—
Poetic Interventions in the
Open City: Homo Viator
and Landscape in Houston
and Randstad, Holland
Stephen Engblom—
A Public Landscape,
Galveston, Texas
Kyle Fisher—
The Feminization of the
American Domestic
Landscape
Richard Graves—
Patterns in the Landscape
Kelvin Hall—
Housing and Its Social
Implications Through
Architecture
Matt Juros—
Architectural Discourse
and Practice at the End of
the 20th Century
John Kisner—
Beyond the Control of
Architecture
Mark Kroeckel—
Acting Space... Following
the Line: Architectures of
the Drawing Act
Petia Morozov—
Materializing the Invisible:
A Return to Form-Making
Alfons Poblocki—
Uncooperative Housing
James W. Powell—
Towards a Complex
Minimal Architecture
through Twentieth Century
Music
Peter Rockrise—
The Interlocutor and the

Metropolis
Christian Schmidt—
Hard Core Urbanism
Rebecca Sternberg—
Tel Aviv: Concrete Beaches
and Fallen Skyscrapers
Niall Washburn—
Recovering Scraps from
the Cutting Edge: Flexible
Theatre Architecture and
the Avant-Garde

Lectures

09.10
Luis Fernandez-Galiano
*Spain 1900-1950: Avante
Garde and Tradition*

09.11
Luis Fernandez-Galiano
Alejandro de la Sota

09.12
Luis Fernandez-Galiano
*Spain 1950-1975: Modernity
under Franco*

10.15
Luis Fernandez-Galiano
*Spain 1975-1980: The
Building of Democracy*

10.16
Luis Fernandez-Galiano
Rafael Moneo

10.17
Luis Fernandez-Galiano
*Spain 1980-1985: A Socialist
Spring*

10.23
Enric Miralles
*Enric Miralles: Intuition and
Process*

11.18
Luis Fernandez-Galiano
*Spain 1985-1990: Years of
Affluence*

11.19
Luis Fernandez-Galiano
Enric Miralles

11.20
Luis Fernandez-Galiano
*Spain 1990-1995: Spectacle
and Crisis*

02.09
Rem Koolhaus
Office for Metropolitan
Architecture, Rotterdam

02.22
Peter Eisenman
Eisenman Architects, New
York

03.12
Rafael Moneo
Rafael Moneo Architects,
Madrid

04.15
**Rofolfo Machado and Jorge
Silvetti**
Machado Silvetti Architects,
Boston

Exhibitions

Enric Miralles: Enric Miralles

*The Byzantine Fresco Chapel:
Francois de Menil*

*Citta Aperta—Open City:
Luciano Rigolini*

274

Faculty office portraits, 1996/97

Sol Lewitt: Complex Forms, Farish Gallery, 1997

Publications
AAR 30
Rem Koolhaas: Conversations with Students
Sanford Kwinter, editor
Second edition, Princeton Architectural Press

AAR 34
Ladders
Albert Pope
Princeton Architectural Press

AAR 36
Buildings
Carlos Jiménez
Princeton Architectural Press

1997

Graduates
M.ARCH.
Laurence David Albert
Katherine Anne Bottom
Stefanie Diehm
Ann M. Doyle
Nick Charles Dragna, Jr.
Brent Richard Dykstra
Eric Blake Hildebrandt
Alison Hart Hill
Keith Alan Koski
Haemin Lee
Lijia Lu
Chad Jermaine Machen
Gary Wayne Machicek
Christopher Peter Nichols
Richard Anthony Odom
David Robin Parke
Carmen Platero Parada
Sara Elizabeth Ridenour
Robert Ramis Sheh
Elizaabeth Rowe Spelman
Nicola Joy Springer
Sharon Ann Steinberg
Rebecca Sternberg
Marc Terrance Swackhamer

Allen Gardiner Symonds
Ivan Yuri Tkachenko
Stephen Eric Traeger
Kerry Colleen Whitehead
Christina Ann Wilson
Allison Claire Zuchman

B.ARCH
Katherine B. Dy
James Michael Evans
Diane Theresa Golomb
Adam T Hayes
Kim Marie Neuscheler
Carice Annette Pingenot
Niel Hanson Prunier
Brent Edward Revis
Stuart Gene Smith
James Morris Spearman, Jr.
Wen-Kai Zhong

Faculty
Merrill Aldrich
Visiting Critic
Natalye Appel
Visiting Critic
Leonard Bachman
Lecturer
Bill Bavinger
Lecturer
Michael Bell
Associate Professor
David Brown
Assistant Professor
William T. Cannady
Professor
John J. Casbarian
Associate Dean and Professor
Joseph Colaco
Lecturer
Louis DeLaura
Lecturer
Farès el-Dahdah
Assistant Professor
Alejandro Ferdman
Lecturer

Alan Fleishacker
Lecturer
Stephen Fox
Lecturer
Wally Ford
Lecturer
James Furr
Lecturer
Elizabeth Gamard
Assistant Professor
Nonya Grenader
Visiting Critic
David Guthrie
Visiting Critic
Dave Hickey
Visiting Cullinan Professor
Mark Holzbach
Lecturer
Carlos Jiménez
Assistant Professor
Keith Krumwiede
Caudill Visiting Lecturer
Sanford Kwinter
Associate Professor
Lars Lerup
Dean and William Ward Watkin Professor
David Lever
Lecturer
Tom Lord
Lecturer
Robert Mangurian
Wortham Visiting Professor
Bruce Mau
Visiting Cullinan Professor
Detlef Mertins
Visiting Critic
Mark Oberholzer
Lecturer
Douglas Oliver
Visiting Critic
Spencer Parsons
Associate Professor
Albert Pope
Wortham Associate Professor

Mary-Ann Ray
Wortham Visiting Professor
Martin Reiner
Lecturer
Lindy Roy
Assistant Professor
Danny Samuels
Visiting Critic
David Todd
Lecturer
Wendy Todd
Visiting Critic
Mark Wamble
Assistant Professor
James Wasley
Lecturer
Frank White
Lecturer
Gordon Wittenberg
Professor

Staff
Doris Anderson
School Administrator
Rob Christie
Woodshop Manager
Molly Cumming
Program Administrator, RDA
Hans Krause
Information Technology Specialist
Dung Ngo
Director of Publications and Exhibitions
Kathleen Roberts
Graduate Coordinator
Barrie Scardino
Managing Editor, Cite
Elaine Sebring
Accounting Assistant
Mary Swift
Office Assistant, RDA
Linda Sylvan
Executive Director, RDA
Janet Wheeler
Office Assistant

Diania Williams
Receptionist

Thesis book, 1997, by Luke Bulman and Kimberly Shoemake

Awards

AIA/AAF Scholarship
Heather Coyne, Matt
Seltzer
AIA School Medal
Annatina Schneider
AIA School Certificate
Craig Eigenberg
Alpha Rho Chi Medal
Cedra Ginsburg
*Berda & Charles Soon Chan
Memorial Scholarship*
Christy Raber
Chillman Prize:
- 1st place
Heidi McDowell
- Honorable Mention
Christina Lee
Darden Award
Ann Doyle
Edward B Arrants Award
Christina Lee
*Gene Hackerman Award
(undergraduate)*
Aline Cautis, Cine Ostrow
*John Crowder Traveling
Fellowship*
Shelly Pottorf
*John T Mitchell Traveling
Fellowship*
James Horn
*Margaret Everson Fossi
Traveling Fellowship:*
- 1st place
Brett Terpeluk
- 2nd place
Brian Burke
*Mary Ellen Hale Lovett
Traveling Fellowship
(graduate)*
Mary Springer
*Mary Ellen Hale Lovett
Traveling Fellowship
(undergraduate)*
Omayya Kanafani, Jason
Millhouse
MN Davidson Fellowship
Annatina Schneider
*Morris R Pitman Award in
Architecture*
Diana Davis
*Ralph S Herman Memorial
Scholarship*
Meredith Hamm, George
Soo
Rice Visionary Project
William Craig
Tau Sigma Delta

Craig Eigenberg, Meredith
Elbaum, Heidi McDowell,
Jason Millhouse, Annatina
Schneider, George Soo
*Texas Architectural
Foundation Scholarships:*
- Jesse H Jones Scholarship
Gail Borden
*- Southwest Terrazzo
Association Scholarship*
Matt Seltzer
*- San Antonio Conservation
Society Award*
James Horn
William Ward Watkin Awards:
- Mary Alice Elliott Award
Meredith Elbaum
- Honorable Mention
Meredith Hamm, Christina
Lee, Annatina Schneider
*- Rosemary Watkin Barrick
Traveling Fellowship, 2nd
place*
Heidi McDowell
*- William Ward Watkin
Traveling Fellowship*
John Mueller

Thesis Titles

Laurence Albert—
Houston Wet
Katherine Bottom—
Traversing the Edge
Stephanie Diehm—
*Die Schleuse Zur
Darstellenden Kunst*
Ann Doyle —
Escape
Brent Dykstra—
Rerailing
Eric Hildebrandt—
*A Ceramics School in
Monte San Savino, Italy (A
Tectonic Intervention*
Nick Dragna—
Riding the Urban Carpet
Alison Hill—
*The Modern Novel as a
Frame of Orientation in
Fragmented Social Worlds:
The Individual in the
Postwar Urban America of*

Saul Bellow
Keith Koski—
Long Point, Houston
Haemin Lee—
New Officetel
Lijia Lu—
*Dwelling as a Cultural
Phenomenon*
Chad Machen—
Manufacturing Facility
Gary Machicek—
A Downtown Superstop
Christopher Nichols—
Permutation
Richard Odom—
*The Fourth Floor:
Reconnecting Houston*
David Parke—
*Dirty Blue on Not-So-White
Walls for the Wittgenstein
House*
Carmen Platero—
A Tomb, A Wall... A City
Sara Ridenour—
Polylectic
Robert Sheh—
Jungle Gym
Elizabeth Spelman—
A Facade Project
Nicola Springer—
*If a House Burns Down
It's Gone, But the Place-
The Picture of It-Stays, And
Not Just in My Rememory
But Out There, in the World*
Sharon Steinberg—
Strip City
Marc Swackhamer—
*Material Investigation:
Plastic*
Ivan Tkachenko—
*On The School of
Architecture*
Stephen Traeger—
Boxing Domesticity
Kerry Whitehead—
Terminal Project
Christie Wilson—
Landscrapes
Allison Zuchman—
Approriating Architecture

Lectures

02.03
David Chipperfield
Recent Work

02.13
Will Bruder
Recent Work

09.24
Dave Hickey
*The Deplorable Consequences
of Architecture as Drawing*

10.29
Dave Hickey
*Hong Kong Aesthetics:
Post-Industrial Architectural
Practices*

11.04
John Claggett
*Approaching the Limit of
Change: The Conceptual
Basis of the Baroque*

11.12
Dave Hickey
*In the Palace of the People:
New Lessons from Las Vegas*

11.24
Beatriz Colomina
*Reflections on the Eames
House*

12.08
Wes Jones
Instramental Form: Openness

Exhibitions

Sol Lewitt: Complex Forms

Kennon Symposium

*Architecture after
Individualism*
The 2nd Kennon Symposium
Organized by Farès el-Dahdah

Participants: George Baird,
Michael Bell, Aaron Betsky,

Peter Cook: *Tongue, Claws and Tail*, Farish Gallery

John Biln, Marc Blanchard, David Brown, Robert Brown, John Casbarian, Yung-Ho Chang, Ti-Nan Chi, Karl Chu, Milton Curry, Farès el-Dahdah, Françoise Gaillard, Elysabeth Gamard, Benjamin Gianni, Jean-Joseph Goux, Carlos Jiménez, Kevin Kennon, Rodolphe el-Khoury, Sanford Kwinter, Sylvia Lavin, Lars Lerup, Greg Lynn, Bruce Mau, Ed Mitchell, Toshiko Mori, Shin Muramatsu, Albert Pope, Mark Robbins, Lindy Roy, Hashim Sarkis, Richard Sommer, Robert Somol, Kay Ngee Tan, Nader Tehrani, Mark Wamble, Allen Weiss, William Williams, Mabel Wilson, Alejandro Zaera-Polo

1998

Graduates
M.ARCH.
Krista Lee Armstrong
Jonathan Michael Baron
Blaine Erickson Brownell
Luke Tucker Bulman
William Carl Craig
Andrew Lyle Cruse
Diana Kay Davis
Branden Hugh Hookway
Gene William Johnston, Jr.

Cathryn Elizabeth King
Mihail Suhail Lari
Hu Li
Criag Bryan McCormick
James Eric Phillips
Michelle Debra Pottorf
Kimberly L. Shoemake
Michael S. Sweebe
Brett Terpeluk
Benjamin Brinkley Thorne

B.ARCH
Gail Peter Borden
Charles Scott Cahill
Heather Eileen Coyne
Caryn Beth Dietrich
Amy Rebecca Farber
Brooke Taylor Johnson
Christina Marie LeTourneau
Matthew David Seltzer
Vicotr H. H. Sheen
Emily Elizabeth Sing
Juliet O'Keeffe Whelan

Faculty
Merrill Aldrich
Visiting Critic
Leonard Bachman
Lecturer
Michael Bell
Associate Professor
Aaron Betsky
Visiting Cullinan Professor
David Brown
Assistant Professor
William T. Cannady
Professor
John J. Casbarian
Associate Dean and Professor
Peter Cook
Visiting Cullinan Professor

Kevin Daly
Visiting Critic
Louis DeLaura
Lecturer
Farès el-Dahdah
Assistant Professor
Alan Fleishacker
Lecturer
Stephen Fox
Lecturer
James Furr
Lecturer
Chris Genik
Visiting Critic
Nonya Grenader
Visiting Critic
Richard Ingersoll
Associate Professor
Carlos Jiménez
Assistant Professor
Donna Kacmar
Wortham Fellow
Keith Krumwiede
Caudill Assistant Professor
Sanford Kwinter
Associate Professor

Lars Lerup
Dean and William Ward Watkin Professor
Tom Lord
Lecturer
Robert Mangurian
Visiting Cullinan Professor
Bruce Mau
Visiting Cullinan Professor
Chris Nichols
Lecturer
Mark Oberholzer
Lecturer
Douglas Oliver
Visiting Critic
Spencer Parsons
Associate Professor
Albert Pope
Associate Professor
Mary-Ann Ray
Wortham Visiting Professor
Danny Samuels
Visiting Professor
David Todd
Lecturer
Mark Wamble
Assistant Professor
Frank White
Lecturer
Walter Widrig
Associate Professor
Kerry Whitehead
Wortham Fellow
Gordon Wittenberg
Professor

Staff
Doris Anderson
School Administrator
Rob Christie
Woodshop Manager
Hans Krause
Information Technology Specialist

RSA Events card, 1998

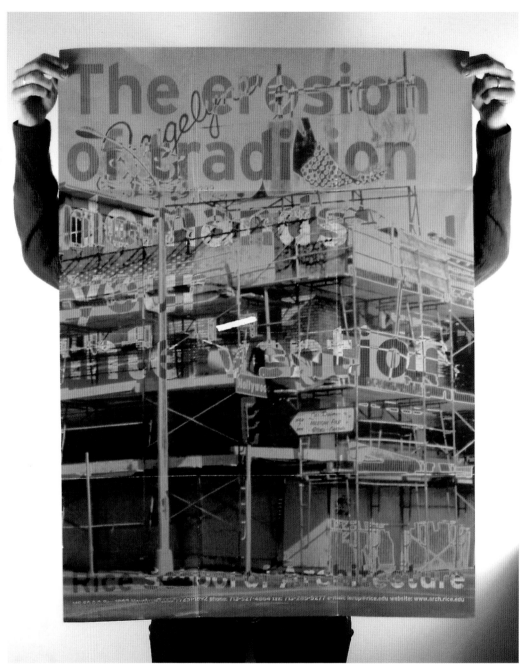

RIce School of Architecture posters, Bruce Mau Design

Site-specific art in Anderson Hall, installed in secrecy overnight, Gunnar Hartmann.

Amanda Lytz
Program Administrator, RDA
Dung Ngo
Director of Publications and Exhibitions
Kathleen Roberts
Graduate Coordinator
Elaine Sebring
Accounting Assistant
Mitchell Shields
Managing Editor, Cite
Mary Swift
RDA Records Coordinator
Linda Sylvan
Executive Director, RDA
Janet Wheeler
Office Assistant
Diania Williams
Receptionist

280

Awards

AIA School Medal
    Christy Raber
AIA School Certificate
    Justus Kessler
Alpha Rho Chi Medal
    Brian Huffines
Berda & Charles Soon Chan
Memorial Scholarship
    Leonard Brewer
Chillman Prize:
- 1st place
    Lian Chang
- 2nd place
    Kyle Martin
Darden Award
    Shelley Pottorf, Diana
    Davis

Making the Zoohemic Cake,
commissioned by Robert
Mangurian and Mary-Ann Ray

Edward B Arrants Award
    Tillie Hatcher
Gene Hackerman Award
(undergraduate)
    Julia Ebner, Nicole Mellado
John Crowder Traveling
Fellowship
    Joseph Meppelink
John T Mitchell Traveling
Fellowship
    Laura Dougherty
Louis Sudler Prize in the Arts
    Christy Raber
Margaret Everson Fossi
Traveling Fellowship:
- 1st place
    Lucia Cheung
- 2nd place
    Rusty Walker
Mary Ellen Hale Lovett
Traveling Fellowship
(graduate)
    Dawn Finley
Mary Ellen Hale Lovett
Traveling Fellowship
(undergraduate)
    Tillie Hatcher, Justus Kes-
    sler, Kyle Martin
Mary Ellen Hale Lovett
Endowed Traveling
Scholarship through the Art &
Art History Department
    Leslie Witt
MN Davidson Fellowship
    Christy Raber
Morris R Pitman Award in
Architecture
    Ana Miljacki

Parrish Traveling Fellowship
(through Weiss College)
    Elizabeth Maletz
Peter I Karp Traveling
Fellowship
    Hite Billes
Ralph S Herman Memorial
Scholarship
    Theodore Calvin, Irene Chu
Rice Visionary Project
    Brian Heiss, Michael
    Morrow
Tau Sigma Delta
    Theodore Calvin, Lian
    Chang, Julia Ebner, Tillie
    Hatcher, Justus Kessler,
    Christy Raber
Texas Architectural Founda-
tion Scholarships:
- Association Administrators
& Consultants, Inc.
    Annatina Schneider
- Paul & Katie Stein
Scholarship
    Itohan Osayimwese
- Grayson Gill Memorial
Scholarship
    Cine Ostrow
- Jesse H Jones Scholarship
    Heidi McDowell
- San Antonio Conservation
Society Award
    Brett Zamore
William Ward Watkin Awards:
- Mary Alice Elliott Award
    Kyle Martin
- Honorable Mention
    David Cunningham, Christy
    Raber

- Rosemary Watkin Barrick
Traveling Fellowship, 2nd
place
    Lian Chang
- William Ward Watkin
Traveling Fellowship
    Jennifer Ferng

Thesis Titles

Krista Armstrong—
    *Exploiting the Edge:
    Infrastructure and
    Development of Sandia
    Pueblo's Southern Border*
Jonathan Baron—
    Measures of Awkwardness
Blaine Brownell—
    *Infratecture: The
    Implementation of a
    Business Substation
    Prototype in the Port of
    Nagoya, Japan*
Luke Bulman—
    *Through Inside: Static
    Distorters of the 24 Hour
    Cycle, An Economic Living
    Toy, 1 Thesis in 6 Pieces*
William Craig—
    *The Road Less Traveled:
    Proposed Additions to the
    Natchez Trace Parkway*
Andrew Cruse—
    The City is Not Architecture
Diana Davis—
    *Architecture of Pestilence:
    Smallpox, Tuberculosis,
    and the Spatial Control of
    Epidemic Disease*
Branden Hookway—
    *Pandemonium: An Essay
    on Predation and
    Modernity*
Gene Johnston—
    *American Wall: The
    Investigation, Evolution,
    and Implementation of an
    Alternative Building System*
Cathryn King—
    *An Architecture of
    Accessibility: An Urban
    House for a Small
    Midwestern Town*
Mihail Lari—
    *Appropriate Housing
    Solutions for the Fast
    Growing Middle Class in
    Karachi*
Li Hu—
    The Edge of City
Craig McCormick—
    *The Image of Space/Space
    of the Image*

James Eric Phillips—
Conflicting Systems: A Mediation of the Natural, the Man-Made, and the In-Between
Michelle Pottorf—
Beating the Bounds
Kimberly Shoemake—
Through Inside: Static Distorters of the 24 Hour Cycle, An Economic Living Toy, 1 Thesis in 6 Pieces
Michael Sweebe—
Fluxbau Architects
Brett Terpeluk—
The Garden in the Machine: Rethinking Nature and History in the Post-Industrial Landscape
Benjamin Thorne—
Tearing A Cleft in the Continuous Surface of Reality

Lectures

01.16
Stan Allen
Recent Work

02.23
Sheila Kennedy
Recent Work

03.09
Ted Krueger
Recent Work

04.13
Sulan Kolatan
Recent Work

04.16
Aaron Betsky
Recent Work

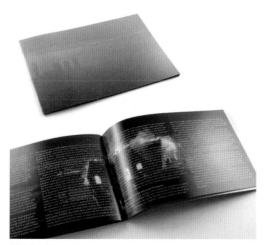

RSA Catalog, 1998

09.08
Josep Muntanola
Professor, Universitat Politecnia de Catalunya, Barcelona
Dialogics of Architecture: the Catalan Experience

09.09
Magda Saura
Professor, Universitat Politecnia de Catalunya, Barcelona
The Architecture of Urban Form

09.21
Peter Cook
Visiting Cullinan Professor in Architecture; Head of Architecture at the Bartlett School of Built Environment at University College, London
Tongue, Claws and Tail

10.28
Kevin Daly and Chris Genik
Principals, Daly, Genik Architects, Long Angeles
Catalog

11.02
James Corner
Associate Professor, University of Pennsylvania, Philadelphia
Disposition

11.09
Dana Cuff
Associate Professor, University of California, Los Angeles
The Provisional City

11.18
Jan Kaplicky
Principal, Future Systems, London
Future Systems: 300 Slides

12.08
Michael Maltzan
Principal, Michael Maltzan Architecture, Inc., Los Angeles
Recently

12.09
Peter Cook
Visiting Cullinan Professor in Architecture; Head of Architecture at the Bartlett School of Built Environment at University College, London
Furry Friends

Exhibitions

Oct 23 – Nov 6
The Eichler Homes: Building the California Dream

Sep 18 – Oct 2
Peter Cook: Tongue, Claws and Tail

Publications

AAR 26
Louis I. Kahn: Talks with Students
Peter C. Papademetriou, editor
Second edition, Princeton Architectural Press

1999

Graduates
M.ARCH.
Joonsuk Ahn
Andrew Shannon Albers
Brian Kelly Burke
YimFunLucia Cheung
Gerard K.H. Chong
Laura Crystal Dougherty
Carlos Eduardo Fighetti

Dawn Finley
Lynn Lucille Fisher
Timothy Brooks Gordon
William Kelly Hall
James Richard Horn
Eliza Howard
Ana Miljacki
Pamela Frances Samuels
David Michael Sisson
Mary Ann Springer
Alane Lynette Truitt
Russell Thompson Walker
Feng Zu
Brett Elliot Zamore

B.ARCH
Aline Nicole Cautis
Craig Allen Eigenberg
Meredith Sue Elbaum
Cedra Manya Ginsburg
Omayya Katarina Kanafani
Christina Sun Lee
Jonathan Clark McNeal
John Helmut Mueller
Cine Justine Ostrow
Thomas Patrick Parker
Nellie Loftus Reid
Annatina Barbara Schneider
George Soo
John Edward Theobald Jr.
Phirozeshah Rumi Titina
Richard Samuel Weiss

Faculty
Tim Barry
Lecturer
John Biln
Cullinan Professor
David Brown
Assistant Professor
Luke Bulman
Visiting Critic
Tom Buresh
Visiting Cullinan Professor
William T. Cannady
Professor
John J. Casbarian
Associate Dean and Professor
Louis DeLaura
Lecturer
Farès el-Dahdah
Assistant Professor
Dawn Finley
Wortham Fellow
Alan Fleishacker
Lecturer
Stephen Fox
Lecturer
James Furr
Lecturer

282

Sleepers, 1998/99

Nonya Grenader
  Visiting Critic
David Guthrie
  Visiting Critic
Carlos Jiménez
  Assistant Professor
Donna Kacmar
  Wortham Fellow
Keith Krumwiede
  Caudill Assistant Professor
Sanford Kwinter
  Associate Professor
Nana Last
  Assistant Professor
Lars Lerup
  Dean and William Ward

  Watkin Professor
Tom Lord
  Lecturer
Robert Mangurian
  Visiting Cullinan Professor
Bruce Mau
  Visiting Cullinan Professor
Chris Nichols
  Lecturer
Mark Oberholzer
  Lecturer
Douglas Oliver
  Visiting Critic
Spencer Parsons
  Associate Professor

Albert Pope
  Wortham Associate
  Professor
Mary-Ann Ray
  Visiting Cullinan Professor
Renny Ramakers
  Visiting Cullinan Professor
Danny Samuels
  Smith Professor
Felicity Scott
  Lecturer
Kimberly Shoemake
  Visiting Critic
Alex Wall
  Visiting Critic

Mark Wamble
  Brochstein Visiting
  Assistant Professor
Frank White
  Lecturer
Walter Widrig
  Associate Professor
William Williams
  Brochstein Visiting
  Assistant Professor
Gordon Wittenberg, AIA
  Professor

Staff
Doris Anderson
  School Administrator
Luke Bulman
  Director of Publications
  and Exhibitions
Hans Krause
  Information Technology
  Specialist
Amanda Lytz
  Program Administrator,
  RDA
Kathleen Roberts
  Graduate Coordinator
Elaine Sebring
  Accounting Assistant
Mitchell Shields
  Managing Editor, Cite

Kimberly Shoemake
Director of Publications
and Exhibitions
Mary Swift
RDA Records Coordinator
Linda Sylvan
Executive Director, RDA
Janet Wheeler
Staff Assistant
Diania Williams
Receptionist

Awards

AIA School Medal
Blair Payson
AIA School Certificate
Jill Dau
Alpha Rho Chi Medal
Tony Hron
Berda & Charles Soon Chan
Memorial Scholarship
Phil Schmunk
Chillman Prize:
- 1st place
Leslie Witt
- 2nd place
Elizabeth Maletz, Joshua
Roberts
Darden Award
Lucia Cheung, Ana Miljacki
Edward B Arrants Award
Gloria Leung
Gene Hackerman Award
(undergraduate)
Kirsten Kinzer, Skye Smith
John Crowder Traveling
Fellowship
Brian Heiss
John T Mitchell Traveling
Fellowship
Michael Morrow
Margaret Everson Fossi
Traveling Fellowship:
- 1st place
project by Kent Fitzsimons,
Jon McNeil
- 2nd place
project by Christina Lee &
Phiroze Titina

Mary Ellen Hale Lovett
Traveling Fellowship
(graduate)
Elizabeth McQuitty, Alex
O'Briant
Mary Ellen Hale Lovett
Traveling Fellowship
(undergraduate)
Jonathan Cherry, Tony
Hron, Elizabeth Maletz
MN Davidson Fellowship
Blair Payson
Morris R Pitman Award in
Architecture
Onezieme Mouton
Ralph S Herman Memorial
Scholarship
Leonard Brewer, Martin
Edwards
Rice Visionary Project
David Sisson
Tau Sigma Delta
Elena Bresciani, Jill Dau,
Elizabeth Maletz, Blair
Payson, Joo Teng, Kindra
Welch, Leslie Witt
Texas Architectural
Foundation Scholarships:
- Association Administrators
& Consultants, Inc.
Irene Chu
- O'Neil Ford Traveling
Fellowship
Christy Raber
- Jesse H Jones Scholarship
Kyle Martin
William Ward Watkin Awards:
- Mary Alice Elliott Award
Cathryn Minium
- Honorable Mention
Jonathan Cherry, Martin
Edwards, Gloria Leung,
Elizabeth Maletz, Blair
Payson
- Rosemary Watkin Barrick
Traveling Fellowship, 2nd
place
Elena Bresciani

- William Ward Watkin Travel-
ing Fellowship
Jill Dau
Ziegler Cooper Award in
Architecture
Justus Kessler

Thesis Titles

Joon Suk Ahn—
Urban Acupuncture: Urban
Park for Houston Down-
town Tunnel System
Andrew Albers—
Many, Many, Many, Many,
Parking Spaces
Brian Burke—
Symbiosis
Lucia Cheung—
Capturing the City/
Spatializing the Captured:
An Animated Documentary
of Hong Kong
Gerard Chong—
Three Bridges and a River
Laura Dougherty—
Starting with Seven
Suburban Houses
Carlos Fighetti—
The Collapsible House
Dawn Finley—
Capsizing the Flagship: A
Study in PHARMETICS
Lynn Fisher—
Amphibious Landscapes
Timothy Gordon—
Aurorium: The Architecture
of a Phenonmenonn
William Hall—
Designing the Store-
Bought Spec-Built Dream
James Horn—
Modulating Sound and
Motion: Electronic and
Physical Membranes for
Urban Dwellers
Eliza Howard—
Immersion
Ana Miljacki—
Incorporaiding City:
Drawing the Belgrade

Rejected poster concept, 1999

Protest 1996/97
David Sisson—
Supaspace: An Exploration
of Architectural Space in
Co-operative Networked
Hyperreal Gaming
Environments
Mary Springer—
washateria/cafeteria,
laundromat/automat
Alane Truitt—
Big Space, Little Place and
11 Retro-fit, Futur-fit
Strategies for Emerging
Airports
Russell Walker—
One room, One buildings,
4 Spaces a Subtext:
Finding the Extraordinary
in the Ordinary
Feng Xu—
Abstraction and Reinter-
pretation in Architecture
Brett Zamore—
House 00

Lectures

02.11
LaMa Architects
Martha LaGess and Michael
McNamara
Letter from Britain

02.15
Abidin Jusno
Post Doctoral Fellow at the
International Center for Ad-
vanced Studies at New York
University
Embodied Nation, Vanish-
ing State: The Making and

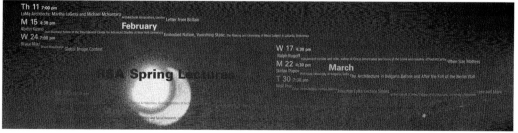

RSA Events card, Spring 1999

RSA Events poster, Fall 1999

*Unmaking of Mass Subject in
Jakarta, Indonesia*

02.24
Bruce Mau
Bruce Mau Design
Global Image Context

03.17
Ralph Rugoff
Independent curator and critic
When Size Matters

03.19
Dolf Schnebli
Dolf Schnebli Architects and
Partner, SAM Architects,
Zurich, Switzerland
*The Patience to be
Contemporary for 49 Years*

03.22
Stefan Popov
Professor, University of
Bulgaria, Sofia
*The Architecture in Bulgaria
Before and After the Fall of
the Berlin Wall*

03.30
Wolf Prix
Coop Himmelb(l)au, Vienna,
Austria
Less and More

04.05
Millika Bose
Post Doctoral Scholar, Ph.D.
Program, College of Archi-
tecture, Georgia Institute of
Technology, Atlanta
*Women's Work Women's
Spaces: A Socio-spatial*

*Analysis of the Slums of
Calcutta, India*

04.14
Edward Soja
Professor of Urban Studies
at the School of Public Policy
and Social Research,
University of California, Los
Angeles
*Thirdspace: Expanding the
Scope of the Geographical
Imagination*

09.20
Bernard Khoury
Interdesign, Beirut

09.27
Mark Linnemann
NL Architects, Amsterdam

10.04
George Ranalli
Principal, George Ranalli
Architects, New York; Dean,
School of Architecture of City
College, CUNY
*Modern Architecture:
Sensuality for the New Age*

10.11
Tom Buresh
Visiting Cullinan Chair, Rice
School of Architecture,
Guthrie + Buresh Architects,
Los Angeles
Programmatic Instability

10.25
Javier Perez-Gil Salcido
Architect, Mexico City
Design: Never-ending Story

11.01
Renny Ramakers
Visiting Cullinan Chair, Rice
School of Architecture, Droog
Design, Amsterdam
Droog Design

11.08
Javier Sanchez
Higuera + Sanchez
Architects, Mexico City
1999 in 1926

11.15
Jose Antonio Aldrete-Haas
Architect, Mexico City
Stones and Half Light

12.01
Constance M. Adams
Space Architect/Human
Factors Engineer, Lockheed
Martin Space Operations
Company, Houston

Final reviews, 1999

Space Architecture: Building
the Future

Frederick Turner
Visiting Cullinan Chair, Rice
School of Architecture;
Founders Professor of Arts
and Humanities, University of
Texas at Dallas
*Natural Classicism: How the
Past Breaks the Shackles
of the Present to Create the
Future*
10.05 – *Beauty, The Cosmo-
logical Constant*
10.06 – *Art in the Age of the
Charm Industries*
10.07 – *Ecological Turbulence
and the New Arcadia*

Edward Dimendberg
Visiting Cullinan Chair, Rice
School of Architecture,
Professor of Film and Video,
and Germanic Languages
and Literatures, University of
Michigan
*After Night Falls: Post-1939
American Urbanism and
Film Noir*
11.04 – *Core Reflections*
11.05 – *Film Noir*
11.11 – *Naked Cities*
11.12 – *Peripheral Visions*

Publications
AAR 37
Pandemonium
Branden Hookway, edited and
presented by Sanford Kwinter
and Bruce Mau

Princeton Architectural Press

AAR 38
Wrapper
Robert Mangurian and Mary
Ann Ray
William Stout Publishers

2000

Graduates
M.ARCH.
Ernesto David Alfara
Aaron Lane Casey
Christopher Matthew Casey
Maria Del Carmen Cruz
Juan Kent Fitzsimons
Brian Wesley Heiss
Jaime A. Lara
Ali Sabet Mahjouri
Joseph Edwin Meppelink
Lee N. Moreau
Michael Miller Morrow
Isabel Rios

B.ARCH
Darshan Amrit
Joseph Hite Billes
Alana Wynne Blum
Loretta Ann Bork
Theodore Osborn Calvin
Lian Bee Chang
Irene I. Chu
David M. Cunningham
Julia Marie Ebner
Jana Jean Edelbrock
Jennifer Hsiao-Mei Ferng
Tilly Suemac Fox Hatcher
James Brian Huffines
Justus Nathaniel Kessler
Mark Stuart Knoke
Lucy Jane Malone
Kyle Layne Martin
Nicole A. Mellando
Christianna Irene Raber
Phirozeshah Rumi Titina

Faculty
Tim Barry
    Lecturer
Aaron Betsky
    Visiting Cullinan Professor
John Biln
    Associate Professor
David Brown
    Assistant Professor
Luke Bulman
    Visiting Critic
William T. Cannady
    Professor

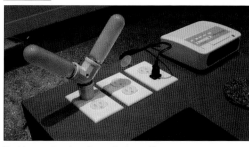

Electric carpet and appliances by Logan Ray

John J. Casbarian
    *Associate Dean and
    Professor*
Louis DeLaura
    Lecturer
Farès el-Dahdah
    Assistant Professor
Dawn Finley
    Visiting Critic
Alan Fleishacker
    Lecturer
Stephen Fox
    Lecturer
James Furr
    Lecturer
Nonya Grenader
    Visiting Critic
David Guthrie
    Visiting Critic
Brian Heiss
    Wortham Fellow
Carlos Jiménez
    Associate Professor
Keith Krumwiede
    Caudill Assistant Professor
Sanford Kwinter
    Associate Professor
Nana Last
    Assistant Professor
Lars Lerup
    *Dean and William Ward
    Watkin Professor*
Tom Lord
    Lecturer
Robert Mangurian
    Visiting Cullinan Professor
Chris Nichols
    Lecturer
Mark Oberholzer
    Lecturer

RSA Catalog, 2000

Douglas Oliver
    Cullinan Professor
Spencer Parsons
    Associate Professor
Jason Payne
    *Brochstein Visiting
    Assistant Professor*
Albert Pope
    *Wortham Associate
    Professor*
Mary-Ann Ray
    Visiting Cullinan Professor
Danny Samuels
    Smith Professor
Dan Sherer
    Visiting Assistant Professor
Kimberly Shoemake
    Visiting Critic
Rives Taylor
    Visiting Lecturer
Jacob van Rijs
    Visiting Cullinan Professor
Mark Wamble
    *Brochstein Visiting
    Assistant Professor*
Frank White
    Lecturer
William Williams
    Visiting Critic
Gordon Wittenberg
    Professor
Kramer Woodard
    Visiting Cullinan Professor

Staff
Doris Anderson
    School Administrator
Luke Bulman
    *Director of Publications
    and Exhibitions*
Rob Christie
    Woodshop Manager
Hans Krause
    *Information Technology
    Specialist*
Amanda Lytz
    *Program Administrator,
    RDA*
Kathleen Roberts
    Graduate Coordinator

RSA Events poster, Spring 2000

Elaine Sebring
  Accounting Assistant
Mitchell Shields
  Managing Editor, Cite
Kimberly Shoemake
  Director of Publications
  and Exhibitions
Mary Swift
  RDA Records Coordinator
Linda Sylvan
  Executive Director, RDA
Janet Wheeler
  Executive Assistant
Diania Williams
  Receptionist

Awards

AIA/AAF Scholarship
  Elizabeth Maletz
AIA School Medal
  Alex Knapp
AIA School Certificate
  Bill Rankin
Alpha Rho Chi Medal
  Sara Stevens

Berda & Charles Soon Chan
Memorial Scholarship
  Chris Kimball
Chillman Prize:
- 1st place
  Sara Stevens
- 2nd place
  Bill Rankin, Kiyomi
  Troemner
Darden Award
  Michael Morrow
Edward B Arrants Award
  Phil Schmunk
Gene Hackerman Award
(graduate)
  Jessica Young
Gene Hackerman Award
(undergraduate)
  Kiyomi Troemner, Maureen
  Hull
John Crowder Traveling
Fellowship
  Gunnar Hartmann
John T Mitchell Traveling
Fellowship
  Angela Loughry

Margaret Everson Fossi
Traveling Fellowship:
- 1st place
  Wyatt Frantom
- 2nd place
  Alex O'Briant & Todd Van
  Varick
- 2nd place
  class project by: Darshan
  Amrit, Hite Billes, Theodore
  Calvin, Lian Chang, Wyatt
  Frantom, Tilly Hatcher,
  Brian Huffines, Justus Kes-
  sler, Peter Koehler, Angela
  loughry, Kyle Martin, Nicki
  Mellado
Mary Ellen Hale Lovett
Traveling Fellowship
(graduate)
  Peter Klein, Cemre
  Durusoy, Todd Van Varick
Mary Ellen Hale Lovett
Traveling Fellowship
(undergraduate)
  Alex Knapp, Taryn Kinney,
  Bill Rankin, Brett Bentson,
  Emily Estes
MN Davidson Fellowship
  Phil Schmunk
Morris R Pitman Award in
Architecture
  Nik Nikolav
Ralph S Herman Memorial
Scholarship
  Brenna Smith, Nu Nu
  Chang, Sara Stevens
Rice Visionary Project
  Darshan Amrit

Tau Sigma Delta
  Brett Bentson, Emily Estes,
  Taryn Kinney, Alex Knapp,
  Bill Rankin, Phil Schmunk
Texas Architectural
Foundation Scholarships:
- Jesse H Jones Scholarship
  Elizabeth Maletz, Blair
  Payson
- Southwest Terrazzo
Association Scholarship
  Elena Bresciani
- San Antonio Conservation
Society Award
  Itohan Osayimwese
William Ward Watkin Awards:
- Mary Alice Elliott Award
  Alex Knapp
- Rosemary Watkin Barrick
Traveling Fellowship, 2nd
place
  Michele Stevenson
- William Ward Watkin
Traveling Fellowship
  Brett Bentson
Ziegler Cooper Award in
Architecture
  Jill Dau

RSA Thesis Book, 2000, by Alex
O'Briant and Todd van Varick

Thesis Titles

Ernesto Alfaro—
  Nuevo Parque Central de
  la Emergencia Nacional,
  Para las Ciudades de
  Tegucigalpa y
  Comayaguela
Aaron Casey—
  Representing Occulted
  Projections: Cultivating

Final reviews poster, Spring 2000

RSA Events poster, Fall 2000

Anamorphic Visions in the Paradise Garden
Chris Casey—
Boxes
Maria del Carmen Cruz—
Compressed Strip: The Deceleration of the Automobile
Juan Kent Fitzsimons—
On the Social Reception of Material Form and Space, or the SUV in the Melee
Brian Wesley Heiss—
Convergence
Jaime Lara—
"Tactic" as a Subversive Act to the "Proper" or "Institutional"
Ali Mahjouri—
There When Hear: Sound, Space and Chance
Joseph Meppelink—
Walltype
Lee Moreau—
Houston Inside, Slowly

Michael Morrow—
mtP: An Urban Tactic
Isabel Rios—
The Ethereal Surface: The Act of Making (Painting + Construction)

Lectures

02.21
Howard Davies
Principal, Atelier Big City, Montreal
Spectacular Subtleties

03.01
Robert Mangurian and Mary-Ann Ray
Visiting Professors, Rice School of Architecture; Principals, Studio Works, Los Angeles
Some Directive for Moving into (this) Next Century or, "You Can't Go Wrong, but it is

Hard to Go Right" Parts One and Two

03. 22
Laurie Hawkinson
Principal, Smith-Miller + Hawkinson Architects, New York
Between Spaces

03.27
Eric Owen Moss
Principal, Eric Owen Moss Architects, Los Angeles
Through a Glass Darkly

04.06
Krzysztof Wodiczko
Artist, New York
Critical Vehicles

04.26
Norman Bryson
Chair of the History and Theory of Art Slade School of Fine Art, University College, London
Seurat and the Scene of Drawing

09.11
Bernardo Gomez-Pimienta
TEN Arquitectos, Mexico City
Architecture of Light

09.18
Aaron Betsky
Craig Francis Cullinan Visiting Professor, Rice School of

Architecture; San Francisco Museum of Modern Art, San Franciso
Architecture Must Burn

10.09
Sean Griffiths
FAT (Fashion, Architecture, Taste), London
Taste Not Space

10.23
Kramer Woodard
Craig Francis Cullinan Visiting Professor, Rice School of Architecture; KEW Architects, Albuquerque, NM
Un-Framing

11.06
Peter Wilson
Architekturburo Bolles+Wilson, Munster, Germany
Mass in the Age of Media

1.13
Donald Bates
Lab Architecture Studio, Melbourne, Australia
Coherence and Difference

12.06
Jacob van Rijs
Craig Francis Cullinan Visiting Professor, Rice School of Architecture; MVRDV, Rotterdam, The Netherlands
KM3/3D City

Exhibitions
200 Years of Dutch Architecture

Digital Design at Gensler

Nuova Architettura: Young Italian Architects

2001

Graduates
M.ARCH.
Manfred Barboza
Jill Nai-Chien Cheng
Cemre Durusoy
Wyatt Jacob Frantom
Kevin Rogers Guarnotta
Gunnar Hartmann
Peter John Koehler
Michael Pavel Kuchkovsky

Long empty hallway, Anderson Hall

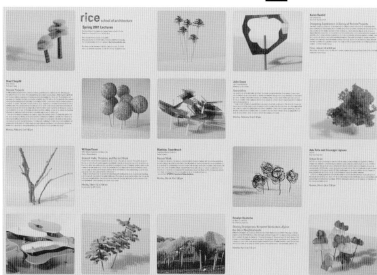

288

RSA Events poster, Spring 2001

Dongxiao Liu
Angela Leigh Loughry
Onezieme Mouton
Alex Kendall O'Briant
Itohan Osayimwese
Logan Adrian Ray
Marie Ivette Rodgriguez
Todd Roy Van Varick
Qiao Zhang

B.ARCH
Leonard Daniel Rehkop
Brewer
Jonathan Sher Cherry
Jill Ann Dau
John Martin Edwards Jr.
Laura Virginia Feist
Anthony J Hron
Kirsten Lee Kinzer

Gloria Dik-Sze Leung
Elizabeth Claire Maletz
Cathryn Janelle Minium
Blair Laurence Payson
Skye Kimberly Smith
Joo Chong Teng
Kindra Anne Welch
Leslie Rae Witt

Faculty
Larry Albert
Visiting Critic
Tim Barry
Lecturer
John Biln
Associate Professor
David Brown
Assistant Professor

Luke Bulman
Visiting Critic
Brian Burke
Visiting Critic
William T. Cannady
Professor
John J. Casbarian
*Associate Dean and
Professor*
Louis DeLaura
Lecturer

Edward Eigen
Visiting Assistant Professor
Fares el-Dahdah
Assistant Professor
Dawn Finley
Assistant Professor
Alan Fleishacker
Lecturer
Stephen Fox
Lecturer
James Furr
Lecturer
Nonya Grenader
Visiting Critic
David Guthrie
Visiting Critic
Brian Heiss
*Wortham Fellow,
Visiting Critic*
Carlos Jiménez
Associate Professor
Keith Krumwiede
Assistant Professor
Sanford Kwinter
Associate Professor
Nana Last
Assistant Professor
Lars Lerup
*Dean and William Ward
Watkin Professor*
Tom Lord
Lecturer
Joe Meppelink
Lecturer
Chris Nichols
Lecturer
Maria Nystrom-Reutersward
Visiting Cullinan Professor
Mark Oberholzer
Lecturer
Alex O'Briant
Wortham Fellow
Douglas Oliver
*Brochstein Visiting
Assistant Professor*
Spencer Parsons
Associate Professor
Jason Payne
*Brochstein Visiting
Assistant Professor*
Albert Pope
*Wortham Associate
Professor*
Danny Samuels
Smith Professor
Blair Satterfield
Visiting Critic
David Sisson
Lecturer
Robert Somol
Visiting Cullinan Professor

Karim Rashid speaking about his installation at Rice Gallery

Rives Taylor
    Visiting Lecturer
Mark Wamble
    Cullinan Professor
Frank White
    Lecturer
Kerry Whitehead
    Visiting Critic
William Williams
    Visiting Critic
Gordon Wittenberg
    Professor

Staff

Doris Anderson
    School Administrator
Luke Bulman
    Director of Publications
    and Exhibitions
Rob Christie
    Woodshop Manager
Lisa Gray
    Managing Editor, Cite
Hans Krause
    Information Technology
    Specialist
Trang Phan
    Program Administrator,
    RDA
Kathleen Roberts
    Graduate Coordinator
Elaine Sebring
    Accounting Assistant
Kimberly Shoemake
    Director of Publications
    and Exhibitions

Mary Swift
    RDA Records Coordinator
Linda Sylvan
    Executive Director, RDA
Janet Wheeler
    Executive Assistant
Diania Williams
    Receptionist

Awards

AIA School Medal
    Chris Kimball
AIA School Certificate
    Gary Tran
Alpha Rho Chi Medal
    Delia Wendel
Berda & Charles Soon Chan
Memorial Scholarship
    Kerim Demirkan
Chillman Prize:
- 1st place
    Joseph Gabriel
- 2nd place
    Emily Kirkland
- Honorable Mention
    Chris Kimball
Darden Award
    Peter Koehler, Angela
    Loughry
Edward B Arrants Award
    Justin Boone
Gene Hackerman Award
(graduate)
    Nicole Blair
Gene Hackerman Award
(undergraduate)
    Emily Kirkland
John Crowder Traveling
Fellowship
    Kayte Young
John T Mitchell Traveling
Fellowship
    Scott Allen
Louis Sudler Prize in the Arts
    Christopher Kimball
Margaret Everson Fossi
Traveling Fellowship:
- 1st place
    Jessica Young

Mary Ellen Hale Lovett
Traveling Fellowship
(graduate)
    Adele Houghton, David
    Stockwell, Janelle Gunther
Mary Ellen Hale Lovett
Traveling Fellowship
(undergraduate)
    Jared Fisher, Kyle
    Humphries, Delia Wendel,
    Gary Tran
MN Davidson Fellowship
    Katie Bennett
Morris R Pitman Award in
Architecture
    Ken Andrews
Ralph S Herman Memorial
Scholarship
    Chris Kimball
Rice Visionary Project
    Elizabeth McQuitty
Tau Sigma Delta
    Miriam Bently, Justin
    Boone, Jared Fisher,
    Joseph Gabriel, Chris
    Kimball, Gary Tran
Texas Architectural
Foundation Scholarships:
- Jesse H Jones Scholarship
    Emily Estes
- Fay Spencer Scholarship
    Sara Stevens
William Ward Watkin Awards:
- Mary Alice Elliott Award
    Delia Wendel
- Honorable Mention
    Carina Dullum, Jared
    Fisher
- Rosemary Watkin Barrick
Traveling Fellowship, 3rd
place
    Kyle Humphries
- Rosemary Watkin Barrick
Traveling Fellowship, 2nd
place
    Chris Starkey
- William Ward Watkin
Traveling Fellowship
    Katie Bennett
Ziegler Cooper Award in
Architecture
    Alex Knapp

Thesis Titles

Manfred Barboza—
    Patterns + Systems: Green
    Parking Systems
Cemre Durusoy—
    Gezi Park Kampanyasi:
    Resurfacing an Urban
    Park/Istanbul/2002-2006

RSA Thesis Book, 2001, by
Scott Allen and Jessica Young

Jill Cheng—
    The Fluid Lattice
Wyatt Frantom—
    Mobilization of the Multi-
    Tasking Machine: Up-
    Cycling the Interstate and
    Defense Highways
Kevin Guarnotta—
    Event Proposed in the
    Form
Gunnar Hartmann—
    A Perceptual Device:
    Locus Moment
Peter Koehler—
    namebrandcorporation
    (venture based informa
    tion/technology & new
    media startup incubator
    infrastructure)
Michael Kuchkovsky—
    Farm Worker Housing/
    Tourist Shelter in Napa
    Valley
Dongxiao Liu—
    Six Houses

Alfred Jacoby exhibition card

Poster for *Moneo: A Celebration*, the 3rd Kennon Symposium, 2001

Angela Loughry—
    Seeing Open Space: An
    Examination of a Spatial
    Anti-Body
Onezieme Mouton—
    protoHouse: Searching For
    New Form
Alex O'Briant—
    Introducing the LiQUid
    House
Itohan Osayimwase—
    Global/Local—
    (Re)Construction and (Re)
    Spatialization in the Post-
    Apartheid Condition
Logan Ray—
    Hive Systems: Explorations
    into the Possibilities and
    Consequences Of
    Behavioral Programming in
    Architectural Spaces
Maria Rodriguez—
    Fibered Interrogarities
Todd Van Varick—
    House Loops: Upcycling
    the Single-Family House
Qiao Zhang—
    Bookstore/Soft Capsule:
    A Retail Prototype for
    Small Independent
    Business

Lectures

01.26
Karim Rashid
Karim Rashid Inc., New York
Designing Experience:
A Survey of Recent Projects

02.05
Brad Cloepfil
Allied Works, Portland
Recent Projects

02.19
Julie Snow
Julie Snow Architects,
Minneapolis, MN
Assemblies

03.12
William Rawn
William Rawn Associates,
Architects, Inc. Boston
Concert Halls, Theatres, and
Recent Work

03.18
Matthias Sauerbruch
Sauerbruch Hutton
Architects, Berlin, Germany
Recent Work

03.26
Ada Tolla and Giuseppe
Lignano
LOT/EK, New York
Urban Scan

04.09
Rosalyn Deutsche
Art Historian and Critic,
New York
Sharing Strangeness:
Krzysztof Wodiczko's Aegis in
the City of Neighborhoods

09.05
Alfred Jacoby
Alfred Jacoby Architects,
Frankfurt, Germany
Recent Work

10.01
Maria Nystrom
Visiting Cullinan Professor,
Rice School of Architecture
and Industrial Design, Lund
University, Lund, Sweden
A Shortcut via Mars – A
Design Journey

10.11
Bell Hooks
Author, New York
House Art: Merging Public
and Private

10.22
Monica Ponce de Leon
Principal, Office dA, Boston
Recent Works

Frank Lloyd Wright exhibition poster

11.05
Marion Weiss and Michael Manfredi
Principals, Weiss/Manfredi
Architects, New York
Surface/Subsurface

11.26
R. E. Somol
Visiting Cullinan Professor,
Rice School of Architecture;
Assistant Professor, Depart-
ment of Architecture and
Urban Design, UCLA;
Principal, PXS, Los Angeles
Absolut® Landscape

Exhibitions
September 6- November 30
In a New Spirit: Synagogues of Germany
The Work of Alfred Jacoby

March 30 - April 20
Frank Lloyd Wright and Stanley Marcus: a Virtual House

Kennon Symposium
Moneo: A Celebration
The 3rd Kennon Symposium
March 24
Organized by Carlos Jimenez

Participants:
Luis Fernandez Galiano,
Stephen Fox, Kenneth
Frampton, Carlos Jimenez,
Lars Lerup, Enrique Miralles,
Stanley Saitowitz, Jorge
Silvetti, Martha Thorne, Elias
Torres, and Kevin Kennon

2002

Graduates
M.ARCH.
Scott Hosmer Allen
David Allan DaPonte
Janelle Marie Gunther
Jessica Payne Harner
Benjamin Herrold Koush
Kwanhee Lee
Jyonghwa Lim
Alistair Colin Lucks
Steven T. Maynard
Elizabeth Burns McQuitty
Nikolai Panteleev Nikolov
JinYeob Park
Minsik Park

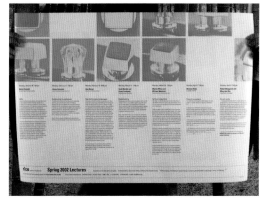

RSA Events poster, Spring 2002

Fani Qano
Jessica Leslie Young

B.ARCH
Brett Bentson
Justin Lee Boone
NuNu Chang
Emily L. Estes
Jonathan Charles Fountain
Maureen Francis Hull
Laura Marie Johnson
Taryn Elyse Kinney
Alexander Ward Nathaniel Knapp
Jeffrey Michael Koffler
Emily Rae Kuchenrither
Jason Arden Millhouse
Katherine Elizabeth Newman
Christina Andrea Noble
William Joseph Rankin
Philip Andrew Schmunk
Sara Kathryn Stevens
Michelle Clare Stevenson
Kiyomi Kohatsu Troemner

Faculty
Larry Albert
Visiting Critic
John Biln
Associate Professor

David Brown
Assistant Professor
Brian Burke
Visiting Critic
William T. Cannady
Professor
John J. Casbarian
Associate Dean and Professor
Brad Cloepfil
Visiting Cullinan Professor
Louis DeLaura
Lecturer

Design charette with students from Lund, Sweden

Farès el-Dahdah
Assistant Professor
Dawn Finley
Assistant Professor
J. Kent Fitzsimons
Assistant Director, Rice School of Architecture-Paris
Alan Fleishacker
Lecturer
Stephen Fox
Lecturer
James Furr
Lecturer
Nonya Grenader
Lecturer
David Guthrie
Visiting Critic
Brian Heiss
Visiting Critic
Carlos Jiménez
Associate Professor
Keith Krumwiede
Assistant Professor
Sanford Kwinter
Associate Professor
Sean Lally
Wortham Fellow
Nana Last
Assistant Professor
Lars Lerup
Dean and William Ward Watkin Professor
Tom Lord
Lecturer

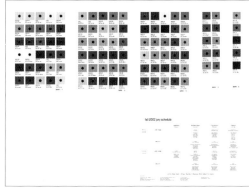

Thesis reviews poster, 2002

Robert Mangurian
  Visiting Cullinan Professor
Michael Morrow
  Visiting Critic
Mark Oberholzer
  Lecturer
Alex O'Briant
  Wortham Fellow
Douglas Oliver
  Brochstein Visiting Assistant Professor
Spencer Parsons
  Associate Professor
Jason Payne
  Assistant Professor
Albert Pope
  Wortham Associate Professor
Mary-Ann Ray
  Visiting Cullinan Professor
Danny Samuels
  Smith Professor
Blair Satterfield
  Visiting Critic
Rives Taylor
  Caudill Visiting Lecturer
Mark Wamble
  Cullinan Professor
Frank White
  Lecturer
Kerry Whitehead
  Visiting Critic
William Williams
  Visiting Critic
Gordon Wittenberg
  Professor

Staff

Doris Anderson
  School Administrator
Luke Bulman
  Director of Publications and Exhibitions
Kent Fitzsimons
  Assistant Director, Rice School of Architecture Paris
Lisa Gray
  Managing Editor, Cite
Hans Krause
  Information Technology Specialist
Chad Loucks
  Woodshop Manager

Kathleen Roberts
  Graduate Coordinator
Carrie Rushing
  Program Administrator, RDA
Elaine Sebring
  Accounting Assistant
Mary Swift
  Membership Coordinator, RDA
Linda Sylvan
  Executive Director, RDA
Lisa Tsokos
  Staff Assistant
Janet Wheeler
  Assistant to the Dean
Diania Williams
  Receptionist

Awards

AIA/AAF Scholarship
  Jared Fisher
AIA School Medal
  David Herman
AIA School Certificate
  Kerim Demirkan
Alpha Rho Chi Medal
  Brian Baldor
Berda & Charles Soon Chan Memorial Scholarship
  Parrish Kyle
Brett Michael Detamore Award in Architecture
  Heidi Werner
Chillman Prize:
- *1st place*
  David Herman

- *2nd place*
  Jennifer Henry
Darden Award
  Elizabeth McQuitty,
  Jessica Young
Edward B Arrants Award
  Heidi Werner
Eleanor & Frank Freed Foundation Traveling Fellowship
  Ben Johanson
Gene Hackerman Award (graduate)
  Naseema Asif
Gene Hackerman Award (undergraduate)
  Gigi Sperber
H Russell Pitman Graduate Fellowship in Architecture
  Kent Fitzsimons
John Crowder Traveling Fellowship
  Lauren Benech, John Montag
John T Mitchell Traveling Fellowship
  Marc Frohn
Louis Sudler Prize in the Arts
  David Herman
Margaret Everson Fossi Traveling Fellowship:
- *1st place*
  Philip Lee
- *2nd place*
  David Stockwell
Mary Ellen Hale Lovett Traveling Fellowship (graduate)

Cope Bailey, Joe Bailey, CJ Hoogland, Brent Linden
Mary Ellen Hale Lovett Traveling Fellowship (undergraduate)
  Kerim Demirkan, Dustin Eshenroder, Jeff Geisinger
MN Davidson Fellowship
  Jennifer Henry
Morris R Pitman Award in Architecture
  Paul Schuette

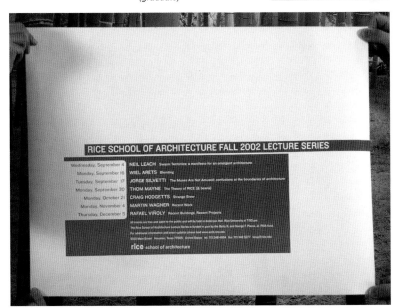

Choose-Your-Own RSA Events poster, Fall 2002

Nikolai Nikolov—
Home-Land
Jin Yeob Park—
Green Void
Minsik Park—
Alternative Spatial
Frameworks in High-
Density Housing
Fani Qano—
Spatial Experiments:
Designing a Space for
Living, Working, Playing
and Sleeping
Jessica Young—
Erasure

Lectures

01.28
Sheila Kennedy
Kennedy/Violich Architects,
Boston
MATx

02.11
James Carpenter
James Carpenter Architects,
New York
Constructing the Ephemeral

02.18
Alan Berger
University of Colorado,Denver
Post-Technological
Landscapes

03.11
Scott Marble and Karen
Fairbanks
Marble Fairbanks, New York
Bootstrapping

03.25
Marion Weiss and Michael
Manfredi
Weiss Manfredi Architects,
New York
Surface/Subsurface

04.01
Michael Rock
2 x 4/AMO, New York
Diagram as Weapon

04.08
Robert Mangurian and
Mary-Ann Ray
Studio Works, Los Angeles
Recent Works

09.04
Neil Leach
Swarm Tectonics: A Manifesto
for an Emergent Architecture

09.16
Wiel Arets
Blending

09.17
Jorge Silvetti
The Muses are not Amused:
Confusions at the Boundaries
of Architecture

09.30
Thom Mayne
The Theory of RICE (and
beans)

10.21
Craig Hodgetts
Strange Brew

11.04
Martin Wagner
Recent Work

12.05
Rafael Vinoly
Recent Buildings, Recent
Projects

Exhibitions

February 18 through March 15
Alan Berger: Reclaiming the
Western American Landscape

Publications

AAR 39
Excluded Middle: Toward a
Reflective Architecture and
Urbanism
Edward Dimendberg
William Stout Publishers

Ralph S Herman Memorial
Scholarship
  Brian Baldor, Ewen Will
Rice Visionary Project
  Brent Linden
Rice Undergraduate Research
Symposium in Architecture
  Seth Clarke
Tau Sigma Delta
  Kerim Demirkan, Dustin
  Eshenroder, Jennifer
  Henry, David Herman,
  Gigi Sperber, Ewen Will
Texas Architectural Founda-
tion Scholarships:
- *Association Administrators*
& Consultants, Inc.
  Gary Tran
- *O'Neil Ford Traveling*
Fellowship
  Giselle Sperber
- *Jesse H Jones Scholarship*
  Chris Kimball
- *E.G. Spencer Memorial*
Scholarship
  Joseph Gabriel
- *Fay Spencer Scholarship*
  Soo Jin Yoo
William Ward Watkin Awards:
- *Honorable Mention*
  Kerim Demirkan, Jessica
  Walitt, Heidi Werner
- *Rosemary Watkin Barrick*
Traveling Fellowship, 3rd
place
  Benjamin Johanson
- *Rosemary Watkin Barrick*
Traveling Fellowship, 2nd
place
  Jennifer Henry
- *William Ward Watkin*
Traveling Fellowship
  David Herman
Ziegler Cooper Award in
Architecture
  Chris Kimball

Thesis Titles

Scott Allen—
The Advantages of Blured
Vision: Uncertainty in
Architectural Production
David Daponte—
Dwelling Engages Dweller
Engages Dwelling
Jessica Harner—
Mel Bochner: Painting
Outside the Frame
Benjamin Koush—
Houston Lives the Life:
Modern Houses in the
Suburbs, 1952-1962
Kwan Hee Lee—
Simplicity and Complexity
through a Progressive
Ordering System
Jyonghwa Lim—
@
Alistair Lucks—
The Demise of the Plan:
New Architecture of the
Real-Time City
Steven Maynard—
You Have Followed Me
Here...
Elizabeth McQuitty—
Structures of Agency:
Contradiction, Parallel,
Paradox

Lars Lerup delivers his semesterly call to arms

RICE SCHOOL OF ARCHITECTURE

SPRING
2003 LECTURE SERIES

FRIDAY, JANUARY 24 AT 5PM □ JASON GRIFFITHS AND ALEX GINO □ GINO GRIFFITHS ARCHITECTS, LONDON □ THESE ARE A FEW OF MY FAVORITE THINGS

MONDAY, FEBRUARY 10 AT 7PM □ OLE BOUMAN □ ARCHIS, AMSTERDAM □ PUBLISHING ARCHITECTURE: CONVERGING PRACTICES

MONDAY, FEBRUARY 24 AT 7PM □ TERENCE RILEY □ MUSEUM OF MODERN ART, NEW YORK □ THIS WILL KILL THAT — ARCHITECTURE AND THE MEDIA

MONDAY, MARCH 3 AT 7PM □ MARK WIGLEY □ SCHOOL OF ARCHITECTURE, COLUMBIA UNIVERSITY, NEW YORK □ HOW OLD IS YOUNG? — THE CONCEPT OF THE YOUNG ARCHITECT

MONDAY, MARCH 17 AT 7PM □ MARIA ELISA COSTA □ ARCHITECT, RIO DE JANEIRO □ BRASILIA IN THE FLESH

WEDNESDAY, MARCH 26 AT 7PM □ SARAH WHITING AND RON WITTE □ WW, CAMBRIDGE □ BOUNCE

MONDAY, APRIL 7 AT 7PM □ LARS SPUYBROEK □ NOX, ROTTERDAM □ MACHINING ARCHITECTURE

All events are free and open to the public and will be held at Anderson Hall on the Rice University campus □ The Spring 2003 Lecture Series is funded in part by the Betty R. and George F. Pierce Jr. FAIA Fund □ For information updates and further information please load www.arch.rice.edu or call 713 348 4864.

rice school of architecture   6100 Main Street   Houston, Texas 77006   USA

RSA Events poster, Spring 2003

2003

Graduates
M.ARCH.
Kenneth Alfred Andrews
Lauren Nicole Benech
Nicole Leeanna Cody Blair
Daniel Stephen Brueggert
Liliana Marcela Garcia
Christopher Joseph Gerrick
Adele Birdsall Houghton
Joshua Isaiah Francis Jones
Namhun Kim
Kyungho Pio Koh
Philip Lee
Norris Alexander Ligon
John Dominic Montag
Victor Manuel Murillo
Karim Khalil Nader
Benjamin Thomas Reavis
Paul Edward Schuette
Kristin Akkerman Schuster
David William Stockwell
Adam J Weiss
Christi Kayte Young
Sven Eric Zbinden
Ozge Zoralioglu

B.ARCH
Katherine Elizabeth Bennett
Miriam Jane Bentley
Carina Mechyl Valerie Coel

Jared Shawn Fisher
Joseph Monroy Gabriel
Kyle Berton Humphries
Christopher Wilson Kimball
Emily Elizabeth Kirkland
Ryan Matthew LeVasseur
Colin Stauss Owen
Brenna Lowrey Smith
Christopher Neal Starkey
Douglas Nevin Subbiondo
Gary Chi Tran
Delia Duong Ba Wendel
Soo Jin Sophie Yoo

Faculty
John Biln
Associate Professor
David Brown
Assistant Professor
William T. Cannady
Professor
John J. Casbarian
Associate Dean and Professor
Louis DeLaura
Lecturer
Farès el-Dahdah
Associate Professor
Dawn Finley
Assistant Professor
J. Kent Fitzsimons
Assistant Director, Rice

2003

School of Architecture-Paris
Alan Fleishacker
Lecturer
Stephen Fox
Lecturer
James Furr
Lecturer
Nonya Grenader
Professor in Practice
David Guthrie
Visiting Critic
Brian Heiss
Visiting Critic
Christopher Hight
Assistant Professor
Richard Ingersoll
Associate Professor
Carlos Jiménez
Associate Professor
Sanford Kwinter
Associate Professor
Sean Lally
Wortham Fellow
Nana Last
Assistant Professor
Lars Lerup
Dean and William Ward Watkin Professor
Tom Lord
Lecturer
Mark Oberholzer
Lecturer
Douglas Oliver
Brochstein Visiting Assistant Professor
Spencer Parsons
Associate Professor
Albert Pope
Wortham Professor
Danny Samuels
Smith Professor
Blair Satterfield
Visiting Critic
Rives Taylor
Caudill Visiting Lecturer
Mark Wamble
Cullinan Professor
Frank White
Lecturer
William Williams
Visiting Critic
Gordon Wittenberg
Professor

Staff
Doris Anderson
School Administrator
Luke Bulman
Director of Publications and Exhibitions

Kent Fitzsimons
Assistant Director, Rice School of Architecture Paris
Lisa Gray
Managing Editor, Cite
Hans Krause
Information Technology Specialist
Chad Loucks
Woodshop Manager
Sara Oussar
Staff Assistant, RDA
Kathleen Roberts
Graduate Coordinator
Carrie Rushing
Program Administrator, RDA
Elaine Sebring
Accounting Assistant
Mary Swift
Membership Coordinator, RDA
Linda Sylvan
Executive Director, RDA
Lisa Tsokos
Staff Assistant
Janet Wheeler
Assistant to the Dean
Lee Wilson
Staff Assistant, RDA
Diania Williams
Receptionist

Awards
AIA/AAF Scholarship
Kerim Demirkan, David Herman
AIA School Medal
David Jefferis
AIA School Certificate
Parrish Kyle
Alpha Rho Chi Medal
Jessica Spiegel
Berda & Charles Soon Chan Memorial Scholarship
Thomas Hardin
Brett Michael Detamore Award in Architecture
Mary Franzosa
Chillman Prize:
- 1st place
Mary Franzosa
- 2nd place
Megan Arendt, Parrish Kyle
Darden Award
Victor Murillo
Edward B Arrants Award
Ryan Indovina

Erin MacKenzie Peck
Freshman Prize in
Architecture
  Etien Santiago
Erin MacKenzie Peck
Architecture Studio Prize
  Erin Porter
Gene Hackerman Award
(graduate)
  Betsy Engler
Gene Hackerman Award
(undergraduate)
  Jessica Spiegel
John Crowder Traveling
Fellowship
  Anthony Sinkewich, Eric
  Leshinsky
John T Mitchell Traveling
Fellowship
  Jason Carney
LF McCollum Fellowship
  Marc Frohn

Louis Sudler Prize in the Arts
  Heather Pfaff
Margaret Everson Fossi
Traveling Fellowship:
- 1st place
  Quyen Luong, Delia Wen-
  del, Kathy Williams
Mary Ellen Hale Lovett
Traveling Fellowship
(graduate)
  John Bacus, Jamie Flatt,
  Reiko Igarashi
Mary Ellen Hale Lovett
Traveling Fellowship
(undergraduate)
  Pranjali Desai, Jared
  Banks, Sharon Floyd
McDermott Fellowship
  Ryan Jones
MN Davidson Fellowship
  Michael Kross

Morris R Pitman Award in
Architecture
  Naseema Asif
Ralph S Herman Memorial
Scholarship
  Parrish Kyle, David Jefferis
Rice Visionary Project
  Philip Lee
Tau Sigma Delta
  Jared Banks, Sharon
  Floyd, Ryan Indovina,
  David Jefferis, Michael
  Kross, Katherine Motchan,
  Heather Pfaff, Jessica
  Spiegel
Texas Architectural
Foundation Scholarships:
- Jesse H Jones Scholarship
  David Herman
- E.G. Spencer Memorial
Scholarship
  David Herman
- Southwest Terrazzo
Association Scholarship
  Jennifer Henry
Watson Fellowship
  Heather Pfaff
William Ward Watkin Awards:
- Mary Alice Elliott Award
  Sara-Ann Logan
- Honorable Mention
  Jared Banks, Sara-Ann
  Logan

- Rosemary Watkin Barrick
Traveling Fellowship, 3rd
place
  Tate Ragland
- Rosemary Watkin Barrick
Traveling Fellowship, 2nd
place
  Seth Clarke
- William Ward Watkin
Traveling Fellowship
  Jing Gu
Ziegler Cooper Award in
Architecture
  Jennifer Henry

Thesis Titles

Kenneth Andrews—
  Catalysis: A Paradigmatic
  Shift in the Production of
  Architectural Morphologies
Lauren Benech—
  Revealing the Trace: or
  How Mr. Grant Mows His
  Lawn
Dan Brueggert—
  Issues in the Develop-
  ment of a Formal Theme –
  or – "How to Make a
  Building Look Good
Liliana Garcia—
  Temporal and Permanent
  Structures

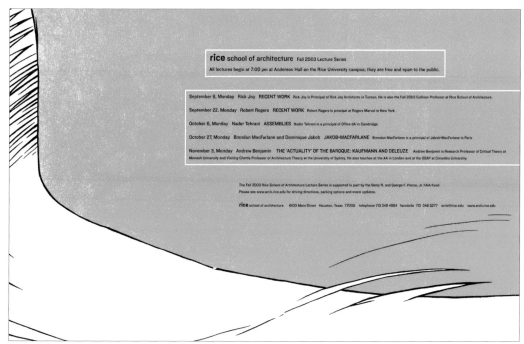

RSA Events card, Fall 2003, inspired by Seuss

Christopher Gerrick—
Fear of the In-Between:
Interstitial "Space in Edgar
Allen Poe's William Wilson
Adele Houghton—
Spatializing Alice, en
passant
Philip Lee—
Living with Topography
John Montag—
By the Sea
Victor Murillo—
Hybrid Sponges
Karim Nader—
The End of a Lighthouse
Ben Reavis—
Garaging the House
Paul Schuette—
The Baytown Museum of
Network Archaeology
Kristin Schuster—
Sea Change
David Stockwell—
Chapter 43: New
Un-Steady States for
Houston
Adam Weiss—
T Traffic: The Commute
Kayte Young—
House/Broken: Debbie
Drechsler's Daddy's Girl
and the Crisis of the House
Sven Zbinden—
Architecture and
Impermanence: The
Re-Thinking of Territories
Ozge Zoralioglu—
Vittoria says: there are
days when a table, or
chair, or book, or a man are
all the same"

Lectures
01.24
Jason Griffiths and Alex Gino
Gino Griffiths Architects,
London
These are a Few of My
Favorite Things

02.10
Ole Bouman
Archis, Amsterdam
Publishing Architecture:
Converging Practices

02.24
Terence Riley
Museum of Modern Art, New
York
This Will Kill That —
Architecture and the Media

03.03
Mark Wigley
School of Architecture,
Columbia University,
New York
How Old is Young? –
The Concept of the Young
Architect

03.17
Maria Elisa Costa
Author, Rio de Janeiro
Brasilia in the Flesh

03.26
Sarah Whiting and Ron Witte
WW, Cambridge
Bounce

04.07
Lars Spuybroek
Nox, Rotterdam
Machining Architecture

09.08
Rick Joy
Principal, Rick Joy
Architects, Tucson; Cullinan
Professor, Rice School of
Architecture
Recent Work

09.22
Robert Rogers
Principal, Rogers Marvel
Architects, New York City
Projects

10.20
Nader Tehrani
Principal, Office dA,
Cambridge
Shish Kebabs and Other
Ongoing Projects

10.27
Dominique Jakob and
Brendan MacFarlane
Prinicpals, Jakob +
MacFarlane, Paris
Jakob+MacFarlane

11.17
Dawn Finley and Mark
Wamble
Principals, Interloop A/D,
Houston
The Rest of the World Exists

GinoGriffiths exhibition an-
nouncement card

Exhibitions
January 23-30
COLLECTION POINT:
GinoGriffiths Architects

February 7-28
RETROSPECTIVE:
William T. Cannady, FAIA,
Architect

2004

Graduates
M.ARCH.
Naseema Luise Asif
John Michael Bacus
Daniel Cope Bailey
Joseph Michael Bailey
Anne Elisabeth Buttyan
Jason Michael Carney
Aidan Dylan Chopra
Marcus Miller Farr
Marc Frohn
Ross Douglas Garland
Eric Harry Hartz
Henry C.J. Hoogland, III
Jan Marlon Jander
Peter Michael Klein
Lina Jisun Lee
Mihael Brent Linden
Christopher Michael
Mechaley
Karlene Jeanette Morgan
Daniel Aaron Nemec
Jennifer Marie Painter
Ji-Min Park
Gage Patton Reese

Hema Srinivasan
Katherine Irene Williams
Sandra Faye Winstead
Zhaoyan Zheng

B.ARCH
Brian Anthony Baldor
Erh-Chun Amy Chien
Kerim Tahsin Demirkan
Dustin Owen Eshenroder
Joey Favaloro
Elizabeth Flaherty Ferrara
Jeffrey Geisinger
Jennifer Leigh Henry
David Lee Herman
Jobie Renee Hill
Benjamin Luke Johanson
Giselle Everett Sperber
Jessica Ilana Walitt
Ewen Fegan Will

Faculty
Larry Albert
Visiting Critic
John Biln
Associate Professor
Barbara Bryson
Lecturer
William T. Cannady
Professor
John J. Casbarian
Associate Dean and
Professor
Farès el-Dahdah
Associate Professor
Dallas Felder
Visiting Critic
Dawn Finley
Assistant Professor
J. Kent Fitzsimons
Assistant Director, Rice
School of Architecture-
Paris
Alan Fleishacker
Lecturer
Stephen Fox
Lecturer

RSA Events poster, Spring 2004

296

Helene Furjan
Assistant Professor
James Furr
Lecturer
Nonya Grenader
Professor in Practice
David Guthrie
Wortham Assistant
Professor
Shirene Hamadeh
Assistant Professor
Brian Heiss
Visiting Critic
Michael Hensel
Visiting Professor
Christopher Hight
Assistant Professor
Carlos Jiménez
Professor
Laura Koehler
Lecturer
Peter Koehler
Lecturer
Sanford Kwinter
Associate Professor
Sean Lally
Hild Visiting Critic
Nana Last
Assistant Professor
Lars Lerup
Dean and William Ward
Watkin Professor
Tom Lord
Lecturer
Robert Mangurian
Visiting Cullinan Professor
Jonathan Marvel
Visiting Professor
Achim Menges
Visiting Professor
Michael Morrow
Visiting Critic
Mark Oberholzer
Lecturer
Douglas Oliver
Professor in Practice
Spencer Parsons
Associate Professor
Albert Pope
Wortham Professor
Mary-Ann Ray
Visiting Cullinan Professor
Robert Rogers
Visiting Professor
Danny Samuels
Smith Professor
Blair Satterfield
Visiting Critic
Vincent Snyder
Visiting Professor
Rives Taylor
Caudill Visiting Lecturer

Screening of *Paris, Texas* outside of Anderson Hall

SURF

Mark Wamble
Cullinan Professor
Frank White
Lecturer
Kerry Whitehead
Visiting Critic
William Williams
Visiting Critic
Gordon Wittenberg
Professor

Staff

Doris Anderson
School Administrator
Mildred Crocker
Accounting Assistant
Kent Fitzsimons
Assistant Director, Rice
School of Architecture
Paris
Hans Krause
Information Technology
Specialist
Chad Loucks
Woodshop Manager
Kathleen Roberts
Graduate Coordinator
Carrie Rushing
Program Administrator,
RDA
Elaine Sebring
Accounting Assistant

Lisa Simon
Managing Editor, Cite
Mary Swift
Membership Coordinator,
RDA
Linda Sylvan
Executive Director, RDA
Sara Oussar Tovar
Staff Assistant, RDA
Janet Wheeler
Assistant to the Dean
Diania Williams
Receptionist
Lee Wilson
Staff Assistant
Lisa Tsokos
Staff Assistant
Jessica Young
Director of Publications
and Exhibitions

Awards

AIA/AAF Scholarship
Michael Kross
AIA School Medal
Thomas Hardin
AIA School Certificate
Ben Regnier
Alpha Rho Chi Medal
Jean Daly, Anna Goodman
Berda & Charles Soon Chan
Memorial Scholarship
Jason Cook
Brett Michael Detamore
Award in Architecture
Jean Daly
Chillman Prize:
- 1st place
Thomas Hardin

- 2nd place
Anna Goodman, Liang Wu
Darden Award
John Bacus, Brent Michael
Linden
Edward B Arrants Award
John Peek
Erin MacKenzie Peck
Freshman Prize in
Architecture
Jacqueline Craig
Erin MacKenzie Peck
Architecture Studio Prize
Stephanie Hsie
Gene Hackerman Award
(graduate)
Kari Smith
Gene Hackerman Award
(undergraduate)
Melissa Biringer
John Crowder Traveling
Fellowship
Betsy Engler, Susanna
Hohmann
John T Mitchell Traveling
Fellowship
Elaine An
LF McCollum Fellowship
Reiko Igarashi
Louis Sudler Prize in the Arts
Thomas Hardin
Margaret Everson Fossi
Traveling Fellowship:
- 1st place
Micah Morgan
- 2nd place
Dan Burkett and Andrea
Dietz

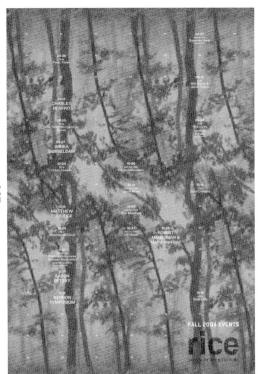

RSA Events poster, Fall 2004

Mary Ellen Hale Lovett
Traveling Fellowship
(graduate)
  Tony Harrington
Mary Ellen Hale Lovett
Traveling Fellowship
(undergraduate)
  Andrew Hamblin, Liang Wu
MN Davidson Fellowship
  Colin Bruce
Morris R Pitman Award in
Architecture
  Sky Lanigan, Quyen Luong
Ralph S Herman Memorial
Scholarship
  Anna Goodman

RSA Thesis book, 2004

Rice Visionary Project
  Sky Lanigan, Judson
  Moore, David Newton
Student Lego Design
Competition
  Jean Daly, Katy Dankberg,
  Anna Gooodman, Mark
  Watabe, Liang Wu
Tau Sigma Delta
  Melissa Biringer, Colin
  Bruce, Anna Goodman,
  Andrew Hamblin, Thomas
  Hardin, Alex Higbee, John
  Peek, Ben Regnier, Lewis
  Swanson, Liang Wu
Texas Architectural
Foundation Scholarships:
- Jesse H Jones Scholarship
  Parrish Kyle
- George F Harrell II Memorial
Scholarship
  Parrish Kyle
Texas Society of Architecture
Competition
  Katy Dankberg, Anna
  Goodman led by Sean Lally
William Ward Watkin Awards:
- Honorable Mention
  Colin Bruce, Tara Teter,
  Liang Wu

2004

- Rosemary Watkin Barrick
Traveling Fellowship, 4th
place
  John Peek
- Rosemary Watkin Barrick
Traveling Fellowship, 3rd
place
  Thomas Hardin
- Rosemary Watkin Barrick
Traveling Fellowship, 2nd
place
  Jeremy Arianpour
- William Ward Watkin
Traveling Fellowship
  Alex Higbee
Willis M Upchurch & Mames R
Kimbrough Scholarship
  Ben Regnier
Ziegler Cooper Award in
Architecture
  David Jefferis

Thesis Titles

Naseema Asif—
  Conversant Transparency
John Bacus—
  Datastructure
Cope Bailey—
  Urban Catalysis: Operative
  Strategies for Jump
  Starting Metropolitan Life
  In Central Houston
Joseph Bailey—
  Frameworks: Background
  Exposition and Movement
Anne Buttyan—
  Play-Back: The Act or
  Process of Replaying a
  Recording
Jason Carney—
  Agencies of Reassurance
Aiden Chopra—
  Play at School
Marcus Farr—
  Hybrid PARK(ing):
  Exploring the Mediation
  Between Infrastructure,
  Architecture, and the Public

Marc Frohn—
  Impresario of Change
Ross Garland—
  Light, Form, Place
Eric Hartz—
  Acoustic Aesthetics:
  A Material Exploration
C.J. Hoogland—
  Artifacts of Nature
Jan Jander—
  Big, Bigger, Vacant
Lina Lee—
  Appropriating (Negative)
  Space
Brent Linden—
  As Found: Light Space
  Situation
Christopher Mechaley—
  The Sacred and the
  Individual
Karlene Morgan—
  Negotiating (Ex)Change
Jennifer Painter—
  Off the Wall: Exploring
  Waterfront Reciprocities of
  Surface and Space
Gage Reese—
  Material Standard
Katherine Williams—
  Action Potentials: Building
  an Urban Landscape
  Through Discrete Moments
Sandra Winstead—
  Shifting the Landscape:
  Preservation Through
  Projection
Zhaoyan Zheng—
  Foreignness: Hybridiza-
  tion and Mutation as
  Design Process

Lectures

01.26
Bart Lootsma
Professor in the a42.org at
the Akademie der Bildenden
Kunste in Nurnberg
Reality Bytes

Softspace exhibition opening

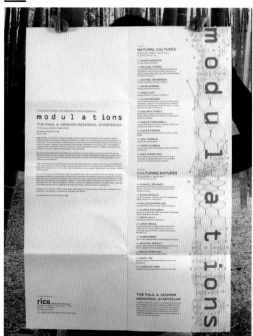

Poster for *Modulations*, the 4th Kennon Symposium, 2004

Exhibition of student work associated with the Kennon Symposium, *Modulations*

02.16
Edwin Chan
Design Partner at Frank O.
Gehry and Associates,
Los Angeles
@foga.com

02.23
Bruno Queysanne
Professor at L'Ecole
d'Architecture de Grenoble,
France
*The Walter Benjamin
Memorial in Portbou:
Doublesense in Architectural
Meaning*

03.08
James Timberlake
Partner at Kieran Timberlake
Associates LLP, Philadelphia
Refabricating Architecture

03.18
Eyal Weizman
Architect, Tel Aviv and
London
The Politics of Verticality

03.22
Mark Goulthorpe
Principal, dECOi Architects,
Paris; Assistant Professor
at MIT
*From Autoplastic to
Alloplastic*

04.05
Mark Cousins
Director of General Studies at
the Architectural Association,
London
Functionalism and Guilt

04.22
Kivi Sotamaa
Partner, Ocean North, London
and Helsinki; Assistant
Professor, Ohio State
University, Columbus
Adventures in Form

09.13
Charles Renfro
Principal, Diller Scofidio +
Renfro, New York;
Assistant Adjunct Professor,
Columbia University
Sight Specific

09.27
Winka Dubbeldam
Principal, Archi-Tectonics,
New York; Professor of
Practice, University of
Pennsylvania
From HardWare to SoftForm

10.18
Matthew Coolidge
Programming Director, Center
for Land Use Interpretation,
Los Angeles
*Interpreting Anthropogeo-
morphology: Projects of
the Center for Land use
Interpretation*

10.28
**Robert Mangurian and
Mary-Ann Ray**
Principals, Studio Works, Los
Angeles; B.A.S.E., Beijing
In Ciphered Rivers

11.08
Aaron Betsky
Director, Netherlands
Architecture Institute,
Rotterdam
*Why Dutch Design Will Save
You*

Exhibitions
Sep 24 – Oct 15
SUPERMUNDANE
Photographs by David
Guthrie

Nov 1 – Nov 24
*6 PACK: Contemporary
Slovenian Architecture*

New design work from 6 young Slovenian architecture offices: Bevk Perovic Arhitekti, Dekleva Gregoric Arhitekti, Elastik, Maechtig Vrhunc Arhitekti, Ofis Arhitekti, and Sadar Vuga Arhitekti

Feb 20 – Mar 12
Softspace
new architectural work from 6 design offices. Participants include dECOi architects (Paris), Jakob + MacFarlane (Paris), Ocean North (London and Helsinki), Open Source Architecture (Los Angeles, Paris, and Tel Aviv), Sean Lally (Houston) and Servo (Los Angeles, New York, Stockholm and Zurich)

Kennon Symposium
Modulations
The 4th Kennon Symposium
November 15
Organized by Christopher Hight

Session 1: *Natural Cultures*
Participants: Aran Chadwick, Michael Hensel, George Jeronimidis, Kevin Kennon, Nana Last, Achim Menges, Una-May O'Reily, Gregg Pasquarelli, Hadas Steiner, Neil Thomas, Mark Wamble, Mike Weinstock

Publications
AAR 40
Row: Trajectories through the Shotgun House
David Brown and William Williams, editors
DAP

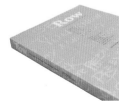

2005

Graduates
M.ARCH.
W. Brent Armstrong
Zeynep Atas
Sharen Malini Bidaisee

Graham Roland Booth
Megan Brady
Dan Burkett
Amy Aileen DaPonte
Andrea Hunter Dietz
Elizabeth Koken Engler
Jamie Susan Flatt-Hickey
Laura Bettina Francisco
Anthony Joseph Harrington
Susanna Marie Hohmann
Ryan Daniel Jones
Patrick Michael Kraft
Jason Scott LaRocca
Quyen Luong
Michael Simon Martinez
Micah Lane Morgan
Brendan Daniel Mulcahy
Matthew Albert Radune
Paul Jeremy Richey
Maya Ling Richter
Thomas Michael Schroeder
Christian Nikirk Sheridan
Kari Jasmine Smith
Melissa Megan Sullivan

B.ARCH
Megan Lee Arendt
Andrea Jill Bacon
Jared Elias Banks
Amy Michelle Byrge
Seth Porter Clarke
Pranjali Desai
Sharon Elizabeth Floyd
Mary Lynn Franzoso
Jing Gu
Audrey Malhiot Handelman
Jennifer Leigh Henry
Ryan David Indovina
David Gilpin Jefferis
Michael Jordan Kross
Parrish Michael Kyle
Sara-Ann Rose Logan
Katherine R. Motchan
Nozomi Nakabayashi
Susan Anne Oehme
Tate Kent Ragland
Jessica Ann Spiegel
Rebeca Ellen Vieyra
Irina Wing Wong
Linnea Elizabeth Wingo

Faculty
Larry Albert
  Visiting Critic
John Biln
  Associate Professor
Barbara Bryson
  Lecturer
William T. Cannady
  Professor
Julien DeSmedt
  Cullinan Visiting Professor

RSA Events poster, Spring 2002

John J. Casbarian
  Associate Dean and
  Professor
Farès el-Dahdah
  Associate Professor
Dallas Felder
  Visiting Critic
Emine Fetvaci
  Lecturer
Dawn Finley
  Assistant Professor
J. Kent Fitzsimons
  Assistant Director, Rice
  School of Architecture-
  Paris
Alan Fleishacker
  Lecturer
Stephen Fox
  Lecturer

Helene Furjan
  Assistant Professor
James Furr
  Lecturer
Nonya Grenader
  Professor in Practice
David Guthrie
  Wortham Assistant
  Professor
Shirene Hamadeh
  Assistant Professor
Brian Heiss
  Visiting Critic
Christopher Hight
  Assistant Professor
Bjarke Ingels
  Cullinan Visiting Professor
Carlos Jiménez
  Professor
Laura Koehler
  Lecturer
Peter Koehler
  Lecturer
Gordana Kostich
  Visiting Lecturer
Sanford Kwinter
  Associate Professor
Sean Lally
  Visiting Critic
Nana Last
  Assistant Professor
Clover Lee
  Assistant Professor

Holiday card, 2005

Lars Lerup
  Dean and William Ward
  Watkin Professor
Tom Lord
  Lecturer
Michael Morrow
  Visiting Critic
Mark Oberholzer
  Lecturer
Douglas Oliver
  Professor in Practice
Spencer Parsons
  Associate Professor
Albert Pope
  Wortham Professor
Danny Samuels
  Smith Professor
Blair Satterfield
  Visiting Critic
Rives Taylor
  Caudill Visiting Lecturer
Mark Wamble
  Cullinan Professor
Frank White
  Lecturer
Kerry Whitehead
  Visiting Critic
Gordon Wittenberg
  Professor

Staff

Doris Anderson
  School Administrator
Cathy Bauer
  Accounting Assistant, RDA
Mildred Crocker
  Accounting Assistant
Kent Fitzsimons
  Assistant Director, Rice
  School of Architecture
  Paris
Kathryn Fosdick
  Program Administrator,
  RDA
Hans Krause
  Information Technology
  Specialist

Chad Loucks
  Woodshop Manager
Raquel Puccio
  Staff Assistant, RDA
Kathleen Roberts
  Graduate Coordinator
Elaine Sebring
  Accounting Assistant
Lisa Simon
  Managing Editor, Cite
Mary Swift
  Membership Coordinator,
  RDA
Linda Sylvan
  Executive Director, RDA
Sara Oussar Tovar
  Marketing Coordinator,
  RDA
Lisa Tsokos
  Staff Assistant
Janet Wheeler
  Assistant to the Dean
Diania Williams
  Receptionist
Jessica Young
  Director of Publications
  and Exhibitions

Awards

AIA/AAF Scholarship
  Anna Goodman
AIA School Medal
  Jason Cook
AIA School Certificate
  Emily Clanahan
Alpha Rho Chi Medal
  Davis Niendorff
Berda & Charles Soon Chan
Memorial Scholarship
  Etien Santiago
Brett Michael Detamore
Award in Architecture
  Axel Weisheit
Chillman Prize:
- *1st place*
  Lindsey Brigati

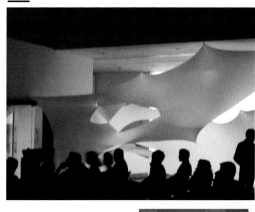

- *2nd place*
  Julia Hager
- *3rd place*
  Stephanie Hsie
- *Honorable Mention*
  Axel Weisheit
Darden Award
  Jonathan LaRocca
Edward B Arrants Award
  Lindsey Brigati
Erin MacKenzie Peck
Freshman Prize in
Architecture
  Van-Tuong Nguyen
Erin MacKenzie Peck
Architecture Studio Prize
  Stephanie Lin
Gene Hackerman Award
(graduate)
  Wendy Gilmartin
Gene Hackerman Award
(undergraduate)
  Emily Clanahan
H Russell Pitman Graduate
Fellowship in Architecture
  Judson Moore
John Crowder Traveling
Fellowship
  Kristine Youngblood
John T Mitchell Traveling
Fellowship
  Matt Geiger
Margaret Everson Fossi
Traveling Fellowship:
- *1st place*
  Joe Kellner and David
  Newton
- *2nd place*
  Catie Newell and Judson
  Moore; Mike Kross
Mary Ellen Hale Lovett
Traveling Fellowship
(graduate)
  Maria Cornejo, Kate Levine
Mary Ellen Hale Lovett
Traveling Fellowship

The second session of
Modulations, the 4th Kennon
Symposium

(undergraduate)
  Erin Porter
MN Davidson Fellowship
  Julia Hager
Morris R Pitman Award in
Architecture
  Reiko Igarashi, Catie
  Newell
Ralph S Herman Memorial
Scholarship
  Mark Watabe
Rice Visionary Project
  Mike Kross
Tau Sigma Delta
  Lindsey Brigati, Emily
  Clanahan, Jason Cook,
  Stephanie Hsie,
  Stephanie Lin, Erin
  Porter, Mark Watabe, Axel
  Weisheit

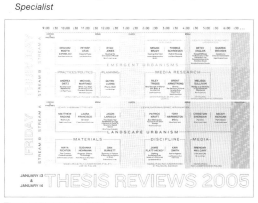

Thesis reviews poster, 2005

Texas Architectural
Foundation Scholarships:
- Charles Lamar & Verda
McKittrick Endowed
Scholarship
  Beatrice Eleazar
- Jesse H Jones Scholarship
  Thomas Hardin
- E.G. Spencer memorial
Scholarship
  John Peek
- Fay Spencer Scholarship
  Melissa Biringer
- George F Harrell II Memorial
Scholarship
  Andrew Hamblin
William Ward Watkin Awards:
- Honorable Mention
  Ruya Saner, Mark Watabe,
  Axel Weisheit
- Rosemary Watkin Barrick
Traveling Fellowship, 4th
place
  Sarah Billington
- Rosemary Watkin Barrick
Traveling Fellowship, 3rd
place
  Stephanie Hsie
- Rosemary Watkin Barrick
Traveling Fellowship, 2nd
place
  Jason Cook
- William Ward Watkin
Traveling Fellowship
  Lindsey Brigati
Ziegler Cooper Award in
Architecture
  Thomas Hardin

Thesis Titles

Zeynep Atas—
  Copy-and-Paste
W. Brent Armstrong—
  Brenta: The Structure
  of Brand-scaping ones
  image(inary)
Sharen Bidaisee—
  Commons

302

RSA Events poster, Fall 2005

Megan Brady—
  Casting the Void
Graham Booth—
  Superblox
Dan Burkett—
  Counterpoint
Andrea Dietz—
  architecture: Appalachia
Elizabeth Engler—
  HomeOwning: An Explora-
  tion of the Possession and
  Personalization of the
  American Dream
Anthony Harrington—
  Bio-City
Susannah Hohmann—
  FeltPET: A Material
  Research Project
Jamie Flatt-Hickey—
  Shifting Arch(text)ure:
  Notes on a Disclosure

Laura Francisco—
  Dovetail Ranch at Ajo
  Valley
Ryan Jones—
  Healing the Circulatory
  Wound
Patrick Kraft—
  Eco-Metropolis™
Jason LaRocca—
  The Snake that Swallowed
  the Egg: A Network of
  Parks for Houston's
  Wasted Spaces
Quyen Luong—
  PHARM_STAD: Fieldworks
  for Somkhele
Michael Martinez—
  Border Crossings
Micah Morgan—
  Park Space
Brendan Mulcahy—
  Like and Like
Matthew Radune—
  Niche Life
Maya Richter—
  The Comfort Consciousness
Thomas Schroeder—
  Hybrid Housing
Christian Sheridan—
  Fat City: A Post-Movement
  Manifesto
Kari Smith—
  Active Agents

Melissa Sullivan—
  Media as a Modality of
  Architectural Discourse:
  Methods/Modes/Medium/
  Activity

Lectures

01.31
Michael Van Valkenburgh
Principal, Michael Van
Valkenburgh Landscape
Architecture, New York;
Professor, Harvard
Graduate School of Design
Hypernatural, Dense, and
Syncopated Parks – 21st
Century Parks as a Fecund
Alternative of Landscape
Minimalism

02.21
Roemer Van Toorn
Architect, Critic,
Photographer, Curator;
Projective Theory and PHD
Coordinator, Berlage Institute,
Rotterdam
After Criticality – The Passion
for Extreme Reality and....It's
Limitations

02.28
Marc Angelil
Principal, Angelil Graham
Pfenninger Scholl
Architecture, Los Angeles
and Zurich; Professor, Swiss
Federal Institute of Technology
(ETH), Zurich
Six Impossible Things Before
Breakfast

03.14
Ben Van Berkel
Principal, UN Studio,
Amsterdam
Design Models, Figments,
and the Origin of the After
Image

04.11
**Bjarke Ingels and Julien
de Smedt**
Principals, Plot, Copenhagen,
Denmark
In Search of a Plot

04.28
Peter Trummer
Architect; Research Coor-
dinator, Berlage Institute,
Rotterdam

Robert Mangurian and Mary Ann Ray studio event

Product opening at Sunset Settings

Population Thinking and
Material Practices

09.26
Paul Lewis
Lewis Tsurumaki Lewis
Architects, New York;
Princeton University School of
Architecture
Opportunism at Play

10.03
Maria Elisa Costa
Architect; former President of
Brazil's Institute for
Historic and Artistic Heritage
About Brasilia

10.05
Bas Princen
Designer; Photographer of
public space, Rotterdam
Landscape and Rubble

10.17-10.21
Manuel Delanda
Street Philosopher
The Role of Cities in New
Social Science

11.07
Sarah W Goldhagen
Harvard University
Graduate School of Design
Kool Houses, Kold Cities

11.14
Preston Scott Cohen
Preston Scott Cohen, Inc.,
Cambridge, MA; Harvard
University Graduate School
of Design
Geometry Betrayed

12.01
Antoine Picon
Professor of the History of
Architecture and Technology,
Harvard University Graduate
School of Design
Architecture and Digial
Culture: Towards a New
Materiality?

Exhibitions
Morphologies, Material
Systems and Performativity:
Proto-Architectures between
Modulations and Mutuality
Installations by the Generative
Proto-Architectures Studio,
a Fall 2004 graduate option
studio, organized by Michael
Hensel and Achim Menges

Kennon Symposium
Modulations
The 4th Kennon Symposium
April 01
Organized by Christopher
Hight

Session 2: *Culturing Natures*
Participants: Manuel Delanda,
Evan Douglis, Keller
Easterling, Ulrika Karlsson,
Sean Lally, John Maeda,
Chris Perry, Michael Speaks,
Bruce Sterling, Mark Yim,
J. Meejin Yoon

Graduates
M.ARCH.
Elaine Moon An
Suzanne Camp Bird
Susan L. Crowe
Kerri Shannon Frick
Malini Leah Fuangvuthi
Joel Harrison Gilliam
Anne Maxine Hawkins
Reiko Igarashi
Joseph Alan Kellner
Sky Lanigan-Durschlag
Eric Jon Leshinsky
Katherine Levine
Stephanie Louise Millet
Judson Wilkins Moore
Cathlyn L. Newell
David William Newton
Robert Matthew Olsen, Jr.
Catherine Annie Peek
Melanie Leanne Pratt
Eric C. Ratkowski
John Michael Robison
Anthony J. Sinkewich
Nagthan Glenn Smith
Ricardo Supiciche
RileyGrant Triggs
Antonio Valadez
Shuo Wang
Michelle Ann Weinfeld
Kristine Marie Youngblood

B.ARCH
Jeremy Darusch Arianpour
Ann MishiAwantang
David Grant Barr
Melissa Diane Biringer
Colin Tyler Bruce
AllanVillanueva Co
Jean Clare Daly
Katherine Anna Dankberg
Kelli Dawn DesRochers
Anna G. Goodman
Andrew Winter Hamblin
Thomas McKinney Hardin
Alexander Robert Higbee
Jennifer Y. Lee
Chester Edward Kimball
Nielsen III
John Michael Peek
Heather Elizabeth Pfaff
Benjamin Lee Regnier
Lewis Tyler Swanson
Tara Kristen Teter
Liang Cai Wu

Faculty
Larry Albert
Visiting Critic

John Biln
Associate Professor
Barbara Bryson
Lecturer
William T. Cannady
Professor
Mary Ellen Carroll
Visiting Cullinan Professor
John J. Casbarian
Associate Dean and
Professor
Farès el-Dahdah
Associate Professor
Dallas Felder
Visiting Critic
Emine Fetvaci
Lecturer
Dawn Finley
Assistant Professor
J. Kent Fitzsimons
Assistant Director, Rice
School of Architecture-
Paris
Alan Fleishacker
Lecturer
Stephen Fox
Lecturer
James Furr
Lecturer
Nonya Grenader
Professor in Practice
David Guthrie
Wortham Assistant
Professor
Shirene Hamadeh
Assistant Professor
Christopher Hight
Assistant Professor
Carlos Jiménez
Professor
Laura Koehler
Lecturer
Peter Koehler
Lecturer
Sanford Kwinter
Associate Professor
Sean Lally
Assistant Professor
Nana Last
Assistant Professor
Clover Lee
Assistant Professor

Holiday card, 2006

RSA Events poster, Spring 2006

RSA Events poster, Fall 2006

Lars Lerup
   Dean and William Ward
   Watkin Professor
Tom Lord
   Lecturer
Michael Morrow
   Visiting Critic
Douglas Oliver
   Professor in Practice
Spencer Parsons
   Associate Professor
Albert Pope
   Wortham Professor
Mary-Ann Ray
   Visiting Professor
Charles Renfro
   Visiting Cullinan Professor
Michael Robinson
   Lecturer
Danny Samuels
   Smith Professor
Blair Satterfield
   Visiting Critic
Rives Taylor
   Caudill Visiting Lecturer
Mark Wamble
   Cullinan Professor
Frank White
   Lecturer
Kerry Whitehead
   Visiting Critic
Gordon Wittenberg
   Professor

Staff
Doris Anderson
   School Administrator
Cathy Bauer
   Accounting Assistant, RDA
Mildred Crocker
   Accounting Assistant
Kent Fitzsimons
   Assistant Director, Rice
   School of Architecture
   Paris
Kathryn Fosdick
   Program Administrator,
   RDA
Susan Guidry
   Staff Assistant
Hans Krause
   Information Technology
   Specialist

Light switch and fire alarm distinction noted

Chad Loucks
   Woodshop Manager
Raquel Puccio
   Staff Assistant, RDA
Kathleen Roberts
   Graduate Coordinator
Elaine Sebring
   Accounting Assistant
Mitchell Shields
   Managing Editor, Cite
Mary Swift
   Associate Director,
   Membership, RDA
Linda Sylvan
   Executive Director, RDA
Sara Oussar Tovar
   Marketing Coordinator,
   RDA
Janet Wheeler
   Project Coordinator

Diania Williams
   Receptionist
Jessica Young
   Director of Publications
   and Exhibitions

Awards
AIA School Medal
   Etien Santiago
AIA School Certificate
   Kristen Smith
Alpha Rho Chi Medal
   Jean-Marc Tribie
Berda & Charles Soon Chan
Memorial Scholarship
   Linh Dan Do
Brett Michael Detamore
Award in Architecture
   Joseph Lim
Chillman Prize:
- 1st place
   Christopher White
- 2nd place
   Etien Santiago
- 3rd place
   Mary Ann Holliday
Darden Award
   Judson Moore
Dean's Staff Appreciation
Award
   Hans Krause
Edward B Arrants Award
   Beatrice Eleazar
   Erin MacKenzie Peck
Freshman Prize in

Architecture
Sohael Chowfla
*Gene Hackerman Award
(graduate)*
Gabby Flores
*Gene Hackerman Award
(undergraduate)*
Mary Ann Holliday
*H Russell Pitman Graduate
Fellowship in Architecture*
Mike Schanbacher
*John Crowder Traveling
Fellowship*
Wendy Gilmartin
LF McCollum Fellowship
Clint Keithley, Paul Morel
Louis Sudler Prize in the Arts
Etien Santiago
*Margaret Everson Fossi
Traveling Fellowship:*
- *1st place*
Jon LaRocca and Ben
Regnier
- *2nd place*
Callie Bailey, Natalia Beard
and Eric Hughes
*Mary Ellen Hale Lovett
Traveling Fellowship
(graduate)*
Phil Baraldi
*Mary Ellen Hale Lovett
Traveling Fellowship
(undergraduate)*

Etien Santiago
MN Davidson Fellowship
Kristen Smith
*Morris R Pitman Award in
Architecture*
Natalia Beard, Nicholas
Risteen
*Ralph S Herman Memorial
Scholarship*
Christian Ervin
*RDA Initiatives for Houston
Grant*
Jean Daly, Katherine
Dankberg and Ben Regnier
Rice Visionary Project
Nick Hofstede
Tau Sigma Delta
Beatrice Eleazar,
Christian Ervin, Izabel
Gass, Mary Ann Holliday,
Etien Santiago, Kristen
Smith, Jean-Marc Tribie
*Texas Architectural
Foundation Scholarships:*
- *Jesse H Jones Scholarship*
Jason Cook, Julia Hager
William Ward Watkin Awards:
- *Honorable Mention*
Brian Love, Divya Pande,
Izabel Gass, Claire
Pritchett, Etien Santiago

- *Rosemary Watkin Barrick
Traveling Fellowship, 3rd
place*
Mary Ann Holliday
- *Rosemary Watkin Barrick
Traveling Fellowship, 2nd
place*
Beatrice Eleazar
- *William Ward Watkin
Traveling Fellowship*
Fede Cavazos and Robert
Crawford
*Ziegler Cooper Award in
Architecture*
Lindsey Brigati

Thesis Titles

Elaine An—
*IAH: Reconstituting the
Coordinates*
Susan Crowe—
*Curating Identity: A new
Rijksmuseum*
Malini Fuangvuthi—
Prosthetic Habitat
Joel Gilliam—
*Soft Zoning: A Flooplain
Development Strategy for
a High Performance Urban
Watershed*
Joseph Kellner—
Entrepot 69

Kerri Frick—
*Thresholds: Gradients of
Activity in a Changing
Landscape*
Reiko Igarashi—
Alley Memphis
Eric Leshinsky—
*Locating Houston's
Museum for Missing Places*
Katherine Levine—
Response Development
Stephanie Millet—
Hospice House
Jud Moore—
*Implement: Interface
Architecture*
Catie Newell—
Site Amplification
David Newton—
*Performative Landscapes:
Strategizing a Man-Made
Geology*
Robert Olsen—
*The Structures of Things to
Come: New Movements in
the Architectural Profession*
Melanie Pratt—
Shadow Urbanism
Eric Ratkowski—
*Detroit: Return of the
Cityzen*
Michael Robinson—
Field of Edges

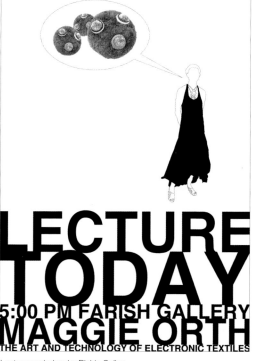

LECTURE TODAY 5:00 PM FARISH GALLERY MAGGIE ORTH
THE ART AND TECHNOLOGY OF ELECTRONIC TEXTILES

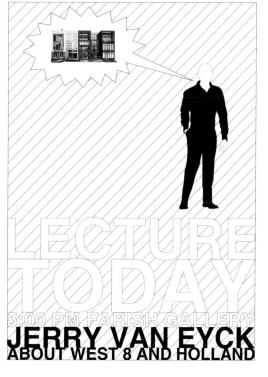

LECTURE TODAY 5:00 PM FARISH GALLERY JERRY VAN EYCK ABOUT WEST 8 AND HOLLAND

Lecture reminders by Richie Gelles

Nathan Smith—
Transpositions CU
Richardo Supiciche—
Building a new Plot
Cartography
Tony Valadez—
Recasting the Convivial
Tool
Shuo Wang—
Enabling Wild Beijing:
Try-out for the Future of
Hyper-Density
Kristine Youngblood—
Digital Space/Physical
Place: Systems for
Community Growth

Lectures

01.23
Neil Denari
Neil M Denari Architects,
Los Angeles; Professor-in-
Residence, UCLA
Formagraphics

02.10
Luis Fernandez-Galiano
Editor, Arquitectura Viva and
AV Monographs, Madrid
The Disorder of Our Time

02.27
Lauro Cavalcanti
Architectural Historian;
Director, Paco Imperial Center
for Landmarks and Contem-
porary Art, Rio de Janiero
Contemporary Architecture
in Brazil

03.06
Paul Lewis
Lewis Tsurumaki Lewis Archi-
tects, New York; Director of
Graduate Studies, Princeton
University School of
Architecture
Opportunism at Play

03.20
Juan Miguel Hernandez Leon
Architect; Dean, Escuela
Tecnica Superior de
Arquitectura de Madrid
(ETSAM)
The Resonance of Place (My
Work with Alvaro Siza)

03.27
Robert Fishman
Professor of Architecture and
Urban Planning, University of
Mimchigan
Cities After the End of Cities

04.10
Francoise Fromonot
Architect and Architectural
Critic, Paris; Associate
Professor, Ecole d'Architecture
de Paris-LaVillette
The Cabbage Patch and the
Stork: Classifying Contempo-
rary Urbanism

04.27
Pierre David
Architect, Paris;
Associate Professor, Ecole
d'Architecture de Marseille
The Great Beyond

10.02
Maggie Orth
Artist & Director of Research,
International Fashion
Machines, Inc.; Visiting
Scientist, Department of
Computer Science, University
of Washington
The Art and Technology of
Electronic Textiles

10.23
Marc Simmons
Partner, Front Inc., New York
Recent Work

11.06
Jerry Van Eych
Partner, West 8 Urban Design
and Landscape Architecture,
Rotterdam
About West 8.....and Holland

11.13
Tom Wiscombe
Principal, EMERGENT, Los
Angeles; Design and
Technology Faculty, Sci-Arc
Parts and Wholes

11.20
Francisco Mangado
Architect, Pamplona;
Professor, Escuela Superior
de Arquitectura de la
Universidad de Navarra
Left-Handed Architecture

RSA Events poster, Spring 2007

12.07
Michelle Addington
Associate Professor, Yale
University School of
Architecture
The Phenomena of the Non-
Visual

Publications
AAR 42
Live Work: The Collaboration
Between the Rice Building
Workshop and Project Row
Houses in Houston, Texas
Nonya Grenader and Danny
Samuels

2007

Graduates
DR.ARCH
Juan Kent Fitzsimons

M.ARCH.
Susan Armsby
Callie Bailey
Natalia Beard
Mercedes Cornejo
James Andrew Corrigan
Dewey Nelson Ervin, Jr.
Gabriela Flores Kearns
Matthew Allen Geiger
Wendy Gilmartin
Joseph Han
Nicholas Hofstede
Eric Hughes
Jonathan LaRocca
Andrea Manning Day
Nicholas Moore Risteen
Michael J. Schanbacher
Sze Min Soo
Claudia Jeanne Ziegler

B.ARCH
Lindsey Leah Brigati
Emily Ann Clanahan
Jason Alexander Cook
Lauren Patricia Eckberg
Cynthia Miller Fishman
Elizabeth Anna Fomby
Julia Chrstina Hager
Stephanie Hsie
Stephanie Shih-Pei Lin
Edgar Rafael Pagan
Erin Elisabeth Porter
Amanda Elspeth Smith
Natalie Diane thurman
Mark M. Watabe

Axel Weisheit
Sarah Yvette Ziegler

Faculty

Larry Albert
Visiting Critic
William T. Cannady
Professor
John J. Casbarian
Associate Dean and
Professor
Farès el-Dahdah
Associate Professor
David Erdman
Visiting Cullinan Professor
Dallas Felder
Visiting Critic
Dawn Finley
Assistant Professor
J. Kent Fitzsimons
Assistant Director, Rice
School of Architecture-
Paris
Alan Fleishacker
Lecturer
Stephen Fox
Lecturer
Cody French
Lecturer
James Furr
Lecturer
Nonya Grenader
Professor in Practice

Holiday card, 2007

David Guthrie
Wortham Assistant
Professor
Shirene Hamadeh
Assistant Professor
Christopher Hight
Assistant Professor
Carlos Jiménez
Professor
Laura Koehler
Lecturer
Peter Koehler
Lecturer
Sanford Kwinter
Associate Professor
Sean Lally
Assistant Professor
Nana Last
Assistant Professor
Clover Lee
Assistant Professor
Lars Lerup
Dean and William Ward
Watkin Professor

Tom Lord
Lecturer
Michael Morrow
Visiting Critic
Douglas Oliver
Professor in Practice
Spencer Parsons
Associate Professor
Albert Pope
Professor
Joe Powell
Lecturer
Michael Robinson
Lecturer
Danny Samuels
Smith Professor
Blair Satterfield
Visiting Critic
Rives Taylor
Lecturer
Mark Wamble
Cullinan Professor
Frank White
Lecturer
Kerry Whitehead
Visiting Critic
Gordon Wittenberg
Professor

Staff

Doris Anderson
School Administrator

Cathy Bauer
Accounting Assistant, RDA
Mildred Crocker
Accounting Assistant
Julie Sinclair Eakin
Executive Editor, Cite
Kent Fitzsimons
Assistant Director, Rice
School of Architecture
Paris
Kathryn Fosdick
Program Administrator,
RDA
Susan Guidry
Staff Assistant
Hans Krause
Information Technology
Specialist
Chad Loucks
Woodshop Manager
Raquel Puccio
Staff Assistant, RDA
Kathleen Roberts
Graduate Coordinator
Mary Swift
Associate Director,
Membership, RDA
Linda Sylvan
Executive Director, RDA
Janet Wheeler
Project Coordinator
Diania Williams
Receptionist

Lecture reminders by Richie Gelles

Jessica Young
    Director of Publications
    and Exhibitions

Awards

AIA School Medal
    Linh Dan Do
AIA School Certificate
    Joseph Lim
Alpha Rho Chi Medal
    Scott Stark
Berda & Charles Soon Chan
Memorial Scholarship
    Megan Mills
Brett Michael Detamore
Award in Architecture
    Jessica Colangelo
Chillman Prize:
- 1st place
    Joseph Lim
- 2nd place
    Danish Kurani
- 3rd place
    Stephanie Squibb
- Honorable Mention
    Sae Hee Kim
Darden Award
    Natalia Beard
Edward B Arrants Award
    Keiko Vuong
Erin MacKenzie Peck
Freshman Prize in
Architecture

Igraine Perkinson, Jessy
Yang
Gene Hackerman Award
(graduate)
    Cary Place
Gene Hackerman Award
(undergraduate)
    Sarah Simpson
H Russell Pitman Graduate
Fellowship in Architecture
    Julia Mandell
John Crowder Traveling
Fellowship
    Paul Kweton
John T Mitchell Traveling
Fellowship
    Ned Dodington
LF McCollum Fellowship
    Viktor Ramos
Louis Sudler Prize in the Arts
    Linh Dan Do
Margaret Everson Fossi
Traveling Fellowship:
- 1st place
    Frank Guittard, Phil Baraldi
    and Stephanie Lin
- 2nd place
    Lindsey Brigati and Axel
    Weisheit
- 3rd place
    Emily Clanahan
Mary Ellen Hale Lovett
Traveling Fellowship

RSA Events poster, Spring 2007

(graduate)
    Nkiruka Mokwe, Paul
    Morel, Justus Pang
Mary Ellen Hale Lovett
Traveling Fellowship
(undergraduate)
    Danish Kurani, Kate
    McPhillips, Julia Siple
MN Davidson Fellowship
    Linh Dan Do
Morris R Pitman Award in
Architecture
    Ryan Byrnes, Joanne Park
Ralph S Herman Memorial
Scholarship
    Doug Shilo

RDA Initiatives for Houston
Grant
    Jonathan LaRocca,
    Heather Rowell
Rice Visionary Project
    Nkiruka Mokwe, Viktor
    Ramos
Tau Sigma Delta
    Linh Dan Do, Danish
    Kurani, Joseph Lim, Kate,
    McPhillips, Kelly Nicholas,
    Sarah Simpson, Julia Siple,
    Keiko Vuong
Texas Architectural
Foundation Scholarships:
- Paul & Katie Stein
Scholarship

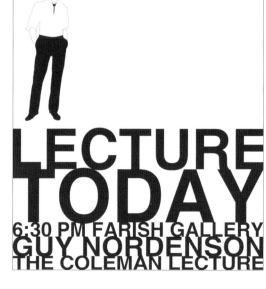

Lecture reminders by Richie Gelles

Hristiyan Petrov
- *Charles Lamar & Verda McKittrick Endowed Scholarship*
Scott Stark
- *O'Neil Ford Traveling Fellowship*
Kelly Nicholas
- *Edwin W and Alyce O Carroll Scholarship*
Jessica Colangelo
William Ward Watkin Awards:
- *Honorable Mention*
Doug Shilo, Sarah Simpson
- *Rosemary Watkin Barrick Traveling Fellowship, 4th place*
Scott Stark
- *Rosemary Watkin Barrick Traveling Fellowship, 3rd place*
Linh Dan Do
- *Rosemary Watkin Barrick Traveling Fellowship, 2nd place*
Keiko Vuong
- *William Ward Watkin Traveling Fellowship*
Joseph Lim
Ziegler Cooper Award in Architecture
Beatrice Eleazar

Thesis Titles

Susan Armsby—
World Roadtrip: Rethinking Road Accommodation for Global Roadtrip Scenarios
Callie Bailey—
The Doomsday Annex: A Living Preservation Index
Natalia Beard—
Waterline: The Future of Alluvial Ubanism in New Orleans
Dewey Ervin—
A Museum for a Small Town
Maria Gabriella Flores—
White Noise

Matt Geiger—
Incrementalism: Re/Inserting into the Homogenous, Block by Block Development of Houston's 4th Ward or How to Put Out a Gentri-fire
Wendy Gilmartin—
Latent City
Nicholas Hofstede—
66°N
Eric Hughes—
Any Given Sunday
Jonathan LaRocca—
The Cook, The Farmer, His Wife and Her Grocer: Plotting a New Urban/Rural Interface
Andrea Manning—
Vertical Zoo
Nicholas Risteen—
Havana (After) Life: Touring the Entropics
Michael Schanbacher—
DE-VOID: Tracing Shadows in the American Desert
Claudia Ziegler—
The Real Monument to Be Built: Contemporary Public Space

Lectures

02.05
Lisa Iwamoto
Principal, Iwamotoscott Architecture, Berkeley, CA
Adaptations

02.12
Charles Rice
Senior Lecturer and B.Arch Course Director, School of Architecture, University of Technology, Sydney
The Emergence of the Interior

02.19
Peter Testa and Devyn Weiser
Principals, Testa & Weiser, Santa Monica; Senior Design Faculty, Sci-Arc
Extreme Networks

03.12
Florian Idenburg
Senior Associate, SAANA, New York; Visiting Lecturer, Princeton University School of Architecture
SAANA's Two Museums in the U.S.

03.26
Hernan Diaz Alonso
Principal, Xefirotarch, Los Angeles; Design Faculty, Sci-Arc
Pitch-Black

04.02
James Carpenter
Principal, James Carpenter Design Associates, Inc., New York
Environmental Refractions

04.09
Kevin Daly and Christopher Genik
Principals, Daly Genik Architects, Santa Monica
Greetings from Silver Lake

04.25
Guy Nordenson
Partner, Guy Nordenson & Associates, Structural Engineers, New York; Professor, Princeton University School of Architecture

09.12
Eric Kuhne
Eric Kuhne & Associates, London
Marketplace of Ideas

09.24
David Erdman
RSA Cullinan Visiting Critic; david clovers, Los Angeles and Houston
Mass Mysteria

10.08
Bob McGhee
RSA Adjunct Professor; Architect and Senior Facilities Officer, Howard Hughes Medical Institute
From the Inside Out

11.12
Detlef Mertins
Chair, Department of Architecture, University of Pennsylvania
Bioconstructivism

11.26
Yung Ho Chang
Head Department of Architecture, MIT; Atelier FCJZ, Beijing
The Project

12.06
Mark Lee
Johnston Marklee & Associates, Los Angeles
Too Dumb for New York, Too Ugly for LA

Publications

AAR 41
Softspace: From a Representation of Form to a Simulation of Space
Sean Lally and Jessica Young, editors
Routledge

AAR 43
The Things They've Done
Wm. T. Cannady, FAIA, editor

2008

Graduates
M.ARCH.
Alexandre Sevan Acemyan
Laura Allen Baird
Lawrence Philip Baraldi
William Ryan Matta Byrnes
John Carr
Jennifer Raylene Chen
Cecilia Martha Elizondo Cardenas
Francis Gevrier Guittard
Ozge Gulec
John Daniel Hettwer
Kevin Patrick Jones
Clint Alan Keithley
Paul Kweton
Rosalynn Yu-Shan Lu
Julia Virginia Mandell
Paul James Morel

309

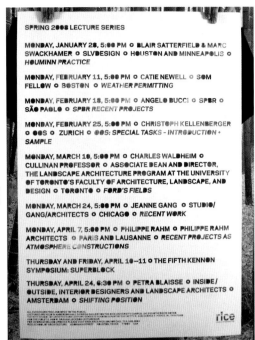

RSA Events poster, Spring 2008

310

Brad Stephan Naeher
Justus Szu-Yi Pang
Joanne Min-Young Park
Amanda McRae Slaughter

B.ARCH
Federico Antonio Cavazos
Ann Min-An Chou
Robert Walton Crawford
Matthew John Crnkovich
Beatrice Ann Eleazar
Christian Anglin Johnson
Ervin
Izabel Ireland Strodtbeck
Gass
Justin Eric Holdahl
Mary Ann Holliday
Julien Boy Jaworski
Charles Barkley Leahy
Brian Trevor Love
Brian John Meinrath
Julie Ann Mulligan
Divya Ratna Pande
Claire Pritchett
Ruya Ipek Saner
Etien Santiago
Kristen Ruth Smith
Jean-Marc Tribie
Christopher Stuart White
Kaileen Y. Yen

Faculty
Andrew Albers
Lecturer

Larry Albert
Visiting Critic
Ernesto Alfaro
Lecturer
Barbara Bryson
Lecturer
William T. Cannady
Professor
John J. Casbarian
Associate Dean and
Professor
Farès el-Dahdah
Associate Professor
Dawn Finley
Assistant Professor
J. Kent Fitzsimons
Assistant Director, Rice
School of Architecture-
Paris
Alan Fleishacker
Lecturer
Stephen Fox
Lecturer
James Furr
Lecturer
Eva Franch
Visiting Wortham Fellow
Nonya Grenader
Professor in Practice
Shirene Hamadeh
Assistant Professor
Christopher Hight
Assistant Professor
Carlos Jiménez
Professor

Rodolphe el-Khoury
Visiting Cullinan Professor
Sanford Kwinter
Associate Professor
Sean Lally
Assistant Professor
Nana Last
Professor in Practice
Clover Lee
Assistant Professor
Lars Lerup
Dean and William Ward
Watkin Professor
Tom Lord
Lecturer
Michael Morrow
Visiting Critic
Douglas Oliver
Professor in Practice
Spencer Parsons
Associate Professor
Chris Perry
Jackson Visiting Critic
Albert Pope
Professor
Joe Powell
Lecturer
Michael Robinson
Lecturer
Danny Samuels
Smith Professor
Blair Satterfield
Visiting Critic
Troy Schaum
Visiting Wortham Fellow

Christopf Spieler
Lecturer
Rives Taylor
Lecturer
Charles Waldheim
Visiting Cullinan Professor
Mark Wamble
Cullinan Professor
Frank White
Lecturer
Kerry Whitehead
Visiting Critic
Gordon Wittenberg
Professor

RED DOG KEEPS HIS EYE ON
YEARS PAST...

Holiday card, 2008

Staff
Doris Anderson
School Administrator
Cathy Bauer
Accounting Assistant, RDA

Mildred Crocker
Accounting Assistant
Kent Fitzsimons
Assistant Director, Rice
School of Architecture
Paris
Kathryn Fosdick
Associate Director,
Programs, RDA
Izabel Gass
Events and Publications
Coordinator
Susan Guidry
Staff Assistant
Hans Krause
Information Technology
Specialist
Chad Loucks
Woodshop Manager
Raj Mankad
Editor, Cite
Raquel Puccio
Staff Assistant, RDA
Kathleen Roberts
Graduate Coordinator
Mary Swift
Associate Director,
Membership, RDA
Linda Sylvan
Executive Director, RDA
Diania Williams
Receptionist

Awards

AIA School Medal
Linh Dan Do
AIA School Certificate
Jessica Colangelo, Megan
Mills
Alpha Rho Chi Medal
Alice Chai
Berda & Charles Soon Chan
Memorial Scholarship
Ethan Feuer
Brett Michael Detamore
Award in Architecture
Karla Wallace
Chillman Prize:
- 1st place
Will Garris
Darden Award
Paul Kweton
Edward B Arrants Award
David Alf
Erin MacKenzie Peck
Freshman Prize in
Architecture
Ryan Botta, Martha Cox,
Aya Matsumoto
Gene Hackerman Award
(graduate)
Quyen Ma

Gene Hackerman Award
(undergraduate)
Van-Tuong Nguyen
H Russell Pitman Graduate
Fellowship in Architecture
Lysle Oliveros
John Crowder Traveling
Fellowship
David Dewane
John T Mitchell Traveling
Fellowship
Katherine Green
LF McCollum Fellowship
Yvette Herrera
Margaret Everson Fossi
Traveling Fellowship:
- 1st place
Amanda Chin, Viktor
Ramos
- 2nd place
Amanda Chin, Beatrice
Eleazar, Nkiru Mokwe
- 3rd place
Curt Gambetta, Brian
Shepherdson
- 4th place
Ernesto Bilbao
Mary Ellen Hale Lovett
Traveling Fellowship
(graduate)
Ernesto Bilbao, Meredith
Epley, Asma Husain,
Kimberly Raborn
Mary Ellen Hale Lovett
Traveling Fellowship
(undergraduate)
David Alf, Alice Chai, Sean
Cowan
MN Davidson Fellowship
Charles Sharpless
Morris R Pitman Award in
Architecture
Curt Gambetta, Cary Place
Ralph S Herman Memorial
Scholarship
Jessica Colangelo
RDA Initiatives for Houston
Grant
Benson Gillespie, Lysle
Oliveros
Rice Visionary Project
Izabel Gass
Tau Sigma Delta
David Alf, Jacquelyn
Cacan, Alice Chai, Jessica
Colangelo, Sean Cowan,
Megan Mills, Van-Tuong
Nguyen, Charles Sharpless
Texas Architectural
Foundation Scholarships:

RSA Events poster, Fall 2008, by Jon LaRocca

- E.G. Spencer Memorial
Scholarship
Linh Dan Do
William Ward Watkin Awards:
- Honorable Mention
Sara Freudensprung
- Rosemary Watkin Barrick
Traveling Fellowship, 4th
place
Van-Tuong Nguyen
- Rosemary Watkin Barrick
Traveling Fellowship, 3rd
place
Jessica Colangelo and
Charles Sharpless
- Rosemary Watkin Barrick
Traveling Fellowship, 2nd
place
Megan Mills
- William Ward Watkin
Traveling Fellowship
Jacquelyn Cacan
Ziegler Cooper Award in
Architecture
Linh Dan Do

Thesis Titles

Alexandre Acemyan—
Mega Distributed Dealer-
ship: Transforming the

Houston Car Dealership
into an Autoscape
Laura Baird—
In Order to Form a More
Perfect Union: A New
Student Center for NYU
Lawrence Baraldi—
Urbanisms of Subsistence:
The Void, the Seed, and
the Splint
William Ryan Byrnes—
Hotel-Beirut Architecture
in the Conflict City
John Carr—
Architecture in 2 ½
Dimensions
Jennifer Chen—
Welcome to the Halfway
House in Prisoner Town,
USA
Cecelia Elizondo—
(re)Program for an Art
District
Francis Guittard—
MegaBank
Ozge Gulec—
New Stockholm Public
Library: An Editable Output

John Hettwer—
Floating: An Infrastructural
Response to Disaster
Kevin Jones—
Prefabricating Flexibility:
Aggregate House
Clint Keithly—
Mo' Pixels, Mo' Prolems:
Institionalizing Street
Artists without Killing Their
Street Cred
Paul Kweton—
DFW-AHC: The future of
physical gambling in the
US
Julia Mandell—
River of Trees: A Floating
Ecotourism Camp in the
Atchafalaya Basin
Paul Morel—
Parliament/Park
Brad Naeher—
Etreating the Megachurch
Joanne Park—
Borderwall: Peace and the
Future of the Korean DMZ
Justus Pang—
The Parking Garage Apart-
ment Park: Accommodating
the Increasing Density of
Los Angeles
Amanda Slaughter—
Closer to Heaven: The
Typology of the Cemetary
Tower

312

Lectures
01.28
**Blair Satterfield and Marc
Swackhamer**
SLVDesign, Houston and
Minneapolis
Houminn Practice

02.11
Catie Newell
SOM Fellow, Boston
Weather Permitting

02.18
Angelo Bucci
SPBR, Sao Paolo
SPBR Recent Projects

02.25
Christoph Kellenberger
OOS, Zurich
*OOS: Special Tasks –
Introduction + Sample*

03.10
Charles Waldheim
Cullinan Professor, Rice
School of Architecture;
Associate Dean and Director,
The Landscape Architecture
Program at the University of
Toronto
Ford's Field

03.24
Jeanne Gang
Studio/Gang/Architects,
Chicago
Recent Work

04.07
Philippe Rahm
Rhilippe Rahm Architects,
Paris and Lausanne
*Recent Projects as
Atmosphere Constructions*

04.24
Petra Blaisse
Inside/Outside, Interior
Designers and Landscape
Architects, Amsterdam
Shifting Position

10.20
Lawrence Barth
Senior Lecturer in Urbanism,
Architectural Association;
Consultant urbanist, London

11.03
**Rodolphe el-Khoury and
Robert Levit**
Partners, Khoury Levit Fong,
Toronto

11.10
Francisco Javier Rodriguez
Principal, r s v p architects,
New York and San Juan; Dean
at the University of Puerto
Rico School of Architecture

11.17
Mark Rakatansky
Principal, Mark Rakatansky
Studio, New York

11.19
**Marcelyn Gow and
Chris Perry**
Partners, servo, an architec-
tural design collaborative with
offices in Europe and the U.S

2008/2009
2009 (half)

Faculty
Andrew Albers
Lecturer
Larry Albert
Visiting Critic
Ernesto Alfaro
Lecturer
Barbara Bryson
Lecturer
William T. Cannady
Professor
John J. Casbarian
Associate Dean and
Professor
Farès el-Dahdah
Associate Professor
Dawn Finley
Assistant Professor
J. Kent Fitzsimons
Assistant Director, Rice
School of Architecture-
Paris
Alan Fleishacker
Lecturer
Stephen Fox
Lecturer
James Furr
Lecturer
Eva Franch
Visiting Wortham Fellow
Nonya Grenader
Professor in Practice
Shirene Hamadeh
Assistant Professor
Christopher Hight
Assistant Professor
Carlos Jiménez
Professor
Rodolphe el-Khoury
Visiting Cullinan Professor
Sanford Kwinter
Associate Professor
Sean Lally
Assistant Professor
Nana Last
Professor in Practice
Clover Lee
Assistant Professor
Lars Lerup
Dean and William Ward
Watkin Professor
Tom Lord
Lecturer
Michael Morrow
Visiting Critic
Douglas Oliver
Professor in Practice
Spencer Parsons
Associate Professor

Chris Perry
Jackson Visiting Critic
Albert Pope
Professor
Joe Powell
Lecturer
Michael Robinson
Lecturer
Danny Samuels
Smith Professor
Blair Satterfield
Visiting Critic
Troy Schaum
Visiting Wortham Fellow
Christopf Spieler
Lecturer
Rives Taylor
Lecturer
Charles Waldheim
Visiting Cullinan Professor
Mark Wamble
Cullinan Professor
Frank White
Lecturer
Kerry Whitehead
Visiting Critic
Gordon Wittenberg
Professor

Staff
Doris Anderson
School Administrator
Cathy Bauer
Accounting Assistant, RDA
Mildred Crocker
Accounting Assistant
Kent Fitzsimons
Assistant Director, Rice
School of Architecture
Paris
Kathryn Fosdick
Associate Director,
Programs, RDA
Izabel Gass
Events and Publications
Coordinator
Susan Guidry
Staff Assistant
Hans Krause
Information Technology
Specialist
Chad Loucks
Woodshop Manager
Raj Mankad
Editor, Cite
Raquel Puccio
Staff Assistant, RDA
Kathleen Roberts
Graduate Coordinator
Mary Swift
Associate Director,
Membership, RDA

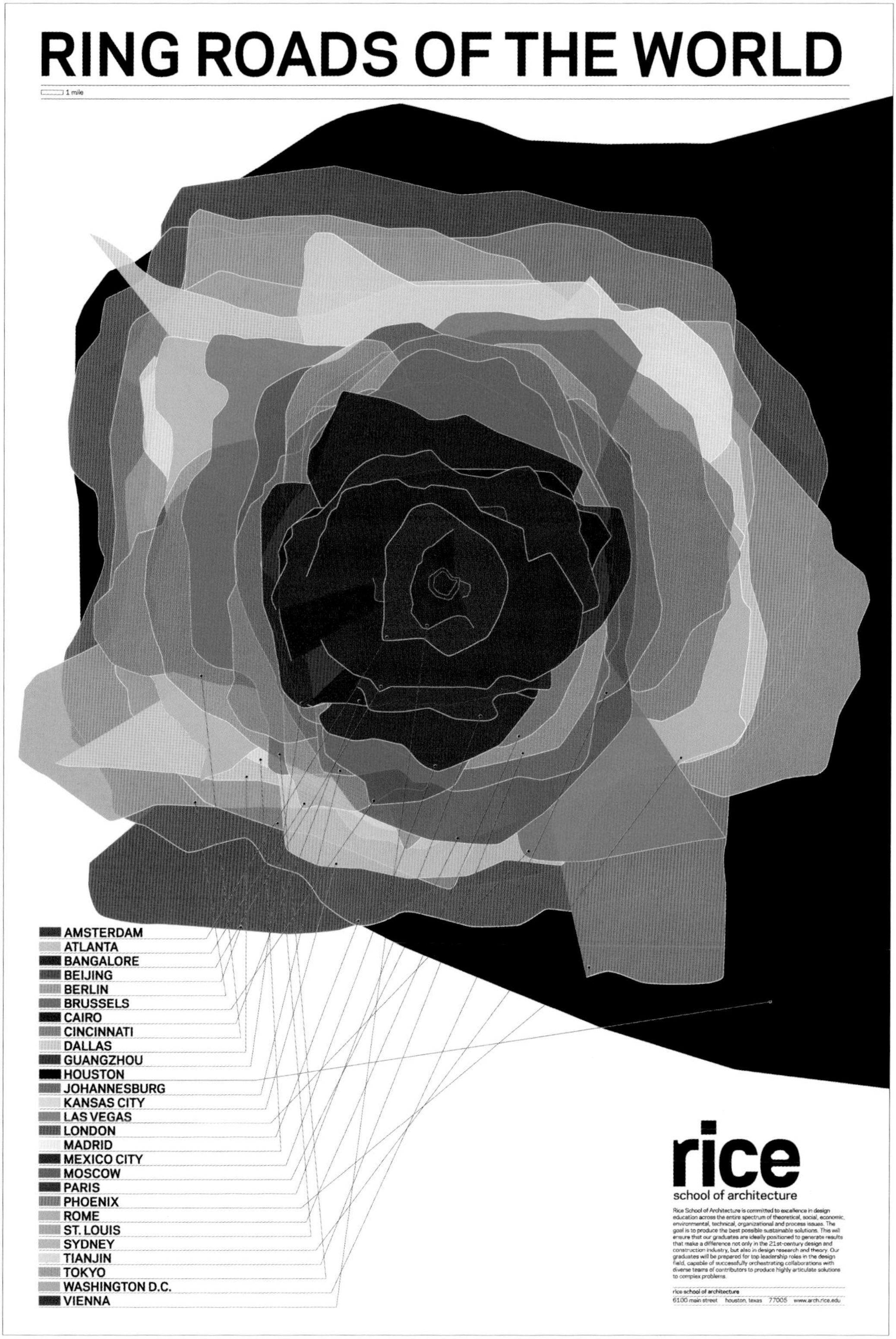

RSA poster, 2009

Linda Sylvan
Executive Director, RDA
Diania Williams
Receptionist

Thesis titles

Michael Binick—
Power Struggle: Explorations of a New Autonomy
María del Mar Ceballos—
Evento-Barrio: Scaping the Wall
W. Amanda Chin—
Manhattan's Annex [the crosstown [of] excess]
Ned Dodington—
Polyspecies Park
Curt Gambetta—
Making Waste Public
Richie Gelles—
Super NAFTA Land!
Katherine Hays—
The Next Step: Recreational Trail Interface
Quyen Ma—
Strip Culture: Emergent Identities in the Suburban Landscape
Nkiru Mokwe—
MTA[Lagos] – mobile transaction architecture: Rethinking the Drive Through Market
Marina Nicollier—
Change of Heart
Lysle Oliveros—
Houston Needs a Mountain

Cary d'Alo Place—
Krumped Control: Constructing the LAPD Interface
Kim Raborn—
The 13th Compound: Co-operative Development of an Industrial Urban Village
Viktor Ramos—
The Continuous Enclave: Strategies in Bypass Urbanism
Heather Rowell—
Driving Forces: Projections of the Car City
Brian Shepherdson—
Hyper Geographic Office: How the Clouds Activate Public Space
Peter Stanley—
Post-Game: Re-appropiating America's Jettisoned Stadia
Leming Yang—
The New Crowd: Subway Station Design with Digital Circulation for the newly Developed Beijing Subway Line 8

Lectures

01.07
Geoff Manaugh
Senior editior, *Dwell* magazine
Cities Gone Wild

01.12
Pier Vittorio Aureli
Co-founder, Dogma, an architectural collective
Without Attributes: Towards a History of Non-Figurative Architecture

01.26
Beatriz Colomina
Architectural historian and theorist; Professor and Founding Director of the Program in Media and Modernity, Princeton University
Blurred Vision: Architectures of Surveillance from Mies to SANAA

02.02
Reinhold Martin
Associate Professor, Columbia University GSAPP; Partner, Martin/Baxi Architects
Utopia's Ghost: Postmodernism Reconsidered

02.16
Stan Allen
Dean and Professor of Architectural Design, Princeton University; Principal, SAA / Stan Allen Architect
Pavilions and Fields: Beyond Landscape Urbanism

02.18
Peter Trummer
Architect and Head of the Associatve Design Research Program, Berlage Institute, Rotterdam
Urbanism in the Age of Bio-Politics

03.16
Felicity Scott
Assistant Professor of Architecture, Columbia University GSAPP; Founding co-editor, *Grey Room*
Code Wars

03.23
Cynthia Davidson
Editor, **Log** and Writing Architecture book series
Publish or Perish? (Architecture in a Media Age)

03.25
Juan Herreros
Principal, Herreros Arquitectos, Madrid; Senior Professor, School of Architecture of Madrid
Civil Architecture

03.30
Richard Ingersoll
Architectural historian; Associate Professor, Syracuse University in Florence, Italy
Toward a Cross-Cultural History of the Built Environment

04.16
Michael Weinstock
Academic Head, Architectural Association; Director of the Emergent Technologies and Design Program, AA; Founding member of The Emergence and Design Group
The Evolution of Form in Nature and Civilisation

Exhibition

March 11 through March 25
Oscar 101 / BPP 51: Eight Projects in Commemoration of Oscar Niemeyer and the Brasilia Pilot Plan
Organized by Farès el-Dahdah

RSA Events poster, Spring 2009

314

Kennon Symposium

Everything Must Move

The 5th Kennon Symposium
March 20 and 21
Organized by Lars Lerup with
Izabel Gass

Participants: John Casbarian,
Yung-Ho Chang, Sir Peter
Cook, Farès el-Dahdah,
Edward Dimendberg, Peter
Eisenman, David Erdman,
Dawn Finley, Luis Galiano,
Christopher Hight, Jeffrey
Inaba, Alfred Jacoby, Carlos
Jiménez, Kevin Kennon,
Sanford Kwinter, Clover Lee,
Lars Lerup, Bart Lootsma,
Francisco Mangado, Robert
Mangurian, Albert Pope, Mary-
Ann Ray, Lars Reutersward,
Stanley Saitowitz, Robert
Somol, Brett Steele, Roemer
van Toorn, Mark Wamble,
Sarah Whiting, Ron Witte

Publications

AAR 44

Everything Must Move:
15 Years at Rice School of
Architecture, 1994-2009

Words

38th floor
1968, May 1968
A
Accident
Act
Action
Activity
Aformal
Agglomeration
Air
Airport
Alibi
Alienation
Allison
Ambiguity
America
Amorphous
Analog
Animation
Answers

Anything
Appropriate
Architecture
Archive
Art
Artifact
Astrodome
Automobile
Autonomy
B
Bayou
Ballardian
Beauty
Big Box
Bigness
Binary thinking
Biology
Blob
Book
Borrowing
Box
Boundaries
Bridge
Building
Business
C
Camera
Capital
Cell
Center
Central Business District
Chair
Chance
Charts and graphs
Chemistry
Chicken scratch
Cinema
Citta Aperta
City
Circuit
Clay
Cleverness
Climactic
Climatic
Clothing
Collective
Comic
Commute
Competition
Complexity
Comprehensive
Computation
Concrete
Constraints
Contour
Conurbation
Co-operation
Coordination
Crime
Cross-Fertilization
Cul de Sac
Culture

Words

D
Democracy
Design
Detention Basin
Developer
Development
Diagram
Digital
Disaster
Discipline
Discussion
Disegno speculativo
Dispersed
Displacement
Dizzying
Domestic
Doris
Drainage
Draw
Dross
Duration
Dynamic
E
Ecology
Economic
Ecosystem
Edge
Emergent
Enclave
End(less)
Energy
Enron
Entertainment
Entropy
Europe
Event
Event Surface
Everything
Ex-urb
Exhibit
Expression
Exuberance
F
Fabrication
Fashion
Fiction
Fiesta
Film
Finance
Find
Fixity
Flat
Flexibility
Flight
Flood
Floodplain
Floor
Flow
Flux
Fold
Footprint
Form

Framework
Freedom
Freeway
Front
Frontier
Function
Furniture
Future
G
Galleria
Gas
Geneology
Gift
Globalization
Go
Good
Gray Space
Gray Zones
Growth
Gulf
Gumbo
H
Hans
Happiness
Hardware
Hedge
High
History
Holey Plane
Horizontal
Housey House
Humidity
Hurricane
Hybrid
Hypermarket
I
Ice House
Identity
Image
Impossible
Improvisation
Incremental
Infiltrate
Influence
Informal
Information
Infrastructure
Inner Loop
Inside/outside
Interior urbanism
Interview
Iteration
J
Joke
Joy
K
Katrina
Knowledge
Kulture
L
Ladder
Landbank

Words

NOW
Lars Lerup

"Architecture has been absorbed by the Metropolis." This daunting proposition by Manfredo Tafuri set the stage for our rethinking of architectural education at the Rice School of Architecture. The year was 1994. Now, we are seeing the results.

Although we are still a professional school grounded in the architectural discipline, the boundaries have shifted. The two opposing poles have been hollowed out and replenished with new content. Concerns have become panoramic. Never focused simply on hardware, or on an obsession with form, architecture at Rice is soft, ambiguous—alive.

We hold that an architect must reflect on his or her work. Reflection then becomes an instrument of design—"architecture is built thought." But it is built as software, program, and attitude as often as it is in steel and glass. Synthesizing thinking and design, the profession finds its place in the university.

The metropolis provides us with a dizzying array of new tools and a steadily shifting worldview that challenge traditional, well-established practices. Relying on its pragmatic approach to the practice and discipline of architecture, Rice has historically faced change with a steady calm. Aware that thinking, learning, and teaching cannot yet be replaced by machines, we still have committed ourselves fully to the electronic revolution, providing students with the latest in soft and hardware. Even as we bid farewell to a mechanical world-view, we recognize that it will be awhile before culture becomes indistinguishable from nature—before we can grow our houses.

Confronted by the sprawl of a postwar city, we have come to see architecture through the lens of the suburban metropolis. Because of its typical characteristics, Houston has remained our primary laboratory: multi-centered, dispersed, and amorphous. The city as we have known it is passé, but the alternatives—somatic clusters in protected enclaves—do not meet our hopes for the emerging metropolis: site that is no longer fixed but always becoming, always in the making and there to be made. In fact, it has already begun: the hollowing out of the city's inner loop has been arrested and replaced by new growth inside. The middle ground (rather than the edge) has become the new frontier.

The introduction of the often harsh realities of the surrounding metropolis—Houstonians cumulatively spend the equivalent of 35 years a day commuting; the money spent on one mile of freeway construction could build 367 houses; 20-25 percent of the population lives on and around the poverty line; the design fee for an average suburban subdivision is 0.03 percent of its construction cost—challenges faculty and students to perform their work in a pragmatic atmosphere. Architectural education has been brought onto the floor of the emerging metropolis.

We lay claim to seven educational innovations, one for each year of the Metropolitan Project:

1. Ideas are more important than form
Experience has shown us that formal eloquence is just that and no more, without ideas. Architecture is built thought. Thinking, reflection, and criticism produce form.

2. The city is conservative and the metropolis is revolutionary
The concept of the city has been so reduced that it applies only to a "lovely Italian hill town"; but much like Adolf Loos' art object, the metropolis is radical, unpredictable, wild.

3. Architecture writes, speaks, thinks, and moves while attempting to form us
Just as Walter Benjamin couldn't think of a photograph without a caption, architecture is steeped in language, thought, labels and

brands. Despite its apparent destiny as stasis, it is always on the move.

4. Architecture arises from capital

Architecture schools seem to be the last to know that architecture does not come from design but from capital. This realization transforms all the formerly boring courses in engineering and finance into exciting courses in design.

5. Binary thinking must die

The mind-body, nature-culture, program-design splits were fundamental to the mechanical worldview. In an age of biology, all such simplicity is erased in favor of the dynamic and complex.

6. Working together

Rice is the open city—la città aperta—a school without trademarks. Working together in teams under the auspices of the Metropolitan Project fosters camaraderie, a common purpose, and better work.

7. Everything moves

Fixed ideas, standard responses, and formulaic rights and wrongs have been replaced by innovation, risk-taking, skepticism, desire, respect for others, and a passion for a better world.

The last bayou

The Corps was here!

A to Z
Lars Lerup and Roemer van Toorn in conversation

A as in Ambiguity

RvT: Just like Stephen Shore's photos of America, you seem to like places and things that are not just unfinished but what Michael Fried has called "unfinishable." I sense that you are interested in situations that can never be fixed up. Somehow you like complexities that cannot be expressed simply in terms of "this is good, and that is bad." It seems that you find these sorts of places and things imaginatively liberating. Combining a surf-board with a bowling ball as a piece of furniture, or provoking us with titles such as "Toxic Ecology," or spinning other theatrical stories seems to indicate that you are interested in ambiguous and even contradictory constellations (at times positively schizophrenic in character). What gives ambiguity (correct me if I am wrong) so much potential?

LL: Leonard Cohen sings: "Forget the perfect offering. There is a crack in everything. That's how the light gets in." Roland Barthes also tells us that "where the garment gapes" is where the erotic has its locus. One of my first books was titled Building the Unfinished. All three offer openings—escapes—futures. The unpredictable.

The ambiguous has been with me from the very beginning—I never knew for sure who either of my grandfathers was. I am drawn to the enigma that never disappears, why I don't know.

So what happens when you insert a bowling ball into a surfboard and call the hybrid table a "floor-mouse"? You get (aside from its tableness) at least three other trajectories, each leading away from tabledom—stealing its genus. Ambiguity opens the object to others by diverting the designer's synthetic intention. But when you try to make it your own, the table figuratively slips away into a bowling alley, or into the tube of a huge wave breaking toward a beach in Hawaii, or into the world of the computer mouse. Meanwhile the supposed table smiles at us ambiguously, Sphinx-like. Because it knows that despite its versatility, it is simultaneously uniquely itself. Slipping out of any orthodox claim on meaning, it belongs to the world.

Architects are hopelessly mired in the perfect object; I guess that prohibits me from claiming the title. Ambiguity is my muse—my escape route—my hope for redemption.

B as in Becoming

RvT: As you have stated elsewhere, you see the dichotomy between city and suburb as a real obstacle to rethinking architecture and with it humanity in our urban age. It is all about the suburban metropolis today, full of unpredictable, wild, and radical becoming. It looks as if——on first sight——that the urban age today, with its end-less city, is producing (by itself now) what you always have been looking for: permanent becom-ing full of ambiguity. What are the risks of such becoming and the potentials of the current urban developments when we understand the city as an entity beyond its fixed form? At times you even celebrate suburbia (stimdross)...

LL: The dichotomy is both conceptual and ac-tual. If we see city/suburb as a Janus face, where the suburb is the "guilty conscience" of the city (since the city couldn't satisfy the fleeing middle class), and thus make the two umbilically connected, a new conscious-ness under the rubric of urbanism emerges.

The radical becoming that I suggest lies dormant in suburbia is embedded in its in-completeness. In its unevolved "stupidity" lies the hope that with time suburbia will shed its adolescence and come of age. Here I (naively?) put my money on IT——on the vir-tual——which is beginning to compensate for suburbia's physical impediments.

J. G. Ballard suggests that suburbia is a "huge petting zoo" full of furry animals. This suggests that suburbia may be infantile in its cheery fluffiness, but one day the cute pets may bite back. So we as urbanists, much like good parents, need to affirm suburbia's well-being by gently petting it, but at the same time urge it to take a larger responsi-bility for the metropolis——an acknowledgment that suburbia, like a mollusk, now lives in attached symbiosis with the city. Only in tandem will city and suburb meet the chal-lenges of the future.

Human foolishness——and suburbia may be one good example——is also our hapless acknowl-edgment that we don't really know where we came from and where we are heading. This leads us back to "A": our destiny is ulti-mately ambiguous.

C as in Critique

RvT: Can we still speak of resistance or critique in architecture? Are you a supporter of the Projective (versus the Critical), as advocated by Bob Somol and Sarah Whiting? Or is there a third position?

LL: If I understand Projective practice cor-rectly, it suggests that you criticize by projecting a better future——deed over word. My own "practice" uses analytical descriptions to project a reading that is akin to deconstruction, revealing "where the garment gapes" or "where the light comes in," while avoiding direct criticism. I must confess that I generally find critique overrated and plagued by self-righteousness. If you look back at my writing, you see that my ambition has been to find "better explanations," and I have rarely, if ever, written about "things" that I don't like (which suggests that I am critical, too, but perform this in privacy and reflect it in my choice of work to consider). I have a distinct affection for interpretation and thus hermeneutics, and see my work as a modest contribution to this field.

I leave criticism to the young and to brilliant critics like Dave Hickey and Michael Sorkin.

D as in Death of Architecture

RvT: At first——on your arrival in America——you seem to "hate" capitalism. Like Manfredo Tafuri, you conclude that architecture is dead, and that our permanent values have lost their permanence and their manifestation in the city fabric. But later——confronted by, and living in, Houston——you start to be less pessimistic. You come to the conclusion that the resistance of traditional architecture in the face of radical mobility demands a rethinking rather than viewing it as an escape. Architecture should no longer be seen as a kind of static enterprise but instead as a form of software. Does this mean that somehow through your experiences in America your idea of architecture has changed? You have been a friend of Aldo Rossi——and today his plea for absolute architecture is returning... What is your "definition" of architecture?

LL: Yes, my evolution from "hating" to ambiguously "accepting" the current conditions is evident——today it is very hard for me to hate. Living in Houston has made me a compliant victim of the Stockholm Syndrome.

Architecture will most certainly remain as long as homo faber exists, while the Architect——as some Foucauldian drawing on the beach——may disappear or be transformed until we no longer recognize it. Architecture therefore is a "moving feast" that architects may choose to forego——in the US they have done a very good job at leaving the responsibility to others: construction managers and market consultants are two examples.

For me everything artificial, soft and hard, is architecture with a small a. At the same time, I would be sad if Architecture with a capital A disappeared. I once

asked Aldo, "What is your favorite architecture?" To which he answered, holding me in his dreamy gaze, "The architecture of my friends." I am afraid I am caught in the same sentimentality. Yet I view proclamations about Architecture's death as premature, not unlike Francis Fukuyama's "end of history."

Despite my deep affection for the vernacular, my long training in the "finer things of bourgeois life" will not leave me until my vision goes. A finely shaped human ankle——male or female——will catch my eye as readily as the rhino-induced shape of an imaginary shell produced by a student.

In the end, my preference is for the broken and the used, not unlike traditional Japanese ideals. However, my own predilections are not messianic; in this sense I have no problem with the practitioners of the absolute.

E as in Education

RvT: Given the current condition of the Metropolis, you have rethought architecture education at the Rice School of Architecture. How do you see the role of the university (as an independent institute educating professional architects as well as public intellectuals who think further than what the client wants), the student, and academic research? Several international schools have abandoned individual (thesis) research and focus instead upon units led by a professor who produces architectural knowledge in collaboration with the students. Mapping the real, along with architectural expertise (technology) and even CAD-generated advanced forms (leading to "blobalization"), has become the trend today. What are the risks and advantages of these trends and shifts of focus in architecture education? And what would you advise the next RSA dean and his/her colleagues to do next? Or is the passion for the real (mapping and technology) enough?

LL: Let me begin by saying that my tolerance for others' preoccupations is considerably greater than my tolerance for my own. Therefore intersubjectivity has dominated my teaching, combined with what I call the "kiss & kick" method. (This is particularly important with American students who often confuse life with art.) Thus "kissing the ego" plus tough, direct, and honest criticism has been my way: i.e., "You are a great person, but the project is not good."

So, in terms of the new, I tolerate it——in fact, encourage it——as long as we don't lose track of the "design activity" so beautifully defined by Herbert Simon. Given that the field of architecture is extremely wide and generous, as educators we must go with this flow. That it helps older people like myself to stay relevant (without really trying) is a side benefit. (In the privacy of my home, I can still drool over minimalism or my preference for the borderline surreal as in the misanthropic interiors of Jean-Michel Frank.)

I am concerned by your suggestion that "making" is being replaced by a passion for the real. My concern stems from my belief that "in order to see, we must act," which, if I am not mistaken, comes from Heinz von Foerster, whose cybernetics is one of my cornerstones. This dictum suggests that we must take the leap before we can really see. Thus making is the vehicle for seeing. This makes architectural education a very important and lucky enterprise. The architect is the embodiment of the homo faber. With due respect for the "real," to abandon this gift is self-destructive.

It is clear that architectural practice is always a teamwork process, making collaborative studios an obvious response. But if this means abandoning the evolution of the self in its own space and time, I beg to differ with the obvious. Especially since all real teams have leaders, and unless you choose a leader in a collaborative studio, the experience remains unreal. I have never understood why we always have to reinvent the wheel. We could use a bit more gracious acknowledgment that the new complexity engulfing us all must be managed and navigated with considerably better tools than simple abandonment of yesterday's activity in favor of today's. Just as sex and food are necessary for a good life, making is a necessary ingredient in a design school—I bet this will never change.

F as in Film

RvT: In a film, each character follows a series of paths, which intersect with the paths of other characters, and the spectator classifies different locations in terms of their spatial, social, and psychological relationships with the characters. The same is true of buildings, but architects seem to take the plot (and its programming) hardly ever seriously. I believe there is so much to learn from film——how architecture in film (and theatre) always gives priority to meaning and use instead of "just" form. What architects forget is that reality is all about our emotional inner life——the chaotic, fierce world full of affects, fears, associations, contradictions, desires, and nightmares. According to Slavoy Zizek[1], cinema is the right medium by which to arrive at the reality in your mind. So what is your favorite film?

LL: There are a couple of interesting dilemmas that appear when we use film as a metaphor for architecture.

Despite all its subplots, a film is determined to drive its narrative to its conclusion. Roman Polanski has said that "movies should make you forget that you are in a movie," and that is not exactly the case with architecture. In film, you have to have a willing subject who is able to abandon life for the movie's reality. The camera movement is the action that awakens the seeing eye. That is why movies are so compelling—so "real."

The architect, however, is only in charge of the setting, not the plot. Buildings need to serve diverging and different narratives. And unfortunately, as Martin Pawley once wrote, "Architecture is not a radio." Architecture cannot create (broadcast) meaning, emotion, or awareness without a willing subject who is able to engage it. The peculiar muteness of a building works in at least two ways. First, it is true that architects ignore the importance of the program and ignore meaning, but when the experience of a building is good, none of those concerns matter: the goodness comes from the interaction between architecture and subject. As is often said (with a slight twist), "a building is only as good as its client"—the client here being the user. Second, the muteness allows for interpretation——action, desire, and determination. Thus, any building can be good provided the subject is inventive enough. A scary thought for the architect who believes he or she determines behavior.

In the end, I don't like to confuse different practices. Architecture is strong enough to survive by itself. This certainty probably stems from my affection for, and belief in, its autonomy (as suggested by its muteness), but also from my long struggles with the various professions that are trying to highjack architecture: social scientists, do-gooders, bankers, psychologists, and artists. The only practitioners I like to share architecture with are philosophers, economists, engineers, and those in the building trades.

Since life flows on and memory lapses are one of my devices to stay young, my favorite films are both forgotten and probably ever changing. My first love must have been *Robin Hood* with Alan Ladd, and a bit later Zbigniew Cybulski in Polanski's *Knife in the Water*, but I have forgotten the plot (remembering only the cool glasses that Zbig wore). Then Ingmar Bergman, over and over again. But my loves, directly connected to my purported generosity, are wide ranging, from Benny Hill to Jean-Luc Godard. Oh, I forgot Rita Hayward. So on the subject of favorites, I am hopeless.

G as in Guilt

RvT: You can make an industry out of guilt——Daniel Libeskind has made a name for himself painstakingly recording the trauma of the twentieth century——but what irritates me is how journalists and those in academia attacked Rem Koolhaas for constructing the mouthpiece of totalitarian China (CCTV in Beijing). Architects cannot afford the luxury of retreating into the comfortable space of the critic, but must get their hands dirty in negotiation with reality. In that sense, all architects are guilty… China, says Rem Koolhaas, is still a state. He claims that this allows him to focus on the public interest——rather than using aesthetics as a cover for the sacrifice of personal principles to a capitalist regime that puts the profit motive above all else. "Money is a less fundamental tenet of their ideology," says Rem Koolhaas. How do you "judge" architecture?

LL: After a decade of self-righteousness exported by our own political and economic systems, it is hard to enter the guilt industry with much enthusiasm, although architecture may have a privileged status in such a debate. Just as I don't believe there is Fascist architecture——only Fascists——commodious building is a plus in any system. It may become trickier if what you design is housing for alleged terrorists in Guantanamo, although you may escape guilt by making humane rooms (albeit for inhumane activities). If we appreciate Rem's project for its commitment to the "public interest," the building is clearly "awesome." But with caveats: what, for instance, have he and the contractors done to diminish the possibility of injury during construction? During 2005, there were some 250,000 work-related accidents in China, clearly a public interest issue. In other words, there are many complex ethical issues intertwined within the fundamentally positive design activity.

How do I judge architecture? When I do, mostly in my mind, I look for "the cracks where the light comes in." I am thinking here of Peter Celsing's central bank in Stockholm, for me one of the most intriguing buildings of the twentieth century. It is full of surprises and strange gaps of reason, beginning at the majestic granite façade. At first appearing solid and heroic, it becomes upon closer scrutiny profoundly unsettling: is it structure or mere surface——carrying or merely hanging? No visual scrutiny helps here; the eye must rely on faith——Hinc Robur et Securitas (In This Rests Our Security), as Swedish paper currency declares. Although I wrote a major research paper on the bank, I never wanted to solve the puzzle, just as I prefer not to know how someone does a card trick. Unfortunately

for me, there are very few if any buildings filled with such enigmatic power. The closest I have found is in the field of painting, especially Giogio de Chirico's oeuvre, both the radical and the neoclassical periods of his work.

Being halbstark, or half-strong (referring to the German word for 1950's adolescent rebels), may be a central tenet in my approach to evaluating architecture. Simultaneous weakness and strength. Wise counsel given that a unified theory of everything has yet to account for gravity.

H as in Hesitation

RvT: For a moment I was not sure which word to choose, but than I understood (from your writings on "The Metropolitan Architect" in *After the City*) that the architect's Hand, his/her principle of Hope, and the architect's House (habitation proper) only get their true meaning through the concept of Hesitation. Without hesitation, there is no life for you, no future, and no architecture worth speaking of. Why is that? And could you perhaps give us some hints as to how to produce hesitation? (Can the tools of hesitation be smooth, striated, violent, and/or representational? In what way are the floor plans, framing of the view, tectonics, etc., different from the "norm"?) What kind of specific freedoms do they produce? Albert Frey's desert house in Palm Springs is indeed amazing, but are there any contemporary architects you can think of who work in this "tradition" too?

LL: To hesitate is to acknowledge that we don't yet know, and the only way to overcome not-knowing is to act in a partial fog. This requires a belief in the self, in fate. Fools and heroes may not notice, or appreciate, this moment of suspended animation. Frey, out there in the hysterically vibrating heat of the desert, knew or just felt how to act or let be. Like a puma, he knew, maybe instinctively, when to strike and when to wait. A very unusual sensibility, it is probably found only among architects whose feet and mind are on the site——the rhino-motored architect is a very different creature. (Are there any new pumas? I think we may be breeding some at Rice.)

I as in Immediacy

RvT: Walter Benjamin speaks about the fact that criticism must change and that the model for this change is the advertisement or, simply, anything that creates a "perceived contact with things"——like the space of the street. This approach (beyond critique) taps into the touch of, and fascination with, everyday life: how people are touched by it, blown away by it, or simply "warmed by the subject" and so desire it. In a more theoretical sense, Benjamin tells us that this critical approach, like advertising, should affect the reader and user through visceral projections of "fragmented" intensity that circumvent any form of contemplation. This intensity (distraction) is something like a "burst of energy" that affects the very life of the subject. What seems privileged in this approach is immediacy, that bolus of direct experience, those lines of flight that cannot be reflected by any dominant social system because they cannot, by definition, exhaust all social experience. The unknown always potentially contains space for alternative intentions that are not yet articulated as social institution or even project. What is the power of the immediate according to you, now that capitalism has discovered the subversive power of everyday life? Several artists, designers, and architects have embraced the everyday and mass culture——like Droog Design and architecture in the Netherlands——but it also has to do with the fascination with cities like Houston, Lagos, and Dubai, and it doesn't stop there. Activism (and with it a return to the sixties), creating networks of participation and interaction among different people, is being advocated nowadays.

LL: Immediacy, proximity, and nearness require what I have called "mechanisms of closeness," or design machines where people and environments are bound together in conspiracy——in common purpose. There seems to be an aversion against such intimacy in American society——a fear of pollution, of losing the self. Yet, at the same time, the ancient distinction between mind and body is being seriously questioned, and subsequently so is the distinction between finite individual and environment. To experience the "burst of energy," there can be no distinction between the dancer and the dance, between the dwellers and the environment. Again we must have collusion——a willing subject.

I am not sure that everyday life has the particular privilege of being more conducive than architecture to such "hot" interaction. So much of our daily life is driven by agendas that literally use the environment merely as a vehicle because their conclusions lie in the immediate future. Thus getting to the coffeehouse is like a jump cut in a movie, a blank, maybe even an annoyance. And the crowd in the street may promote some togetherness, but unless there is a hot spot——a "flock-event," i.e., suddenly you encounter Baudelaire with a turtle on a leash——this too is just a blank. In my world humans have to awaken the environment by colluding in its promises, not the other way around.

J as in Joke (and Joy)

RvT: Whatever happened to humor, parody, and laughter in architecture? I think architecture takes itself much too seriously, and the critics are even worse. I do know that you enjoy the humor of much contemporary Dutch architecture. I am curious to find examples and a definition of the potential of jouissance in architecture, and I would be thrilled if you could speculate upon what architectural laughter could activate.

LL: Beginning with Celsing's bank, I think it is clear that architecture can provoke "curiosity + puzzlement," while standing in front of the world's longest bridge, tallest building, or longest pool may result in "awe." Looking at Rossi's school in Bologna, Italy, brings out "melancholy," and Coop Himmelb(l)au's "apartment on fire" in Vienna prompts "immediacy." But "laughter" seems much harder to find. Of course, if you turn to roadside architecture, Fast Food Ducks and Giant Sausages evokes "mirth," and when arriving in Vegas, you can even feel "hilarity." But I think you are asking for more. The Lacanian version of jouisssance in contradistinction to plaisir, or enjoyment, is hard to grasp in English (maybe for prudish reasons since jouisssance has sexual connotations). Jacques Lacan opposes the two to suggest that Freud's pleasure principle limits rather than promotes and enhances jouisssance, which in turn pushes pleasure to the point where it slips into pain.

Again architecture has its media constraints, illustrated by its muteness, and since I side with life rather than art, architecture fails me in this particular pursuit.

K as in Kitsch

RvT: "When I hear the word 'culture,' I reach for my gun," Joseph Goebbels once said. "When I hear the word 'culture,' I reach for my checkbook," says the cynical producer in Jean-Luc Godard's film Le Mépris. And a leftist slogan inverts Goebbels's statement: "When I hear the word 'gun,' I reach for culture." Indeed culture has become mainstream, almost as big an industry as the military. In that sense the subversive quality of the avant-garde (and its pleasure principle) has become a potent energy source for the creative class, from Andy Warhol to Damien Hirst, and the experience economy it is running. No wonder that "starchitects" and their iconic buildings are celebrated these days. How would you position architecture once it becomes part of this mass culture of kitsch? Does kitsch have potential? Should we ignore the spectacle-ization of life altogether——return to silence and autonomy——or rework it from within, look for the gaps, ride its waves like a buccaneer?

LL: Kitsch as a way for the elite to separate themselves from those with bad taste has suffered inflation. Now "bad taste" is so prevalent that the word kitsch may have lost its punch. I don't see much hope for kitsch, first because it has lost its ability to differentiate, and second because, when it does distinguish the good from the ugly, it is still just bad taste. My analytical affection for suburbia may have influenced my thought here, since everything built there is "as if"—whether English Tudor, French Provincial, or Spanish Hacienda—but when you look closer at houses built within these narrow stylistic confines, you find innovation that makes it almost okay.

The celebrity culture is, of course, deeply longing for more celebrity, now at any cost. Among the momentarily chosen—every year someone is airbrushed away and replaced by some new phenomena—one senses an internal bonhomie that reveals the volatility, vacuity, and fear of fading behind such fame. Having been a backbencher in the reality shows featuring practitioners of the Bilbao Effect, I have concluded all you need is Charlie Rose and a coterie of Peters, Jacques, and Zahas, all indulging in blogging vivante—and always acting as if there is no audience. Here bad taste has reached its nadir: the only one who seems to remain unscathed is Charlie Rose. The only feeling left for us sitting in darkness is envy and loss. The venerable architectural discipline has been reduced to providing endless bandwidth to the personality cult. Kitsch has been replaced by vanity.

A commodious Tudor, basking in bucolic suburban splendor, is far more consequential to millions of suburbanites than the recent Olympic "Bird's Nest" stadium, whose image on our TV screens will now be beamed up to the advertising world to sell perfumes and puff pastry. So if I have to make a bet on kitsch, its central locus is still Dallas—silence in this light seems wonderful.

L as in Lars Lerup

RvT: Today's neo-conservatism (and fundamentalism) makes us believe that strangers——i.e., the immigrant——can only bring harm. I believe the opposite is true: it is the immigrant——the unknown knocking at the door, that which is new to us——who brings innovation. Innovation starts when we are part of at least two cultures. In what sense did the power of exile produce innovation for you? After all, you were Swedish American of the Year in 2004. And how can we understand the cultural interdependence (exchange) between America and Europe (besides noting America's obvious problems of imperialism). And last but not least, what are your next steps into the future after leaving your deanship?

LL: As you probably know by now, I reject most categorical arguments. Thus, I have trouble with your premises. Immigrants like myself may work hard, and be occasionally effective, but we are also lost souls. We have lost our culture, our language, our bearings, to become chameleons capable of turning any color. My personal loss has been considerable, leaving me with an ever-returning melancholy for a lost paradise. First, I found an American Utopia That Never Fails to Disappoint the European in Me, and simultaneously Sweden faded in favor of that Utopia's constant volatility. So I became a navigator in search of a harbor. And at all my landfalls, I have found unusual acts of both cruelty and kindness in all populations regardless of their status.

When I look out my office window here at Rice University, I know that most of the Mexican-Americans that cleaned up the campus after Hurricane Ike have no power at home, no ice and no water, and no schools open for their children. As in New Orleans, FEMA is doing a spotty job. Hovering over their heads is also a set of anti-immigrant policies recently evolved in a country that would not exist without immigrants. Clearly absurd. During a recent visit in Sweden, I saw rows of idle Iraqi immigrants twirling their worry-beads, amply supported by the Swedish welfare system and worrying about the demise of their own country. Clearly absurd.

Here is where I resort to pensiere debole, or weak thought, suggesting that human existence—immigrant or otherwise—is a cold that we can never overcome but must learn to cope with until it kills us. The notion that either of the Left/Right political duality has some dormant potential to solve our deeply imbedded weakness is, of course, absurd. Consumerism will heal all wounds, at least momentarily, while catastrophes like Ike will awaken us—at least momentarily.

M as in Myth

RvT: I think there exists an unbridgeable distance between arguments, which appeal to our capacity to become enthusiastic, and our feeling for concrete, practical aims. A growing mytho-aesthetic dimension has made our Western culture inoffensive to an extent we have never seen before. Of course, says Franco Moretti, "inoffensive does not mean useless. But here it is a usefulness with a different function from that usually attributed to culture." The usefulness of architecture produced by the cultural industry includes the theories (discourses) of academia, the many exhibitions, the mappings of reality as found, and the publications and symposia on architecture and the city, etc. In our civilization, we do not use culture to orient ourselves––for good or for evil––but instead we live in order to consume culture. And I agree with Moretti, who says that "this consumption is no longer useful to assure a 'consensus' centering on the values capable of directing the individual's behavior in those fields which we consider fundamental––political life and, especially, work––but rather to empty those fields of all symbolic value: to reduce them to mere means lacking all intrinsic value. The frantic vogue-driven curiosity which dominates within the system of mass culture is symmetrical and complementary to the bored and slightly obtuse indifference nourished with regard to work and politics."[2] We seem to enjoy the fruits of late capitalism as a sort of miracle without asking too many questions. The gap between culture and politics has become grotesque. The Right acts big, while the Left has lost its hopes and aspirations to give significance to the world. Do you agree with me that this "talking shop" culture is a rather disquieting state of affairs? Aren't we in need of alternative forms of social, political, and ethical engagement: experiments and experiences that are useful and even offensive in character? Shouldn't we develop another "Mythical Method" that can be useful for the world? Perhaps you can speak of examples/ideas/methods that work toward this direction today (a fruitful mix between myth and reality; if I remember well, the last chapters in your new book are about this too).

LL: Architecture has always had a mythic dimension because of its future orientation. Architecture has never been possible without hope. In this sense I feel that architecture is insulated from politics––when you assess a palace for a dictator, the building itself is guilt-free, even if its construction used resources that could have fed the poor. This argument is, of course, very dicey, yet I must admit to subscribing to it. Here I am probably deeply Rossian, or better Tafurian, who thought that the paper architecture of the New York Five or "whites" was okay in the face of the collapsed project of the Left. The very positivity of making is profoundly human––once the dictator has been toppled, the palace will be a school for the disadvantaged.

My favorite writers, Jorge Luis Borges and J. G. Ballard, write about possible worlds that have not yet arrived but very likely will. I like the fulcrum between reality and myth, since it is the source of interpretation––my own core business. Is it useful for the world? Beats me. But I will say this: B&B have made my life a lot more interesting.

N as in Nature
RvT: All the fashionable buzzwords I associate with green politics I find highly problematic. They take ideology out of the equation of political life. Al Gore 's plea against global warming––although his facts are "correct"––avoids any debate about the logic of late capitalism itself. Instead of being Red, the Left has become Green, celebrating consensus and management (just like the Third Way politics of Tony Blair) as if it is just a matter of fine-tuning the motor of neoliberalism. What is your concept of Nature? How green are you? How toxic (political) is your ecology?

LL: Nature as we have conceived it during my lifetime no longer exists. Progress has seen to that. Now life is a complex fusion between Nature and culture. In some areas one of the two dominates. In the case of the city, culture dominates, particularly so in the traditional city. The suburban city may be a place where both equally rule.

Your political concerns seem to stem from the need to find and challenge the culprit destroying Nature. Having seen the Baltic's gradual dying, largely because the Left (Russia) has slowly but surely polluted it, suggests to me that "human progress" rather than "political ideology" lies behind its demise. (The armchair leftists who sit in comfortable seats all over the Western world are to be neither counted on nor blamed since they have zero power.)

The green issue is much larger and more complex than the squabble between political ideologies. Of course, this does not mean that this greening is not a highly charged political issue, and that capitalists without a conscience, just like state industries without one, will not do everything in their power to ship (or sell) their pollutants down the river. Being both a pragmatist and skeptic, I believe it is necessary to "build as naturally as possible," rather than use "sustainability" as the goal—sustainability is unattainable and always will be since we don't really know what it means. If you allow me a metaphor: "Society, whether steered by the Left or the Right (or anything in-between), is a very large ship that will take enormous effort to turn." So those in power have to exercise both patience and cunning to do the turning. Toxic events, like the one I am sitting through at this moment (Hurricane Ike), are sobering and will result

in change, so if you have any heavenly connections, ask them to "bring it on."

O as in Oppression

RvT: Antonio Negri's choice for O in his alphabet (Negri on Negri)[3] is the word Oppression. He
states that oppression has become invisible. One
no longer knows where to look for oppression. One
finds oneself suffering from a kind of mental block
regarding the definition of oppression. New forms
of immaterial oppression can be found in the
media, new technologies, and the service sectors,
or emerging from the flexibility and ferocious
mobility of the labor market. "The big difficulty,"
says Negri, "is that it is no longer possible to
identify a specific form of oppression capable of
provoking an equally specific form of resistance.
Perhaps the term oppression should be replaced
by exclusion, or perhaps by destitution, suffering, or poverty." And "Oppression is so nebulous
that it can't be named, so diffuse and so gray
that responding to it is hard. (...) The same army
drops bombs, propaganda, packages of medicine
and supplies: liberation or oppression?" This is
difficult to answer, says Negri. "What we have to
do is find a way to dispel the fog of oppression,
to invent new alternatives, to learn to struggle
against an invisible enemy, a non-identifiable op-
pressor." How do you see this? Are there invisible
enemies in architecture? Should we indeed teach
students to fight, built alternatives, and dispel
the fog of oppression in architecture?

LL: Michel Foucault suggested a long time
ago that centralized power is now atomized
and that the "disciplinary society" lives
in (and is performed by) all of us. Closely
associated with discipline, oppression (as
Negri suggests) comes in a multitude of
versions, from family to society. Having
struggled philosophically with the oppressive consequences of architectural form,
as played out in my book *Planned Assaults*,
I have come to believe that, yes, we will
stumble over Marcel Duchamp's coat hanger
nailed to the floor (Trebuchet, 1917), but
real oppression comes from human beings em-
ploying architectural form to oppress each
other. Any building can be turned into
a torture chamber. Meanwhile, form itself
retains autonomy by virtue of "not being
a radio."
   In terms of teaching, I do not believe
that we should teach students guerrilla
tactics, but we should stick to excava-
tion, deconstruction, hermeneutics, and
analysis to allow them to freely project. We
must refrain from oppression, in this case
ideological oppression, and rely instead on
"caring for others"——rather than "speaking

for others," which Foucault saw as the worst
of sins.

P as in Post-Modernism

RvT: While I champion your idea of ambiguity and
your deliberate method of postponing judgment
when you excavate reality (as in Houston), it is
less clear to me where you stand. After all, no
regime is more in love with the multiple and the
dynamic than late capitalism. Ambiguity can be
easily misunderstood as the ultimate postmodern
jouissance: to "enjoy," to realize your potential,
to take delight in all manner of ways, from intense
sexual pleasures through social success and
spiritual self-fulfillment. Ambiguity can also be associated with Gianni Vattimo's "weak thought": the
interpretation-is-all celebration of difference,
otherness, and endless diversity. Alain Badiou said
somewhere that our worlds lack a "point," that we
have arrived at "atonal" worlds. Anything that im-
poses a principle of "ordering" into the world, the
point of a simple decision (yes or no), has disappeared in our confused reality. Simply put, then:
Are you a postmodernist or do you believe that
a new social order is already latent within our
existing condition? Is another modernity perhaps
arising from the creative destruction inherent in
capitalism itself? Can your idea of ambiguity——as
part of the open city (open work)——have a social
direction or enforce a standpoint? (I know you
are fully aware that the very forces that make
for human misery and oppression can also make for
emancipation and well-being, but what do we need
beyond what postmodernism advocates?)

LL: Many years ago Vattimo told me after he
heard my lecture on the Parthenon that I
was "more postmodern than he." Since then
I have come to realize that it is harder to
know oneself than to have coherent views
of others. So I think that you——in a subtle
way——are suggesting that I am hopelessly
postmodern, a sufferer of "weak thought."
It is also clear that my public persona is
much more provocative than my private self,
where I am instead hopelessly bourgeois——often even snobbish. I like these two states,
since invariably one feeds the other. Both
states are informed by "a hope for liberty
for all"——for freedom——and by an intense
need to be intersubjective, a need that has
often driven me to take other people's views
much more seriously than my own. I became a
teacher because I like to be on the stage,
but also because I am deeply interested in
others' thought. If this makes me postmodern, so be it.

Q as in Quasi Object

RvT: Architects love to talk about objects. It is their matter-of-fact world, while users are more concerned with what objects produce. With the term "quasi-object," the continuing interplay between objects and people is emphasized by thinkers such as Bruno Latour and Michel Serres. It is mentally easier to divide humans from objects, but I do believe we have to start to understand objects as comprehensive and interdependent, in much the way you also speak of the erasure of the distinction between subject and object. We too often have looked to the world and declared: people are alive, while objects are dead; people can think, while objects just lie there. In fact, this taxonomical division blinds us to the ways in which, and means by which, objects do change us, and it obscures the areas where architecture can intervene to reshape things. For that reason I prefer to talk about the quasi-object instead of the classical object. Those quasi-objects are both social and technical. Agency is the key to understanding and creating them. The quasi-object establishes and enables relations through its assemblages and aesthetic complexity. Quasi-objects invite the user to complete them through action——by relating to them in movement. In that sense they also have a moral obligation: after all, they need to be used. How do you see the architecture object? Some of your furniture designs seem to act like quasi-objects (*Room*, 1999): they migrate into the field of the sensory, one that is tactile, auditory, and visual. Meanwhile your housing designs, like the Nofamily House, Love/House, Texas Zero (*Planned Assaults*, 1987), "function" like sentences, creating fiction (drama) out of familiar narratives. Did your perception of the object change over time, from telling stories (representation) to enacting events (presence)...?

LL: I am entirely in agreement here. I find the idea of quasi-objects extremely useful. One of my fundamental beliefs, as I have said, comes from cybernetics and Heinz von Foerster's dictum that "in order to see, we must act." This makes it clear that our existence is driven—indeed motivated by—action, by leaps of faith. It suggests in turn that inanimate objects are incredibly important because they may help us to see things in new and inspiring ways. In this sense I am all for the exploration of new form. Maybe more intriguingly, objects can be more or less "quasi." An all too familiar object becomes just a servant in our daily errands——a mere tool to be used up—while unfamiliar objects are more alive, more tentative, more ambiguous, and therefore more "quasi," suggesting that new form is essential for our advancement. As you say, these objects begin to infiltrate us and become more lifelike, more like verbs...

R as in Ruins

RvT: Cities are full of fabricated memories at the expense of the original experience. Hidden and controversial memories of a place often disappear. Peter Eisenman's recent war memorial in Berlin not only dismantles but also neutralizes much of war's horror with its formal architectural gesture. He creates a ruin without memory. What role does the memory of the city——the idea of history——play in your work? Walter Benjamin in his Arcades project represents and critiques the bourgeois experience of the nineteenth century and, in so doing, liberates the suppressed "true history" that underlies the ideological mask. Benjamin finds the lost time(s) embedded in the space of things. In your "Toxic Ecology," you represent and critique the urban landscape of the twenty-first century in Houston in a similar manner and, in doing so, propose possible routes to come. What kind of potential ruin is Houston? And how should we understand memory in this middle landscape?

LL: It is interesting that you call Eisenman's Berlin project "a ruin without memory," since I see it as the opposite: a dead city where everything is petrified and turned into inanimate matter—truly frozen music. For me, every horror from the ultimate hurricane to the Nazi tortures can be read here in its most dour form. The undulating, seemingly unstable ground, giving all the gray boxes a more or less precarious tilt, reveals how ephemeral everything is. Is this not the ultimate purpose of memory—to remind us, and to remind us collectively? Every time I have been there, masses of people are wandering through, and everyone but the youngest ones look thoughtful. As I have said above, often the more abstract an object is, the more it becomes a true quasi-object.

If Houston loses power in all its various forms, it will look like Eisenman's project.

S as in Suburbanization

RvT: With globalization, a certain cosmopolitanism has arrived in our lives, something the elite in the nineteenth century could only dream of in their Parisian cafés. The human condition has itself become cosmopolitan, says Ulrich Beck. "A sense of boundarylessness, an everyday, historically alert, reflexive awareness of ambivalences in a milieu of blurring differentiations and cultural contradictions emerges. It reveals not just the 'anguish' but also the possibility of shaping one's own life and social relations under conditions of cultural mixture." The result of this cosmopolitanism is a patchwork of urbanities who are quasi-cosmopolitan and simultaneously provincial; their central characteristic is their rejection of traditional relations of responsibility. Beck calls it "banal cosmopolitanism." The modest, familiar, local, circumscribed, or stable——in short, our protective shell——is becoming the site of broadly universal experience; place, whether it be Houston or Moscow, Stockholm or Amsterdam, becomes the locus of encounters and interminglings——or alternatively of anonymous coexistence and the overlapping of possible worlds with global dangers. All of this requires us to rethink the relation between place and the world. What we need, according to Beck, and I fully agree with him, is a new cosmopolitan outlook where the intermingling between us and them, the national and the international, the provincial and the global, is developed through a new political vision. Am I correct that your new book, *Toxic Ecology...*, instead of discounting the world of suburbia as an arena of action, sees it as a potential place for just such a political vision, a place full of ingredients to counter banal cosmopolitanism? Do you see Houston as the powerhouse of the political?

LL: Yes, you are correct. I am fully aware that my suggestion that software (IT) will reanimate the stolid carcass of suburban hardware and that a new quasi-urbanity will result is extremely naïve and hopeful. In fact, I believe that "urban form" is much less localized than it used to be. It is now possible to "be human" all across the inhabited landscape, from the totally wired tractor that plows fields in Kansas to the apartment in New York. Is this banal? Well, intellectuals have always had a tendency to view whatever happens outside their own sphere as banal. Given that this "banal cosmopolitanism" is actually what will elect a new president in my country, I am less inclined to see it that way. (By the way, my book is now renamed *One Million Acres and No Zoning*, which may be interpreted as a stepping away from toxicity to increased neutrality.)

T as in Technology
RvT: Two kinds of "technologies" in particular have reemerged in architecture: one is mapping (data-buildings), and the other is parametric design (blobalization). What are the potentials and risks of such new technologies in architecture (beyond its caricaturing)? Does the future of a progressive architecture depend on the development of innovative (computational) technologies?

LL: Knowing well that hammers can be used both to build houses and also to kill, I am sure that new misuses of technology will be possible and will take place. The fact is that the new technologies can probably wreak more havoc than a hammer. So firewalls become more urgent.

I have in all of my adult life been unimpressed by fads and purported salvations of any kind. So I remain relatively unmoved by hysterical reactions to these new technologies. In the end, we are humans, which means that we will commit horrible crimes as well as acts of utter selflessness, all in an unpredictable order——with or without new technology.

U as in Ugliness and Urgencies
RvT: Two (related) questions:
1. Rem Koolhaas once said, "Talk about beauty and you get boring answers, but talk about ugliness and things get interesting." What's your concept of the Ugly and the Beautiful?
2. Do you believe architecture should relate to the urgencies of the world? On the one hand, we are lost in paradise; the upper middle class has no idea how to dance now that it has everything (too much beauty avoiding the ugly). On the other hand, the public sphere has been sold to private corporations, and most of the world population lives in urban slums. Public housing is a lost cause to fight for as architect. What kind of urgencies could architecture help to resolve? And is your concept of ambiguity a part of the solution?

LL: Well, I think you caught me! Let me put it simply: "When architects gave up designing housing, we lost Architecture." And I lost interest and moved on to urbanism. Redemption lies in waiting. In fact, any building designed to house a collectivity is part of this redemption (although I am skeptical as to whether museums should be counted here). I therefore take Rem's suggestion to mean that architects should take on the ugliness——these forgotten domains of hospitals, supermarkets, post offices, public housing, slums, motels, new towns, back offices, suburbia, etc.

My own sense of beauty is still fully intact; it took years to construct and hovers, as I have said, somewhere between minimalism and Japanese traditional design culture. Broken beauty is far more beautiful than its undamaged other. So, since so much is broken, my aesthetic pleasures are still abundant.

V as in Violence
RvT: I agree with Chantal Mouffe and Jacques Rancière that the political only emerges when disagreement (dissensus) is part of the system you build. A certain foreignness (violence) is needed to liberate the user from within. Through

disagreement within a system, and not just op-position or critique, a final answer can be avoided and a liberating kind of agonism realized. How exclusion——i.e., what you experience standing in front of a the Berlin Wall——can make you wonder what happens on the other side (while demystifying the role of institutional powers), or how a strange (violent) form by virtue of its inconsumerability can provoke you to complete it in movement (like the CCTV building in China by OMA), all can push you to look beyond the cliché. Voyeurism, the perversion of the look, framing the view, can be yet another act of violence. Should architecture indeed be violent? Or is violence a force located elsewhere that architecture can capitalize upon?

LL: Just as I don't believe that there is Fascist architecture (Giuseppe Terragni), I do believe there are Fascists (Benito Mussolini). Your elaboration above is a bit too obscure for me to really understand. Clearly I think "foreignness" is of utmost importance to my sense that action precedes seeing, while at the same time I think arch-itecture is too mute to be violent, leaving it always a bit clumsy and lumbering.

W as in Words

RvT: Are words still essential for architecture? Should an architect still write, or can she or he do without it? Theory had its moment (we know it all)…, and it's time for practice experiments now (America needs change),… while the media (the world of images) tells it all…

LL: Well, for a wordsmith it is really hard to think that we no longer need words. And this by now long dialogue between you and me is in itself a piece of architecture——the only architecture I get to do. So, I hope not. As for the real architects, well, of course they must attach words to what they design, since those words are the preambles of the actions later taken by the dwellers.

X as in SeX

RvT: Architecture is——like the political arena today——often forced to "sex it up." How do you see the relation between sex (desire) and architecture? What are its risks and advantages? Frank Gehry's pornofication does lure visitors in, but it is nothing like the giant "Hon-en Katedral" sculpture installation, which Niki de Saint Phalle designed in 1968 in Stockholm, where you entered via her vagina, or…

LL: When I as a young man "entered" Niki's sculpture sprawled outside the Moderna Museet in Stockholm, I never thought of myself as a phallus. Neither do I see Bilbao as

pornography. In fact, I seem to always have trouble with the metaphoric. I like the real thing and respect the media constraints that give all our different practices their peculiar autonomy. On the other hand, in-toxications breaking through from one to the other are both possible and occasionally very exciting… ambiguity returns.

Y as in Youth

RvT: The period before and after May '68 was a very rich, liberating, stimulating, and creative moment in history. Many things were discovered. To speak with the voice of Friedrich Nietzsche: a collective in history did shoot a liberating arrow through space, and eventually it will fall even if it must pass through a desert for a while. Do you see anything new emerging——moving through our desert of the real today? And what inspires you most, including examples of the young, the fresh, and the cool?

LL: Since I count myself as a child of the sixties, I have considerable nostalgia for that peculiar window of opportunity. I also feel that this era still lives in me in the form of both a certain youthfulness and an often naïve hope. Mix this with my deep skepticism/pragmatism, and you have a fac-simile of the Lerupian apparatus. (I see my hair's refusal to either fall out or turn gray as a sign of the aforementioned youth and hope.)

Z as in Zigzag

RvT: Linear developments, or points in space, no longer seem to make sense. Today we prefer to model reality through folds, multitudes, black holes, assemblages, flow dynamics, and quantum theory. Several mathematicians[4] have shown that puff pastry is a rather accurate model to explain what happens. Puff pastry contains all possibili-ties, both positive and negative, in a topological mix that initially doesn't allow any clear division to occur. The pastry develops (puffs up) in a layered mix of jumping points, which travel adventitiously away from each other only to——nobody knows when and which detours they took——meet again. Many recent practices in architecture behave and even look like puff pastry. Although these creations often resemble a large croissant, it is not always a matter of literal form, but instead one of a refined system of layers that are stuck on top of or under each other, or assembled in a heap. It is an architecture of the free section, where ceilings become floors, walls become hills, rooms turn into fields, etc. And we, the user and the program, are the freely moving raisins in the puff pastry. It is up to us to make all kinds of possible ends meet through our zigzag route. The

334

puff pastry concept is a porous, compact, and
performative construction in which mass moves
fluently. Oppositions and paradoxes are applied
in different mixtures. It is a game where the
puff pastry concept (re)activates all manner of
ambiguities and unintended consequences through
a rather "primitive" form that can be constantly
infiltrated and reevaluated. The puff pastry concept is construction as infrastructure, in which
different sorts of circuits both can be built and
can appear spontaneously. It is a heterogeneous
landscape where the walls and floors act as a kind
of foam. The puff pastry concept allows a greater amount of complexity in use and programming.
It is specific and undetermined at the same time.
What do you think of the many contemporary puff
pastry concepts full of zigzag routes that are
enacting ambiguity? As in the work of Foreign Office
Architects, MVRDV, Diller & Scofidio, Eisenman,
Greg Lynn, Lars Spuybroek (NOX), UN Studio (Ben
van Berkel), and many others. Is the puff pastry
indeed the route to take, or are we in need of
another kind of zigzag-enacting ambiguity?

LL: Need I say more? I leave the cooking to
you. In a puff of smoke, our just completed
Abecedarium is blown into the eyes of our
readers. While they cough, I am going for
dessert—but it will probably be low-fat va-
nilla ice cream with a snifter of Courvoisier
to motivate the digestion. Pastry is too rich
for my aging constitution.

1. See also his 2006 BBC series "The pervert's guide to the
cinema."
2. Franco Moretti, "From the Waste Land to the Artificial Paradise,"
in *Signs Taken for Wonders* (London: Verson, 1983).
3. *Negri on Negri: In Conversation with Anne Dufourmentelle* (New
York and Oxford: Routledge, 2004).
4. For instance, George David Birkhoff, Vladimir Arnold, and
Stephen Smale.

****

**LARS LERUP is the dean and William Ward Watkin
Professor of Architecture at Rice School of Architecture.**

**ROEMER VAN TOORN is head of the Projective Theory
Program at the Berlage Institute.**

Commuter electrogram

Texas time

Bladerunner city

5

↓Architecture: An Imposition upon Reality or Reshuffling of Worlds?

Christopher Hight, Sean Lally and Michael Robinson

Critics, Undergraduate Core Studios, 2002–08

342

Architecture is inevitably a form of Paranoid Critical activity... Architecture = the imposition on the world of structures it never asked for and that existed previously only as clouds of conjecture...
—Rem Koolhaas, Delirious New York

What is a diagram? It is the display of the relations between forces which constitute power... The diagram or abstract machine is the map of relations between forces, a map of destiny, or intensity, which proceeds by primary non-localizable relations and at every point passes through every point.
—Gilles Deleuze and Felix Guattari

Does architecture IMPOSE itself upon a preexisting Reality? Or is it possible to pursue a related but slightly different tack also suggested by Koolhaas in the same text, one that treats our own known reality as a deck of cards in which each card is a FACT, and their sequence, a map or diagram of our World (the hand we are dealt).

Can we reshuffle the deck of an often disappointing hand? Can we construct alternative rules that are nevertheless coherent? That is, take the same set of FACTS and reorder them into different sequences, different maps of alternative but possible WORLDS? Is architecture an imposition, a criticism of Reality, or a projective practice of potentials latent within the present?

Generic Cities

The generic has at least two senses. The first is the typical sense of the "general," the "unbranded" and ubiquitous neutral condition. Often this is also seen as "without qualities," but the generic is never non-ordered; it is in fact an evolved relationship of ordering between specific forces and logics of combination, economies, and ideologies. The typical office plan (Koolhaas) is an example, as is the "generic city" that surrounds us. The generic, then, has a sense of the "genre" or topological genus: a class of things that all share a certain specificity in a combination that yields certain spatial qualities and organizational possibilities and hinders others. Therefore, the generic also points toward the "generative" conditions that one finds and one can create. One needs to shift from understanding the generic as an opposite to the "signature" to understanding it as a generative diagram of the relationship between things that can produce variations beyond itself, a genre of formal relations between material, structure, space, and affect. This is not so far from Aldo Rossi's idea of the "type," but at a more abstract,

pre-tectonic set condition, one that does not always already foreclose on the space of architectural innovation into known or historical assemblies. By relating the same set of relationships differently, or by rearranging the value placed on them, or by adding new ones, new "generics" can be produced.

Perhaps the most famous and prevalent of such prototypes is the Maison Dom-ino by Le Corbusier, which was not simply a local structural system for a single house, but the spatial/material diagram from which one could construct a global diagram for an entire city: the Ville Radieuse. It was at once architecture and infrastructure. Indeed, this diagram may be considered the dominant diagram of the generic city of Houston itself, endlessly replicated as strip malls, loft apartments, and office towers. However, the inadequacies of both Le Corbusier's Radiant City and its later common deployment (or, for that matter, successful examples of its deployment, such as Brasilia) reveal that such generics are not enough; they require specification and differentiation. The success of the Maison Dom-ino lies in the fact that its diagram can have almost any "architecture" hung upon it, from modern to historic to kitsch. Thus it reveals not only the power of the opposition between the generic and the formally specific, but also its deleterious effects. Although it is an exceedingly successful and powerful diagram, it should not be reified or naturalized as exhausting the specifications of architecture. Indeed, for something to become an object of architectural knowledge, it necessarily must leave the realm of the generic and enter a greater degree of specificity regarding the genealogies of the discipline and the relationship between material performance and subjective affect.

The generic in design might be specified according to the class of affects it produces, including organization, both spatial and phenomenological. The "effect" is understood as a trait of the object and is seen as a one-way transfer, as in a "special effects" or thrill ride. It "affects" you... and produces an effect, i.e., fear. The effect tends toward the spectacular. The affect, on the other hand, suggests a two-way operation, in which that which produces affects is then informed by the effects that the affective response produces. The affect transforms the target or subject in an empowering way. When combined with the concept of the generic, what we get are prototypes that are "generative" of conditions through the specificity of affects and can be adapted to specific conditions.

Ultimately in the third-year studio, each team of students produces projections for alternative "generics" out of which other Worlds can be woven at the junction of architecture, infrastructure, and urbanism. Utilizing contemporary concepts of morphogenesis, physical computation, and digital modeling, we operate upon "generic" conditions, performing simple operations to simple materials to produce complex spatial affects that can serve as generic diagrams (in the sense of the generative and the genre) for the relationship of matter, space, and organization.

The first exercise divides the class in two, half of which work through processes of differentiation of a

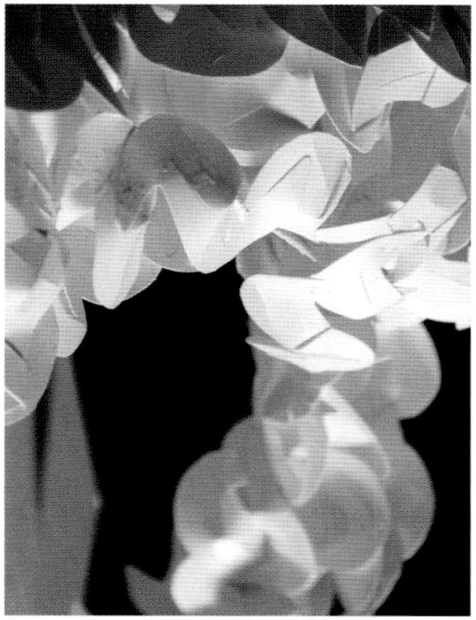
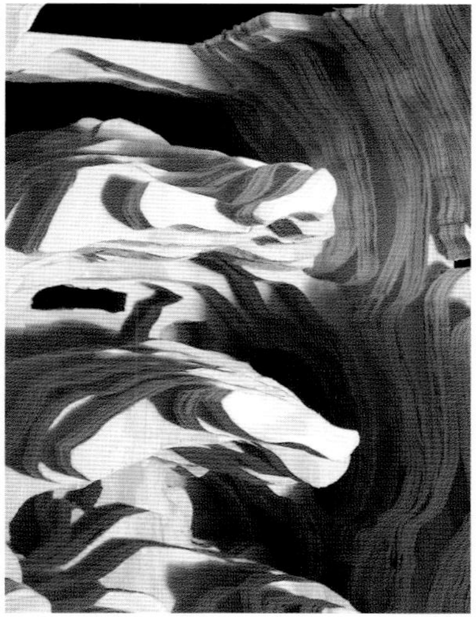
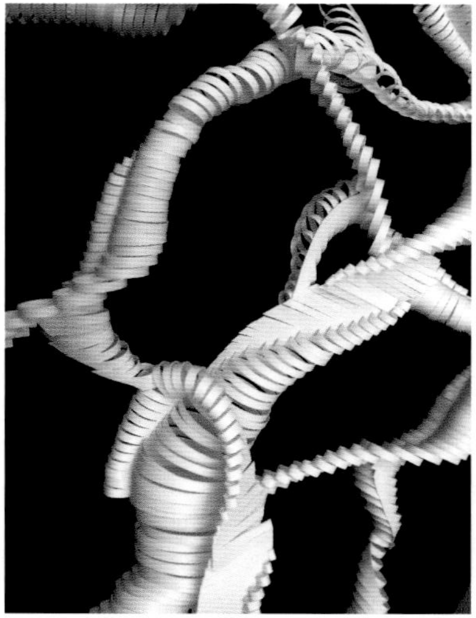
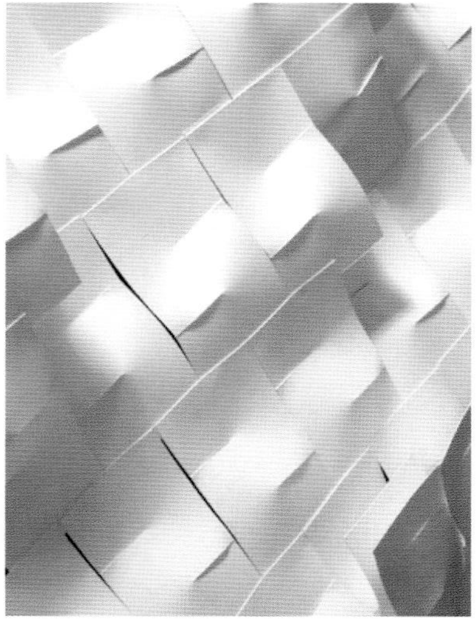
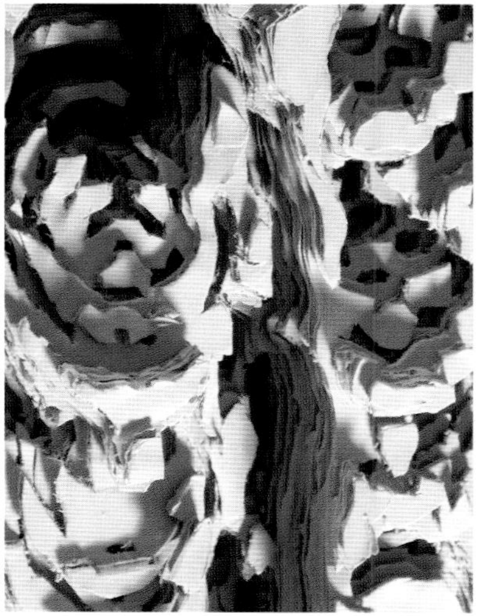
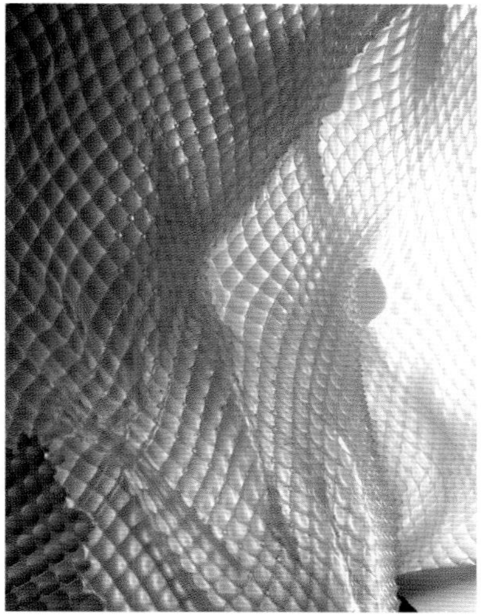
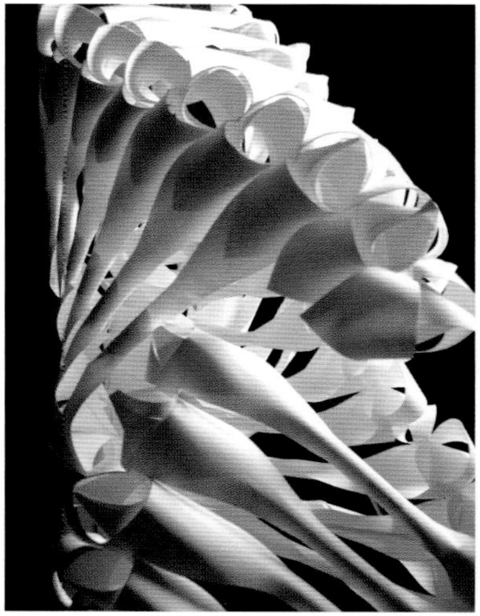
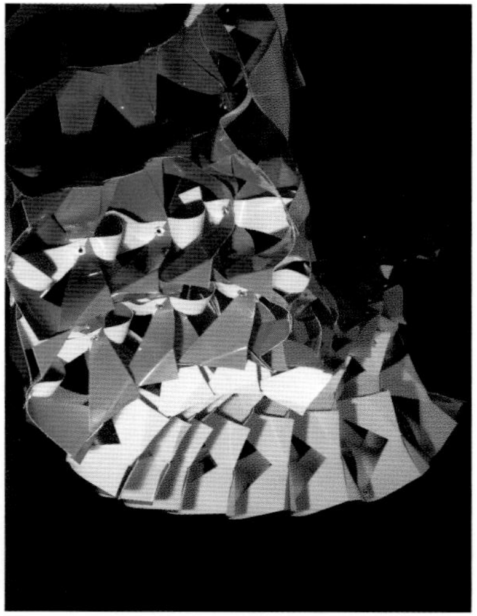

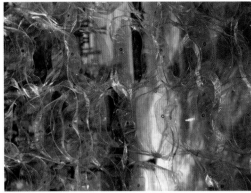

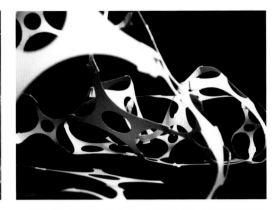

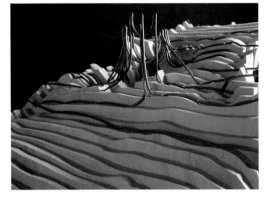

continuous surface; the other half integrates discontinuous elements into a surface. The primary material is paper: through a series of operations, such as slicing, folding, punching, and bundling, different performative capacities and organizational strategies are developed (all associated with historical means of differentiating surfaces in architecture, i.e., the Gothic bundling of lines, the Renaissance punching of the wall, the Baroque folding of vaults). These operations are linked through connection logics, such as tabbing, weaving, laminating, and tying. These techniques and operations are deployed not only through physical models but also through graphic representations that often require notional devices and graphics by the students, not simply for documentation and recording but also for exploration and design for future operations.

While students and faculty alike tend to refer to this semester as the "digital sequence" of their core education, in reality the use of the computer during this sequence is simply a placeholder of terminology for a sequence whose underpinning is really the alternate methods of representations and operations, and the importance that these tools play in translating and building our design intentions. The translation between construction and representation, and from one media or platform to another, becomes a mechanism for exploration and innovation of architectural concepts as material actualizations.

The course has evolved over six years as we continually seek variable testing grounds for these endeavors; however, the underlying principles have remained the same. Scales have shifted, sites in

Houston have changed, and different programs have been explored as parameters for exploration within the laboratory-based format. Because we, as instructors, were educated in a manner that emphasized critical and projective reevaluation of accepted conventions, our task and responsibility revolves around framing disciplinary issues and potentialities opened through the materials practices and processes.

CHRISTOPHER HIGHT is an assistant professor at Rice School of Architecture.

SEAN LALLY is an assistant professor at University of Illinois at Chicago School of Architecture. He was an assistant professor at Rice School of Architecture from 2002-08.

MICHAEL ROBINSON is a lecturer at Rice School of Architecture.

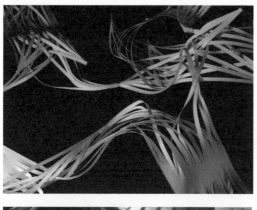

Final review of research and design proposals

Not yesterday,

not tomorrow,

only today
can be
given form.

—Ludwig Mies van der Rohe, 1923

↓Intensive Expansion

Jason Payne
Critic, Graduate Option Studio, 2002

Once one develops matter rich enough to produce emergent effects of architectural value, the focus tends to amplify the qualitative, substantive aspects of material organizations. At the same time, conceptual and representational issues tend to be forced out. When we were young and saw in the cloud overhead a bear or a unicorn, we all saw those animals at the expense of the matter of the cloud itself. Conversely, the meteorologist's insistence upon seeing the cloud in terms of vector analysis gets closer to the truth of the matter, so to speak, in that the animal simile is no longer visible. It is not visible because it cannot be conceived of in terms of vectors—it has been forced out. Vectors weren't invented to describe images of discrete concepts that came before them and will exist after them. Vectors and similar geometries—designed to carry certain techniques and tactics within them—describe flows, effects, and atmospheres that are much closer to their own constitution. These geometries are actually like what they describe, and because of this, they move beyond passive description into a condition that is partially real. Further, they are literally tied to the body they inhabit in both space and time, moving as it moves (as opposed to vanishing from the surface and, perhaps, reappearing as some other image). These more dynamic geometries allow us to work in the elusive zone that exists between the diagram and the building. Historically, there has been a methodological gulf between where the diagram ends and the building begins. Now we might actually occupy and design within that previously inaccessible space.

The first phase of the project involves the construction of an acrylic container that acts as a controlled environment for the study of gelatinous or particulate matter. Each project thus sets out to demonstrate a particular form of behavior or structural/organizational tendency. The term structural should be understood in its broadest sense. It need not be a literal or "hard" object or set of objects floating in the atmospheric material. It could be as simple as the folds formed as a gelatinous atmosphere is piled into the container. The second phase of this experiment is at least as critical as the first. This phase involves documenting the behaviors, organizations, and structures observed in the model. Modes of documentation must capture the system's growth over time. This suggests seriality. It also requires the use of methods of representation from disciplines outside of architecture. Areas of study involving growth and mutation such as biology, fluid dynamics, physics, and engineering are likely methodological reservoirs.

The documentation of a system through dynamic geometries generates a complex model unto itself. The process for the construction of these geometries first involves capturing images of a system's behavior at various stages in its "lifespan," then extracting the geometries from these images. The extraction of a geometry does not involve tracing representations of the original image, but rather replacing the image of the system with geometries capable of further behavior. Ultimately, the documentation models a system's principles of behavior.

JASON PAYNE is a principal at Hirsuta and an assistant professor at University of California at Los Angeles Architecture and Urban Design. He was an assistant professor at Rice School of Architecture from 2000-02.

347

GELATINOUS ATMOSPHERE

METHODOLOGICAL GULF

THE ANIMAL SIMILE IS NO LONGER VISIBLE

Acrylic containers act as a controlled environment for the study of gelatinous or particulate matter

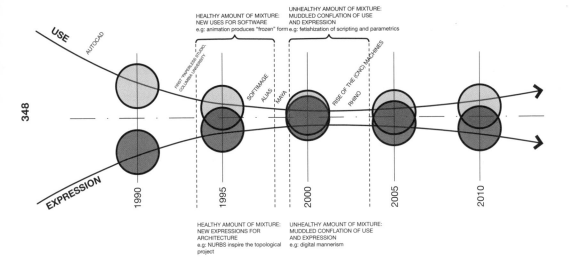

348

What Mattered Then Still Matters Now:
Reflections on Intensive Expansion, Rice University, 2002

The diagram above describes the overlapping, often conflated relationship between the use and expression of technology that has emerged with the evolution of "digital design" since the early nineties. As we know, tools of representation always exert their own degree of influence over expression. Some of architecture's better moments, in fact, have been those points at which the introduction of new technologies and protocols for description drove their subject toward new objectives. In this way, the designed form always owes something of its morphology to the way in which it is drawn, rendered, and modeled.

The handful of designers pioneering the engagement with advanced modeling software in the early nineties, most notably those associated with Bernard Tschumi's Paperless Studio initiative at Columbia University (Greg Lynn, Jesse Reiser, Stan Allen, Hani Rashid, etc.), were quite conscious of the productive influence tools of expression could have on form. Their collective training within the schools and studios of some of the masters of late twentieth-century representation led to the enthusiastic promotion of active interference between emerging technologies and the organizations they described. This polemic reached its greatest discursive clarity sometime around 1995 in a series of projects and studios aimed at the "productive misuse" of digital modeling software, particularly animation software, that convinced a generation of younger designers that a new course had been set. It was clear that the emerging paradigm required renewed, conscious engagement with tools of representation, harnessing their potential for influence over morphological expression.

There was, however, a sober caveat attached to the credo of creative misuse: do it, but do it judiciously, a simple but powerful warning to keep track of the degree to which we would allow disciplinary conventions to bend under the influence of emerging, experimental modes of expression. Were it not for the enormous amount of production that ensued, this cautionary note would surely have been observed. Instead, immersed in the sea change of optimism borne on a wave of massive generative potential (our own disciplinary version of a Cambrian Explosion), the growing Hydra of digital design lost track of the difference between its new tools and the subject of their expression. We were in a zone of befuddlement, a confused place in which it was no longer clear when the tool drove the expression or when the expression drove the tool. It appeared that a kind of digital mannerism had taken root whereby our earlier critical-experimental commitment, despite its awkward uncertainties, was eclipsed by the formal and aesthetic expertise that had, quite naturally, developed along the way. Before long it appeared that all that really mattered was the image itself: that the work "looked" digitally expert. Projective experimentation was replaced by virtuoso performance.

It was in this context that the studio Intensive Expansion took place at Rice School of Architecture in 2002. Sparing the reader a detailed description of the studio's objectives and methodologies, suffice it to say here that our approach was akin to that found in certain subjects involving material form derived of complex dynamics... hydrodynamics, for example. Here, despite increasing use of digital simulations to quantify and describe material behaviors like turbulence, there still exists the need for physical (analog) experimentation. Real material behavior still exceeds the capacity of computation to fully capture its description. Our studio took a similar approach to the development of complex architectural form, mixing digital and analog technique in an effort to avoid the momentum toward mannerism described above and keep the problem open. This proved difficult, awkward,

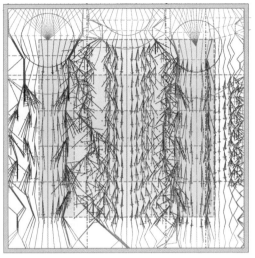

↑**CONTENTS: part A and part B of polyurethane elastomer in various durometers / four mylar sheets / mold release agent**

Lay out mylar sheets on large flat surface, apply mold release agent and let dry. Mix parts A and B of poly-urethane elastomers, make two pots total each with a different durometer rubber. Carefully pour mixed rubbers on to mylar sheets allowing only the edges to blend, float to thin layer using a spatula, putty knife or other useful spreading tool. Let rubber cure, and remove from Mylar sheets. Trim uneven edges to make rectangular sheets twice the size of the largest surface of the acrylic box. Fold rectangular sheets in an accordion manner, stuff into box, and spread out pleats to fill volume of box. The rubbers will bend, fold, stick, rub, unify, separate, slip, fall, according to the durometer and local internal pressures caused by the variations in thickness in the sheet material and the densities that form from being forced into internal expansion.

KEN ANDREWS / Graduate Option Studio, 2002

↑**CONTENTS: twenty packets of gelatin / water / two aluminum rods 1/8" diameter / one large jar of molasses**

Gelatin and water were heated and set to cure in the box for approximately two hours until near coagulation. Two rods were then inserted into the gelatin, one at two inches from the side of the box, the other at one inch from the side of the box. Molasses was poured into the box at each rod and introduced to the gelatin environment. This allowed the molasses to enter the gelatin substance at a control point. The idea was to study how the introduced liquid reacted both to the gelatin environment and to an edge condition. The purpose of the second phase was to study under decelerated conditions the branching behavior of a thick substance in a gelatinous environment. The translucency of the molasses also made it possible to study the details of the branches. The organic nature of the ingredients used in the experiment led to the breakdown of the contents of the box over the course of two weeks.

LAUREN BENECH / Graduate Option Studio, 2002

and messy, but at least it was real. Perhaps not by coincidence, it was at this time that early moves toward material fabrication of digital form began to take hold of our imagination. A kind of "correction" in the market of digital design discourse, the rise of fabrication reclaimed the mandate of the real in the development of form and, happily, worked toward conscious recalibration of the relation between tools of expression and expression itself.

—Jason Payne

→ **Queens Museum Ramp**

In 2001 the Department of Design and Construction of the City of New York sponsored a competition for the expansion of the Queens Museum of Art; the program's charge involved the physical expansion of the museum within the existing perimeter walls of the building and the reconfiguration of existing spaces. This project provides a useful test bed for a number of issues critical to current architectural thinking and practice. These include the evolving role of cultural institutions in society, the differences and similarities between traditional and emerging forms of art, the increasingly problematic relationship between exhibition space and exhibited artifact, the dynamics of crowd behavior and public gathering, and the problems and possibilities involved in retrofitting buildings.

Strategies for the physical and conceptual expansion of the Queens Museum of Art must shape the museum's future as a leading institution for the exhibition of emerging and alternative forms of art and performance. In concert with this, extensive infrastructures must be provided to promote various forms of public gathering: complexes within the existing envelope that comprise layered sets of structures, the spaces and surfaces of which amplify and express the dynamics inherent in large groups of people. In this way, the museum's infrastructure draws upon the patterns, rhythms, and formations generated through crowd behavior to create visible yet transitory structures within and around those of the built environment. Exhibition, then, becomes an activity immersed within a larger, more variegated field of public gathering.

A single, yet robust architectural system performs as the project's primary infrastructural device. As such, it is poised to accept new information and organizations as regards public circulation and the display of artwork. While these infrastructures are actual systems comprising form,

structure, program, space, and effect, they should also be understood as strategies. Strategic infrastructures do more than just solve a problem. They consciously promote certain forms of occupation and distribution, and deny others. They may also give rise to sensibilities. Further, these systems develop to take advantage of potential relationships and resistances between themselves and the existing perimeter walls and building structure.

DAVID STOCKWELL / Graduate Option Studio, 2002

The work pursued in my 2002 studio Intensive Expansion at Rice School of Architecture found itself enmeshed in the rapidly expanding, turbulent gas cloud of a digital design movement that was billowing toward some form of disciplinary definition. It was an atmosphere fraught with competing polemics, with their associated "key questions" (matter or data? technique or effect?), sensibilities (facet or fold?), generations (tail-end baby boom or Gen X?), and techniques and procedures (animation? rendering? parametrics? prototyping?). Origins and lineages, too, were uncertain. The fast rise of the North American "Columbians," a kind of academic street gang of recent Columbia University graduates religiously devoted to extreme process and increasingly complex formal expression, was confronted by the programmatically focused, graph-and-chart-wielding "Dutch" resistance. Ever-closer combat resulted in a somewhat messy exchange of weaponsfire on the battlefield... already, for example, we had seen the exchange of the fillet and the NURB.

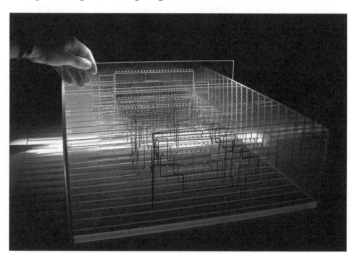

Acrylic wireframe sectional model

Existing Queens Museum of Art perimeter with new infrastructure strategy

Clearly, things were murky. The only thing that did seem clear was how very productive, provocative, and fun things had become (much to the chagrin of those who don't like fun, who don't see the generative potential of play). Anyhow.
—Jason Payne

→ Generative Proto-Architectures

Michael Hensel and Achim Menges

Critics, Graduate Option Studio, 2004

MICHAEL HENSEL and ACHIM MENGES are partners at OCEAN. They were Visiting Cullinan Professors at Rice School of Architecture in 2004.

→ Aggregate System

This project looks at the constraints and potentials of an aggregate system, defined as a modulated system that is differentiated through the manipulation of (1) the element, (2) the pouring condition, and (3) the environmental constraints. Interaction among these three conditions determines the configuration and performative response of the whole system.

Establishing only these three constraint conditions ensures the results rely solely on a process of self-organization. Aggregate systems are an extremely sensitive technique of integrating discrete and repeated components into a whole. (Even the internal joint of each element relies only on friction and tension.) The configuration is likely to respond to any alteration, adjusting the entire arrangement in response to new conditions.

The constant alteration within the system and its ability to easily reconfigure itself necessitates a long and changing involvement in the designers' and the participants' role. Aggregate systems in general appear difficult to control and inconsistent in exact performance output. There are, however, emergent tendencies that generate opportunities for design and response.

In this particular study, the element was designed to encourage an interlocking effect among components, as well as the potential for multiple configurations,

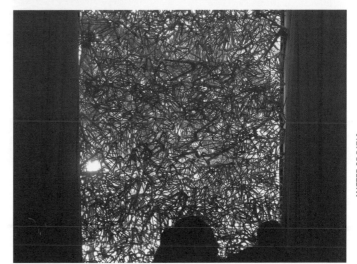

Installation of aggregate system

or families, constructed out of the same base unit. Once an element configuration and its related families of design were formulated, the system tendencies were studied through numerous experiments that included analyzing emergent shapes, collapse points, shifting characteristics, and load-bearing tests.

The larger issues that this system discussed in terms of architecture and methods of construction included sensitive reaction-intrinsic forces; the reliance on, and potentials of, redundancy; an accelerated time scale of construction deterioration; and the demands of human interaction.
ANNE HAWKINS, CATHLYN NEWELL / Graduate Option Studio, 2004

→ Modulated Component Assembly

As metal rods bend across geometrically located and fixed positions, a differentiated material system unfolds, capturing, organizing, and redirecting energy. This system explores the behaviors and potentials of accelerated and decelerated deflection and torque in a modulated component assembly.

Focusing on macro-diameter steel threaded rods as the primary material for study, the project tested several assembly configurations, each experimenting with the specifications of the component parts, considering the relations between parametric definitions aligned with geometric and topological logics, as well as construction processes.

Moving from the development of a selected component, research and testing explored the proliferation of the system into larger regional and global assemblies, further integrating and expanding on the system's articulation and response to various environmental conditions.

JUDSON MOORE, MICHAEL ROBINSON / Graduate Option Studio, 2004

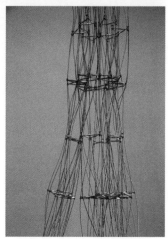

Assembly and installation of modular component system

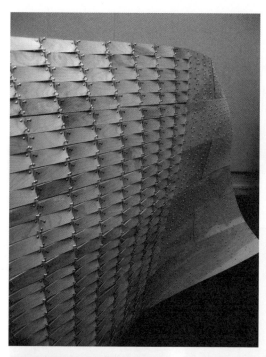

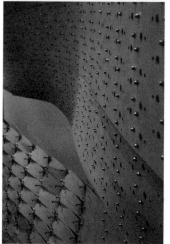

Assembled system generates a variable surface

↑ Meta-Patch

Meta-Patch is a proliferated Halbzeug, or off-the-shelf, component system. The project began with the design of a singular component and led to a phase involving the thorough mapping and analysis of the unfolding behavior of sets of components.

The study focused on how the behavior of multiple components could be affected by changing sets of variables at three scales: the scale of the component, the scale of a region of components, and the scale of the entire assemblage.

The second phase of the project involved the analysis of the performance of the assembly in relationship to a context containing people, other structures, and environmental conditions. The project became a search to find ways that a Meta-Patch assembly could create heterogeneous zones of performativity to satisfy a range of activities, a single activity, or particular structural requirements.

DAVID NEWTON, JOSEPH KELLNER / Graduate Option Studio, 2004

→ Symbiosis

Between Wheat and Rigid Sails

Houston is not known for its abundance of moving air. It is, however, recognized for its reputation of high humidity and inclement temperatures. Houston's large downtown core only accelerates this problem, serving as an "urban heat island." As within any urban center with tall buildings, points of increased air speed are created by the "concrete canyon" phenomenon. Houston, like New York City or Chicago, has these locations. However, as a city Houston suffers more from "wind shadow" than from increased wind velocity, especially on downtown's northwest side, the area currently reconstructing itself as an "outdoors" Houston. Consideration of how to ameliorate these circumstances has initiated a path that explores two differing technological arenas: wind harnessing for transportation and wind dissipation for agriculture.

Boat sails have evolved to make increasingly efficient use of wind by translating moving air into kinetic mobility. In the case of traditional cloth sails, this exchange is greatest when the sail profile is "full," or in a state presenting its largest dimensional cross section. The variance in surface length over the two sides of the full sail causes air to pass over at differing accelerated speeds. This disparity creates a dual positive and negative pressure on opposite sides of the sail and produces a directional force. Effectively, a sailing vessel is both pushed and pulled along through its ability to "catch" air when conducive air speeds are present. This same cloth sail becomes problematic when these air velocities drop and the desired sail profile cannot be obtained. Borrowing technology from airplanes, sailing vessels have begun to incorporate the aerodynamic advantage of full wing cross sections called "rigid sails."

Recent advancements in rigid sail technology have brought together the mobility of the cloth sail and the stability of the airplane wing, and have engineered a vertical wing that is attached to the boat hull. The primary advantage of the rigid sail is its ability to maintain a three-dimensional profile regardless of ambient air speed. Internal ribbing, like that of an airplane wing, keeps a thin membrane stretched taut over the profile of the ribs. The cross section can also be symmetrical, depending on the intended use, and permits propulsion even during extremely slow air velocities. Accelerated airflow moving along the surface of the wing performs similarly to air moving across cloth sails, especially when the wings are organized in tandem or in dense groups. The rigid sail is a hybrid and, as a three-dimensional airfoil, has possibilities beyond its current use. The interest here is not in its ability to translate airflow into propulsion, but rather in its ability to stimulate air velocity while channeling it toward a target.

In a related exercise, the agricultural industry has employed its own unique version of "wind catching." Through continual Darwinian adjustments, plants have evolved to make use of the wind. Seed dispersion is often what benefits from this natural evolution. This project focuses on the plant *X Triticosecale Wittmack*, a genetically altered extension of the wheat family.

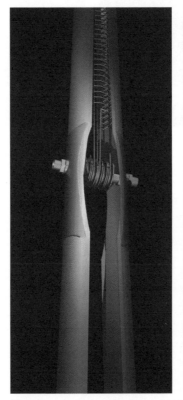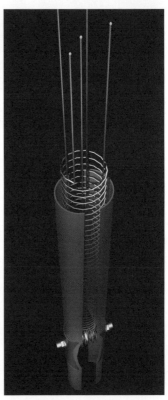

Urban air garden (top) and details of environmental prosthetic (bottom)

X Triticosecale Wittmack, more commonly known as triticale, is a hybrid of the parent plants wheat (*Triticum aestivum*) and rye (*Secale cereale*). This bioengineered plant was originally designed for its ability to resist erosion, primarily that of adjacent crops.

Mechanically, triticale works as a bipartite system: the seed head and the stem. Holding a collection of 200-plus individual seeds, the thick seed head creates a vertical "wind sock" designed to catch moving air. Each seed extends an array of

fifteen to thirty stiff hairs that enable reproduction through aerial dispersion. Effectively, each seed has its own sail. These seeds grow in a dinergic spiral within the upper six to eight inches of each stalk, and as such exemplify a natural representation of the Fibonacci number series. The stem is proportionally thin and scored with continuous miniature "flutes." This provides each plant with its own structurally dynamic column, which flexes and redistributes wind energy into its root foundation. Together, the two parts

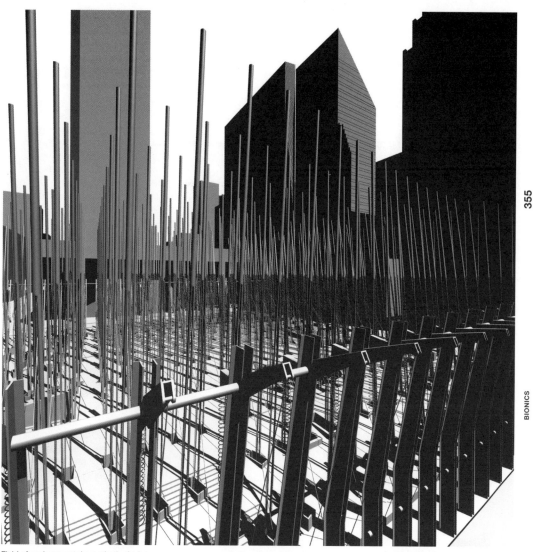

Field of environmental prosthetic devices

both shield and absorb wind energy while simultaneously registering a visual response.

Unlike the rigid sail, triticale does not work well individually. So, triticale is always grown in ribbon formations, like its parent plant wheat, that then collectively work as a windbreak. It is this spatial arrangement and density through planting that make triticale successful, much like the rigid sails placed in tandem. "Wind rows," as they are commonly known, are a result of the empirical derivation of wind speed (exposure) and machinery width. Designed to negate harmful air movement, "wind rows" are planted in alternating strips running perpendicular to the common flow of air. These rows

run intermittently alongside primary crops and protect them by creating wind shadows. The collective stands of the individual plants work in unison to decrease the negative influence of moving air on adjacent crops: an environmental prosthetic.

Bionics pursues the development of artificial systems based on the study of biological systems. Recent technology has changed the trajectory of prosthetic design from one satisfied to emulate nature, to one that aims to extend nature beyond its original capabilities. Still, the success or failure of these systems travels hand in hand with each design's ability to negotiate a relationship with its host or surroundings. In other words,

adaptability is paramount, whether it be between the gate of a bipedal robot and its terrain or between a prosthetic leg and its connection.

In the case of triticale, the flexibility of the stem and seed head allows for its ascendancy. In the case of the rigid sail, it is its ability to realign itself to directional airflow that ultimately makes it useful. I am outlining a potential symbiogenetic "next step" for each of these hybrids.

As discussed earlier, the microclimate of downtown Houston is an inhospitable urban heat island for most of the calendar year. As a result, pedestrian activity is minimal, and life outside the underground tunnels and interior atriums is sparse. Regardless, Houston has felt compelled to create an outdoor downtown. With the construction catalyst of the "open air" ballpark, the Sesquicentennial Park, and Bayou Place, as well as Rice Hotel and other residential loft spaces, Houstonians are actively engaging the outdoors in downtown. The fact remains that many of these places lie within the wind shadow of our signature skyline, which (unlike in many other major cities) creates stagnate, not accelerated, air.

I am positing the sowing of an "urban air garden," cultivated for the downtown condition. Its crop: an environmental prosthetic working in tandem with the oscillating flows of its context. Its yield: increased airflow. Modeled on the aerodynamic properties of rigid sails and triticale, this environmental graft will seek to redistribute air movement from an overhead strata. The spatial distribution will look to an inversion of the strategy of "wind rows"—not reducing but increasing air speeds while deflecting them toward the pedestrian level.

Although Houston has a prevailing wind condition, the dynamics of the downtown airflow and temperature, as well as seasonal variations, requires a behavioral overlay to the program. Adaptability will be key to the success of this device. Like the swaying of wheat in a field, this environmental prosthetic will manage moving air while registering a visual barometric response.

BRIAN BURKE / M.Arch. Thesis, 1999 / Carlos Jiménez, director

Brian Burke's thesis offers an inspired and insightful transformation of Houston's generic parking structure. It turns the typical concrete monolith into a malleable field to harness the wind. It becomes not only a newfound energy resource but also a compelling urban structure, casting and emitting surprising shadows and sounds. The parking structure turns into a full-time participant in the life of the city, subverting the inert and temporal equation that upholds the primacy of the car.

—**Carlos Jiménenz** is the principal of Carlos Jiménez Studio. He is a professor at Rice School of Architecture.

↓Towards a Vegetal Infrastructure

Dynamic/Green is an infrastructural proposal that responds to the call to eliminate, or at least mitigate, environmental contamination in the soil, air, and water in Harris County using plants. A variety of plants were chosen based on their particular ability to absorb contaminants. Plants will be deployed to various sites all over Harris County, and then arranged on the site using a system of containers.

Given the large number of plastic containers needed for Dynamic/Green, consideration was given to selecting a plastic with awareness of its recycling ability. Initial benefits of a recyclable choice include reduced processing temperatures, thereby reducing energy costs during production, as well as increased tensile and flexural strength. In comparison to mineral-filled plastics, so-called agro-plastics also have a lower specific gravity, resulting in both material savings during production and reduction of shipping costs after production.

One eight foot by eight foot wide container is made by bolting together four plastic panels. Each panel is thermoformed from

a single of inch and a half thick "agro-plastic". Each container is adjustable within a fifteen degree pivot as well as being fitted

for both irrigation and drainage

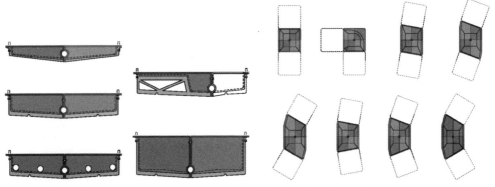

Various container profiles

Plan view of container modules in possible arrangements.

Containers deployed along a highway

Nursery enclosure

Growing the plants and the initial stages of soil remediation will happen at various Superfund sites in Harris County. Greenhouses and nurseries at these locations will allow for proper development of seasonal plants as well as an environment for maintenance, display, and temporary storage before deliveries to destinations. Both greenhouse and nursery enclosure systems are fabric structures that can be set up seasonally and attached to a series of connected containers.

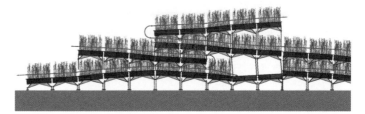

Container drainage system allows for control of drainage flow and collection of runoff water to be cycled into irrigation system. Due to significant seasonal changes of rainfall of Houston, the proportion of water-containers to plant-containers varies from season to season. Containers are adjusted locally to allow for the direction, accumulation, and isolation of drainage water from plant at different remediation phases.

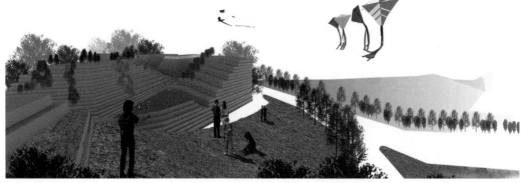

Phase one: monumental index

Implementation of Dynamic/ Green is contingent upon collaboration among diverse interest groups. In addition to federal, state, and local government intervention, large conglomerations and private businesses may allocate resources in exchange for business and tax incentives.

PHILIP LEE / Graduate Option Studio, 2001 / Mark Wamble, critic
[See also *The Circuit and the Cell*, page 81]

↗ Houston Needs a Mountain: Toward a New Monumentality

Landfills have always been the large voids in the city fabric; they are disguised and hidden from the public's view. This proposal offers an alternative to the current typology by reorganizing, restructuring, and redesigning the wastescape in order to reinsert it back into the city like a new, grafted, participatory organ.

Landfills are containers of time-stamped consumption and archived local historical events. By studying the cross sections of the cellular landmass, one can trace the archeology of our recent past human life, activities, technology, fads, and catastrophes. Landfills are no longer smelly piles of trash; once they are reorganized in a performative structure, the resulting

Phase two: a choreographed land(fill)scape

Phase three: garbage as ritual

wastescape will be the new epicenter of learning, archiving, recreation, migration routes, and alternate energy opportunities.

Phase One: Monumental Index
The typical landfill takes its mountainous form from a constant stacking and layering of daily to annual deposits. The proposal of phase one is to use the current methodology, but reorganize the trash into an index. Each trash mountain is a signifier of the region's annual consumption. Its autonomy not only suggests an awareness of the sheer volume the visitor is confronted with, but creates a new

monument that contains the history of our recent past.

Phase Two: A Choreographed Land(fill)scape
Phase two proposes the separation of garbage types according to their anticipated decay lifetimes. Due to the lack of oxygenation below 35 feet (oxygenation is needed for decay), the architecture built into the garbage brings air and water into the depths of the fill. With the ability to change diameters, apertures, and containment, the wastescape can be choreographed for multiple programmatic uses, introducing new natural processes. Phase two is regarded as the garden of the

project—wetlands, migration stop-offs, lot farming, flower cultivation—and becomes the leisure space for the phase to come.

Phase Three: Garbage as Ritual
The days of leaving trash on the curb are over. Phase three proposes a new ritual of garbage disposal: as the community sees the transformation the landfill has produced, members will want to be participants in its creation. The infrastructure is designed for automobile access, and each area of the structure segregates a different type of garbage for recycling or conversion into alternate energies. The dead zone of rotting garbage and off-gassing wasteland is no longer; the stereotypes of the local dump have been reversed to become an asset to the community. The vertical landfills create density and shrink the footprint of the old horizontal typology. Urban housing units may be attached to the infrastructure, offering spectacular views of Houston, wetlands, gardens, and the activities they support.

LYSLE OLIVEROS / M.Arch. Thesis, 2009 / Michael Morrow, director

↓Vertical Zoo

Situated alongside traditional zoo typologies in a zoological network, the Vertical Zoo takes advantage of typical features of tower design, specifically strategies related to structure, circulation, program orientation, and skin, to create dramatically different interior spaces

Vertical Zoo surrounded by Tokyo's dense urban environment

that support a completely atypical tower program—a zoo. The various subsystems of the vertical type are systematized to allow for variation and flexibility. From skin to circulation to mechanical systems, the Vertical Zoo focuses the visitor's attention both on the various bioclimates that house animal habitats and on their juxtaposition to the surrounding urban context.

Situated in an extremely dense urban environment, the Vertical Zoo examines how the most successful zoological exhibit to date, the immersion exhibit, can continue the evolution of the zoological institution through a stacked organization. The immersion exhibit has been the most successful exhibit type to date because of its focus on animal health and welfare, its ability to provide the zoo visitor with an engaging, educational experience, and its ability to bring a natural setting to an urban environment. However, this exhibit model is difficult to implement in rapidly growing cities because of its large space requirements.

Exterior view of the Vertical Zoo

Entering the Tundra zone, showing two types of circulation systems

688'-0" Desert Chaparral bio-climatic zone, at the top of the tower

By taking advantage of vertical space, the Vertical Zoo is able to occupy an urban site, allowing for a zoo presence in the city and for improved visitor accessibility. The Vertical Zoo's stacked organization reconsiders the spatial orientation of the immersion exhibit and creates a more efficient model. Although the zoo's site is only 2.4 acres, 70 percent of the program is dedicated to exhibit space, compared to traditional zoos where exhibit space is typically only 10 percent of the total program. Additionally, the vertical organization results in a more energy-efficient model by taking advantage of rising heat and falling water, organizing exhibits vertically according to bioclimatic needs.

The Vertical Zoo uses a system of distributed structural cores that terminate at different heights through the building, accommodating the diverse loading conditions and spatial configurations of the various climatic zones. A dynagrid structure is used to unite these cores, creating super columns. This arrangement requires less structural steel, can more adequately support uneven loading conditions, and enables the unimpeded movement of light into the

building. Further, the cores enclose the extensive mechanical support the zoo program requires, while the dynagrid structure extends out from the cores to form the framework for the secondary structure. The latter structure is what directly supports the exhibit armature and visitor circulation.

The zoo program requires the interaction of multiple, simultaneously occurring circulation routes. To accomplish this, the Vertical Zoo uses a two-pronged circulation system consisting of a primary, "fast" element and a secondary, "slow" element. The exhibit

platforms, conceived of as plates that overlay a steel skeletal frame, act as a framework for the ground-cover and vegetation that will later fill out the exhibit space. The platforms can support various ground conditions, ranging from steep, rocky, mountainous terrain to shallow, wet areas filled with soft matter such as mud or sand. The platforms are not designed for a specific animal inhabitant, but rather support conditions typical of a particular bioclimatic zone.

A double-layer skin system, consisting of a glass exterior and a wire mesh interior, creates different

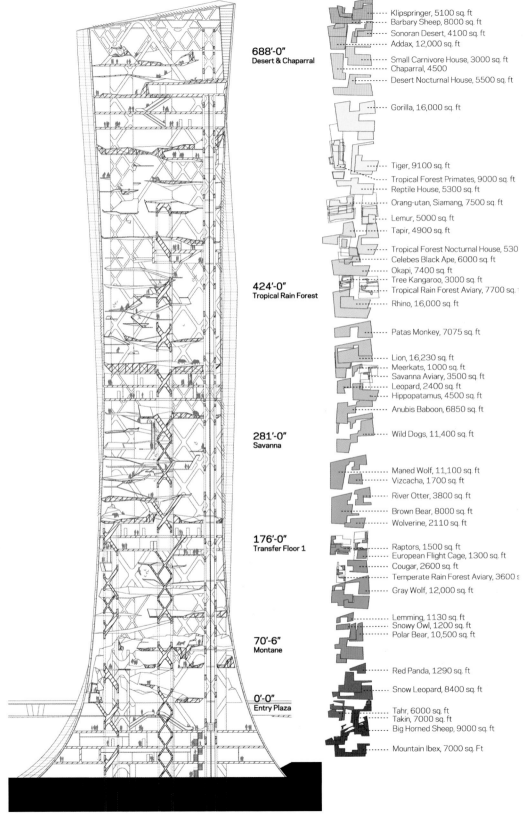

688'-0"
Desert & Chaparral

Klipspringer, 5100 sq. ft
Barbary Sheep, 8000 sq. ft
Sonoran Desert, 4100 sq. ft
Addax, 12,000 sq. ft
Small Carnivore House, 3000 sq. ft
Chaparral, 4500
Desert Nocturnal House, 5500 sq. ft

Gorilla, 16,000 sq. ft

Tiger, 9100 sq. ft
Tropical Forest Primates, 9000 sq. ft
Reptile House, 5300 sq. ft
Orang-utan, Siamang, 7500 sq. ft
Lemur, 5000 sq. ft
Tapir, 4900 sq. ft
Tropical Forest Nocturnal House, 530
Celebes Black Ape, 6000 sq. ft
Okapi, 7400 sq. ft
Tree Kangaroo, 3000 sq. ft
Tropical Rain Forest Aviary, 7700 sq.
Rhino, 16,000 sq. ft

424'-0"
Tropical Rain Forest

Patas Monkey, 7075 sq. ft

Lion, 16,230 sq. ft
Meerkats, 1000 sq. ft
Savanna Aviary, 3500 sq. ft
Leopard, 2400 sq. ft
Hippopotamus, 4500 sq. ft
Anubis Baboon, 6850 sq. ft

Wild Dogs, 11,400 sq. ft

281'-0"
Savanna

Maned Wolf, 11,100 sq. ft
Vizcacha, 1700 sq. ft
River Otter, 3800 sq. ft
Brown Bear, 8000 sq. ft
Wolverine, 2110 sq. ft

176'-0"
Transfer Floor 1

Raptors, 1500 sq. ft
European Flight Cage, 1300 sq. ft
Cougar, 2600 sq. ft
Temperate Rain Forest Aviary, 3600 s
Gray Wolf, 12,000 sq. ft

Lemming, 1130 sq. ft
Snowy Owl, 1200 sq. ft
Polar Bear, 10,500 sq. ft

70'-6"
Montane

Red Panda, 1290 sq. ft

Snow Leopard, 8400 sq. ft

0'-0"
Entry Plaza

Tahr, 6000 sq. ft
Takin, 7000 sq. ft
Big Horned Sheep, 9000 sq. ft

Mountain Ibex, 7000 sq. Ft

Building section and animal / climatic zone floor plate distribution

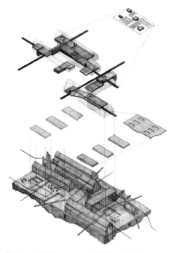

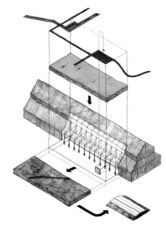

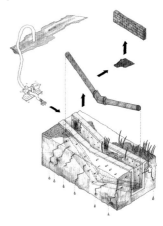

Diagram of the general relationship between the existing industrial infrastructure, ecological sinks, and pedestrian circulation.

Ecological sinks penetrate infrastructural thickets, allowing for permeation of sunlight and ventilation, introducing a potential field of biomass.

Removal of derelict pipes and spigots allows for a network of new "leaky" irrigation troughs that use existing pumping facilities to siphon water from the adjacent river and allow it to circulate through the site.

opportunities for the regulation of the interior environment and for views both outwards and inwards. These different conditions are achieved through the arrangement of the glass and mesh components of the skin. Additionally, an operable skin is provided for climatic zones that can be maintained open to Tokyo's climate.

ANDREA MANNING / M.Arch. Thesis, 2007 / Clover Lee, director

↗ The Garden in the Machine

Following in the wake of accelerated technological advancement are often detrimental economic and environmental consequences. As older industrial facilities become obsolete, newer technologies look toward virgin land for growth. In turn, the industrial city, once the recipient of generous corporate taxation and the beneficiary of a stable workforce, is now saddled with social unrest, economic stagnation, and vast tracts of infrastructure-laden land. Such is the case with the vacated Bethlehem Steel plant in Bethlehem, Pennsylvania.

The mutations of naturally occurring ecologies reported in the contaminated areas of Bethlehem Steel confound romantic ideals

Section through existing Steel Plant buildings and new ecological zones

of nature as an autonomous phenomenon external to the interventions of humankind. The Bio-Remedial Park (above) is structured by landscapes characterized by the levels of contamination existing in their soils. The present ecologies, although of different varieties, will eventually give way to indigenous flora and fauna as the land is purified.

At the root of this thesis is the conviction that regeneration of this site needs to be approached as a multidimensional phenomenon that touches upon the organic, the economic, and the chemical. As such, a kind of petri dish can be created

where physical entropy and the erosion of memory coexist with economic and ecologic growth. This thesis defines a new beginning by bridging the cleft between growth and decay. The history of this site, its entropic future, and the beginnings of a new history are conflated into a single continuum.

BRETT TERPELUK / M.Arch. Thesis, 1998 / Michael Bell, director

Brett Terupulek's work ultimately diagrammed the residual chemical contamination at Bethlehem Steel's closed plant in Allentown, Pennsylvania. But it was both a diagram of former industry—a factory and its

FLORA AND FAUNA

ECOLOGICAL SINKS

WILD DOGS

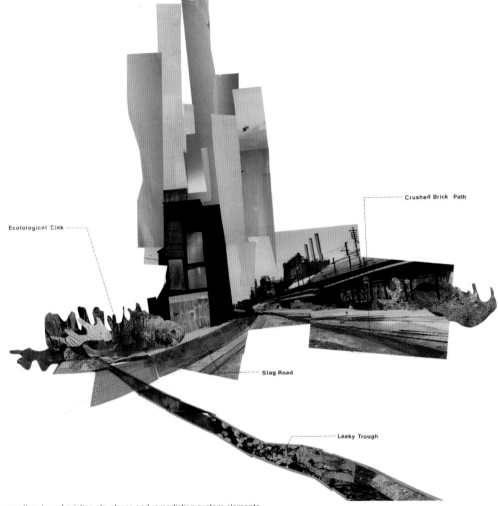

Ecolological Eink

Crushed Brick Path

Slag Road

Leaky Trough

Perspective view of existing structures and remediation system elements

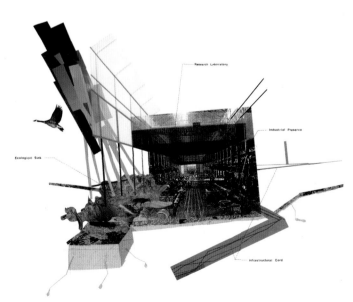

Research Laboratory

Industrial Preserve

Ecological Sink

Infrastructural Cord

Interior view of existing and proposed structures

labor (a lament for lost work, the demise of an economic social engine)—and a diagram accessing former flows. He saw the sinking contamination and culled from its weight a still, even formal, image of a very slow flowing, yet continuous, history. The past was STILL in motion.

Terupulek read Robert Smithson's work about the experience of Houston's vacuous expanses of leftover lands (still hardly recovered from the oil bust of the eighties). He was seeing prehistories with modern eyes that attempted to both avert the crisis and allow it to dilate his vision. The present was expanded into a material history that had never lost its continuity even if it was near some elastic limits.

Terupulek's was a plan project, recovering weights of residual oil settled into the earth on the site (contamination). The work struggled with the projective aspects of what to do with Bethlehem Steel—how to avoid a theme park and how not to reconvene a labor project or a new factory. It was a huge success, though, in terms of moving the temporality of the diagram toward a form of materiality... to having both. The predatory metropolis and a resistance to it are here, but it is also based on an intuition of material that promises a projective and temporal habitation. To be there is to understand the literal weight of what was, a history that is not still and thus is not as prone to capture.

—**Michael Bell** is an associate professor at Columbia Graduate School of Architecture, Planning and Preservation and a principal at Visible Weather. He was an associate professor at Rice School of Architecture 1994-1999.

→Staging Bands

This urban research laboratory investigated the emerging spaces, phenomena, and experiences of collectivity in our splintered metropolis: the spaces of the multitude. We were concerned with urban forms and spaces as registers of (often bottom-up) post-Fordist processes. Crucial were the transformations in the regimes of power and subjects, and their implications for the repertoire of urban typologies and concepts: peer-to-peer urbanisms, distributed systems of control, "smart mobs," zones of "commonality," celebrations of the deviant productivity of habit (and, alternatively, the normalization of the carnivalesque), the oxymoronic dwellings of the archipelago economy, and the social cluster. The triangulated relationship between landscape, urbanism, and networked information infrastructures calibrated our work. The city of Houston's proposed downtown park was the site, in both geographic and conceptual senses, for our investigations. We had the opportunity to directly engage the actors and forces that are guiding this project.

The city of Houston has secured a piece of land in the downtown area adjacent to a convention center and basketball arena. The land has the potential to become an exemplary public space, yet it has been a field of political, economic, and formal indeterminacy. Responding to

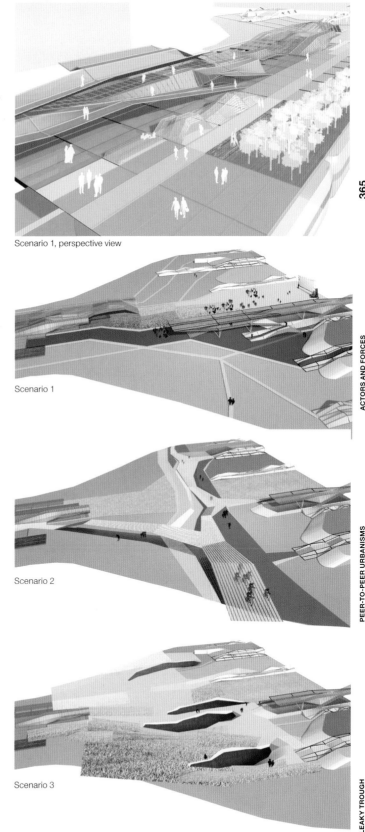

Scenario 1, perspective view

ACTORS AND FORCES

Scenario 1

PEER-TO-PEER URBANISMS

Scenario 2

LEAKY TROUGH

Scenario 3

the indefinite nature of the site, this project proposes a park focused on staged connections rather than on static programs. It designates initial charges that attach to areas of high pedestrian density, forming lasting connections to other monitored events over time. These charges or connections, such as tunnels, a skywalk, and embedded electronic networks, for example, create the possibility for flexible forms on the site. From shade and seating at the edge of an open playing field to more specific and embedded, permanent programs, the park intermeshes material surfaces and programmatic density.

ERIC HUGHES, NATASHA BEARD, ANDREW CORRIGAN / Graduate Core Studio, 2005 / Christopher Hight, Sean Lally, critics

↓Growing Atmospheres

The proposed program takes advantage of Houston's subtropical climate to produce nine acres of highly productive hydroponic, or soil-less, farmland. By choosing plant varieties suited to Houston's climate, this open-air urban farm produces year round without the expensive heating and cooling required by hydroponic facilities in other climates. Lifting the farm above the urban fabric provides an opportunity to generate "microclimates," or local atmospheric zones, and frees up the ground plane for more traditional park activities. Like a rainforest canopy, the density of the vegetation above determines the character of the growth below, allowing for the creation of exciting, unique park spaces. Additionally, by utilizing the abundance of green space available in Houston to grow local produce and increase the usability of parks in the summer months, we can reduce the energy impact of a lower-density city while retaining its advantages.

JOSEPH LIM / Undergraduate Vertical Studio, 2007 / Spencer Parsons, critic

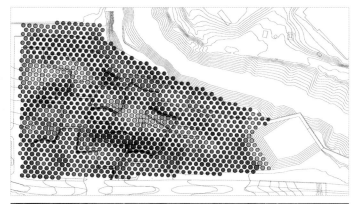

Higher density planting generates more shaded area during summer months. Scenario for mid-July above.

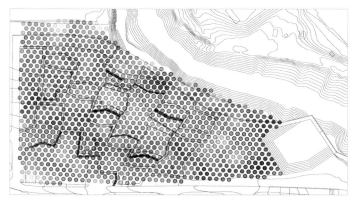

Low density planting allows more sunlight penetration during colder months. Scenario for mid-February above.

↓Potential Futures

Sean Lally

Critic, Graduate Option Studios, 2007-2008

The main objective here isn't to question the role of process, to seek new and previously unseen representational techniques, or to outline a new manifesto to solve all others. Like light from a flashlight, the efforts are bound to bounce off of a few things on their way to the objective across the room. The work is mindful of the methods and strategies that offer the resultant opportunities, but is always looking forward, continually glimpsing into countless potential futures—not only for evaluation, but for instigating new events. With such an approach, these projects act as facilitators to jumpstart future endeavors, ones that can be absorbed by additional associations in order to create opportunities and speculations that offer more than their own end product. As we question the role we are playing in the design of tomorrow, we acknowledge the power and proclivities of the tools and techniques we deploy and the information they quantify. And while the toolsets at our disposal seem to grow faster, stronger, and more efficient every year, we need to remain mindful that our reliance on technology is often an excuse for a weak imagination. Our fascination and attention must extend beyond the protocols, tools and research to the potentialities and implications they provide. As designers, when our discussions fall into a defense of process and contemporaneity, we slip into a model of design practice that's self referential and defined by protocols instead of opportunities. Design today is the search for these opportunities, not the scrutiny of the paths that get us there! The research and work here is a generator of speculation and a reservoir for potentialities to be tapped when needed. Not for manifestos and proclamations but for inclinations and instincts as we tackle new projects still to come.

The work illustrated here is an attempt to question a rather fundamental and all too often ignored discussion in architectural education and design; what constitutes a physical boundary and edge in the spatial organizations we as architects create? The work investigates a realm of materiality associated with energy as it pertains to defining and constructing physical boundaries in our built domain. As these are often oversimplified and pigeon holed as either qualitative 'effects' or as part of a preconceived and efficient 'sustainable design', the projects address these 'material energies' which in themselves are rarely heralded as an opportunity for design innovation with broader spatial and organizational implications in the foreground. Such innovation in design at our local—as well as urban and regional—environments is most fruitful not at the level of the structural engineer's attempts to design better walls, but when it seeks to investigate a broader spectrum of materiality when questioning something as fundamental as what constitutes a boundary when organizing activity in architecture. Because ENERGY is addressed as a design material to be exploited during the design phase, the work inevitably crosses disciplines ranging from architecture and landscape architecture into issues encompassed in the broader domain of urban planning; as these materials are not mutually exclusive to a building, a landscape, or city organization.

Many of these projects and study exercises operate as full-scale investigations, not only through software simulations but by the deployment of physical prototypes and fabrication, intended to show deviations in results between the software and the physical tests. These investigations question those materials at the architect's disposal that are useful in the quantifying and instrumentalizing phases in the design process. The results indicate an approach to research that is not a product in and of itself, but rather one where the investigation is only as important as where it leads us next. The work is less about being fully executable 'complete' projects and more about a strategy of design that seeks a 'proof of concept'—a verification of a strategy that shows a potential for its future project endeavors.

Each of these projects relies on their inherent role as generators for future opportunities and speculations. The projects seek to increase the feedback between the choices we make and the evaluation of their prospects as we sieve through options and entertain daydreams of the imagination. If what we as designers are looking for is an ability to heighten and amplify the feedback loop between the ideas we generate, our ability to test and gather information about its feasibility and it's potential for success or failure, than the discussion becomes one less about the methods deployed in design and more about the spatial and social implications such work provides and instigates. It is the attempt to increase the rate of return that increases our decision-making abilities and knowledge base in the pursuit of design innovation. We strive to maximize those 'eureka moments' during the design process that propel us forward and beyond our previously linear trajectory. The work is an act of instigation with friends and accomplices rather than a search for a captive audience to digest and reflect upon our tactics.

This essay originally appeared in *AD: Energies, New Material Boundaries*, John Wiley & Sons, 2009.

SEAN LALLY is an assistant professor at University of Illinois at Chicago School of Architecture. He was an assistant professor at Rice School of Architecture from 2002-08.

MATERIAL ENERGIES

HYDROPONIC FARMLAND

SUBTROPICAL CLIMATE

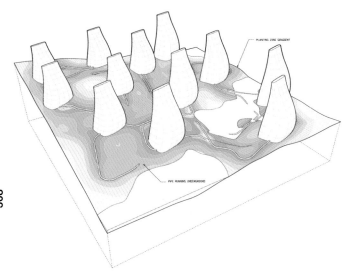

Botanical Garden rooftop showing the twelve distinct growing environments

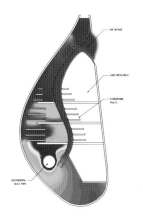

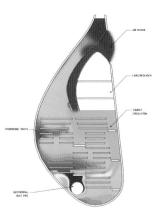

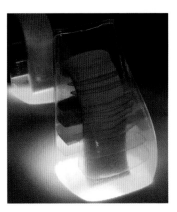

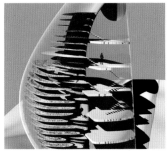

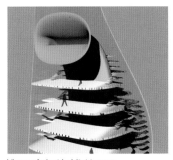

Views of plant habitat towers

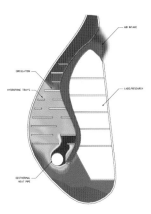

Hydroponic trays are arranged to create three climatic zones. The trays at the base of the tower gather geothermal heat, creating a hot zone. Heat dissipates as it rises, offering cooler zones towards the top of the tower.

↑ Reykjavik Botanical Garden

Reykjavík Botanical Garden is a hybrid system, utilizing Iceland's abundant geothermal energy resources to serve a series of convection loops, which create microclimates for varied plant growth. Heat is taken directly from the ground and piped up across the landscape into a system of towers. The geothermal distribution system, operating at ground level, is exploited in order to warm the earth's surface and increase the plantable area. Zones of heat radiate out from the pipes, creating a new climate layer with variable conditions based on the number of pipes and their proximity to each other. These exterior plantings are mostly native to Iceland, but the amplified environment allows a wider range of plant species than would normally be possible, informing the role and opportunity of this particular Botanical Garden. Visitors will experience plantings never before seen in Iceland and

travel through new climates throughout the site. Geothermal wells extract steam from volcanic fissures within the earth, and this steam is directly pumped through pipes on the site. This network of interwoven pipes feeds twelve towers, each of which siphons off a portion of the available heat, which rises within each tower and in turn draws in cooler air from outside in a convection loop. The towers contain a catalogued variety of plants from many of the world's climates. A system of intake tubes and chambers modulate the heat flow to hydroponic growing trays and research laboratories. The towers in the landscape are each slightly different, creating twelve distinct growing environments simply by rearranging the hydroponic trays and the air intake systems within the towers.

ANDREW CORRIGAN, JOHN CARR / Graduate Option Studio, 2007

Prototype of cooling module

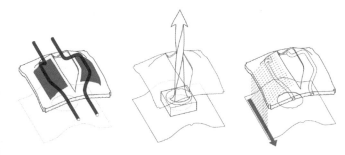

Coolant is delivered through the curved panel while air is directed upwards by a small fan to produce turbulence, resulting in cooling. Condensation is collected and redistributed for other domestic uses.

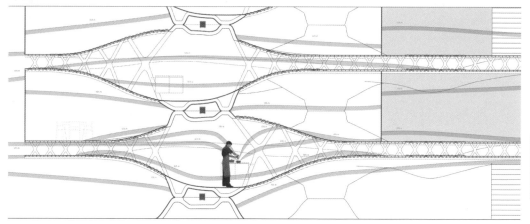

Section showing the field of distributed air processing units that comprise both floor and ceiling surfaces.

→ Living in Coils

This project, located in Houston, proposes a model of living organized around the movement and humidity of air. The map of humidity within the city recalls the contrasts of Nolli's map, though here the contrast is drawn between internal conditioned space and external atmosphere. Air conditioning and the waterproofing of materials work to fortify the home against the intrusion of water vapor, creating a homogeneous environment of hard programmatic enclosures. This reinforces an organization of living that we wish to criticize, at the scale both of the unit and of the city. In this project, humidity is thought of as a generative force, rather than a nuisance, imagining an environment where the affective qualities of air movement and moisture content engender soft boundaries and unit cohabitation through air exchange.

In the conventional home environment, air is processed at a discrete and centralized point in order to achieve homogeneous qualities of smell, temperature, and humidity, which are distributed to distinct volumes of residential program. The

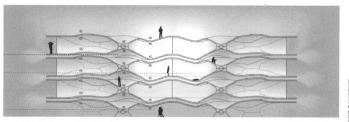

System allows for a variety of domestic activities in the multi-unit arrangement while meeting individual thermal demands

point-fed distribution of the conventional air-conditioning unit is here supplanted with a field of distributed air processing units that comprise both floor and ceiling surfaces. The interior of the prototypical unit draws air across its cooled upper surfaces, removing water vapor through

condensation and collecting it in channels. Fields of these units hover above vapor-producing activities, pulling air upward and softly emitting it into the environment above. By modulating both the intensity of these fields and the volumetric sizes of atmosphere they work to define, patterns of

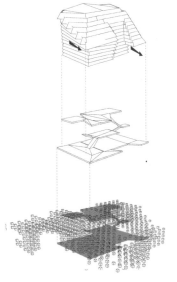

Convective unit system and its aggregate behaviors

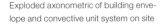

Conditioning strategy includes sculpted floor plates, convective units, and louvers

Exploded axonometric of building envelope and convective unit system on site

domestic living are created. Self-interested
cells of conditioned space become an
ecology of conditions.
**CURT GAMBETTA, BRIAN
SHEPHERDSON / Graduate Option
Studio, 2008**

↑ We Do Not Live in a Mono-Climatic World.

The project proposes a way of living in
close relation to our local environments, in
this case by constructing an urban-scale
convective flow. Three systems operate
to this end: (1) an array of heat-collecting
pods directs large-scale convective flow
across the site, (2) the external skin of
each residential unit is a system of louvers,

affording residents the ability to tap into the
larger environmental system, and (3) interior
partitions direct air circulation to areas of
specific residential needs. Modeling software
was used during the course of the studio
to develop and test the performance of
both individual pods and the system as a
whole. A combination of digital fabrication
techniques was then used to prototype each
pod at full scale. The pods comprise three
parts: An aluminum-filled epoxy-resin base
collects and radiates heat; a vacuum-formed
acrylic top captures and directs convective flow; and the lattice structure where
these two pieces sit provides system-wide
aggregation and control. Residential living
is rewritten to become complicit with larger,
augmented macro-environmental conditions. Now existing in a semi-nomadic state,
program relocates within the building at different times of the day and year. Convection
and air pressure become full participants as
materials for controlling and celebrating a
new way of life in the convective flow.
**NED DODINGTON, BRIAN LOVE /
Graduate Option Studio, 2008**

→ Ambiguous Etiologies

Ambiguous Etiologies is a reconfigurable,
modular lattice system that minimizes
Wyoming's large temperature swings
between summer and winter to create a
year-round inhabitable outdoor space. The
pavilion harnesses water, wind, and snow to
create a landscape of differentiated spatial
zones. During the frigid winter months, the
components' semi-porous aggregations
act as snow fences, slowing down drifting
snow enough for it to accrue into moguls.
These mounds, or "fetches," of snow are
calibrated to accumulate behind and in front
of the fences to a size that is proportionately
scaled to the pavilion's human occupants.
The hollow modules comprising these
fences act in conjunction with the fetches
to insulate the space and reduce wind chill.
Furthermore, nichrome, a heating metal al-
loy, is spliced into the modules' connections
to warm the inhabitable spaces downwind.
These space heaters, many buried within
the mounds, are activated just before the
hot summer months to melt the stored
snow and ice into a series of upwind pools.

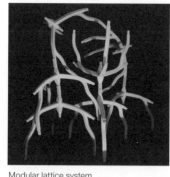

Modular lattice system

Breezes blow over these pools, cooling the pavilion, while the fences now provide shade not readily available on the barren plains. The pavilion contemporaneously shapes its climate and is shaped by it.

The orchestration of these complex and inseparably entwined spatio-temporal forces necessitated using digital and analog feedback loops at the scale of the module and the pavilion. These loops tested the structural stability and electrical conductivity of the modules, as well as the aerodynamics, heat output, and insulating capacity of different component aggregations and their fetches. The growth of these various distributions' fetches was simulated with a digital script derived from government-funded snow fence research data. The feedback from these different trials was constantly integrated into each other's data as well as the design of the module and its arrangement. This generative design process simultaneously affected and was affected by the aforementioned performance criteria.

The pavilion challenges the understanding of space as a "discrete multiplicity" and instead approaches architecture as the dynamic distribution of intensive material properties: light, heat, density, turbulence, pressure. Ambiguous Etiologies acknowledges architecture's full immersion in the flux of material energies, revealing the absurdity of dialectic categories such as the "natural" and the "artificial," or the "landscape" and the "building." This project is an engine for the organization of matter.

FEDERICO CAVAZOS, ROBERT CRAWFORD / Undergraduate Vertical Studio, 2006

Aggregations of lattice system units act as snow fences

velocity

inlet mass flow: .00025 in/s

temperature

environment: 5 degrees F

Nichrome: 200 degrees F

connection type 3

connection type 6

connection type 10

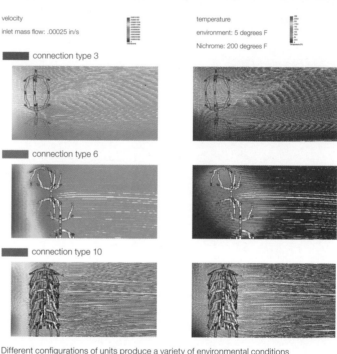

Different configurations of units produce a variety of environmental conditions

"...but sunsets are better."

White knight

Above the smog line

The electric forest

7

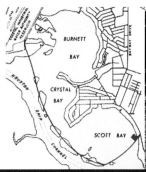

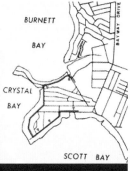

A levee protecting the three bays surrounding Brownwood had been proposed by 1961, after Hurricane Carla. Built along islands formed from Ship Channel dredging, it could turn Scott, Crystal, and Burnett Bays into freshwater lakes.

But 12 years have passed, Brownwood has continued to sink and flood, and the levee project -- estimated to cost $10 million -- is still being studied.

Seeking more immediate relief, Baytown hatches its own scheme: a smaller, seven-foot-high roadway dike within Brownwood itself.

Flooding after sustained southeast winds, Bayshore Dr., Brownwood subdivision, April 1972. Photo by Ed Malcik. Courtesy *Baytown Sun*.

Plan of Brownwood subdivision showing roadway dike and pump locations, January 1975. Courtesy U.S. Army Corps of Engineers, Galveston District.

Plan of proposed levee or floodwall around Burnett, Crystal, and Scott Bays, January 1975. Courtesy U.S. Army Corps of Engineers, Galveston District.

→ Houston Wet

Imagine a city with the mission of making life possible where it wasn't—yet.

In Houston, this idea predates the founding of NASA, the building of the giant air-conditioned expanse of the Astrodome, even the discovery of oil. It was present at the city's founding. Houston was a real-estate scam, the artificial instant capital of an invented republic, a booming metropolis—and a great international port—just where it would seem most unlikely: in the middle of a damp and sweltering coastal plain.

Houston Wet is a documentary that attempts to identify Houston's role in some of the immense transformations that have rearranged the American landscape over the last thirty years: the seeming homogenization of urban, suburban, and exurban areas; the increasing isolation of people and buildings from their natural surroundings; and the rise of generic approaches to specific problems.

Houston Wet paints a picture of this city as a giant war zone

The flag is a last-minute addition to the flight of Apollo 11. There is little time to spare.

Apollo 11 Saturn V rocket drives itself along crawlerway to the launch pad, Kennedy Space Center, Florida, May 1969. Courtesy NASA.

and laboratory. Over a period of more than 150 years, Houstonians have fought steadily escalating battles against nature just to be able to live here. In the course of those battles, we have learned from our mistakes, developing and appropriating successively more complex techniques with which to isolate ourselves not only from the particular hazards of this soggy land, but also from hazards that might exist in any environment.

In other locations, parallel battles have yielded building practices

that we might term "appropriate" or even "indigenous" because they inscribe the particular qualities of the region in the architecture itself.

But in Houston local or regionally developed technologies have always been eagerly abandoned when more powerful, more generic solutions developed elsewhere could be imported. Generic solutions have been applied so persistently in Houston that they have established themselves as a significant aspect of the local culture. Here, the attempt to insulate

It is an incomplete defense. Bayfront homes will get no protection. But by this time, some of them have already been abandoned.

Bayfront house rented by the Atkisson family, Brownwood subdivision, 1973. Sign reads "WHO NEEDS A LEVEE? If you wake up in time, you probably may escape the tide waters via the dike (Bayshore Dr.), says owner, Clyde Tacker." Courtesy Harris-Galveston Coastal Subsidence District.

Three years after it is approved, the levee is finally built. It is both protector and escape route: a road that is a wall.

West Bayshore, North Bayshore, and South Bayshore Drives, Mapleton Ave., and parts of Crow Road and Brownwood Drive -- all perimeter roads -- are elevated. They will form a bulwark against the bay.

Construction on raised West Bayshore Drive, Brownwood subdivision, 1973. Brown family home is at far left. Photo by Keith Thompson. Courtesy *Baytown Sun*.

The road turns out to be a blessing...

Suspended walkway connecting house to raised perimeter road, Brownwood subdivision, 1970's. Courtesy Harris-Galveston Coastal Subsidence District.

When Armstrong and Aldrin rehearse their lunar surface activities, the flag plays no role. It isn't ready yet. Later, Kinzler will train Armstrong separately.

Astronauts Aldrin and Armstrong during lunar surface training, Building 9, MSC, April 1969. Courtesy NASA.

There is no mention of the flag on the lunar-surface-activity checklist sewn onto the astronauts' cuffs. It is not ready in time.

Checklist sewn onto Neil Armstrong's EVA suit, July 1969. Courtesy NASA.

It is July 15, 1969, the day before Apollo 11 is to launch, and the flag is not even packed.

Apollo 11 flag prepares for its journey, MSC, July 15, 1969. Courtesy NASA.

human life from any and all hazards has staked a strong claim as the appropriate, if not quite indigenous, way of life for the city.

Houston Wet is a browse-able mythology: it is a set of ideas and a small collection of illustrated stories about a place. The stories portray this city at its extremes.

The first story follows the remarkable history of Brownwood subdivision, a once-elite neighborhood just outside the city limits that slowly sank into the surrounding bay. Eventually it was abandoned and turned into a marsh preserve. The second story details how NASA engineers altered and repackaged the American flag so that it could be planted on the moon.

Each story is divided into chapters and illustrated with archival photographs, displayed filmstrip-style on the Houston Wet website. A separate series of exhibits describes themes common to the two stories. Links between the stories and exhibits allow website visitors to trace their own paths between idea and narrative.

LARRY ALBERT / M.Arch. Thesis, 1997 / Albert Pope, director

… and a curse.

Mr. and Mrs. Joseph Beam take a boat ride through Brownwood subdivision, September 1973. Courtesy Harris-Galveston Coastal Subsidence District.

The raised road is supposed to sit seven feet above sea level, but ends up being raised only to five-and-a-half feet. According to some reports, the problem occurs because construction crews base their measurements on elevation readings from a few years earlier -- and the land has continued to sink since then.

Raised perimeter road, West Bayshore Drive, Brownwood subdivision, 1970's. Courtesy Harris-Galveston Coastal Subsidence District.

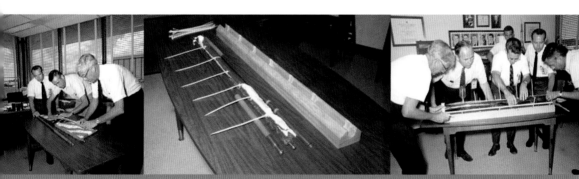

A group including Jack Kinzler, Dave McCraw, Tom Moser, and Chief of Quality Assurance Jack Jones assemble in Kinzler's office at the Manned Spacecraft Center to prepare the flag for its journey to the moon.

First they fold the flag according to a procedure developed by Billy Drummond, head of the MSC parachute shop.

Tom Moser, Billy Drummond, and Jack Kinzler pack the flag in Kinzler's office, July 15, 1969. Courtesy NASA.

A wooden cradle and plastic ties help them hold the flag together at each step.

Flag assembly with cradle during packing, MSC, July 15, 1969. Courtesy NASA.

They place the flag, temporarily bound with ties, in the aluminized thermal wrap.

Yes -- Jack Kinzler says later -- "it took all those hands to pull and fold the flag and stuff it into the heat shield."

Jack Kinzler, Jack Jones, Dave McCraw, Tom Moser, and Billy Drummond stuff the flag in Kinzler's office, MSC, July 15, 1969. Man in back is unidentified. Courtesy NASA.

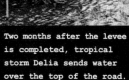

City funds pay for raising the road, but not for any way to remove water that falls behind it. Every drop will have to be pumped out. So members of the Brownwood Civic Association -- a group begun, in less stressful times, as a social organization -- collect funds from homeowners themselves to pay for five old rice-field pumps.

The pumps have float switches. They will turn on automatically whenever there is flooding, to send water back to the bay.

Brownwood rice-field pump aimed toward the San Jacinto Monument, 1980's. Courtesy Harris-Galveston Coastal Subsidence District.

Two months after the levee is completed, tropical storm Delia sends water over the top of the road.

Flooding after Delia, Crow & Mapleton, Brownwood subdivision, September 1973. Courtesy *Baytown Sun*.

Rice-field pump, perimeter road, viewed from the bay, Brownwood subdivision, 1976. Photo by Kathy Callahan. Courtesy Brownwood Civic Association Archives.

Thermaflex insulation goes on the ends of the poles, inside the brackets.

Then comes the tricky part: wrapping new ties around the aluminum wrap and removing the inner ties around the flag, while keeping everything tight.

Dave McCraw, Billy Drummond, and Jack Kinzler wrestle with flag ties as Jack Jones and Tom Moser look on in Kinzler's office, MSC, July 15, 1969. Courtesy NASA.

Then they attach the Velcro rip strip...

Billy Drummond, Dave McCraw, and Jack Kinzler align Velcro strips as Tom Moser and Jack Jones (just off camera) look on, Kinzler's office, MSC, July 15, 1969. Courtesy NASA.

...wrapping it around the package...

Jack Jones, Tom Moser, Billy Drummond, Dave McCraw, and Jack Kinzler wrap the flag in Kinzler's office, MSC, July 15, 1969. Courtesy NASA.

Water fills the subdivision like a giant bowl.

And then it sits.

Plan of proposed levee or floodwall around Burnett, Crystal, and Scott Bays, January 1975. Courtesy U.S. Army Corps of Engineers, Galveston District.

Plan of proposed levee or floodwall around Burnett, Crystal, and Scott Bays, January 1975. Courtesy U.S. Army Corps of Engineers, Galveston District.

... and taking it out of the block to remove the last set of ties.

They stuff the insulated package into the metal shroud. "Normally," says Kinzler, "you'd never see five or six guys in an office packing something."

Next comes the pip-pin assembly. Clips go onto the ends of the brackets, then are connected to a temporary rail -- a stand-in for the ladder -- so everything won't come apart before it's attached to the Lunar Module.

Billy Drummond, Dave McCraw, and Jack Kinzler remove ties from the flag package as Jack Jones (off camera) and Tom Moser look on in Kinzler's office, MSC, July 15, 1969. Courtesy NASA.

Jack Jones, Tom Moser, Billy Drummond, Dave McCraw, and Jack Kinzler fit the flag into its shroud, MSC, July 15, 1969. Courtesy NASA.

Tom Moser and Jack Jones watch Dave McCraw and Jack Kinzler attach the flag to its ladder substitute in Kinzler's office, MSC, July 15, 1969. Courtesy NASA.

It has nowhere to go.

Except through the pumps, slowly, out again to the bay.

Plan of proposed levee or floodwall around Burnett, Crystal, and Scott Bays, January 1975. Courtesy U.S. Army Corps of Engineers, Galveston District.

Plan of proposed levee or floodwall around Burnett, Crystal, and Scott Bays, January 1975. Courtesy U.S. Army Corps of Engineers, Galveston District.

And the package is complete. As soon as it is packed, Kinzler, George Low (now Apollo Program manager), his secretary, and the flag assembly fly a specially chartered Lear jet to Kennedy Space Center in Florida.

At 4 a.m. -- less than six hours before liftoff -- Kinzler installs the flag onto the underside of the Lunar Module ladder, following an 11-step procedure he has written out. The spacecraft sits on top of the Saturn V rocket that will propel it into outer space.

And at 9:37 a.m., Apollo 11 is launched.

Apollo 11 Saturn V blasts off past a U.S. flag, KSC, July 16, 1969. Courtesy NASA.

The flag, ready for takeoff on Apollo 11, Jack Kinzler's office, MSC, July 15, 1969. Courtesy NASA.

Searchlights illuminate Apollo 11 Saturn V rocket on the launch pad, July 1969. Courtesy NASA.

Houston's Buffalo Bayou is a sanctuary, international port, catchment basin, military depot, petrochemical complex, bird million people have gathered forty-mile reservoir, wildlife recreational zone, open sewer, industrial wasteland, shipyard, sanctuary, around which four in savage exploitation.

According to the Houston Department of Public Works, no public or private utility in the Houston area, including even the freeway system, will cost as much in the years to come as an adequate drainage system.

→ Bayou/City

Albert Pope
Critic, Graduate Core Studio, 2001

Founded on the banks of Buffalo Bayou in 1863, Houston exploded some sixty years later when a hurricane destroyed both Galveston and the shipping monopoly that it possessed. Having recently secured its place in the global economy, the city has been forced to reconsider its own backyard. Houston is essentially a very large, discontinuous stretch of asphalt and concrete set in the costal wetlands of southeast Texas, along the western arc of the gulf of Mexico.

In this regard, the city might best be described as a series of overlaps: local trade upon global economy, subdivision upon ecosystem, freeway upon floodplain, park upon retention basin, bird sanctuary upon commercial mall. Superimpositions of these competing, often clashing forces have created a city where conventional categories are meaningless and boundaries have ceased to exist.

For example, the city's insistence on dominating natural forces has muddled any meaningful distinction between the man-made and the natural. Seemingly over-endowed with moisture, Houston extracts water from the ground for agriculture and industry. While aquifers are tapped indiscriminately and neighborhoods sink below sea level, the low-lying landscape is subject to ever-catastrophic magnitudes of flooding. Described by politicians and insurance agents as "Acts of God," such flooding can be attributed to no such obvious force. With the paving over of wetlands,

dramatic shifts in weather patterns, extraction of ground water, the flooding of fields for recreational hunting, rogue hurricanes in the Gulf of Mexico, who can possibly separate the workings of the man-made world from the workings of the natural world?

As conceptual limits collapse, however, the bayous continue to be paved, the ship channel continues to be dredged, the aquifers continue to be depleted, and subdivisions continue to rise from the fifty-year floodplains.

Yet for all of Houston's attempts to deny such paradoxes, the metropolis coexists with the environment in strange and sometimes beautiful ways. Agricultural manipulation of the Katy Prairie has resulted in the establishment North America's largest population of migratory birds. Environmental legislation has seen a wealthy housing subdivision sink into the bay and devolve back into wetlands under the care and supervision of Exxon. Large islands, some two miles in diameter, have been created from dredging material, attracting the most threatened species of the biological region. Accelerating economies of scale in the shipping industry have turned obsolete port facilities into the largest and most surreal landscapes of industrial archeology virtually overnight.

More often than not, what makes these new, hybrid environments beautiful is the very absence of conventional classification. The Bayou thus forms a significant site in the ongoing reorganization of the man-made and the natural world. It establishes a new conceptual frontier that is at once, both urban horizon and natural edge.

Bolivar Pass. This man-modified inlet connects the Houston Ship Channel to the Gulf of Mexico. The round island at the bottom of the image was produced entirely by dredging material.

Urban Frontier

At the meeting of the natural and the urban the world comes into existence, which is to say that there exists in real space—concrete and localizable—a convergence that creates a fundamental cultural distinction. The natural cannot be defined without the urban and the urban cannot be defined without the natural. This is another way of saying that nature is not a transcendent value existing as an essence beyond historical circumstances. The natural is something that is reinvented every day and such reinvention is the meaning of urban frontier.

Singularity

The urban frontier is a singularity in that it defines the qualities of the urban and the natural while belonging to neither.

Monoculture

Historically, the urban frontier was recognized to be the built-up edge or line of new urban construction. Over the past half-century this singular, built-up edge has disappeared. The urban frontier has exfoliated from a finite line into a boundless field. It is a zone, a sprawl, a periphery, a region of uncontrolled growth, and it is everywhere. Today, the sprawl of the urban frontier replaces the urban/natural duality. While most people understand that new cities have become zoned, franchised, sterile and one-dimensional, few agree on the causes of this transformation. We would argue that these qualities are the direct effect of a duality collapsing into a singularity. In the contemporary city, the line between the natural and the urban has consumed the categories that it once sustained. The city has been transformed into an all-pervasive monoculture of franchise stores, production housing, corporate office parks, and engineered thoroughfares. The elements of this monoculture have, quite simply, de-polarized the world.

Inner Horizon

If a peripheral urban monoculture has superseded the structuring dichotomies of the past, then what remains of the urban and the natural and the decisive line that

Pre-war

1945

porosity

1970

1995

< Katy Prairie

Downtown Houston >

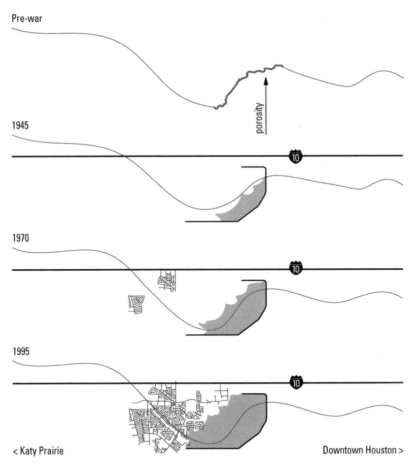

Resonance. Houston is shielded by a reservoir. Upstream, suburban development and the reservoir ecosystems (woodlands, wetlands, and prairies) are more intimately connected. Spurred by a burgeoning economy and an abundant supply of surface water, these two systems grow towards each other, while planners amplify a formal disconnection with a paired ditch and wall. Urban growth thus requires an equal and opposing adjustment of the natural. The reservoir is the counterpoint, the void produced by an urban solid.

creates them? Is there a line existing today that could be identified as an urban horizon or natural edge? It is possible to imagine that the urban horizon has imploded inward and appears, not on the periphery, but inside the city reclaiming the edge of a former frontier. The work presented on these pages was predicated on the possibility that some form of inner horizon has opened up inside the contemporary city. One thinks of imploded worlds where an urban frontier is reconstituted internally such as bombed cities (postwar Rotterdam and Berlin), or abandoned cities (medieval Rome), but it is mostly to be found as the lines of dereliction and redevelopment that have moved through western cities over the last 50 years. The question posed in the studio asked if the natural and the urban could be reconstituted along the lines of an inner horizon.

Bayou/City
The studio only scratched the surface, uncovering just a few of the possible intersections between the natural and the urban as they were found down the length of the forty mile bayou. The more we uncovered, the more we suspected that there existed an infinite number of such intersections and that every drawing or photograph we made of the bayou constituted, in itself, a section through the strange reordering of the natural and the urban. Some of these intersections were beautiful, some were catastrophic, some were highly profitable, and most are entropic. Some of them exist today as they existed before history, some are so new, and present so confounded a juncture, that they lack the conceptual framework by which they can even be seen.

Thoreau
We tend to think of the natural only in highly idealized, "Thoreauvian" terms. While such a restricted conception of the natural is recent, it is completely entrenched in our thought. Understood as something behind the gates of a national park, nature today is something to which we are conceptually blind. Thus it is that we look at the most fantastic of engagements between the natural and the man-made—dams, strip mines, quarries,

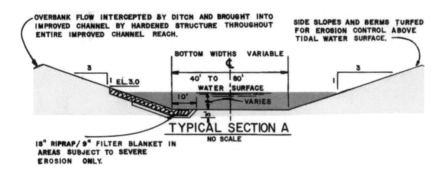

OVERBANK FLOW INTERCEPTED BY DITCH AND BROUGHT INTO
IMPROVED CHANNEL BY HARDENED STRUCTURE THROUGHOUT
ENTIRE IMPROVED CHANNEL REACH.

SIDE SLOPES AND BERMS TURFED
FOR EROSION CONTROL ABOVE
TIDAL WATER SURFACE.

BOTTOM WIDTHS VARIABLE

40' TO 80'
WATER SURFACE

TYPICAL SECTION A
NO SCALE

18" RIPRAP/ 9" FILTER BLANKET IN
AREAS SUBJECT TO SEVERE
EROSION ONLY.

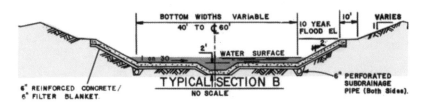

BOTTOM WIDTHS VARIABLE
40' TO ₵ 60'

10 YEAR
FLOOD EL

VARIES

WATER SURFACE

TYPICAL SECTION B
NO SCALE

6" REINFORCED CONCRETE/
6" FILTER BLANKET.

6" PERFORATED
SUBDRAINAGE
PIPE (Both Sides).

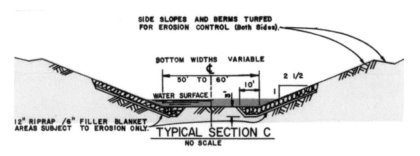

SIDE SLOPES AND BERMS TURFED
FOR EROSION CONTROL (Both Sides).

BOTTOM WIDTHS VARIABLE

50' TO 60'

WATER SURFACE

TYPICAL SECTION C
NO SCALE

12" RIPRAP /6" FILLER BLANKET
AREAS SUBJECT TO EROSION ONLY.

Bayou Rectification. Following the tremendously devastating flood of 1935, the Houston Chamber of Commerce immediately initiated a comprehensive study of flood and drainage problems in Houston and Harris County. The Flood Control Committee realized that the peak flows resulting from the unusually high rainfall intensities of the region's flat coastal plain were substantially greater in areas of intense urbanization than in natural watershed conditions. A series of surveys and engineering plans culminated in the construction of the Barker and Addicks Reservoirs in 1945.

refineries, irrigation projects, Superfund sites, international ports—yet we never see ourselves. Instead, we see only what we choose to see, that limited part of nature we can confidently and respectfully engage: ski slopes, climbing routes, sailing harbors, million-dollar views, four thousand meter summits, nature trails, hang gliding ports, natural history museums, and white sand beaches. In other words, our relation to the natural is utterly symbolic. We "conquer" nature respectfully, we "preserve" it deferentially, and we preach sustainability all the while plundering resources with virulent technologies applied on a massive scale. Nature has altogether ceased being something to which we are bound in a pitiless struggle (as if this had ever stopped being the bottom line). Thoreau famously said, "in wildness is the preservation of the world." As if the wild, so conceptually remote from the reality of an urban bayou, could ever constitute the terms of our survival. Meanwhile, we clog the parking lots of gourmet coffee shops with our safari vehicles but remain ill-equipped to grasp the irony—the catastrophic terms of our alienation.

Quiet Catastrophe

The city is not only a product of the mind, whether the mind be that of an engineer, a developer, a politician, or an urban designer. This is merely a conceit. By definition, the city is impure; it is clogged with matter. No matter how we might idealize its outward aspect, or refine its basic elements there is no escape from matter. There is no escape from the physical nor is there any escape from the mind. The two are in a constant collision course. You might say that the city is like a catastrophe. It is a quiet catastrophe of mind and matter.
—Robert Smithson

NASEEMA ASIF, COPE BAILEY, AIDAN CHOPRA, ROSS GARLAND, JAN JANDER, KATHERINE SCHOENFELDER, SADIA SHIRAZI / Graduate Core Studio, 2001 / Albert Pope, Alex O'Briant, critics

ALBERT POPE is the Gus Sessions Wortham Professor of Architecture at Rice School of Architecture.

Standardized Channelization. Water flows easily and rapidly through the portions of paved bayou. In heavy rains, this channel might be overflowing. The cracks in the concrete indicate the forces that even the Army Corps of Engineers can't stop.

→Bayou Research Facility
The program for a Bayou Research Facility requires a large percentage of public space, prompting the design of a park that incorporates the entire site. Both the site-scaled bar building and the landscape, which is highly designed and artificial using vegetation to function architecturally by defining space and encouraging circulation, retain their own character, at times converging, but in the end remaining separate systems that serve to highlight each other by their difference. While the building structure remains fixed, various programs extend outwards and activate the site as paths take the visitor along prescribed routes (prescribed but not enforced, as one acknowledges the unexpected possibilities that can arise from divergence). The site presents specific moments rather than generalized landscape as it is not intended that the visitor experience the entire facility in one visit; smaller vignettes exist, encouraging multiple visits and prompting the visitor to adopt various roles.
JENNIFER HENRY / Undergraduate Option Studio, 2002 / Spencer Parsons, critic

↓Strategies for a County Park and Detention Basin

Mark Wamble

Critic, Graduate Option Studio, 2000

Architectural strategies rely upon system form. Processes that incorporate interactions between new and pre-existing procedures, methods, and protocols make the delivery of a system form to a site both complex and compelling. That architecture can be formal, yet invisible to the unadjusted eye, evidences the extent to which we live in a dynamic and transforming world where the ability to engage requires more than a strong sense of what will ultimately prevail—or what constitutes an architectural result. The eye that sees architecture, sees in-progress.

The subject of this studio was to design a public park for East Harris County, Precinct Two. The provisional name for this project was Beltway 8 Park as the proposed site is located in the southeast quadrant of the intersection of Beltway 8, the middle of three freeways that encircle the Houston metropolitan area, and Texas Highway 90. The site, and the land surrounding the site, is undeveloped.

As growth in the area continues it is anticipated that the park will become an important spatial and economic center for East Harris County. The Harris County Parks Department is responsible for developing a program and agenda for the use of the site, accommodating public needs as they evolve. This project was proposed on behalf of the Parks Department to develop a public park program and design.

Land for the site is leased to the Parks Department for a stipulated period of time. It is owned by the Harris County Flood Control District, one of the most important, albeit invisible, public infrastructures of the gulf region. In Houston, economic growth and public safety are assured by the development of infrastructures that monitor and divert floodwaters as they rise and fall due to variables in rainfall and surface water absorption. It is the responsibility of Flood Control to oversee this infrastructure. Though it is difficult to overstate its importance, the existence of Flood Control is virtually unknown. Through the development of Beltway 8 Park, it is hoped the role of this infrastructure can be demonstrated to the public.

Of the 172 acres that make up the park site, approximately 80 percent of the surface area is engineered to flood. During periods of heavy rain the park is transformed, becoming a floodwater detention basin for occupied and developing East Harris County. The detention area captures surface water, holds it in a 10 foot deep by 140 acre hole—the same land dedicated to become public park—then slowly releases the water back into nearby creeks and bayous where it can be re-absorbed or directed to the gulf.

While it seems to have few physical traits, there are both consequences and opportunities when altering the geometric and material qualities of the detention basin and surrounding slope. The goal of the studio

Aerial view of Beltway 8 Detention Basin at Beltway 8 and Texas Highway 90. This 140 acre detention basin, elevation minus 10 feet, provides Carpenter's Watershed with flood relief approximately five times annually. Current plans to increase capacity in this and other basins throughout Harris County represent an ongoing process where flood control infrastructure and private development evolve together.

was to develop a park that operates during wet and dry conditions, taking advantage of both the temporary and periodic presence of water, and its absence, to become a permanent aspect of the park.

Timing is everything. Initiation of the design process was like running to catch a moving bus — it's motion, and the designer's, had to converge. As such, awareness of the temporal dimension — as a synchronic and diachronic component of development — helped to coordinate investigations of the existing site into a broad-impact point of view. While it will be almost impossible to predict when the site will flood, it is inevitable that it will (and has).

The studio made extensive use of scenario planning as outlined by Global Business Network, an institute concerned with patterns of economic change, variability and mutability. Our interest in scenario planning broadened to include spatial and material dimensions into the economic matrix in order to span the timing scale of the park and park site. Design proposals were evaluated on the fitness of the system form with regard to how it was illustrated across different time-scales, integrating itself into plausible and productive scenarios for the present and future occupation of the site.

MARK WAMBLE is a principal at Interloop—Architecture. He is a Cullinan Visiting Professor at Rice School of Architecture.

[See also *The Circuit and the Cell*, page 81]

The coincidence of property edge, where the legal limit of ownership begins, and spatial intent, where the shaping of the landscape is boundless has long afflicted architecture. Would the unraveling of legal, spatial, material, and operational edges have productive consequences?

1. **Interpretation:** park keys into adjacent land

2. **Truncation:** park extensions and additions are detached

3. **Acquisition/Reclamation:** park extensions reclaim zones in adjacent property

4. **Navigation:** automobile access follows edges

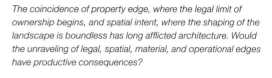

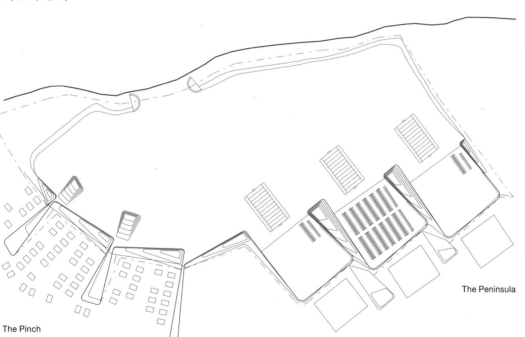

The Peninsula

The Pinch

↑ Plotting Economics — Provisional Edges

The site plan displays the two types of edge conditions—the pinch and the peninsula—conceived as organizational devices that could potentially support different activities and relationships with adjacent development. The plan anticipates future residential development (along the edges of the pinch) and retail development (along the edges of the peninsula) with a strategy for shared parking surfaces within the edge of the basin between the park and the adjacent development.

The pliant property line allows key lines of organization and operation to form a multidimensional edge between the detention basin and adjacent property. Softening of this boundary could result in shifts in the conventional relationships of flood control, parks, and private development.

JANELLE GUNTHER / Graduate Option Studio, 2000

Insofar as material choices can be applied to design, the role of matter has been to support and reinforce spatial objectives. Can material determine spatial objectives?

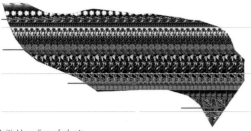

Initial banding of plants

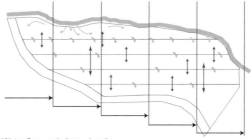

Water flow and plant migration

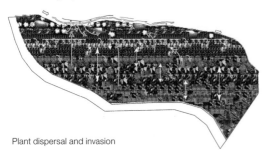

Plant dispersal and invasion

Anaerobic Patterns. The combination of flood events and plant behaviors produce dynamic form and organization of program across the site buffer zone. Planting strategies are no longer determined by a formal garden-like approach, but look to behavioral tendencies inherent in the behaviors of the imported nature itself for organization. However, the reproductive success and dispersal throughout the park of the planting is determined in part by the degree of development and growth of the surrounding metropolis. This is not a token green space but a dynamic, performative exhibit.

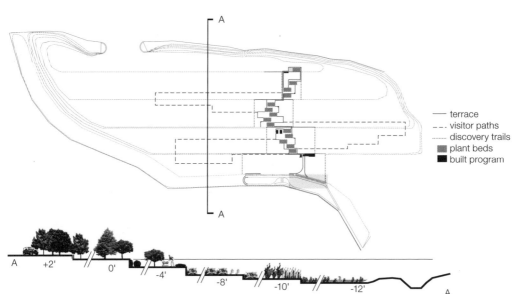

terrace
visitor paths
discovery trails
plant beds
built program

↑ Material Ranges—Anaerobic Patterns

Here a park becomes an exhibit of a restored wetland ecosystem. Wetland plants are deployed across the site in sections, creating a gradient along the bands. These rows will be visible for many years, but over time will blend into an organic field to be determined by the forces at work on the site. As this blending occurs, the zones and types of species will become more diverse due to dispersal and invasion. New wetland species will emerge, some original species will be replaced, and the ecosystem will eventually find a dynamic balance. Visitors experience the site by moving alternately across the bands and along them, taking in framed views of specific locations and wide, vast views of the landscape.

JESSICA HARNER / Graduate Option Studio, 2000

Potential flood levels create a dynamic park program. Each level has a landscaped area that is marked in contrast to the actual wetland planting areas, which are not marked. Terraces contain programs oriented to the visitor in combination with program that is integral to the operation of the site. The operational program creates nodes of interest. These nodes suggest a snaking visitor path along the bands of plant material. Abbreviated section showing conditions at each level, pertaining to potential degree of wetness during flood events.

Form without intention confounds much of what architecture would stand for when measured against values that privilege utility and commodification. Can form persist unprovoked?

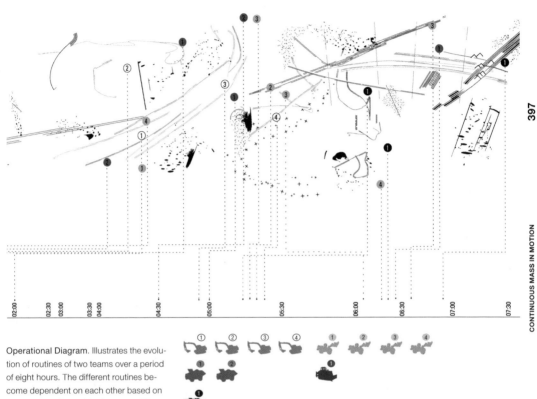

02:00 02:30 03:00 03:30 04:00 04:30 05:00 05:30 06:00 06:30 07:00 07:30

Operational Diagram. Illustrates the evolution of routines of two teams over a period of eight hours. The different routines become dependent on each other based on hierarchical relationships between different tools used in the earth-shaping process. Once begun, the process continuously shapes the land.

↑ In Form—Material Routines, Unsettled Form

John Dewey in his 1896 article "The Reflex Arc" states that behavior cannot be analyzed into elemental components. He asserts that the world is one uninterrupted, continuous mass in motion. There is nothing that reacts, nothing that is response. There is just change in the system of tensions.

As an imaginary topographical model, the routine describes a virtual circuit or pathway of formal causes and effects. The purpose of the routine is to liberate: routines can be malleable and responsive; they do not have to be of any utilitarian value, nor are they always part of a totalizing procedure that proscribes the way in which each routine is to be performed. The park comprises a series of temporally modified landscapes that exist in numerous possible shapes. Routines begin to give shape to the park through construction methods and the movement of equipment.

NIK NIKOLOV / Graduate Option Studio, 2000

Can architecture plausibly expand its own definition of space to include the terms of engagement with the geometric/material, and the temporal? If the answer is yes, what tools will we use to work with this space, or occupy it?

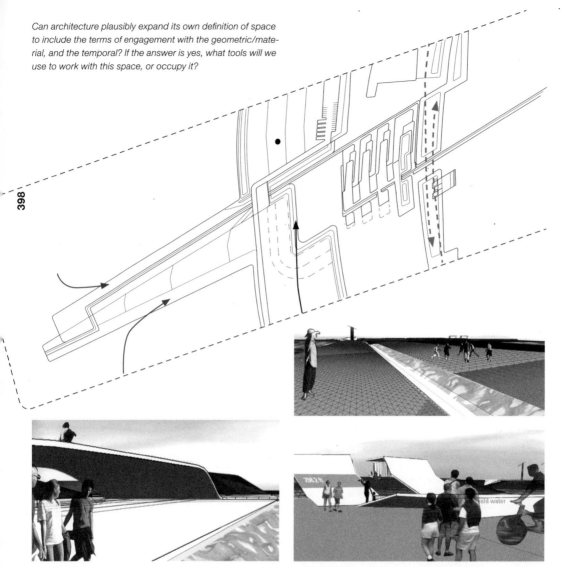

Segues and extensions into adjacent property provide an extended frontality to the park by creating more surface area of frontage. As an amenity to adjacent development scenarios, the segues could influence the form and program of the park's neighbors. As the area shifts towards becoming a center, the park is poised to receive adjacent constructions. The edges of the park thicken and the boundary softens as front yards, back yards, and parking develop.

Over time biological changes reveal an infrastructural history of the park. The inner edge of the basin is designed to expand

in three phases in order to accommodate increased flood water volume due to development and subsequent decrease in porous surfaces. By smoothing earth away from the gently sloped edge of the basin and compacting this earth into berms with a smaller footprint, the basin capacity can increase significantly through each of the three expansion phases (about 2.3 acre-feet per phase). As earth is smoothed from the bank and moved to one of the sequential receptor surfaces, it goes through a material evolution. The resultant berms develop visible age differentials due to the material qualities of their surfaces and the valleys between them.

↑ Spatial Encounters—Geometry/Temporality/Terms of Engagement

Identifying three scenarios of potential adjacent development (banding, interlocking, and wedging) leads to further study of movement patterns entering the site. Routine movement and activity occur along the portions of the park that extend into adjacent areas of development. Within these general paths of movement are spaces of higher programmatic intensity where pauses of different duration might occur.

The clustering of these pauses in particular areas of the site leads to the possibility of nesting programs within those areas, based on duration of occupation. The clusters then have a permanence associated with them according to their location on the dynamic site. Given this dynamism, some edges are identified as stable and others are "on deck" for removal due to the need for flood basin expansion.

JESSICA YOUNG / Graduate Option Studio, 2000 / Mark Wamble, critic

↓Hybrid Sponges

When one studies an ecosystem, from the rain forest to a small prairie, one sees a system that is interdependent with other systems. It is not one species, but a group of species that have the ability to live amicably with their field mates. Nature works as a polycultural system, one where all the components are in continuous interaction, allowing different environments to adapt to several conditions.

In contrast, the existing urban drainage system in Houston and its man-made infrastructures work as separate parts of a monoculture that is reflected in the design of a system of regional, site-specific, small or individual detention basins.

These isolated structures have been designed to deny the environment that surrounds them. At the same time, the construction industry is repeating the same house, shopping mall, gas station, and office building throughout the whole city, creating an expansive asphalt and concrete field that depends upon the constancy of human maintenance and a drainage infrastructure that does not accept the laws of nature. The ground in Houston is characterized by its low permeability rate due to layers of heavy marine clays that do not easily absorb or release water. This condition, combined with the standard manner of building construction, is pushing Houston's drainage system (natural or artificial) to the limits, increasing the possibility of more frequent urban flooding. These conditions point out the shortcomings of a singular,

monocultural approach to working with complex conditions.

In order for the city's water management system to work as a polyculture, the project proposes a complementary tower system to help control urban floods. The existing system of flood plains, detention basins, and their water sources (the bayou in some cases) will be used to locate a new infrastructural element, which will extract water vertically like a system of artificial pores. These towers will act as "hybrid sponges," an extension of the bayou that will attract and store water. In this way artificial elements will begin to complement natural systems, developing a smarter, more flexible system. This polycultural infrastructure will also help to generate new land uses within a community, which will become the platform for new alternatives of development, like housing. New

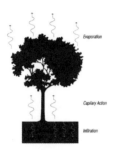

Evaporation

Capilary Action

Infiltration

How nature regulates the water excess? By infiltration, capilary action and evaporation.

The Tree is a kind of live sponge that sucks water by capilary action and holds it until water is evaporated.

Intertwine system that works with a group of pores that perform as veins that transport liquids through the sponge.

In order to be filled, the sponge attract water to the edges.

Tree as sponge

Capillary action is defined as the movement of water within the spaces of a porous material due to the forces of adhesion, cohesion and surface tension. Capillary action occurs because water is sticky—water molecules stick to each other and to other substances, such as glass, cloth, organic tissues and soil.

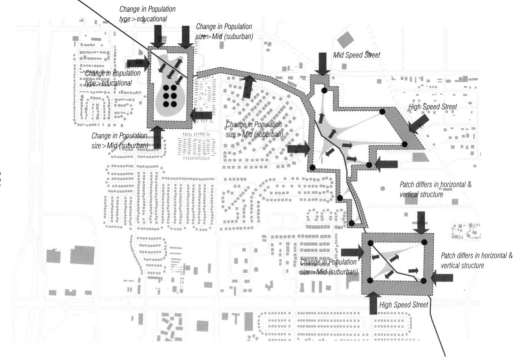

Plan of interconnected water collection and retention systems

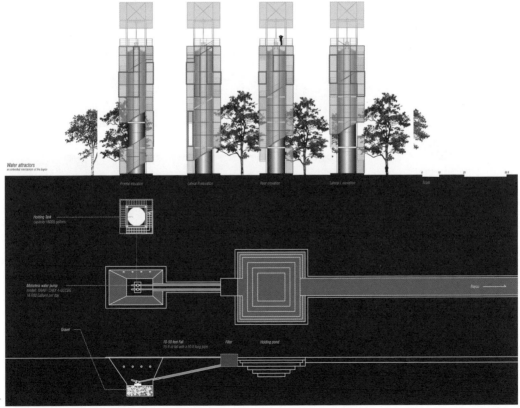

Elevation, plan, and below-grade section of water attractors

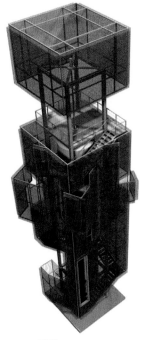

Regular Appearance

80% Full

100% Full. Water is going to be keep untill the flood is over. There is two release alternatives:1. Return the water to the bayou, or 2. Use it to reforest the tower surroundings by an irrigation system.

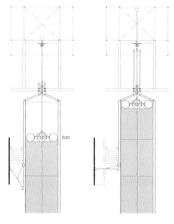

floats

Section of water collection tank in tower

Absorb and Release: When the panels are open, the capillary action is revealed, tanks are full. The towers will release the water in three ways: 1. The water can be used for irrigation purposes to reforest the tower's surroundings and to minimize the effects of expansive soil erosion with a year-round watering that will regulate moisture throughout the rainy and dry seasons. 2. In the long term, the water can be treated to provide the community with drinking water. 3. The water can be returned to the bayou after flood waters recede.

homes will use land from the buy-out program of the Harris County Flood Control District, properties exchanged for the ones in danger of being flooded. This exchange will maintain population density, while giving families the option to stay in their community.

VICTOR MURILLO / M.Arch. Thesis, 2003 / Keith Krumwiede, director

Victor Murillo's project presents us with an imaginative and much needed infrastructure for addressing the flooding threats that continually besiege Houston. A new tower—a vertical sponge that siphons the flooding waters from their destructive course. How welcome to have these hybrid sponges across the flat landscape, protecting its vulnerable ecosystems from erosion and devastation. The ever-present problem of water retention and detention acquires a new reading, perhaps a more effective and appropriate one than the customary

solutions preferred by an ossified core of bureaucrats and engineers.
—**Carlos Jiménez** is the principal of Carlos Jimenez Studio. He is a professor at Rice School of Architecture.

Aerial view of the entire park network

↑ The Snake that Swallowed an Egg: A Network of Parks for Houston's Wasted Spaces

In a privatized city, open land is wasted land. Houston suffers from a lack of public open space. What it does have is a glut of wasted space. I propose to restore Houston's blighted, abandoned, and under-utilized sites to productive, public use as cultural parks. Bayous, railroads, pipelines, and electric lines string and stitch everything together. Brownfields and other abandoned industrial sites, along with parks, are points and mats along these lines. This is the network. The parks stitch and bulge, like a snake that swallowed an egg.

Using the bayou system along vacant industrial sites, Harris County Flood Control properties, and the city's existing parks as available land, this project seeks to create new public space. Additionally, the project aims to address some of Houston's other issues, including flooding and pollution.

The park organizes itself as a 7.3 mile linear strand along Buffalo Bayou, passing through a diverse collection of neighborhoods, with nodes of program that occasionally expand outwards. The linear strand is composed of three larger parks. A Bayou Path runs along Buffalo Bayou, connecting the three parks to other regions of the city. The Fifth Ward Bayou Park has been designed in more detail, as a case study.

The network is an open-ended system that has the ability to grow as the city develops more public parks. The Bayou Path can extend farther along Buffalo Bayou, or split and follow other bayous. Abandoned rail lines and pipeline easements can also serve as linear paths, while other larger wasted sites, such as landfills, can continue to be reclaimed and transformed into new parks.

Each park is comprised of a series of raised islands surrounded by a continuous meadow-furrow. Natural high points become the "islands," which are safe from flooding during Houston's heaviest storm runoff. These high points are raised using soil excavated from the furrows. This minimizes the amount of earth that needs to be trucked off-site. The irregular edges of the islands and furrows slow runoff, allowing more water to infiltrate the soil and decreasing runoff into the bayou. The islands closer to the bayou also redirect and slow the flow of the bayou, increasing infiltration. The stone gabions and plantings along the bayou create even more surface area that slows the water and decreases the energy of the flows, while strengthening the banks to minimize erosion. Additionally, the plants filter many pollutants. The pockets of the meadow-furrow are designed to hold storm runoff and to flood, aiding in potential absorption. Due to these conditions, the usable area of the park fluctuates depending on flooding conditions, which causes furrows to be alternately submerged or exposed.

Pollution Remedy

The entire park is planted with grasses and plants that remediate certain hazardous materials. With a federal superfund site located just a few blocks away, the northeast side of the park is heavily planted with plants that can eliminate the arsenic, lead, petroleum, copper, zinc, nickel, along with other extremely

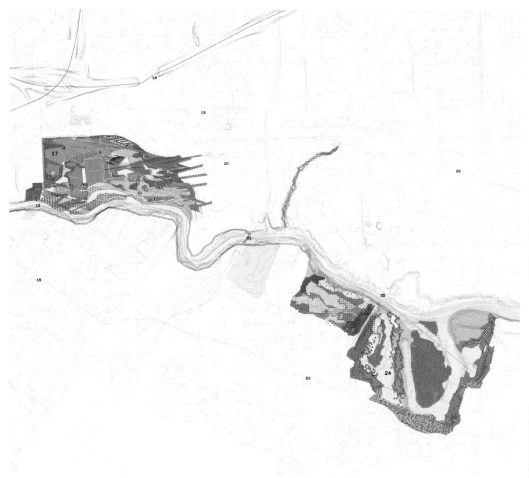

Two parks along the linear strand—the Fifth Ward Bayou Park and the Lockwood Oxbow Lake Park

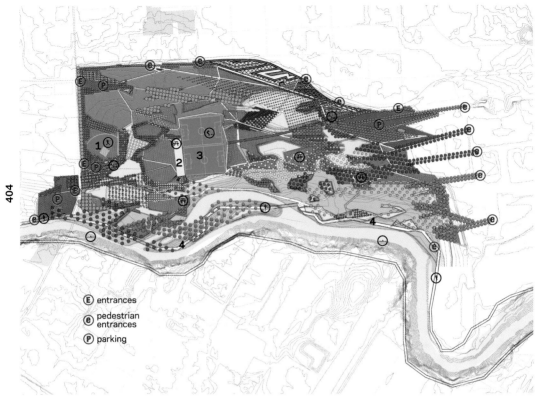

(E) entrances

(e) pedestrian entrances

(P) parking

Fifth Ward Bayou Park plan: 1. Little League and softball field; 2. Pavilion with roof and screen; 3. Events field; 4. Bayou path

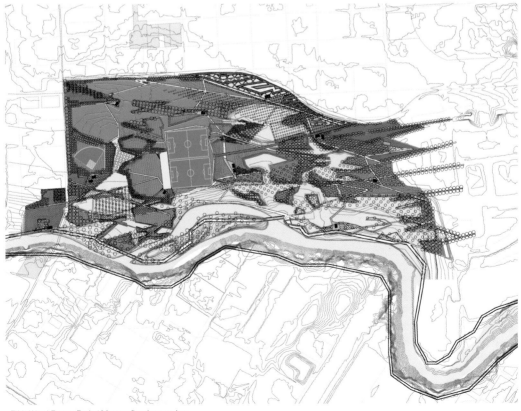

Fifth Ward Bayou Park 100-year flood zone plan

View of the bayou path at Fifth Ward Bayou Park

toxic chemicals that are present in the ground. Meadows and open spaces are planted with grasses that not only filter out chemicals by slowing the polluted runoff, but the grasses used are selected based on the chemicals present in that runoff, so that the water can be treated as well. In addition to soil and water, air pollution, especially ozone, is also a concern. Potato, alfalfa, and cotton plants have been shown to exhibit a resistance to the harmful affects of ozone in areas where there are increased levels of ozone pollution. Studies have also shown that increased levels of ascorbate in these plants helps in detoxifying ozone. Additionally, the increased number of trees will absorb more heat-trapping CO_2 from the air, increase the amount of shade, and decrease the amount of hard-scape (impermeable surfaces), subsequently contributing to a lower air temperature in the city.

Focused Plan: Fifth Ward Bayou Park

Just east of downtown, the Fifth Ward Bayou Park is located on the north side of Buffalo Bayou, south of Clinton Drive on the grounds of former industrial properties and adjacent to Halliburton's main headquarters. A few blocks to the northeast is the federal superfund site, and immediately adjacent to the east side is the Halliburton site. Green "fingers" extend from the park deep into Halliburton's parking lot, encouraging workers to take lunchtime or post-work strolls, jogs, or picnics in the park.
JASON LAROCCA / M. Arch. Thesis, 2005 / Doug Oliver, director

→ Erasure

Houston's landscape is inherently wet. Historically and at present the control of this wetness has occurred most dominantly through the channelization and movement of water across the landscape, resulting in the veinlike organization of infrastructural bayous. Although once naturally occurring waterways, in their current state they are a system of altered and engineered channels designed for efficient performance.

The implications of the creation of such an infrastructure are many. As an alternative, the principal method of control could favor the movement of water through the earth rather than across it, resulting in a landscape that begins to look and perform much differently and with increasing complexity.

This design proposal investigates a situation where speculative, non-structural methods of flood control interface with the governmental acquisition of private residential property through a buyout program for repetitively flood-damaged homes in a strategy to create open space for recreation. Non-structural methods of control would favor a return to a model of percolation, which involves the slowing of water flow as opposed to its conveyance, and the (re)introduction of permeable materials to the landscape in place of asphalt and rooftops. The project takes the position that design should promote active and responsive relationships to and between the inherently variable conditions of a site—such as those discussed—while simultaneously

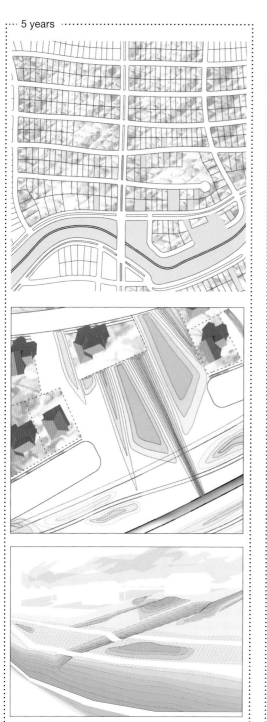

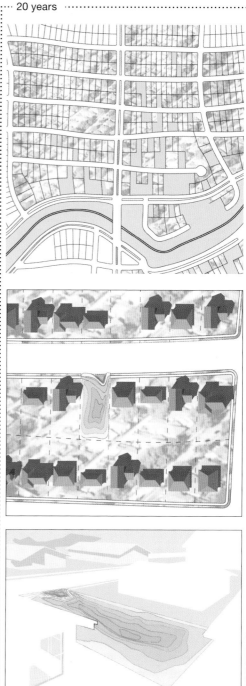

··· 5 years ···

··· 20 years ···

proposing and creating new dynamic conditions. Like the water that flows over and through it, this landscape is always in fluid transformation, be it in terms of physical growth (through the accretion of lot-sized plots of land), in terms of entropy (through the natural softening and morphing of the landscape), or in terms of political and economic parameters (through the interactivity of the federal to local level agencies involved). In such a scenario, the designer must project futures through variable states in a system that never reaches a point of crystallization (through time) and never settles on one scale of effects and implications (in space).

JESSICA YOUNG / M.Arch. Thesis, 2002 / Keith Krumwiede, director

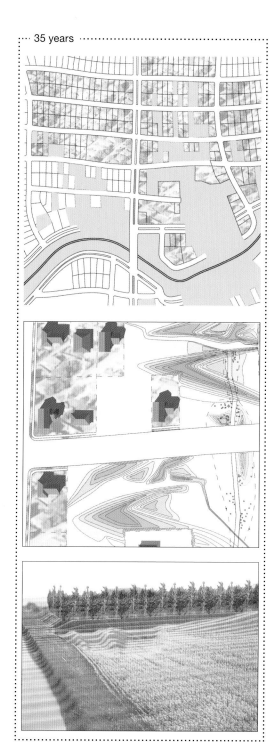

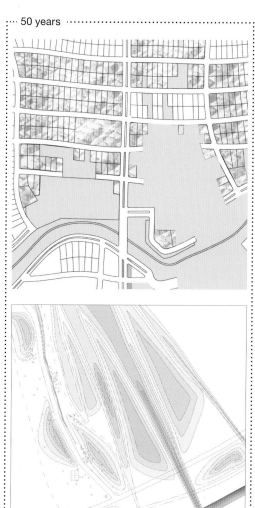

BUYOUT PROGRAM

LOT-SIZED PLOTS

AGENT #1 focuses on maximizing the potential of the parking lot to capture various forms of energy moving across the site. This process occurs above and below the parking surface, leaving it undisturbed, but increasing the economic value of the parking lot.

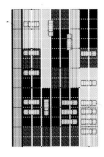

AGENT #2 focuses on laying infrastructure for activity on the site. This activity may come in the form of permanent future development or through temporary re-appropriation. Market value and demand become the transformative forces in this agent.

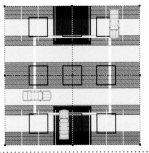

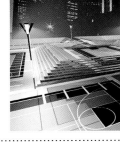

AGENT #3 focuses on the movement of water across the site. It is especially sensitive to water quantities, flood plains, and drainage networks.

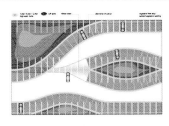

AGENT #4 focuses on establishing a local environment that will be amenable to flora. This results in a local ecology ties dynamically to parking activity. In this way, smaller zones are created within the agent, decreasing perceived scale.

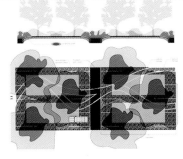

↑Park Space: Seeding Diversity in the Surface Parking Lot Population of Houston

The current view of surface parking lots as simple surfaces has led to a stagnation of articulation and a collective acceptance of banality in parking lot design. The singular nature of this articulation is compounding the negative effects exerted by parking on the city and causing the underutilization of surface parking space on the whole. This thesis proposes a design schematic for the surface parking lot population of Houston that promotes a more symbiotic integration between this population and other environmental systems within the city. Sub-populations of existing or potential sites, derived directly from like sets of local environmental conditions, serve as entry points for the introduction of new parking lot agents designed to develop dynamically alongside changes in local and global environmental conditions. To begin the effort of diversification, sub-populations are carved out of the global population of surface parking lots. Each sub-population is derived from a specific set of values related to the environmental conditions common to those sites that comprise it. It is from these sets of values that the

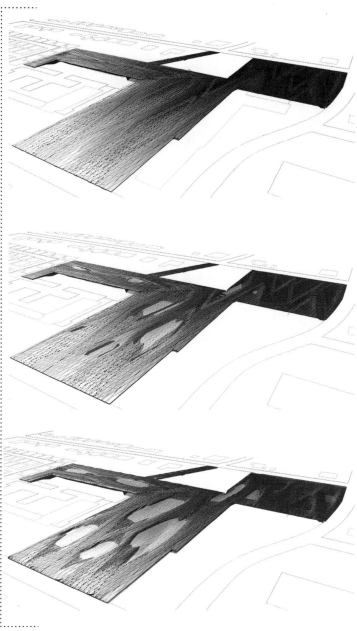

As part of Agent #3, the Soft Spot is an infrastructural sinkhole designed to deflect, over time, with regards to water quantities and usage. An open-web polymer structure, filled with gravel, forms the upper skin of the parking lot. This allows for the surface to retain parking function while it deflects. As the surface changes swales are formed, which may eventually cause the alteration of the format of the parking lot, developing portions into water retention areas. If usage increases, however, a resurfacing of the swales will prevent a loss of parking volume and will develop, instead, interior water detention ponds. Based on a 12-year development cycle, Agent 3 is designed in dynamic relationship to the environmental conditions of duration, water quantity, and car usage. The three images here depict three points in the development cycle, showing the gradual deformation of the parking lot's surface.

new agents are designed. These sub-populations also serve as the entry points for the introduction of new agents into the global population. As groups of like agents begin to colonize a sub-population, they may begin to exert an aggregate effect on environmental conditions at a more global level.
MICAH MORGAN / M.Arch. Thesis, 2005 / Helene Furjan, director

A perceived excess—surface parking lots—was combined with perceived deficits—flood management

techniques, farmers market and flea market areas, community playing fields—in a strategy that catalyzed a redevelopment of downtown Houston. The project was systemic, operating as a parametric system that responded to shifting market demands, allowing for recalibration of the parking lot's operation over time. For instance, certain lots were seeded with water retention and detention areas, permitting the lots to operate as a network of flood remediation zones. Detention areas permit parking to coexist (water is temporarily held through section

construction), while retention areas develop as wetland strips; the percentage of each is scaled to changing parking needs.
—**Helene Furjan** is an assistant professor at University of Pennsylvania School of Design. She was an assistant professor at Rice School of Architecture from 2004-05.

Biofuel farms on unused space at Escobedo Airport

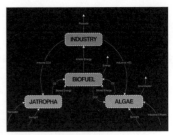

System of biofuel production

Expansion of biofuel farm in phases

→Carbon Nation

Carbon Nation allows the maquiladora economy of Monterrey to continue to prosper while it addresses the environmental degradation that is characteristic of heavy industry. An open-loop system uses two by-products of manufacturing—untreated or undertreated wastewater and carbon dioxide—along with the abundant sunshine and long growing season of the low-latitude site to produce energy. In keeping with Monterrey's civic desire to move its economy from manufacturing to high technology, Carbon Nation proposes to gradually reconfigure underused land at the General Mariano Escobedo International Airport into a laboratory for the production of biofuels.

Unused space at the airport is reclaimed to farm two of the highest-yielding sources of biofuel, algae and jatropha—both non-food crops that do not require arable land, which could otherwise be used for farming. Funding for the construction of the algae cultivation infrastructure comes from two sources: the sale of energy produced and the sale of carbon cred-

its through the "clean development mechanism" (established under the Kyoto protocol) to Monterrey manufacturers who provide harvested carbon dioxide to Carbon Nation.

The evapotranspiration rate of jatropha is low enough that the average annual rainfall in Monterrey will sustain its growth without irrigation, Jatropha is also effective in preventing soil erosion. Rainfall runoff and untreated wastewater coming as a by-product from manufacturing will be collected in ponds and used to compensate for evaporation in the algae cultivation process. Two abundant waste products, carbon dioxide and urea, are used to feed the algae, which is the known organism most effective at storing the energy of sunlight in a lipid-based form, which can then be directly substituted for petroleum or refined for use in other applications.

Windmills are present on Carbon Nation's site. Instead of converting the wind energy to electricity, however, the windmills' function is purely mechanical: the windmills' power turbines cause the water to flow through the algae habitats, which is a necessity for

algae growth. They also operate the centrifuges used to extract the single-celled organisms from the water in which they grow. That way, the kinetic energy harvested from the wind blowing across the long, flat site can contribute to Carbon Nation's overall productivity.

The layout of the site is based on the cellular structure of a eukaryotic algae species and allows for organic expansion in phases. Although the airport is surrounded

by abundant arid scrubland, Carbon Nation acknowledges the potential need for Monterrey Airport to
expand beyond its current two-runway configuration.
Additionally, although the algae ponds are a potentially
lucrative source of green energy, there is an initial cost
associated with their construction. Thus, a system
modeled after the propagation of algae cells allows for
the expansion of the algae cultivation system (as well
as the airport itself) as economic and social conditions
mandate.

BRIAN MEINRATH / Graduate Option Studio, 2008 /
Charles Waldheim, critic

For many designers across a range of disciplines, landscape has recently emerged as a model for contemporary
urbanism. This is particularly true of North American cities
that continue to disperse as a result of mature industrial
decentralization and the effects of economic transformations associated with globalization.

The ongoing consolidation of industrial capacity in
North America, now associated with global capital markets
and flexible labor relations, was envisioned by modern
urbanists and industrialists nearly a century ago. With
regard to the automobile industry, none other than Henry
Ford predicted, in the first decades of the twentieth century,
that the traditional city would not survive and that the
decentralization of industry would reshape settlement
across the continent. Ford's decision to relocate production
outside the city in favor of more competitive and flexible
arrangements of capital, material, and labor signaled what
can now be understood as a century of decentralization led
by economic forces. This process continues apace today as
over seventy metropolitan areas in the U.S. are experiencing
some degree of disinvestment, depopulation, and decay.

This studio extended my teaching and research on the
role of landscape as an element of urban order in the context of globalization. Students in the studio were invited
to pursue design proposals for sites associated with the
automobile industry maquiladoras in the north of Mexico.
As research in support of those projects, we surveyed recent
literature on the topics of landscape urbanism, industrial
decentralization, and the global economy. Of particular
interest to our work were contemporary models for the eco-
industrial park. These precedents informed proposals for
the economic and ecological restructuring of maquiladora
sites through projects of landscape urbanism.

Our work in the design studio examined the role of the
automobile industry in North American urbanization,
the present status of its commitments, and its various
potential futures. This research focused on design proposals for the Metalsa maquiladora site outside Monterrey.
The studio examined multiple scenarios for the Metalsa
factory and surrounding sites, and explored emergent
understandings of landscape urbanism as a potentially
useful set of practices available to design professionals
across disciplines. Particularly significant were economic,
ecological, and social strategies based on agrarian models
for exurban form.

—**Charles Waldheim** is the Associate Dean at University
Toronto's Faculty of Architecture, Landscape and Design. He
was a Visiting Cullinan Professor at Rice School of Architecture
in 2008.

AGRAIAN MODELS FOR EXURBAN FORM

ORGANIC EXPANSION

ALGAE AND JATROPHA

Moist prairie redux (flood retention pond)

Toxic Ecology: The Struggle Between Nature and Culture in the Suburban Mega-City

Lars Lerup

First, let me make a note about the last part of the subtitle. Suburban cities—dominated by the single-family house and an alphabet of supporting solitaires of shopping centers, high schools, and gas stations—are proliferating at a dizzying rate all over the world. Much like franchise fast food chains and hotels, these generic suburban cities look alike and function pretty much the same way, suggesting that they form one giant megacity no longer just attached to existing older cities but spread to form an autonomous urbanization operating globally—conceptually like the largest living organism, the Oregon fungus, that, although tattered, sprawls over thousands of acres.[1] Urban sprawl is no longer just a nuisance but an empire. But it is a peculiar empire since it is motivated by the escape from the City, built around a single family life style, and lived as communities without propinquity, suggesting that as of now they are but a giant real estate empire oblivious not only to its societal purpose but to its own impact. One of which is environmental.

There are haunting similarities between an ocean's inundation of a city or, as in the case of The Netherlands, a country and the reckless spread of the suburban city. Both tend to annihilate the other—Nature washing away culture, and culture usurping Nature, respectively. That Nature has little understanding of culture is not surprising (though what may be surprising is how desperately Nature attempts to adapt to change). Culture, however, sees Nature as an obstacle, as a burden, and as an enemy that can be overcome only by increasingly aggressive technological interventions. Yet the technologically enhanced errand into the wilderness has failed. Even the giant computer-steered steel gates that hold back the North Sea at the *Maeslant* barrier may be inadequate to the task, particularly in light of the steady pressure from raising waters in the oceans, global warming and other side effects of "population growth"—the abstract euphemism for "the spread of the city." Nature can never be held back by technology. There will always be another storm, another earthquake, another heat wave—with a force always greater than anticipated. Nature and culture are today hopelessly intertwined—one cannot escape the other—and the time has come for culture to make room for Nature.

The *Megacities Lecture of 2005* uses the case study of Houston, Texas, to examine an attenuated city that in its ruthless expansion has mutilated an ancient landscape, following a development philosophy that sooner or later will have dire consequences for its citizens. Although this case study has been developed over several years and not as the result of the recent disaster in the bordering states of Louisiana, Alabama and Mississippi, the effects of Hurricane Katrina make the case all the more urgent.

Houston: Bayou City

Houston, much like the Netherlands and New Orleans, lies "low" at the mouth of watersheds: the San Jacinto River (plus some twenty bayous) is a corollary to the Rhine-Meuse-Scheldt and the Mississippi Rivers, respectively. In Houston the low land forms a vast moist prairie, irrigated by a delta of bayous—marshy, sluggish bodies of water—that serve as tributaries to the river. However, the attenuated city has long since permanently altered this delicate ecosystem. In fact, "altered" is not the right verb—it should be "annihilated"! Scanning the new landscape, we can discern a morphology that appears closely attached to the geography of points, lines, and planes. This morphology, a vast attenuated body mostly consisting of an alphabet of solitary buildings embedded in more or less artificial planes, occasionally erupts into megashapes, including the Field Room, where our case begins.

The Field Room

Aside from the million-fold repetition of the single-family house, one similarity among all suburban cities is the dominant presence of Nature: *suburban dispersion*— the stretched distance between buildings—means that Nature is ever present. The actual specifics of the landscape and the climate are different in most suburban cities, but conceptually they are the same: the presence of Nature is what makes Suburbia Suburbia. Houston is no different.

Absolutely flat, the plane here appears both *thin* (stretching across a giant, shallow delta threaded with bayous) and *thick* (reaching up to the endless Zohemic Canopy of trees that is completely integrated with, and dependent on, the naturally irrigated soil). The Field Room, with the flat surface plane as its floor and the underside of the canopy as its ceiling, is the common environmental denominator for all dwellers in Houston. An endlessly faceted "inside" filled with highly mobile inhabitants surrounded by a predominantly hot and humid climate, the Field Room is crisscrossed by a delta of bayous, and by the grids, spokes, and bands of highways and streets. The Field Room is ground zero, the datum of all space in Houston. Unconsciously all Houstonians live *inside* and according to this datum. The cooled interiors of their buildings and cars are just *further* inside, forming a progression of fundamental interiority that marks a radical climatic bifurcation between hot and cold: this is a gigantic step away from the smoothness of the once contiguous and moist prairie that constituted the original *Houston Field*.[2]

The Field Room is a compromised concept. Its endless contiguity in Houston occurs because the ground plane is literally flat, so in conceptual terms the Field Room is *wide open*. (In some imaginary past, long before it was a room, this vast field may have been truly enchanted.) However, with rampant suburbanization the smoothness of the Field Room exists now only as a concept. No longer really open and smooth, the Field Room today suffers all manner of balkanization. This paradox between concept and reality is important, since in light of current practices, particularly in the counties of suburban cities, there is reason to argue for the existence of an Open City. Umberto Eco in *The Open Work* makes a useful historical distinction when he defines the modern conception of a field as follows:

The notion of "field" is provided by physics and implies a revised vision of the classic relationship posited between cause and effect as a rigid, one-directional system: now a complex interplay of motive forces is envisaged, a configuration of possible events, a complete dynamism of structure.[3]

The current relative openness of Houston suggests that the Field Room is still a place of possibility. Again I refer to Eco's work:

The notion of "possibility" is a philosophical canon, which reflects a widespread tendency in contemporary science: the discarding of a static, syllogistic view of order, and a corresponding devolution of intellectual authority to personal choice and social context.[4]

Coincidentally, this is also an apt description of Houston's individualist entrepreneurship and its relative openness for those with the right "tools." The partitioning of the original Houston Field into a Field Room was and is an ongoing and complicated affair. The "walls"—physical as well as virtual, actual and imagined, cast in concrete and forever on the move—hint at the radical *geomorphologic* shift that occurs once the *equation* of urbanization is introduced into the *biology* of Nature.

The Uncanny Relationship

Seen historically, as one of the most prominent megashapes, the Field Room is a *disfigured ecology* with many often contradictory and opposing forces at work and with an assortment of goals at stake. A majority of those in the *social ecology* may seek environmental quality, but first must come access, security, and—if deemed necessary by the metropolitans—isolation. The *economic ecology* in turn ruthlessly seeks new markets, expanded profits, flexible labor markets, and freedom from government intervention. The *natural ecology* may oppose all these interests and propose instead to create a local closed ecology in total balance, where all energy outputs equal the inputs. In the meantime the *political ecology* attempts to gather a majority of votes by pleasing as many of these forces as possible, despite the fact that the truly invasive and one-dimensional public aspects of the *economic ecology* with its various engineering projects—buildings, roads, and other forms of infrastructure—remains a major agent of disfigurement in what we commonly understand an ecology to be (i.e., something organic and well-functioning).

The various relationships among all the ecologies described above are unclear and further complicated by the more generic rub between human action (artifice) and Nature. Artifice has historically been oblivious to Nature, seeing it only as an obstacle and as an endless resource to be used up: an engineering project driven by Pert charts and spreadsheets is singular in focus, notoriously linear, and blind to anything but its own mission. For example, Houston's flooding project until recently was a single-purpose utility whose only mission was to deliver surface runoff water downstream. The relentless pursuit of this narrow goal turned the delicate bayou system into a crude open-ditch delivery system, replete with concrete channels and retention ponds. The *potential synergy between artifice and Nature* was completely ignored. Even more disconcerting, the potential benefits of interactions among the flooding project, the huge housing project, and the freeway project were also ignored—each enterprise was left to its own. This schizophrenic internal comportment reveals the fundamental hubris of all such single-minded enterprises—"each to its own" means no responsibility beyond the job at hand.

Not only is the total lack of feedback between the artifice of the enterprise ecology and Nature disheartening, but it shows how unevolved human intervention in the natural environment still is. Watching the leaf-blowers—the myriads of roving gardeners with protective headgear wielding their aggressive little machines while chasing a pile of leaves onto the neighbor's lot—is not just to witness an act of utter futility but also to note what comes with the rejection of native plants in favor of plants that can be chased down and dominated. This not only destroys the ancient ecology but also allows the domestication of the entire ecological system—the destruction of the wild in favor of an *image* of Nature.[5] In the suburban mind, Nature should be controlled, wearing a fixed smile just as rigidly held as that of the living room glimpsed behind the picture window. The waking beast of complexity and confusion may be stirring in the relative coolness and dappled shadows of the once-enchanted forest, but for now all problems, like the mess of leaves, are simply being pushed down the road.

The citizen's relationship to this conflict between Nature and culture is obscure and abstract since Nature remains out of sight in the City—pushed downstream. Consequently, the true battleground between Nature and artifice lies in the suburban metropolis. Among the many such battlegrounds in suburbs everywhere, Houston's may very well be the most deceptive because of its paradoxical sense of bucolic calm. Houston's footprint, like that of some new-fangled athletic shoe, hits the ground selectively—for example, leaving patches of beautiful trees untouched. Yet the repercussions of suburbanization on this highly sensitive prairie have been, to put it mildly, catastrophic and all encompassing. The battle in all suburban cities over a better environment may be the most dramatic and consequential of those fought in the world's growing metropolises—the mother-battle of all other battles.

The remaining battles will surely seem minor in light of the battle for our life space.

Ironically, we seem to know much more about the trees and their connection to the moist ground than we know about the freeway and its connection to the trees, or about the relation between the concrete chutes that have replaced the bayous and the sapped field that the chutes attempt to drain. Basically, we are pretty much devoid of tools or algorithms to explain the interaction between the built and the grown. Despite the existence of city gardeners and studies in urban forestry, the interdisciplinary science project involving engineers and biologists together has never evolved. The suburban metropolis is facing a much greater challenge in the next hundred years than it faced in the hundred years it took to build it, and the dearth of new ideas for bridging this gap between Nature and the artifice of Suburbia is troubling.

Meanwhile, ironies multiply. Despite the long journey, the "errand into the wilderness" that has now stopped halfway—here on a vast plane with its mixture of houses and trees—is further away from a Nature-culture reconciliation than when it was a lonely block house in its clearing. Suburban Nature itself has changed. The fat squirrels running up the oak tree outside my window are more domesticated and well-adjusted to human cohabitants and their offal than the Brahma bulls on the Texas prairie beyond. Likewise, the fauna has adjusted to meet the new conditions. We might say that Nature has taken her first steps towards an amalgamation, a meeting halfway, with artifice. At the same time, unfortunately, there is no evidence that the suburban project is adjusting to do its part. Where is the new flow-arresting yet drivable surface material that would allow a deluge to slowly evaporate on the streets via the trees (the myriad natural pumps that make up the Zohemic Canopy) instead of being rushed post-haste by solid asphalt and concrete pavements into the waiting chutes of the former bayou? Where are the biodegradable petroleum products that would improve on the soil rather than kill it?

We are still far away from an intelligent *artificial nature*, a relationship between Nature and artifice that is uncanny, or mysteriously linked along slurred boundaries. Instead the relationship is still one of separation and unfamiliarity, in the sense of the German *unheimlich* (which in turn is probably derived from *heim*, or home). We remain far from Nature's home and will not draw closer unless we rethink our relations radically.

Field Preparations

Among a wide array of suburban cities, Houston may be the poorest in providing public goods and services, particularly when it comes to open space. However, if the entire Field Room were to be seen as a public good (now unevenly attended to by mostly private interests), Houston would suddenly be at the forefront of cities boasting natural public amenity. How does one produce such a change in perception and subsequent action? Adjusting and improving the technical aspects of the suburban project is comparatively easy. The

hard bit is to convince its citizens and their politicians of the urgency of providing public goods in a largely privatized suburban environment. But there are some changing perceptions among the citizenry that may provide useful inroads.

In today's times of heightened awareness of health, nutrition, and exercise, a better life implies a productive relationship between humans and Nature. So far the Field Room has relied entirely on private interests and Nature's own generosity for its enhancement, while the public domain has remained in the pragmatic hands of engineers and concerned citizens—with mostly uninspired support from city officials. The highway and flooding projects have dominated the latter agenda. Clearly both of these projects have been beneficial for the economy; in fact, despite the consequences of suburban gridlock typical of most such cities, a new highway is a lightning rod for development. As Jonathan Rauch writes: "…public capital…often has the important benefit of stimulating private investment and thus economic growth. Build a road, and development follows."[6] John McMillan, a professor in the Stanford Business School, agrees with author Jeff Mudrick when he suggests that "public investment is needed for education, transport, communications, research, child care and health care."[7]

Houston's inner loop, like so much about this city, seems a perfect case study for arguing that public capital will not only build a better Field Room but also enhance the economy of the metropolis. McMillan writes, still in reference to Mudrick's book:

First, we need a further spread of communications for expanding markets. Critical to renewed growth. Second, since inequality is counterproductive, aid to the poor would promote growth. Third, public investment in education, transportation and research is needed if the market economy is to be fully productive.[8]

Simply put, an awakened citizenry would urge their politicians to invest in the public domain, which in turn would stimulate private investment. This would entail cultivating an open city form with an articulated "barrier-free" public domain. I use "barrier-free" in its most generic sense: an environment open to all citizens by providing access and activity opportunity for everyone, young and old. But this openness must be embedded deeply in the conflicted relationship between human activity and Nature's way. The lines of this relationship at this time are radically drawn, fundamentally obstructing one from the other. We must therefore begin at the philosophical end with a thought experiment. We will then turn to some of the pragmatics to bring the citizens back to the fields of the suburban city.

On Instability

The first order of business in this thought experiment is the "flooding project" and its potential transformation from an engineering enterprise to a *soft, or natural, machine* for cooperation between Nature and culture. Clearly this proposition is ambitious (even foolhardy), particularly in light of the general pessimism that surrounds the return of serious public investment to our cities. Texans' aversion to government and increased taxes makes the experiment all the more doubtful. Yet, public opinion is changing in Houston, where a majority now thinks environmental issues must be solved by planning (albeit still without raising taxes). Because the bayou is clearly not the freeway, and saving the bayou will not improve the commute, a coupling of road and water systems is necessary for both synergetic and political reasons. The occasional gush of water sluicing down the bayou is a useful metaphor for the experiment, since its churning wake will stir its neighboring waters in many diverse directions.

Addressing the flooding project requires close attention to the natural peculiarities and accidents of development. Few of the adverse consequences of technological striations are intended, but they instead are spin-offs of the raucous market system. However, if any of the operating ecologies in the Field Room becomes truly stressed, coalitions will certainly form, requiring everyone to turn seriously to *tending the Field Room* itself. Catastrophic events in the Field Room's ecology, especially flooding, are not farfetched. The erratic transformation of the original Houston Field has erased many of the distinguishing characteristics of the moist soil prairie. At one time the immediate bayou environment had a distinct and complex micro-ecology, creating bands of biodiversity easily distinguished from the more impoverished "in betweens." The subsequent transformation has left only occasional and sad remnants of this glorious era of natural spatiality and difference.

One might say that the Field Room suffers from ecological distinction envy. Although many still beautiful trees make up the increasingly haggard canopy, the bayous are rarely in view. Aside from some idiosyncratic leftover stretches of "untouched" bayou, the moist prairie ecology is no longer visible or available to experience. Development emphasizes access and fluidity, but ignores the creation of difference, while other patterns, both social and economic, create striations that encourage isolation rather than environmental complexity. The lack of a "there, there" is rampant. Its bayous and trees reduced to the merely decorative, the Field Room stumbles along on its trajectory towards total environmental darkness.

Despite the downward trend in the environment, the artificially constrained Field Room, formed by the canopy of trees and the field of bayous, is an ecological niche of enormous potential. The struggle to realize this potential is probably the most important metropolitan venture at hand. If *stillness* is the typical condition of the ever-present suburban subdivision, the *Field Room* is the typical state of Houston. However, the total lack of relationship between the invasive suburban project and the Field Room is often the very thing that blocks the completion of this metropolitan ambition. To succeed, we must continue the evolution of this *already existing artificial nature*—this "uncanny" blend—which will require adaptations not just by Nature but also by artifice.[9]

Artifice is plainly visible in the form of the meandering concrete chute that has effectively eclipsed the bayou. Only a frozen grimace of its former natural self is left in the "meander." A bayou dies when the last concrete is poured and the chute begins to set. The seepage from the concrete into the bayou bed is negligible: separated from the bayou ecology, the chute is on its own algorithmic errand. The separation between Nature and culture thus is complete, and the death of the bayou is final. Yet the occupants of the Field Room still speak as if the bayou were alive and well, even when the fissured relationship between Nature and culture, appearing here in the total separation between chute and bayou bed, is crystal clear. What if that separation were uncanny? What if we could not easily distinguish between Nature and culture, thus slurring the human desire to prohibit flooding with Nature's way of mediating it? How can we assure that uncanny condition?

To approach this uncanny state of "permanent instability," we must return to the ecology of the bayou. The ancient Houston Field was an endless moist prairie, not quite flat, but articulated with peaks and water-filled valleys, or small ponds. Since the marine clay—the gumbo soil—that makes up most of the soil has virtually no permeability, Nature had to get rid of excess water in two primary ways: through evaporation (on surfaces and trees) and by runoff into the bayous. The small ponds pocking the articulated field served as a billion tiny retention ponds that eventually became many tiny rivulets collected in a handful of larger bayous that flowed to a river and on to the sea. The flow of water was quite slow: both runoff and evaporation worked in tandem to get rid of excess rainfall.

When farmers settled on the prairie, rice became the preferred agricultural crop because of the moist soil system. However, the Houston Field was more like a swamp with trees than a continuously flooded marsh. Consequently, the rice farmers pushed the old moist prairie to become a wetland—the beginning of *artificial nature*. Here is also where the fragmentation of that great Field began: when we add to these individual farms the attendant railroads, and later the freeways and roads, the old Houston Field was soon gone. Rice production has since decreased radically for reasons having to do with the global economy and labor, while urbanization has replaced the rice levees in a further striation of the ancient Field.

The environmental changes have been manifold. Although similar to the heavy marine clay in not allowing water to penetrate, the concrete pavement of the roads and parking lots has multiplied the flooding problem.[10] When the smooth surfaces of concrete and asphalt replace the topsoil of grasses and trees, the clay is compacted even more and penetration is stopped for good. The fauna has changed, too, this time for the better. Waterfowl, such as ducks and geese, now spend the winter in the many wetlands created by rice cultivation, showing that Nature readily adapts when artificial nature skews the whole environment—suggesting that humans could, too.

One such fruitful adaptation would be to slow, rather than speed up, the flow of runoff water. Until recently, flood control engineers have diminished the importance of evaporation and tried instead to speed up runoff by paving the bayous, ignoring the function of trees and grass, and by using streets and parking lots as part of the water delivery system. But to reverse that trend (and make a Nature-like adaptation) is nearly impossible in Houston, where recent polls show traffic congestion as the overriding problem, with pollution only beginning to appear on the public radar as a serious concern (this in one of the most polluted metropolitan areas in the country). To bring the bayous into the spotlight on a stage where the citizenry is preoccupied with convenience will be an uphill struggle. Yet by mixing the Field Room's struggle for survival with our daily lives—by blurring these traditionally binary worlds into one messy, uncanny one—we take a huge step forward towards an integrated life world.

Rethinking the Engineering Project

Suburbanites seem hopelessly linked with activity. We don't just walk in the park; we jog or take the kids to the playground. There is no time for loafing—even leisure must be purposeful! These attitudes are deeply ingrained in suburban life, possibly reflecting a distinctive American history that still affects suburban culture in the US.

Culture has a major influence on the way we think, behave, and identify ourselves. Houston's development culture, which is shared by most suburban cities, is characterized by pragmatism and (maybe more importantly, if less obviously) by a military attitude. The young Dwight D. Eisenhower's early forays into linking the country's coasts and his subsequent work as President may have helped to instill in the nation's development culture a certain military discipline—a drive to get the job done. In fact, this attitude may have been common to everyone attempting to settle this vast country—there was simply no time for reflection. The military mission with its tendency to ignore collateral damage is the perfect development model because it simplifies problems by concentrating on the mission.

Individual entrepreneurs have motivated, invented, and undertaken development in Houston.[11] "Flying by the seat of their pants," rather than operating from complete knowledge, they have produced hit-or-miss developments in ventures that are risky because there are so many unknowns. The best one can do is to tightly control the internal aspects of the mission and hope for the best. This military view seems to dominate most suburban public enterprises as well (enterprises that are, like all military ventures, deeply political.) The freeway project, the flooding project, and the typical subdivision share a highly focused single-mindedness; this relentless interiority is invariably coupled with a disregard for the larger context. However, when all these myopic and self-serving missions agglomerate, the collateral damage begins to show, and when this happens, the time has come to rethink and to retool.

One of the most severe consequences of this military-style development is the environmental damage. Reconstruction of a natural setting that is already far gone is a major undertaking. This refocusing on the relation between landscape and development—between Nature and artifice—will require us to unlearn the single-minded engineering approach. And as I suggest below, a new artfulness may be a first step towards a fully bio-technical approach—an artfulness that allows us to playfully reinvent both Nature and our approach to it.

Despite the bucolic *appearances* of the Field Room, its bearings have been shaken by the often devastating effects of development. The dominance of engineering practices in the suburban metropolis is never seriously questioned because, aside from raking leaves, most human endeavors are blind to the complex underlying ecology. As a result, their actions drive wedges into a potentially integrated techno-organic system. Now, however, some people are waking up to the problem. Because the realization of this complex problem has been late in coming, change will require a conceptual retooling—a new worldview that removes the technological axis of perception. The previously predominant view of the environment as a problem in need of efficient technical solutions has collapsed—Nature, biology, information science, and new engineering have pulled the carpet out from under it. Engineering rationality as the only navigational device has lost its standing. A certain artfulness is required instead, one that solicits the help of both Nature and culture.

How do we gain access to this new artfulness, an artfulness that displaces the false assuredness of all engineering work on Nature? How do we learn how to live with the uncertainty that artfulness brings? How do we see the replacement of the former engineering project as a grand project, still largely in the hands of humans? And how do we divert the public's preoccupation with the daily commute to the larger public improvement project of rebuilding the Field Room? The task is to push for a sea change in public opinion that couples personal interests with a deep activist commitment to the metropolitan environment. Further, we must realize that the grand project we propose is not just technical and ecological, but rhetorical as well, in that it must, very simply, be convincing.

Again, the overriding task is not just to rethink but to *rebuild the Field Room*, reaching a *slurred and uncanny* relationship between artifice and Nature, while simultaneously making the Field Room a much better place to be—a truly public living room. The rebuilding is clearly not a return to the Houston Field, which is not only impossible but not desirable. The joining of suburbanization and prairie instead must find a new ground somewhere obscurely between Nature and artifice. I need to emphasize the necessity of this "obscurity": at this point no one knows what the new state of artificial nature really is, particularly since it can no longer be viewed as a series of objects—a freeway, a park, or a transportation link—but is a *field in process*, a metabolism in which all those previous objects must lose some significant aspects of their former integrity and become links in the anabolic and catabolic functions of building energy, consuming it, and rejecting its residues.

The Invention of a New Bayou

First, let it be said that in the last two or three years (as in many cities), there have been a remarkable number of attempts to improve on the environment, and in Houston's case several important bayou proposals are under way. There may be reasons to be cautiously optimistic, although pretty much the same military attitude is likely to dominate these projects, too. Because it is hard to radically rethink, I believe we need to take an approach that makes clear that the project of bringing Nature and culture closer must start with just that: a radical rethinking.

We must literally *reinvent* Nature, possibly first as a form of spectacle. In the 1830's, Charles Durande of Louisiana celebrated his daughter's wedding by importing a million spiders from China to spin their webs in the trees on his Pine Alley estate, while his servants dusted the spider webs with gold and silver (imported from California). It is hard to think of a more artful, yet gentle enhancement of Nature, but our view changes in light of the descendents of those Chinese spiders spinning their webs as we speak. Human intention joins Nature in a process with equal measures of cooperation and uncertainty—will coexistence emerge or will the Chinese spiders overpower their Louisiana cohorts? And here lies the modern crux: we know now that introducing foreign species is almost always disastrous to the natural environment. No, a modern spectacle to kick off the rebuilding the Field Room, specifically the bayous, must stay native but be as seductive and artful as Durande's gesture.

In 1997, Olafur Eliasson, a Danish artist, ran five gallons of water per hour from a faucet in the outer wall of a museum in Johannesburg, South Africa, letting it flow into the street and across the yards of adjacent houses. In this way, municipal water was surreptitiously returned to Nature to begin the formation of a new creek. Back in the Field Room, resuming our thought experiment, let us say that Eliasson selects for his next work of art a leftover field—a leapfrogged lacuna—close to a bayou. He digs scores of tiny shallow pools or potholes, then opens an adjacent faucet to let water run through the lacuna. A tiny rivulet forms as the small pools connect, then it finds its way to the nearby bayou. Is the initial purposelessness of the action (art for art's sake) eventually rendered purposeful by its surreptitious (uncanny) transformation into Nature—whether a boon for the horticulturist or an environmental disgrace? Can culturally "created" water become a natural creek or, as in our case, a Houston bayou? Can we return an act of art to Nature? Tiny (artful) bayous effectively bring metropolitans back to the beginning as an ancient bayou is rediscovered. The process of creating a bayou brings it out of the background—out of its taken-for-granted condition. A dozen bayous and their tributaries provide a literal sea change. Swept away, the metropolitans float along.

Environmental art, with artists like Eliasson and his elder Robert Smithson, points repeatedly at natural cycles, at origins, at entropy, at bio-logics, and at effects. This artful way of engaging Nature seems to be in search of something more consequential than the mere buzz of phenomena. If we were to link the effects of all this process art into an array or geography, assembling them on an imaginary field, a map appears.[12] The geography of such a map suggests a much wider territory of possibilities than any one project.

If a map of the climatic conditions of the Field Room were produced, it too would open broader possibilities. It would add to the metropolitan's binary Field Room the real climate, with its juxtaposition of cold fronts from Canada and equally persistent hot and humid fronts from the Gulf of Mexico, whose battles high above the canopy often result in torrential rains. This new map also reveals the contradiction and intense tension between the natural and the artificial, including the clumsy attempts by the artificial to adjust to the natural. Temperatures outside rise and fall precipitously, sometimes thirty degrees in one hour, while the indoor thermostats attempt desperately to stay at seventy-two degrees. These schizophrenic conditions in the Field Room tell us how difficult it is to calibrate human occupation and actual climate.

Alfred Wegener, the German inventor of the theory of continental drift, in devising his theory hovered intently for days on end over globes and geological maps.[13] The drifting apart of continents is similar to Eliasson's escaping water project: it takes a concerted understanding of movement to reestablish the origins of continents or water. Plate tectonics are of course more massive than a minor inundation outside a South African museum or a major one in our Field Room thought experiment, but in both cases phenomena are running away from their origins. And in viewing environmental artists' larger project as a map that may not know its origin or its future, Wegener's visionary leap comes in handy. It seems clear that only a visionary leap will make us stop and take another path.

Although other works by Eliasson and Smithson resemble art objects in that they are original pieces that sit isolated in museums, most have a *renegade dimension*, as if the objects were in some form of self-denial or in the process of an act of self-annihilation. Indeed, Eliasson's machines seem to be processes first and objects second. Objects are usually opaque and point inward toward their own authenticity, while processes point away from themselves toward a largely unpredictable future. *Processes are radical, while objects are conservative.* Shifting our attention away from peculiar elements in the Field Room to the process that underlies its climate, health, and future is a radical intention.

This intention is also radical in the sense that it leads away from a concentration on the individual to seeing all of us *in* Nature. The first time I sensed that art may have devised an escape route from the hegemony of complete control, from authorship, was in my encounter with Joseph Beuys's *Olive Stones* in a museum in Turin, Italy. The large blocks of stone comprising the

419

Beuys work sat in an old castle, and in the next room was a gold vessel by James Lee Byars. As I recall, both works overlooked a park. At first I thought the floor around Beuys's stones was simply stained, but then I realized that the stones were emitting olive oil in a slow trickle. (It reminded me of a childhood story about a boy who stood up to a giant by squeezing the rennet out of a cheese that he said was a stone.) I might not have understood the functional aspects of these stones, but I could imagine the castle in some distant future inundated with olive oil. In the same way, the Field Room is dynamic, less an object than its trickling process, a potential inundation that eludes control. We must go with the flow and abandon notions of the static, the binary, and the fixed in favor of the dynamic and the relative.

Synomorphy

When we introduce the articulated *Field Room* into the climatic diagram, with its concerted effort to defy the temperature's dizzying peaks and vertiginous drops, a peculiar *synomorphy*, a similarity in form, appears. Writing about the volcano Vesuvius near Naples in southern Italy, Susan Sontag articulates the coincidence between human feeling and natural processes, which has application in the Field Room as well:

Maybe it is not the destructiveness of the volcano that pleases most, though everyone loves a conflagration, but its defiance of the law of gravity to which every inorganic mass is subject. What pleases first at the sight of the plant world is its vertical upward direction. That is why we love trees. Perhaps we attend to a volcano for its elevation, like ballet. How high the molten rocks soar, how far above the mushrooming cloud. The thrill is that the mountain blows itself up, even if it must then like a dancer return to earth; even if it does not simply descend—it falls, falls on us. But first it goes up, it flies. Whereas everything pulls, drags down. Down.[14]

The Field Room produces that same mixed drama of beauty and fear when it floods. New perspectives come into focus: the canopy of tall trees is huge but eventually an inefficient umbrella, and the former hog wallows in abandoned fields that have become suburban lacunas turn into treacherous lakes all in the matter of minutes. Below freeway underpasses eighteen-wheelers and SUVs are swallowed up, while the bayous overflow to inundate entire neighborhoods. Water and lava—depth and height—reveal in their oscillations a new geography in the making.

Nature and culture, now on almost equal terms, side-by-side or superimposed, here begin to coincide. Again it is a synomorphy that emerges behind this vista dominated by a field of oscillations, with its multiplicity of peaks and valleys smoothly or steeply ascending, descending, and cutting across seemingly idiosyncratic domains. It begins with our bodies and their rhythms, particularly our breath going in and out. Around us, the night smoothly gives way to day in the steady circadian cycle. In the Field Room,

the *activity surface* fluctuates from activity (stim) to lack thereof (dross), while the *climatic spectrum* (not always smoothly) moves from hot/humid to cold/dry and back. At the same time, the *traffic patterns* dispersed through the open street grid, concentrated and speeded up in the Speedzones, are superimposed by another oscillation reflecting the daily commute.

Similar rhythms are revealed in the vacillation of open and built space. Studying the lacunas of open land left by leapfrogging development gives us a natural history of the Field Room that shows the transformation of the Houston Field from moist prairie to artificial prairie—and the beginning of an historical oscillation. In the past, the original moist prairie with its occasional trees and bayous existed in a natural symbiosis—a balance between evaporation and gradual runoff. Today, the newly refurbished Hermann Park has returned to this natural symbiosis. Now imagine a new archipelago created in every front and back yard, the replacement of concrete parking lots with a pavement yet to be invented that allows slow runoff, and the use of plastic grids to firm up grass surfaces. Further imagine native grasses and new gardening techniques replacing Bermuda grass, lawnmowers and leaf blowers, and the fixed smile of Suburbia falters.

This geography of oscillations suggests a new conceptual domain where a group of different disciplines meets, each bringing its particular subculture (or oscillation) to bear on a common problem. This multidisciplinary coming together elevates pragmatics over ideals, since each discipline must give up some territory (belief) to engage with others for the benefit of all. Much communication and translation must take place. The single-minded mission becomes in this "trading zone" of the Field Room rapidly obsolete. To forestall stalemate, common ground must be found, while the pragmatics of the *project* rule the day. In light of this emphasis on pragmatics, one of the most daunting challenges for all involved is to realize that in the Field Room there is no *telos*, no final end of things. The truly pragmatic thinkers interpret reality solely on the basis of itself (a desirable goal that most architects, myself included, have problems adhering to).

This *trading zone of oscillation* is provocative, suggesting that the oscillatory synomorphy conceals a common ground to be revealed by a future state when Nature and culture reach some yet unknown equilibrium. The hope is that an affinity can be found between the ins and outs of our bodies (of nature or of life itself) and some future technology: an alchemy of self, community, life, technology, and Nature. We are clearly not there yet! However, the outlines of this desirable, possibly attainable future are there: dynamic, self-correcting processes where the "highly artificial" cohabits and sometimes fuses with the "almost natural" in endless alternation—building, erasing, and rebuilding vistas of astonishing beauty and intelligence.

Exit the Fixed Smile

Not typically, but fortuitously for my discussion, three types of landscapes lie before me as I stand at the window on the eighteenth floor. To my right, a newly refurbished public park (one of only a few inside the loop) boasts a public golf course. Next to the park and right below me, squeezed between a wide drive and a new development, lies a swath of green with a simple brick structure and on-site parking shaded by a corrugated tin roof (civilization's substitute for a canopy of trees), which borders pastures divided by rows of trees and decrepit fences—what J. B. Jackson would call a vernacular landscape. And to my left, a smoothly bulldozed swath of raw soil lies dead, occupied by two idle bulldozers. The park, constructed with the latest understanding of how to create a sustainable ecology, features smooth hills and connected, barely articulated valleys (for evaporation), a piece of exemplary artificial nature that shows how a group of organized and dedicated citizens can push a ragged lacuna back to something resembling the myth of Houston Field. (Unfortunately, the sophistication displayed in that leisure landscape is as rare as snow in Houston.) Next to it, the vernacular landscape with its agricultural striations drawn in close cooperation with the Zohemic Canopy is an example of the vintage Field Room. However, in light of the bulldozers next door, that landscape's days are numbered. Finally, the raw, not yet smooth field has been left unbuilt because of rain. It will wait for evaporation four days longer than the park, but soon work will resume.

The spectrum between the leisure landscape and the treeless suburban ground zero dramatically illustrates Suburbia's two opposing strategies. One heads back toward the moist prairie, and the other rushes toward more of the concrete and housing that serve as pawns in the area's huge Monopoly Game. To radically reverse that game is the thrust of this thought experiment. The Field Room, roughly comprising a vernacular landscape (albeit a modern vernacular), can still be pushed away from the Monopoly Game and towards the leisure landscape of the new park. The careful construction of an artificial ecology would follow, including the dispersion of public amenities—from cool rooms to mini parks. Radically changed, inner loop life would become a complex mixture of leisure, work, and domesticity. And since most of the destroyed bayous are in the less wealthy wards of the city, a simultaneous socioeconomic rehabilitation would take place. The relentless fixed pursuits we've seen in the past, radically exposed to each other and to the nature of the Field Room, would have to find their own oscillations to enter productively into this dynamic trading zone.

After we summarily wipe off Suburbia's fixed smile, the many, more or less interconnected oscillations from Nature to activity will most certainly unsettle the fabricated calm of the current Field Room. Many chaotic undercurrents will reveal themselves, keeping the new "gardeners" busy and occasionally flummoxed. But we must finally break free of the engineering hubris that has made acceptable the blind pursuit of narrow missions resulting in the persistent ill treatment of the natural setting. No longer is it possible to conquer Nature: when it comes to this precious irreplaceable resource, conquering has gone out of style. Modern practice is now a matter of meticulous calibrations of resources and energies to arrive at the least friction— and the least damage to all involved. Time has shown that pure engineering solutions to complex societal problems outlived their usefulness a long time ago. Engineering must finally realize that to serve society is the primary goal of all professional culture.

Although Houston is both a unique and dramatic example of the collision between Nature and culture, it is clear that all suburban cities suffer various forms of Nature-culture collision and that all of these have to be rethought. The spectacular deserts of Nevada and Arizona or the already greatly transformed plains of the Dutch Randstad are all in their dire straits, problematising the lack of sophistication when it comes to the treatment of the very ground of our existence. We must begin afresh. We must learn how to welcome the wild. Anything short of this welcome, and we face an amalgamation of Nature and culture that amounts to no less than a toxic ecology.

Toxic Ecology

Mobility, the driving force behind suburbanization, has more than one dark side that is largely ignored in everyday life. This speedy darkness emits a surplus in the form of unforeseen consequences. Steadily proliferating, these consequences begin to emerge as a toxic ecology. And there appear to be no tools in the suburban arsenal to deal with this negative condition. Suburbia is in this sense still in its adolescence. By extrapolation we can briefly and fleetingly imagine the ultimate demise of the suburban city.

A huge toxic event—a tropical storm or, worse, a major hurricane—rolls in over the horizon, exposing the entire attenuated city to its wrath. In turn triggering an obnoxious collusion among escaped environmental toxins, polluted drinking water, epidemic sickness, and rising stress levels, both behind the barricades in the gated communities and in the poverty-stricken wards, the huge 500-year flood inundates a vast area of the city, including a total submersion of the newly revamped Medical Center—Ebola floating in the streets—and the new Downtown. All the discrete problems of the city coalesce.

WEEKS OF EXTREME OZONE ALERT, WITH EVERYONE CONFINED TO THE IN-DOORS AND CHILDREN AND ELDERLY FILLING THE HOSPITALS,

ARE FOLLOWED BY A 500-YEAR HURRICANE,

THAT RESULTS IN WEEKS OF SEVERE FLOODING, FAR BEYOND THE ASSIGNED FLOOD PLAINS,

SIMULTANEOUSLY, THE DRINKING WATER SUPPLY COLLAPSES, INSTIGATING AN EPIDEMIC HEALTH CRISIS...

WITH PROLONGED BLACK-OUTS
AND SHELTER DESTRUCTION CAUSED
BY DEVASTATING WINDS.

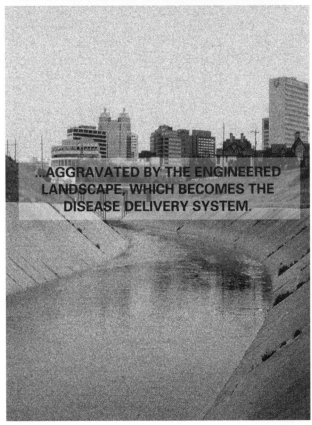

...AGGRAVATED BY THE ENGINEERED
LANDSCAPE, WHICH BECOMES THE
DISEASE DELIVERY SYSTEM.

AND THE ALREADY GATED COMMUNI-
TIES BECOME VOLUNTARY PRISONS.

A COLLATERAL TRAGEDY:
ESCAPED ENVIRONMENTAL TOXINS,
POLLUTED DRINKING WATER, EPIDEM-
IC SICKNESS, RISING STRESS LEVELS –
TOTAL INNUNDATION!

Awakening

The projected scenario shows how the domino effect of the most obvious dark consequences will play out in one suburban city. Through actions triggered by a natural event, the alphabetic city will suddenly form its own sinister grammar and the toxic ecology will break its bounds (no longer mere annoyance) and strike back—hard. Each suburban city has its own hidden scenario—some worse than others. All such scenarios are characterized by the collusion of natural and artificial events. Los Angeles has its earthquakes, Phoenix its heat and drought, Houston and New Orleans their hurricanes, Mexico City its thermal inversions, and Randstad Holland its inundations. Because of its size and complexity, the suburban metropolis is now shaping its own environment—constructing its own ecology. All are tainted by certain levels of inherent toxicity.

Once a major toxic event happens, even the somnolent suburban city will wake up. We can be sure of that. And once the initial shock has abated, citizens will go to work, hand in hand with the public sector and the marketplace. This awakening took place in Holland after the disaster of 1953, and it is taking place, as we speak, in Louisiana and Mississippi in the wake of Hurricane Katrina. In the embryonic stages of the exhilarating aftermath of the ultimate stim, a spontaneously formed public domain will strike back at the calamity by projecting a better future. The pragmatic spirit that informed the heady postwar era may return. All the actors in this spectacle will be at their best. Suddenly they will think outside the box—outside the root components of the alphabet city—by doing their thinking together and therefore publicly. And in the process of getting together, they may realize that the true concern is not the calamity but their threatened humanity. Until the toxic event, the alphabet city has (comfortably) been the alienated city, maybe the city of seemingly insurmountable distance, and clearly the city of some acceptable environmental ailments. But now its euphoric era is over. Wrapped in its private preoccupations, the self may have thrived, but the real reason for having a city—to live and work together, often face to face—has been obscured. This realization is the silver lining.

When the waters of the Gulf of Mexico and the North Sea clash with the seas of urbanization in the southern United States and in the Low Countries, they do so with a vengeance. And one is always implicated in the other. Culture's habit, especially as it can be seen in the US, is to employ radical technologies, often in response to disastrous encounters between weather and city. Such measures—invariably stopgap measures—use military metaphors and strategy. The Army Corps of Engineers is somehow always implicated, whether in the levies surrounding New Orleans or in the paved bayous in Houston. No one seems to have noticed that engineering has changed its mission and left its constraining autonomy behind to join forces with biology. Perhaps an Ecology Corps of Engineers should replace its military predecessor.

Blaming technology, engineering, and engineers will of course get us nowhere. Citizens and their representatives are the real culprits. We in turn must confront our hopelessly unevolved modernity—our insatiable urge to escape by frenetically driving away from whatever haunts us in our super-powered machines. A true modernity will reverse the obsession with artifice and technology, and turn towards a new bio-mimetics in which *learning with Nature* rather than defeating it will be our aspiration. As in our aboriginal past, we must again "give room to our oceans, rivers, and deltas." In a slurred relationship between Nature and culture, we will learn how to live an evolutionary existence forever on the run *towards* rather than away from our manufactured monsters.

1. *Armillaria ostoyae* or the honey fungus grows in the soil around tree roots in the Malheur National Forest in the Blue Mountains in eastern Oregon. The controversy around weather this fungus is one organism suits my metaphor well since a suburb in Houston may not look like a suburb in the Randstad its metabolism may be the same—or in another case, the opposite—same form but different metabolism.
2. The Houston Field is the original ecological condition that rapid urbanization has transformed into the more "civilized" Field Room.
3. Umberto Eco, *The Open Work* (Cambridge: Harvard University Press, 1989), p. 14-15.
4. Ibid.
5. Houston is an important way station for the yearly migration of literally millions of birds. With a return to native plants, more birds would land in the Field Room, and the suburban metropolis would take a step closer to an integration of Nature and culture.
6. Jonathan Rauch, "Taking Stock," *The Atlantic* (Jan.-Feb. 2003): p. 119.
7. John McMillan, "Come Back, New Economy," review of *Why Economies Grow* by Jeff Mudrick, *New York Times Book Review*, 27 Jan. 2003, p. 23.
8. Ibid.
9. The silver lining resulting from Tropical Storm Allison was a substantial FEMA grant to the Harris County Flood Control District to map the entire city to better predict flooding—far beyond FEMA's usual supply of emergency shelter, food, and blankets. Will Meyer and Jacob Spenn of the District now have a very precise digital model to play out various flooding scenarios in ways that will help guide development. In contradistinction to previous practices, the District is now ahead of development, particularly at the edge of suburban expansion. In these areas at least, a thousand feet of right-of-way surrounds future runoff channels (neo-bayous?). Combined in these right-of-ways are recreational amenities, detention, and runoff, marking a clear evolution in the military mentality that led to the traditional canalization. The almost natural bayou meander is even returning as a feature in the planning process. However, remedying the earlier and consistent destruction of the bayou ecology has yet to be tackled—a restoration that will take much more design, political, and economic ingenuity than is required when building at the edge.
10. It should be pointed out that penetration in the gumbo soil is dismal, so the key here is time. Prairie grass slows down runoff and, combined with hog wallows, allows all flooding deterrents to work in tandem: time, penetration, and evaporation. Tarmacs allow none of these measures their space and time.

11. Given that most really successful entrepreneurial missions have been partnerships with the state or federal government, the mythological individual Houston developer may be a misnomer. However, even in these elaborate partnerships between the private and the public, the military attitude prevails.

12. Such a map, or field, of Eliasson's eighteen projects would include fog, thickets of branches, a billowing blue plastic wall, light, smoke, rainbows, dripping or splashing water, igloos, wave machines, mirrors, windows, and of course ice.

13. Alfred Wegener, *Origins of Continents and Oceans* (New York: Dover Publications, 1966).

14. Susan Sontag, *The Volcano Lover: A Romance* (New York: Vintage, 1993), p. 32.

This essay originally appeared in *Megacities Lecture 8*, Kenniscentrum Grote Steden, 2005.

LARS LERUP is the dean and William Ward Watkin Professor of Architecture at Rice School of Architecture.

Highway harbor

Gas guzzlers at rest

Suburban quilting

→ ¡SUPER NAFTA LAND! Connecting the "Third Space"

The Mexico/U.S. border is a line of division between two nations and a moment of connection between the local communities along the border, specifically between sister cities. These competing (often directly conflicting) interests of the border region at the federal and local scales have created a dynamic, hybridized, and rapidly growing regional zone known as "Amexica" or the "third space." The emergence and potential of this "third space" as an economic engine and potential immigration buffer has been jeopardized by U.S. policies toward Mexico such as the Secure Fence Act of 2006, which insists on understanding the border as a line, rather than recognizing its reality as a blurred zone of transition. This project proposes building a thickened, connective infrastructural corridor landscape to unite the sister cities (in place of the divisive 700 miles of fence currently under construction by the U.S. government) and generate the resources and conditions for an independent, neutral border nation to emerge.

Free trade agreements such as NAFTA open up borders for goods and capital, but restrict the flow of the people and labor that generate this value. This selective filtering creates the bottlenecks in economic migration that paradoxically first cause the binational border cities to form and grow rapidly, but then actively thwart any subsequent development through divisive measures applied at the federal level to keep both sides split along an increasingly anachronistic political line. ¡SUPER NAFTA LAND! is a critique of the increasingly militarized linear border as nothing more than ineffective, if deadly and expensive, political theater, and presents an alternative model of establishing border regions as independent binational

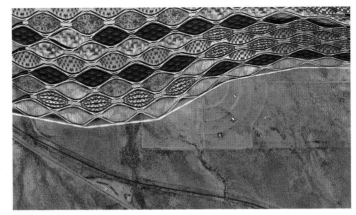

Connective landscape links sister cities along border

zones of productivity, trade, and culture that grant to people and architecture the same freedoms that the products of their labor are already granted.

RICHIE GELLES / M.Arch. Thesis, 2009 / Carlos Jiménez, director

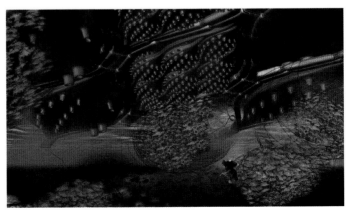

Underwater connective border condition

Sectional view of connective landscape

Blurred zone of transition along border

Interior perspective of newly created public and market space.

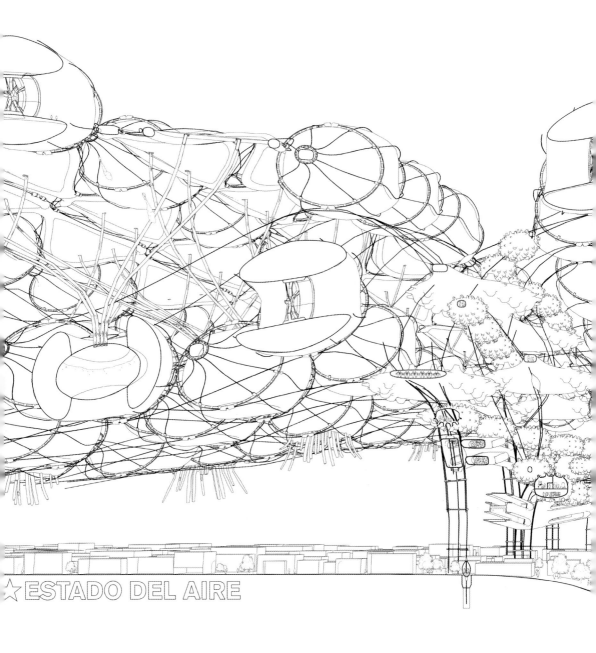

☆ ESTADO DEL AIRE

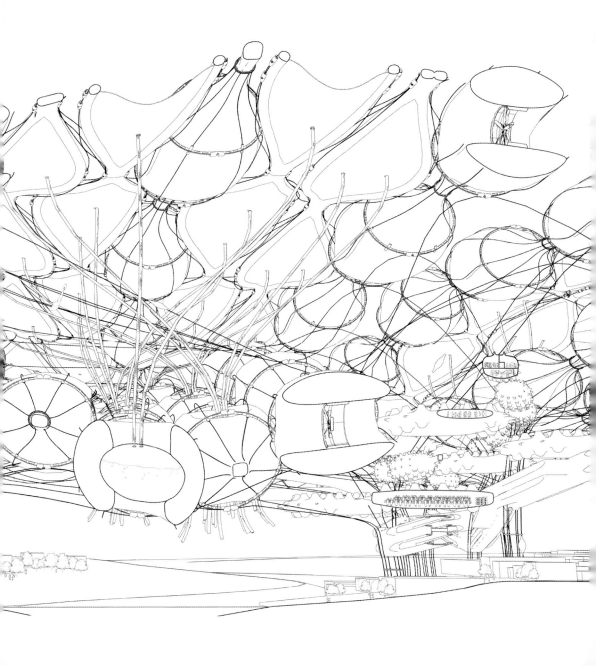

Party Like It's 1999: Postcards from the Edge
Proposal for intelligent growth of Galveston's seawall
**ALBERTO GOVELA and ASMA HUSAIN / Graduate Core
Studio, 2008 / Christopher Hight, Michael Robinson,
critics**

↓Last Resorts

Christopher Hight and Michael Robinson

Critics, Graduate Core Studio, 2008

In the wake of hurricanes Katrina, Rita, and Ike, we focused on Galveston as a case study along the global littoral. This resort community was once one of the most important ports in North America. Wiped out by a hurricane in 1905, the entire island was raised over ten feet and the city was rebuilt with an epochal seawall. The seawall was steadily added to until it was over ten miles long; it was a triumph of modern engineering, a powerful example of modern top-down approaches to infrastructure that did not so much conserve the island as recreate its social reality.

The city never recovered economically, as the port and petrochemical industry had in the meantime been relocated to the port of Houston, twenty miles inland. The seawall has, however, allowed Galveston to exist for a hundred years in an uncanny post-histoire eddy as a fragile place of tourism, historicism, and leisure. This is especially apparent at a time when the Gulf Coast is booming as the last reasonably priced, developable coastal real estate in North America. Galveston is also now the second largest cruise ship terminal in the U.S. In that regard, Galveston's current urban condition is emblematically an afterimage of the polis. The island represents the largest developable stretch of undervalued coastal real estate remaining in North America.

The seawall is quite literally and conceptually an infrastructural line that attempts to delineate natural forces (coastal ecology, storms, erosion) and human representations (tourism, landscape, branding, historicism). Currently, subsidence and rising sea levels are shortening its projected lifespan, which raises interesting questions as to the future of the city. Moreover, because its role is seen largely as a barrier against nature, the seawall is underdeveloped in terms of cultural and economic operations.

In a broader sense, we can understand the line of the seawall as merely the largest example of the entropic infrastructures of erosion, dredging, and land "reclamation" that characterize the Gulf Coast, especially Galveston Bay, and that now determine its ecosystem. New, ongoing projects in the Bay are attempting to combine its continual need for dredging with pollution remediation and the restoration of the marshlands. The new islands of dredged material filter the sandy water into more tourist-friendly surf and produce habitats for the fauna that drive ecotourism. It is not much of a projection to imagine resort communities as well.

As a result of our research with coastal engineers and geologists, the studio proposes appliances for re-envisioning the seawall at Galveston and for the possibility of constructing new bio-political territories in the Gulf Coast. Along the line of the seawall, architecture conservation, environmental conservation, and tourism collide; our task is to project ways in which these forces can be intertwined. The littoral—or waterland edge—is rearticulated as a zone of mediation between ecological, social, economic-political agencies and their exchanges. We explore how one might integrate socioeconomic pressures and environmental forces of coastal development through innovative large-scaled architectural proposals that integrate infrastructure and landscape into its design sensibility.

CHRISTOPHER HIGHT is an assistant professor at Rice School of Architecture.

MICHAEL ROBINSON is a lecturer at Rice School of Architecture.

Hurricanes. Erosion. Subsidence. Why on earth would anyone want to build near the coast? In the aftermath of Hurricane Ike (and in years prior), and with our knowledge of the perpetual dynamics of barrier islands, we have sought to propose new modes of occupying the coastline. At the same time, this allows us to recalibrate how architects might be instrumental to the world. When, exactly, was it that the public forgot that we operate with organization and synthesis rather than merely styles and ornaments? The immediacy of a shifting environment gives urgency to some of the fundamental questions shaping our discipline and helps to rearticulate our ontological status: How does architecture ground itself? What is this desire for permanence? How does architecture interface with other disciplines? In attempting to synthesize landscape ecology, development, urbanism, architecture, and infrastructure with the coastal environment, the studio works across multiple scales of space and time to analyze and project new possible worlds that are latent in both the geographies of the coast and the fuzzy areas of our discipline.
—Michael Robinson

Plan of new wetlands recreational loop on Galveston's bay side

Existing development and future development sites

↑ Fluctuating Territories

Fluctuating Territories is an architectural response to the slurry conditions of Galveston's bay edges. This restless landscape is in a constant state of flux—sea or land, wet or dry. As one of the most productive wetland ecosystems in the world, the bays of Galveston play a crucial role in the local economy, especially the commercial fishing and eco-tourism industries. This proposal repositions the focus away from the beachfront and toward the bay's edge.

The design explores the natural cycles and processes that are present in the surrounding landscape and apparent in the ambient and latent qualities of the site. Wetlands are amplified, which accentuates the intensifying propagation of valuable wetland products and expansion of nesting sites for migratory birds. Visitors are introduced to these phenomena with a heightened sensitivity through architecture occupying the augmented edge.

Proposed new recreational loop

The architecture can be seen as sequences of thick edges and deep surfaces floating along the West Bay edge, forming a recreational loop. Nodes of highly intensified activity (programs) are strategically positioned throughout the loop. Programs can be classified as controlled, static, or in flux; they are embedded within, placed above, and inserted below the surface, depending on the nature of the activity. By varying the anatomy of each module, different programs can be accommodated.

NORTH KEERAGOOL, KATHRYN PAKENHAM / Graduate Core Studio, 2008

Proposed new recreational nodes

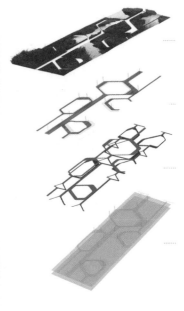

Exploded axonometric of system

System of thick edges and deep surfaces float along the West Bay edge

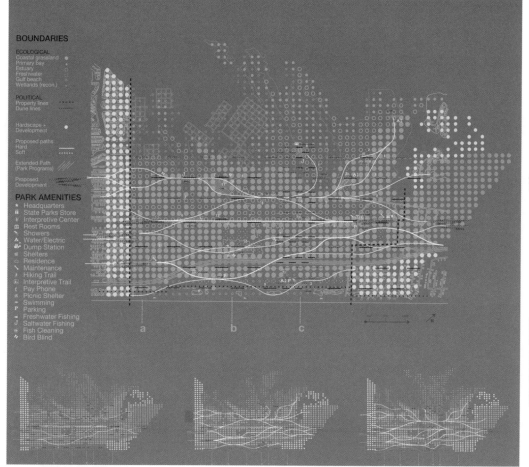

BOUNDARIES

ECOLOGICAL
Coastal grassland
Primary bay
Estuary
Freshwater
Gulf beach
Wetlands (recon.)

POLITICAL
Property lines
Dune lines

Hardscape +
Development

Proposed paths
Hard
Soft

Extended Path
(Park Programs)

Proposed
Development

PARK AMENITIES
* Headquarters
* State Parks Store
* Interpretive Center
* Rest Rooms
* Showers
* Water/Electric
* Dump Station
* Shelters
* Residence
* Maintenance
* Hiking Trail
* Interpretive Trail
* Pay Phone
* Picnic Shelter
* Swimming
* Parking
* Freshwater Fishing
* Saltwater Fishing
* Fish Cleaning
* Bird Blind

a   b   c

Site organizational diagrams

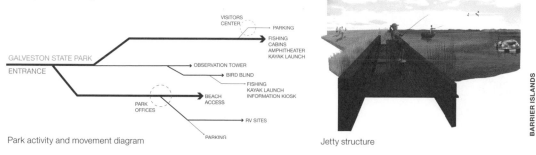

VISITORS
CENTER ———→ PARKING

→ FISHING
CABINS
AMPHITHEATER
KAYAK LAUNCH

GALVESTON STATE PARK
ENTRANCE   → OBSERVATION TOWER
                            → BIRD BLIND
                                → FISHING
                                KAYAK LAUNCH
                                INFORMATION KIOSK
                  BEACH
PARK   ACCESS
OFFICES
                            → RV SITES

PARKING

Park activity and movement diagram

Jetty structure

↑ Cross Currents

Hurricanes can create widespread destruction, disrupt local economies, and take an emotional and human toll on population. But to the barrier islands of the Gulf Coast of the United States, hurricanes are a natural and necessary event. Planning a sustainable future for Galveston, Texas, relies on accepting the barrier island's predisposition for hurricanes.

Through dynamic modeling of hurricane conditions, it is possible to begin mapping the particular areas of the island vulnerable to damage from a major storm. Interventions in these locations, specifically the state park, have to discover a way to allow for the natural forces of a major storm. In the future, the landscape of Galveston will adapt to natural and artificial forces. It will shift along

a non-linear timeline initiated by natural disasters and framed by a collective social memory.

Subverting the traditional view of a jetty as a structure extending out into the water to catch sediment, jettylike structures are instead layered in a field within the existing landscape to mitigate the undesirable physical and social implications of a major hurricane. As the natural habitats of the island shift according to storm patterns, the jetties represent a site-specific material response to the natural phenomena. A denser field of small jetties, set within the wider jetty system, strategically located in the probable path of a washover, helps minimize the physical scarring of the island. As new jetties are revealed and ones previously exposed are stranded, program and paths coupled with them relocate and shift across time to survive. Certain programmatic elements, such as housing, rest on

A selection of jetty types showing combinations of materials and elevation organizations

top of the jetties to further allow the natural habitats of the island to flow around and between the jetty system as needed.

Following the paths woven between the jetties and through the park, people are better able to interact with the park as well as to move from their neighborhood to adjacent communities on the island. The park is a place of cross-pollination that weaves seemingly disparate criteria together and acknowledges several different and specific types of interaction with the site. Rather than generate an autonomous utopian environment, or seek to make one size fit all, this intervention is satisfied to allow a messy, but structured suturing of park, housing, recreation, and infrastructure with the temporal qualities of the site.

TESS HILGEFORT, MEGAN SPRENGER / Graduate Core Studio, 2008

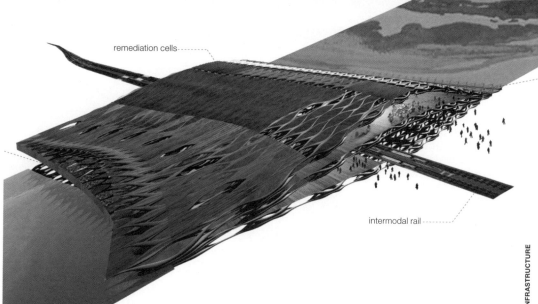

remediation cells

intermodal rail

Complex of wetland and port facilities allowing for a flexible boundary between cultural and natural ecology

↓Performative Landscapes

Performative Landscapes examines and strategizes the production of artificial wetlands, port facilities, and recreational and commercial fishing areas by using the excess dredge material generated by the Houston Ship Channel. Performative Landscapes seeks to propose a developmental tool kit and set of logics that will guide the growth of new wetlands and foster the production of integrated, rather than fragmented, program along Galveston Bay. The primary goal of the project is to produce a design method, or a generative seed, that can be used to develop new and integrated man-made and natural systems along the coast and in Galveston Bay. The thesis concentrates on the advancement of a design analytic and a design method geared towards ecological and relational thinking. These two tools are derived and inspired by the concept of self-organization in material systems and the operational searching method of the genetic algorithm as defined by David E. Goldberg.

At the edge of Houston's dense urban mat, suburban and industrial clusters flake off and fragment into the undeveloped countryside, each

securing a moment of partial autonomy until the dense mat, driven by its market forces, can eventually catch-up, absorb these forward advancements, and dispatch yet others further ahead. Like viral particles hop-scotching through a body, these clusters advance, projecting the city's material and spatializing logics into the dense ecological webs of the coastal wetlands, replacing multi-performative ecological infrastructure with the mono-performative, mineralized tissues of the modern city. In this exchange, soft systems are traded for hard. The spongy, wetland-floor meshworks are replaced by hard, mineralized strata such as asphalt, concrete and compacted earth. Speed is exchanged for slowness, and in so doing, natural protection from erosion, flood and pollution is sacrificed, along with scenic beauty and wildlife habitat. This dynamic ensues on a programmatic level, as well, as field logics are supplanted by exclusionary fragmentation, moving from a logic of gradients and blends to one of hard boundaries and homogeneity.

This clash between organizing and categorizing diagrams has lead to an environmental, social, and economic crisis in and along Galveston Bay. In the last 30 years alone the Bay area has lost over 30,000 acres of wetlands. With this

sobering reduction in wetlands, pollution in the bay has risen to dangerous levels as storm water run-off, no longer filtered or detained by wetland meshworks, is drained directly into the bay from the city's hardened surfaces. This process has tended to increase the amount of freshwater, disturbing salinity levels within the bay and causing high mortality rates among valuable species. Consider as well the bird and fish species loss caused by projected wetland destruction, and it becomes clear that an environmental crisis looms over Galveston Bay. Harm to the bay threatens to destroy one of the Gulf Coast's most productive fishery and nursery areas for the growth of Blue Crab, White and Brown Shrimp, and the prey species for many other commercial fishing species, as well as the habitat for many large and endangered birds.

Alongside these environmental problems, social and economic imbalances abound as the city haphazardly deploys port facilities and chemical facilities alongside (and in some cases on top of) residential communities and scenic recreation areas. This organizing diagram essentially operates by placing homogenized, discrete, programmatic objects in the wetland field, denying any integration between the new built environment and the existing natural environment. The solution to such juxtapositions, when deemed necessary, is the clumsy erection of 20-feet high earthen berms to block views and sounds emanating from the ports, or the appropriation of storm water wetlands on 15 percent of the cleared land. The social and economic costs of this form of urbanism include high cancer rates, decreased tourism, decreased commercial fishing revenue, decreased home value, fractured communities, and mountains of legal costs from lawsuits to stop new port development.

The situation presented is not an isolated dynamic. All along the gulf coasts, from Houston to New Orleans, building in the littoral region, in soft meshwork spaces, is continually problematic. Counter to this defunct form of urbanism, Performative Landscapes seeks to develop systems of soft infrastructures that explore the potentials of wetlands meshworks logics for the creation of an inclusive coastal planning strategy. What new social, legal, spatial and economic organizations will emerge from a serious and prolonged engagement with the wetland meshwork and its material logics?

Soft Infrastructures—The Cell

Along the Gulf Coast there is an excess production of clays, silts, sands, and shells from the dredging of the shipping channels. Once this material is removed from the ocean floor, disposal always becomes a question. In Galveston Bay, there is a federally funded program to use the material to build artificial wetlands and recreational areas

Inner and outer bags and core of the cell

in order to begin to replace some of the area lost over the last 30 years, seeking to construct over 8,000 acres of wetlands. The plan currently calls for the construction of 140-acre containment cells to contain and consolidate the dredge that is deposited into them. The levy walls of these cells, constructed mainly of imported stone, are solid and continuous except for the occasional drainage pipe that allows the contaminated water from the dredge to drain into the bay.

To develop an inclusive coastal design and planning strategy, Performative Landscapes seeks to appropriate this man-made flow of material towards the production of a hybrid landscape, of both cultural and natural value, that is engendered with the material and organizational logics endemic to wetland meshworks. The project begins with the development of a soft infrastructural component for dredge retention, erosion protection, wetland generation, and foundational support needs. The

design of the local cell of the system employs the use of water, air or liquefied dredge pressure to effect a geometric, adaptational deformation of its rigid elements. The cell is composed of four rigid hollow spine elements that are attached to bag system capable of being filled with the water, air, or liquefied dredge material. The inflated volumes protect against erosion, making imported stone no longer necessary. The system, when proliferated, then acts as a material collection mat that can inform self-organized silting and accumulation densities.

The Cell and the Assemblage

A material phylogram describes the parameters involved in the design of the sub-local cell. The phylogram works as a generative center that maps and relates the material and geometric variations that may be employed in order to elicit a specific performance. For instance, the four hollow, rigid spines of the sub-local cell can be made with a variety of materials, from structural steel to

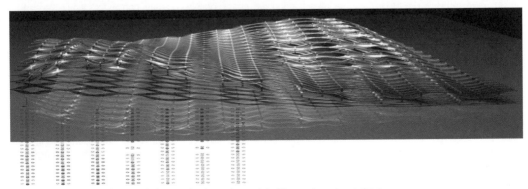

Proliferation of component into mats induces regional curvature and double curvature, shown above

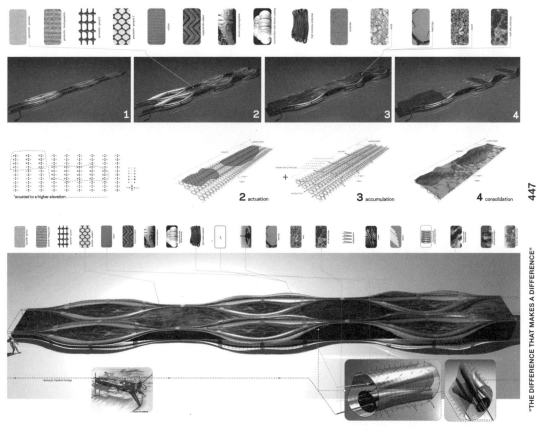

2 actuation + 3 accumulation 4 consolidation

Various performances of the mat system, which result in elevational differences, and their subsequent material states

polypropylene, depending on the use of the cell and the performance needed. The thickness of the hollow tube wall then varies depending on desired curvature or load bearing capacity. When the component is proliferated into a line, a regional curvature may be induced in the x-y and the x-z planes by specific actuation patterns in the bags. When these lines are then proliferated into a surface, double curvatures may be induced.

The Difference that Makes the Difference

The component system, when deployed in a mat configuration, takes advantage of self-organizing silting and accumulation dynamics by varying its density and spacing of elements, its elevational profiles, its global and regional curvatures, and its porosity (through the extent to which its bags are filled). In doing so, the system seeks to obtain a soft control of the location of elevational profiles, island morphology,

water channel densities, pond densities, and cove densities. All of these factors of soft control are fundamental in encouraging various types of ecosystems in the bay. The "difference that makes a difference," to use Gregory Bateson's phrase, is in this case a small range (50 centimeters) of elevational difference along and in the bay which produces several different types of wetlands, all of which perform differently. The major performances the project attempts to elicit are chemical remediation (to decontaminate dredge material), aquacultural productive wetlands (for commercial and recreational fishing), and large and endangered bird habitat (to attract eco-tourism and bird watching enthusiasts). The system may also provide foundational support, depending on the density of the elements, and may begin to suggest the possibility of deployment as a building system, producing varying degrees of enclosure

and various hybrid spaces between the strata of the system.

The proliferated mats have several possible fill conditions. First, the mats may rest on the bay floor and create topography through actuation with water to various heights from that datum. Second, the mats may be actuated with air, making them buoyant and producing a floating meshwork of wetlands and port facilities, rising from the datum of the water line. Third, the mats may be filled by pumping dredge through the hollow spines.

Global Deployments

At the global and regional scales the project proposes a comprehensive and inclusive design strategy, as well as a developmental tool kit, that can integrate the production of wetland habitats, remediation wetland complexes, recreational areas, and port facilities. The developmental tool kit, as presented thus far, allows this multiplicity of performances to be strategized and

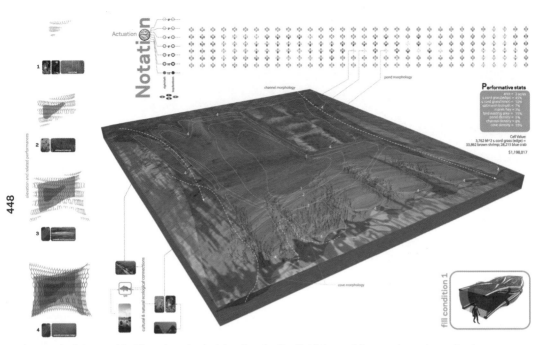

An example of a larger patch of the system, showing integration of wetland habitat, remediation complex, and recreational area.

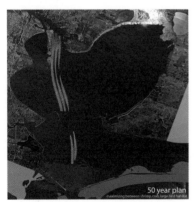

A 50-Year plan that seeks to maximize shrimp, crab, and large bird habitat

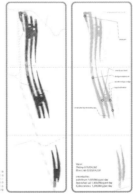

produced in various hybrid modes through one material component system, displacing the mono-performative and clumsy deployment of traditional levy and pier construction in typical wetland/port production. This material system, designed from the cell and proliferated into mats, also suggests an alternative diagram for global deployments.

Performative Landscapes seeks to create an entangled boundary condition, integrating the production of a complex of wetland and port facilities that has the ability to grow and decay as the market requires, while allowing for a flexible boundary between cultural and natural ecology, where port facilities may dissolve into recreational wetlands, and vice versa.

Performative Meshworks in the Phenotype

The 50 year plan diagram situates itself over the central flow attractors of ocean currents in the bay, balancing the salinity levels while strategically directing the currents over a field of wetlands meshworks, tuning pollution levels. The geometric and material logics of the component system allow for varied and differentiated cross flow porosity while the sub-local components are proliferated into mats that form local cells. When this local cell is linked to other local cells a regional complex is produced.

Shifting focus from the mechanics of the skeleton to the complex of natural and cultural activities occurring at the site, the performance that this system hopes to develop and entangle in its differentiated lattice mat becomes clearer. The single unit of the phenotype of the local cell was designed as a toolkit of performative generics—remediation, bird habitat, recreational/commercial fishing, port facilities, and dredge consolidation cells. Each generic cell was tuned to encourage, through soft control, target ranges of water channel, pond and cove densities, as well as specific elevational ranges to encourage various wetland types and their associated fish and bird populations. In controlling the distribution of specific types of wetlands, collateral performances such as remediation, eco-tourism, and commercial and recreational fishing are encouraged as well. The 50-year plan is one phenotype amidst a multitude, and is geared specifically towards developing an emergent performance that maximizes the economics of fishing by encouraging shrimp and blue crab species, while at the same time acting as remediation tissue for the bay. In this scheme, the far west line of cells are a dredge consolidation and remediation band, functioning as a spillway for the deposit of newly dredged material. From these consolidation cells excess water and liquefied dredge flow into the next line of cells which are dedicated to further remediation. The easterly line of cells is then populated with cell generics that foster specific wetland conditions, encouraging the growth of shrimp and crab species, and some generics that foster large bird habitat and recreational fishing.

DAVID NEWTON / M. Arch Thesis, 2006 / Christopher Hight, Director

→River of Trees

This thesis is an exercise in design for extreme hydrological conditions. River of Trees envisions a houseboat ecotourism community in the Atchafalaya Basin of southern Louisiana. A million acres of uninhabited soggy beauty, the Atchafalaya River Swamp is the main floodway for the Mississippi River, receiving overflow from the Mississippi's massive watershed year round. As a result the swamp is a constantly changing floodscape of rising and falling waters.

As the story of the Atchafalaya demonstrates, it does not work to approach such sites as if we can control them. The levee system, meant to ensure a stable future for coastal Louisiana, has instead choked the natural processes that once sustained the region's wetland ecosystems. Traditional engineering solutions like the levee system, which cast nature as finite and quantifiable, either fail outright or produce unforeseen complications. How do we design for unstable and erratic water conditions and the delicate natural situations they sustain? And how can designing for such conditions allow us to envision more mutable modes of living?

River of Trees installs a system of fixed piers that act on water flow in the swamp, slowing the current to facilitate ecological processes. The piers act as a datum, registering the changing water levels against their unchanging structure. At the

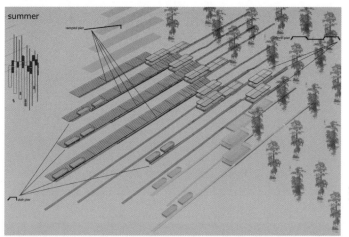

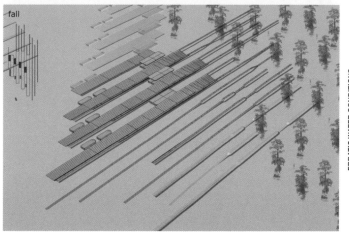

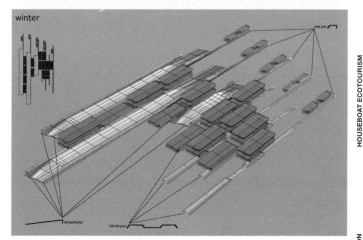

Summer, fall, and winter configurations, from top to bottom

same time, floating barges move amongst the piers as the water rises and falls, reorganizing the camp seasonally across the site.

JULIA MANDELL / M. Arch. Thesis, 2008 / Christopher Hight, director

ERRATIC WATER CONDITIONS   HOUSEBOAT ECOTOURISM   ENTANGLED BOUNDARY CONDITION

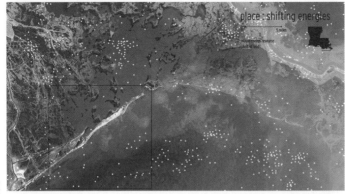

The test site, on the Louisiana coast

The assembled system deployed along the coastline

→Site Amplification

Site Amplification takes the role of site to the extreme by using design as a way of amplifying the shifting conditions of a place. Such an approach aims to harness and direct these shifting intensities into a productive entanglement of site and design, therefore removing the possibility of considering site as a given context. This method treats site as an active input into a sensitive system that anticipates and registers the momentary energies of a site.

The project that emerges is an assembly system that registers and amplifies the role of the varying conditions—from calm to extreme—of a site. This particular instance is a test of a coastal situation that encounters drastic changes in water levels and wave intensities due to weather situations both near and far, geographically, from the site. The entire assembly produces different visual and spatial affects as it harnesses and redirects the energy. This renders time of storms, or seemingly disastrous situations, quite advantageous in the production of energy, as well as a constantly changing visual and spatial registration of the natural phenomenon ingrained in the site. It is therefore a challenge to our notion of site and an amplification of the site's potential.

This particular instance is a coastal entanglement. It is a tenuous and precarious assembly that, in its integration and performance with the site, amplifies the shifting conditions visually and spatially, while simultaneously providing energy to the vicinity, and when produced in excess, possibly beyond the local site. This design is entangled with the anticipation of the changing site characteristics, mainly those of the shifting water levels and wave aggression. The result is a new site experience, a visual and spatial register generated through the interplay of altering conditions, most closely linked to the weather.

The approach to this investigation involved studying a very dynamic site as a cue to how to proceed in the amplification of site. A site that lends itself to this method is the Louisiana coast. These variable notions of site, in particular the conditions of the water and the weather, are crucial to the existence and use of the area. Weather and its behavior as a larger network condition brings about different gradients of change to a specific locale, from calm and typical to that of extreme. Weather is compounded on top of other gradient shifts. Such gradient shifts are brought by cyclical changes such as the shifts in tides, and that of day and night. Each aspect of the shift develops its own patterns and contributions to the experience of the site, together making the complex network.

The overall composition, although seemingly quite complex, is constructed of individual components, sensitive and responsive to their own immediate context, but with the capability of being networked together. When compounded, the system as a whole, entangled into the site, develops a new site atmospheric. How the entanglement with the site shifts these components is at the core of how energy is actually created. This is simple electromagnetic induction, which works by harnessing relative movement. Apart from the actual technical working of the piece, the performance of each pod relies on its own sensing of the exact locale in which it is placed. This registration and collection of energy reveals itself in the form of a glow, a slow pulse, that relates to the amount of energy stored. As more energy is created, the pulse increases until the pod reaches maximum capacity for storage. It then discharges all of its energy to be moved to a larger storage area, found in an electrical target convergence platform.

The design of the pod allows for four points of connection on the same layer. The method of stacking allows the sectional and planimetric variations to occur. For any layout, a base layer of sensitivity over an area is generated as the first layer.

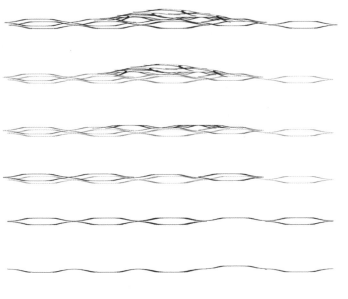

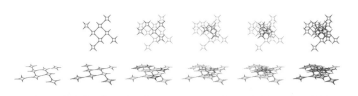

The base component tubes (above) contain water, electrical technology and lights. Pod assembly and stacking methods (left)

Hypothetical snapshots of the effect of the generated glow in a small portion of entanglement. These perspectives also indicate the results of the design's spatial consideration. The configuration of the larger network in relationship to the water level determines the exposure or submergence of the system. The water level, the time of day, the stored energy, the density of pods, and the wave aggression all contribute to the effect of the overall site atmospheric.

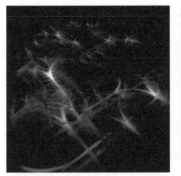

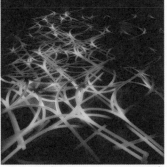

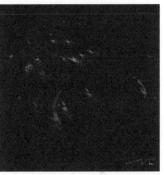

a

b

c

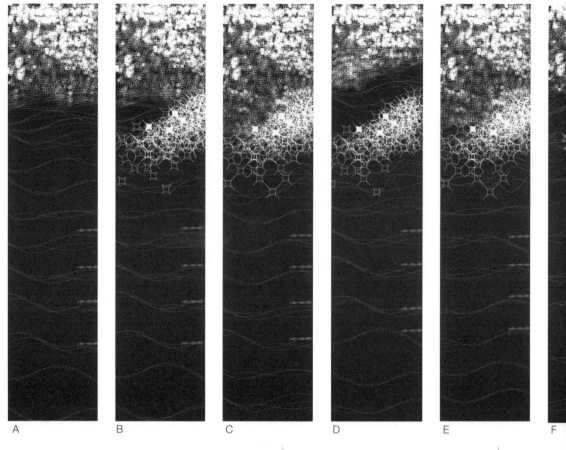

This series of representations looks at the performance of a portion of an entanglement during various water levels and aggressions. Here the energy the substrate of water is carrying, the exposure of the coastal entanglement in plan, and its relationship to land are represented. The series below is an indication of the relative levels of activation of the network system. It is a basic indication of what is participating in the energy transfer and the degree of intensity that is being registered.

Then stacks are added based on the desired amount of sectional variation, recalling that sensitivity is established to be productive on the base level under normal calm conditions, and the stacking anticipates responses at varying water level depths and aggressions.

A. As Is: The site acting without the designed entanglement. There exists an energy transfer between the water and the land. Any addition acts as a filter, and an amplification of what is occurring. The coastal entanglement is the new visual and spatialization of the 'as is' situation

B. Mean Sea Level

C. Low Tide

D. High Tide

E. Low Tide: Typical conditions characterized by simple shifts and exposures, subtly changing what is exposed. The scale that is most drastically effected is that of the pedestrian. Exposure and submergence as well as nearness to land access would provide very different moments spatially based on even the subtlest shifts in water level. While it will appear only subtle in this view, it would be quite drastic to be out there, have a connection, and then it is gone.

F. Storm Afar: This demonstrated the idea that the network is extended and responsive to a scale much beyond itself. For example, a storm afar brings new gradients to this specific site. Interestingly, this specific area receives more power in response to what may be happening farther away.

G. Local Storm: The regulation and amplification of a storm existing at that immediate site. The system is less exposed but still many of the pods are operating and even pulling on the rest of the system. In this event, occupation and stability become less and less an issue as registration and energy transfer are

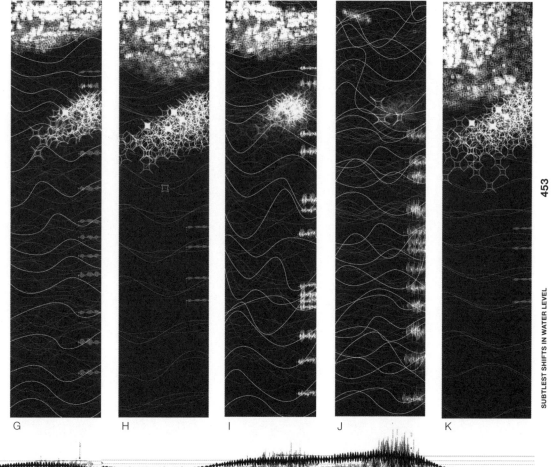

SUBTLEST SHIFTS IN WATER LEVEL

G   H   I   J   K

ENERGY TRANSFER

brought into the forefront of the system's condition.

H. Calm: Post-storm, this condition would provide an ongoing amplification of the storm condition, in particular a very visual activation of the entanglement in comparison to the pre-storm condition. Further, it becomes apparent that the placement of this entanglement will have an effect on how the site develops. One can speculate that because the land shifts and takes on new patterns during a storm, by placing a large configuration of pods near land there will be a dampening of the quantity of energy that will hit the land.

I. Immense Storm: An increase in the gradients of intensity, thus the energy quantity. This condition sets up a strange anxiety or hopefulness and comfort, that even in the storm this will provide some sense of advantage. As a note, the system itself is not looking to save any land, just gain energy during all intensities.

J. High Categorical Stom (disaster): The entire system is wildly sucked under and released. The current continues to shift and pull the system. Much energy is created and damage is very likely.

K. Reset: By default, from all of the aggression the system just faced,

there exists a new relationship and configuration, providing new registrations, and accessibilities across the system in its entirety.

CATHLYN NEWELL / M. Arch Thesis, 2006 / Clover Lee, Director

AS IS

Post categorical-storm entanglement

+ 1 month

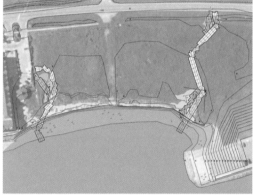

+ 6 months

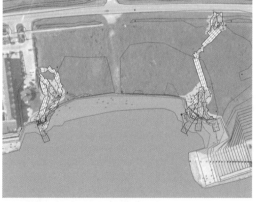

+ 48 months

↑Sea Change, or Impending Dune

The slow disaster of shoreline erosion has been met with various human attempts to control the relationship between Galveston Island and the Gulf of Mexico. In territorializing the island as private property, people are sacrificing the main economic draw (the beach), as the sandbar is increasingly expected to behave like a stable landmass. Private property rights and public beach access clash as the difference between the land and the sea refuses to manifest itself as a line drawn through space.

There is latent potential within the land itself to work with a beach access infrastructure that operates as a mesh. Such a system can transgress problematic territorial boundaries and mark out multiple processes of reterritorialization as they occur on the site. In this way, the forces at work in shaping the island can become culturally relevant in a constructive way, altering the human relationship with the land.

The proposed beach access infrastructure takes the form of a system of geotextile panels in order to take

advantage of the natural abilities of a mesh structure to strategically mediate the behavior of both people and a slurry. There are three panel types, each corresponding to different conditions within the slurry. Each panel is anchored in the slurry at only two points: the centers of the short edges. As a result, the panel is able to radically deform to accommodate the current configuration of the landscape and the total panel construction, thus remaining viable as a system of beach access. The combination of unidirectional pleats, spring straps, and a dimensionally stable edge ribbon creates specific deformational behaviors that both impact the smoothness of the resulting configuration and add significant sectional characteristics. As an infrastructure, the paths must be maintained at the county level. As paths become no longer traversable, new panels must be connected to the system. The result is a constantly self-configuring system of pathways that operate according to the physical principles of the ecology.
KRISTEN AKKERMAN SCHUSTER / M.Arch. Thesis, 2003 / Nana Last, director

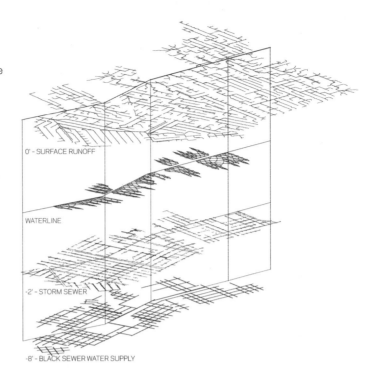

0' – SURFACE RUNOFF

WATERLINE

-2' – STORM SEWER

-8' – BLACK SEWER WATER SUPPLY

The integration of the landscape into the urban watershed, showing a fragment of the Waterline network diagram in exploded axonometric.

↗ Waterline: The Future of Alluvial Urbanism in New Orleans

Throughout the history of New Orleans the paradigms of mechanical and fluid were projected as opposing modes of thought in the attempts to render the inhospitable, dynamic site suitable for urbanism. The city's devastation in hurricane Katrina is a reminder that top-down infrastructural practices have failed to freeze the unstable ground and, in fact, may have increased the city's vulnerability by encouraging unlimited growth. A reconstruction strategy that perpetuates a mode of occupation irreverent of the fragile geographical reality will inevitably lay the groundwork for future disasters.

This thesis seeks to develop an alternative vision by surrendering a high-risk area in the city to the fluvial landscape. As a system of passive water management controls interspersed with islands of resilient program, the new territory will be a catalyst for the city's recovery between major catastrophic events by alleviating seasonal flooding and operating as a bio-remediating filter for toxic runoff.

The project site emerged through the examination of historical superimposition of urban control systems on the geologic conditions underlying the New Orleans area. Parts of the same continuum, they set up systems of primary and secondary surface differentiation. At the locales where the two systems are in misalignment with each other conflict in the social strata is generated, and consequently is generative to uncovering hidden potentialities of those locales.

The project becomes an investigation into the architectural and spatial implications presented by the incorporation of a fluvial landscape into an urban setting. At the foundation of the approach is a willingness to give up some degree of control by surrendering considerable stretches of the site to the presence of water. Pertaining to the integrity of the city, the system of constructed wetlands will be activated in three ways. First, as an excellent bio-filter, it will continuously treat the toxic urban runoff before it gets discharged into the canal, and it will remediate local soils to make them suitable for human occupation. Second, it will absorb the overflow of seasonal rains. Third, in the event of a Katrina-type catastrophe, it can provide islands of elevated ground while maintaining a territorial continuity with its context in the aftermath.

There are three scales and modes of operation that together orchestrate the fluvial processes of the project and its spatial effects. The global design operations deal with delineating the perimeter of the constructed wetland basin. Its configuration and extents are determined by the points of intersection of areas at the lowest elevation and existing run off management networks—both active

A fragment of the Waterline network diagram in plan showing the formation of detention basins

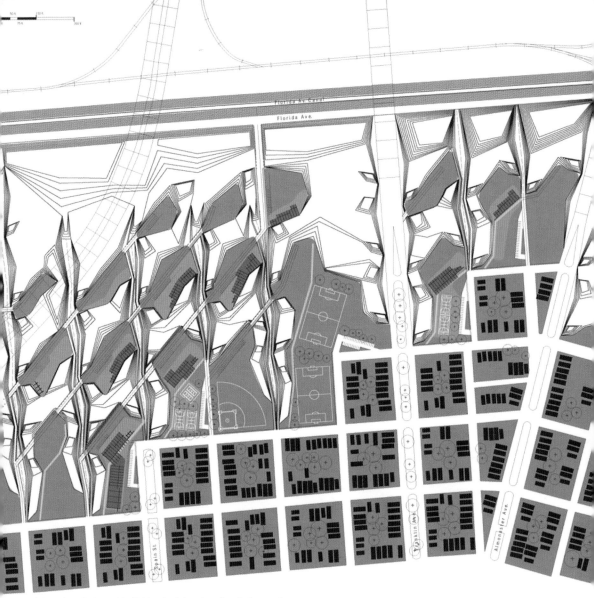

Integration of urban grid with island patchwork on the site fragment

(storm sewer) and passive (surface flows). Regionally, the edge is modified to maintain continuity along vital urban corridors. Locally, finer adjacencies to the neighborhoods, port and transportation infrastructure determine sizing and programmatic content.

The site's technological mesh is completely integrated and plays a crucial role in the functionality of the city's hydro-management networks. The more detailed understanding of the operations comes from breaking it down into components—network into chains, and chains into modules. When the modules are organized into chains, the landscape acquires a soft gradient that accepts water table fluctuations.

The field of detention basins gets interspersed with islands of elevated dry land, each roughly the size of a city block. The geometry of connectivity that emerges is driven by the regularities of urban accessibility. The process of differentiation creates a language of soft-scape and hard-edges that construct shallow ponding areas, networks of connectivity, and raised program areas with hard program and/or buildings anchored to the edge. Architectural elements, and another works, emerge out of the landscape, as they are grounded in their performance as part of the water retention system. Integration of architectural foundation systems and infrastructural levy systems is the key technical problem through which the language of the built envelopes emerges. Waterline hardscape finds its tectonic expression in steel sheet piling technology. A thin steel wall comes out of the ground to create a resilient framing system and an unyieldingly defiant architectural façade. This is then an infrastructure designed to be domesticated.

NATALIA BEARD / M. Arch Thesis, 2007 / Christopher Hight, Director

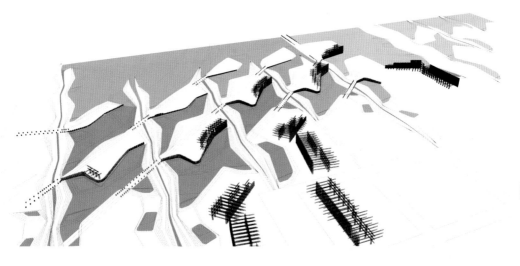

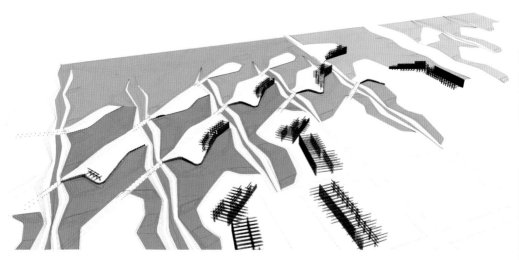

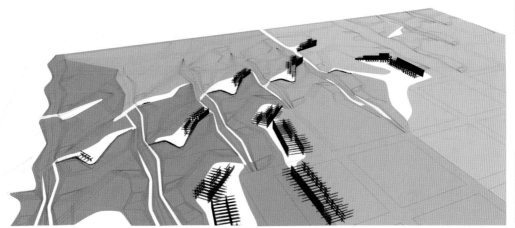

Three water stages, showing a perspective view of a chain of modules, normal conditions, partial flood, and total inundation.

Integration of urban grid with island patchwork on the site fragment

Weird wetlands

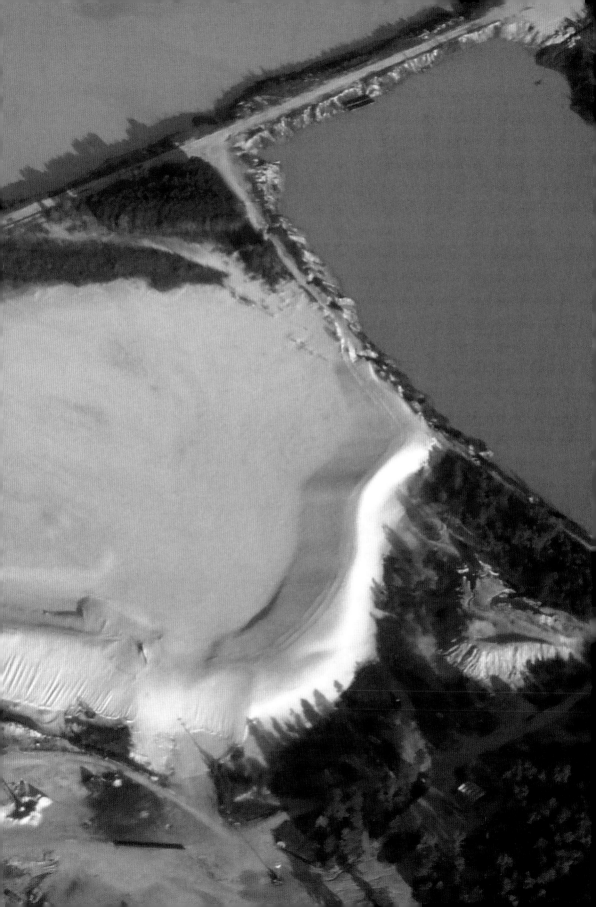

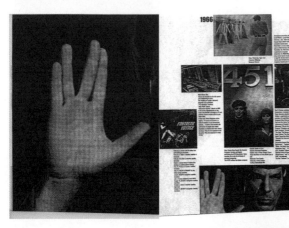

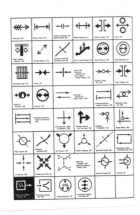

packet

switching

networks

↑ Spooling...

Write a story about the end of the 20th century.

STUDIO MEMBERS: Angelo Directo, John Clegg, Sherry Line, Eric Stotts, Sharon Steinberg, Andrew Cruse, Joy Yoder, Ari Seligmann, David Parke, Nick Dragna, Richard Odom,

Meredith McCree, Branden Hookway / Graduate Option Studio, 1998 / Sanford Kwinter and Bruce Mau, critics

Lars Lerup changed my life. He invited me to become part of a community of intellectuals willing to look hard at the possibilities in the cultural practice of architecture. He allowed me, without any documented qualification beyond

my high school diploma, to join him and his colleagues at Rice University on a journey of exploration and speculative innovation. He bent every rule in the book, and some that aren't in the book, to create a fertile ground where I could collaborate on teaching for the first time with my friend and beloved provocatuer Sanford Kwinter. Together, under the tender brutality that defines Lars Lerup's generous

AN EXTREME IMAGE ECOLOGY

Satellite
Television
Computer
Disney

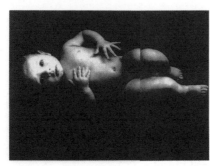

Bar Code Baby

by Sherry Y. Lin

Henry Ford's fact'ry
changed how we labor.
Now there is time
and money to savor.
Assembly lines helped
to make things cost less,
Which forced us to change
our diet and dress.

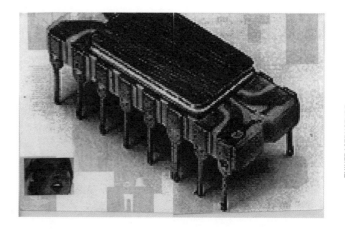

encouragement, we did an experiment in collaborative intellectual and aesthetic production. That first project, Spooling, set the model for many of my projects to follow, and eventually led to the development of the Institute without Boundaries and the Massive Change project. Not only did Lars allow me to deepen my research with Sanford Kwinter, but through my work as the Cullinan Professor, I also collaborated

with some extraordinary students, among them Luke Bulman and Brandon Hookway, who went on to publish *Pandemonium*, a project that had its origin in Spooling.

Years later, it is the time I spent at Rice, thanks to Lars Lerup, that continues to resonate and reverberate through my life, my work, and my ideas.

—**Bruce Mau** is the chairman of Bruce Mau Design. He was a Visiting Cullinan Professor at Rice School of Architecture from 1996-99.

➔ Pages 468-69: excerpt, Eric Stotts: The Last Twenty Minutes / Graduate Option Studio, 1996 / Sanford Kwinter and Bruce Mau, critics

resistance. The cityscape around me suddenly became a diagram: the columns, mullions, decks of car parks, television aerials, microwave towers, all in some way diagramming their resistance to the force of gravity. A force which must simultaneously be resisted and accepted.

The constructions around me resonated with potential energy, hundreds of millions

8:48: The members of The Reorganized Oasis of Love Evangelical Church sit silently

: of eyes dart nervously, watching the blips on the enormous big-screen TV,

of minute oppositions all averaging to zero.

incoming Armageddon on the satellite map generated by their new Trinity Satellite,

onous orbit miles above Atlanta (or is it the New Jerusalem?) Jesse Jones,

Only rarely does one of these constructions

minister, rants furiously as he struggles to complete his hastily abbreviated sermon

entitled, "This is God's Way of Saying 'I Told You So.'" Rex, caught between a

receive the necessary energy to transform it-

ature and a welling sense of regret for temptations not acted upon, can sense Janice

Her smell overwhelms him as images flood back of sermons past. Rex is

self, to disintegrate into its various compo-

crossed tightly, straining to suppress the pregnant erection which always seemed to

against his Sans-a-belt slacks at only the most inopportune moments -

nents of heat, light, and sound. How excit-

for example. As the feverish pitch of Reverend Jones increases, the members moan

ught somewhere between terror and ecstasy. The sweat pours off of Rex's

ing to realize this potential, not necessarily

the satellite image blurs in his mind, his hand creeping ever so tentatively towards

h.The words of Jesus (translated) echo through his head: "Father, forgive them,

w not what they do" as Janice's thighs spread ever so slightly under the pressure of his trembling hand...

Flying the Bullet,
or
When Did the
Future Begin?
Sanford Kwinter

A. Toward an Extreme Architecture

To convert optimism into danger and to make that danger speak; this set of operations arguably has always been the core of Rem Koolhaas's architectural program, even as far back as the "Voluntary Prisoners of Architecture" project of 1972. Yet never has it been expressed quite so explicitly as here, in this deceptively small, manifesto-like book, which opens with just such a blunt proclamation: "Architecture is a *dangerous* profession." And although this phrase emerges modestly and deliberately at the outset, with little pretence to impress, the words do not fail, by book's end, to bring home both the dramatic affirmations and the wild defiances implicit in their message. The Koolhaas optimism, then, is twofold: it states not only that architecture must turn away from the comfortable vanity and narcissism that continue to protect it from the hazardous realities of historical becoming, but also that architectural speculation must pragmatically refocus on "discovering [new] potential in existing conditions," on "aligning, and finding articulation for, the inevitable transformations and forces of modernization."[1] For Koolhaas, the posture of optimism forms no less than an "obligation," indeed a "fundamental position," for any architecture[2]; Serious architecture must actually *desire* to be dangerous. Yet the critical question nevertheless remains: How actually to become dangerous? Seen through OMA's work, at least one answer would read in the following manner: Architecture becomes dangerous when it forgoes all that is "pregiven"—in this case fixed types and predetermined matter—when, rather, it takes the actual flow of historical conditions as its privileged materiality (not the habitual discrete domains of geometry, masonry, stone, and glass) and works these, adapts these through transformations and deformations, in order to engender and bind its form. The effect of danger derives here from the fact that this radical view of materiality is a perfectly active, fluid and mobile one: it describes a materiality that actually moves and changes as it is worked, one that envelops and releases its own spontaneous properties or traits, carries its own capacities to express itself in form—all beyond the arbitrary reach of external control. This is why for Koolhaas truly radical optimism is incompatible with utopianism: Optimism recognizes an inherent propensity or directedness in any disposition of historical things (even the post-historical "fragments" or the passive drift of cultural "plankton" to which Koolhaas alludes), a direction or propensity that may be drawn

out and *followed*, while utopianism remains imprisoned with in the moral universe of what "ought" to be, and so can call on no materiality whatever on which to impress its chimerical shape. Optimism and danger, very simply, are affirmations of the wildness of *life*—of the life that resides even in places and things—while utopianism remains an affirmation of the stillborn universe of the metaphysician's *Idea*: transcendent, fixed, and quixotically indifferent to the vivid roilings of a historical world. To follow the movements of matter, to seize the prodigious blooms of "work" that emerge "for free" at certain critical moments in matter's free and irregular flow, is to collaborate with, and actually develop, the unfoldings of a vitalist universe, to tap both its powerful inevitability and its vast, though subtle, *potential*; to merge with that fluid universe, to both guide and be guided by its unchallengeable, inexhaustible, but fully intuitable efficacy. All technology depends at one level or another on the harnessing of just these types of potential forces, although for the most part we have forgotten that that is where its power and poetry lie. Thus modern techno-science happily operates on an arid continuum of numbers (or on skillfully reduced matter-models designed to behave like a pristine, controlled numerical milieu), willfully oblivious that the flow of numbers through equations only approximately reproduces, yet certainly entirely derives from, the more primitive and far more inventive flows of real matter. Though these processes today remain largely hidden from us, the pre-modern "arts" of intuition—ancient (and most current) metallurgy, nautical and telluric wayfinding, agriculture, plant pharmacology, astronomy, medical semeiotics, etc.—all depended on the ability to apprehend multiple dynamic trajectories in space-time as distinct stratifications in a single organic ensemble. The trick, then as now, is to grasp both together—both the whole and the nested passages that we moderns analytically refer to as "parts"—to know that materiality is but a continuous production of properties vigorously yet compliantly seeking to integrate into new complexes, alloys, and alliances. By manipulating the focus, viscosity, direction, and "fibrosity" of these material flows, complex natural or artificial reactions take place, and from this, the "new" and the unexpected suddenly become possible. All *techne* is at bottom the husbanding and manipulation of these fluid relations to produce new shapes of order.

Although this fluid art of variation and husbandry is by no means "lost," it is clearly no longer the province of modern thinking.[3] As the world continues to vary and flow, to aggregate, self-organize, and to re-break apart, most modern humans operate within a gridded metaworld of abstraction, ratiocination, and the crudest approximations to nature that even the most massive number-crunching devices cannot exceed. As a result most modern architecture draws its form, not from the topological world of fluid materiality, but from the rigid metaworld of ideality, of hubristic (naive) machinism, and of dead geometry. This arrested world, blind to the dimensions of time, produces an equally blind architecture, an architecture thrown from the metaworld into the real one, like a lead boot into time's refreshing river. There are simply no corresponding hooks or currents to keep it afloat.

While almost anything workaday—though also mediocre—is possible from within such a schema, everything exceptional, all true innovation, necessarily draws from the other side. Whatever depends on rote repeatability or on a uniformity of relations in space and time to achieve its effect will find its cause well supported by the time- and material-blind world of abstract operations. The "new"—by definition that which deviates or departs from what has already appeared—is, however, the offspring of creative, material instabilities cultivated beyond the looking-glass of the grid; it seems that we cannot help but explain novelty to ourselves (although this almost certainly betrays a false consciousness) as a dispatch from a mythical "outside." But this "outside" is in fact everywhere, all around us, indeed ours for the conjuring up. In the modern world we witness it most acutely in "extreme" conditions of performance, in real-time engagement with a wildly mobile environment in frenetic material flux. All extreme sports for example—skysurfing, bungee ballet, base jumping, BMX, speedclimbing, etc.—have for an ethos the concept of *a limit that must be reached and inhabited*, a performative destination known as "the ragged edge."[4] It is not by accident that such images abound: the liminal condition is in fact a communicative interface where rational information processing (i.e. planning) breaks down under the weight of too many, and too quickly shifting, variables, where it then gives way to spontaneous material intelligences ("intuition" in philosophy, "universal computation" in science), to the archaic way of proceeding by feel and by flow and by following the grain of the world unfolding—to the process of *becoming material* oneself. It is said that at the edge we encounter danger, but this is just another way of saying that there we are forced to communicate critically with a great many dimensions at once.

Nowhere is the necessity of opening oneself up, and remaining attuned, to a multiplicity of dimensions more critical than in the world of aerial combat. Since the enumeration of German ace Oswald Boelcke's eight "dicta" of 1916, the principles of aerial warfare have undergone refinement, but they have not changed. Tactical rules for mobile weaponry were, of course, already both commonplace and remarkably sophisticated as developed over centuries of marine warfare by French, Spanish, and especially British admirals. But naval maneuvers, for all their elegance and complexity, lack two a priori dimensional constraints that strongly condition aerial ones. Although in the maritime milieu one must account not only for the positions of enemy ships, their relation to land and nearby fleets, supply times, and routes, but for wind and water currents as well, the entire choreography plays itself out on a single surface, in only two dimensions of space. Also, the use of strategic immobility remains a clear, and still effective, option in sea control, and has been so from the time of the famous Beachy Head battle between the Earl of Torrington and the Comte de Tourville in 1690, when the former, although he lost the battle for Britain (and

most of the Dutch fleet under his command), invented the doctrine of the "fleet in being," according to which one deploys one's forces geometrically in such a way as to paralyze action yet project a continuous threat. Combat in the air, of course, takes place fully in three spatial dimensions, and immobility does not figure as an option—one chooses simply to engage the enemy, or not. But these are still only rudimentary givens. Aerial warfare has its own specific features, of which speed, or total fluidity, is the primary one.

For Koolhaas, the concept of "America" has always loomed large. It not only has served enormous aesthetic ends but has played a major role in generating both the novelty and the radicality in OMA's work (especially in the primarily European context with which it has dealt), and has provided a coherent theoretical framework through which the OMA office has come to understand and harness, for speculative architectural and urbanistic ends, the volatile processes of late-capitalist modernization. For Koolhaas, America, although deeply studied and assimilated into his work, has always strategically been kept at a "dangerous"—and therefore creative—distance: it has been constituted and skillfully maintained as the necessarily ragged, mythical gateway to the destabilizing, novelty-inducing outside. Koolhaas's America (Houston, Atlanta, Manhattan) would come to represent the whoosh of matter in free action, wellspring of the new, provenance of everything that has ever carried the wishful promise of "the future"—a strange and extreme milieu domain of pure movement free of historical drag. It was this America that actually invented the hyper-future, precisely because only America could invent the outside of the outside. Europe invented "Amerika" as *their* future and outside, but America invented the new frontiers—outer space and the insane warp speed that was meant to take them there—as theirs. Speed and space were the new materials of which the future would be made.

Among architects, then, Koolhaas is the true American, for he is the only one to have attempted to engage the absolute and pure future. And yet, from where does this strange idea of a pure future come? After the Second World War, America rode a manic wave of cocksureness, not so much for having won a war as for having realized the hubristic technological achievement that made such a claim possible in the first place: the Manhattan Project and its colossal, savage product, the Atom Bomb. The American air force played a crucial role in choreographing this complex, two-year long gesture, which was said to be capable of ending all wars; its pilots had also performed brilliantly in many critical battles in both the European and Asian theaters. Returning home after the war, the flying aces were celebrated as godlike heroes, and the warmasters soon decided that the sci-fi, bigger-than-real postwar future would be ushered in on their shoulders (and at the risk of their necks). To maintain America's technological (geopolitical) edge, it was decided that two fundamental space-time "barriers" would have to be torn down: a manned aircraft would need to fly beyond the outer limit of the earth's atmosphere (280,000 feet), and the so-called sonic wall Mach 1 (660 to 760 miles per hour)—the speed beyond which, it was commonly believed, any aircraft would disintegrate—had somehow to be surpassed. These linked achievements laid the foundations for what the general public would soon deliriously come to know as the space race.

There was one pilot whose wartime dogfighting skills and natural aircraft handling abilities were legendary, indeed considered by some to be supernatural. For these reasons Chuck Yeager was chosen after the war to spearhead the classified supersonic project, and by October 1947 he had broken the proverbial sound barrier, against the advice and conventional wisdom of many physicists. But Yeager could know what no physicist ever could: he was a pure creature of movement and speed, among the most instinctive pilots the air force has ever seen. "The only pilot I've ever flown with who gives the impression that he's part of the cockpit hardware, so in tune with the machine that instead of being flesh and blood, he could be an autopilot. He could make an airplane talk."[5] In the space-time world of the dogfight, where Yeager's instincts were trained, everything takes place right at the limit, perhaps even a little beyond. To survive "you've got to fly an airplane close to the ragged edge where you've got to keep it if you really want to make that machine talk." Knowing the critical tolerances of the aircraft in a variety of violent, dangerous maneuvers was everything. One had to know exactly "where the outside of the envelope was… [to] know about the part where you reached the outside and then *stretched* her a little… without breaking through."[6] Aerial dogfighting, more than anything else, is like space-time arbitrage: one must exploit discrepancies that appear between parallel flows (the twisting vectors of adversarial aircraft). But these flows are so far from equilibrium—so stretched—that the critical discrepancies must be snatched from any dimension that is not already totally strained to the max. No one knew this "fine feathered edge" better than Yeager.[7]

There are many ways to inhabit space, and so there are many ways to handle an airplane. In Koolhaas, I will want to claim, we bear witness not only to a remarkable architectural project traditionally defined but to the emergence of a new way of holding social and economic space a ltogether, for which, in architecture, there are no real precedents at all.[8] Koolhaas's work, with its fierce, stark geometries and imperious logic, is in many senses an *extreme architecture*, and bears philosophical and ontological kinship with all extremity (even virtual or unrealized) in all domains of cultural activity. What these extreme states and activities have in common is sudden precipitation and total blending of diverse materialities, of wild fluxes, in an organic computational ensemble that defies both predetermination and "hard," or rational, control ("If you have to think, you're dead," according to a common fighter pilot's slogan). In simpler terms, extreme activities involve the mobilization of every interacting part in a field, so that every movement of every part instantaneously changes the conditions of the unfolding of the whole. The

edge of the envelope is where time (relations) gains the computational upper hand over space (things).

In Yeager's world, the sky is a totally kinetic domain. One could say that Koolhaas's work is to classical architecture exactly what the dogfight is to formation flying. In the air, formations establish rigid, homogeneous structures of movement and relationship. They inject a uniformity into space by fixing intervals and relative speeds, and arrest natural variation and all developmental routines. Even the earth, the sun, and the horizon are drawn into this meticulous stratification, for they are all interpreted as stable, on their own and in relation to one another: the earth's varying features serve as guides on which to project fixed routes, the horizon equilibrates gravity like a regulating line, and the sun offers a fixed point to triangulate position and the progress of linear movement. In air-to-air combat this space becomes not only liquid but turbulent: the sun, the earth, and the horizon spin, volley, and fly—in a phrase, they go ballistic. The pilot episodically *uses* these elements (and their ballistic pathways) to hide against, to blind the opponent, or to create vertiginous relationships of weaving, gyrating motion. The cardinal rule for survival in aerial combat: *Never become predictable*. What better slogan for the creation of a truly modern—and wild—architecture? Imagine a fighter (History/Capital) on your tail. You are forced into evasive maneuvers to avoid getting "locked" on the radar intercept screen. Do you now follow guidebook escape routes? Regularly shaped oscillating trajectories? Do you carve desultory, fluctuating lines across a single, even skewed plane? Certainly not. The true problem is how to avoid any regular repetitive behavioral pattern (how to depart the space you are in entirely)? The simple but not obvious solution is: *Explode into all dimensions at once*. Easier to say than to do? Perhaps, but far from impossible. All three of the projects Koolhaas has presented here—the multiple, focused confluences of communication, transport, and capital flows of the Zeebrugge vortex; the plucked and twisted, then re-embedded, positive-negative and scoop-the-loop structures of the Bibliotheque de France; the psychoplastic amplifications of image and infrastructure in the Karlsruhe Art and Media Center—represent exactly such controlled explosions of active materiality into invisible but adjacent co-dimensions. [End encounter number one: History/Capital disengages, peeling off into a long arc, circling back to re-engage later in a different tactical scenario.]

In November 1994, Yeager published a brief article on air-combat tactics. The article consisted of three short paragraphs, each outlining what might be referred to as three new "dicta" on how to expand the elastic "edge" of any "envelope."[9] Before examining these dicta, it is worth pointing out how the envelope concept is itself significant. The term's origin almost certainly derives from military ergonomic milieus, a context in which "envelope" always implies at least three things: the idea that a human-machine interface constitutes a next-order synthetic unity; the idea of a homeostatically contained group of forces in flux that form a temporary, fluid, but *historical* ensemble; and the idea that this unity or ensemble is an organic one, that it is defined *performatively*, and possesses its own global tolerances and parameters. The envelope, by definition, is a communicative, active apparatus. No wonder it has for years been a favorite term in Koolhaas's lexicon. A Koolhaas project, for better or worse, is never an eternal or stable solution to a "classic" problem, nor does it pretend to be. Rather, it is a provisional, elastic resolution of a compound conjunctural *situation*. His solutions have half-lives, they are temporally and historically determined, they move with the stream of the world and so build in flexibility and allow for immense programmatic turnover. They are more fully products of their n-dimensional *epoch* than of their time-blind (world-blind!), literal *site*. The Koolhaas work, like the aerial encounter, is composed in a purely tactical arena, formed in an abstract envelope of concrete historical (cosmopolitan) fluids.

B. The Full Metal Jacket

See more than your opponent sees: Yeager dictum number 1. For the flyer this can mean only one thing: free the eyes of objects and the habits that follow from object-oriented vision. Yeager shows how to retrain one's focus to take in all of space, to see everything. (When asked what made him such an exceptional flyer, Yeager used to answer, "I had the best eyes.") For the architect, this means take your focus to infinity, do not linger on objects but rather enter the space tactilely and prospect the space in search of breaking developments. Scan for changes and fluctuations, then respond as if part of a cycle, as if you had always been a causal part of those flows. This dictum works well with the more classic exhortation to "spot the enemy first." Arbitrage, here as everywhere, is the process that makes the emerging difference critical—the symmetry break that "seeds" space, allowing form to rush in. For Yeager, as for Koolhaas, history, even material history, is all about thresholds. This is because in free matter, energy and information become perfectly coextensive fluxes, the translation of one into the other is simultaneous, and events are "computed" instantly. Matter, like history, is an aggregate, partly fluid and partly solid, a "colloid" or liquid crystal that shifts its pattern rhythmically in relation to the flow of inputs and outputs that traverse it. The shifts are distributed like stages with triggers that are tripped when variables extend beyond their local "equilibria," or envelopes. The pilot must learn to enter this domain as free matter, to become computationally coextensive with the aggregate's unfolding, so that all reaction is instantaneous ("If you have to think, you're dead"). Koolhaas's technique is to ride these thresholds as well. After all, "threshold" is just another name for that privileged eventfilled place at the edge of the envelope.[10] In the present book, he defines at least six thresholds or emergences, potential or already realized: *congestion*, short of which the "metropolitan" effect would not exist; a new concept of Europe, its new modalities of collecting, storing, and deploying energy based on a sudden "explosion of scale," and the multiple

reorganizations that take place around it; *bigness*, the umbrella theme that typifies all "quantum" phenomena in the late-modern landscape, where changes in scale and size produce not only changes in degree but changes in kind (new qualities); *dissociation of interior and exterior*, which become not only autonomous programs and domains to be developed freely, but free-floating values (exteriority folded within buildings; interiorities, as in a Riemannian manifold, locally and promiscuously defined); *sheer mass as affect or trait*, a density-volume relationship, like Jorge Silvetti's "Colossal,"[11] that speaks a forgotten language, like a lost tribe of the Beautiful suddenly come home; and *rootlessness*, the severing of relations with slow and deep unfoldings (the old-world swells of "ground" and "place") and the reterritorialization—inevitable if regrettable—onto the "fast, cheap, and out of control" ethos of late-modern capital, demographics, and globalization.[12]

Yeager's third dictum (allow me to save the second for last): *Use all four dimensions*. A poor pilot (and a mediocre architect) thinks of space as a discrete manifold of two-dimensional sheets in a variety of different axes and orientations. An average pilot (and a better architect) thinks in terms of three dimensions in continuum. In a dogfight, however (or in the space of the late twentieth century), a precise and especially a plastic sense of time is critical. What most pilots don't understand, Yeager tells us, is that "by controlling the throttle, they're controlling time."[13] Time, of course, is not simply one dimension among others; it is *the dimension out of which all other dimensions unfold*. It is adjacent to everything, it presses at every edge, assigns every threshold, opens onto every becoming. How long does it take to get from point A to point B? That question is at the basis of modern material space, although not in the sense of a simple translatory trajectory. In a four-dimensional manifold, space, quite simply, is alive. Points A and B are no longer simple coordinates in a Newtonian *lattice* ("simple location," in Whitehead's terminology), but vectors in a Lagranian *mesh* (Whitehead's proto-"organism"). What this means is that every movement drags local space along with it—local conditions with a high degree of correlation with their surroundings—so that every displacement of location is simultaneously a transformation of kind. In the dogfight—an extreme activity par excellence, because time becomes so material you can taste it—the variables become so multiplied that the very concept of aerial tactics essentially evaporates.[14] All that is left is a very rapid game of "relative motion and time-distance problems." This new, Lagrangian space is one of compound correlations or, in aerial combat, of "multiple tactics." For example, with several enemy and friendly aircraft in play, you must, in a given situation, determine whether you can take an enemy off your wingman's tail even while another is already coming, and gunning at you. You must compute the "energy" differential in each "frame": can your relative motion get you into range to take out one aircraft before the relative motion of the fighter on your tail can get into range to take you? In such a situation, it must be remembered, speed determines every coordinate (not "simple location"), yet velocity remains only a relative value. The game is to exploit differentials, and to produce them when needed, continually, and indeed literally, out of thin air. For example, forcing an opponent to overspeed is even more effective than flying pirouettes around him. This logic explains why the slower Russian and Chinese MiGs had tighter turning radiuses, why they enveloped a different spectrum of traits or "materiality," and why this made them lethal to many much faster aircraft. In encounters such as high-speed turns, for example, the appearance of significant G forces introduced a new internal envelope, with new tolerances that offered a new material dimension that could be exploited, a new envelope to be feathered or stretched. The envelope of fluids that presents itself to the fighter pilot is not simply one of multiple mobile elements—the diverse aptitudes of his own airplane, the positions and energy levels of terrain, horizon, sky, sun, enemy, co-wingmen, etc.—whose coordination must be precisely tracked; it is one of compound relationships all woven together in hyper-time. The architect who grasps this grasps the bizarre truth of both the dogfight and of late capitalism all at once: the agent who triumphs is the one who makes best use of his aircraft and weapons within the constraints of its performance envelope. One must fly one's airplane closer to the edge of the envelope (without exceeding it) than the opponent—History/Capital—flies its. One materiality against another, in the same world, with freedom hovering alongside disaster, just at the edge. Optimism and danger: two heads on the shoulders of a single beast.

This brings us to the final problem of integrating gunnery into the flight system, and with it Yeager's final, most mystical, dictum: *Fly the bullet*. Learning to see and learning to shoot, it turns out, are extremely similar problems, the latter at an order of magnitude and complexity a full step above the former. Yet as we move up the ladder of complexity, we also move up the ladder of integration: more elements in interaction but with a smoother overall shape. Lars Lerup has written of "mega shapes," algorithmic ghosts buried in geometrical systems that offer themselves to the intuition, albeit parceled over time.[15] Others have spoken of strange emergences, where "prehensions" occur replete with control mechanisms that remain demonstrably stable but cannot be located in the system's parts. This is the case even with simple swarm and flock activity in animal continuums. Again, the smoothness of the flow-shape is what strikes both the mind and the eye. This smoothness actually derives from the intense *directedness* that is built into material systems. One could again invoke the theoretical intricacies of the Lagrangian mesh, but for such a complex problem duty obliges one to develop a much simpler model. We are again dealing with relative motion and time/distance computation: how to make the bullet find the enemy aircraft, or rather, how to make the bullet meet its target, in time and not only in... when that rendezvous must clearly take place in the unknowable future! This was the same problem, at another level, on which

Norbert Wiener worked during World War II and which led to the science of cybernetics. But long before the science of cybernetics there was the art of cybernetics. Now the art remains superior to the science in most extreme (hypertemporal) situations and milieus, and so it is the art that both the pilot and the visionary architect pursue. How, then, to fly the bullet? Well, Yeager was probably a natural:

In the midst of a wild sky, I knew that dogfighting was what I was born to do. It's almost impossible to explain the feeling: it's as if you were one with that mustang, an extension of that damned throttle... You were so wired into that airplane that you flew it to the limit of its specs... You felt that engine in your bones, felt it nibbling toward a stall, getting maximum maneuvering performance achieved mostly by instinctive flying: you knew your horse.[16]

No, this is not mysticism; it is computational metallurgy. We all know that metals are liquids whose flow has been arrested. Precisely where and by what sequence of operations we arrest them determines how these metals will behave, what they look like, and what qualities they possess. The closer we bring them to extreme states—that is, liquid, compressed, or hot—the more qualities or properties they "speak." Arresting their various flows is a process achieved through painstaking operations, separating this one off, letting these others continue on for one or two more measures. Artisans in all materials follow and exploit the found material pattern and structure that presents itself as "potential"—the work for free spoken of above. Even fish tap the vortexes in their aquatic environment in a similar way to achieve greater than 100 percent locomotor efficiency. Mostly, though, this work emerges at confluences, where communication and information exchange between systems is at its most intense.

Yeager has taught generations of pilots how to fly and be effective in the air. There is no doubt that these techniques, these modes of extracting effects from unfolding configurations, are transmissible. Fly the bullet: "In order to lead the [enemy] plane [on its time path so your bullets will meet it]. you have to be able to make the aircraft an extension of your body."[17] Now the submerged art of cybernetics has always said, Your airplane is metal. Your flight path is metal. (Our cities, no doubt, are metal!) Of course the airplane is very complex metal, exceptionally highly organized and, of course, full of life. Now that it is "hot" enough that is, far enough from equilibrium and therefore close to the envelope's edge—hadn't we really ought to let its own metallic nature speak? The entire encounter now, including your nervous system, is a metallic one (action-potential cycles of Na^+, K^+ and Cl^-) and we must let its metal speak as well. All that remains is to *enter* the imbroglio and *follow* the flow. But to do this we must first forget the airplane.[18] As your focus opens, the airplane is drawn inside you (the universe is metal!).[19] Yeager:

Don't even think about turning. Just turn your head or your body and let the plane come along for the ride. When you take aim, fly the bullet into position.[20]

That's it. Ignore the plane, just fly the bullet into position. The sweep of your head and the arc along which your buttocks swing on the cockpit seat form a single computational matrix with the tangent from your guns. Total continuity, total extension into time. There is no room here for number crunching, no room for computers, no room for auto-override. "Forget planning," Koolhaas tells us, "Forget the plane," says Yeager. And we know they are right, because the essence of successful dogfighting, despite radical technological developments, has not changed since World War I.[21] When Koolhaas cautiously promotes "a forward-looking extrapolation"[22] as an alternative to fixing rules, you know he is looking for just this extension into the future and into time. Koolhaas's city is the metallic city (Karlsruhe—the tungsten and phosphorus of the cathode ray tube; Paris—silver bromide and Technicolor chemistry of optical image processing; Zeebrugge—the sheet metal of train, boat and automobile). It is the *cybernetropolis* of "the open" and of the ragged edge. To fly the bullet is to prime matter with action potential (ionic differentials allowing signals to propagate long distances through the nervous system by exploiting local interactions), with continuums of influence transmitted ahead of them like shock waves into time.[23] When Koolhaas talks of the possibility of generating virtual congestion by eschewing the usual radial connections in favor of circulation and of serial—or massively parallel—links in a megalopolis condition (what he calls "bridge connections"), it is just this "action potential" in the urban axons that he is exploiting. To fly the bullet is to endow the material field with directedness—all that, and yet nothing mystical, nothing more.

Koolhaas commits to the bullet and its mysteriously correlated trajectory when he commits to the "vitality," however strange, of what *is*. Vitality *is* materiality, and materiality, like Nietzsche's Will to Power, must always engage other units of itself. Oswald Boelcke makes an important point about Nature as well as dogfighting when in dictum number 6 he says, "If your opponent dives on you, do not try to evade his onslaught, but fly to meet it." Koolhaas, to the horror of many bystanders in the so-called "Resistance," has largely adopted this activist creed.

Vitality, then, is a field property, a quality of active ensembles (of "excitable media" in the biological sense, the "wild sky" in Yeager). and is not reduceable or locatable in the living system, be it that of the city, the organism, or the hyper-field of the dogfight. Life may be defined as a pattern sustaining itself over time, a control system that regulates a sequence of processes that follow mysteriously from one another. In this organismal view of things that, I would claim, we see in both Yeager and Koolhaas, and indeed at every ragged edge through which the future intrudes, there can be no *horror vacuii*. The void, as Koolhaas recognizes, is the very source of novelty, of creative

potential, because it is both indeterminate *and* correlated (directed but not predetermined).[24] To fly the bullet is to allow the vector, once released, to inhabit itself; it is the interval in the throes of becoming substance. In the organismal view of the world, interval *is* substance, an active plastic medium projected ahead of the present, and which in turn receives it. We do not know in advance what it will be, because it is pure formation (potential) without form.

Only when architecture fully grasps the intuition of continuity and of relation as a pragmatics and as a physics will it have become *extreme*. At that moment, however distant, we may well find that, in architecture, the future did in fact begin with Koolhaas.

Notes

1. Rem Koolhaas, *Rem Koolhaas: Conversations with Students*, Architecture at Rice 30. (Houston and New York: Architecture at Rice and Princeton Architectural Press, Second Edition, 1996) p. 65.
2. Rem Koolhaas, *Rem Koolhaas: Conversations with Students*, Architecture at Rice 30. (Houston and New York: Architecture at Rice and Princeton Architectural Press, Second Edition, 1996) p. 53.
3. On husbandry or the "pastoral" in urban systems generally, and in Koolhaas specifically, see my "Politics and Pastoralism," *Assemblage 28* (1995).
4. Other extreme sports such as the triple Ironman, ultra-deep-sea diving with liquid inhalants, or unassisted oxygen-less ascents to the peak of Everest are also extreme by virtue of their "catastrophic" use of the human body's performance envelope-pushing it to the edge of unconsciousness so that an "autopilot" mechanism must kick in.
5. Major Gen. Fred J. Ascani. in Chuck Yeager, *Yeager*, (New York: Bantam Books, 1985).
6. Yeager; Tom Wolfe, *The Right Stuff*. (New York: Bantam Books, 1979).
7. Yeager, who flew only winged aircraft (even the F-104 had seven-foot-long razor wings) or ones that took off under their own power (not including the X-10 experiments of the 1940's). never actually flew beyond the absolute atmospheric boundary (280,000 feet). but he unquestionably prepared the way. He was the first American to probe the extreme edge of the NF-104's envelope (a conventional atmosphere-dependent aircraft) by flying it above 100,000 feet, a test flight that all but cost him his life. Nonetheless, Yeager routinely took his students up beyond the first atmospheric boundary (70,000 feet) where the sky goes black and silent but the air's molecular structure still sustains aerodynamic buoyancy-to give them a taste of the "outside"—that is, of *space*.
8. Sant'Elia, Hilberseimer, and certain early Soviet revolutionaries are among the only figures whose work comes to mind.
9. General Chuck Yeager, "How to Win a Dogfight," *Men's Health*, November 1994. My thanks to Brian Boigon for alerting me to this article.
10. "Class four behaviour" in Stephen Wolfram; "poised systems" and "edge of chaos" in Chris Langton and Stuart Kaufmann; "separatrices" and "catastrophe sets" in Ralph Abraham and René Thom; "bifurcation regimes" and "far from equilibrium states" of chaologists and thermodynamicists; "singularities" in Deleuze and Guattari; "flow" in

Csikszentmihalyi and optimal experience theorists; "one-over-f" systems in signal theory; the state of "highest or fulfilled tension" in Zen Buddhist disciplines… the list is beautiful, and long.

11. Jorge Silvetti, "The Seven Wonders of the World" a lecture delivered at the Rhode Island School of Design, 1982.

12. Koolhaas's own *mot d'ordre* here is "fuck context." Cf. "Bigness" in Rem Koolhaas, *S,M,L,XL* (New York: Monacelli Press, 1996).

13. "How to Win a Dogfight." Emphasis supplied.

14. Peter Kilduff with Lieutenants Randall H. Cunningham and William P. Driscoll, "McDonnell F-4 Phantom," in *In the Cockpit*. ed. Anthony Robinson (London: Orbis, 1979). My thanks to Jesse Reiser for bringing this text to my attention.

15. Lars Lerup, "Stim and Dross," *Assemblage 25* (1994).

16. Yeager.

17. "How to Win a Dogfight."

18. Similarly, in the art of juggling, the flexible control of multiple non-linear variables (hands, balls and their trajectories) to maintain a solid pattern is properly achieved only by keeping the eye *off* the ball, that is, by letting touch, memory, and more importantly, natural rhythmic attractors (coupled oscillator phenomena) deep in the body's bio-schema take over regulating the movements. There is a musical materiality that juggling calls out of the body. The structure of these pattern relationships is just beginning to undergo experimental notation in what is known as "site swap theory." See Peter J. Beek and Arthur Lewbel, "The Science of Juggling," *Scientific American*, November 1995.

19. "Not everything is metal, but metal is everywhere. Metal is the conductor of all matter… *Non-organic Life* was the invention, the intuition of metallurgy." Gilles Deleuze and Felix Guattari, *A Thousand Plateaus* (Minneapolis: University of Minnesota Press, 1987). The entire discussion of materiality here is indebted to this work, especially the chapters "On Nomadology" and "The Geology of Morals."

20. "How to Win a Dogfight."

21. The RIO (radio intercept officer), who sits directly behind the pilot in most advanced fighters today and who is responsible for managing the weapons systems, has an entirely computerized cockpit. In front, however, computors are often little more than a liability; in aerial combat there never has been such a thing as a pushbutton war. Even today, bomber pilots seek maximum override capability against automated pilot functions, giving the pilot maximum control over critical "edge" maneuvers. The role of computers, more often than not, is to filter and minimize the flow of numerical data to the pilot's nervous system.

22. Rem Koolhaas, *Rem Koolhaas: Conversations with Students*, Architecture at Rice 30. (Houston and New York: Architecture at Rice and Princeton Architectural Press, Second Edition, 1996) p. 47.

23. Kinematic wave theory, applied to traffic flow studies, has shown that pulses, or traffic shock waves, form on highway traffic clusters. These waves travel backward or forward along the flow entirely independent of, and at a speed greater than, that of any individual automobile or the velocity of the group flow.

24. Rem Koolhaas, *Rem Koolhaas: Conversations with Students*, Architecture at Rice 30. (Houston and New York: Architecture at Rice and Princeton Architectural Press, Second Edition, 1996) p. 63.

This essay originally appeared in *Rem Koolhaas: Conversations with Students*, **Architecture at Rice 30, co-published with Princeton Architectural Press, Second Edition, 1996.**

SANFORD KWINTER is an associate professor at Rice School of Architecture.

Super-Houston

Peter Cook

Strange that Super-Houston is the one scheme that has been born directly out of an academic base. Over many years of teaching I have been consciously reluctant to force a piece of design out of the formality of the seminar or the studio program (except for the Brisbane Towers, which only used the same site as the students and not much more).

I had already spent a few days in Houston here and there and had benefited from Reyner Banham's frequent observations and inevitable comparisons with Los Angeles. I had sweated my way across a campus in the heat and stickiness of September. I had dashed for air-conditioned cover in a car or lobby and then shivered with cold. I had been guided elegantly and amusingly by Stephen Fox through the glades of River Oaks or across into Pasadena, following one's nose as it became more and more aware of the cloying presence of oil in the air. I had walked purposefully down avenues, as a good European, in search of a drugstore; having been told, "It's just a few blocks," I found that it was a sweaty two miles. I had wallowed in the very calmness of the enclave that surrounds Renzo Piano's Menil Collection. I had lined my eye up onto Carlos Jiménez's miniature sets of related pavilions and paths of recognition by which he determined his small house pavilions. In other words, despite the seeming endlessness of Houston, there could be sweet moments, but fazed by the apparent lack of sequence in the urban experience. My task was to conduct morning seminars on a loose series of topics and to respond to Rice's articulate graduate students who had already rumbled by attraction to Los Angeles. Moreover, the architecture school of Rice University was heavily infused with persuasive talent that had moved over from California: Lars Lerup, Albert

Pope, and their followers who found themselves making constant reference back and forth from the features of Houston to those of the San Fernando Valley, Orange County, and Beverly Hills, as had Reyner Banham before them. "So, Mr Cook, how do you regard the two cities?" My response was instinctive:

To really place Houston, you have to construct a chain of inspirational models. Let's say:

1. the Italian hill town
2. London
3. Los Angeles
4. Houston... and then conjecture something beyond that, with the same level of contradiction... let's say
5. Super-Houston...

and I became stuck on the idea for a good two years.

The chain is a personal one, for the Italian hill town had been the love for many of my teachers' generation and for some older English friends, and therefore existed as an irritation as well as an objective model. London was there as my daily reminder that cities are circumstantial and paradoxical—and certainly not all that they seem. Los Angeles had remained my running dream, temptation, and revelation, for so much of its sociology is reminiscent of London and even of the British suburban world. Yet its endless provocation of Dream—denial of the Dream—Dream again, kept one on one's intellectual toes. But then Houston? Surely challenging one to delve, to seep into the simultaneous and languid acceptance of both fate and terror suggested by those ambiguous Larry McMurtry characters. A major challenge to spot the most subtle of variations of detail, of nuances, of hints.

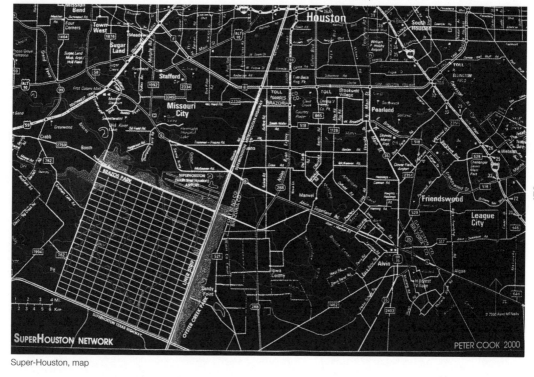

SuperHouston Network

PETER COOK 2000

Super-Houston, map

In a drive down Westheimer one comes upon the first cluster of outlets—maybe a Burger King, a Walgreens, a Buy-Rite arranged just clear of the highway and given the usual appliqué styling. Three miles further on, the next cluster of Burger King, Walgreens, but Buy-Rite possibly replaced by a 7-Eleven. Three miles further and the King has moved a few jumps down in the strip, Walgreens is still there and Buy-Rite has reappeared. The architecture (for that is what it must be, must it not, since there are pilasters, corners, and well-mannered edges?) has subtly evolved. They are rarely repeat buildings and the arrangements are particular. But the themes go on. The presence of trees with housing peeking out beneath is as subtle in its conscious market appeal as are the details of the shops. It lacks the layered quality of Los Angeles; it has far fewer remnants of the 1930's, 1940's, or 1950's Googie architecture and even fewer remnants of old enterprise. In all of this I exclude downtown, for the Houston that fascinates me is the *treed* city. By which I mean the half of the urbanized area where almost continuous tree cover does not prevent a continuity of two-story buildings.

Anyhow, downtown is determined to provide corporate identity and cultural identity markers: the opera, the symphony, and many world headquarters. Yet its rival, the Galleria, is more fascinating, for it acts as a mall (and an unusually long one at that) and as a magnet. It has drawn a cluster of other enterprises around it, rather like a downtown would have done in the 1920's. It has nearly enough variety within it to act as a "city," but not quite enough, and this remained in my mind as a working reference when I came to develop the Liner element of Super-Houston.

Returning to London between two spells of Rice seminars, I knew that I had to creatively get in there and draw this Super-Houston. I was inspired as much by the puzzlement and dismay that had set upon me when, having enjoyed a good haircut, I could not just stroll down the strip beyond the hairdressers: there wasn't one. After a long browse in one of Houston's excellent bookstores I couldn't just mosey over to the record store or even a candy store or even... it just wasn't there. Even restaurant patterns could be confusing: a well-located but over-popular coffee shop could leave you stranded, as there was no rival or clone across the way, as in other cities. Rice Village excepted, you had to know and you had to network.

So there were two experiences running around in my mind: tree cover and scattered networking. Plus the inevitability of the car: not the staccato pattern of dash-and-weave that we have in most other cities. More a knowing glide that makes physical the pleasantries of much Texan conversation. It intrigued me too much to let it go.

The Network

Super-Houston must start from the traffic network and a positive attitude toward it. It must offer the ultimate in added value and take the last ounce of strain out of traveling. So why not bug the streets with induction and monitoring electronics? Fit a small device to every local car (and have them available to rent at the edge of town), so that you can let the steering go on automatic pilot. You can dial for a morning's run : "kids," "school," "groceries," "nail bar," "therapist," "Uncle Joe"... the network of streets is in a series of one-way routings. Arriving at the school, you would have a

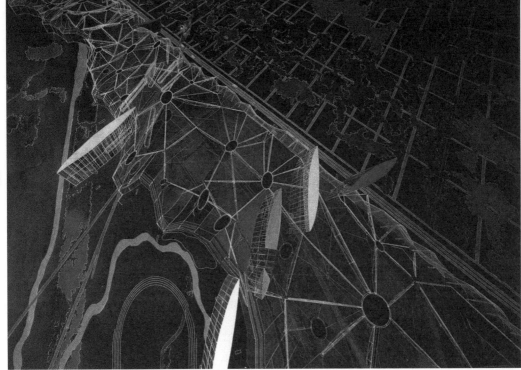

Super-Houston, aerial view of the liner

reminder signal for waves and pleasantries. Arriving at the grocery store, you silently and uninvolvedly gain a parking slot, similarly for the nail bar and therapist (you don't want him to watch you neurotically fidgeting the car into place, do you?). But for Uncle Joe, there is a half-minute warning signal so that you can get in the mood: do the old traditional drive-up, window down, wave-and-holler arrival.

Alternating with the driving streets are an equal number of pathways for the encouragement of jogs, early-morning and evening walking, and small-scale ball games: not all exercise needs a gym. These pathways are of course a rerun of the swathes in the Layer City and a memory of the Arcadian atmosphere that can be created beneath good tree cover and among hedges.

At greater intervals, somewhere between a kilometer and a mile, there have to be larger gatherings of through-routes, and at an even larger interval the equivalent of freeways with combinations of guided and unguided tracks. As the scheme developed, it suggested that a ten-mile square of Super-Houston could straddle the low hills and rivulets at the southwestern edge of the existing city.

Over these ten miles we can enjoy something similar in atmosphere to McMurtry's description of "the well-tamed forests of River Oaks." Swathes of trees and clearings, an even spread of middle-income houses, and some slightly more show-off houses in among them. Small watercourses snaking their way through, but not sufficiently grand or constant to cause any ceremony or interruption in the general spread. Similarly, there needs to be some occasional splitting

open of the run of building, enough to host a public park or playing fields, but definitely nothing too special. The establishment of an evenness greater than that of Houston itself sets up the ultimate tease: to determine event where there is none. To proliferate the same and then invite the inhabitant to suss out the particular. You can always find the particular in the Yellow Pages or on the Internet—if you know what you are looking for. And even if you don't—you can get a vicarious urge to do something, visit something or someone, buy something by scanning down through these seemingly bland sources of information.

To someone who has surely exposed himself as a place-inspired, thing-inspired, event-inspired designer, this pursuit of the bland can be recognized as a self-tease but also a conscious exercise in reassembling the criteria of action. The temporary detachment of mannerism from event is stimulating and intriguing. Centuries of conscious and physical celebration—of looking, stopping, starting, worshiping, selling, or even just passing over a river—have given architects the excuse to articulate day-to-day life and freeze the values of a monarchy or a civilization in stone.

And anyway, what the hell?

This essay originally appeared in *The City, Seen as a Garden of Ideas*, The Monacelli Press, 2003.

PETER COOK is a principal of CRAB studio. He was a Visiting Cullinan Professor at Rice School of Architecture in 1998.

Super-Houston, typical housing, axonometric

Super-Houston, view to a village along the freeway

Seven Aphorisms
Lars Lerup

Aphorism 1
The contemporary metropolis, or rather that which has replaced the metropolis, surrounds us but is invisible, escaping the gaze of the architect whose knowledge of the metropolis was calibrated for another time and place. At Rice School of Architecture, we are committed to retooling our profession to engage the vast field of urban flows in which we wade.

Aphorism 2
Thirty years ago architects were told they had lost the ability to affect the development of the metropolis. And we believed it, rushing headlong into oblivious irrelevance and headless professionalism as we abandoned our fiduciary responsibilities in even the most modest of proposals. At Rice we seek to reinvest architecture into the pragmatics of space by radically innovating the conditions and objects of the architect's practice.

Aphorism 3
Form has become the refuge of the architectural scoundrel, whose seeks to hide in it from the forces which are rapidly hunting his discipline down.

Aphorism 4
Space, rather than form, is the subject-matter through which architecture can begin to track the multiplicitous forces which configure the contemporary built environment. This space is neither uniform, empty or static. It is a flux-space through which all the heterogeneous dynamics of the metropolitan field and the suburban

ecology manifest. The forms of the city are the momentary calci-fications of these spatial dynamics.

Aphorism 5

The "alphabetization" of the architect's knowledge and practice in modernity, its segmentation into discrete objects and competencies, must be reversed by investment in the connectivity of these elements. Ecological ethics are not just about environmentalism but about understanding the complex topology of effects, agents and phenom-ena that traverse all boundaries and borders of the built environment. Gradients rather than walls, fields rather than plots, links rather than nodes, hybrids rather then essences, slurries rather than names.

Aphorism 6

The impending environmental calamity, for which the city will be a primary site, is at once the architect's last hope and greatest challenge.

Aphorism 7

We hope to engender a performative understanding of the built environment as a dance of matters, forces, ideas, things, economies, subjects.

LARS LERUP is the dean and William Ward Watkin Professor of Architecture at Rice School of Architecture.

Leaving
Aaron Betsky

More and more, we have come to realize that we live in a landscape that does not consist of a natural terrain gridded by humans and given coherent shape through the contrast between what has grown and what we have made. Instead, we live in an extensive territory of mixed character that coheres around nodes. The hybrid terrain is touched, if not shaped, every-where by technology, from the acres of asphalt that take up over half the surface area in most urban areas to the climate changes our technology has produced, affecting the most remote rain forest. Within this miasmic hybrid landscape, the concentrated nodes consist of us, as conscious human beings, but also our social products, especially those where we have concen-trated the most intense technology, which extends us out into that landscape inside cocoons that less and less resemble traditional types such as clothes, cars, homes, or office buildings. We live in a world of stim and dross.

Dross is what most of us understand as sprawl, which is not just the physical sprawl that has dissolved cities, suburbs, exurbs, and agricultural areas into a mess of continually developing ugliness, but also the sprawl of the internet, the sprawl of our global information-based society, and even the sprawl of our bodies. It is the messy reality where the promised center cannot hold. Stim is what is left of coherence and consciousness, of value and reason, but it is also quite simply those places where we are protected from the elements and others, those places where we gather, those moments of crystallized concentration and awareness that make sense out of all and shine forth in dross.

These terms, coming out of Lars Lerup's analysis of the landscape of sprawl he learned to navigate once he moved to Houston in 1994, have given shape to what otherwise is an abstract and troubling physical real-ity. To understand this environment, we must draw not just on the tools of architecture and planning history, nor merely, on the one hand, on an analysis of topography or, on the other hand, on the intricacies of human relations as they have occurred (history), are occurring (sociology), or may occur (economy). Instead, we have to develop ways of understanding that are not only multidisciplinary, but also poetic, which is to say, that create palimpsest landscapes covering the diurnal realities we traverse but barely ever notice.

To do so, we construct evocative models or phrases, of which Lars Lerup and the Rice School of Architecture have been particularly productive in the last few decades: ladders, slow space, stim and dross, the city escaping from itself. All of these encapsulate much larger and more complex develop-ments into mimetic and multivalent phrases that have the power to give these developments visual and narrative form.

What we need, and what Rice has started to become, is a research and design facility for the future of the designed environment.

What is still lacking in such an academic stim, perhaps, is the physical form that might act as a built critique of the situation we find ourselves in today. We know that buildings may not be enough anymore to create the kinds of cocoons that shelter us and make us feel at home, and yet are open to and even invite social relations, but we are not quite sure what is. As the current analysis is still being generated from the traditions of architecture, a clear idea has yet to emerge of how to escape from the sticks and stones that have until now constrained the manner in which that discipline reveals, domesticates, and makes specific the technology that allows us to inhabit the modern territory. Lars Lerup's project remains at present the most con-centrated attempt to research, reveal, understand, name, evoke, and remake the world of stim and dross. We are grateful for this work, but it is unfinished, and much work is to be done. Lars Lerup leaves us with a stimulating starting point in an exploration of our drossy reality.

AARON BETSKY is the director of the Cincinnatti Art Museum. He was a Visiting Cullinan Professor at Rice School of Architecture in 2000.

Acknowledgments

This book would not have been possible without fifteen years of effort by a multitude of people: students, faculty, staff and administration working to make Rice School of Architecture the vibrant institution that it is. Our thanks to everyone who has participated in that "long haul."

Special thanks are especially warranted to those who truly went out of their way to help us make this publication possible: David Brown, Stephen Fox, Izabel Gass, Brian Wesley Heiss, Carlos Jiménez, and Albert Pope.

Photography plays an important part in this book. We want to express extended thanks to George O. Jackson, Alex Knapp, Lars Lerup, Bas Princen and Geoff Winningham whom together show us Houston and the diffuse city in ways we haven't seen it before or may in the future.

Everybody knows how important Doris Anderson is to the school, and this endeavor has made it even clearer.

John J. Casbarian has at key moments helped us to make connections to the longer history of Rice that have helped this project become broader in vision and deeper in reach.

Lars Lerup: Well, what can we say? It's been a long, strange trip and we're glad we made it with you.

This book was funded in part with a generous gift by H. Ralph and Susan K. Hawkins, of Dallas, Texas.

Photo Credits

Luke Bulman
60-1, 256-9

Farès el-Dahdah
219

J. Kent Fitzsimons
24-5

Stephen Fox
106-9, 153-5

**Brian Wesley Heiss
and Michael Morrow**
282

Christopher Hight
343-5

George O. Jackson
158-9, 162-3, 244, 251-5, 264-5, 336-
41, 372-9

Alex Knapp
Pages 26-7, 56-9, 62-3, 75, 88-9, 120-1,
164-5, 264-7, 260-1, 266-7

**Houston Postcards/ Independent
Study, 2002 / Alex O'Briant, advisor**
...Houston faces two possibilities—first,
to try to follow, as best it can, the model
laid out by other cities; second, and
perhaps more interesting, to attempt
to redefine the rules by which identity
is created. To do this would require
the abandonment of nostalgia as the
primary focus of identity. While many
other cities have taken great interest
In preserving their history, Houston is
remarkable because of its complete dis-
interest in the past. The city is disposed
and recycled in a way that is paralleled
in no other major American metropolis.
The logics of the market economy have
more to do with the shape of Houston
than with other cities of its size, in part
because there has never been collective
interest in large scale civic projects.
Houston is always looking forward,
without a rear view mirror, and would
do well to exploit this fascination with
the new. It is a city that has never been
interested in the master plan handed
down from above ...

Lars Lerup
54-5, 90-1, 118-9, 122-5, 160-1, 248,
262-3, 320, 412-3, 428-33, 462-5

Chad Loucks
98, 101, 155 (bottom), 198

Michael Morrow
274

Alex O'Briant
64-5

Bas Princen
1-7

Luciano Rigolini
22-3

Danny Samuels
100, 103

Tony Valadez
99

Lew Watts
104-5

Geoff Winningham
243, 388

**Unless noted, project photos
are taken by their designer.**